Perspectives on Ethics

Perspectives on Ethics

Judith A. Boss

Center for the Study of Human Development, Brown University

Mayfield Publishing Company
Mountain View, California
London • Toronto

Library of Congress Cataloging-in-Publication Data
Perspectives on ethics / [edited by] Judith A. Boss.
      p.   cm.
   Includes index.
   ISBN 1-55934-970-0
   1. Ethics.   I. Boss, Judith A.,
BJ1012.P435   1997
17—dc21   97-41495
                              CIP

Manufactured in the United States of America
10 9 8 7 6 5 4 3 2

Sponsoring editor, Ken King; production editor, Melissa Kreischer; manuscript editor, Jennifer Gordon; design manager, Jean Mailander; text designer, Ellen Pettengell; cover designer, Donna Davis; manufacturing manager, Randy Hurst. Cover art by Joseph Albers © ARS, TN/Tate Gallery, London/Art Resource, NY. The text was set in 10/12 Sabon by TBH Typecast, Inc. and printed on acid-free 45# Glatfleter Restorecote by Malloy Lithographing, Inc.

Text credits appear at the back of the book on pages 485–486, which constitute an extension of the copyright page.

 This book is printed on recycled paper.

To my daughter Alyssa, on the occasion of her graduation from law school as valedictorian of her class

Contents

Preface xi

Introduction xv

CHAPTER ONE
The Study of Ethics 1
Robert Coles, "The Disparity Between Intellect and Character" 3
Mencius, "The Natural Goodness of Humans" 8
Christina Hoff Sommers, "Where Have All the Good Deeds Gone?" 13
Sheila Mullett, "Shifting Perspective: A New Approach to Ethics" 17
Kōshō Mizutani, "Buddhist Tradition and Modernity" 23
Chapter Applications 27

CHAPTER TWO
Ethical Relativism 29
Ethical Subjectivism 29
Jean-Jacques Rousseau, *Émile* 31
Mary Wollstonecraft, *A Vindication of the Rights of Woman* 39
Jacob Javits and A. M. Rosenthal, "Study of the Sickness Called Apathy" 44
Stephen A. Satris, "Student Relativism" 51
Cultural Relativism 54
Herbert Spencer, *The Principles of Ethics* 57
Ruth Benedict, "A Defense of Cultural Relativism" 62
Ibn Khaldun, *The Muqaddimah* 67
Marilyn Frye, *"Oppression"* 71
Daniel Jonah Goldhagen, *Hitler's Willing Executioners* 80
Dr. Martin Luther King, Jr., "Letter from a Birmingham Jail" 87

William H. Shaw, "Relativism in Ethics"   92
Chapter Applications   97

CHAPTER THREE
Morality and Religion   105
Qu'ran   107
Mohandas K. Gandhi, "The Moral Teaching of the *Bhagavad Gita*"   110
Excerpts from Genesis, Exodus, and Matthew, *Holy Bible*   118
Lippman Bodoff, "God Tests Abraham, Abraham Tests God"   124
Plato, *Euthyphro*   129
Thomas Aquinas, *The Summa Theologica*   140
Friedrich Nietzsche, *Beyond Good and Evil* and *The Joyful Wisdom*   147
Kai Nielsen, "Religious Ethics Versus Humanistic Ethics"   154
Chapter Applications   164

CHAPTER FOUR
Beyond Relativism:
Conscience and Moral Development   170
James Q. Wilson, *The Moral Sense*   172
Lawrence Kohlberg, *The Philosophy of Moral Development*   185
Carol Gilligan, *In a Different Voice*   193
Virginia Held, "The Meshing of Care and Justice"   203
Mark Twain, *The Adventures of Huckleberry Finn*   208
Eagle Man, "We Are All Related"   211
Chapter Applications   217

CHAPTER FIVE
Ethical Egoism   225
Plato, *The Republic*   227
Edward O. Wilson, *On Human Nature*   234
Ayn Rand, *The Fountainhead*   241
Mary Midgley, *Can't We Make Moral Judgements?*   248
Jean Hampton, "The Wisdom of the Egoist: The Moral and Political Implications of Valuing the Self"   252
Chapter Applications   269

CHAPTER SIX

Utilitarianism 274

Mo Tzu, *Universal Love* 275

Jeremy Bentham, *An Introduction to the Principles of Morals and Legislation* 281

John Stuart Mill, *Utilitarianism, Liberty, and Representative Government* 288

Peter Singer, *Animal Liberation* 295

Bernard Williams, "A Critique of Utilitarianism" 302

Chapter Applications 306

CHAPTER SEVEN

Deontology 314

Immanuel Kant, *Fundamental Principles of the Metaphysic of Ethics* 315

The Analects of Confucius 326

Sissela Bok, *Lying: Moral Choice in Public and Private Life* 331

William David Ross, *The Right and the Good* 343

John Rawls, *A Theory of Justice* 349

Chapter Applications 356

CHAPTER EIGHT

Rights Ethics 364

John Locke, *Two Treatises of Civil Government* 366

Karl Marx, "The Jewish Question" 377

Gustavo Gutierrez, *The Power of the Poor in History* 381

United Nations, "The Universal Declaration of Human Rights" 388

Jeane Kirkpatrick, "Establishing a Viable Human Rights Policy" 395

Joel Feinberg, *Rights, Justice, and the Bounds of Liberty* 401

Chapter Applications 411

CHAPTER NINE

Virtue Ethics 419

Aristotle, *Nicomachean Ethics* 421

Confucius, *The Doctrine of the Mean* 435

P. Don Premasiri, "The Relevance of the Noble Eightfold Path to Contemporary Society" 441

The Instruction of Ptahhotep 450

David Hume, *An Enquiry Concerning the Principles of Morals* 453

Nel Noddings, *Caring: A Feminine Approach to Ethics and Moral Education* 460

Alasdair MacIntyre, *After Virtue: A Study in Moral Theory* 469

Chapter Applications 477

Credits 485

Index 487

Preface

Many students in an introductory-level ethics course perceive the subject as irrelevant to their lives. This obstacle is caused largely by courses and texts that focus exclusively on theory. Also, students often lack the analytical tools necessary to understand the complex theories in philosophical readings. Ethics courses that are lean in theory and focus on issues, on the other hand, tend to leave students feeling that morality is all relative. In addition, multiculturalism and the increasing awareness of the impact of human activities and decisions on the environment have made professors and students more aware of the inadequacies of traditional approaches to making moral decisions.

Perspectives on Ethics is intended to overcome these obstacles by guiding students through the theoretical readings while at the same time anchoring moral theory in real life through the use of discussion questions and case studies. Although traditional Western moral philosophy forms the core of the book, this reader also integrates selections from non-Western traditions and other disciplines in an effort to address the true richness of moral analysis.

THE ORGANIZATION OF THE BOOK

The Introduction

Many students feel overwhelmed when they first encounter philosophical writings. The introduction helps alleviate this anxiety by providing students with the critical thinking skills necessary for understanding and critically analyzing the readings. Critical thinking questions at the beginning of each section reinforce these skills.

The Reading Selections

The selections in this book include readings from traditional Western moral philosophy as well as readings that represent non-Western, multicultural, feminist, religious, anthropological, sociobiological, psychological, legal, and literary perspectives. The readings work together as an interrelated whole, each elaborating on and reinforcing themes brought up in other readings. At the same time, enough readings are included so they can be used selectively.

The Nine Chapters

The readings are divided into nine chapters. These chapters are arranged in approximate order of a person's moral development which moves from ethical relativism to universal moral principles. The following is a brief summary of each section:

1. The opening chapter raises questions about the study of ethics and the need for ethics education.

2. The second chapter introduces the reader to moral theories based on ethical relativism. This section is further subdivided into ethical subjectivism (morality is relative to the individual), and cultural relativism (morality is relative to the culture).

3. Chapter 3 explores the relationship between morality and religion. In particular, this chapter addresses the question of whether morality is relative to religion and God's commands, or whether it is based on universal moral values that exist independently of religion and God.

4. The readings in Chapter 4 deal with conscience and moral development. The notion of moral development requires us, as moral agents, to strive to go beyond the types of ethical relativism discussed in the two previous chapters.

5. Chapters 5 through 9 cover moral theories which regard morality as universal. Chapter 5 introduces students to ethical egoism, the view that morality is doing that which is in our best self-interests. In this chapter students are encouraged to expand their thinking beyond their own self-interests without, at the same time, minimizing the moral importance of their own interests and lives.

6. Chapter 6 is on utilitarian theory. Utilitarians believe that the morality of an action is determined solely by its consequences. The readings in this chapter include the utilitarian theory of Chinese philosopher Mo Tzu as well as Western utilitarian theories. While consequences are important, students learn that an adequate moral theory cannot be based on consequences alone.

7. Deontology, one of the most popular moral theories, is the subject of Chapter 7. Deontologists regard duty as the basis of morality. In this chapter students learn about the different types of moral duties and their relevance to real-life issues such as suicide, self-esteem, lying, and distributive justice.

8. There are two main branches of rights ethics, the subject of Chapter 8. Natural rights ethicists claim that rights stem from our human nature; other rights ethicists say that rights are derived from duties. This chapter looks at the implications of these different theories on rights.

9. The final chapter is on virtue ethics. Almost all moral theories contain a strand of virtue ethics as well as rights ethics. Virtue ethics is sometimes regarded as the highest form of moral theory. Virtue requires not only that we do what is

right but that we *be* good people; which brings us back to Aristotle's deeply-held conviction (one also held by this author) that "the ultimate purpose in studying ethics is not as it is in other inquiries, the attainment of theoretical knowledge; we are not conducting this inquiry in order to know what virtue is, but in order to become good, else there would be no advantage in studying it."

The theories in the chapters are organized in the same order that they appear in a person's moral development—beginning with ethical relativism and ending with the theories based on universal moral principles. Because so many college students still subscribe to ethical relativism, considerable attention is given to these theories.

Each chapter, like the readings within the chapters, builds on the previous sections. The readings on morality and religion are included in their own section since the religious ethics ranges the whole gamut from ethical relativism (divine command theory) to universalist ethics (natural law theory). The section on conscience and moral development acts as a bridge between ethical relativism and theories based on universal moral principles. One of the primary purposes of this book is to help the student make the journey across this bridge.

The Critical Reading and Discussion Questions

The chapter introductions and questions provide the primary structure that weaves the topics together. Each reading in *Perspectives on Ethics* is preceded by a short introduction and a set of critical thinking questions. Discussion questions are included at the end of each reading; these questions require the student to think deeper about the arguments and concepts raised in that particular reading. The discussion questions also encourage students to relate these concepts to other readings in the book as well as to real-life moral issues in their own lives.

Chapter Applications

Each chapter ends with several case studies relating to the set of readings. The majority of case studies are based on real-life events. These case studies provide students with an opportunity to apply moral theory to real-life issues such as jealousy, deception, greed, euthanasia, hate speech on campuses, abortion and fetal rights, homelessness, child labor, political asylum, family obligations, and economic justice. Some of the case studies involve moral dilemmas that force students to defend a particular position on a controversial issue. Discussion of real-life moral dilemmas has been shown to enhance a student's ability to engage in effective moral reasoning. On the other hand, exclusive focus on dilemmas runs the danger of leaving students with the impression that there are no right and wrong answers and that morality is all relative. Therefore, other cases focus on issues that are fairly straightforward but which require introspection and reflection.

ACKNOWLEDGMENTS

I would like to thank the reviewers for their suggestions: Donna Bestock, Skyline College; David Cheney, Bridgewater State University; Lucia Palmer, University of Delaware; Robert Pring, Herkimer County Community College; and Maurine Stein, Prairie State College.

Thanks also to my editor, Ken King, for his enthusiastic support, his many helpful suggestions, and for keeping me on my toes when it came to keeping on schedule. I would also like to thank Melissa Kreischer, production editor, for her patience, cheerfulness, and efficiency, and Marty Granahan, permissions editor, for her greatly-appreciated assistance in obtaining permissions for the reading selections. I am very grateful for the support from my colleagues at Brown University, especially Dr. William Damon, professor of Moral Education, for his advice on the chapter on moral development, and Dr. Victor Caston, professor of philosophy, for his very helpful suggestions on the section on Aristotle. In addition, I would like to express my appreciation to Nanette Kelley, reference librarian at Roger Williams University Law School, for assisting me with my research, and to Dr. Mel Topf, communications professor at Roger Williams University, for his encouragement and feedback throughout the project. I would also like to thank my wonderful assistant, James Nuzum, who was always willing to go that extra mile when we had a deadline looming before us. Last, but not least, my very deepest gratitude goes to my daughter Alyssa Boss, to whom this book is dedicated, for her unflagging enthusiasm, for her willingness to carefully proof-read the earlier drafts, and for her many helpful comments.

Introduction

As a philosophical discipline, ethics is the study of the values and guidelines by which we live, as well as the justification of these values and guidelines. Ethics does not rely simply on personal opinion or the acceptance of customs and guidelines of a particular group or culture. Rather, philosophical ethics requires analysis and evaluation of these guidelines in light of universal principles. This aids the development of critical thinking skills and, thus, the ability to make better moral judgments.

There is no way to avoid making moral judgments. Every day we are confronted with situations in which we have to decide what is the correct course of action. Even inaction may constitute a decision by default. Whatever decision we make we do so for reasons. Some of these reasons are better than others. We've all heard the proverb "The road to hell is paved with good intentions." One goal of an ethics course is to help you discern which reasons are better so you can make considered moral decisions—ones you are less likely to regret later.

In addition to individual decision making, effective participation in a democracy requires that you first be able to engage in critical thinking and dialogue. Critical thinking is a process that can help you determine if a particular claim is true or, at least, more likely to be true than competing claims. By improving your critical thinking skills, you will be better prepared to make good decisions in your life and avoid being swept along by the prevailing opinion. People who are adept at critical thinking are less likely to be taken in by faulty reasoning and more likely to make satisfactory moral decisions in their own lives.

WHAT IS A MORAL THEORY?

Moral philosophers constantly ask questions such as: "What kind of life should I live?" "How can I know what is good?" "What are my obligations and rights?" "Do we have free will?" "Why should I be moral?" "What is the source of morality?" "How can I justify my moral beliefs?" "Do I have a moral obligation to non-human beings and the rest of nature?" "Are people basically good or are they basically selfish?" and "What happens when moral principles come into conflict?" Moral theories provide a coherent structure by which to analyze and answer these and other important questions.

This reader will introduce you to some important moral theories that have shaped people's behavior and analysis of moral issues throughout the world. You may ask how reading about something as abstract as moral theory can help you make a better moral decision. What do moral theories have to do with real life? A moral theory is not just a collection of abstract musings. It also concerns action, the consequences of action, and our motives and our character. In analyzing and explaining moral concepts, moral theories provide us with a justification for which actions and norms are morally right or wrong. A good moral theory, in other words, provides moral principles for guiding our behavior and shaping our character.

Even though moral theories may remain unarticulated, they shape our world view and our interpretation of experiences. For example, most U.S. adults identify morality with cultural norms and customs. The theory underlying this assumption is known as *cultural relativism*. Cultural relativism as a theory is wrought with inconsistencies and problems; it leaves no room for the concept of social reform and encourages mindless conformity to convention.

In seeking answers to questions about the meaning of life and the nature of goodness, moral philosophers go beyond conventional answers. Sometimes analysis will reveal that what at first appeared to be a coherent moral insight is nothing more than the result of cultural tradition—such as Eurocentrism or a belief that men are more rational than women.

As with scientific theories, some moral theories do a better job than others at answering these questions. It is up to us to learn how to discern which theories are best. Theories, by their very nature, also oversimplify. Sometimes theories contain fragments of truth that, when combined with other theories, can enrich our understanding of morality. In this chapter you will learn how to evaluate the merits and weaknesses of a particular moral theory.

This book divides moral theories into two broad categories: ethical relativism and universalist theories. Each category is based on a different set of assumptions about the ultimate source of morality. Ethical relativism claims that morality is created by people. Universalist theories, on the other hand, claim that morality is the same for all people and that people discover rather than create morality. Theories claiming that morality is relative tend to be weaker and less consistent. However, because so many people base their moral decisions on ethical relativism, it is important that we study these theories if only to learn how to recognize their weakness.

The construction of a moral theory may progress through several stages. A philosopher, after reflection and listening to critiques of his or her theory, may rework the theory or even abandon it altogether. One of the simplest, and the weakest, moral theories is ethical subjectivism, which claims that morality is all a matter of personal opinion. Cultural relativism, which enjoyed popularity among some scholars in the first part of this century, fell out of favor following World

War II. The strongest moral theories are those that claim that morality is universal. Interestingly, people's moral reasoning tends to evolve over the course of their lifetime from ethical subjectivism to cultural relativism to a belief in universal moral principles.

CRITICAL READING SKILLS

Like many students, you may feel overwhelmed when you first encounter philosophical writings. This reader will provide you with the critical thinking skills necessary for understanding and critically analyzing the readings. Critical reading skills provide a framework by which you may test different theories and lines of reasoning. Keep in mind that you are not approaching the readings empty-handed. You have been making moral judgments all your life. Following are some recommendations for effective critical reading.

Preparing to Read

1. *Set aside enough time.* Readings in moral philosophy form a whole, with each part building on the other. Therefore, you should allow enough time to read through each selection without interruption. Part of the task of the moral philosopher is to prod the reader into asking questions and reexamining his or her values and lifestyle. To get the most out of each reading, also plan to set aside time between readings to reflect on the arguments that are presented.

2. *Get in the right frame of mind.* The first step in critically reading moral philosophy is to take on the perspective of the philosopher. Critical reading is not passive. Rather, it requires the participation of the reader. According to educator Charles Fries, critical reading and making social judgments involve "the cultivation of a whole array of techniques [including] understanding, thinking, reflecting, imagining, judging, evaluating, analyzing and reasoning."[1]

Taking the perspective of a philosopher means first setting aside your own prejudices and preconceptions in order to be objective. Philosophers adopt as their starting point an attitude of qualified skepticism. As a philosopher you should question your own beliefs as well as the beliefs of others.

3. *Be aware of your own reactions to the readings and various theories.* Being objective requires controlling, or at least being aware of, your emotional reactions to the readings. Most of us hate to be proven wrong and will use defense mechanisms, known as resistance, to avoid having our cherished world views challenged. These defense mechanisms include anger, boredom, distractions, superficial tolerance, and avoidance. For example, you may find yourself turning on the television or radio while reading a particular selection. These types of resistance may keep you from thinking in depth and, hence, engaging in critical reading. If you are aware of these reactions, you can take steps to work through these defenses when reading a particular section.

4. *Learn how to recognize arguments.* Learning how to recognize and ana-lyze an argument is at the heart of critical reading. The majority of selections in this reader present an argument to support a particular theory or position on a moral issue. The goal of the writer is to convince you, the reader, that his or her theory or position is the correct or best one.

In order to determine if a particular argument is good, you first have to be able to identify the flow of reasoning. Reasoning proceeds from the premises to a con-clusion. The premises are propositions that offer reasons or support for a partic-ular position or conclusion. The conclusion is that proposition that is supported by the premises. The conclusion in writings from moral philosophy may be a the-ory, such as "morality is relative to culture" or a position on an issue, such as "abortion is immoral."

The ability to analyze arguments and to recognize faulty reasoning is impor-tant in the study of ethics. *Logic,* the study of correct and incorrect reasoning, provides people with the methods and skills to formulate sound moral arguments as well as to distinguish good arguments from poor arguments. If you have not had a course in logic, there are several logic books, as well as some ethics books, that explain how to recognize and break down arguments.

5. *Read the critical reading questions.* Before you start reading, look over the critical reading questions at the beginning of the selection. These questions serve as guideposts that point out the important ideas in the reading. They will also make it easier for you to answer the discussion questions at the end of each read-ing selection.

The First Reading: Identifying the Key Parts

Breaking down each selection into its essential parts will make the readings more manageable. Most writings in moral philosophy include two main parts: (1) the main argument with its conclusion and premises and (2) the explanations and clarifications of key terms and concepts used in the argument. Some readings may also include background material or examples of application of the theory. It is usually easiest to begin with the main argument because this generally forms the focal point of the reading. A summary of the main argument is often found in the first paragraph or two of the reading.

1. *Identify the conclusion.* The purpose of most philosophical writing is to support a particular position. This position is known as the *thesis statement* or *conclusion.* In critical reading, begin by identifying the conclusion of the main argument. The conclusion is often stated at the beginning of the writing and then restated again at the end. If you are having trouble identifying the conclusion or thesis, ask yourself, "What is the main purpose of the argument? What is the writer trying to prove? What position is the writer trying to get me, the reader, to accept?"

Sometimes arguments contain terms known as *conclusion indicators*. Conclusion indicators include terms such as *therefore, thus, hence, it follows that, for this reason,* and *consequently,* which can help you identify the conclusion. For example, in Book One of Aristotle's *Nichomachean Ethics,* the thesis statement or conclusion appears in the second sentence: "We may therefore assent to the view which has been expressed that 'the good' is 'that at which all things aim.'"

In critical reading it is usually helpful to underline or highlight the conclusion. Even philosophers sometimes stray from their original argument! If the conclusion is clearly marked, you, as a critical reader, will be less likely to be thrown off by any distractions.

2. *Identify the premises.* Premises in moral arguments include both (a) descriptive statements about facts and (b) prescriptive statements about what ought to be. Ethics goes beyond science and observation. We cannot go directly from a descriptive statement about how things are to a prescriptive statement about how things ought to be. Instead, moral judgments and values—such as "do not lie," "be fair," and "do no harm"—need to be brought into the picture when making decisions about the right course of action. Definitions of key terms may also appear in premises. In a good argument, the writer tries to use only premises that are uncontroversial and readily accepted by most rational people. This is because if one of the premises is factually wrong or unacceptable to a reader, the conclusion itself may also be untrue or unacceptable.

Ethical arguments do not stand on their own but are grounded in other philosophical assumptions about matters such as the role of humans in the universe, the existence of free will, and the nature of moral knowledge. If you are not sure what the argument's premises are, ask yourself questions such as "What assumptions does the writer make regarding human nature and the place of humans in the world?" "What assumptions does the writer make about the nature of society?" "What facts or moral principles does the writer use to support his or her position?" If you are having trouble identifying the premises, try looking for premise indicators. Words such as *because, since,* and *for* may signal the presence of a premise. However, as with conclusion indicators, not all premises are conveniently preceded by a premise indicator.

Aristotle offers a premise for his conclusion in the very first sentence of his *Nichomachean Ethics:* "It is thought that every activity, artistic or scientific, in fact every deliberate action or pursuit, has for its object the attainment of some good." This premise is based on Aristotle's observation about human nature that humans engage in activities in a purposeful way. In critical reading, however, you should never simply accept a premise without first assessing whether it is true. For example, is Aristotle's observation or assumption that all human behavior is purposeful correct? Not all Eastern philosophers agree with this interpretation of human activity.

Bracket or mark each of the premises. If you have any questions about a premise, put a question mark beside it so you can go back later and examine it more closely. Sometimes a particular premise may be followed by a long explanation of the premise. This may clear up some of your initial doubts about the premise. A premise may also appear again later in the argument. You may want to write a quick summary of each premise in the margin of the page so you can keep track of them.

Some philosophers, such as Aristotle, may digress during the course of the argument to address objections and counterarguments. This is in part because the *Nichomachean Ethics,* like some of the other writings in this book, were probably lecture notes and, therefore, more abbreviated than a polished literary writing. This is not to say that the argument is not as good as others; it just means that it involves a more open-ended approach with give-and-take discussion.

Premises that the writer considers to be obvious are sometimes unstated. In critical reading it is important that you learn how to read between the lines. Although some of the unstated assumptions or premises may be relatively innocuous, others—particularly those concerning human nature—tend to be based on cultural and religious biases rather than empirical data. If there are any unstated assumptions, you should make note of them as well.

3. *Identify the key terms and their definitions.* Constructing sound moral judgments involves clearly defining and explaining the key terms. Terms such as *person, happiness, good, rational,* and *right* are notoriously ambiguous with different shades of meaning to different people. For this reason it is important that philosophers clarify how they are using these terms, and they must use these terms in a consistent manner throughout their argument. In critical reading, ask yourself if the key terms in the argument have been clearly defined.

In the reading from the *Nichomachean Ethics,* Aristotle goes to considerable lengths to define the term *good.* He begins by using the generally accepted definition that *good* is "happiness." However, this leaves him having to define the term *happiness,* which he does in his usual skillful manner. Indeed, simply being able to clarify these terms is often a notable achievement in itself!

The Second Reading: Critical Analysis

Once you have identified the various parts of the reading, you are ready to subject it to critical analysis. In going back over the reading, ask yourself the following questions:

1. *Are the key terms and concepts clearly defined?* Are definitions omitted, or are they too vague to be useful? Are you satisfied with the definitions used? For instance, are you satisfied with Aristotle's definitions of *good* and *happiness?* Are the key terms used in a consistent manner throughout the reading? In the Platonic dialogue *Euthyphro,* for example, Euthyphro keeps changing the meaning of the term *impiety* during the course of his argument. Socrates, being the astute philosopher he is, challenges Euthyphro on this point by asking him to clarify the definition of this key term.

2. *Are the premises acceptable?* An argument may be logically flawless. However, some of its premises may be based on incorrect data. Many people blend fact and opinion. It is important to distinguish between the two. Can the descriptive premises be supported? In discussions of moral issues, writers often back up their conclusions with empirical claims such as "capital punishment acts as a deterrent to future crime" or "same-sex marriages will weaken the structure of the traditional family." When you see statements such as these, do not simply assume that the writer has done his or her research. Remember, as a philosopher you are adopting the position of a skeptic. Ask yourself if the writers back up the statement with facts.

For example, Ayn Rand, in her theory of rational egoism, claims that productive work makes people happy. The premise is critical to her whole argument. However, is the claim empirically correct? Does she cite any studies to back up her claim, or is this premise simply based on her personal opinion? Aristotle, on the other hand, claims that virtuous people are the happiest. Can his claim be verified? Check it out. In fact, if you look at the studies on happiness, you will find that Aristotle's claim has more empirical support than does Rand's.

Also look at the prescriptive premises. Are the moral principles and sentiments used in the premises acceptable? Although people may disagree on the application of general moral principles, the acceptance of the basic principles themselves is often uncontroversial—even across cultures. More often, the problem with a theory is that some important moral principles have been omitted or not taken seriously. For example, utilitarians believe that morality can be reduced to one principle: "Actions are right in proportion as they tend to promote happiness, wrong as they tend to produce the reverse of happiness."[2] As a result utilitarians have been accused of failing to give sufficient weight to the principle of justice and to issues of personal autonomy.

3. *Do the premises support the conclusion?* The premises form the foundation of the argument. In a good argument, the premises must be strong enough to support the conclusion. A well-constructed argument, like a well-built house, must be able to withstand challenges. If the premises are weak, the whole argument can collapse like the proverbial house built on sand.

If any of the key premises are based on incorrect data or unacceptable prescriptive statements, the whole argument is weak, no matter how compelling the conclusion may seem. If any of the premises are false, the conclusion may also be false.

An argument can also be weak because it contains fallacies. When an argument is psychologically or emotionally persuasive but logically incorrect, it contains what logicians call an *informal fallacy.* Examples of informal fallacies include:

- Attacking the character of people who disagree with one's position
- Using a factual statement from someone who is not an authority in the field under discussion

- Appealing to popular opinion
- Making generalizations based on insufficient or atypical cases
- Changing the topic to a related subject
- Claiming something is moral simply because it is natural

People are most likely to resort to fallacies when they are uncertain of their position. Being able to recognize fallacies will make you less likely to fall for them.

The conclusion must be based on the premises. Sometimes the conclusion may say too much. It may make assertions that go far beyond anything stated in the argument. This does not mean that the conclusion is false, just that it is unsubstantiated. When a conclusion is not properly supported by the premises, you should reject the argument.

4. *Is the argument consistent?* Consistency is the hallmark of reason. Consistency requires that our reasons be universal unless there is a compelling difference between situations that renders the reason inapplicable. The notion of universality is captured in the concept of ought. We *ought* not to kill unless there is a compelling reason to do so. Self-defense is an instance of a situation where the rule "do not kill" may be inapplicable. The personal pleasure someone may get from killing, on the other hand, is not a compelling reason for overriding the command "Do not kill."

In deciding whether an argument is consistent, ask yourself if the writer applies the principles put forth in the theory to everyone. The notion of impartiality is found in almost all moral systems. Impartiality requires that everyone's interest count the same and that everyone be treated with equal respect. Impartiality rules out giving preferential treatment to or discriminating against a certain group. If a philosopher argues that different groups should receive different treatment, then he or she must provide justification for deviating from the principle of impartiality. For example, such a justification is important in discussions involving the moral status and rights of non-human animals, unborn humans, and the environment. If the writer cannot provide good reasons for differential treatment, then the requirement of impartiality should not be set aside.

Sometimes the premises themselves contain contradictions. For example, Jean-Jacques Rousseau claims that virtue is one thing for men and another for women. Mary Wollstonecraft, in her criticism of Rousseau's moral theory, accuses him of being inconsistent in his definition of virtue. Some ethical relativists—although claiming that moral principles are relative and differ from person to person—may also try to sneak in universal moral principles, such as tolerance, through the back door. When writers claim both that there *are* universal moral principles and that there are *no* universal moral principles, they are being logically inconsistent. If the theory contains inconsistencies and internal contradictions, it should be rejected.

5. *What are the implications of the theory, and are these implications acceptable?* Some moral theories have unstated implications that most people find unacceptable. According to emotivists, for example, moral statements are neither

true nor false but merely expressions of feelings. One of the implications of this theory is that the actions of the Nazis during World War II were neither right nor wrong but merely morally neutral expressions of their feelings.

Cultural relativists, who equate morality with cultural norms, also have a problem with horrific events such as the Holocaust. Daniel Goldhagen examines some of these implications in the selection from *Hitler's Willing Executioners*. Because the implications of these two theories are unacceptable to most rational people, both theories fell out of favor with scholars after World War II.

6. *Does the theory offer practical guidance for living the good life?* Moral theories do not exist apart from real life. A good theory offers practical sugges- tions for how we should act and live a better life. According to Aristotle, for instance, the ultimate purpose of studying ethics is in order to become good.

Ask yourself if the theory provides practical guidelines for making everyday moral decisions. Also ask whether these guidelines are within human capability. Sometimes the guidelines, such as universal love, are too vague and abstract to be useful in actual application. Just as a house without windows or doors may be structurally sound, some moral theories, although logically consistent, offer little guidance for living our lives. Jeremy Bentham's utilitarianism and Confucian ethics, in contrast, are concerned primarily with offering guidelines for making practical moral decisions.

7. *Does the theory work in unusual situations or when there is a conflict between moral values?* A theory should also provide guidelines for resolving a conflict between moral values and help in discussing controversial moral issues. Many theories are fine for dealing with relatively straightforward situations. However, their weakness becomes evident when we try to apply them to unusual situations or to a moral dilemma.

For example, Immanuel Kant, in his insistence that moral principles never come into conflict, has been criticized for not taking sufficient account of situa- tions where lying, to use an example, may be the only way to save a life. Utilitar- ianism has also been criticized for allowing the execution of an innocent person if it will restore social harmony. Whether these criticisms are justified is up to you, as a critical reader, to decide.

8. *Does the theory pass the test of publicity?* The test of publicity requires that rational persons, and especially those who will be affected by the theory or position, agree with it. Confucius refers to this as the *principle of reciprocity:* "Do not do unto others as you would not want others to do unto you." To share the perspective of those affected by a theory, we must use our imagination to put ourselves in their place. For example, in deciding the morality of same-sex mar- riage, one of the questions you should ask yourself is which position you would find most acceptable from a moral point of view if you were gay or lesbian. The Golden Rule, which is basic to so many moral positions, is an example of a moral principle that passes the test of publicity. Slavery, as a moral position, would not pass the test of publicity.

9. *Does the theory fit with our most fundamental moral beliefs and intuitions?* This last question involves some soul-searching. A theory's description of morality and human nature should be consistent with our human experience. A good theory also does not inadvertently permit actions that we would find repugnant. If a theory is at variance with our most fundamental moral beliefs and intuitions, we have to either reject the theory or rethink the validity of our own beliefs.

10. *Is it a good theory or argument?* Go back over your answers to the previous nine questions. Some of the theories may have elements that are stronger than others. If this is the case, examine the theory to see if it has parts that can be salvaged. Ask yourself if the argument can still stand on its own if you weed out the weak, contradictory, and fallacious premises. In reworking a theory, also make sure that it is still consistent. If the theory cannot be salvaged or reworked, then it should be rejected.

Following these recommendations will help you develop your critical reading skills, which in turn will help you better understand and enjoy the readings in this book. In addition, being able to critically read moral theories will enable you to make better moral decisions in your own life.

NOTES

[1] Charles C. Fries, *Linguistics and Reading* (New York: Holt, Rinehart & Winston, 1962), p. 118.

[2] John Stuart Mill, "Utilitarianism" in Mary Warnock, ed., *Utilitarianism and On Liberty* (Cleveland: Meridian Books, 1962), p. 257.

CHAPTER ONE

The Study of Ethics

The ultimate purpose in studying ethics is not as it is in other inquiries, the attainment of theoretical knowledge; we are not conducting this inquiry in order to know what virtue is, but in order to become good, else there would be no advantage in studying it.

Aristotle, *Nicomachean Ethics*

Ethics includes the study of the values and guidelines by which we live, as well as the justification of these guidelines. The U.S. system of higher education was founded with ethics education as one of its primary goals. At the time our country was founded, ethics education was viewed as the key to the progress of humanity.

Ethics education, however, is no longer a priority in college. The tremendous success of science and technology in the late nineteenth and early twentieth centuries led to a declining concern about teaching broader questions of human values and morality. In response, modern academic ethicists have tended more and more to limit ethics education to the purely theoretical. In popular culture, emotivism and relativist theories of morality gradually replaced theories that were grounded in a belief in universal moral values.

Recently some educators have started questioning the wisdom of removing ethics education from the realm of everyday experience. Increased crime and racism among young people and a decline in altruistic behavior during the college years have become sources of concern and even alarm on many campuses.[1] In trying to develop more effective ethics courses, college teachers are increasingly looking for direction from the traditional philosophers, such as Aristotle, as well as from Eastern philosophies and feminist ethics.

The theme of ethics education is found in many writings on moral philosophy. The selection of readings in this section is only a small sampling of the different approaches to ethics education. The readings were chosen to provide a well-rounded picture of some of the diverse approaches to ethics education.

In the first selection, "The Disparity Between Intellect and Character," Harvard educator and psychiatrist Robert Coles highlights some of the deficiencies in our current approach to ethics education on college campuses.

The second reading in this section is "The Natural Goodness of Humans" from the *Works of Mencius*. Confucian philosopher Mencius believes that humans are innately good. Moral education, Mencius argues, entails nurturing our natural goodness.

In the next article, "Where Have All the Good Deeds Gone?" Christina Hoff Sommers concludes that contemporary ethics courses focus too much on public policy and too little on individual morality. The fourth selection is from Sheila Mullett's essay, "Shifting Perspective: A New Approach to Ethics." Many feminist ethicists reject what they call "male" abstract reasoning as the primary way of experiencing moral value in the world. Mullett argues that moral character can only fully develop through actual experience.

The final selection in this chapter offers another perspective on ethics education. Non-Western moral philosophies, such as Buddhism, are now part of many college ethics courses. In his article "Buddhist Tradition and Modernity," Kōshō Mizutani argues that Buddhist ethics are relevant to modern ethics education. Like many of the ancient Greek philosophers, most Eastern philosophers view ethics first and foremost as a way of life—an active engagement in the pursuit of the good life. Buddhist ethics has provided inspiration and practical guidance for several modern reform movements, including those led by Gandhi and Martin Luther King, Jr.

NOTES

[1] Alexander W. Astin, *What Matters in College?* (San Francisco: Jossey-Bass, 1993).

Robert Coles

The Disparity Between Intellect and Character

Robert Coles is a professor of psychiatry and medical humanities at Harvard University. In 1973, Coles won a Pulitzer Prize for his book *Children of Crisis*. In this reading, Coles reflects on the shift in the mission of colleges over the last century from character development to intellectual growth. He then asks how we as members of the college community can bridge the growing gap between character and intellect.

CRITICAL THINKING QUESTIONS

1. Why does Coles think colleges are paying less attention to character or moral development than they did a century ago?
2. What does Coles mean by "character"? How is character reflected in students' attitudes and actions?
3. What is the distinction between knowing what is good and becoming a good person?

Over 150 years ago, Ralph Waldo Emerson gave a lecture at Harvard University, which he ended with the terse assertion: "Character is higher than intellect." Even then, this prominent man of letters was worried (as many other writers and thinkers of succeeding generations would be) about the limits of knowledge and the nature of a college's mission. The intellect can grow and grow, he knew, in a person who is smug, ungenerous, even cruel. Institutions originally founded to teach their students how to become good and decent, as well as broadly and deeply literate, may abandon the first mission to concentrate on a driven, narrow book learning—a course of study in no way intent on making a connection between ideas and theories on one hand and, on the other, our lives as we actually live them.

Students have their own way of realizing and trying to come to terms with the split that Emerson addressed. A few years ago, a sophomore student of mine came to see me in great anguish. She had arrived at Harvard from a Midwestern, working-class background. She was trying hard to work her way through college, and, in doing so, cleaned the rooms of some of her fellow students. Again and again, she encountered classmates who apparently had forgotten the meaning of

"The Disparity Between Intellect and Character," *The Chronicle of Higher Education*, September 22, 1995, p. A68.

please, of *thank you*—no matter how high their Scholastic Assessment Test scores
—students who did not hesitate to be rude, even crude toward her.

One day she was not so subtly propositioned by a young man she knew to be
a very bright, successful pre-med student and already an accomplished journalist.
This was not the first time he had made such an overture, but now she had
reached a breaking point. She had quit her job and was preparing to quit college
in what she called "fancy, phony Cambridge."

The student had been part of a seminar I teach, which links Raymond Carver's
fiction and poetry with Edward Hopper's paintings and drawings—the thematic
convergence of literary and artistic sensibility in exploring American loneliness,
both its social and its personal aspects. As she expressed her anxiety and anger to
me, she soon was sobbing hard. After her sobs quieted, we began to remember
the old days of that class. But she had some weightier matters on her mind and
began to give me a detailed, sardonic account of college life, as viewed by someone vulnerable and hardpressed by it. At one point, she observed of the student
who had propositioned her: "That guy gets all A's. He tells people he's in Group
I [the top academic category]. I've taken two moral-reasoning courses with him,
and I'm sure he's gotten A's in both of them—and look at how he behaves with
me, and I'm sure with others."

She stopped for a moment to let me take that in. I happened to know the
young man and could only acknowledge the irony of his behavior, even as I
wasn't totally surprised by what she'd experienced. But I was at a loss to know
what to say to her. A philosophy major, with a strong interest in literature, she
had taken a course on the Holocaust and described for me the ironies she also
saw in that tragedy—mass murder of unparalleled historical proportion in a
nation hitherto known as one of the most civilized in the world, with a citizenry
as well educated as that of any country at the time.

Drawing on her education, the student put before me names such as Martin
Heidegger, Carl Jung, Paul De Man, Ezra Pound—brilliant and accomplished
men (a philosopher, a psychoanalyst, a literary critic, a poet) who nonetheless
had linked themselves with the hate that was Nazism and Fascism during the
1930s. She reminded me of the willingness of the leaders of German and Italian
universities to embrace Nazi and Fascist ideas, of the countless doctors and
lawyers and judges and journalists and schoolteachers, and, yes, even members of
the clergy—who were able to accommodate themselves to murderous thugs
because the thugs had political power. She pointedly mentioned, too, the Soviet
Gulag, that expanse of prisons to which millions of honorable people were sent
by Stalin and his brutish accomplices—prisons commonly staffed by psychiatrists
quite eager to label those victims of a vicious totalitarian state with an assortment
of psychiatric names, then shoot them up with drugs meant to reduce them to
zombies.

I tried hard, toward the end of a conversation that lasted almost two hours, to
salvage something for her, for myself, and, not least, for a university that I much
respect, even as I know its failings. I suggested that if she had learned what she
had just shared with me at Harvard—why, *that* was itself a valuable education
acquired. She smiled, gave me credit for a "nice try," but remained unconvinced.

Then she put this tough, pointed, unnerving question to me: "I've been taking all these philosophy courses, and we talk about what's true, what's important, what's *good*. Well, how do you teach people to *be* good?" And she added: "What's the point of *knowing* good, if you don't keep trying to *become* a good person?"

I suddenly found myself on the defensive, although all along I had been sympathetic to her, to the indignation she had been directing toward some of her fellow students, and to her critical examination of the limits of abstract knowledge. Schools are schools, colleges are colleges, I averred, a complaisant and smug accommodation in my voice. Thereby I meant to say that our schools and colleges these days don't take major responsibility for the moral values of their students, but, rather, assume that their students acquire those values at home. I topped off my surrender to the *status quo* with a shrug of my shoulders, to which she responded with an unspoken but barely concealed anger. This she expressed through a knowing look that announced that she'd taken the full moral measure of me.

Suddenly, she was on her feet preparing to leave. I realized that I'd stumbled badly. I wanted to pursue the discussion, applaud her for taking on a large subject in a forthright, incisive manner, and tell her she was right in understanding that moral reasoning is not to be equated with moral conduct. I wanted, really, to explain my shrug—point out that there is only so much that any of us can do to affect others' behavior, that institutional life has its own momentum. But she had no interest in that kind of self-justification—as she let me know in an unforgettable aside as she was departing my office: "I wonder whether Emerson was just being 'smart' in that lecture he gave here. I wonder if he ever had any ideas about what to *do* about what was worrying him—or did he think he'd done enough because he'd spelled the problem out to those Harvard professors?"

She was demonstrating that she understood two levels of irony: One was that the study of philosophy—even moral philosophy or moral reasoning—doesn't necessarily prompt in either the teacher or the student a determination to act in accordance with moral principles. And, further, a discussion of that very irony can prove equally sterile—again carrying no apparent consequences as far as one's everyday actions go.

When that student left my office (she would soon leave Harvard for good), I was exhausted and saddened—and brought up short. All too often those of us who read books or teach don't think to pose for ourselves the kind of ironic dilemma she had posed to me. How might we teachers encourage our students (encourage *ourselves*) to take that big step from thought to action, from moral analysis to fulfilled moral commitments? Rather obviously, community service offers us all a chance to put our money where our mouths are; and, of course, such service can enrich our understanding of the disciplines we study. A reading of *Invisible Man* (literature), *Tally's Corners* (sociology and anthropology), or *Childhood and Society* (psychology and psychoanalysis) takes on new meaning after some time spent in a ghetto school or a clinic. By the same token, such books can prompt us to think pragmatically about, say, how the wisdom that Ralph Ellison worked into his fiction might shape the way we get along with the children we're tutoring—affect our attitudes toward them, the things we say and do with them.

Yet I wonder whether classroom discussion, *per se,* can't also be of help, the skepticism of my student notwithstanding. She had pushed me hard, and I started referring again and again in my classes on moral introspection to what she had observed and learned, and my students more than got the message. Her moral righteousness, her shrewd eye and ear for hypocrisy hovered over us, made us uneasy, goaded us.

She challenged us to prove that what we think intellectually can be connected to our daily deeds. For some of us, the connection was established through community service. But that is not the only possible way. I asked students to write papers that told of particular efforts to honor through action the high thoughts we were discussing. Thus goaded to a certain self-consciousness, I suppose, students made various efforts. I felt that the best of them were small victories, brief epiphanies that might otherwise have been overlooked, but had great significance for the students in question.

"I thanked someone serving me food in the college cafeteria, and then we got to talking, the first time," one student wrote. For her, this was a decisive break with her former indifference to others she abstractly regarded as "the people who work on the serving line." She felt that she had learned something about another's life and had tried to show respect for that life.

The student who challenged me with her angry, melancholy story had pushed me to teach differently. Now, I make an explicit issue of the more than occasional disparity between thinking and doing, and I ask my students to consider how we all might bridge that disparity. To be sure, the task of connecting intellect to character is daunting, as Emerson and others well knew. And any of us can lapse into cynicism, turn the moral challenge of a seminar into yet another moment of opportunism: I'll get an A this time, by writing a paper cannily extolling myself as a doer of this or that "good deed"!

Still, I know that college administrators and faculty members everywhere are struggling with the same issues that I was faced with, and I can testify that many students will respond seriously, in at least small ways, if we make clear that we really believe that the link between moral reasoning and action is important to us. My experience has given me at least a measure of hope that moral reasoning and reflection can somehow be integrated into students'—and teachers'—lives as they actually live them.

DISCUSSION QUESTIONS

1. Do you agree with Coles that our colleges do not place enough emphasis on character development? Illustrate your answer with examples from your own college experience.
2. How would you have responded to Coles's student had you been in his shoes? Do you think her dissatisfaction with the moral quality of college life is justified? Explain why.
3. What sort of goals are appropriate for an ethics class?
4. Would Coles agree with the quote by Aristotle at the beginning of this chapter that states that the only advantage in studying ethics is to become good people? Do you

agree with Aristotle that this should be the primary purpose of ethics education? Support your answer.

5. Do colleges have a moral obligation to provide ethics education? If so, discuss ways in which you could change the college experience to encourage the development of virtue in students as well as in the rest of the college community.

The Natural Goodness of Humans

Mencius (390–305 B.C.E) is one of the foremost Confucian philosophers. Mencius lived at the same time as the Greek philosopher Plato, although, as far as we know, the two never heard of each other. Mencius was a traveling scholar who devoted himself primarily to the instruction of princes and rulers of China.

In the following selection from the *Works of Mencius,* Mencius attempts to explain the origin and nature of human goodness. True goodness is intimately connected to being true to oneself. His doctrine of the original goodness of human nature had many detractors who believed that humans are basically evil and have to be shaped into being good.

CRITICAL THINKING QUESTIONS

1. What is Mencius's view of human nature? Are people innately good or innately self-interested? What evidence does Mencius use to support this view?
2. What, according to Mencius, is the basis of true morality?
3. Why do people feel distress at the sight of another person's suffering?
4. What, according to Mencius, are the four innate feelings? How are these related to morality? Do we have a moral obligation to develop these four innate feelings?
5. What is the meaning of Mencius's analogy between a benevolent person and an archer? Is learning how to be moral a skill similar to that of being a good archer?
6. How does Mencius explain the presence of evil in the world?
7. Why is self-examination an integral part of our moral education and moral development according to Mencius?

Book II, Part I

VI. 1. Mencius said, "All men have a mind which cannot bear *to see the sufferings of* others.

"The Natural Goodness of Humans," from the *Works of Mencius,* in *The Chinese Classics,* Part I, translated by James Legge (New York: John B. Alden, Publishers, 1891).

2. "The ancient kings had this commiserating mind, and they, as a matter of course, had likewise a commiserating government. When with a commiserating mind was practised a commiserating government, the government of the empire was *as easy a matter* as the making anything go round in the palm.

3. "When I say that all men have a mind which cannot bear *to see the sufferings of* others, my meaning may be illustrated thus:—even now-a-days, if men suddenly see a child about to fall into a well, they will without exception experience a feeling of alarm and distress. *They will feel so,* not as a ground on which they may gain the favour of the child's parents, nor as a ground on which they may seek the praise of their neighbours and friends, nor from a dislike to the reputation of *having been unmoved by* such a thing.

4. "From this case we may perceive that the feeling of commiseration is essential to man, that the feeling of shame and dislike is essential to man, that the feeling of modesty and complaisance is essential to man, and that the feeling of approving and disapproving is essential to man.

5. "The feeling of commiseration is the principle of benevolence. The feeling of shame and dislike is the principle of righteousness. The feeling of modesty and complaisance is the principle of propriety. The feeling of approving and disapproving is the principle of knowledge.

6. "Men have these four principles just as they have their four limbs. When men, having these four principles, yet say of themselves that they cannot *develope them,* they play the thief with themselves, and he who says of his prince that he cannot *develope them,* plays the thief with his prince.

7. "Since all men have these four principles in themselves, let them know to give them all their development and completion, and the issue will be like that of fire which has begun to burn, or that of a spring which has begun to find vent. Let them have their complete development, and they will suffice to love and protect all within the four seas. Let them be denied that development, and they will not suffice for a man to serve his parents with." . . .

VII. . . . 3. "From the want of benevolence and the want of wisdom will ensue the entire absence of propriety and righteousness;—he who is in such a case must be the servant of other men. To be the servant of men and yet ashamed of such servitude, is like a bow-maker's being ashamed to make bows, or an arrow-maker's being ashamed to make arrows.

4. "If he be ashamed of his case, his best course is to practice benevolence.

5. "The man who would be benevolent is like the archer. The archer adjusts himself and then shoots. If he misses, he does not murmur against those who surpass himself. He simply turns round and seeks *the cause of his failure* in himself." . . .

Book VI, Part I

VI. 1. The disciple Kung-too said, "The philosopher Kaou says, '*Man's* nature is neither good nor bad.'

2. "Some say, '*Man's* nature may be made to practise good, and it may be made to practise evil, and accordingly, under Wan and Woo, the people loved what was good, *while* under Yew and Le, they loved what was cruel.'

3. "Some say, 'The nature of some is good, and the nature of others is bad. Hence it was that under such a sovereign as Yaou there yet appeared Swang; that with such a father as Koo-sow there yet appeared Shun; and that with Chow for their sovereign, and the son of their elder brother besides, there were found K'e, the viscount of Wei, and the prince Pe-kan.

4. "And now you say, 'The nature is good.' Then are all those wrong?"

5. Mencius said, "From the feelings proper to it, it is constituted for the practice of what is good. This is what I mean in saying that *the nature* is good.

6. "If men do what is not good, the blame cannot be imputed to their natural powers."

7. "The feeling of commiseration belongs to all men; so does that of shame and dislike; and that of reverence and respect; and that of approving and disapproving. The feeling of commiseration *implies the principle* of benevolence; that of shame and dislike, the principle of righteousness; that of reverence and respect, the principle of propriety; and that of approving and disapproving, the principle of knowledge. Benevolence, righteousness, propriety, and knowledge, are not infused into us from without. We are certainly furnished with them. *And a different view* is simply from want of reflection. Hence it is said, 'Seek and you will find them. Neglect and you will lose them.' Men differ from one another in regard to them;—some as much again as others, some five times as much, and some to an incalculable amount:—it is because they cannot carry out fully their *natural* powers.

8. "It is said in the Book of Poetry,

'Heaven in producing mankind,
Gave them their various faculties and relations with their specific laws.
These are the invariable rules of nature for all to hold,
And all love this admirable virtue.'

Confucius said, 'The maker of this ode knew indeed the principle *of our nature!*' We may thus see that every faculty and relation must have its law, and since there are invariable rules for all to hold, they consequently love this admirable virtue.'

VII. 1. Mencius said, "In good years the children of the people are most of them good, while in bad years the most of them abandon themselves to evil. It is not owing to their natural powers conferred by Heaven that they are thus different. The abandonment is owing to the circumstances through which they allow their minds to be ensnared and drowned *in evil*.

2. "There now is barley.—Let it be sown and covered up; the ground being the same, and the time of sowing likewise the same; it grows rapidly up, and when the full time is come, it is all found to be ripe. Although there may be inequalities *of produce*, that is owing to the *difference of the* soil, as rich or poor, to the *unequal* nourishment afforded by the rains and dews, and to the different ways in which man has performed his business *in reference to it*. . . .

Book VII, Part I

IV. 1. Mencius said, "All things are already complete in us.

2. "There is no greater delight than to be conscious of sincerity on self-examination.

3. "If one acts with a vigorous effort at the law of reciprocity, when he seeks for *the realization of* perfect virtue, nothing can be closer than his approximation to it."

V. 1. Mencius said, "To act without understanding, and to do so habitually without examination, pursuing the proper path all the life without knowing its nature;—this is the way of multitudes."

VI. Mencius said, "A man may not be without shame. When one is ashamed of having been without shame, he will *afterwards* not have *occasion for* shame."

VII. 1. Mencius said, "The sense of shame is to a man of great importance.

2. "Those who form contrivances and versatile schemes distinguished for their artfulness, do not allow their sense of shame to come into action.

3. "When one differs from other men in not having this sense of shame, what will he have in common with them?"

DISCUSSION QUESTIONS

1. Do you agree with Mencius that human nature is originally virtuous? What evidence does he offer to support his position? Are you satisfied with his argument?
2. Discuss whether, as well as how, the teachings of Mencius are relevant to moral education in the contemporary Western world. How might Robert Coles respond to Mencius's ideas on human nature and moral philosophy?
3. In our "If it feels good, do it" culture, guilt—what Mencius refers to as shame—is seen as an undesirable feeling. However, Mencius believes that shame is important. Do you agree? In what ways does guilt motivate you to correct past wrongs? If guilt does motivate us to be more moral, should the cultivation of appropriate guilt be part of a college ethics curriculum? Use specific examples to illustrate your answer.

4. Is the obligation to develop the "four innate feelings" part of the goal of most ethics curriculums? Is this obligation an appropriate goal for a college ethics class? How might this goal be reflected in an ethics curriculum?

5. Discuss whether Mencius's explanation of the presence of evil in the world is consistent with his fundamental premise that human nature is originally virtuous. How is the presence of evil in the world reflected on the college campus? What might Mencius suggest as a means of educating students to be more morally sensitive?

6. What role, according to Mencius, does our upbringing and education play in our moral development? Discuss the implications of Mencius's teachings for ethics education for children.

7. What does Mencius mean when he says "All things are already complete in us"? What, according to Mencius, is the connection between morality, self-examination, and integrity? Do you agree that self-examination is essential to moral development? Support your answer.

8. How might Mencius answer the question "Why be moral?" Are you satisfied with his answer? How would you answer the question?

Christina Hoff Sommers

Where Have All the Good Deeds Gone?

Christina Hoff Sommers (b. 1950) teaches philosophy at Clark University in Massachusetts. In the following selection she expresses alarm at the growing lack of concern for individual morality. She suggests that the fault is due, in part, to the current focus of moral education on public policy rather than private ethics.

CRITICAL THINKING QUESTIONS

1. What is Miller House? Who lives there?
2. Do the residents of Miller House, in Sommers's view, live a good life? If not, why not?
3. What, according to Sommers, makes someone a virtuous person?
4. How, according to Sommers, has the concept of volunteerism in our culture changed over the past years? What argument does Sommers use to support her position?
5. To what does Sommers attribute the decline in private morality?
6. What does Sommers mean by a "moral amateur"?
7. In what ways does Sommers find the current ethics curriculum inadequate?

Miller House is an old-age home in a well-to-do Boston suburb. As in many other homes for the elderly, conditions are grim. No matter how cold it is outside, old men sit downcast on the front porch. Sometimes one of them wanders over to a nearby fast-food restaurant where he will sit alone at a table for hours. One resident, Mr. Kelly, recently slipped out the front door and did not stop walking for three days. The police picked him up forty miles away, dazed from lack of sleep and still clutching his cardboard suitcase, and brought him back.

Mr. Richards, age eighty-four, sleeps more than twenty hours a day, waking only for meals and cigarette breaks. He hates Miller House. "I don't like fish cakes," he says. "We have them all the time and the director makes me eat them."

"Where Have All the Good Deeds Gone?" *Hastings Center Report,* August 1982, pp. 13–14.

For the past seven years Miss Pickins, who is ninety-one, has lived in Miller House. Last year her doctor ordered her to stop smoking. This upset a daily routine she had enjoyed—coffee and cigarettes in the lounge downstairs with the men. She became depressed, lost interest in leaving her room, and now spends most of her time there alone. The woman who runs the home makes Miss Pickins keep the sound of her radio so low that she cannot hear it. Once she did not finish her dessert, and as punishment she no longer gets any. These little injustices keep her in a constant rage.

Simone de Beauvoir has said, "By the fate it allots to its members who can no longer work, society gives itself away." Who is to blame for the fate that has been allotted to Miss Pickins, Mr. Kelly, and Mr. Richards? It is fashionable to condemn civic agencies and the government. But government agencies are responsible for enforcing standards of cleanliness and safety: should we also require that they meet standards of good-heartedness and neighborliness? What the Miller residents need is kindly attention: someone to talk to them, to take an interest in them, and to mitigate the little cruelties that seem always to tempt those in charge of helpless people. Should the state pay a social worker twenty dollars to make sure Miss Pickins gets her dessert? A few concerned neighbors could transform the residence into a much happier place. But that is not going to happen.

One reason, no doubt, is that a lot of people are uncaring and irresponsible, but far more important is the attitude of the responsible private individuals who no longer see themselves as the seat of moral initiative. Good deeds have been given over to experts: the acts that constitute the social morality of our time are being performed by paid professionals in large public agencies. Helping the needy, the sick, and the aged has become an operation whose scale and character leave little room for the virtuous private person. Our ancestors in their idiosyncratic charitable endeavors look like moral amateurs.

Professionals who do use volunteers see them as incipient professionals. The assistant manager of the Greater Boston Red Cross observes: "Volunteers are there but you have to offer them something . . . career benefits and resumé experience." The Children's Museum of Boston offers the potential volunteer entries for a curriculum vitae—a volunteer fund raiser is called a "corporate membership marketing specialist"; someone who helps paint walls, a "maintenance assistant." Since professionals look down on amateurs, executives of social institutions feel forced to counter the stigma of amateurism by conferring on the volunteer a quasi-professional status. The loss of confidence in private moral initiative is part of a general derogation of amateurism, a phenomenon that Christopher Lasch has called the "atrophy of competence."

The notion that it is unrealistic to depend on the private generosity of volunteers is cynical and false. Volunteer programs are doing very well in such areas as the prevention of suicide, care for battered women, food distribution to the needy (Meals on Wheels), and care for lonely children (Big Brother, Big Sister). The Little Brothers is an obscure private organization in Boston that arranges for volunteers to visit and cheer up lonely old people. The visitors provide them with so-called nonessential services such as regular weekly visits, flowers, and gifts on birthdays, and occasional weekend trips to Cape Cod. The program is small, but catching on; it is a paradigm of what is needed and what can only be done by direct moral initiative. Unfortunately, not many Americans are active in such programs, preferring to believe that institutional solutions suffice.

Is it excessive to say that our society has become more morally passive? After all, the past few decades have seen the growth of liberal ideals and their realization in social programs that have benefited great numbers of people. Also, private moral initiative is not sufficient to guarantee a decent life to citizens in a complex society like our own. Without social security, Medicaid, and board of health regulations, the Miller residents would be much worse off.

The political diversion of moral energies, however, has given rise to a new kind of hypocrisy. It is now possible to consider ourselves morally exemplary simply because we adhere to an enlightened set of social principles. We may vote in accordance with these principles, but they require nothing of us personally; we need never lift a finger to help anyone and we need take no active part in social reform movements. We can even permit ourselves to be ruthless in relations with other people. Because morality has been sublimated into ideology, great numbers of people, the young and educated especially, feel they have an adequate moral identity merely because they hold the "right" views on such matters as ecology, feminism, socialism, and nuclear energy. They may lead narrow, self-indulgent lives, obsessed with their physical health, material comforts, and personal growth, yet still feel a moral advantage over those who actively work to help the needy but who are, in their eyes, ideologically unsound.

The problems that arise from the imbalance of private morality and public policy transcend questions of liberal left versus conservative right. Where the left is directly responsible for the false and unworkable doctrine that ethics is reducible to public policy, the right wishes to dismantle crucial institutions that protect people's rights to a sustainable existence. Conservatives too believe that one may discharge moral duties by holding and advocating "correct" views on public policy (against busing and gun control, for prayers in the school and the death penalty). If the extreme right proves effective, the indigent will have lost such protection as public policy now provides—and this in a society whose members have lost the will and the way to be their brothers' keeper. Moreover, in any number of situations direct action is simply inappropriate (housing for the elderly or disaster relief are prime examples) and the need for concerted social effort and sound public policy is clear. But being right and effective in social ethics is only half of the moral life; and the growing belief that it is more than half should be combated and dispelled. Courses in ethics might be one place to begin.

A glance at a typical anthology of a college course in ethics reveals that most of what the student will read is directed toward analyzing and criticizing policies on such issues as punishment, recombinant DNA research, abortion, and euthanasia. Since the student is not likely to be personally involved in, say, inflicting the death penalty on anyone, the point is to learn how to form responsible opinions. Inevitably the student gets the idea that applying ethics to modern life is mainly a matter of being for or against some social policy. And since many of the articles read like briefs written for a judge or legislator, before long the student loses sight of him- or herself as a moral agent and begins to think like a proto-jurist or legislator.

The net effect of identifying normative ethics with public policy is to justify the moral passivity of the individual. But private benevolence continues to be badly needed in all areas of social concern. The paid functionaries who have virtually excluded the unpaid, well-meaning person are in no position to replace or repair the bonds that have been weakened by the atrophy of private moral initiative. Intellectuals, too, have lost their nerve. Consider the following, from Simone de Beauvoir's *The Coming of Age:*

> Once we have understood what the state of the aged really is, we cannot satisfy
> ourselves with calling for a more generous "old age policy," higher pensions,
> decent housing, and organized leisure. It is the whole system that is at issue and
> our claim cannot be otherwise than radical—change life itself.

Here is the mysterious and ultimately despairing demand of the contemporary social philosopher who has lost sight of the morally concerned citizen. The concrete need is not for revolutionizing society, perhaps not even for reforming it, but for finding a way to reach people like Miss Pickins and the other residents of Miller House.

DISCUSSION QUESTIONS

1. Do you agree with Sommers that ethics classes are currently focusing too much on public policy and too little on private morality?
2. Discuss whether Sommers does an adequate job in supporting her conclusion that the current emphasis on public policy has had a direct negative impact on a sense of personal moral responsibility.
3. Do you agree with Sommers that our society has become morally passive? Is this true of the students and faculty on your campus? Would Coles agree with Sommers? Discuss whether we have a moral responsibility, to the extent that Sommers claims, to care for people who are in need.
4. Discuss how Sommers might structure ethics courses so that people become more responsible for others in need, such as the residents of Miller House.
5. Discuss whether Sommers would agree or disagree with Mencius that people are naturally good. Should ethics education consist of teaching students the nature of goodness and moral responsibility, or should ethics education be concerned with nurturing our natural goodness?

Sheila Mullett

Shifting Perspective: A New Approach to Ethics

Many feminist ethicists reject the focus on analytical thinking that characterizes so much of Western philosophy. Ethical education, they maintain, can be done only within a particular social context. In the following selection, Canadian philosopher Sheila Mullett offers a process, which she calls a feminist methodology, for doing ethics where our actual experiences and relationships provide the foundation for moral analysis and moral action. Mullett argues that moral character can only fully develop through actual experience.

Although Mullett does not reject reason, she points out that our actual experiences and relationships are also an important source of moral knowledge. Mullett's feminist perspective also requires that we recognize our own complicity in destructive social arrangements as well as our responsibility to care for others and to engage in responsible social action.

CRITICAL THINKING QUESTIONS

1. What are the three dimensions of Mullett's perspective?
2. What is moral sensitivity? How do we cultivate moral sensitivity?
3. What is ontological shock? What role does it play in the way we experience the world around us?
4. What is praxis? What is its link to both theory and action?
5. What is the role of positive caring in feminist ethics?
6. Why is collective awareness or consciousness important in moral decision making?
7. Why is listening to other people's stories important to Mullett?

FEMINIST ETHICS

Feminist ethical theory calls for a complex alteration of consciousness. There are three dimensions to this perspective, which might be labeled (1) "moral sensitivity"; (2) "ontological shock"; and (3) "praxis."

"Shifting Perspective: A New Approach to Ethics," in *Feminist Perspectives: Philosophical Essays on Method and Morals,* edited by Lorraine Code, Sheila Mullett, and Christine Overall (Toronto: University of Toronto Press, 1988), pp. 114–117, 120–124. Notes have been omitted.

1. Moral sensitivity: Feminist moral consciousness begins with an anguished awareness of violence, victimization, and pain. The highly developed capacity of human beings to avoid painful experience, to ignore, suppress, deny, and forget the agonies of life, is shifted aside and they fill our consciousness. We lose our moral callousness and see the violence around us: "It is astonishing to note the profound silence in ethics regarding violence against women—rape, battering, child sexual abuse and incest. The exceptions are few, recent and feminist. This silence must be broken."

Until we acquire this painful awareness of suffering we inadvertently perpetuate it: "good people, nice people, people of good will, whom I do not hesitate to call 'moral' in the ordinary sense of that term, myself included, all participate in and perpetuate, even extend and legitimate, violence against women simply by going about our business in an ordinary way. We do so primarily by our quotidian participation in social patterns and institutions which make up the bulk of everyday life."

This significant feature of this consciousness of pain is that it is made possible, in part at least, by a new attitude towards the social arrangements which contribute to suffering.

2. Ontological shock: This new attitude is not a passive acceptance of misery but a commitment to "reformulating our actions and thought." It is not merely a lament, but a transformation of the way the social milieu is present in our experience: "Women have long lamented their condition, but a lament, pure and simple, need not be an expression of feminist consciousness. As long as their situation is apprehended as natural, inevitable, and inescapable, women's consciousness of themselves, no matter how alive to insult and inferiority, is not yet feminist consciousness."

Feminist consciousness involves a double perspective: we see the situation as it is in the present, and as it is understood and interpreted within the existing social context, while, at the same time, viewing it in terms of a state of affairs not yet actual, in terms of possibility, "in which what is given would be negated and radically transformed." "Feminists are not aware of different things than other people, they are aware of the same things differently." Bartky calls this a state of "ontological shock" because it involves a displacement of the world we have taken for granted, it opens up whole new areas of ambiguity and uncertainty and requires continuous attempts to formulate new possibilities for action. In short it puts everything into question. It involves, "first, the realization that what is really happening is quite different from what appears to be happening; and second, the frequent inability to tell what is really happening at all."

In this perspective thought and feeling are blended. We experience the suffering of women and our own suffering as intolerable, and we experience the shock of seeing the "normal" categories of interpretation shift before a perception of almost inchoate possibilities of social transformation.

3. Praxis: A collective understanding of the transformative possibilities within a given social context. The third characteristic of the feminist ethical perspective

is that it is disclosed, however dimly and with however much shock, in a collective awareness. We shift from seeing the world as an individual moral agent to seeing it through the eyes of a "we." It is not my moral perspective that I come to understand better but the emerging moral perspective of countless others committed to changing the structures in which we live our lives. We struggle to delineate the conditions under which we can develop forms of attachment that also serve as avenues to self-affirmation. We search for forms of collective action which can lead to the transformation of existing social structures. When people are: "truly committed to liberation, their action and reflection cannot proceed without the action and reflection of others." "Authentic thinking, thinking that is concerned about *reality,* does not take place in ivory tower isolation, but only in communication."

There are several ideas embedded in the notion of praxis. First, there is the idea that our perception of reality emerges in our efforts to transform it. We must perceive our state "not as fated and unalterable, but merely as limiting." This might be expressed as the idea that thought and action are inseparably linked in ethics. Second, there is the idea that this transformative perception is a collective one, emerging out of shared attempts to understand what is going on and to discern possibilities. This might be expressed as the view that in the development of a moral perspective self and others are inseparably linked. And third, there is the idea that the reality which we wish to focus upon as moral agents is a socially constructed reality, one which has not yet emerged but which may emerge out of our efforts. This might be expressed as the view that imagination is a crucial component of a moral perspective: "We need to imagine an alternative human world so as to act in the present as if it had already begun to emerge and its anticipated norms had begun to bind us."

We can now see how a feminist moral philosophy presents a radically altered picture of the moral agent, who is depicted as constructing a moral perspective within the context of a collective endeavour to transform existing social arrangements. The moral perspective is thus depicted as multi-dimensional and incomplete. It is not something that can be fully grasped as it is in the process of being discerned. The attempts to articulate the obscurely discerned possibilities contribute to the construction of the perspective. It is inchoate and affected by our articulations of it. And, it requires attention to one's deepest sense of what is worthwhile. But feminist ethics goes one step farther than this and sees this deep sense as something that emerges in a collective consciousness. . . .

AN EXAMPLE OF "POSITIVE" CARING IN AN OPPRESSIVE CONTEXT

A description by Helen Levine of her experience as a patient in a psychiatric hospital illustrates these criteria of "positive" caring as well as the shift of perspective that constitutes the crucial dimension of morality. She was hospitalized for severe depression in an institution in which all doctors and senior administrators were male. These were some of the experiences she recorded in her journal. During the initial interview there was no visible concern for what she might be experiencing. She was handed a typed set of rules and regulations with no explanations. Privileges, such as walking out in the grounds or playing badminton, had to be earned. Patients, all female in this ward, were told what to do in minute detail. She was administered two powerful anti-depressants, as well as muscle relaxants and sleeping pills, at the beginning in full dosage, even though she was totally unaccustomed to medication of any sort. She was dizzy, dazed, and trembling from the medication and her vision was blurred. She noted many instances in which other patients were treated with scorn, indifference, or outright insult. One older woman was left to wait and suffer alone so that "she would not become dependent." Another woman was forced to undergo shock treatment against her will. Only one nurse spent time talking with Helen. Others simply handed out the medication. At one point, when she was sobbing and planning to leave, members of the staff criticized her for being demanding and hysterical. The ward was run in an authoritarian way and the ward meeting of patients turned out to be an occasion for nurses to complain about small infractions of the rules (patients putting their feet on the coffee table, which is not "ladylike"). No real grievances were aired by patients because of fear of repercussions. During her stay in this institution where patients were treated as passive recipients of orders and medication, she began to talk with some of the other patients. Talking with P she discovered a woman who had put her husband through college and could not concentrate now that it was her turn to study. She had been told there is too much "child" in her, not enough "adult." After talking with C, laughing about the absurdity of their daily humiliations, she found her to be an interesting, observant, self-educated woman. They began to do yoga together. Other women began to talk and share their fear. Fear of shock treatments, fear of being sent to the large provincial hospital, fear of loss of privileges if they complained. They began to have sing songs.

In this demoralizing social context we can identify some of the features of "positive" caring and many of the features of the emerging feminist perspective: (1) "Moral sensitivity." She was aware of the suffering of her fellow patients as well as her own. She did not ignore the demoralizing social relations between staff and patients. She listened with sympathy to the accounts of all the other patients. (2) She experienced "ontological shock" not just lament, in her recognition of the oppressive domination of the patients and her understanding that this is not the only possible way the situation could be structured. She saw the situation through the double perspective of seeing the present as unacceptable in light of the possibilities which are repressed. (3) Her perspective could be characterized as a form of praxis insofar as it emerged from shared experience and common efforts to help one another and to alter the social situation (educate the staff by giving her doctor *Women and Madness* by Phyllis Chesler, encourage more physical activity and fitness, engage in discussions and sing songs and yoga, etc.). In this sense she contributed to the development of a collective consciousness of possibility in the midst of appalling oppression and weakness.

Further, in this case we can see the emergent paradigm of caring. Her caring for her friends on the ward had several characteristics. (1) It was fulfilling turning her away from self-pity and despair, and was not extracted in exchange for economic support or done out of guilt or desire to fill her "role." (2) It was an expression of her particularity and could not have been done by a hired person. It was her sensitivity and her ability to understand the social context of the oppression of her friends as well as her interest in exercise, yoga, music, and humorous caricature of the situation that constituted her individual expression of herself in her caring. (3) It was not the expression of a social division of roles in which expressive and nurturing behaviour is relegated to one social class while instrumental behaviour is reserved for another class of human beings. She was not acting in her role as psychiatric social worker at the time of this example. (4) It was reciprocated. (5) It emerged in the context of conversations and actions that loosened the restricting effect of the predefined roles of "female psychiatric patient" on the experience of herself and her friends.

CONCLUSIONS

One of the concerns of feminists has been to figure out how we could maintain our traditional concern with caring without the powerlessness associated with that concern. We have seen that an ethics of caring can fail to address that issue. The anguished feminist consciousness can deal with this shortcoming by producing the double perspective that consists in seeing the ways in which caring relations are distorted by the existing power relations and superimposing upon that picture imaginative possibilities of transformation. The feminist is thus aware of the distortions of caring and at the same time aware of the possibility of change. But the imaginative search for possibilities of transformation is a dynamic project and not a completed vision. The feminist perspective that I am describing does not produce a set of moral paradigms but rather focuses on the process of generating such paradigms. It is an experimental consciousness, a method of paying attention to suffering, a toleration of ambiguities.

Our experience with caring has, of course, prepared us for this double consciousness, for part of caring is precisely the ability to apprehend the world through the eyes of the other. The double perspective of feminism is characterized by the ability to see and feel the limitations of the present while imagining alternatives to it. It also involves relinquishing the perspective of a solitary moral agent operating alone and contributing to the construction of a consensual perspective by a process of sharing experiences and seeking to articulate and explain these experiences so as to generate new categories of interpretation.

The feminist perspective is a double one in yet another way. It involves recognition and acknowledgment of one's own complicity with the destructive social arrangements, through exchanging caring for economic support, through the moral callousness of denying suffering, or through excesses of rage and narcissism to which the psyche is prone, while at the same time balancing this consciousness with a view of the possibilities of increased moral sensitivity. It is easy to give in to rage and just as easy to give in to apathy. The double perspective I am describing is one in which one recognizes and experiences the inclination to withdraw into rage or apathy while at the same time seeing that what is required is continued presence of mind within the contexts of oppression. This presence of mind was evinced by Helen Levine when she held firm in the face of powerful incentives to rage and self-pity, while she was drugged and master-minded in a psychiatric hospital. Grimly clinging to the possibility that things could be different she survived powerful inner resistance as well as nearly overwhelming collusion by those who were determined to invalidate her perception of the situation.

Any act we perform is either a confirmation of the existing social arrangements or a move away from them. Helen Levine could have submitted to the therapy passively. What prevents us from seeking new social arrangements? First, failing to see the destructiveness of the social context, i.e., oblivion or ignorance; second, denying or suppressing the painful view of the context, i.e., "moral callousness"; third, despairing because one feels entirely alone; fourth, being overwhelmed by rage, and the paralysis that ensues; fifth, experiencing self-pity, again a matter of feeling separated from others. It takes imagination to see our connection with others and to see how our social arrangements are continually reinforced by daily choices and actions. Because we imagine our situation to be unalterable we fail to undertake the experiments that might enable us to reconstruct our familiar settings. . . .

This is the challenge of shifting perspectives in moral life and in moral theory.

DISCUSSION QUESTIONS

1. Do you agree with Mullett that we have to actually experience pain and suffering—whether in our own lives or the lives of those around us—before we will take steps to change the social arrangements that cause the suffering? Illustrate your answer using examples from your life.
2. Psychologists have noted that most young people go through a period of crisis when they leave their families and go away to college. To what extent does this crisis involve ontological shock? How has your view of the world and other people changed since entering college? If you have experienced such a crisis, to what extent has it led to a commitment to reformulate your thoughts and actions? Illustrate your answer with specific examples.
3. Describe an instance of praxis in your own life. How did praxis, in this case, build on collective experience and understanding? What role did ontological shock and moral sensitivity play in leading you to take action?
4. Do you agree with Mullett regarding the importance of "positive caring" in overcoming oppressive social arrangements? Can positive caring be taught in an ethics class? Support your answer.
5. Discuss whether Sommers would approve of Mullett's approach to ethics education. Does Mullett pay sufficient attention to what Sommers calls private morality?

Kōshō Mizutani

Buddhist Tradition and Modernity

The basic moral teachings of Buddhism reflect the experience and insight of the historic Buddha as he engaged in his own search for freedom and wisdom. In Buddhist philosophy, ethics is not separate from other philosophical inquiries. Instead, morality and wisdom are integrated in a vision of a way of life based on compassion and universal love for all living beings.

In the final selection for Chapter 1, Japanese philosopher Kōshō Mizutani points out ways in which Buddhist ethics offers practical guidance for modern life as well as for ethics education. Buddhism's emphasis of tolerance and concern for all life has had a profound influence not only on human rights movements but also on the current environmental and animal rights movements.

CRITICAL THINKING QUESTIONS

1. What are the two characteristic features of Buddhism?
2. What is Dharma, and what is its relevance to ethics?
3. What is the Buddhist view of human nature?
4. What do Buddhists mean by "compassion"? Why is compassion so important in Buddhist ethics?
5. According to Mizutani, what does Buddhist ethics have to offer contemporary society?

Buddhism has been criticized for an alleged lack of a dynamic ethic able to deal with everyday, actual problems in life. Whenever the topic of Buddhist ethics arises, this alleged weakness is almost always mentioned. For example, Confucianists judge Buddhism to be escapist because it neglects the role of human relationships in maintaining order within families and society. On the other hand, Christians have criticized Buddhism for its pessimistic worldview that sees life as simply an agonizing episode. Such pessimism, it is argued, deprives us of the strength necessary to pursue social justice. Thus, some philosophers regard Confucianists as advocates of social morals and Christianity as an ethical religion

---

"Buddhist Tradition and Modernity," in *Buddhist Ethics and Modern Society,* edited by Charles Wei-hsun Fu and Sandra W. Wawrytko (New York: Greenwood Press, 1991), pp. 6–11. Notes have been omitted.

that puts God's love in practice, yet maintain that Buddhism lacks a firm grasp of the nature of history and society.

In the face of such criticism, Buddhist scholars have produced ethical arguments based on Buddhist metaphysics, while other Buddhists have worked toward realizing Buddhist ethics in the real world. Currently Buddhism is not only a code of ethics for Buddhists, but also an ethics that should guide the education of the young and help ordinary people in everyday life. I submit that a study of Buddhism that emphasizes its ethical aspects will be the most important task facing Buddhists in the twenty-first century.

THE FOUNDATION OF BUDDHIST ETHICS

There are two characteristic features of Buddhism. The first is that from its beginning Buddhism emphasized ethics, as clearly demonstrated in such early texts as the *Nikāya, Dhammapada,* and *Sutta-nipāta.* Second, both rationality and tolerance are intrinsic to Buddhism. As Buddhism spread, it avoided an outright conflict with the indigenous religions it encountered, and rather sought to understand them. Because of its commitment to tolerance, it assumed various forms, depending on the culture and country it met. As for its rationality, Mahāyāna Buddhism contains philosophical thoughts that continue to challenge contemporary thinkers.

Buddhism's point of origin is Buddha's *bodhi,* which is nothing but the self-consciousness of Dharma. Buddhism's essence is Dharma, as indicated by the fact that it is also referred to as Buddha's Dharma. This is illustrated in the following quotation: "When one realizes Dharma, one realizes Buddha; and when one realizes Buddha, one realizes Dharma." The practical aspects of Dharma can serve as a guide for action, for "Dharma" can mean habit, custom, or duty. Buddhist ethics is rooted in this practical aspect of Dharma. An everyday ethics as a guide for action has been developed by Buddhism and still is embraced today. There are numerous ways of putting Dharma into practice. . . .

ETHICAL PRACTICE

At the heart of numerous Buddhist ethical practices is *maitreya-karunā,* compassion or mercy. The role of compassion in Buddhism can be compared to the role of love in Christianity. Compassion makes human relationships genuine. Without compassion, ethics becomes powerless and empty.

The first step toward putting the spirit of compassion into practice is giving (*dāna*). *Dāna* is not only important to Buddhists in the struggle for their salvation, it is also important for laypersons. The four *samgraha-vastu* and the six *pāramitā,* systematized in Mahāyāna Buddhism, both represent the practical ethic summarized in a famous Buddhist text: "Refrain from all evil; do anything good; and thus purify the mind: this is Buddha's teaching." The straightforward essence of Buddhism is contained in this verse, which is frequently cited in Buddhist texts. The importance of ethics to Buddhism, then, is clear.

To denounce Buddhism by saying that it is escapist or pessimistic is simply a misconception. In fact, Buddhism encourages people to do good and to refrain from wrongdoing. Of course, to complete their training, it is unavoidable that Buddhists hide themselves from the world. However, after completing their rigorous training, they return to the world, for the ultimate purpose of Buddhists is to save others. Mahāyāna Buddhism claims that the ideal society and the cultivation of personality are the primary purposes of Buddhism, and has striven consistently to improve societies and cultivate members of those societies.

THE ROLE OF BUDDHISM
IN CONTEMPORARY SOCIETY

The above remarks demonstrate that Buddhist ethics are essential in any society. It is not a simple task to describe today's societies and the challenges they will meet as we move toward the twenty-first century. I would like to focus on three of these challenges that can be met by the application of Buddhist ethics: internationalization, the information explosion, and the growing percentage of older people.

Internationalization continues to accelerate, and cultural syntheses among various nations occur constantly, while the traditions and customs of the individual nations remain intact. Buddhist ethics can justify its position as a universal ethics by considering human problems from the human point of view. It can provide the motive force for leading us toward the achievement of world peace and well-being for all human beings.

Another notable trend is the rapid growth of information. Technological development has caused sweeping changes in both industrial societies and those that seek to industrialize. One consequence has been the alienation of humanity —machines are overwhelming people. This technological development also has had devastating effects on Nature. Both the free competition of capitalism and the tight control of power in socialistic societies have left people in a state of continual struggle. Skepticism is growing, and uncontrolled desire is wreaking havoc on humanity. Ethics must be established in both economic and political contexts; reason and common sense must be restored in order that we can have faith in the value of each individual. The ideas of *pratitya-samutpāda* and *śūnyatā* offer a ground for meeting these pressing needs.

One of the major challenges facing Japan as well as other nations in the twenty-first century is that of coping with an aging population. Buddhist philosophy provides an ethical foundation not only for family relationships and social welfare, but also an ethical foundation for medical ethics and bioethics. Hospice care, euthanasia, brain death, and organ transplantation are but a few examples of the problems we face. The four *samgraha-vastu* mentioned earlier are of particular importance here. *Dāna, priya-akhyana, artha-caryā,* and *samanā-arthatā* are virtues based on self-sacrifice. They seek to unify people in this age of isolation and alienation. We must recognize the importance of this orientation in contemporary society.

I have mentioned several reasons why we can expect Buddhist ethics to play a significant role in the twenty-first century. Buddhism is concerned with the everyday life of ordinary people and accords respect to each individual. In this sense Buddhist study can be regarded as the study of human nature. Some have predicted that the future ideal for humanity will be provided not by Western thought, but rather by Oriental philosophy, particularly Buddhist thought. And so it is that the value of Buddhism is presently undergoing reevaluation throughout the world.

Ethics is grounded in human relationships. Society consists of the same relationships. Education and social welfare (politics and economics) are both needed for the improvement of social conditions. Education aims at the cultivation of personality; politics and economics strive to achieve an ideal society. I am confident that Buddhist ethics can provide us with a brilliant future by providing a firm foundation for education and social welfare. As a Buddhist, I hereby dedicate myself to promoting the move toward future societies based on the Buddhist ideal.

DISCUSSION QUESTIONS

1. Do you agree with Mizutani that Buddhism offers a dynamic and practical ethics for modern life? Support your answer.
2. Discuss the Buddhist concept of Dharma in light of your own moral development. What is the relation between Dharma and the Western concept of conscience?
3. What effect would an ethics that calls for universal concern for all living beings have on your lifestyle? Use specific examples to illustrate your answer.
4. What effect would adopting Buddhist ethics have on formulating national and international policy? In particular, what practical guidance could it give us for solving domestic and international conflicts? Use specific examples to illustrate your answer.
5. Compare and contrast Mullett's view of ethics education with the Buddhist view.
6. Would a Buddhist ethicist agree with Aristotle that the purpose of ethics education is not so much to teach theory as to make us good people? Support your answer.

Chapter Applications

1. Mandating Community Service in Schools

Community service as part of a program of ethics education has been found to have a positive effect on students' moral behavior and ability to engage in moral reasoning. Because of the benefits of community service, a growing number of high schools and colleges are making it a requirement for graduation.

Scott Bullock, a lawyer in Washington, DC, argues that requiring community service is an infringement on the liberty rights of students. "Mandatory community service is for criminals," he told a newspaper reporter. "Voluntary community service is for citizens."

Others defend the requirement because of the benefits it provides to students and the community. "Most kids don't want to do calculus either," Mayor Michael Capuano of Somerville, Massachusetts, points out in defense of the requirement; "but we make them do it because it's good for them."[1]

Discussion Questions

1. Compare and contrast the views of Bullock and Capuano regarding the rights of students to choose their own course requirements.

2. Should schools be trying to influence the character of their students? Or should moral education be beyond the purview of schools? Support your answer. Discuss how Robert Coles might answer this question.

3. Do you agree with Bullock that requiring service learning is an infringement on students' liberty rights?

4. Would Christina Hoff Sommers be more likely to agree with Bullock or Capuano regarding mandatory community service for students? Support your answer.

2. Teaching Civility

"Rudeness reigns in many aspects of our society," writes Laura Pappano of the Murray Research Center at Radcliffe College. "People today routinely backbite, browbeat, and tailgate."[2] According to a 1996 Gallup poll, 89 percent of Americans believe that incivility is a serious problem, and 78 percent think the problem has become worse in the last ten years. Sixty percent of those polled admitted to "shouting, cursing, or making gestures at drivers who upset them."[3]

Two years ago the Massachusetts Registry of Motor Vehicles decided to do something about driver incivility. The registry began requiring people who have five driving violations to take a Highway Safety Council course before they could get their license back. The course basically focuses on being a more civil driver.

The Registry of Motor Vehicles is not the only institution to join the civility crusade. Colleges, government agencies, and think tanks are also setting rules and offering retreats on how to behave in a more respectful and civil manner. Educator William Damon, of Brown University, believes that part of the problem is that we are expecting less and less of our young people.[4] Some people are suggesting that civics education, which used to be a standard part of the public school curriculum, be brought back into the schools and colleges, or at least be required of students who repeatedly engage in uncivil behavior.

For example, in January 1997, Kim Messer and Jeanie Mentavlos, two of the four women attending the Citadel, announced that they were leaving the 154-year-old formerly all-male military academy in South Carolina. The two women claimed that they had been sexually harassed and viciously hazed by some of the male students. Despite a court-ordered plan to ensure the women's safety, allegedly they had been smeared with fingernail polish and then set on fire. They also had their mouths washed out with cleanser.[5]

Several male cadets have already been implicated. However, the problem of uncivil behavior toward female cadets is fairly pervasive at the Citadel. School officials and lawyers involved in the Citadel case are debating how to handle cases such as these, as well as how to prevent future occurrences of gross incivility.

Discussion Questions

1. Do you think that people are becoming more disrespectful and uncivil? Is this true on your campus? If so, why do you think this is happening?

2. What is meant by "civility"? How is civility related to being a moral person? What is the difference, if any, between ethics education and civics education? Explain.

3. Discuss whether the prevalence of incivility in contemporary society disproves Mencius's theory that people are innately good.

4. Should civics education be required for all college students? Should it be required for students who repeatedly engage in disrespectful behavior? What advice might a Buddhist ethicist offer for cultivating civility and compassion on our campuses? Discuss your answer in light of the Citadel case.

NOTES

[1] Tony Pelton, "Mayor, Students Spar Over Service," *The Boston Globe,* May 10, 1996, pp. 31, 33.

[2] Laura Pappano, "The Crusade for Civility," *The Boston Globe Magazine,* May 4, 1997, pp. 17, 38.

[3] Ibid., p. 36.

[4] Ibid., p. 44.

[5] Elizabeth Gleick, "And Then There were Two . . . ; Claiming Sexual Harassment and Vicious Hazing, Half the Female Cadets Quit the Citadel," *Time,* January 27, 1997, p. 38.

CHAPTER TWO

Ethical Relativism

There is one thing a professor can be absolutely certain of; almost every student entering the university believes, or says he believes, that truth is relative.

Allan Bloom, *The Closing of the American Mind*

Ethical relativism is one of the most popular moral theories among college students. Ethical relativists believe that because there is disagreement among people on moral questions, there are no universal moral principles. Instead, ethical relativists hold that ethical values are created by, or are relative to, the people who hold the beliefs.

There are two main types of ethical relativism: (1) ethical subjectivism and (2) cultural relativism. Both theories claim that humans, either individually or collectively, are the ultimate measure of what is right and what is wrong. Ethical subjectivism states that morality is simply the expression of individual opinions. Cultural relativism, on the other hand, claims that societal norms, rather than the opinions of isolated individuals, form the basis of morality. The divine command theory, a third variation of ethical relativism, will be covered in Chapter 3 on morality and religion.

Relativist theories are the weakest of the moral theories covered in the reader. However, because so many people believe that these theories are true, and act in accordance with this belief, it is important that we study them to analyze their weaknesses—and their strengths.

Ethical Subjectivism

Ethical subjectivism is the philosophical theory that morality is created by or relative to the individual person. According to this theory, there are no objective moral truths—only individual opinions or preferences. Therefore, people can never be mistaken about what is moral or immoral. What is right for you may be wrong for me, depending on our respective feelings.

Ethical subjectivism, for the most part, is a Western phenomenon and an outgrowth of Romantic Sentimentalism, which thrived during the late eighteenth through the mid-nineteenth centuries. Romantic Sentimentalism emphasizes the inner person and is based on the assumption that humans by nature are good.

The first selection is from the writings of Swiss philosopher and Romantic Sentimentalist Jean-Jacques Rousseau. Rousseau is one of the few philosophers who advocated ethical subjectivism, or what he calls the law of the heart. In his book *Émile*, Rousseau applies this moral theory to the education of Émile.

In the second reading taken from *A Vindication of the Rights of Woman*, British philosopher Mary Wollstonecraft challenges Rousseau's version of ethical subjectivism. She notes that ethical subjectivism is not as liberating as it may first appear.

In the next selection, "Study of the Sickness Called Apathy," U.S. Senator Jacob Javits and journalist A. M. Rosenthal relate the case of Kitty Genovese—a young woman who was murdered while her neighbors stood by and did nothing —to civil rights and civic duty. A shared notion of civic duty, which is based on a belief in a community or universal standard of morality, does not exist in the context of ethical subjectivism.

In the final selection, "Student Relativism," Stephen Satris argues that the relativism espoused by today's college students is not even a philosophical position. Instead, he claims that student relativism is a defense mechanism for avoiding thinking about philosophical issues.

Jean-Jacques Rousseau

Émile

Swiss philosopher Jean-Jacques Rousseau (1712–1778) espoused ethical subjectivism. Unlike most of the philosophers of his time who regarded reason as the path to truth, Rousseau exalted feeling over reason. When it came to morality, he believed in "the law of the heart." According to this law, we can discover goodness by retreating to pure inner feelings. It is only in this radical subjectivism that true moral goodness abides.

Rousseau's romantic depiction of the noble savage as morally superior to the civilized European was never generally accepted. Although Rousseau was tremendously influential as a social and political philosopher, his moral theory contains many inconsistencies.

In the following reading, Rousseau applies ethical subjectivism to the education of a hypothetical student Émile. Rousseau then goes on to describe the moral education of Sophy, who is to become Émile's wife.

CRITICAL THINKING QUESTIONS

1. What is Rousseau's view of human nature?
2. What does Rousseau think about the role of society in shaping morality?
3. What is the purpose of education? Where should parents and teachers look for guidance in educating their children?
4. What, according to Rousseau, is the law of nature, and what is its relation to morality?
5. Why does Rousseau value liberty so highly in a child's moral education?
6. How does Rousseau define virtue? What makes a person virtuous?
7. How, according to Rousseau, do men and women differ? What is the relevance of this difference to their moral education?

"The Law of the Heart," from *Émile,* translated by Jules Steeg (Boston: D. C. Heath & Co., 1894, Books I–IV) and *Émile,* translated by Barbara Foxley (London: J. M. Dent & Sons, 1974, Book V). Notes have been omitted.

THE OBJECT OF EDUCATION

Coming from the hand of the Author of all things, everything is good; in the hands of man, everything degenerates. Man obliges one soil to nourish the productions of another, one tree to bear the fruits of another; he mingles and confounds climates, elements, seasons; he mutilates his dog, his horse, his slave. He overturns everything, disfigures everything; he loves deformity, monsters; he desires that nothing should be as nature made it, not even man himself. To please him, man must be broken in like a horse; man must be adapted to man's own fashion, like a tree in his garden. . . .

Plants are improved by cultivation, and men by education. If man were born large and strong, his size and strength would be useless to him until he had learned to use them. They would be prejudicial to him, by preventing others from thinking of assisting him; and left to himself he would die of wretchedness before he had known his own necessities. We pity the state of infancy; we do not perceive that the human race would have perished if man had not begun by being a child.

We are born weak, we need strength; we are born destitute of all things, we need assistance; we are born stupid, we need judgment. All that we have not at our birth, and that we need when grown up, is given us by education.

This education comes to us from nature itself, or from other men, or from circumstances. The internal development of our faculties and of our organs is the education nature gives us; the use we are taught to make of this development is the education we get from other men; and what we learn, by our own experience, about things that interest us, is the education of circumstances. . . .

Watch nature carefully, and follow the paths she traces out for you. She gives children continual exercise; she strengthens their constitution by ordeals of every kind; she teaches them early what pain and trouble mean. The cutting of their teeth gives them fever, sharp fits of colic throw them into convulsions, long coughing chokes them, worms torment them, repletion corrupts their blood, different leavens fermenting there cause dangerous eruptions. Nearly the whole of infancy is sickness and danger; half the children born into the world die before their eighth year. These trials past, the child has gained strength, and as soon as he can use life, its principle becomes more assured.

This is the law of nature. Why do you oppose her? Do you not see that in thinking to correct her you destroy her work and counteract the effect of all her cares? . . .

THE EDUCATION OF ÉMILE

Result. The Pupil at the Age of Ten or Twelve

Supposing that my method is indeed that of nature itself, and that I have made no mistakes in applying it, I have now conducted my pupil through the region of sensations to the boundaries of childish reason. The first step beyond should be that of a man. But before beginning this new career, let us for a moment cast our eyes over what we have just traversed. Every age and station in life has a perfection, a maturity, all its own. . . . When he tells you what he has been thinking or doing, he will speak of the evil as freely as of the good, not in the least embarrassed by its effect upon those who hear him. He will use words in all the simplicity of their original meaning.

We like to prophesy good of children, and are always sorry when a stream of nonsense comes to disappoint hopes aroused by some chance repartee. My pupil seldom awakens such hopes, and will never cause such regrets: for he never utters an unnecessary word, or wastes breath in babble to which he knows nobody will listen. If his ideas have a limited range, they are nevertheless clear. If he knows nothing by heart, he knows a great deal from experience. If he does not read ordinary books so well as other children, he reads the book of nature far better. His mind is in his brain, and not at his tongue's end. He has less memory than judgment. He can speak only one language, but he understands what he says: and if he does not say it as well as another, he can do things far better than they can.

He does not know the meaning of custom or routine. What he did yesterday does not in any wise affect his actions of to-day. He never follows a rigid formula, or gives way in the least to authority or to example. Everything he does and says is after the natural fashion of his age. Expect of him, therefore, no formal speeches or studied manners, but always the faithful expression of his own ideas, and a conduct arising from his own inclinations.

You will find he has a few moral ideas in relation to his own concerns, but in regard to men in general, none at all. Of what use would these last be to him, since a child is not yet an active member of society? Speak to him of liberty, of property, even of things done by common consent, and he may understand you. He knows why his own things belong to him and those of another person do not, and beyond this he knows nothing. Speak to him of duty and obedience, and he will not know what you mean. Command him to do a thing, and he will not understand you. But tell him that if he will do you such and such a favor, you will do the same for him whenever you can, and he will readily oblige you; for he likes nothing better than to increase his power, and to lay you under obligations he knows to be inviolable. Perhaps, too, he enjoys being recognized as somebody and accounted worth something. But if this last be his motive, he has already left the path of nature, and you have not effectually closed the approaches to vanity. . . .

Leave him at liberty and by himself, and without saying a word, watch what he does, and how he does it. Knowing perfectly well that he is free, he will do nothing from mere thoughtlessness, or just to show that he can do it; for is he not aware that he is always his own master? . . .

Result. The Pupil at the Age of Fifteen

I think these explanations will suffice to mark distinctly the advance my pupil's mind has hitherto made, and the route by which he has advanced. You are probably alarmed at the number of subjects I have brought to his notice. You are afraid I will overwhelm his mind with all this knowledge. But I teach him rather not to know them than to know them. I am showing him a path to knowledge not indeed difficult, but without limit, slowly measured, long, or rather endless, and tedious to follow. I am showing him how to take the first steps, so that he may know its beginning, but allow him to go no farther.

Obliged to learn by his own effort, he employs his own reason, not that of another. Most of our mistakes arise less within ourselves than from others; so that if he is not to be ruled by opinion, he must receive nothing upon authority. Such continual exercise must invigorate the mind as labor and fatigue strengthen the body. . . .

Émile has little knowledge, but it is really his own; he knows nothing by halves; and the most important fact is that he does not now know things he will one day know; that many things known to other people he never will know; and that there is an infinity of things which neither he nor any one else ever will know. He is prepared for knowledge of every kind; . . .

Émile is industrious, temperate, patient, steadfast, and full of courage. His imagination, never aroused, does not exaggerate dangers. He feels few discomforts, and can bear pain with fortitude, because he has never learned to contend with fate. He does not yet know exactly what death is, but, accustomed to yield to the law of necessity, he will die when he must, without a groan or a struggle. Nature can do no more at that moment abhorred by all. To live free and to have little to do with human affairs is the best way of learning how to die.

In a word, Émile has every virtue which affects himself. To have the social virtues as well, he only needs to know the relations which make them necessary; and this knowledge his mind is ready to receive. He considers himself independently of others, and is satisfied when others do not think of him at all. He exacts nothing from others, and never thinks of owing anything to them. He is alone in human society, and depends solely upon himself. He has the best right of all to be independent, for he is all that any one can be at his age. He has no errors but such as a human being must have; no vices but those from which no one can warrant himself exempt. He has a sound constitution, active limbs, a fair and unprejudiced mind, a heart free and without passions. Self-love, the first and most natural of all, has scarcely manifested itself at all. Without disturbing any one's peace of mind he has led a happy, contented life, as free as nature will allow. Do you think a youth who has thus attained his fifteenth year has lost the years that have gone before? . . .

We have reached the last act of youth's drama; we are approaching its closing scene.

It is not good that man should be alone. Émile is now a man, and we must give him his promised helpmeet. That helpmeet is Sophy. . . .

THE EDUCATION OF SOPHY*

Sophy, or Woman

Sophy should be as truly a woman as Émile is a man, *i.e.*, she must possess all those characters of her sex which are required to enable her to play her part in the physical and moral order. Let us inquire to begin with in what respects her sex differs from our own.

But for her sex, a woman is a man; she has the same organs, the same needs, the same faculties. The machine is the same in its construction; its parts, its working, and its appearance are similar. Regard it as you will the difference is only in degree.

Yet where sex is concerned man and woman are unlike; each is the complement of the other; the difficulty in comparing them lies in our inability to decide, in either case, what is a matter of sex, and what is not. General differences present themselves to the comparative anatomist and even to the superficial observer; they seem not to be a matter of sex; yet they are really sex differences, though the connection eludes our observation. How far such differences may extend we cannot tell; all we know for certain is that where man and woman are alike we have to do with the characteristics of the species; where they are unlike, we have to do with the characteristics of sex. Considered from these two standpoints, we find so many instances of likeness and unlikeness that it is perhaps one of the greatest of marvels how nature has contrived to make two beings so like and yet so different.

These resemblances and differences must have an influence on the moral nature; this inference is obvious, and it is confirmed by experience; it shows the vanity of the disputes as to the superiority or the equality of the sexes; as if each sex, pursuing the path marked out for it by nature, were not more perfect in that very divergence than if it more closely resembled the other. A perfect man and a perfect woman should no more be alike in mind than in face, and perfection admits of neither less nor more.

In the union of the sexes each alike contributes to the common end, but in different ways. From this diversity springs the first difference which may be observed between man and woman in their moral relations. The man should be strong and active; the woman should be weak and passive; the one must have both the power and the will; it is enough that the other should offer little resistance.

When this principle is admitted, it follows that woman is specially made for man's delight. If man in his turn ought to be pleasing in her eyes, the necessity is less urgent, his virtue is in his strength, he pleases because he is strong. I grant you this is not the law of love, but it is the law of nature, which is older than love itself.

---

*Book V is from *Émile*, translated by Barbara Foxley (London: J. M. Dent & Sons, Ltd., 1974). Steeg's translation is for Books I–IV.

If woman is made to please and to be in subjection to man, she ought to make herself pleasing in his eyes and not provoke him to anger; her strength is in her charms, by their means she should compel him to discover and use his strength. The surest way of arousing this strength is to make it necessary by resistance. Thus pride comes to the help of desire and each exults in the other's victory. This is the origin of attack and defence, of the boldness of one sex and the timidity of the other, and even of the shame and modesty with which nature has armed the weak for the conquest of the strong.

Who can possibly suppose that nature has prescribed the same advances to the one sex as to the other, or that the first to feel desire should be the first to show it? What strange depravity of judgment! The consequences of the act being so different for the two sexes, is it natural that they should enter upon it with equal boldness? How can any one fail to see that when the share of each is so unequal, if the one were not controlled by modesty as the other is controlled by nature, the result would be the destruction of both, and the human race would perish through the very means ordained for its continuance?

Women so easily stir a man's senses and fan the ashes of a dying passion, that if philosophy ever succeeded in introducing this custom into any unlucky country, especially if it were a warm country where more women are born than men, the men, tyrannised over by the women, would at last become their victims, and would be dragged to their death without the least chance of escape. . . .

Thus the different constitution of the two sexes leads us to a third conclusion, that the stronger party seems to be master, but is as a matter of fact dependent on the weaker, and that, not by any foolish custom of gallantry, nor yet by the magnanimity of the protector, but by an inexorable law of nature. For nature has endowed woman with a power of stimulating man's passions in excess of man's power of satisfying those passions, and has thus made him dependent on her goodwill, and compelled him in his turn to endeavour to please her, so that she may be willing to yield to his superior strength. Is it weakness which yields to force, or is it voluntary self-surrender? This uncertainty constitutes the chief charm of the man's victory, and the woman is usually cunning enough to leave him in doubt. In this respect the woman's mind exactly resembles her body; far from being ashamed of her weakness, she is proud of it; her soft muscles offer no resistance, she professes that she cannot lift the lightest weight; she would be ashamed to be strong. And why? Not only to gain an appearance of refinement; she is too clever for that; she is providing herself beforehand with excuses, with the right to be weak if she chooses.

The experience we have gained through our vices has considerably modified the views held in older times; we rarely hear of violence for which there is so little occasion that it would hardly be credited. Yet such stories are common enough among the Jews and ancient Greeks; . . .

See how we find ourselves led unconsciously from the physical to the moral constitution, how from the grosser union of the sexes spring the sweet laws of love. Woman reigns, not by the will of man, but by the decrees of nature herself; she had the power long before she showed it. That same Hercules who proposed to violate all the fifty daughters of Thespis was compelled to spin at the feet of Omphale, and Samson, the strong man, was less strong than Delilah. This power cannot be taken from woman; it is hers by right; she would have lost it long ago, were it possible.

The consequences of sex are wholly unlike for man and woman. The male is only a male now and again, the female is always a female, or at least all her youth; everything reminds her of her sex; the performance of her functions requires a special constitution. She needs care during pregnancy and freedom from work when her child is born; she must have a quiet, easy life while she nurses her children; their education calls for patience and gentleness, for a zeal and love which nothing can dismay; she forms a bond between father and child, she alone can win the father's love for his children and convince him that they are indeed his own. What loving care is required to preserve a united family! And there should be no question of virtue in all this, it must be a labour of love, without which the human race would be doomed to extinction.

The mutual duties of the two sexes are not, and cannot be, equally binding on both. Women do wrong to complain of the inequality of man-made laws; this inequality is not of man's making, or at any rate it is not the result of mere prejudice, but of reason. She to whom nature has entrusted the care of the children must hold herself responsible for them to their father. No doubt every breach of faith is wrong, and every faithless husband, who robs his wife of the sole reward of the stern duties of her sex, is cruel and unjust; but the faithless wife is worse; she destroys the family and breaks the bonds of nature; when she gives her husband children who are not his own, she is false both to him and them, her crime is not infidelity but treason. To my mind, it is the source of dissension and of crime of every kind. Can any position be more wretched than that of the unhappy father who, when he clasps his child to his breast, is haunted by the suspicion that this is the child of another, the badge of his own dishonour, a thief who is robbing his own children of their inheritance. Under such circumstances the family is little more than a group of secret enemies, armed against each other by a guilty woman, who compels them to pretend to love one another.

Thus it is not enough that a wife should be faithful; her husband, along with his friends and neighbours, must believe in her fidelity; she must be modest, devoted, retiring; she should have the witness not only of a good conscience, but of a good reputation. In a word, if a father must love his children, he must be able to respect their mother. For these reasons it is not enough that the woman should be chaste, she must preserve her reputation and her good name. From these principles there arises not only a moral difference between the sexes, but also a fresh motive for duty and propriety, which prescribes to women in particular the most scrupulous attention to their conduct, their manners, their behaviour. Vague assertions as to the equality of the sexes and the similarity of their duties are only empty words; they are no answer to my argument.

It is a poor sort of logic to quote isolated exceptions against laws so firmly established. Women, you say, are not always bearing children. Granted; yet that is their proper business. Because there are a hundred or so of large towns in the world where women live licentiously and have few children, will you maintain that it is their business to have few children? And what would become of your towns if the remote country districts, with their simpler and purer women, did not make up for the barrenness of your fine ladies? There are plenty of country places where women with only four or five children are reckoned unfruitful. In conclusion, although here and there a woman may have few children, what difference does it make? Is it any the less a woman's business to be a mother? And do not the general laws of nature and morality make provision for this state of things? . . .

DISCUSSION QUESTIONS

1. Is Rousseau's assumption about the goodness of human nature borne out by empirical evidence? Use examples to support your answer.
2. Do you agree with Rousseau that virtue is different for men and women? Can he consistently maintain this position while still supporting ethical subjectivism? Support your answer.
3. Does Rousseau's moral theory give practical guidelines for how to live our lives and educate our children? If so, what are some of these guidelines? Are the guidelines he gives consistent with his support of ethical subjectivism?
4. Compare and contrast Rousseau's and Mencius's views of human nature. How do their respective views influence their ideas about ethics education? Which of the two philosophers has the more convincing description of human nature?

Mary Wollstonecraft

A Vindication of the Rights of Woman

English philosopher Mary Wollstonecraft (1759–1797) wrote *A Vindication of the Rights of Woman,* in part, in response to Rousseau's ethical subjectivism and belief that the state of nature is preferable to civilization. In the following selections from her book, Wollstonecraft discusses the role of reason in moral decision making. She argues that socialization works to make women more dependent and emotional rather than rational. She also points out how Rousseau's version of ethical subjectivism, although claiming to be based on freedom of expression, can be used to oppress women by arguing that virtue is different for women because women have a different nature.

CRITICAL THINKING QUESTIONS

1. What, according to Wollstonecraft, is the role of reason in making moral judgments? Is reason necessary for virtue?

2. How does Wollstonecraft respond to Rousseau's argument that the state of nature is morally preferable to civilization?

3. On what grounds does Wollstonecraft claim that Rousseau is being inconsistent?

4. Why does Wollstonecraft argue that there must be one eternal standard of virtue? How does this differ from Rousseau's concept of virtue?

5. Why does Wollstonecraft reject Rousseau's claim that virtue is different for men and women?

Chapter I
The Rights and Involved Duties of Mankind Considered

In the present state of society it appears necessary to go back to first principles in search of the most simple truths, and to dispute with some prevailing prejudice every inch of ground. To clear my way, I must be allowed to ask some plain questions, and the answers will probably appear as unequivocal as the axioms on which reasoning is built; though, when entangled with various motives of action, they are formally contradicted, either by the words or conduct of men.

"Morality Is More Than Feeling: A Response to Rousseau," from *A Vindication of the Rights of Woman* (London: Walter Scott, 1892). Notes have been omitted.

In what does man's pre-eminence over the brute creation consist? The answer is as clear as that a half is less than the whole; in Reason.

What acquirement exalts one being above another? Virtue; we spontaneously reply.

For what purpose were the passions implanted? That man by struggling with them might attain a degree of knowledge denied to the brutes; whispers Experience.

Consequently the perfection of our nature and capability of happiness, must be estimated by the degree of reason, virtue, and knowledge, that distinguish the individual, and direct the laws which bind society: and that from the exercise of reason, knowledge and virtue naturally flow, is equally undeniable, if mankind be viewed collectively.

The rights and duties of man thus simplified, it seems almost impertinent to attempt to illustrate truths that appear so incontrovertible; yet such deeply rooted prejudices have clouded reason, and such spurious qualities have assumed the name of virtues, that it is necessary to pursue the course of reason as it has been perplexed and involved in error, by various adventitious circumstances, comparing the simple axiom with casual deviations.

Men, in general, seem to employ their reason to justify prejudices, which they have imbibed, they can scarcely trace how, rather than to root them out. The mind must be strong that resolutely forms its own principles; for a kind of intellectual cowardice prevails which makes many men shrink from the task, or only do it by halves. Yet the imperfect conclusions thus drawn, are frequently very plausible, because they are built on partial experience, on just, though narrow, views. . . .

The civilization of the bulk of the people of Europe is very partial; nay, it may be made a question, whether they have acquired any virtues in exchange for innocence, equivalent to the misery produced by the vices that have been plastered over unsightly ignorance, and the freedom which has been bartered for splendid slavery. . . .

Impressed by this view of the misery and disorder which pervaded society, and fatigued with jostling against artificial fools, Rousseau became enamoured of solitude, and, being at the same time an optimist, he labours with uncommon eloquence to prove that man was naturally a solitary animal. Misled by his respect for the goodness of God, who certainly—for what man of sense and feeling can doubt it!—gave life only to communicate happiness, he considers evil as positive, and the work of man; not aware that he was exalting one attribute at the expense of another, equally necessary to divine perfection.

Reared on a false hypothesis his arguments in favour of a state of nature are plausible, but unsound. I say unsound; for to assert that a state of nature is preferable to civilization, in all its possible perfection, is, in other words, to arraign supreme wisdom; and the paradoxical exclamation, that God had made all things right, and that error has been introduced by the creature, whom he formed, knowing what he formed, is as unphilosophical as impious.

. . . How could that energetic advocate for immortality argue so inconsistently? Had mankind remained for ever in the brutal state of nature, which even his magic pen cannot paint as a state in which a single virtue took root, it would have been clear, though not to the sensitive unreflecting wanderer, that man was born to run the circle of life and death, and adorn God's garden for some purpose which could not easily be reconciled with his attributes. . . .

Rousseau exerts himself to prove that all *was* right originally: a crowd of authors that all *is* now right: and I, that all will be right.

But, true to his first position, next to a state of nature, Rousseau celebrates barbarism, and apostrophizing the shade of Fabricius, he forgets that, in conquering the world, the Romans never dreamed of establishing their own liberty on a firm basis, or of extending the reign of virtue. Eager to support his system, he stigmatizes, as vicious, every effort of genius; and, uttering the apotheosis of savage virtues, he exalts those to demi-gods, who were scarcely human—the brutal Spartans, who, in defiance of justice and gratitude, sacrificed, in cold blood, the slaves who had shewn themselves heroes to rescue their oppressors.

Disgusted with artificial manners and virtues, the citizen of Geneva, instead of properly sifting the subject, threw away the wheat with the chaff, without waiting to inquire whether the evils which his ardent soul turned from indignantly, were the consequence of civilization or the vestiges of barbarism. . . .

It is the pestiferous purple which renders the progress of civilization a curse, and warps the understanding, till men of sensibility doubt whether the expansion of the intellect produces a greater portion of happiness or misery. But the nature of the poison points out the antidote; and had Rousseau mounted one step higher in his investigation, or could his eye have pierced through the foggy atmosphere, which he almost disdained to breathe, his active mind would have darted forward to contemplate the perfection of man in the establishment of true civilization, instead of taking his ferocious flight back to the night of sensual ignorance. . . .

Children, I grant, should be innocent; but when the epithet is applied to men, or women, it is but a civil term for weakness. For if it be allowed that women were destined by Providence to acquire human virtues, and by the exercise of their understandings, that stability of character which is the firmest ground to rest our future hopes upon, they must be permitted to turn to the fountain of light, and not forced to shape their course by the twinkling of a mere satellite. . . .

. . . the most perfect education, in my opinion, is such an exercise of the understanding as is best calculated to strengthen the body and form the heart. Or, in other words, to enable the individual to attain such habits of virtue as will render it independent. In fact, it is a farce to call any being virtuous whose virtues do not result from the exercise of its own reason. This was Rousseau's opinion respecting men: I extend it to women, . . .

. . . Rousseau declares that a woman should never, for a moment, feel herself independent, that she should be governed by fear to exercise her *natural* cunning, and made a coquettish slave in order to render her a more alluring object of desire, a *sweeter* companion to man, whenever he chooses to relax himself. He carries the arguments, which he pretends to draw from the indications of nature, still further, and insinuates that truth and fortitude, the cornerstones of all human virtue, should be cultivated with certain restrictions, because, with respect to the female character, obedience is the grand lesson which ought to be impressed with unrelenting rigour.

What nonsense! when will a great man arise with sufficient strength of mind to puff away the fumes which pride and sensuality have thus spread over the subject! If women are by nature inferior to men, their virtues must be the same in quality, if not in degree, or virtue is a relative idea; consequently, their conduct should be founded on the same principles, and have the same aim. . . .

. . . I see not the shadow of a reason to conclude that their virtues should differ in respect to their nature. In fact, how can they, if virtue has only one eternal standard? I must therefore, if I reason consequentially, as strenuously maintain that they have the same simple direction, as that there is a God.

. . . But Rousseau, and most of the male writers who have followed his steps, have warmly inculcated that the whole tendency of female education ought to be directed to one point:—to render them pleasing. . . .

He [Dr. Gregory] advises them to cultivate a fondness for dress, because a fondness for dress, he asserts, is natural to them. I am unable to comprehend what either he or Rousseau mean, when they frequently use this indefinite term. If they told us that in a pre-existent state the soul was fond of dress, and brought this inclination with it into a new body, I should listen to them with a half smile, as I often do when I hear a rant about innate elegance.—But if he only meant to say that the exercise of the faculties will produce this fondness—I deny it.—It is not natural; but arises, like false ambition in men, from a love of power. . . .

His [Rousseau's] ridiculous stories, which tend to prove that girls are *naturally* attentive to their persons, without laying any stress on daily example, are below contempt.—And that a little miss should have such a correct taste as to neglect the pleasing amusement of making O's, merely because she perceived that it was an ungraceful attitude, should be selected with the anecdotes of the learned pig.

I have, probably, had an opportunity of observing more girls in their infancy than J. J. Rousseau—I can recollect my own feelings, and I have looked steadily around me; yet, so far from coinciding with him in opinion respecting the first dawn of the female character, I will venture to affirm, that a girl, whose spirits have not been damped by inactivity, or innocence tainted by false shame, will always be a romp, and the doll will never excite attention unless confinement allows her no alternative. Girls and boys, in short, would play harmlessly together, if the distinction of sex was not inculcated long before nature makes any difference.—I will go further, and affirm, as an indisputable fact, that most of the women, in the circle of my observation, who have acted like rational creatures, or shewn any vigour of intellect, have accidentally been allowed to run wild—as some of the elegant formers of the fair sex would insinuate. . . .

Women are every where in this deplorable state; for, in order to preserve their innocence, as ignorance is courteously termed, truth is hidden from them, and they are made to assume an artificial character before their faculties have acquired any strength. Taught from their infancy that beauty is woman's sceptre, the mind shapes itself to the body, and, roaming round its gilt cage, only seeks to adorn its prison. Men have various employments and pursuits which engage their attention, and give a character to the opening mind; but women, confined to one, and having their thoughts constantly directed to the most insignificant part of themselves, seldom extend their views beyond the triumph of the hour. But were their understanding once emancipated from the slavery to which the pride and sensuality of man and their short-sighted desire, like that of dominion in tyrants, of present sway, has subjected them, we should probably read of their weaknesses with surprise. . . .

It is time to effect a revolution in female manners—time to restore to them their lost dignity—and make them, as a part of the human species, labour by reforming themselves to reform the world. It is time to separate unchangeable morals from local manners. . . .

I wish to sum up what I have said in a few words, for I here throw down my gauntlet, and deny the existence of sexual virtues, not excepting modesty. For man and woman, truth, if I understand the meaning of the word, must be the same; yet the fanciful female character, so prettily drawn by poets and novelists, demanding the sacrifice of truth and sincerity, virtue becomes a relative idea, having no other foundation than utility, and of that utility men pretend arbitrarily to judge, shaping it to their own convenience.

Women, I allow, may have different duties to fulfil; but they are *human* duties, and the principles that should regulate the discharge of them, I sturdily maintain, must be the same.

To become respectable, the exercise of their understanding is necessary, there is no other foundation for independence of character; I mean explicitly to say that they must only bow to the authority of reason, instead of being the *modest* slaves of opinion. . . .

DISCUSSION QUESTIONS

1. What does Wollstonecraft mean when she says that Rousseau "celebrates barbarianism"? Do you agree with her critique of Rousseau's moral theory?
2. Is Wollstonecraft correct in her claim that there is only one eternal standard of virtue? Or do you agree with Rousseau and the ethical subjectivists that virtue is different for different people?
3. Wollstonecraft accuses Rousseau, despite his apparent disdain for culture, of actually being a cultural relativist when it comes to his ideas about women and morality. Is her criticism of Rousseau justified?
4. To what extent does our culture have different ideas of what it means to be a virtuous man and what it means to be a virtuous woman? Are these different expectations justified? Support your position.
5. Is it possible to separate our natural moral feelings from those that grow out of our life as social beings? Support your answer. How would Rousseau and Wollstonecraft each respond to this question?

Jacob Javits and A. M. Rosenthal

Study of the Sickness Called Apathy

Jacob Koppel Javits (1904–1986), U.S. Senator from New York, was one of
the leading Republican senators in the 1960s and 1970s and a strong advocate of civil rights. In his statement before the Senate on civil rights legislation, Javits raises the case of Kitty Genovese who was murdered outside her
apartment in New York City while thirty-eight witnesses did nothing. The
selection also includes excerpts from a *New York Times* article by journalist
A. M. Rosenthal.

The Kitty Genovese case raises the question of whether there are certain
obligations and civic responsibilities that are morally binding despite what
we may personally feel.

CRITICAL THINKING QUESTIONS

1. Did Genovese have an expectation that the witnesses should help
   her?
2. How did the witnesses respond to Genovese's cries for help?
3. Why did the assailant leave the scene twice before coming back to
   kill Genovese?
4. What reasons did the witnesses offer for not calling the police?

. . . [O]ne item which has turned up in this civil rights debate has to do with a
shocking incident which occurred in Kew Gardens, in Queens County, N.Y., on
the night of March 13. A young woman was stabbed to death, and it developed
that 38 of her neighbors had seen her stabbed or heard her cries and not one of
them called the police or tried to save her life. I have joined those who have not
only deplored this apathy, but called it shocking, and requiring our searching
attention. . . .

In view of this, I would like to commend to my colleagues a penetrating article
by A. M. Rosenthal, metropolitan editor of the New York Times, in last Sunday's
New York Times magazine. This article, "Study of the Sickness Called Apathy,"
deplores the "metropolitan masochism" and "sadistic search for a target" which
followed the publication of that story. It makes the point that there are various

---

"Study of the Sickness Called Apathy," *Congressional Record*. S10149 (May 6, 1964) (Statement of
Senator Javits).

forms of apathy, that some forms of apathy exist in villages and towns and other forms of apathy exist in great cities. And Mr. Rosenthal pointedly adds:

> The self-protective shells in which we live are determined not only by the difference between big cities and small. They are determined by economics and social class, by caste and by color, and by religion and by politics.

The apathy displayed by the incident in Kew Gardens, tragically deplorable as it was, cannot be oversimplified and written off as some big city problem. Apathy is a sickness which afflicts many aspects of our society in many ways. I am reminded, for example, of a moving book, entitled "A Time To Speak," just published in the past 2 weeks. It was written by Charles Morgan, Jr., a courageous Birmingham, Ala., lawyer and it concerns the church bombing which killed four Negro Sunday schoolchildren. Mr. Morgan writes that this bombing was "a storm warning of the death in life that awaits any community where the good people remain silent in the face of hatred, lawlessness, intolerance, and bigotry."

In short, the question of apathy is a complex subject; it is reflected in various ways in North and South, and in both large and small towns. I urge my colleagues to read this searching article by A. M. Rosenthal in the New York Times Sunday magazine of May 3. I ask unanimous consent that it be printed in the Record at this point.

There being no objection, the article was ordered to be printed in the Record, as follows:

STUDY OF THE SICKNESS CALLED APATHY (BY A. M. ROSENTHAL)

> It happens from time to time in New York that the life of the city is frozen by an instant of shock. In that instant the people of the city are seized by the paralyzing realization that they are one, that each man is in some way a mirror of every other man. They stare at each other—or, really, into themselves—and a look quite like a flush of embarrassment passes over the face of the city. Then the instant passes and the beat resumes and the people turn away and try to explain what they have seen, or try to deny it.
>
> The last 35 minutes of the young life of Miss Catherine Genovese became such a shock in the life of the city. But at the time she died, stabbed again and again by a marauder in her quiet, dark, but entirely respectable, street in Kew Gardens, New York hardly took note.
>
> It was not until 2 weeks later that Catherine Genovese, known as Kitty, returned in death to cry the city awake. Even then it was not her life or her dying that froze the city, but the witnessing of her murder—the choking fact that 38 of her neighbors had seen her stabbed or heard her cries, and that not one of them, during that hideous half hour, had lifted the telephone from the safety of his own apartment to call the police and try to save her life. When it was over and Miss Genovese was dead and the murderer gone, one man did call—not from his own

apartment but from a neighbor's, and only after he had called a friend and asked her what to do.

The day that the story of the witnessing of the death of Miss Genovese appeared in this newspaper became that frozen instant. "Thirty-eight," people said over and over. "Thirty-eight."

It was as if the number itself had some special meaning, and in a way, of course, it did. One person or two or even three or four witnessing a murder passively would have been the unnoticed symptom of the disease in the city's body and again would have passed unnoticed. . . .

For in that instant of shock, the mirror showed quite clearly what was wrong, that the face of mankind was spotted with the disease of apathy—all mankind. But this was too frightening a thought to live with and soon the beholders began to set boundaries for the illness, to search frantically for causes that were external and to look for the carrier.

There was a rash of metropolitan masochism. "What the devil do you expect in a town, a jungle, like this?" Sociologists and psychiatrists reached for the warm comfort of jargon—"alienation of the individual from the group," "megalopolitan societies," "the disaster syndrome."

People who came from small towns said it could never happen back home. New Yorkers, ashamed, agreed. Nobody seemed to stop to ask whether there were not perhaps various forms of apathy and that some that exist in villages and towns do not exist in great cities. . . .

There are two tragedies in the story of Catherine Genovese. One is the fact that her life was taken from her, that she died in pain and horror at the age of 28. The other is that in dying she gave every human being—not just species New Yorker—an opportunity to examine some truths about the nature of apathy and that this has not been done.

Austin Street, where Catherine Genovese lived, is in a section of Queens known as Kew Gardens. There are two apartment buildings and the rest of the street consists of one-family homes—red brick, stucco or wood-frame. There are Jews, Catholics, and Protestants, a scattering of foreign accents, middle-class incomes.

On the night of March 13, about 3 a.m., Catherine Genovese was returning to her home. She worked late as manager of a bar in Hollis, another part of Queens. She parked her car (a red Fiat) and started to walk to her death.

Lurking near the parking lot was a man. Miss Genovese saw him in the shadows, turned and walked toward a police callbox. The man pursued her, stabbed her. She screamed, "Oh my God, he stabbed me. Please help me. Please help me."

Somebody threw open a window and a man called out: "Let that girl alone." Other lights turned on, other windows were raised. The attacker got into a car and drove away. A bus passed.

The attacker drove back, got out, searched out Miss Genovese in the back of an apartment building where she had crawled for safety, stabbed her again, drove away again.

The first attack came at 3:15. The first call to the police came at 3:50. Police arrived within 2 minutes, they say. Miss Genovese was dead.

That night and the next morning the police combed the neighborhood looking for witnesses. They found them, 38.

Two weeks later, when this newspaper heard of the story, a reporter went knocking, door to door, asking "Why, why?"

Through half-opened doors, they told him. Most of them were neither defiant nor terribly embarrassed nor particularly ashamed. The underlying attitude, or explanation, seemed to be fear of involvement—any kind of involvement.

"I don't want my husband to get involved," a housewife said.

"We thought it was a lovers' quarrel," said another woman. "I went back to bed."

"I was tired," said a man.

"I don't know," said another man.

"I don't know," said still another.

"I don't know," said others.

On March 19, police arrested a 29-year-old business-machine operator named Winston Moseley and charged him with the murder of Catherine Genovese. He has confessed to killing two other women, for one of whose murders police say they have a confession from another man.

Not much is said or heard or thought in the city about Winston Moseley. In this drama, as far as the city is concerned, he appeared briefly, acted his piece, exited into the wings.

A week after the first story appeared, a reporter went back to Austin Street. Now the witnesses no longer wanted to talk. They were harried, annoyed; they thought they should keep their mouths shut. "I've done enough talking," one witness said. "Oh, it's you again," said a woman witness and slammed the door.

The neighbors of the witnesses are willing to talk. Their sympathy is for the silent witnesses and the embarrassment in which they now live.

Max Heilbrunn, who runs a coffeehouse on Austin Street, talked about all the newspaper publicity and said his neighbors felt they were being picked on. "It isn't a bad neighborhood," he said.

And this from Frank Facciola, the owner of the neighborhood barbershop: "I resent the way these newspaper and television people have hurt us. We have wonderful people here. What happened could have happened anyplace. There is no question in my mind that people here now would rush out to help anyone being attacked on the street."

Then he said: "The same thing [failure to call the police] happens in other sections every day. Why make such a fuss when it happens in Kew Gardens? We are trying to forget it happened here."

A Frenchwoman in the neighborhood said: "Let's forget the whole thing. It is a quiet neighborhood, good to live in. What happened, happened."

Each individual, obviously, approaches the story of Catherine Genovese, reacts to it, and veers away from it against the background of his own life and experience, and his own fears and shortcomings and rationalization.

It seems to this writer that what happened in the apartments and houses on Austin Street was a symptom of a terrible reality in the human condition—that only under certain situations and only in response to certain reflexes or certain beliefs will a man step out of his shell toward his brother.

To say this is not to excuse, but to try to understand and in so doing perhaps eventually to extend the reflexes and beliefs and situations to include more people.

To ignore it is to perpetuate myths that lead nowhere. Of these the two most futile philosophically are that apathy is a response to official ineptitude ("The cops never come on time anyway"), or that apathy is a condition only of metropolitan life.

Certainly police procedures must be improved—although in the story of Miss Genovese all indications were that, once called into action, the police machine behaved perfectly.

As far as is known, not one witness has said that he remained silent because he had had any unpleasant experience with the police. It is a pointless point; there are men who will jump into a river to rescue a drowner; there are others who will tell themselves that a police launch will be cruising by or that, if it does not, it should.

Nobody can say why the 38 did not lift the phone while Miss Genovese was being attacked, since they cannot say themselves. It can be assumed, however, that their apathy was indeed of a big-city variety. It is almost a matter of psychological survival, if one is surrounded and pressed by millions of people, to prevent them from constantly impinging on you and the only way to do this is to ignore them as often as possible.

Indifference to one's neighbor and his troubles is a continued reflex of life in New York as it is in other big cities. In every major city in which I have lived—in Tokyo and Warsaw, Vienna and Bombay—I have seen, over and over again, people walk away from accident victims. I have walked away myself.

Out-of-towners, and sometimes New Yorkers themselves, like to think that there is something special about New York's metropolitan apathy. It is special in that there are more people here than anyplace else in the country—and therefore more people to turn away from each other.

For decades, New York turned away from the truth that is Harlem or Bedford-Stuyvesant in Brooklyn. Everybody knew that in the Negro ghettos, men, women, and children lived in filth and degradation. But the city, as a city, turned away with the metropolitan brand of apathy. This, most simply, consists of drowning the person-to-person responsibility in a wave of impersonal social action.

Committees were organized, speeches made, budgets passed to "do something" about Harlem or Bedford-Stuyvesant—to do something about the communities. This dulled the reality, and still does, that the communities consist of individual people who ache and suffer in the loss of their individual prides. Housewives who contributed to the NAACP saw nothing wrong in going down to the daily shape-up of domestic workers in the Bronx and selecting a maid for the day after looking over the coffle to see which "girl" among the Negro matrons present looked huskiest.

Now there is an acute awareness of the problems of the Negroes in New York. But again, it is an impersonal awareness, and more and more it is tinged with irritation at the thought that the integration movement will impinge on the daily personal life of the city.

Nor are Negroes in the city immune from apathy—toward one another or toward whites. They are apathetic toward one another's right to believe and act as they please; one man's concept of proper action is labeled with the group epithet "Uncle Tom." And, until the recent upsurge of the integration movement, there was less action taken within the Negro community to improve conditions in Harlem than there was in the all-white sections of the East Side. It has become fashionable to sneer at "white liberals"—fashionable even among Negroes who for years did nothing for brothers even of their own color.

In their own sense of being wronged, some Negroes of New York have become totally apathetic to the sensitivities of all other groups. In a night club in Harlem the other night, an aspiring Negro politician, a most decent man, talked as how the Jewish shopkeepers exploited the Negroes, how he wished Negroes could "save a dollar like the Jews," totally apathetic toward the fact that Jews at the table might be as hurt as he would be if they talked in clichés of the happy-go-lucky Stepin Fetchit Negro. When a Jew protested the Negro was stunned—because he was convinced he hated anti-Semitism. He did in the abstract.

Since the Genovese case New Yorkers have sought explanations of their apathy toward individuals. Fear, some say—fear of involvement, fear of reprisal from goons, fear of becoming mixed up with the police. This, it seems to this writer, is simply rationalization.

The self-protective shells in which we live are determined not only by the difference between big cities and small. They are determined by economics and social class, by caste and by color, and by religion, and by politics.

If I were to see a beggar starving to death in rags on the streets of Paris or New York or London I would be moved to take some kind of action. But many times I have seen starving men lying like broken dolls in the streets of Calcutta or Madras and have done nothing.

I think I would have called the police to save Miss Genovese but I know that I did not save a beggar in Calcutta. Was my failing really so much smaller than that of the people who watched from their windows on Austin Street? And what was the apathy of the people of Austin Street compared, let's say, with the apathy of non-Nazi Germans toward Jews?

Geography is a factor of apathy. Indians reacted to Portuguese imprisoning Goans, but not to Russians killing Hungarians.

Color is a factor. Ghanaians reacted toward Frenchmen killing Algerians, not toward Congolese killing white missionaries.

Strangeness is a factor. Americans react to the extermination of Jews but not to the extermination of Watusis.

There are national as well as individual apathies, all inhibiting the ability to react. The "mind-your-own-business" attitude is despised among individuals, and clucked at by sociologists, but glorified as pragmatic national policy among nations.

Only in scattered moments, and then in halting embarrassment, does the United States, the most involved nation in the world, get down to hard cases about the nature of governments with which it deals, and how they treat their subject citizens. People who believe that a free government should react to oppression of people in the mass by other governments are regarded as fanatics or romantics by the same diplomats who would react in horror to the oppression of one single individual in Washington. Between apathy, regarded as a moral disease, and national policy, the line is often hard to find.

There are, it seems to me, only two logical ways to look at the story of the murder of Catherine Genovese. One is the way of the neighbor on Austin Street—"Let's forget the whole thing."

The other is to recognize that the bell tolls even on each man's individual island, to recognize that every man must fear the witness in himself who whispers to close the window.

DISCUSSION QUESTIONS

1. Did the assailant do anything morally wrong in killing Kitty Genovese? Discuss how an ethical subjectivist would answer this question. Are you satisfied with this answer?

2. Did the witnesses have a moral obligation to call the police? Was the fact that they did not feel like calling the police morally relevant? Discuss how an ethical subjectivist would respond to these questions. Are you satisfied with the answers?

3. We cannot avoid moral judgments. Even inaction involves a moral decision on our part. Are the witnesses, in this regard, morally responsible for the murder of Kitty Genovese?

4. Discuss whether ethical subjectivism offers satisfactory guidelines for resolving situations in which people's feelings come into conflict. In this case, Kitty Genovese's desire to live came into conflict with the assailant's desire to kill her. When the feelings of different individuals come into conflict, who, in most cases, gets to act on their feelings? Who benefits most from ethical subjectivism? Support your answer with specific examples.

5. A New York Times journalist referred to the thirty-eight witnesses as "good people" and "respectable, law-abiding citizens."* What moral standard is he using to make this judgment? Do you agree with this journalist?

6. Do we set our moral standards too low in the United States? To what extent, in your view, has the popularity of ethical subjectivism in our culture contributed to people's reluctance to "get involved" or to "pass moral judgments"? Should we have a Good Samaritan law that legally requires bystanders to assist people in critical need when they can safely do so?

---

*Martin Gansberg, "38 Who Saw Murder Didn't Call Police," in Christina Hoff Sommers and Fred Sommers, *Vice and Virtue in Everyday Life* (Fort Worth, TX: Harcourt Brace Jovanovich, 1993), pp. 51–54.

Stephen A. Satris

Student Relativism

Many, if not most, college students say they believe that morality is all relative. In his article on student relativism, Clemson University philosophy professor Stephen Satris suggests that the relativism of college students, what he calls SR, is not a genuine philosophical position but a way of avoiding analysis of one's opinions. Because of this, SR can hinder moral development and the acquisition of critical thinking skills in students.

CRITICAL THINKING QUESTIONS

1. What does Satris mean by student relativism (SR)?
2. What distinguishes SR from ethical relativism or ethical subjectivism?
3. When are students most likely to engage in SR?
4. Why, according to Satris, is SR so prevalent among college students today?

In this paper I offer an analysis of, and suggest some methods for dealing with, a quite particular and peculiar problem in teaching philosophy. It is, perhaps, not a problem essential to the discipline or to its teaching, but it is nevertheless one of the most serious, pervasive, and frustrating problems confronting most philosophy teachers today. I speak of the problem of student relativism—or, SR for short.

I

What is SR? It is a phenomenon or perhaps a cluster of phenomena manifested in statements such as the following.

> There is really nothing true or false—or nothing really good or bad—it's all relative. One person has an opinion or feeling, and another person has a different one.

Stephen A. Satris, "Student Relativism," *Teaching Philosophy* 9 (Sept. 1986) (3): 193–200. Some notes have been omitted.

> What is true for one person might not be true for another. After all, who's to say?
> Everybody has their own feelings.*

Quite a number of variations on these statements are open. One has only to replace *good or bad* by *right or wrong, feelings* by *values,* or *true* by *good,* in order to see the possibilities.

My suggestion, then, is that SR is not relativism, if by relativism one means a philosophical position characterized by holding that truth in some arena or field of inquiry (such a morality, science, religion)—or perhaps truth in all fields—is relative to the beliefs of individuals or social groups. Bluntly stated, my thesis is that SR is not the same as some such philosophical position because it is simply not a position at all. To have a position (and especially a philosophical position) it is necessary in some sense to engage with questions and issues. A position is something that one arrives at or achieves with respect to those questions or issues. But it is the mark of SR that it does not engage with questions or issues, but aims to avoid them. It is not achieved, but taken in hand—much as a weapon—should the questions or wonder of philosophy threaten. . . .

In fact, SR is not particularly linked with philosophical discussions of relativism. It can occur at any time, although it does seem to be associated with morality, religion, and philosophy itself. ("Philosophy—that's all just opinions, isn't it?") It is certainly not necessary to include a unit on relativism in order to elicit SR from a class. SR might arise at any time: on the first day, the last day, or any day in between. Perhaps its most disappointing appearance occurs after the course is over, although, mercifully, most instructors are then spared an encounter with it. SR is like an eraser that one might take up and use at any time in order to eliminate all points of meaning and relevance. . . .

Particular care must be taken to remember that those who seem to express a liberal attitude are not necessarily liberals. The point again is one of non-disclosure rather than the profession of principles such as those of liberalism or tolerance. This became clearer in my own class when we began to discuss human sexuality. Here, for example, most of the same students who evinced SR were the strongest homophobes. Those who insisted that human excellence lay in doing what feels right to or for one's own self were among the least tolerant of non-standard sexual relationships. Again, when the class addressed itself to questions about God and religious belief, the most conservative Christians were among those who had earlier expressed (and continued to express) SR. It became increasingly plausible to believe that the liberalism and tolerance that might seem to be (perhaps the best) part of SR are really demands or pleas that the hearer be liberal or tolerant toward the (still mysteriously undisclosed but usually disappointingly conventional) opinions, values, feeling, etc. of the speaker.

Here, SR is primarily a method of protection, a suit of armor, which can be applied to one's own opinions, whatever they may be—but not necessarily to the opinions of others. "Who's to say?" is not an expression of one's own intellectual

---

*These expressions and their variants appear both singly and in clusters. The ungrammatical "their" is characteristic.

humility, broadmindedness, or unwillingness to condemn others. Rather, it is an expression of the idea that no one step forward and judge (and possibly criticize) one's own opinions. One would not like that. One says it is impossible. One's own opinions are proper and acceptable just by virtue of their being "felt" as one's own. No further scrutiny, judgment, or improvement is to be allowed or tolerated.* . . .

Often a student will enunciate a series of expressions of SR ("What's true for one person might not be true for another," "Who's to say?", etc.), flying from one to the other, sometimes adding the patently false statement that no two people's opinions ever agree, or the more nervously aggressive remark that no one can say that another person's point of view is wrong. This generally happens for two reasons. First, the expressions of SR serve as a kind of charm or chant that is intended to bring the invincible suit of armor into being. Secondly, when initial statements or remarks have failed to close the conversation, this litany relentlessly applies the locking system to the mind. For this is precisely the purpose of most of these statements: to prevent or close off dialogue and thought. The full stop at the end of expressions of SR is considered absolutely final, unless the speakers themselves follow the remark with another from the enchanted set. Any questions are rhetorical ones, designed to introduce silence. I call these remarks "conversation stoppers." In them, one hears the sound of a door, a mind, locking shut. I've had students who said these things while walking out the door and leaving.

It is my belief then, and the argument of this paper, that SR is fundamentally misdiagnosed when it is viewed as a philosophical position, and that it is no position at all but rather a powerful, elaborate, and at times devious defense mechanism for protection against having to maintain any position or make any serious critical (reflective) effort. It is not then primarily an intellectual problem to be put right merely by making certain information available, drawing some useful distinctions, and/or providing some good arguments. Since it is a failure of will as much as of intellect, the difficulty is not to make good certain deficiencies of thinking (say, through technical mastery of informal fallacies) but to *initiate* critical reflection. This, if true, does not make the problem easier to deal with, but more difficult.

If SR is an eraser, then the hand that reaches for the eraser must somehow be stayed. The suit of armor—really emperor's clothing—must be recognized for what it is. The chanting of SR must be stopped, its spell broken. One must be brought to realize that one is in a real world, not a fantasyland of platitudes and complacency.

II

If the problem of SR is anything like what I have described, how then can it be effectively dealt with? I do not think that there are any guaranteed methods here; nevertheless, beginning with more traditional approaches and moving gradually away from these, I shall suggest some possibilities.

---

*With the forthrightness made possible by anonymity, the author of a collegiate graffito I recently saw wrote: "Kill anyone who makes me question my values."

A philosophically generous view which assumes (perhaps merely for pedagogical purposes) that an expression of SR is indeed a genuine philosophical thesis *might*—in spite of all that I have said—be effective. The SR, if it is a protective covering, might be just a very thin surface phenomenon that has been picked up and found useful. Generally, in this country, public education from kindergarten through high school explicitly promotes the use of protective devices such as SR. Students learn from teachers and peers how to fall back upon SR in nearly all non-scientific matters of controversy or evaluation, e.g., in matters of religion, morals, politics, and non-scientific argument in general. Many people come out of a public school background having learned that "value judgment" or "controversial issue" simply *means* a judgment or issue with respect to which there is no right response or answer and about which (since it's all a matter of personal opinion and not of scientific fact) we may all conveniently believe as we wish while remaining error-free. . . .

DISCUSSION QUESTIONS

1. Do you agree with Satris that student relativism (SR) is not the same as ethical relativism or ethical subjectivism? Support your answer.
2. How does a person expressing SR act when his or her moral position is challenged? How does this differ from the way a true ethical subjectivist would respond to a challenge?
3. Have you ever engaged in SR? If so, give some specific examples. When are you most likely to engage in SR? What might you do to make yourself less likely to fall back on SR?
4. Discuss ways, if any, in which SR can interfere with students' moral development and ability to think critically about moral issues.
5. To what extent have your earlier education experiences, as well as your college experience, encouraged SR? How can ethics education counter SR?
6. Has the prevalence of SR contributed to the type of moral apathy that characterized the witnesses in the Kitty Genovese murder? Contrast Satris's discussion of SR with Sommers's explanation of moral apathy in the United States. Which person makes the most convincing argument?

Cultural Relativism

Cultural relativists, like ethical subjectivists, maintain that standards of right and wrong are created by people. However, rather than being relative to isolated individuals, they maintain that morality is created by cultures or societies. Public opinion, not private opinion, determines what is right and wrong. There are no objective universal moral standards that hold for all people in all cultures. Morality instead is nothing more than socially approved customs.

Cultural relativists are not merely arguing that *some* moral values are relative to the culture. Rather, they maintain that *all* moral values are nothing more than cultural customs. Because there are no universal moral values, the moral values of one culture cannot be judged to be any better or worse than those of any other culture. Morality not only differs from culture to culture but may also change within a culture over time, much like laws and fashions. In order to know what is right or wrong, we only have to ask what are the norms and customs of our culture or society at this point in history.

Although the great majority of world philosophers reject cultural relativism, it is still a popular moral theory among nonphilosophers. Studies find that 90 percent of adults in the United States equate morality with cultural norms of right and wrong. According to developmental psychologists such as Lawrence Kohlberg and Carol Gilligan, people do not progress to a higher stage of moral reasoning until they see the inadequacies of their current method of making moral judgments. Because most college students never progress beyond cultural relativism, considerable attention will be given to this theory and, in particular, to its weakness and implications.

The modern version of cultural relativism emerged primarily as a protest against colonial imperialism and the degraded view of primitive society that was used to justify it. During the eighteenth and nineteenth centuries, Europe and the United States adopted expansionist policies. To justify these policies, Darwin's theory of evolution was reinterpreted by Social Darwinists such as Herbert Spencer to "scientifically" validate the takeover of "primitive" societies.

The first selection is from Herbert Spencer's *Principles of Ethics* (1897). According to Spencer, just as animals progress over time to more complex life forms, so too does humanity evolve culturally over time from the ignorant savage cultures to the intelligent and morally civilized Christians. The imposition of European morality and lifestyles on non-Western cultures, consequently, was justified as morally benefiting these primitive people.

In the second selection from "Anthropology and the Abnormal," anthropologist and cultural relativist Ruth Benedict (1887–1948) disputes Spencer's moral theory. She argues instead that no culture's morals are any better, or any worse, than those of any other.

Ibn Khaldun, in the next selection from *The Muqaddimah,* takes a stand against cultural relativism. Although he believes that we can pass moral judgments on other cultures, he does not adopt the hierarchical view of the Social Darwinists. Ibn Khaldun argues instead that nomadic cultures are morally superior to the sedentary urban cultures of the civilized world.

Cultural relativism not only rules out passing moral judgment on other societies and our society's past practices, it also precludes passing moral judgment on existing customs and norms within our own society. Because most adults equate morality with the norms of their culture, oppressive practices and customs are less likely to be noticed than those from the past that are no longer socially acceptable.

In the next selection from *The Politics of Reality,* Marilyn Frye rejects cultural relativism and, in particular, the cultural values and customs that oppress women. The selection from Frye also illustrates how cultural norms are most often the norms of those who have the power to make laws and enforce customs.

The selection from Daniel Goldhagen's recent book *Hitler's Willing Executioners* (1996) explores the implications of cultural relativism for how we define the moral community. Cultural relativism defines the moral community in ethnocentric cultural terms. There are no universal human rights. Beings have moral value only because their society grants them this status. Those who are not in the moral community (like the Jews in Nazi Germany) are denied the respect and opportunities afforded to those who are included.

Cultural relativism, if taken seriously as a moral theory, can be deadly. Goldhagen's book in particular illustrates how most people uncritically justify even destructive cultural norms, such as anti-Semitism, as morally acceptable. If cultural relativism is the correct moral theory, then it is morally acceptable, and perhaps even morally obligatory, to discriminate against certain groups of people such as women, Jews, and Hispanics, if that is the law or custom of the society.

In the next selection, "Letter from a Birmingham Jail," civil rights leader Martin Luther King, Jr., rejects cultural relativism and instead argues that there are certain universal moral principles regarding respect for the dignity and equal rights of all people that must be acknowledged by a good society. When a society's laws are inconsistent with these universal principles, King argues, civil disobedience may be the morally appropriate response.

Cultural relativism fell out of favor among scholars after World War II. Even the most ardent cultural relativists found they could not justify the horrors of the Holocaust and the anti-Semitism that fueled it as a morally acceptable cultural norm no matter how generally accepted it was in German society. In the final article on relativism in ethics, William Shaw argues that neither type of relativism —ethical subjectivism and cultural relativism—can be justified.

Herbert Spencer

The Principles of Ethics

In the first selection from *The Principles of Ethics,* English philosopher and Social Darwinist Herbert Spencer (1820–1903) defends a moral theory based very loosely on Darwin's theory of the survival of the fittest. Interestingly, the notion of evolution as progress was developed by the Social Darwinists and not by Darwin himself. The belief in progress had become firmly entrenched in the Western psyche during the Enlightenment of the eighteenth century. Rousseau's romantic notion of the noble savage—the natural person unaffected by the restrictions of modern society—was never generally accepted and was easily usurped by the Social Darwinist's view of savages as morally inferior forms of human life.

CRITICAL THINKING QUESTIONS

1. How does Spencer define the term *justice?*
2. What is the relation, according to Spencer, between the degree of organization in a society and the degree of justice practiced in that society? What premises does Spencer use to support his position?
3. Why does Spencer claim that more sedentary agricultural cultures are more morally advanced than hunting and gathering cultures?
4. What is the relation between offensive wars and the Darwinian principle of survival of the fittest?
5. What is the relation between aggression, cooperation, and level of civilization, according to Spencer?
6. What are the steps, according to Spencer, in the evolution of justice from its "universal simple form" to the justice found in civilized societies?

HUMAN JUSTICE

§257. The contents of the last chapter foreshadow the contents of this. As, from the evolution point of view, human life must be regarded as a further development of sub-human life, it follows that from this same point of view, human justice must be a further development of sub-human justice. For convenience the

The Principles of Ethics, Vol. II (New York: D. Appleton and Co., 1897), pp. 17–23, 47–48.

two are here separately treated, but they are essentially of the same nature, and form parts of a continuous whole. . . .

§258. The truth that justice becomes more pronounced as organization becomes higher, which we contemplated in the last chapter, is further exemplified on passing from sub-human justice to human justice. The degree of justice and the degree of organization simultaneously make advances. These are shown alike by the entire human race, and by its superior varieties as contrasted with its inferior.

We saw that a high species of animal is distinguished from a low species, in the respect that since its aggregate suffers less mortality from incidental destructive agencies, each of its members continues on the average for a longer time subject to the normal relation between conduct and consequence; and here we see that the human race as a whole, far lower in its rate of mortality than nearly all races of inferior kinds, usually subjects its members for much longer periods to the good and evil results of well-adapted and ill-adapted conduct. We also saw that as, among the higher animals, a greater average longevity makes it possible for individual differences to show their effects for longer periods, it results that the unlike fates of different individuals are to a greater extent determined by that normal relation between conduct and consequence which constitutes justice; and we here see that in mankind, unlikenesses of faculty in still greater degrees, and for still longer periods, work out their effects in advantaging the superior and disadvantaging the inferior in the continuous play of conduct and consequence. . . .

. . . it is manifest that both the greater differences of longevity among individuals, and the greater differences of social position, imply that in civilized societies more than in savage societies, differences of endowment, and consequent differences of conduct, are enabled to cause their appropriate differences of results, good or evil: the justice is greater.

§259. More clearly in the human race than in lower races, we are shown that gregariousness establishes itself because it profits the variety in which it arises; partly by furthering general safety and partly by facilitating sustentation. And we are shown that the degree of gregariousness is determined by the degree in which it thus subserves the interests of the variety. For where the variety is one of which the members live on wild food, they associate only in small groups: game and fruits widely distributed, can support these only. But greater gregariousness arises where agriculture makes possible the support of a large number on a small area; and where the accompanying development of industries introduces many and various co-operations.

We come now to the truth—faintly indicated among lower beings and conspicuously displayed among human beings—that the advantages of co-operation can be had only by conformity to certain requirements which association imposes. The mutual hindrances liable to arise during the pursuit of their ends by individuals living in proximity, must be kept within such limits as to leave a surplus of advantage obtained by associated life. . . .

§260. We saw that among inferior gregarious creatures, justice in its universal simple form, besides being qualified by the self-subordination which parenthood implies, and in some measure by the self-restraint necessitated by association, is, in a few cases, further qualified in a small degree by the partial or complete sacrifice of individuals made in defence of the species. And now, in the highest gregarious creature, we see that this further qualification of primitive justice assumes large proportions.

No longer, as among inferior beings, demanded only by the need for defence against enemies of other kinds, this further self-subordination is, among human beings, also demanded by the need for defence against enemies of the same kind. Having spread wherever there is food, groups of men have come to be everywhere in one another's way; and the mutual enmities hence resulting, have made the sacrifices entailed by wars between groups, far greater than the sacrifices made in defence of groups against inferior animals. . . . Still, it must be regarded as an obligation to the extent to which the maintenance of the species is subserved by the maintenance of each of its groups.

But the self-subordination thus justified, and in a sense rendered obligatory, is limited to that which is required for defensive war. Only because the preservation of the group as a whole conduces to preservation of its members' lives, and their ability to pursue the objects of life, is there a reason for the sacrifice of some of its members; and this reason no longer exists when war is offensive instead of defensive.

It may, indeed, be contended that since offensive wars initiate those struggles between groups which end in the destruction of the weaker, offensive wars, furthering the peopling of the Earth by the stronger, subserve the interests of the race. But even supposing that the conquered groups always consisted of men having smaller mental or bodily fitness for war (which they do not; for it is in part a question of numbers, and the smaller groups may consist of the more capable warriors), there would still be an adequate answer. It is only during the earlier stages of human progress that the development of strength, courage, and cunning, are of chief importance. After societies of considerable size have been formed, and the subordination needed for organizing them produced, other and higher faculties become those of chief importance; and the struggle for existence carried on by violence, does not always further the survival of the fittest. The fact that but for a mere accident Persia would have conquered Greece, and the fact that the Tartar hordes very nearly overwhelmed European civilization, show that offensive war can be trusted to subserve the interests of the race only when the capacity for a high social life does not exist; and that in proportion as this capacity develops, offensive war tends more and more to hinder, rather than to further, human welfare. In brief we may say that the arrival at a stage in which ethical considerations come to be entertained, is the arrival at a stage in which offensive war, by no means certain to further predominance of races fitted for a high social life, and certain to cause injurious moral reactions on the conquering as well as on the conquered, ceases to be justifiable; and only defensive war retains quasi-ethical justification. . . .

THE FORMULA OF JUSTICE

§272. After tracing up the evolution of justice in its simple form, considered objectively as a condition to the maintenance of life; after seeing how justice as so considered becomes qualified by a new factor when the life is gregarious, more especially in the human race; and after observing the corresponding subjective products—the sentiment of justice and the idea of justice—arising from converse with this condition; we are now prepared for giving to the conclusion reached a definite form. . . .

§274. . . . an instructive comment is yielded by the facts of social progress. For they show that, in so far as justice is concerned, there has been an advance from the incorrect interpretation to the correct interpretation.

In early stages we see habitual aggression and counter-aggression: now between societies and now between individuals. Neighbouring tribes fight about the limits to their territories, trespassing first on one side and then on the other; and further fights are entailed by the requirement that mortality suffered shall be followed by mortality inflicted. In such acts of revenge and re-revenge there is displayed a vague recognition of equality of claims. This tends towards recognition of definite limits, alike in respect of territory and in respect of bloodshed; so that in some cases a balance is maintained between the numbers of deaths on either side.

Along with this growing conception of inter-tribal justice goes a growing conception of justice among members of each tribe. At first it is the fear of retaliation which causes such respect for one another's persons and possessions as exists. The idea of justice is that of a balancing of injuries—"an eye for an eye and a tooth for a tooth." This remains the idea during early stages of civilization. After justice, as so conceived, ceases to be enforced by the aggrieved person himself, it is this which he asks to have enforced by the constituted authority. The cry to the ruler for justice is the cry for punishment—for the infliction of an injury at least as great as the injury suffered, or, otherwise, for a compensation equivalent to the loss. Thus the equality of claims is but tacitly asserted in the demand to have rectified, as far as may be, the breaches of equality.

How there tends gradually to emerge from this crude conception of justice the finished conception of justice, it seems scarcely needful to explain. The true idea is generated by experience of the evils which accompany the false idea. Naturally, the perception of the right restraints on conduct becomes clearer as respect for these restraints is forced on men, and so rendered more habitual and more general. Men's incursions into one another's spheres constitute a kind of oscillation, which, violent at the outset, becomes gradually less with the progress towards a relatively peaceful state of society. As the oscillations decrease there is an approach to equilibrium; and along with this approach to equilibrium comes approach to definite theory of equilibrium.

Thus that primitive idea of justice in which aggression is to be balanced by counter-aggression, fades from thought as fast as it disappears from practice; and there comes the idea of justice here formulated, in which are recognized such limitations of conduct as exclude aggressions altogether.

DISCUSSION QUESTIONS

1. Is the analogy between human and nonhuman ("lower") animals and civilized humans and primitive humans valid? Does it support Spencer's argument?

2. Is Spencer's argument that longevity in lifespan promotes justice empirically sound? Does he offer any data to back up his assumptions?
3. Are you satisfied with Spencer's definition of the term *justice?* Does he use the term consistently throughout the reading?
4. What evidence does Spencer offer to back up his claim that there is less aggression and more cooperation in civilized societies? Are you satisfied with his argument?
5. On what grounds does Spencer claim that civilized societies are less likely to engage in offensive wars? Do his premises support this conclusion?
6. Spencer reinterpreted Darwin's theory of the survival of the fittest to "scientifically" validate the takeover of primitive societies. Is Spencer's belief in evolution as progress empirically justified? To what extent does the notion of progress inform our thinking about so-called less developed nations today?
7. The imposition of European mortality on non-Western cultures was justified by Spencer and the Social Darwinists as benefiting primitive people. To what extent is Social Darwinism still used today to justify the imposition of the moral values of the mainstream culture on developing and undeveloped nations, as well as on marginalized people within our own society? Is it morally justifiable to impose mainstream moral values on others? Use specific examples to support your answer.

Ruth Benedict

A Defense of Cultural Relativism

Many notable anthropologists and sociologists disagreed with Spencer's Social Darwinism. They argued instead that morality is relative to the particular history and environment of each culture. American anthropologist Ruth Benedict (1887–1948) was one of the most articulate defenders of cultural relativism. In her article "Anthropology and the Abnormal," Benedict uses her extensive anthropological research to support her conclusion that cultural relativism provides the correct description of morality.

CRITICAL THINKING QUESTIONS

1. What, according to Benedict, is the source of moral values?
2. What is Benedict's view of human nature?
3. Does Benedict regard civilization as a higher form of social order than primitive societies?
4. How is Benedict using the term *abnormal?*
5. What, according to Benedict, is the relationship between what is normal and what is good?
6. What examples of cultural traits and attitudes does Benedict use to support her conclusion?

Modern social anthropology has become more and more a study of the varieties and common elements of cultural environment and the consequences of these in human behavior. For such a study of diverse social orders primitive peoples fortunately provide a laboratory not yet entirely vitiated by the spread of a standardized world-wide civilization. Dyaks and Hopis, Fijians and Yakuts are significant for psychological and sociological study because only among these simpler peoples has there been sufficient isolation to give opportunity for the development of localized social forms. In the higher cultures the standardization of custom and belief over a couple of continents has given a false sense of the inevitability of the particular forms that have gained currency, and we need to turn to a wider survey in order to check the conclusions we hastily base upon this near-universality of familiar customs. Most of the simpler cultures did not gain

"A Defense of Cultural Relativism," from "Anthropology and the Abnormal," *The Journal of General Psychology* (10): 59–82. Notes have been omitted.

the wide currency of the one which, out of our experience, we identify with human nature, but this was for various historical reasons, and certainly not for any that gives us as its carriers a monopoly of social good or of social sanity. Modern civilization, from this point of view, becomes not a necessary pinnacle of human achievement but one entry in a long series of possible adjustments.

These adjustments, whether they are in mannerisms like the ways of showing anger, or joy, or grief in any society, or in major human drives like those of sex, prove to be far more variable than experience in any one culture would suggest. . . .

As a matter of fact, one of the most striking facts that emerge from a study of widely varying cultures is the ease with which our abnormals function in other cultures. It does not matter what kind of "abnormality" we choose for illustration, those which indicate extreme instability, or those which are more in the nature of character traits like sadism or delusions of grandeur or of persecution, there are well-described cultures in which these abnormals function at ease and with honor, and apparently without danger or difficulty to the society. . . .

It is clear that culture may value and make socially available even highly unstable human types. If it chooses to treat their peculiarities as the most valued variants of human behavior, the individuals in question will rise to the occasion and perform their social rôles without reference to our usual ideas of the types who can make social adjustments and those who cannot.

Cataleptic and trance phenomena are, of course, only one illustration of the fact that those whom we regard as abnormals may function adequately in other cultures. Many of our culturally discarded traits are selected for elaboration in different societies. Homosexuality is an excellent example, for in this case our attention is not constantly diverted, as in the consideration of trance, to the interruption of routine activity which it implies. Homosexuality poses the problem very simply. A tendency toward this trait in our culture exposes an individual to all the conflicts to which all aberrants are always exposed, and we tend to identify the consequences of this conflict with homosexuality. But these consequences are obviously local and cultural. Homosexuals in many societies are not incompetent, but they may be such if the culture asks adjustments of them that would strain any man's vitality. Wherever homosexuality has been given an honorable place in any society, those to whom it is congenial have filled adequately the honorable rôles society assigns to them. Plato's *Republic* is, of course, the most convincing statement of such a reading of homosexuality. It is presented as one of the major means to the good life, and it was generally so regarded in Greece at that time.

The cultural attitude toward homosexuals has not always been on such a high ethical plane, but it has been very varied. Among many American Indian tribes there exists the institution of the berdache. . . , as the French called them. These men-women were men who at puberty or thereafter took the dress and the occupations of women. Sometimes they married other men and lived with them. Sometimes they were men with no inversion, persons of weak sexual endowment who chose this rôle to avoid the jeers of the women. The berdaches were never regarded as of first-rate supernatural power, as similar men-women were in Siberia, but rather as leaders in women's occupations, good healers in certain diseases, or, among certain tribes, as the genial organizers of social affairs. In any case, they were socially placed. They were not left exposed to the conflicts that visit the deviant who is excluded from participation in the recognized patterns of his society.

The most spectacular illustrations of the extent to which normality may be culturally defined are those cultures where an abnormality of our culture is the cornerstone of their social structure. It is not possible to do justice to these possibilities in a short discussion. A recent study of an island of northwest Melanesia by Fortune . . . describes a society built upon traits which we regard as beyond the border of paranoia. In this tribe the exogamic groups look upon each other as prime manipulators of black magic, so that one marries always into an enemy group which remains for life one's deadly and unappeasable foes. They look upon a good garden crop as a confession of theft, for everyone is engaged in making magic to induce into his garden the productiveness of his neighbors'; therefore no secrecy in the island is so rigidly insisted upon as the secrecy of a man's harvesting of his yams. Their polite phrase at the acceptance of a gift is, "And if you now poison me, how shall I repay you this present?" Their preoccupation with poisoning is constant; no woman ever leaves her cooking pot for a moment untended. Even the great affinal economic exchanges that are characteristic of this Melanesian culture area are quite altered in Dobu since they are incompatible with this fear and distrust that pervades the culture. They go farther and people the whole world outside their own quarters with such malignant spirits that all-night feasts and ceremonials simply do not occur here. They have even rigorous religiously enforced customs that forbid the sharing of seed even in one family group. Anyone else's food is deadly poison to you, so that communality of stores is out of the question. For some months before harvest the whole society is on the verge of starvation, but if one falls to the temptation and eats up one's seed yams, one is an outcast and a beachcomber for life. There is no coming back. It involves, as a matter of course, divorce and the breaking of all social ties. . . .

An even more extreme example, because it is of a culture that has built itself upon a more complex abnormality, is that of the North Pacific Coast of North America. The civilization of the Kwakiutl. . . , at the time when it was first recorded in the last decades of the nineteenth century, was one of the most vigorous in North America. It was built up on an ample economic supply of goods, the fish which furnished their food staple being practically inexhaustible and obtainable with comparatively small labor, and the wood which furnished the material for their houses, their furnishings, and their arts being, with however much labor, always procurable. They lived in coastal villages that compared favorably in size with those of any other American Indians and they kept up constant communication by means of sea-going dug-out canoes.

It was one of the most vigorous and zestful of the aboriginal cultures of North America, with complex crafts and ceremonials, and elaborate and striking arts. It certainly had none of the earmarks of a sick civilization. The tribes of the Northwest Coast had wealth, and exactly in our terms. That is, they had not only a surplus of economic goods, but they made a game of the manipulation of wealth. It was by no means a mere direct transcription of economic needs and the filling of those needs. . . .

Every society, beginning with some slight inclination in one direction or another, carries its preference farther and farther, integrating itself more and more completely upon its chosen basis, and discarding those types of behavior that are uncongenial. Most of those organizations of personality that seem to us most incontrovertibly abnormal have been used by different civilizations in the very foundations of their institutional life. Conversely the most valued traits of our normal individuals have been looked on in differently organized cultures as aberrant. Normality, in short, within a very wide range, is culturally defined. It is primarily a term for the socially elaborated segment of human behavior in any culture; and abnormality, a term for the segment that that particular civilization does not use. The very eyes with which we see the problem are conditioned by the long traditional habits of our own society.

It is a point that has been made more often in relation to ethics than in relation to psychiatry. We do not any longer make the mistake of deriving the morality of our own locality and decade directly from the inevitable constitution of human nature. We do not elevate it to the dignity of a first principle. We recognize that morality differs in every society, and is a convenient term for socially approved habits. Mankind has always preferred to say, "It is morally good," rather than "It is habitual," and the fact of this preference is matter enough for a critical science of ethics. But historically the two phrases are synonymous.

The concept of the normal is properly a variant of the concept of the good. It is that which society has approved. A normal action is one which falls well within the limits of expected behavior for a particular society. Its variability among different peoples is essentially a function of the variability of the behavior patterns that different societies have created for themselves, and can never be wholly divorced from a consideration of culturally institutionalized types of behavior.

Each culture is a more or less elaborate working-out of the potentialities of the segment it has chosen. In so far as a civilization is well integrated and consistent within itself, it will tend to carry farther and farther, according to its nature, its initial impulse toward a particular type of action, and from the point of view of any other culture those elaborations will include more and more extreme and aberrant traits.

Each of these traits, in proportion as it reinforces the chosen behavior patterns of that culture, is for that culture normal. Those individuals to whom it is congenial either congenitally, or as the result of childhood sets, are accorded prestige in that culture, and are not visited with the social contempt or disapproval which their traits could call down upon them in a society that was differently organized. On the other hand, those individuals whose characteristics are not congenial to the selected type of human behavior in that community are the deviants, no matter how valued their personality traits may be in a contrasted civilization.

The Dobuan who is not easily susceptible to fear of treachery, who enjoys work and likes to be helpful, is their neurotic and regarded as silly. On the Northwest Coast the person who finds it difficult to read life in terms of an insult contest will be the person upon whom fall all the difficulties of the culturally unprovided for. The person who does not find it easy to humiliate a neighbor, nor to see humiliation in his own experience, who is genial and loving, may, of course, find some unstandardized way of achieving satisfactions in his society, but not in the major patterned responses that his culture requires of him. If he is born to play an important rôle in a family with many hereditary privileges, he can succeed only by doing violence to his whole personality. If he does not succeed, he has betrayed his culture; that is, he is abnormal. . . .

DISCUSSION QUESTIONS

1. Does the anthropological data used by Benedict support her conclusion that morality is culturally relative? How else might cultural variability be explained?
2. Benedict once said, "Most individuals are plastic to the molding force of the society into which they are born." To what extent are you simply a product of your upbringing and societal influences? Does Benedict's view of human nature allow room for individuality and independent thought?
3. How might Benedict explain the moral convictions of social reformers, such as the American abolitionists, who argue that the values of their own culture are immoral? If morality is the same as cultural norms, isn't this impossible?
4. Is what is normal in our society the same as what we consider good, as Benedict claims? Are there instances where people might consider what is normal as less than morally desirable? Illustrate your answer with examples.
5. Was Benedict being logically consistent when she criticized colonialism and the takeover of simpler non-Western societies? Can cultural relativism be used as an argument for colonialism, given that colonialism and expansionism were cultural norms in much of Europe as well as in the United States during the nineteenth century?
6. Are you satisfied with the range of examples used by Benedict to support her theory? Can Benedict's theory satisfactorily explain more extreme cultural customs and practices, such as slavery, female genital mutilation, apartheid, and Nazism? Are there some cultural customs that fall outside the limits of moral decency? If so, how might we draw the line between the morally acceptable and morally unacceptable cultural customs while still maintaining respect for other cultures' customs?
7. Compare and contrast Benedict's moral theory with that of Herbert Spencer. Are cultural relativism and Social Darwinism the only two possible ways of explaining differences in moral values between cultures? Support your answer.

Ibn Khaldun

The Muqaddimah

Modern cultural relativists like Ruth Benedict disagreed with the prevailing view that Western cultures were morally superior to non-Western cultures. In the selection from *The Muqaddimah,* North African philosopher Ibn Khaldun turns the tables on this argument by arguing that sedentary cultures are morally *inferior* to simpler nomadic cultures. The customs of nomadic cultures, he claims, enhance our good traits whereas those of sedentary and urban cultures encourage immorality. In this sense, Khaldun takes a position that contrasts with those of both Benedict and Spencer.

Ibn Khaldun (1332–1406) was born in Tunisia to Yemenite Arab parents. A noted historian, scholar, and philosopher, *The Muqaddimah* by Khaldun is said to be one of the greatest books ever written on world history and philosophy.

CRITICAL THINKING QUESTIONS

1. What, according to Khaldun, is the goal of civilization? Does Khaldun think this is a worthwhile goal? If not, why not?

2. What are some of the customs associated with a sedentary culture that Khaldun argues contribute to moral corruption?

3. Why does Khaldun think that city life in particular corrupts people's character?

4. Why is a nomadic lifestyle, according to Khaldun, more conducive to the development of moral virtues?

Reason and tradition make it clear that forty years mean the end of the increase of an individual's powers and growth. When a man has reached the age of forty, nature stops growing for a while, then starts to decline. It should be known that the same is the case with sedentary culture in civilization, because there is a limit that cannot be overstepped. When luxury and prosperity come to civilized people, it naturally causes them to follow the ways of sedentary culture and adopt its customs. As one knows, sedentary culture is the adoption of diversified luxuries, the cultivation of the things that go with them, and addiction to the crafts that

"The Moral Corruption of Sedentary Cultures," in *The Muqaddimah,* translated by Franz Rosenthal (Princeton, NJ: Princeton University Press, 1969), pp. 285–289. Notes have been omitted.

give elegance to all refinements, such as the crafts of cooking, dressmaking, building, and (making) carpets, vessels, and all other parts of (domestic) economy. For the elegant execution of all these things, there exist many crafts not needed in desert life with its lack of elegance. When elegance in (domestic) economy has reached the limit, it is followed by subservience to desires. From all these customs, the human soul receives a multiple stamp that undermines its religion and worldly well-being. It cannot preserve its religion, because it has now been firmly stamped by customs that are difficult to discard. (It cannot preserve) its worldly (well-being), because the customs (of luxury) demand a great many things and (entail) many requirements for which (a man's) income is not sufficient. . . .

. . . The expenditure of sedentary people, therefore, grows and is no longer reasonable but extravagant. The people cannot escape this because they are dominated by and subservient to their customs. All their profits go into their expenditure. One person after another becomes reduced in circumstances and indigent. Poverty takes hold of them. Few persons bid for the available goods. Business decreases, and the situation of the town deteriorates.

All this is caused by excessive sedentary culture and luxury. They corrupt the city generally in respect to business and civilization. Corruption of the individual inhabitants is the result of painful and trying efforts to satisfy the needs caused by their (luxury) customs; (the result) of the bad qualities they have acquired in the process of satisfying (those needs); and of the damage the soul suffers after it has obtained them. Immorality, wrongdoing, insincerity, and trickery, for the purposes of making a living in a proper or an improper manner, increase among them. The soul comes to think about (making a living), to study it, and to use all possible trickery for the purpose. People are now devoted to lying, gambling, cheating, fraud, theft, perjury, and usury. Because of the many desires and pleasures resulting from luxury, they are found to know everything about the ways and means of immorality, they talk openly about it and its causes, and give up all restraint in discussing it, even among relatives and close female relations, where the Bedouin attitude requires modesty (and avoidance of) obscenities. They also know everything about fraud and deceit, which they employ to defend themselves against the possible use of force against them and against the punishment expected for their evil deeds. Eventually, this becomes a custom and trait of character with most of them, except those whom God protects.

The city, then, teems with low people of blameworthy character. They encounter competition from many members of the younger generation of the dynasty, whose education has been neglected and whom the dynasty has neglected to accept. They, therefore, adopt the qualities of their environment and company, even though they may be people of noble descent and ancestry. Men are human beings and as such resemble one another. They differ in merit and are distinguished by their character, by their acquisition of virtues and avoidance of vices. The person who is strongly coloured by any kind of vice and whose character is corrupted, is not helped by his good descent and fine origin. Thus, one finds that many descendants of great families, men of a highly esteemed origin, members of the dynasty, get into deep water and adopt low occupations in order to make a living, because their character is corrupt and they are coloured by wrongdoing and insincerity. If this (situation) spreads in a town or nation, God permits it to be ruined and destroyed. This is the meaning of the word of God: "When we want to destroy a village, we order those of its inhabitants who live in luxury to act wickedly therein. Thus, the word becomes true for it, and we do destroy it."

A possible explanation of this (situation) is that the profits (the people) make do not pay for their needs, because of the great number of (luxury) customs and the desire of the soul to satisfy them. Thus, the affairs of the people are disordered, and if the affairs of individuals one by one deteriorate, the town becomes disorganized and falls into ruin. . . .

Among the things that corrupt sedentary culture, there is the disposition toward pleasures and indulgence in them, because of the great luxury (that prevails). It leads to diversification of the desires of the belly for pleasurable food and drink. This is followed by diversification of the pleasures of sex through various ways of sexual intercourse, such as adultery and homosexuality. This leads to destruction of the species. It may come about indirectly, through the confusion concerning one's descent caused by adultery. Nobody knows his own son, since he is illegitimate and since the sperm (of different men) got mixed up in the womb. The natural compassion a man feels for his children and his feeling of responsibility for them is lost. Thus, they perish, and this leads to the end of the species. Or, the destruction of the species may come about directly, as is the case with homosexuality, which leads directly to the nonexistence of offspring. It contributes more to the destruction of the species (than adultery), since it leads to no human beings being brought into existence, while adultery only leads to the (social) nonexistence of those who are in existence. Therefore, the school of Mâlik is more explicit and correct with regard to homosexuality than the other schools. This shows that it understands the intentions of the religious law and their bearing upon the (public) interest better (than the other legal schools).

This should be understood. It shows that the goal of civilization is sedentary culture and luxury. When civilization reaches that goal, it turns toward corruption and starts being senile, as happens in the natural life of living beings. Indeed, we may say that the qualities of character resulting from sedentary culture and luxury are identical with corruption. Man is a man only inasmuch as he is able to procure for himself useful things and to repel harmful things, and inasmuch as his character is suited to making efforts to this effect. The sedentary person cannot take care of his needs personally. He may be too weak, because of the tranquillity he enjoys. Or he may be too proud, because he was brought up in prosperity and luxury. Both things are blameworthy. He also is not able to repel harmful things, because he has no courage as the result of luxury and his upbringing under the impact of education and instruction. He thus becomes dependent upon a protective force to defend him.

He then usually becomes corrupt with regard to his religion, also. The (luxury) customs and his subservience to them have corrupted him, and his soul has been stamped by habits of luxury, as we have stated. There are only very rare exceptions. When the strength of a man and then his character and religion are corrupted, his humanity is corrupted, and he becomes, in effect, transformed into an animal.

It is in this sense that those government soldiers who are close to Bedouin life and toughness are more useful than those who have grown up in a sedentary culture and have adopted its character traits. This can be found in every dynasty. It has thus become clear that the stage of sedentary culture is the stopping point in the life of civilization and dynasties. . . .

DISCUSSION QUESTIONS

1. Do you agree with Khaldun that certain types of cultures are more conducive to the development of virtue? Illustrate your answer with examples.
2. If certain types of cultures are morally superior to others, then cultural relativism must be rejected. Does Khaldun present a convincing refutation of cultural relativism?
3. In what ways have social influences in your own life contributed, for better or worse, to the development of your character? Have you ever rejected any of your family's values on moral grounds? Have you ever rejected any of your cultural values as immoral? On what grounds?
4. Khaldun is especially critical of the corrupting influence of city life. Is the high crime rate and poverty associated with cities in the United States a direct result of city living? Support your answer. What public policies might Khaldun suggest implementing to cope with the problems and corruption currently plaguing so many U.S. cities?
5. Would we, as Americans, be better off by going back to a simpler lifestyle? How might you change your own lifestyle so it is more conducive to the development of a virtuous character?
6. How might Khaldun respond to Spencer's argument regarding the moral superiority of sedentary European societies as opposed to simpler hunting and gathering cultures? Which of the two do you think presents the stronger argument for his position? Support your answer.
7. Discuss how Benedict might respond to Khaldun's argument that the customs of sedentary cultures are morally corrupting. Would she be more likely to agree with Khaldun's position? Support your answer.

Marilyn Frye

Oppression

Feminist philosopher Marilyn Frye, in her essay "Oppression," rejects the cultural values and customs that oppress women. In doing so she rejects the basic premise of cultural relativism, which identifies morality with custom. Frye also argues in her essay that because many of us uncritically assume that customs must be morally correct, people can be oppressed without even being aware of it.

CRITICAL THINKING QUESTIONS

1. How does Frye support her claim that women are oppressed in our culture?
2. Why does Frye reject the statement that men are also oppressed in our culture?
3. How does Frye use the analogy between oppression and living in a birdcage to support her thesis? Are people who live in "birdcages" necessarily aware of their restrictions?
4. Who, according to Frye, defines women's role in our culture?
5. Why do some people claim that women are not oppressed by our culture?
6. What, according to Frye, does the category of "man" stand for in this culture? How does it differ, in terms of position in the moral community, from the category of "woman"?

It is a fundamental claim of feminism that women are oppressed. The word "oppression" is a strong word. It repels and attracts. It is dangerous and dangerously fashionable and endangered. It is much misused, and sometimes not innocently.

The statement that women are oppressed is frequently met with the claim that men are oppressed too. We hear that oppressing is oppressive to those who oppress as well as to those they oppress. Some men cite as evidence of their oppression their much-advertised inability to cry. It is tough, we are told, to be masculine. When the stresses and frustrations of being a man are cited as evidence that oppressors are oppressed by their oppressing, the word "oppression"

"Oppression," in *The Politics of Reality: Essays in Feminist Theory* (Trumansburg, NY: The Crossing Press, 1983), pp. 1–16.

is being stretched to meaninglessness; it is treated as though its scope includes any and all human experience of limitation or suffering, no matter the cause, degree or consequence. Once such usage has been put over on us, then if ever we deny that any person or group is oppressed, we seem to imply that we think they never suffer and have no feelings. We are accused of insensitivity; even of bigotry. For women, such accusation is particularly intimidating, since sensitivity is one of the few virtues that has been assigned to us. If we are found insensitive, we may fear we have no redeeming traits at all and perhaps are not real women. Thus are we silenced before we begin: the name of our situation drained of meaning and our guilt mechanisms tripped.

But this is nonsense. Human beings can be miserable without being oppressed, and it is perfectly consistent to deny that a person or group is oppressed without denying that they have feelings or that they suffer. . . .

I

The root of the word 'oppression' is the element 'press'. *The press of the crowd; pressed into military service; to press a pair of pants; printing press; press the button.* Presses are used to mold things or flatten them or reduce them in bulk, sometimes to reduce them by squeezing out the gasses or liquids in them. Something pressed is something caught between or among forces and barriers which are so related to each other that jointly they restrain, restrict or prevent the thing's motion or mobility. Mold. Immobilize. Reduce.

The mundane experience of the oppressed provides another clue. One of the most characteristic and ubiquitous features of the world as experienced by oppressed people is the double bind—situations in which options are reduced to a very few and all of them expose one to penalty, censure or deprivation. For example, it is often a requirement upon oppressed people that we smile and be cheerful. If we comply, we signal our docility and our acquiescence in our situation. We need not, then, be taken note of. We acquiesce in being made invisible, in our occupying no space. We participate in our own erasure. On the other hand, anything but the sunniest countenance exposes us to being perceived as mean, bitter, angry or dangerous. This means, at the least, that we may be found "difficult" or unpleasant to work with, which is enough to cost one one's livelihood; at worst, being seen as mean, bitter, angry or dangerous has been known to result in rape, arrest, beating and murder. One can only choose to risk one's preferred form and rate of annihilation. . . .

Women are caught like this, too, by networks of forces and barriers that expose one to penalty, loss or contempt whether one works outside the home or not, is on welfare or not, bears children or not, raises children or not, marries or not, stays married or not, is heterosexual, lesbian, both or neither. Economic necessity; confinement to racial and/or sexual job ghettos; sexual harassment; sex discrimination; pressures of competing expectations and judgments about *women, wives* and *mothers* (in the society at large, in racial and ethnic subcultures and in one's own mind); dependence (full or partial) on husbands, parents or the state; commitment to political ideas; loyalties to racial or ethnic or other "minority" groups; the demands of self-respect and responsibilities to others. Each of these factors exists in complex tension with every other, penalizing or prohibiting all of the apparently available options. . . .

The experience of oppressed people is that the living of one's life is confined and shaped by forces and barriers which are not accidental or occasional and hence avoidable, but are systematically related to each other in such a way as to catch one between and among them and restrict or penalize motion in any direction. It is the experience of being caged in: all avenues, in every direction, are blocked or booby trapped.

Cages. Consider a birdcage. If you look very closely at just one wire in the cage, you cannot see the other wires. If your conception of what is before you is determined by this myopic focus, you could look at that one wire, up and down the length of it, and be unable to see why a bird would not just fly around the wire any time it wanted to go somewhere. Furthermore, even if, one day at a time, you myopically inspected each wire, you still could not see why a bird would have trouble going past the wires to get anywhere. There is no physical property of any one wire, *nothing* that the closest scrutiny could discover, that will reveal how a bird could be inhibited or harmed by it except in the most accidental way. It is only when you step back, stop looking at the wires one by one, microscopically, and take a macroscopic view of the whole cage, that you can see why the bird does not go anywhere; and then you will see it in a moment. It will require no great subtlety of mental powers. It is perfectly *obvious* that the bird is surrounded by a network of systematically related barriers, no one of which would be the least hindrance to its flight, but which, by their relations to each other, are as confining as the solid walls of a dungeon.

It is now possible to grasp one of the reasons why oppression can be hard to see and recognize: one can study the elements of an oppressive structure with great care and some good will without seeing the structure as a whole, and hence without seeing or being able to understand that one is looking at a cage and that there are people there who are caged, whose motion and mobility are restricted, whose lives are shaped and reduced.

The arresting of vision at a microscopic level yields such common confusion as that about the male door-opening ritual. This ritual, which is remarkably widespread across classes and races, puzzles many people, some of whom do and some of whom do not find it offensive. Look at the scene of the two people approaching a door. The male steps slightly ahead and opens the door. The male holds the door open while the female glides through. Then the male goes through. The door closes after them. "Now how," one innocently asks, "can those crazy womenslibbers say that is oppressive? The guy *removed* a barrier to the lady's smooth and unruffled progress." But each repetition of this ritual has a place in a pattern, in fact in several patterns. One has to shift the level of one's perception in order to see the whole picture.

The door-opening pretends to be a helpful service, but the helpfulness is false. This can be seen by noting that it will be done whether or not it makes any practical sense. Infirm men and men burdened with packages will open doors for able-bodied women who are free of physical burdens. Men will impose themselves awkwardly and jostle everyone in order to get to the door first. The act is not determined by convenience or grace. Furthermore, these very numerous acts of unneeded or even noisome "help" occur in counterpoint to a pattern of men not being helpful in many practical ways in which women might welcome help. What *women* experience is a world in which gallant princes charming commonly make a fuss about being helpful and providing small services when help and services are of little or no use, but in which there are rarely ingenious and adroit princes at hand when substantial assistance is really wanted either in mundane affairs or in situations of threat, assault or terror. There is no help with the (his) laundry; no help typing a report at 4:00 a.m.; no help in mediating disputes among relatives or children. There is nothing but advice that women should stay indoors after dark, be chaperoned by a man, or when it comes down to it, "lie back and enjoy it."

The gallant gestures have no practical meaning. Their meaning is symbolic. The door-opening and similar services provided are services which really are needed by people who are for one reason or another incapacitated—unwell, burdened with parcels, etc. So the message is that women are incapable. The detachment of the acts from the concrete realities of what women need and do not need is a vehicle for the message that women's actual needs and interests are unimportant or irrelevant. . . .

One cannot see the meanings of these rituals if one's focus is riveted upon the individual event in all its particularity, including the particularity of the individual man's present conscious intentions and motives and the individual woman's conscious perception of the event in the moment. It seems sometimes that people take a deliberately myopic view and fill their eyes with things seen microscopically in order not to see macroscopically. At any rate, whether it is deliberate or not, people can and do fail to see the oppression of women because they fail to see macroscopically and hence fail to see the various elements of the situation as systematically related in larger schemes.

As the cageness of the birdcage is a macroscopic phenomenon, the oppressiveness of the situations in which women live our various and different lives is a macroscopic phenomenon. Neither can be *seen* from a microscopic perspective. But when you look macroscopically you can see it—a network of forces and barriers which are systematically related and which conspire to the immobilization, reduction and molding of women and the lives we live.

II

The image of the cage helps convey one aspect of the systematic nature of oppression. Another is the selection of occupants of the cages, and analysis of this aspect also helps account for the invisibility of the oppression of women.

It is as a woman (or a Chicana/o or as a Black or Asian or lesbian) that one is entrapped.

"Why can't I go to the park; you let Jimmy go!"
"Because it's not safe for girls."

"I want to be a secretary, not a seamstress; I don't want to learn to make dresses."

"There's no work for negroes in that line; learn a skill where you can earn your living."

When you question why you are being blocked, why this barrier is in your path, the answer has not to do with individual talent or merit, handicap or failure; it has to do with your membership in some category understood as a "natural" or "physical" category. The "inhabitant" of the "cage" is not an individual but a group, all those of a certain category. If an individual is oppressed, it is in virtue of being a member of a group or category of people that is systematically reduced, molded, immobilized. Thus, to recognize a person as oppressed, one has to see that individual *as* belonging to a group of a certain sort.

. . . [P]hysical confinement and segregation of the group as a group is not common to all oppressive structures, and when an oppressed group is geographically and demographically dispersed the perception of it as a group is inhibited. There may be little or nothing in the situations of the individuals encouraging the macroscopic focus which would reveal the unity of the structure bearing down on all members of that group.*

A great many people, female and male and of every race and class, simply do not believe that *woman* is a category of oppressed people, and I think that this is in part because they have been fooled by the dispersal and assimilation of women throughout and into the systems of class and race which organize men. Our simply being dispersed makes it difficult for women to have knowledge of each other and hence difficult to recognize the shape of our common cage. The dispersal and assimilation of women throughout economic classes and races also divides us against each other practically and economically and thus attaches *interest* to the inability to see: for some, jealousy of their benefits, and for some, resentment of the others' advantages.

To get past this, it helps to notice that in fact women of all races and classes *are* together in a ghetto of sorts. There is a women's place, a sector, which is inhabited by women of all classes and races, and it is not defined by geographical boundaries but by function. The function is the service of men and men's interests as men define them, which includes the bearing and rearing of children. The details of the service and the working conditions vary by race and class, for men of different races and classes have different interests, perceive their interests differently, and express their needs and demands in different rhetorics, dialects and languages. But there are also some constants.

Whether in lower, middle or upper-class home or work situations, women's service work always includes personal service (the work of maids, butlers, cooks,

---

*Coerced assimilation is in fact one of the *policies* available to an oppressing group in its effort to reduce and/or annihilate another group. This tactic is used by the U.S. government, for instance, on the American Indians.

personal secretaries),* sexual service (including provision for his genital sexual needs and bearing his children, but also including "being nice," "being attractive for him," etc.), and ego service (encouragement, support, praise, attention). Women's service work also is characterized everywhere by the fatal combination of responsibility and powerlessness: we are held responsible and we hold ourselves responsible for good outcomes for men and children in almost every respect though we have in almost no case power adequate to that project. The details of the subjective experience of this servitude are local. They vary with economic class and race and ethnic tradition as well as the personalities of the men in question. So also are the details of the forces which coerce our tolerance of this servitude particular to the different situations in which different women live and work.

. . .

Barriers have different meanings to those on opposite sides of them, even though they are barriers to both. The physical walls of a prison no more dissolve to let an outsider in than to let an insider out, but for the insider they are confining and limiting while to the outsider they may mean protection from what s/he takes to be threats posed by insiders—freedom from harm or anxiety. A set of social and economic barriers and forces separating two groups may be felt, even painfully, by members of both groups and yet may mean confinement to one and liberty and enlargement of opportunity to the other.

The service sector of the wives/mommas/assistants/girls is almost exclusively a woman-only sector; its boundaries not only enclose women but to a very great extent keep men out. Some men sometimes encounter this barrier and experience it as a restriction on their movements, their activities, their control or their choices of "lifestyle." Thinking they might like the simple nurturant life (which they may imagine to be quite free of stress, alienation and hard work), and feeling deprived since it seems closed to them, they thereupon announce the discovery that they are oppressed, too, by "sex roles." But that barrier is erected and maintained by men, for the benefit of men. It consists of cultural and economic forces and pressures in a culture and economy controlled by men in which, at every economic level and in all racial and ethnic subcultures, economy, tradition—and even ideologies of liberation—work to keep at least local culture and economy in male control.†

The boundary that sets apart women's sphere is maintained and promoted by men generally for the benefit of men generally, and men generally do benefit from its existence, even the man who bumps into it and complains of the inconvenience. That barrier is protecting his classification and status as a male, as superior, as having a right to sexual access to a female or females. It protects a kind of citizenship which is superior to that of females of his class and race, his access to

---

*At higher class levels women may not *do* all these kinds of work, but are generally still responsible for hiring and supervising those who do it. These services are still, in these cases, women's responsibility.

†Of course this is complicated by race and class. Machismo and "Black manhood" politics seem to help keep Latin or Black men in control of more cash than Latin or Black women control; but these politics seem to me also to ultimately help keep the larger economy in *white* male control.

a wider range of better paying and higher status work, and his right to prefer unemployment to the degradation of doing lower status or "women's" work.

If a person's life or activity is affected by some force or barrier that person encounters, one may not conclude that the person is oppressed simply because the person encounters that barrier or force; nor simply because the encounter is unpleasant, frustrating, or painful to that person at that time; nor simply because the existence of the barrier or force, or the processes which maintain or apply it, serve to deprive that person of something of value. One must look at the barrier or force and answer certain questions about it. Who constructs and maintains it? Whose interests are served by its existence? Is it part of a structure which tends to confine, reduce and immobilize some group? Is the individual a member of the confined group? Various forces, barriers and limitations a person may encounter or live with may be part of an oppressive structure or not, and if they are, that person may be on either the oppressed or the oppressor side of it. One cannot tell which by how loudly or how little the person complains.

IV

Many of the restrictions and limitations we live with are more or less internalized and self-monitored, and are part of our adaptations to the requirements and expectations imposed by the needs and tastes and tyrannies of others. I have in mind such things as women's cramped postures and attenuated strides and men's restraint of emotional self-expression (except for anger). Who gets what out of the practice of those disciplines, and who imposes what penalties for improper relaxations of them? What are the rewards of this self-discipline?

Can men cry? Yes, in the company of women. If a man cannot cry, it is in the company of men that he cannot cry. It is men, not women, who require this restraint; and men not only require it, they reward it. The man who maintains a steely or tough or laid back demeanor (all are forms which suggest invulnerability) marks himself as a member of the male community and is esteemed by other men. Consequently, the maintenance of that demeanor contributes to the man's self-esteem. It is felt as good, and he can feel good about himself. The way this restriction fits into the structures of men's lives is as one of the socially required behaviors which, if carried off, contribute to their acceptance and respect by significant others and to their own self-esteem. It is to their benefit to practice this discipline.

Consider, by comparison, the discipline of women's cramped physical postures and attenuated stride. This discipline can be relaxed in the company of women; it generally is at its most strenuous in the company of men.* Like men's emotional restraint, women's physical restraint is required by men. But unlike the case of

---

* Cf., *Let's Take Back Our Space: "Female" and "Male" Body Language as a Result of Patriarchal Structures,* by Marianne Wex (Frauenliteratureverlag Hermine Fees, West Germany, 1979), especially p. 173. This remarkable book presents literally thousands of candid photographs of women and men, in public, seated, standing and lying down. It vividly demonstrates the very systematic differences in women's and men's postures and gestures.

men's emotional restraint, women's physical restraint is not rewarded. What do we get for it? Respect and esteem and acceptance? No. They mock us and parody our mincing steps. We look silly, incompetent, weak and generally contemptible. Our exercise of this discipline tends to low esteem and low self-esteem. It does not benefit us. It fits in a network of behaviors through which we constantly announce to others our membership in a lower caste and our unwillingness and/or inability to defend our bodily or moral integrity. It is degrading and part of a pattern of degradation.

Acceptable behavior for both groups, men and women, involves a required restraint that seems in itself silly and perhaps damaging. But the social effect is drastically different. The woman's restraint is part of a structure oppressive to women; the man's restraint is part of a structure oppressive to women.

V

One is marked for application of oppressive pressures by one's membership in some group or category. Much of one's suffering and frustration befalls one partly or largely because one is a member of that category. In the case at hand, it is the category, *woman*. Being a woman is a major factor in my not having a better job than I do; being a woman selects me as a likely victim of sexual assault or harassment; it is my being a woman that reduces the power of my anger to a proof of my insanity. If a woman has little or no economic or political power, or achieves little of what she wants to achieve, a major causal factor in this is that she is a woman. For any woman of any race or economic class, being a woman is significantly attached to whatever disadvantages and deprivations she suffers, be they great or small.

None of this is the case with respect to a person's being a man. Simply being a man is not what stands between him and a better job; whatever assaults and harassments he is subject to, being male is not what selects him for victimization; being male is not a factor which would make his anger impotent—quite the opposite. If a man has little or no material or political power, or achieves little of what he wants to achieve, his being male is no part of the explanation. Being male is something he has going *for* him, even if race or class or age or disability is going against him.

Women are oppressed, *as women*. Members of certain racial and/or economic groups and classes, both the males and the females, are oppressed *as* members of those races and/or classes. But men are not oppressed *as men*.

. . . and isn't it strange that any of us should have been confused and mystified about such a simple thing?

DISCUSSION QUESTIONS

1. Draw a diagram of the moral community as portrayed by Frye. Discuss to what extent this moral community is a cultural construct.
2. Does Frye make a convincing argument regarding the existence of the oppression of women in our culture? Support your answer using examples from her article as well as from your own experience.

3. Is Frye's analogy between being a member of an oppressed category such as "woman" and living in a birdcage convincing? To what extent do existing cultural norms create barriers in your own life? To what extent are these barriers culturally relative to your gender, race, or ethnic group? Illustrate your answer with specific examples.

4. According to Frye, even what appear to be gallant customs, such as opening doors for women, can reinforce oppressive and immoral cultural norms by reinforcing the cultural message that woman are incapable. Do you agree with Frye? Compare and contrast the position of Frye with that of Mary Wollstonecraft in the selections from her book *A Vindication of the Rights of Woman* in an earlier section.

5. Is it possible to be oppressed by cultural customs without even realizing it? How about the subservient wife who claims she is happy always putting the needs of her husband and children before her own?

6. To what extent does Frye bring in universal moral principles to justify her argument that women are oppressed in our society? What are some of these principles? Could someone argue that women are oppressed without going outside of cultural relativism? Or is it necessary to use another standard against which to judge our culture? If so, what is this standard and where does it come from?

Daniel Jonah Goldhagen

Hitler's Willing Executioners

In his book *Hitler's Willing Executioners*, Harvard scholar Daniel Goldhagen argues that the persecution of the Jews in Germany before and during World War II was not the act of a few Nazis. Anti-Semitism and the exclusion of Jews from the moral community, he claims, was the prevailing norm in German culture at the time. Because it was socially acceptable to be anti-Semitic, the majority of Germans willingly participated in the Holocaust.

Goldhagen's book clearly shows the connection between people's moral reasoning and their actions. It also shows how cultural definitions of moral community are to a large extent politically and economically motivated and serve to maintain the status quo. As such, his book presents a powerful warning against the potential dangers of cultural relativism.

CRITICAL THINKING QUESTIONS

1. Who does Goldhagen hold responsible for the Holocaust?
2. How did German society at the time of the Holocaust define their moral community?
3. Why does Goldhagen dismiss the conventional views of the Holocaust that placed responsibility in the hands of a few people?
4. What role did prevailing cultural norms play in motivating people to participate in the Holocaust?
5. Does Goldhagen support cultural relativism?

During the Holocaust, Germans extinguished the lives of six million Jews and, had Germany not been defeated, would have annihilated millions more. The Holocaust was also the defining feature of German politics and political culture during the Nazi period, the most shocking event of the twentieth century, and the most difficult event to understand in all of German history. The Germans' persecution of the Jews culminating in the Holocaust is thus the central feature of Germany during the Nazi period. It is so not because we are retrospectively shocked by the most shocking event of the century, but because of what it meant to Germans at the time and why so many of them contributed to it. It marked their departure from the community of "civilized peoples." This departure needs to be explained. . . .

Hitler's Willing Executioners (New York: Knopf, 1996), pp. 4–23. Notes have been omitted.

We must therefore refocus our attention, our intellectual energy, which has overwhelmingly been devoted elsewhere, onto the perpetrators, namely the men and women who in some intimate way knowingly contributed to the slaughter of Jews. We must investigate their deeds in detail and explain their actions. It is not sufficient to treat the institutions of killing collectively or singly as internally uncomplicated instruments of the Nazi leadership's will, as well-lubricated machines that the regime activated, as if by the flick of a switch, to do its bidding, whatever it might have been. The study of the men and women who collectively gave life to the inert institutional forms, who peopled the institutions of genocidal killing must be set at the focus of scholarship on the Holocaust and become as central to investigations of the genocide as they were to its commission.

These people were overwhelmingly and most importantly Germans. While members of other national groups aided the Germans in their slaughter of Jews, the commission of the Holocaust was primarily a German undertaking. Non-Germans were not essential to the perpetration of the genocide, and they did not supply the drive and initiative that pushed it forward. To be sure, had the Germans not found European (especially, eastern European) helpers, then the Holocaust would have unfolded somewhat differently, and the Germans would likely not have succeeded in killing as many Jews. Still, this was above all a German enterprise; the decisions, plans, organizational resources, and the majority of its executors were German. Comprehension and explanation of the perpetration of the Holocaust therefore requires an explanation of the Germans' drive to kill Jews. Because what can be said about the Germans cannot be said about any other nationality or about all of the other nationalities combined—namely no Germans, no Holocaust—the focus here is appropriately on the German perpetrators.

. . . They were Germans acting in the name of Germany and its highly popular leader, Adolf Hitler. Some were "Nazis," either by reason of Nazi Party membership or according to ideological conviction; some were not. Some were SS men; some were not. The perpetrators killed and made their other genocidal contributions under the auspices of many institutions other than the SS. Their chief common denominator was that they were all Germans pursuing German national political goals—in this case, the genocidal killing of Jews. To be sure, it is sometimes appropriate to use institutional or occupational names or roles and the generic terms "perpetrators" or "killers" to describe the perpetrators, yet this must be done only in the understood context that these men and women were Germans first, and SS men, policemen, or camp guards second.

A second and related task is to reveal something of the perpetrators' backgrounds, to convey the character and quality of their lives as genocidal killers, to bring to life their *Lebenswelt*. What *exactly* did they do when they were killing? What did they do during their time as members of institutions of killing, while they were not undertaking killing operations? Until a great deal is known about the details of their actions and lives, neither they nor the perpetration of their crimes can be understood. The unearthing of the perpetrators' lives, the presentation of a "thick," rather than the customary paper-thin, description of their actions, as important and necessary as it is for its own sake, lays the foundation for the main task of this book's consideration of them, namely to explain their actions.

It is my contention that this cannot be done unless such an analysis is embedded in an understanding of German society before and during its Nazi period, particularly of the political culture that produced the perpetrators and their actions. This has been notably absent from attempts to explain the perpetrators' actions, and has doomed these attempts to providing situational explanations, ones that focus almost exclusively on institutional and immediate social psychological influences, often conceived of as irresistible pressures. The men and women who became the Holocaust's perpetrators were shaped by and operated in a particular social and historical setting. They brought with them prior elaborate conceptions of the world, ones that were common to their society, the investigation of which is necessary for explaining their actions. This entails, most fundamentally, a reexamination of the character and development of antisemitism in Germany during its Nazi period and before, which in turn requires a theoretical reconsideration of the character of antisemitism itself. . . .

The study of the perpetrators further demands a reconsideration, indeed a reconceiving, of the character of German society during its Nazi period and before. The Holocaust was the defining aspect of Nazism, but not only of Nazism. It was also the defining feature of German society during its Nazi period. No significant aspect of German society was untouched by anti-Jewish policy; from the economy, to society, to politics, to culture, from cattle farmers, to merchants, to the organization of small towns, to lawyers, doctors, physicists, and professors. No analysis of German society, no understanding or characterization of it, can be made without placing the persecution and extermination of the Jews at its center. The program's first parts, namely the systematic exclusion of Jews from German economic and social life, were carried out in the open, under approving eyes, and with the complicity of virtually all sectors of German society, from the legal, medical, and teaching professions, to the churches, both Catholic and Protestant, to the gamut of economic, social, and cultural groups and associations. Hundreds of thousands of Germans contributed to the genocide and the still larger system of subjugation that was the vast concentration camp system. Despite the regime's half-hearted attempts to keep the genocide beyond the view of most Germans, millions knew of the mass slaughters. Hitler announced many times, emphatically, that the war would end in the extermination of the Jews. The killings met with general understanding, if not approval. No other policy (of similar or greater scope) was carried out with more persistence and zeal, and with fewer difficulties, than the genocide, except perhaps the war itself. The Holocaust defines not only the history of Jews during the middle of the twentieth century but also the history of Germans. While the Holocaust changed Jewry and Jews irrevocably, its commission was possible, I argue, because Germans had *already* been changed. The fate of the Jews may have been a direct, which does not, however, mean an inexorable, outgrowth of a worldview shared by the vast majority of the German people. . . .

The conventional explanations [of the Holocaust] *assume* a neutral or condemnatory attitude on the part of the perpetrators towards their actions. They therefore premise their interpretations on the assumption that it must be shown how people can be brought to commit acts to which they would not inwardly assent, acts which they would not agree are necessary or just. They either ignore, deny, or radically minimize the importance of Nazi and perhaps the perpetrators' ideology, moral values, and conception of the victims, for engendering the perpetrators' willingness to kill. Some of these conventional explanations also caricature the perpetrators, and Germans in general. The explanations treat them as if they had been people lacking a moral sense, lacking the ability to make decisions and take stances. They do not conceive of the actors as human agents, as people with wills, but as beings moved solely by external forces or by transhistorical and invariant psychological propensities, such as the slavish following of narrow "self-interest." The conventional explanations suffer from two other major conceptual failings. They do not sufficiently recognize the extraordinary nature of the deed: the mass killing of people. They *assume* and imply that inducing people to kill human beings is fundamentally no different from getting them to do any other unwanted or distasteful task. Also, none of the conventional explanations deems the *identity* of the victims to have mattered. The conventional explanations imply that the perpetrators would have treated any other group of intended victims in exactly the same way. That the victims were Jews—according to the logic of these explanations—is irrelevant.

I maintain that any explanation that fails to acknowledge the actors' capacity to know and to judge, namely to understand and to have views about the significance and the morality of their actions, that fails to hold the actors' beliefs and values as central, that fails to emphasize the autonomous motivating force of Nazi ideology, particularly its central component of antisemitism, cannot possibly succeed in telling us much about why the perpetrators acted as they did. Any explanation that ignores either the particular nature of the perpetrators' actions —the systematic, large-scale killing and brutalizing of people—or the identity of the victims is inadequate for a host of reasons. All explanations that adopt these positions, as do the conventional explanations, suffer a mirrored, double failure of recognition of the human aspect of the Holocaust: the humanity of the perpetrators, namely their capacity to judge and to choose to act inhumanely, and the humanity of the victims, that what the perpetrators did, they did to these people with their specific identities, and not to animals or things.

My explanation—which is new to the scholarly literature on the perpetrators —is that the perpetrators, "ordinary Germans," were animated by antisemitism, by a particular *type* of antisemitism that led them to conclude that the Jews *ought to die*. The perpetrators' beliefs, their particular brand of antisemitism, though obviously not the sole source, was, I maintain, a most significant and indispensable source of the perpetrators' actions and must be at the center of any explanation of them. Simply put, the perpetrators, having consulted their own convictions and morality and having judged the mass annihilation of Jews to be right, did not *want* to say "no." . . .

Interpreters of this period make a grave error by refusing to believe that people could slaughter whole populations—especially populations that are by any objective evaluation not threatening—out of conviction. Why persist in the belief that "ordinary" people could not possibly sanction, let alone partake in wholesale human slaughter? The historical record, from ancient times to the present, amply testifies to the ease with which people can extinguish the lives of others, and even take joy in their deaths.

No reason exists to believe that modern, western, even Christian man is incapable of holding notions which devalue human life, which call for its extinction, notions similar to those held by peoples of many religious, cultural, and political dispensations throughout history, including the crusaders and the inquisitors, to name but two relevant examples from twentieth-century Christian Europe's forebears. Who doubts that the Argentine or Chilean murderers of people who opposed the recent authoritarian regimes thought that their victims deserved to die? Who doubts that the Tutsis who slaughtered Hutus in Burundi or the Hutus who slaughtered Tutsis in Rwanda, that one Lebanese militia which slaughtered the civilian supporters of another, that the Serbs who have killed Croats or Bosnian Muslims, did so out of conviction in the justice of their actions? Why do we not believe the same for the German perpetrators?

. . . Perhaps the most important is whether or not it is assumed, as the rule has been for most interpreters of this period, that Germany was more or less a "normal" society, operating according to rules of "common sense" similar to our own. For people to be *willing* to slaughter others, in this view, they must be moved by a cynical lust for power or riches or they must be in the grip of a powerful ideology that is so self-evidently false that only the disturbed few could actually succumb to it (aside from those who cynically exploit it for power). The majority of modern people, simple and decent, may be pushed around by these few—but not won over.

Alternatively, this period can be approached without such assumptions, and instead with the critical eye of an anthropologist disembarking on unknown shores, open to meeting a radically different culture and conscious of the possibility that he might need to devise explanations not in keeping with, perhaps even contravening his own common-sense notions, in order to explain the culture's constitution, its idiosyncratic patterns of practice, and its collective projects and products. This would admit the possibility that large numbers of people, in this case Germans, might have killed or been willing to kill others, in this case Jews, in good conscience. Such an approach would not predetermine the task, as virtually all previous studies have done, to be the explanation of what could have forced people to act against their will (or independent of any will, namely like automatons). Instead, it might be necessary to explain how Germans came to be such potential willing mass killers and how the Nazi regime tapped this disastrous potentiality. This approach, which rejects the anthropologically and social-scientifically primitive notion of the universality of our "common sense," guides this inquiry.

Central and generally unquestioned methodological and substantive assumptions that have guided virtually all scholarship on the Holocaust and its perpetrators are jettisoned here, because such assumptions are theoretically and empirically unsustainable. In contrast to previous scholarship, this book takes the actors' cognition and values seriously and investigates the perpetrators' actions in light of a model of choice. This approach, particularly with regard to the Holocaust, raises a set of social theoretical issues that, however briefly, must be addressed.

The perpetrators were working within institutions that prescribed roles for them and assigned them specific tasks, yet they individually and collectively had latitude to make choices regarding their actions. . . .

. . . No matter what category of action a person's act is properly classified as, the person's attitude towards his act, and his motivation to undertake it, is still important, for it renders the act itself one thing or another. This "objective" categorization needs to be supplemented by a subjective one of motivation. A variety of motives is compatible with acting under orders, with showing initiative, with committing "excesses," or with doing a job well or badly. Most important is the question of whether or not the perpetrators believed their treatment of the Jews to be just and, if so, why.

The motivational dimension is the most crucial for explaining the perpetrators' willingness to act, and to a great extent is a product of the social construction of knowledge. The types of actions that a person is willing to carry out—whether only those directly ordered, those that take initiative, those that are excessive, and those that are the product of zealousness—are derived from a person's motivation; but the person's actions do not *necessarily* correspond to his motivations, because his actions are influenced by the circumstances and opportunities for action. Obviously, without opportunity, a person's motivation to kill or to torture cannot be acted upon. But opportunity alone does not a killer or torturer make. . . .

Explaining the perpetrators' actions demands, therefore, that the perpetrators' phenomenological reality be taken seriously. We must attempt the difficult enterprise of imagining ourselves in their places, performing their deeds, acting as they did, viewing what they beheld. To do so we must always bear in mind the essential nature of their actions as perpetrators: they were killing defenseless men, women, and children, people who were obviously of no martial threat to them, often emaciated and weak, in unmistakable physical and emotional agony, and sometimes begging for their lives or those of their children. Too many interpreters of this period, particularly when they are psychologizing, discuss the Germans' actions as if they were discussing the commission of mundane acts, as if they need explain little more than how a good man might occasionally shoplift. They lose sight of the fundamentally different, extraordinary, and trying character of these acts. The taboo in many societies, including western ones, against killing defenseless people, against killing children, is great. The psychological mechanisms that permit "good" people to commit minor moral transgressions, or to turn a blind eye even to major ones committed by others, particularly if they are far away, cannot be applied to people's perpetration of genocidal killing, to their slaughter of hundreds of others before their own eyes—without careful consideration of such mechanisms' appropriateness for elucidating such actions.

Explaining this genocidal slaughter necessitates, therefore, that we keep two things always in mind. When writing or reading about killing operations, it is too easy to become insensitive to the numbers on the page. Ten thousand dead in one place, four hundred in another, fifteen in a third. Each of us should pause and consider that ten thousand deaths meant that Germans killed ten thousand individuals—unarmed men, women, and children, the old, the young, and the sick—that Germans took a human life ten thousand times. Each of us should ponder what that might have meant for the Germans participating in the slaughter. . . .

. . . [U]nderstanding the beliefs and values common to German culture, particularly the ones that shaped Germans' attitudes towards Jews, is the most essential task for explaining the perpetration of the Holocaust. . . . [There was] the development in Germany well before the Nazis came to power of a virulent and violent "eliminationist" variant of antisemitism, which called for the elimination of Jewish influence or of Jews themselves from German society. When the Nazis did assume power, they found themselves the masters of a society already imbued with notions about Jews that were ready to be mobilized for the most extreme form of "elimination" imaginable.

DISCUSSION QUESTIONS

1. Did the existence of longstanding and socially accepted norms of anti-Semitism, in Goldhagen's view, morally justify the Holocaust? What arguments does Goldhagen use to reject cultural relativism?
2. What universal moral principles does Goldhagen claim are binding regardless of cultural norms? Do you agree that these principles should override cultural norms? How would Benedict respond to Goldhagen's claim?
3. Given that 90 percent of U.S. adults are cultural relativists, could (or has) an event like the Holocaust occur in the United States? Why are most Americans more horrified by the Holocaust than they are by our history of slavery and treatment of Native Americans?
4. How would you define the term civic *responsibility?* Discuss whether civic responsibility necessarily entails going along with cultural norms and laws. Support your answer.
5. Discuss the implications for ethics education of Goldhagen's observations about people's uncritical willingness to conform to cultural norms.

Dr. Martin Luther King, Jr.

Letter from a Birmingham Jail

People who go against their own cultural norms and laws are, according to cultural relativists, immoral by definition. This puts cultural relativists in the awkward position of having to argue that a social reformer who breaks the law is no different than a common criminal.

American civil rights leader and social reformer Martin Luther King, Jr. (1929–1968) believed that there were universal moral principles by which a society could be judged. An advocate of nonviolent civil disobedience as a means of bringing about social change, King was thrown into the Birmingham City Jail for his participation in a nonviolent demonstration. This letter was written in response to a statement issued by a group of clergy in which they criticized King's illegal actions.

The following year, in 1964, King was awarded the Nobel Peace Prize for his work in trying to bring about racial equality in the United States. King was assassinated in Memphis, Tennessee, in 1968.

CRITICAL THINKING QUESTIONS

1. Why were the clergy critical of King's illegal actions?
2. How did King justify his civil disobedience?
3. What are the four basic steps of nonviolent civil disobedience?
4. How does King respond to the accusation that his illegal actions were untimely?
5. On what grounds does King claim that segregation is an unjust law?
6. What criteria does King use to distinguish between a just and an unjust law?

MY DEAR FELLOW CLERGYMEN,

While confined here in the Birmingham City Jail, I came across your recent statement calling our present activities "unwise and untimely." Seldom, if ever, do I pause to answer criticism of my work and ideas. If I sought to answer all of the

---

"Letter from a Birmingham Jail," *Where Do We Go from Here? Chaos or Community?* (New York: HarperCollins, 1965, 1991).

criticisms that cross my desk, my secretaries would be engaged in little else in the course of the day, and I would have no time for constructive work. But since I feel that you are men of genuine goodwill and your criticisms are sincerely set forth, I would like to answer your statement in what I hope will be patient and reasonable terms. . . .

. . . I am in Birmingham because injustice is here. Just as the eighth century prophets left their little villages and carried their "thus saith the Lord" far beyond the boundaries of their hometowns, and just as the Apostle Paul left his little village of Tarsus and carried the gospel of Jesus Christ to practically every hamlet and city of the Graeco-Roman world, I too am compelled to carry the gospel of freedom beyond my particular home town. Like Paul, I must constantly respond to the Macedonian call for aid.

Moreover, I am cognizant of the interrelatedness of all communities and states. I cannot sit idly by in Atlanta and not be concerned about what happens in Birmingham. Injustice anywhere is a threat to justice everywhere. We are caught in an inescapable network of mutuality, tied in a single garment of destiny. Whatever affects one directly affects all indirectly. Never again can we afford to live with the narrow, provincial "outside agitator" idea. Anyone who lives inside the United States can never be considered an outsider anywhere in this country.

You deplore the demonstrations that are presently taking place in Birmingham. But I am sorry that your statement did not express a similar concern for the conditions that brought the demonstrations into being. I am sure that each of you would want to go beyond the superficial social analyst who looks merely at effects, and does not grapple with underlying causes. I would not hesitate to say that it is unfortunate that so-called demonstrations are taking place in Birmingham at this time, but I would say in more emphatic terms that it is even more unfortunate that the white power structure of this city left the Negro community with no other alternative.

In any nonviolent campaign there are four basic steps: (1) Collection of the facts to determine whether injustices are alive (2) Negotiation (3) Self-purification and (4) Direct Action. We have gone through all of these steps in Birmingham. There can be no gainsaying of the fact that racial injustice engulfs this community. . . .

CREATIVE TENSION

You may well ask, "Why direct action? Why sit-ins, marches, etc.? Isn't negotiation a better path?" You are exactly right in your call for negotiation. Indeed, this is the purpose of direct action. Nonviolent direct action seeks to create such a crisis and establish such creative tension that a community that has constantly refused to negotiate is forced to confront the issue. It seeks so to dramatize the issue that it can no longer be ignored. I just referred to the creation of tension as a part of the work of the nonviolent resister. This may sound rather shocking. But I must confess that I am not afraid of the word tension. I have earnestly worked and preached against violent tension, but there is a type of constructive nonviolent tension that is necessary for growth. Just as Socrates felt that it was necessary to create a tension in the mind so that individuals could rise from the bondage of myths and half-truths to the unfettered realm of creative analysis and objective appraisal, we must see the need of having nonviolent gadflies to create the kind of tension in society that will help men to rise from the dark depths of prejudice and racism to the majestic heights of understanding and brotherhood. So the purpose of the direct action is to create a situation so crisis-packed that it will inevitably open the door to negotiation. We, therefore, concur with you in your call for negotiation. Too long has our beloved Southland been bogged down in the tragic attempt to live in monologue rather than dialogue.

One of the basic points in your statement is that our acts are untimely. Some have asked, "Why didn't you give the new administration time to act?" The only answer that I can give to this inquiry is that the new administration must be prodded about as much as the outgoing one before it acts. . . . My friends, I must say to you that we have not made a single gain in civil rights without determined legal and nonviolent pressure. History is the long and tragic story of the fact that privileged groups seldom give up their privileges voluntarily. Individuals may see the moral light and voluntarily give up their unjust posture; but as Reinhold Niebuhr has reminded us, groups are more immoral than individuals.

We know through painful experience that freedom is never voluntarily given by the oppressor; it must be demanded by the oppressed. Frankly, I have never yet engaged in a direct action movement that was "well timed," according to the timetable of those who have not suffered unduly from the disease of segregation. For years now I have heard the word "Wait!" It rings in the ear of every Negro with a piercing familiarity. This "Wait" has almost always meant "Never." . . . We have waited for more than three hundred and forty years for our constitutional and God-given rights. . . . I guess it is easy for those who have never felt the stinging darts of segregation to say, "Wait." But when you have seen vicious mobs lynch your mothers and fathers at will and drown your sisters and brothers at whim; when you have seen hate-filled policemen curse, kick, brutalize and even kill your black brothers and sisters with impunity; when you see the vast majority of your twenty million Negro brothers smothering in an airtight cage of poverty in the midst of an affluent society; when you suddenly find your tongue twisted and your speech stammering as you seek to explain to your six-year-old daughter why she can't go to the public amusement park that has just been advertised on television, and see tears welling up in her little eyes when she is told that Funtown is closed to colored children, and see the depressing clouds of inferiority begin to form in her little mental sky, and see her begin to distort her little personality by unconsciously developing a bitterness toward white people; when you have to concoct an answer for a five-year-old son asking in agonizing pathos: "Daddy, why do white people treat colored people so mean?"; when you take a cross country drive and find it necessary to sleep night after night in the uncomfortable corners of your automobile because no motel will accept you; when you are humiliated day in and day out by nagging signs reading "white" and "colored"; when your first name becomes "nigger" and your middle name becomes "boy" (however old you are) and your last name becomes "John," and when your wife and mother are never given the respected title "Mrs."; when you are harried by day and haunted at night by the fact that you are a Negro, living constantly at tip-toe stance never quite knowing what to expect next, and plagued with inner fears and outer resentments; when you are forever fighting a degenerating sense of "nobodiness"; then you will understand why we find it difficult to wait. There comes a time when the cup of endurance runs over, and men are no longer willing to be plunged into an abyss of injustice where they experience the blackness of corroding despair. I hope, sirs, you can understand our legitimate and unavoidable impatience.

BREAKING THE LAW

You express a great deal of anxiety over our willingness to break laws. This is certainly a legitimate concern. Since we so diligently urge people to obey the Supreme Court's decision of 1954 outlawing segregation in the public schools, it is rather strange and paradoxical to find us consciously breaking laws. One may well ask, "How can you advocate breaking some laws and obeying others?" The answer is found in the fact that there are two types of laws: There are *just* and there are *unjust* laws. I would agree with Saint Augustine that "An unjust law is no law at all."

Now what is the difference between the two? How does one determine when a law is just or unjust? A just law is a man-made code that squares with the moral law or the law of God. An unjust law is a code that is out of harmony with the moral law. To put it in the terms of Saint Thomas Aquinas, an unjust law is a human law that is not rooted in eternal and natural law. Any law that uplifts human personality is just. Any law that degrades human personality is unjust. All segregation statutes are unjust because segregation distorts the soul and damages the personality. It gives the segregator a false sense of superiority, and the segregated a false sense of inferiority. To use the words of Martin Buber, the great Jewish philosopher, segregation substitutes an "I-it" relationship for the "I-thou" relationship, and ends up relegating persons to the status of things. So segregation is not only politically, economically and sociologically unsound, but it is morally wrong and sinful. Paul Tillich has said that sin is separation. Isn't segregation an existential expression of man's tragic separation, an expression of his awful estrangement, his terrible sinfulness? So I can urge men to disobey segregation ordinances because they are morally wrong.

Let us turn to a more concrete example of just and unjust laws. An unjust law is a code that a majority inflicts on a minority that is not binding on itself. This is the difference made legal. On the other hand a just law is a code that a majority compels a minority to follow that it is willing to follow itself. This is sameness made legal.

Let me give another explanation. An unjust law is a code inflicted upon a minority which that minority had no part in enacting or creating because they did not have the unhampered right to vote. Who can say that the legislature of Alabama which set up the segregation laws was democratically elected?

Throughout the state of Alabama all types of conniving methods are used to prevent Negroes from becoming registered voters and there are some counties without a single Negro registered to vote despite the fact that the Negro constitutes a majority of the population. Can any law set up in such a state be considered democratically structured?

These are just a few examples of unjust and just laws. There are some instances when a law is just on its face and unjust in its application. For instance, I was arrested on Friday on a charge of parading without a permit. Now there is nothing wrong with an ordinance which requires a permit for a parade, but when the ordinance is used to preserve segregation and to deny citizens the First Amendment privilege of peaceful assembly and peaceful protest, then it becomes unjust.

I hope you can see the distinction I am trying to point out. In no sense do I advocate evading or defying the law as the rabid segregationist would do. This would lead to anarchy. One who breaks an unjust law must do it *openly, lovingly* (not hatefully as the white mothers did in New Orleans when they were seen on television screaming "nigger, nigger, nigger"), and with a willingness to accept the penalty. I submit that an individual who breaks a law that conscience tells him is unjust, and willingly accepts the penalty by staying in jail to arouse the conscience of the community over its injustice, is in reality expressing the very highest respect for law.

Of course, there is nothing new about this kind of civil disobedience. It was seen sublimely in the refusal of Shadrach, Meshach and Abednego to obey the laws of Nebuchadnezzar because a higher moral law was involved. It was practiced superbly by the early Christians who were willing to face hungry lions and the excruciating pain of chopping blocks, before submitting to certain unjust laws of the Roman empire. To a degree academic freedom is a reality today because Socrates practiced civil disobedience.

DISCUSSION QUESTIONS

1. Why was King's act of civil disobedience incompatible with cultural relativism?
2. Compare and contrast King's concept of "creative tension" to Sheila Mullett's concept of "ontological shock." What role do both play in praxis?
3. Do you agree with King that civil disobedience is sometimes the morally appropriate response to an unjust law? Illustrate your answer with examples from history.
4. To what extent do you as well as other people put off responsibility for actively working to bring about social reform by saying it's not the right time yet? Do you agree with King that the advice "Wait" often means "Never"? Use specific examples to illustrate your answer.
5. How would a cultural relativist respond to King's claim that segregation is unjust? Are you satisfied with the cultural relativist's response?
6. Are there any current laws that you regard as unjust (as opposed to merely inconvenient)? Explain why you regard that law as unjust. What are you doing to get the law changed?

William H. Shaw

Relativism in Ethics

The final reading in this chapter is by philosopher William Shaw, who sum-
marizes some of the problems with ethical relativism. In this paper, Shaw
concludes that neither ethical subjectivism nor cultural relativism are defensi-
ble as moral theories.

CRITICAL THINKING QUESTIONS

1. Why, according to Shaw, does the fact of variance in individual or
   cultural interpretations of morality not necessarily imply ethical
   relativism?

2. What, according to Shaw, do most people really mean when they
   say they support ethical subjectivism?

3. Which theory, ethical subjectivism or cultural relativism, does
   Shaw think is the weaker of the two and why?

4. What empirical data does Shaw use to back up his arguments?

5. Identify the premises Shaw uses to support his conclusion that
   ethical subjectivism cannot be justified as a moral theory.

6. Identify the premises Shaw uses to support his conclusion that cultural relativism cannot be justified as a moral theory.

7. To what extent do the premises for the two arguments overlap?

The peoples and societies of the world are diverse; their institutions, fashions,
ideas, manners, and mores vary tremendously. This is a simple truth. Sometimes
an awareness of this diversity and of the degree to which our own beliefs and
habits mirror those of the culture around us stimulates self-examination. In the
realm of ethics, familiarity with strikingly different cultures has led many people
to suppose that morality itself is relative to particular societies, that right and
wrong vary from culture to culture.

This view is generally called "ethical relativism"; it is the normative theory
that what is right is what the culture says is right. What is right in one place may
be wrong in another, because the only criterion for distinguishing right from

"Relativism in Ethics," from "Relativism and Objectivity in Ethics," in John Arthur, *Morality and
Moral Controversies,* 3rd ed. (Englewood Cliffs, NJ: Prentice-Hall, 1993), pp. 16–19. © 1980 by
William H. Shaw.

wrong—the only ethical standard for judging an action—is the moral system of the society in which the act occurs. Abortion, for example, is condemned as immoral in Catholic Spain, but practiced as a morally neutral form of birth control in Japan. According to the ethical relativist, then, abortion is wrong in Spain but morally permissible in Japan. The relativist is not saying merely that the Spanish believe abortion is abominable and the Japanese do not; that is acknowledged by everyone. Rather, the ethical relativist contends that abortion is immoral in Spain because the Spanish believe it to be immoral and morally permissible in Japan because the Japanese believe it to be so. There is no absolute ethical standard, independent of cultural context, no criterion of right and wrong by which to judge other than that of particular societies. In short, morality is relative to society.

A different sort of relativist might hold that morality is relative, not to the culture, but to the individual. The theory that what is right and wrong is determined by what a person thinks is right and wrong, however, is not very plausible. The main reason is that it collapses the distinction between thinking something is right and its actually being right. We have all done things we thought were right at the time, but later decided were wrong. Our normal view is that we were mistaken in our original thinking; we believed the action to have been right, but it was not. In the relativist view under consideration, one would have to say that the action in question was originally right, but later wrong as our thinking changed—surely a confused and confusing thing to say! Furthermore, if we accept this view, there would be no point in debating ethics with anyone, for whatever he thought right would automatically be right for him, and whatever we thought right would be right for us. Indeed, if right were determined solely by what we took to be right, then it would not be at all clear what we are doing when we try to decide whether something is right or wrong in the first place—since we could never be mistaken! Certainly this is a muddled doctrine. Most likely its proponents have meant to emphasize that each person must determine for himself as best he can what actually is right or to argue that we ought not to blame people for acting according to their sincere moral judgments. These points are plausible, and with some qualifications, perhaps everyone would accept them, but they are not relativistic in the least.

The theory that morality is relative to society, however, is more plausible, and those who endorse this type of ethical relativism point to the diverseness of human values and the multiformity of moral codes to support their case. From our own cultural perspective, some seemingly "immoral" moralities have been adopted: polygamy, homosexuality, stealing, slavery, infanticide, and the eating of strangers have all been tolerated or even encouraged by the moral system of one society or another. In light of this, the ethical relativist feels that there can be no nonethnocentric standard by which to judge actions. We feel the individuals in some remote tribe are wrong to practice infanticide, while other cultures are scandalized that we eat animals. Different societies have different rules; what moral authority other than society, asks the relativist, can there be? Morality is just like fashion in clothes, beauty in persons, and legality in action—all of which are relative to, and determined by, the standards of a particular culture.

In some cases this seems to make sense. Imagine that Betty is raised in a society in which one is thought to have a special obligation to look after one's maternal aunts and uncles in their old age, and Sarah lives in a society in which no such obligation is supposed. Certainly we are inclined to say that Betty really does have an obligation that Sarah does not. Sarah's culture, on the other hand, may hold that if someone keeps a certain kind of promise to you, you owe him or her a favor, or that children are not required to tell the truth to adults. Again, it seems plausible that different sorts of obligations arise in Sarah's society; in her society, promisees really do owe their promisors and children are not wrong to lie, whereas this might not be so in other cultures.

Ethical relativism explains these cases by saying that right and wrong are determined solely by the standards of the society in question, but there are other, nonrelativistic ways of accounting for these examples. In Betty's society, people live with the expectation that their sister's offspring will look after them; for Betty to behave contrary to this institution and to thwart these expectations may produce bad consequences—so there is a reason to think she has this obligation other than the fact that her society thinks she has it. In Sarah's world, on the other hand, no adult expects children to tell the truth; far from deceiving people, children only amuse them with their tall tales. Thus, we are not required to be ethical relativists in order to explain why moral obligations may differ according to the social context. And there are other cases in which ethical relativism seems implausible. Suppose Betty's society thinks that it is wicked to engage in intercourse on Sundays. We do not believe it wrong of her to do so just because her society thinks such conduct is impermissible. Or suppose her culture thinks that it is morally reprehensible to wear the fur of rare animals. Here we may be inclined to concur, but if we think it is wrong of her to do this, we do not think it so because her society says so. In this example and the previous one, we look for some reason why her conduct should be considered immoral. The fact that her society thinks it so is not enough.

Ethical relativism undermines any moral criticism of the practices of other societies as long as their actions conform to their own standards. We cannot say that slavery in a slave society like that of the American South of the last century was immoral and unjust as long as that society held it to be morally permissible. Slavery was right for them, although it is wrong for us today. To condemn slave owners as immoral, says the relativist, is to attempt to extend the standards of our society illegitimately to another culture. But this is not the way we usually think. Not only do we wish to say that a society is mistaken if it thinks that slavery (or cannibalism, cruelty, racial bigotry) is morally permissible, but we also think we have justification for so saying and are not simply projecting ethnocentrically the standards of our own culture. Indeed, far from mirroring those standards in all our moral judgments, we sometimes criticize certain principles or practices accepted by our own society. None of this makes sense from the relativist's point of view. People can be censured for not living up to their society's moral code, but that is all; the moral code itself cannot be criticized. Whatever a society takes to be morally right really is right for it. Reformers who campaign against the "injustices" of their society are only encouraging people to be immoral—that is, to depart from the moral standards of their society—unless or until the majority of society agrees with the reformers. The minority can never be right in moral matters; to be right it must become the majority.

This raises some puzzles for the theory of ethical relativism. What proportion of a society must believe, say, that abortion is permissible for it to be morally acceptable in that society—90 percent? 75 percent? 51 percent? If the figure is set high (say 75 percent) and only 60 percent of the society condone abortion, then it would not be permissible; yet it would seem odd for the relativist to say that abortion was therefore wrong, given that a majority of the population believes otherwise. Without a sufficient majority either way, abortion would be neither morally permissible nor impermissible. On the other hand, if the figure is set lower, then there will be frequent moral flip-flops. Imagine that last year abortion was thought wrong by 51 percent of the populace, but this year only 49 percent are of that opinion; that means, according to the relativist, that it was wrong last year, but is now morally permissible—and things may change again. Surely, though, something is wrong with majority rule in matters of morality. In addition one might wonder what is to count, for the relativist, as a society. In a large and heterogeneous nation like the United States, are right and wrong determined by the whole country; or do smaller societies like Harlem, San Francisco, rural Iowa, or the Chicano community in Los Angeles set their own moral standards? But if these are cohesive enough to count as morality generating societies, what about such "societies" as outlaw bikers, the drug culture, or the underworld? And what, then, does the relativist say about conflicts between these group moralities or between them and the morality of the overall society? Since an individual may be in several overlapping "societies" at the same time, he may well be receiving conflicting moral instructions—all of which, it would seem, are correct according to the relativist.

These are all questions the relativist must answer if he is to make his theory coherent. To raise them is not to refute relativism, of course, since the relativist may be able to explain satisfactorily what he means by "society," how its standards relate to those of other groups, and what is to count as moral approval by a given society. However the relativist attempts to refine his theory, he will still be maintaining that what is right is determined by what the particular society, culture, or group takes to be right and that this is the only standard by which an individual's actions can be judged. Not only does the relativist neglect to give us a reason for believing that a society's own views about morality are conclusive as to what is actually right and wrong, but also his theory does not square with our understanding of morality and the nature of ethical discourse. By contending that the moralities of different societies are all equally valid, the relativist holds that there can be no nonethnocentric ground for preferring one moral code to another, that one cannot speak of moral progress. Moralities may change, but they do not get better or worse. If words mean anything, however, it seems clear that a society that applauded the random torture of children would be immoral, even if it thought such a practice were right. It would simply be mistaken, and disastrously so. Since this is the case, ethical relativism must be false as a theory of normative ethics. . . .

Reason-giving is essential to the nature of morality, at least as we understand it. Suppose that Smith and Jones both think that incest is immoral. Smith, when challenged, argues that it is unnatural, harmful to the family unit, and psychologically destructive to the individuals involved. Each of these reasons can be pursued in greater detail: For example, what is "unnatural," and is the unnatural always immoral? And we can raise other relevant issues with Smith about, say, consent, age, or individual rights. Jones, on the other hand, offers no reasons and does not assent to those Smith gives. When pressed, Jones merely says, "I don't need to give a reason; incest is simply wrong." At this point, one may doubt that Jones is making a moral judgment. He may well be troubled by the thought of incest; it may agitate him; he may be adamant in condemning it. But if he resists offering a justification for his opinion, we shall very likely refuse to recognize it as a moral position at all.* Instead, we would suspect that he is only expressing a personal quirk or emotional reaction. The point I am making about our practice of morality—namely, that reason-giving and argumentation are essential to it—is attested to by the fact that prejudice frequently dresses itself in the language of reason. We recognize that the racist is only rationalizing his visceral bias when he attempts to justify segregation with spurious theories of racial differences, but his effort to so justify his prejudice at least acknowledges the fact that one must have reasons to back one's views if they are to count as a moral position in the first place—let alone be taken seriously.

Two related points are relevant here. The first is that not only are reasoning and argumentation basic to our practice of morality, but only certain sorts of reasons are countenanced by it. If Jones were to offer, as a justification of his judgment that incest is immoral, the reason that the idea is too gross for him to contemplate, or if a racist were to try to justify segregation by pointing to the skin color of the group he disdains, their "arguments" would simply be ruled out of bounds. By contrast, appeals to other sorts of considerations—for example, the rights of the persons involved, fairness, or the happiness produced—are perfectly appropriate and often suffice to establish at least the *prima facie* rightness or wrongness of the action. In other words, within moral discourse there are certain standard moves and relevant considerations—acknowledged by the vast majority of those who engage in it—just as there is an accepted framework of legal principles, policies, rules, and precedents on which a lawyer can and must draw in making his case.

The second point is that the relevant standards are fairly clear and can be applied with a reasonable claim to objectivity. Within the complex institution of morality it is not the case that it is all subjective, that all judgments are equal. There are criteria, and they can be interpreted and applied with a substantial degree of objectivity—just as judges can decide cases, teachers grade essays, or referees call penalties with a legitimate claim to be doing so correctly and objectively. And mistakes can be made: the fact that a judge's decision can be appealed

---

*Reasons are construed broadly here, so that one who claimed such a judgment was self-evident, axiomatic, or an intuitive moral insight would be offering a kind of justification for it. How plausible the justification is, is another matter.

implies that there are accepted standards against which it can be measured. Within our society we do not see eye to eye on everything, but our considered and reflective moral judgments do enjoy extensive agreement. Moral life is, to a large extent, a common life. We have a feel for morality; we understand what constitutes a legitimate moral position and what counts as a moral argument; we share certain institutional practices as well as paradigms of moral and immoral, just and unjust, conduct. There are agreed-upon standards in our moral practice, and within limits most moral determinations can be said to be correct or incorrect, justified or unjustified. . . .

DISCUSSION QUESTIONS

1. Why does Shaw say that if people really accepted ethical subjectivism there would be "no point in debating ethics with anyone"? Is this a necessary implication of ethical subjectivism? Support your answer.
2. Explain why, according to Shaw, "reason-giving" and "objectivity" are essential to morality. Do you agree with Shaw's arguments on these points?
3. How would Shaw respond to the emotivist claim that moral statements are neither true nor false but simply expressions of our feelings?
4. Do you think Shaw effectively dismisses ethical relativism? How might a cultural relativist such as Benedict respond to Shaw's arguments?

Chapter Applications

1. Killer Craig Price: "Mortality Is a Private Choice"

When the police arrived at the Heaton home in Warwick, Rhode Island, they found three mutilated bodies. Joan Heaton, 39, had been stabbed by a knife eleven times, strangled, and bitten in the face. Her daughter Jennifer, 10, had been stabbed sixty-two times. Melissa, 8, had been stabbed eight times and her skull crushed. "We think of what these little kids went through . . . that screaming . . . that unmerciful attack," Police Captain Kevin Collins shudders, recalling that grisly night in September 1989.[1]

Fifteen-year-old Craig Price, who lived in the neighborhood, was arrested shortly after the bodies were found. Police later discovered that two years earlier Price had murdered another neighbor. He also had a record of assaults, burglaries, and other crimes.

Does Price think what he did was immoral? When asked about the murders, Price shrugged his shoulders and responded: "Morality is a private choice." According to Police Captain Kevin Collins, who witnessed Price's confessions to the four murders, "He just loves to kill. There's no doubt . . . that he's going to kill again."[2]

Because Price was 15, he could not be tried as an adult. Under Rhode Island law, the maximum sentence for juveniles, regardless of their crime, is detention in the training school until they are 21.

Fear over Price's release prompted community groups to take out national advertisements to warn people about what was happening. Under increasing community pressure to keep Price in prison, state prosecutors won an assault case against Price for threatening a guard at the training school. Price is currently in prison for the assault.

Discussion Questions

1. Did Price do anything immoral? Support your answer. How would an ethical subjectivist respond to this question? How would a person acting on student relativism (SR), to use Satris's term, most likely respond to this question?

2. Does the fact that Price feels that morality is a private choice and that he acted on his feelings, vindicate him? If Price had regretted what he had done —rather than "loving it"—would it have made his actions more or less immoral? Discuss how an ethical subjectivist would answer these questions.

3. Price was no more corrupted by society than most youth his age. There was nothing unusual about his background; he came from what seemed to be a good family and lived in a middle-class neighborhood. Was Price's action in killing the family consistent with Rousseau's "law of the heart"? How might Rousseau explain people like Price?

4. In our culture we generally believe that children are not morally responsible for their actions. This cultural norm is reflected in the Rhode Island law. If morality is the same as cultural norms, on what grounds might people protest his release at age 21? Are they immoral to do so? Support your answer.

2. *Child Labor*

On a television show in the summer of 1996, Kathie Lee Gifford confessed that her Walmart outfits were made in Honduras by children earning 31 cents an hour. She tearfully vowed that she would try to clean up her purchasing act.

Our international economy is impacted daily by other cultures. Many of the products we use in the United States, such as clothing, athletic equipment, toys, jewelry, and home accessories, are made in sweatshops by child labor in other countries. Some of these children are slaves; others may be blinded or maimed for crying or for trying to return home.

Basketball superstar Michael Jordan, who earns up to $20 million dollars a year to endorse Nike sneakers, which are allegedly made in sweatshops in Indochina, disclaimed any moral responsibility for the manner in which the sneakers are manufactured. "My job with Nike," he told *Time* magazine, "is to endorse the product. Their job is to be up on that."[3]

Discussion Questions

1. If child labor is an acceptable norm in a culture, does that make it morally acceptable to purchase goods made by children in that culture, or do we as individuals have a moral responsibility to avoid buying products that are made by child labor? If so, is this only because child labor is no longer an acceptable custom in our culture? Support your answer. Discuss how a cultural relativist such as Ruth Benedict would respond to these questions.

2. Is Michael Jordan correct in claiming that the moral responsibility lies entirely with the companies who produce the products? Does the fact that we are ignorant of the origin of the products we purchase excuse us from contributing to the perpetuation of the practice? Support your answer.

3. Modern multinational corporations are unfettered by national borders. When the cultural norms of the home corporation and those of the country in which they operate come into conflict, by which norms should the corporations abide? Can cultural relativism offer guidance for deciding what norms should direct their business practices?

4. Although many people are opposed to child labor, others argue that workers, including child labor, in Third World sweatshops actually benefit from their own exploitation because it is better than starving to death. Does the fact that poverty is the norm in some places morally justify multinational companies paying marginal wages?

3. Head-Hunting

Head-hunting and cannibalism as cultural customs seem to have been concentrated in New Guinea and the Solomon Islands. Head-hunters gained prestige by taking and displaying human heads. The head-hunter would catch his victim using a long spiked pole with a loop at the end.[4]

Among some tribes, head-hunting was part of the initiation of boys into manhood. A young man was not considered ready to marry until he had at least one trophy. Although members of one's group were generally immune from becoming each others' trophy, wives from other tribes were considered fair game in some tribes. Indeed many tribes were terrified of the cannibal and head-hunting tribes that would sometimes travel up to 200 miles for human heads.

Sixteen-year-old Omba had been captured the previous year from another head-hunting tribe and given in marriage to one of the men in the tribe. One day when she was working in the garden some young unmarried men began gathering around her, whispering and laughing. Suddenly one of the youths grabbed a pole that was on the ground and lunged forward. As Omba shrieked and began to run, he threw the loop over her head and, giving it a jerk, severed her spinal cord. The other young men in the group congratulated him on his trophy.

Discussion Questions

1. Are cannibalism and head-hunting morally justified if they are a cultural norm? Discuss how you might respond if Omba had managed to escape and came to you for help. Would it be immoral for you to try to save her life? Support your answer.

2. Cultural customs, like cultures, do not exist in isolation. Many Melanesian tribes did not engage in head-hunting and cannibalism. However, they lived in constant terror of raiders and were frequently forced to flee for their lives. Discuss how a cultural relativist might respond regarding the morality of a cultural custom, such as head-hunting, that prevented another culture from pursuing the values that were important to them.

3. During the nineteenth and early twentieth centuries, several missionaries went to Melanesia where they tried to convert the natives to more peaceful ways. Although some of these missionaries were promptly killed by the natives, others managed to convince the natives that cannibalism and head-hunting were immoral. Were the missionaries wrong for trying to change the moral values of the natives? Support your answer.

4. Seeking Asylum from Cultural Customs

Seventeen-year-old Fauziy Kasinga fled her native home in Togo, Africa, and is seeking asylum in the United States. Asylum is granted to people who can show that they have a well-grounded fear of persecution based on race, religion, nationality, political belief, or membership in a social group. Kasinga believes that she is being persecuted because of her gender and is seeking asylum in an attempt to avoid arranged marriage and female circumcision.

Kasinga is not the only person seeking asylum from the customs of her culture. Since 1900 some 200,000 Salvadorans fleeing war in their country have enjoyed temporary amnesty in the United States. However, in December 1994, the Salvadoran refugee-protection program came to an end when the Clinton administration declared that El Salvador's human rights situation had improved significantly. Mario Davila, a Salvadoran organizer with the American Friends Service Committee, is opposed to returning the refugees. "Many of the agreements have been broken and the military continues to abuse human rights," he says.[5]

Discussion Questions

1. Are the customs of female circumcision and arranged marriages morally justified in Togo? How would a cultural relativist respond to this question? How would Marilyn Frye respond? Which answer do you find most satisfactory?

2. Can granting asylum for people who are fleeing the customs of their culture be morally justified using cultural relativism? Relate your answer to both the case of Kasinga and the case of the El Salvadoran refugees.

3. How do we determine if a particular cultural practice is a norm or custom? Discuss whether behavior in wartime, such as the death squads in El Salvador, reflect the customs of the culture or the breakdown of the culture. How should we respond to people seeking asylum from punishment for engaging in civil disobedience because they considered the laws of their country unjust?

4. Discuss which position Martin Luther King, Jr., would most likely take regarding the deportation of Salvadoran refugees. What advice might King give to Salvadorans who are facing deportation?

5. Although female circumcision is illegal, routine male circumcision—which was initially introduced in the late nineteenth century to discourage masturbation—is still an accepted custom in the United States. Routine circumcision of males has been discontinued in all other Western nations and is even illegal in some. However, in the United States about half of all newborn infant boys undergo routine nontherapeutic circumcision—a procedure that can be traumatic and painful. Discuss whether the fact that male circumcision is a custom morally justifies it.

6. During the early and mid-nineteenth century, Canada offered political asylum to people fleeing slavery in the United States. They also offered immigration status to conscientious objectors and to draft dodgers during the Vietnam War. Was it immoral for the Canadians to interfere with the customs of our culture? Or did they have a moral obligation to offer asylum because slavery was considered immoral in Canada?

5. *Immigrants and the Moral Community*

The ending of the refugee protection program for Salvadorans followed on the heels of California's Proposition 187, which denied education and health benefits to illegal immigrants. California Governor Pete Wilson, a supporter of the measure, argues that it was "designed not to control immigration, legal or illegal, but rather to make sure that state social services money went only to immigrants who were legally in California."[6]

However, the proposition has been accompanied by an anti-immigrant—legal or illegal—backlash. For example, in 1994 there was a 35 percent increase in anti-Asian hate crimes nationwide.[7]

Part of the backlash is attributed to the growing number of immigrants coming into the United States. According to the U.S. Bureau of the Census, the percentage of foreign-born residents in the United States has doubled since 1970 and is now higher than it has been in over fifty years.[8] Many people are fearful that the immigrants will take jobs from Americans as well as increase the cost of social services.

Discussion Questions

1. Under cultural relativism people only have moral value—are members of the moral community—if society grants them this status. Are immigrants members of the moral community? Do they deserve the same protection as citizens?

2. Do we have a right to protect our way of life from outsiders? What are the limits of this right? Use specific examples to illustrate your answer.

3. The great majority of people in the United States believe that we do not have a moral obligation to pay for the education and health care of those living in foreign countries. Is it fair that U.S. tax-payers be made to pay for the education and health needs of immigrants who are here in this country illegally? On the other hand, is it fair that children's access to education and basic health care be based on the status and actions of their parents?

4. The prevalence of anti-immigrant sentiment has been attributed to a "growing nativism and racial intolerance."[9] Some liberals point out that refugees from countries such as El Salvador and Haiti are treated differently than political refugees from European cultures. However, is this morally relevant to a cultural relativist? If the majority of people in the United States are opposed to immigration, especially from non-European countries, and this opposition is expressed in the law, does this make intolerance in this case moral? Support your answer. Discuss how a cultural relativist would answer these questions.

5. Some conservatives argue that tolerance for diversity embodied in multiculturalism is an upper-class, academic ideal that ignores the realities of the problems associated with mass immigration. They argue that immigration should be limited and immigrants assimilated into mainstream U.S. culture. If our common U.S. culture is destroyed, these conservatives maintain, law and order will soon crumble. Do you agree?

6. *"Yes Virginia, There Is a Santa Claus"*

The practice of giving gifts and telling children stories about a mythical figure like Santa Claus is widespread throughout Western nations. However, what makes the U.S. practice different is that Santa Claus is portrayed as a real person who actually makes a physical appearance. Today almost all parents in the United States strongly approve of telling their children that Santa Claus is a real person.[10]

Studies show that two-thirds of parents use Santa Claus to get their children to behave. The Santa custom has also been justified on the grounds that telling children that Santa is a real person isn't really a lie because young children don't know the difference between reality and fantasy. However, children as young as 4 years clearly know the difference between reality and fantasy and also recognize that they "have a duty toward adults not to lie."[11] Studies have also found that children will treat Santa Claus as a fantasy figure, rather than a real person, unless their parents tell them otherwise.

When a group of twenty-one sixth-grade students was asked to write an essay on whether it was right for their parents to tell them Santa was a real person, half of the youngsters said no. Another seven students expressed mixed feelings. "It's a lie and parents shouldn't lie to their children," one student wrote.[12] Five students pointed out that lying hurts children's feelings. Several wrote that they were uncomfortable with their parents using Santa as a threat or bribe to get them to behave.

Others have fond memories of the days when they believed. One girl stated that she was "impressed with how they [her parents] had tricked me for four years." Others pointed out that children who did not believe would be considered "oddballs." "What if your kids go to day care and tell everyone [Santa isn't real]," one concerned child wrote, "and they tell their parents? It might start an argument or fight."[13]

Discussion Questions

1. In our culture lying is generally regarded as morally wrong. What is a lie? Is telling children that Santa Claus is a real, living person a lie? Is the Santa story a justified lie? Support your answer.

2. Does the fact that it is a tradition to tell children that Santa is a real, living person morally justify continuing this tradition, or does the tradition have to be justified on different grounds? What other considerations are morally relevant in this case?

3. Lying restricts peoples' autonomy by placing limits on their ability to make informed decisions about their lives. On the other hand, are children really oppressed by a custom if they enjoy participating in that custom? Support your answer.

4. Compare and contrast the Santa custom to situations in which lying to adults is justified on similar grounds.

5. Under what circumstances, if any, is lying justified? Use specific examples to support your answer.

NOTES

[1] Jill Smolowe, "Not in My Backyard!" *Time,* September 5, 1994, p. 59.

[2] John Larrabee, "At 21, R.I. Serial Killer Soon Will Go Free," *USA Today,* June 6, 1994.

[3] Nancy Gibbs, "Cause Celeb," *Time,* June 17, 1996, pp. 28–30.

[4] Based on information in Timothy Severin, *Vanishing Primitive Man* (New York: American Heritage, 1973), pp. 257–267.

[5] Mike Zielinski, "Salvadorans Confront Deportation (Temporary US Amnesty Program Ends)," *The Progressive,* February 1995 59(2): 14.

[6] B. Durmmond Ayres, Jr., "California Immigration Law Is Ruled to Be Partly Illegal," *The New York Times,* November 21, 1995, p. A10.

[7] Kenneth B. Nobel, "Attacks Against Asian-Americans on the Rise, Especially in California," *The New York Times,* December 13, 1995, p. B13.

[8] Steven A. Holmes, "Surprising Rise in Immigration Stirs up Debate," *The New York Times,* August 30, 1995, p. A1.

[9] Kenneth B. Nobel, "Attacks Against Asian-Americans on the Rise, Especially in California," *The New York Times,* December 13, 1995, p. B13.

[10] See Judith A. Boss, "Is Santa Claus Corrupting Our Children's Morals?" *Free Inquiry,* Fall 1991, pp. 24–27.

[11] Jean Piaget, *The Moral Judgment of the Child* (New York: The Free Press, 1965), p. 166.

[12] Judith Boss, "No, Virginia, There Is No Santa Claus. Someone's Been Lying to You," *Free Inquiry,* Spring 1992, p. 52.

[13] Ibid.

CHAPTER THREE

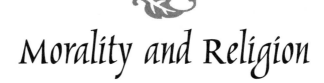

Morality and Religion

Do the gods love holiness because it is holy, or is it holy because the gods love it?

Plato, *Euthyphro*

Many people associate morality with religion. This raises the question of the nature of this association. Is morality dependent on religion, or does it exist independently of religion?

The divine command theory maintains that morality is relative to religion or God's commands. Just as morality for the cultural relativist is relative to cultural norms, for the divine command theorist morality is relative to what God commands or wills. There are no independent, universal moral standards by which to judge God's commands. No other justification is necessary for an action to be right other than God's commanding it.

Most theologians and ethicists, including natural law ethicists, disagree with the divine command theory. They argue instead that, whereas religious teachings may affirm universal moral principles, morality exists independently of religion or God's commands.

Moral instruction and codes are incorporated in the canons of the four major world religions—Judaism, Christianity, Hinduism, and Islam. Buddhism is sometimes included as one of the world religions. However, Buddhism is a philosophy rather than a religion because belief in God or in a transcendent being is not part of their world view. Confucianism, likewise, is a philosophy rather than a religion.

The study of the sacred scriptures is important, in part, because it teaches right from wrong. Many people base their moral behavior on the rules laid down in holy books such as the *Holy Bible* and the *Qu'ran*. However, this does not necessarily imply that the moral guidelines could not exist independently of these religions. Whether morality is, in fact, dependent on religion is up for debate.

The first group of readings represent the heart of the moral teachings of the world religions. The first selection is from the *Qu'ran*, the holy book of the Islam religion. Like many fundamentalist Christian groups, Muslims regard morality as inseparable from religion.

Hinduism does not have one central scripture as do the other three world religions. Instead, the teachings of Hinduism are found throughout several books. In the second selection Mohandas Gandhi discusses some of the moral teachings of his favorite Hindu holy book—the *Bhagavad Gita*.

The next group of selections are taken from the *Holy Bible*. In both the Jewish and mainstream Christian religions, the basic moral principles are held to be universal and discoverable through other means, such as reason or intuition.

The fourth selection from Lippman Bodoff's essay "God Tests Abraham, Abraham Tests God" explores the question of whether the story of Abraham and Isaac is an example of the divine command theory.

In the next reading from Plato's *Euthyphro,* Socrates questions the logic of the divine command theory. "Do the gods love holiness [morality] because it is holy," he asks Euthyphro, "or is it holy [moral] because the gods love it?"

In the selection from *The Summa Theologica,* Catholic philosopher and theologian Thomas Aquinas explains and defends natural law theory. According to Aquinas, God is the creator of moral (natural) law. However, unlike the divine command theorists, who regard morality as relative to God, Aquinas grounds morality in rational human nature. Rather than being relative to God's commands or one's particular religion, morality, Aquinas argues, is the same for all humans.

In the next selection from his works *Beyond Good and Evil* and *The Joyful Wisdom,* Friedrich Nietzsche contends that we have to go beyond conventional societal and religious views of good and evil. Nietzsche is an outspoken critic of all forms of cultural relativism. However, he is especially critical of traditional bourgeois Christian morality, which, he claims, forms the basis of modern Western morality.

In the final selection from "Religious Ethics Versus Humanistic Ethics," Kai Nielsen turns both the divine command theory and Aquinas's theologically based version of natural law theory upside-down. Nielsen argues instead that religious beliefs about morality and the goodness of God are dependent on human moral understanding rather than on any religious beliefs.

Qu'ran

Islam is the predominant religion in northern Africa, western and central Asia, as well as several nations in south and southeast Asia. Islam is also growing rapidly in the United States. The number of adherents to the Muslim faith in the United States is now slightly higher than the Jewish population.

Many Muslims believe that morality is dependent on God. God is the absolute sovereign. The supreme good in Islam is faith in the one God and submission to him. Indeed, the word *Islam* means "submission" in Arabic. To the Muslims, the *Qu'ran* is literally the revealed word of God as spoken to Mohammed by the angel Gabriel in the seventh century. The *Qu'ran* is divided into 114 suras, or chapters. Three of these suras are included in the readings. The first sura is recited daily at each of the five times of prayer. Sura 90 describes the two paths people can take in life: the easy path of vice or the more difficult path of virtue. Sura 96 tells of the creation of humans by Allah and the subsequent rebelliousness of humans.

CRITICAL THINKING QUESTIONS

1. What or who, according to the *Qu'ran*, is the ultimate source of morality and the ultimate judge?
2. What are some of the attributes of God?
3. Why should we obey the commands of God?
4. What happens to people who think they can be independent of God?
5. What is the difference between the path of virtue and the path of vice?
6. Why is the path of virtue more difficult?
7. According to the *Qu'ran*, why should we choose the path of virtue over the path of vice?

Sura 1

In the name of Allah, the Beneficent, the Merciful.

1. Praise be to Allah, Lord of the Worlds,

Qu'ran, Suras 1, 90, and 96. In *The Meaning of the Glorious Koran,* translated by Mohammed Marmakude Pickthall (London: George Allen & Unwin Ltd.).

2. The Beneficent, the Merciful.
3. Owner of the Day of Judgment,
4. Thee [alone] we worship; Thee [alone]we ask for help.
5. Show us the straight path,
6. The path of those whom Thou hast favored;
7. Not [the path] of those who earn Thine anger nor of those who go astray.

Sura 90

"THE CITY"

In the name of Allah, the Beneficent, the Merciful.

1. Nay, I swear by this city—
2. And thou art an indweller of this city—
3. And the begetter and that which he begat,
4. We verily have created man in an atmosphere:
5. Thinketh he that none hath power over him?
6. And he saith: I have destroyed vast wealth:
7. Thinketh he that none beholdeth him?
8. Did We not assign unto him two eyes
9. And a tongue and two lips,
10. And guide him to the parting of the mountain ways?
11. But he hath not attempted the Ascent—
12. Ah, what will convey unto thee what the Ascent is!—
13. [It is] to free a slave,
14. And to feed in the day of hunger
15. An orphan near of kin,
16. Or some poor wretch in misery,
17. And to be of those who believe and exhort one another to perseverance and exhort one another to pity.
18. Their place will be on the right hand.
19. But those who disbelieve Our revelations, their place will be on the left hand.
20. Fire will be an awning over them.

Sura 96

THE FIRST REVELATION

In the name of Allah, the Beneficent, the Merciful.

1. Read: In the name of thy Lord who createth,
2. Createth man from a clot.
3. Read: And thy Lord is the Most Bounteous,
4. Who teacheth by the pen,
5. Teacheth man that which he knew not.
6. Nay, but verily man is rebellious
7. That he thinketh himself independent!

DISCUSSION QUESTIONS

1. Are the attributes of God described in the *Qu'ran* what we would consider moral traits? If God had the opposite attributes, would He still be worthy of worship? How might a Muslim answer this question?
2. What characterizes a life of virtue, according to the *Qu'ran*? Compare this to your idea of a life of virtue. Does your idea of virtue depend on a belief in God or on reading the *Qu'ran* or another holy book? Explain.
3. If the path of vice is easier, why should we choose the path of virtue? Are you satisfied with the answer given in the *Qu'ran*? Why do you act morally when it would be easier for you to act immorally? To what extent are your reasons religiously based?
4. Do you agree that God's commands are the ultimate source of morality? Would it be possible for God to command you to live a life of vice, as defined in the *Qu'ran*? How might a Muslim answer this question?
5. Praying, which includes the repetition of the first sura five times a day, is central to the moral life of the Muslim. Is there a connection between prayer and morality? Can we be moral without ever praying? How would a Muslim most likely answer this question? Do you agree with the answer?
6. How do moral teachings in scripture differ from religious teachings? Are the moral teachings of the *Qu'ran* meant only for Muslims or are they meant to apply universally to all people? Support your answer.

Mohandas K. Gandhi

The Moral Teaching of the Bhagavad Gita

Mohandas Gandhi (1869–1948), also known as Mahatma ("Great Lord"), led the independence movement in India from 1919 to 1947 when independence was finally granted by the British. His method of nonviolent resistance has had a profound influence on subsequent reformers such as Martin Luther King, Jr.

In this selection Gandhi debates whether the teachings of the *Bhagavad Gita* can be reconciled with the moral principle of *ahimsa* (nonviolence). The *Bhagavad Gita* was put together over two thousand years ago and is India's most important religious text. The *Bhagavad Gita* is a record of a dialogue between Arjuna, a great warrior, and his charioteer Krishna, who is an incarnation of ultimate reality. The teachings of the *Bhagavad Gita* provide readers with a vision of Dharma (righteous living). The verses cited by Gandhi in the second reading are included at the end of the reading.

CRITICAL THINKING QUESTIONS

1. What does Gandhi mean when he says that the *Bhagavad Gita* is evolving?
2. How has the term *sacrifice* traditionally been used in Hinduism? How does Gandhi interpret this term?
3. How does Gandhi interpret the Hindu god Krishna's praise of war in the second chapter of the *Bhagavad Gita*?
4. On what grounds does Gandhi support his claim that nonviolence is not merely a Christian moral principle?
5. Why does Gandhi believe that *ahimsa* is an implicit moral teaching of the *Bhagavad Gita*?
6. What advice does the *Bhagavad Gita* give the reader for living a righteous life?

Teaching of Hinduism

Referring to my recent articles on the English peace movement led by Canon Sheppard, a friend writes:

"Teaching of Hinduism," "The Teaching of the Gita," and "Central Teaching of the Gita" in *Hindu Dharma* (Ahmedabad, India: Navajivan Publishing House, 1959), pp. 177–181.

"I hold the view that independently of the context of the *Gita* and the preliminary conversation between Arjuna and Shri Krishna, Hinduism does not stand decisively for non-violence in regard to organized invasion. It would be straining too much to interpret all our best scriptures in this way. Hinduism no doubt holds the spirit of compassion and love as the very highest duty for man. But it does not preach what you or the pacifists preach, and it is no good straining everything into an allegory for this object."

I have admitted in my introduction to the *Gita* known as *Anasaktiyoga* that it is not a treatise on non-violence nor was it written to condemn war. Hinduism as it is practised today, or has even been known to have ever been practised, has certainly not condemned war as I do. What, however, I have done is to put a new but natural and logical interpretation upon the whole teaching of the *Gita* and the spirit of Hinduism. Hinduism, not to speak of other religions, is ever evolving. It has no one scripture like the Quran or the Bible. Its scriptures are also evolving and suffering addition. The *Gita* itself is an instance in point. It has given a new meaning to *karma, sannyasa, yajna,* etc. It has breathed new life into Hinduism. It has given an original rule of conduct. Not that what the *Gita* has given was not implied in the previous writings, but the *Gita* put these implications in a concrete shape. I have endeavoured in the light of a prayerful study of the other faiths of the world and, what is more, in the light of my own experiences in trying to live the teaching of Hinduism as interpreted in the *Gita,* to give an extended but in no way strained meaning to Hinduism, not as buried in its ample scriptures, but as a living faith speaking like a mother to her aching child. What I have done is perfectly historical. I have followed in the footsteps of our forefathers. At one time they sacrificed animals to propitiate angry gods. Their descendants, but our less remote ancestors, read a different meaning into the word "sacrifice" and they taught that sacrifice was meant to be of our baser self, to please not angry gods but the one living God within. I hold that the logical outcome of the teaching of the *Gita* is decidedly for peace at the price of life itself. It is the highest aspiration of the human species.

The *Mahabharata* and the *Ramayana,* the two books that millions of Hindus know and regard as their guides, are undoubtedly allegories as the internal evidence shows. That they most probably deal with historical figures does not affect my proposition. Each epic describes the eternal duel that goes on between the forces of darkness and of light. Anyway I must disclaim any intention of straining the meaning of Hinduism or the *Gita* to suit any preconceived notions of mine. My notions were an outcome of a study of the *Gita,* the *Ramayana,* the *Mahabharata,* the *Upanishads,* etc.

Harijan, 3-10-'36

The Teaching of the Gita

[Dr. Kagawa is a student of religions. He wanted to know how Gandhiji's *ahimsa* teaching could be reconciled with the *Bhagawadgita*. Gandhiji said it could not be discussed in a brief interval, but he would ask him to read his introduction to the *Gita* where he had answered the question. The answer had come to him as part of his experience, and the interpretation was, as he thought, not laboured in any way.

—M.D.

Dr. Kagawa: I am told you recite the *Bhagawadgita* daily?

Gandhiji: Yes, we finish the entire *Gita* reading once every week.

Dr. Kagawa: But at the end of the *Gita* Krishna recommends violence.

Gandhiji: I do not think so. I am also fighting. I should not be fighting effectively if I were fighting violently. The message of the *Gita* is to be found in the second chapter of the *Gita* where Krishna speaks of the balanced state of mind, of mental equipoise. In 19 verses at the close of the 2nd chapter of the *Gita*, Krishna explains how this state can be achieved. It can be achieved, he tells us, after killing all your passions. It is not possible to kill your brother after having killed all your passions. I should like to see that man dealing death—who has no passions, who is indifferent to pleasure and pain, who is undisturbed by the storms that trouble mortal man. The whole thing is described in language of beauty that is unsurpassed. These verses show that the fight Krishna speaks of is a spiritual fight.

Dr. Kagawa: To the common mind it sounds as though it was actual fighting.

Gandhiji: You must read the whole thing dispassionately in its true context. After the first mention of fighting, there is no mention of fighting at all. The rest is a spiritual discourse.

Dr. Kagawa: Has anybody interpreted it like you?

Gandhiji: Yes. The fight is there, but the fight as it is going on within. The Pandavas and Kauravas are the forces of good and evil within. The war is the war between Jekyll and Hyde, God and Satan, going on in the human breast. The internal evidence in support of this interpretation is there in the work itself and in the *Mahabharata* of which the *Gita* is a minute part. It is not a history of war between two families, but the history of man—the history of the spiritual struggle of man. I have sound reasons for my interpretation.

Dr. Kagawa: That is why I say it is your interpretation.

Gandhiji: But that is nothing. The question is whether it is a reasonable interpretation, whether it carries conviction. If it does, it does not matter whether it is mine or X. Y. Z.'s. If it does not, it has no value even if it is mine.

Dr. Kagawa: To my mind Arjuna's ideas are wonderful. Krishna has found some excuse for him, and it was natural and necessary before Christianity.

Gandhiji: This interpretation is even historically wrong. For Buddha existed long before the Christian era, and he preached the doctrine of non-violence.

Dr. Kagawa: But Arjuna's views seem to me to be superior to Krishna's.

Gandhiji: Then according to you the disciple was greater than the master!

Dr. Kagawa: But I agree with your teaching of non-violence. I shall read the *Gita* again, bearing your interpretation in mind.

Harijan, 21-1-'39

Central Teaching of the Gita

"Is the central teaching of the *Gita* selfless action or non-violence?"

"I have no doubt that it is *anasakti*—selfless action. Indeed I have called my little translation of the *Gita Anasaktiyoga*. And *anasakti* transcends *ahimsa*. He who would be *anasakta* (selfless) has necessarily to practise non-violence in order to attain the state of selflessness. *Ahimsa* is, therefore, a necessary preliminary, it is included in *anasakti,* it does not go beyond it."

"Then does the *Gita* teach *himsa* and *ahimsa* both?"

"I do not read that meaning in the *Gita*. It is quite likely that the author did not write it to inculcate *ahimsa,* but as a commentator draws innumerable interpretations from a poetic text, even so I interpret the *Gita* to mean that if its central theme is *anasakti,* it also teaches *ahimsa*. Whilst we are in the flesh and tread the solid earth, we have to practise *ahimsa*. In the life beyond there is no *himsa* or *ahimsa*."

"But," said Balasaheb Kher, "Lord Krishna actually counters the doctrine of *ahimsa*. For Arjuna utters this pacifist resolve:

'Better I deem it, if my kinsmen strike,
To face them weaponless, and bare my breast
To shaft and spear, than answer blow with blow.'

"And Lord Krishna teaches him to 'answer blow with blow'."

WHAT TO DO?

"There I join issue with you," said Gandhiji. "Those words of Arjuna were words of pretentious wisdom. 'Until yesterday,' says Krishna to him, 'you fought your kinsmen with deadly weapons without the slightest compunction. Even today you would strike if the enemy was a stranger and not your own kith and kin!' The question before him was not of non-violence, but whether he should slay his nearest and dearest."

Harijan, 1-9-'40

[Following are the verses from the *Bhagavad Gita,* which Gandhi cites in the second reading.]

53

When your meditating mind, now bewildered
by conflicting views of Revelation,

Shall stand firm, unmoved in concentration,
*   then will you attain Discipline.*

54

Arjuna: *Please describe the man of firm judgment*
*   who is established in concentration.*
How would a man of firm mind speak,
*   or sit, or move about?*

55

The Lord: *A man is of firm judgment*
*   when he had abandoned all inner desires*
And the self is content,
*   at peace with itself.*

56

When unpleasant things do not perturb him
*   nor pleasures beguile him,*
When longing, fear, and anger have left,
*   he is a sage of firm mind.*

57

That man has a firm judgment
*   who feels no desire toward anything.*
Whatever good or bad he incurs,
*   he never delights in it nor hates it.*

58

When on all sides he withdraws his senses
*   from the sensual world,*
As a tortoise draws in its legs,
*   his judgment has become stable.*

59

The realm of the senses recedes
*   for the person who fasts.*
Only an inclination, a flavor, lingers.
*   That leaves him only when he has seen the highest.*

60

Even the wise man who exerts himself
*   to attain perfection*

Has senses that harass him
   and carry away his mind.

61

One should sit down, restraining all senses,
   intent on me.
Whoever controls his senses
   has a firm judgment.

62

A man gets attached to what the senses tell him
   if he does not turn his mind away.
Attachment gives rise to desire,
   desire to anger.

63

Anger leads to a state of delusion;
   delusion distorts one's memory.
Distortion of memory distorts consciousness,
   and then a man perishes.

64

But when a man wholly governing himself
   is roaming the sensual world
With his senses under control, freed
   from likes and dislikes, he attains clarity.

65

In clarity, he is liberated
   from all unpleasantness,
For the judgment of clear-minded men
   is unerringly steadfast.

66

The undisciplined does not meditate;
   he has no means of mental realization.
And there is no peace for one without such means.
   Without peace, how can there be happiness for him?

67

For when a man allows his mind to obey
   the whims of the senses,

It destroys his judgment
like a storm destroys a ship.

68

Therefore, O Warrior,
having your senses entirely withdrawn
From the world of the senses
means attaining a steadfast judgment.

69

The man of self-control is awake
in what is night for all creatures;
And when they are awake,
it is night for the seer.

70

The sea gathers the waters;
It fills and fills itself . . .
Its equilibrium
Is undisturbed.
So also
The man into whom
All desires enter—
Not he who goes after desires—
Finds peace.

71

The man who has given up all desire
and moves about without wanting anything,
Who says neither mine *nor* I,
wins peace.

72

This, Son of Pṛthā, is divine stability.
Whoso reaches it is not again confused.
Whoso abides in it even at death
gains the freedom that is God's.

DISCUSSION QUESTIONS

1. Gandhi believed that the Hindu religion offers moral guidelines. Discuss whether, in Gandhi's view, these guidelines are peculiar to Hinduism or whether they are meant to serve as universal moral principles.

2. How does Gandhi justify his giving new meaning to the moral teachings of the *Bhagavad Gita?* In light of what criteria does Gandhi, or anyone, interpret the moral teachings of scripture? What does this say about the origin of morality?
3. Which does Gandhi think is more important—religion or morality? Support your answer.
4. Why does Gandhi disagree with Dr. Kagawa when Kagawa says that the *Bhagavad Gita* "recommends violence"? Which person do you think presented the strongest argument?
5. Does the selection from the *Bhagavad Gita* support nonviolence as a way of life, as Gandhi argues?
6. Compare and contrast the moral teaching in the *Bhagavad Gita* with those of the *Qu'ran.*
7. Discuss ways in which Gandhi and Kagawa exemplify the perspective of the philosopher in their discussion. Use specific examples to support your answer.

Excerpts from Genesis, Exodus, and Matthew

Holy Bible

These selections from the *Holy Bible* are taken from *The New Oxford Annotated Bible with the Apocrypha*, edited by Herbert G. May and Bruce M. Metzger and published by Oxford University Press, 1977.

The first chapter of Genesis contains the creation story. According to this story, humans beings are a special creation made in the image of God. The rest of creation was given to humans for our use. This anthropocentric view of humans has had a profound effect on Western ethics.

In Genesis 22, Abraham is tested by God, who commands Abraham to sacrifice His son Isaac. This passage is sometimes used as an example of the divine command theory.

The next passage, the Decalogue (Ten Commandments), is taken from Exodus. The Decalogue is based on a legalistic or familial view of morality in which God the Father sets down the laws for His children.

In the New Testament there is a shift away from a legalistic model of morality to one of a model spiritual life. Christian moral teachings are represented in the Sermon on the Mount and other short teachings of Jesus from the Gospel of Matthew. In these readings Jesus presents guidelines for living the moral life.

CRITICAL THINKING QUESTIONS

1. What is the view of human nature and the relation of humans to God?
2. Why did God ask Abraham to sacrifice His son Isaac?
3. How did Abraham respond to God's command?
4. Why, according to this passage, did the Jews have an obligation to God?
5. Which of the Ten Commandments deal with moral issues and which deal with religious issues? On what grounds do you distinguish between the two?
6. To whom was Jesus speaking in the Sermon on the Mount?
7. Who, according to Jesus, is blessed?
8. What is the relation between the laws of the prophets and the moral teachings of Jesus?
9. How, according to Jesus, should we treat our enemies?

Holy Bible, Genesis 1:26–31, 22:1–18; Exodus 20:1–17; Matthew 5:1–20, 38–48, 6:19–23; 7:1–5, 15–20.

Genesis 1:26–31

Then God said, "Let us make man in our image, after our likeness; and let them have dominion over the fish of the sea, and over the birds of the air, and over the cattle, and over all the earth, and over every creeping thing that creeps upon the earth." 27 So God created man in his own image, in the image of God he created him; male and female he created them. 28 And God blessed them, and God said to them, "Be fruitful and multiply, and fill the earth and subdue it; and have dominion over the fish of the sea and over the birds of the air and over every living thing that moves upon the earth." 29 And God said, "Behold, I have given you every plant yielding seed which is upon the face of all the earth, and every tree with seed in its fruit; you shall have them for food. 30 And to every beast of the earth, and to every bird of the air, and to everything that creeps on the earth, everything that has the breath of life, I have given every green plant for food." And it was so. 31 And God saw everything that he had made, and behold, it was very good. And there was evening and there was morning, a sixth day.

Genesis 22:1–18

After these things God tested Abraham, and said to him, "Abraham!" And he said, "Here am I." 2 He said, "Take your son, your only son Isaac, whom you love, and go to the land of Mori'ah, and offer him there as a burnt offering upon one of the mountains of which I shall tell you." 3 So Abraham rose early in the morning, saddled his ass, and took two of his young men with him, and his son Isaac; and he cut the wood for the burnt offering, and arose and went to the place of which God had told him. 4 On the third day Abraham lifted up his eyes and saw the place afar off. 5 Then Abraham said to his young men, "Stay here with the ass; I and the lad will go yonder and worship, and come again to you." 6 And Abraham took the wood of the burnt offering, and laid it on Isaac his son; and he took in his hand the fire and the knife. So they went both of them together. 7 And Isaac said to his father Abraham, "My father!" And he said, "Here am I, my son." He said, "Behold, the fire and the wood; but where is the lamb for a burnt offering?" 8 Abraham said, "God will provide himself the lamb for a burnt offering, my son." So they went both of them together.

9 When they came to the place of which God had told him, Abraham built an altar there, and laid the wood in order, and bound Isaac his son, and laid him on the altar, upon the wood. 10 Then Abraham put forth his hand, and took the knife to slay his son. 11 But the angel of the Lord called to him from heaven, and said, "Abraham, Abraham!" And he said, "Here am I." 12 He said, "Do not lay your hand on the lad or do anything to him; for now I know that you fear God, seeing you have not withheld your son, your only son, from me." 13 And Abraham lifted up his eyes and looked, and behold, behind him was a ram, caught in a thicket by his horns; and Abraham went and took the ram, and offered it up as a burnt offering instead of his son. 14 So Abraham called the name of that place

The Lord will provide; as it is said to this day, "On the mount of the Lord it shall be provided."

[15] And the angel of the Lord called to Abraham a second time from heaven, [16] and said, "By myself I have sworn, says the Lord, because you have done this, and have not withheld your son, your only son, [17] I will indeed bless you, and I will multiply your descendants as the stars of heaven and as the sand which is on the seashore. . . .

Exodus 20:1–17

And God spoke all these words, saying,

[2] "I am the Lord your God, who brought you out of the land of Egypt, out of the house of bondage.

[3] "You shall have no other gods before me.

[4] "You shall not make for yourself a graven image, or any likeness of anything that is in heaven above, or that is in the earth beneath, or that is in the water under the earth; [5] you shall not bow down to them or serve them; for I the Lord your God am a jealous God, visiting the iniquity of the fathers upon the children to the third and the fourth generation of those who hate me, [6] but showing steadfast love to thousands of those who love me and keep my commandments.

[7] "You shall not take the name of the Lord your God in vain; for the Lord will not hold him guiltless who takes his name in vain.

[8] "Remember the sabbath day, to keep it holy. [9] Six days you shall labor, and do all your work; [10] but the seventh day is a sabbath to the Lord your God; in it you shall not do any work, you, or your son, or your daughter, your manservant, or your maidservant, or your cattle, or the sojourner who is within your gates; [11] for in six days the Lord made heaven and earth, the sea, and all that is in them, and rested the seventh day; therefore the Lord blessed the sabbath day and hallowed it.

[12] "Honor your father and your mother, that your days may be long in the land which the Lord your God gives you.

[13] "You shall not kill.

[14] "You shall not commit adultery.

[15] "You shall not steal.

[16] "You shall not bear false witness against your neighbor.

[17] "You shall not covet your neighbor's house; you shall not covet your neighbor's wife, or his manservant, or his maidservant, or his ox, or his ass, or anything that is your neighbor's."

Matthew 5:1–20, 38–48

Seeing the crowds, he [Jesus] went up on the mountain, and when he sat down his disciples came to him. [2] And he opened his mouth and taught them, saying:

[3] "Blessed are the poor in spirit, for theirs is the kingdom of heaven.

[4] "Blessed are those who mourn, for they shall be comforted.

[5] "Blessed are the meek, for they shall inherit the earth.

6 "Blessed are those who hunger and thirst for righteousness, for they shall be satisfied.

7 "Blessed are the merciful, for they shall obtain mercy.

8 "Blessed are the pure in heart, for they shall see God.

9 "Blessed are the peacemakers, for they shall be called sons of God.

10 "Blessed are those who are persecuted for righteousness' sake, for theirs is the kingdom of heaven.

11 "Blessed are you when men revile you and persecute you and utter all kinds of evil against you falsely on my account. 12 Rejoice and be glad, for your reward is great in heaven, for so men persecuted the prophets who were before you.

13 "You are the salt of the earth; but if salt has lost its taste, how shall its saltness be restored? It is no longer good for anything except to be thrown out and trodden under foot by men.

14 "You are the light of the world. A city set on a hill cannot be hid. 15 Nor do men light a lamp and put it under a bushel, but on a stand, and it gives light to all in the house. 16 Let your light so shine before men, that they may see your good works and give glory to your Father who is in heaven.

17 "Think not that I have come to abolish the law and the prophets; I have come not to abolish them but to fulfil them. 18 For truly, I say to you, till heaven and earth pass away, not an iota, not a dot, will pass from the law until all is accomplished. 19 Whoever then relaxes one of the least of these commandments and teaches men so, shall be called least in the kingdom of heaven; but he who does them and teaches them shall be called great in the kingdom of heaven. 20 For I tell you, unless your righteousness exceeds that of the scribes and Pharisees, you will never enter the kingdom of heaven.

. . .

38 "You have heard that it was said, 'An eye for an eye and a tooth for a tooth.' 39 But I say to you, Do not resist one who is evil. But if any one strikes you on the right cheek, turn to him the other also; 40 and if any one would sue you and take your coat, let him have your cloak as well; 41 and if any one forces you to go one mile, go with him two miles. 42 Give to him who begs from you, and do not refuse him who would borrow from you.

43 "You have heard that it was said, 'You shall love your neighbor and hate your enemy.' 44 But I say to you, Love your enemies and pray for those who persecute you, 45 so that you may be sons of your Father who is in heaven; for he makes his sun rise on the evil and on the good, and sends rain on the just and on the unjust. 46 For if you love those who love you, what reward have you? Do not even the tax collectors do the same? 47 And if you salute only your brethren, what more are you doing than others? Do not even the Gentiles do the same? 48 You, therefore, must be perfect, as your heavenly Father is perfect.

Matthew 6:19–23

19 "Do not lay up for yourselves treasures on earth, where moth and rust consume and where thieves break in and steal, 20 but lay up for yourselves treasures in heaven, where neither moth nor rust consumes and where thieves do not break in and steal. 21 For where your treasure is, there will your heart be also.

[22] "The eye is the lamp of the body. So, if your eye is sound, your whole body will be full of light; [23] but if your eye is not sound, your whole body will be full of darkness. If then the light in you is darkness, how great is the darkness!

Matthew 7:1–5, 15–20

[1] "Judge not, that you be not judged.

[2] For with the judgment you pronounce you will be judged, and the measure you give will be the measure you get. [3] Why do you see the speck that is in your brother's eye, but do not notice the log that is in your own eye? [4] Or how can you say to your brother, 'Let me take the speck out of your eye,' when there is the log in your own eye? [5] You hypocrite, first take the log out of your own eye, and then you will see clearly to take the speck out of your brother's eye.

[15] "Beware of false prophets, who come to you in sheep's clothing but inwardly are ravenous wolves. [16] You will know them by their fruits. Are grapes gathered from thorns, or figs from thistles? [17] So, every sound tree bears good fruit, but the bad tree bears evil fruit. [18] A sound tree cannot bear evil fruit, nor can a bad tree bear good fruit. [19] Every tree that does not bear good fruit is cut down and thrown into the fire. [20] Thus you will know them by their fruits.

DISCUSSION QUESTIONS

1. Discuss how the Judeo-Christian view of human nature, as expressed in Genesis, has influenced the Western views of morality and the moral community. What evidence is offered in Genesis to support this view of human nature? Are you satisfied with the evidence?

2. Is the story of Isaac an example of the divine command theory? Does the response "It was God's command" morally justify taking the lives of other people? How can we tell if a person is telling the truth when they say "It was God's command"?

3. Did Abraham do the morally right thing in taking Isaac to the mountains to sacrifice him? Discuss the answer to this question from the perspective of Isaac as well as Isaac's mother Sarah.

4. Are the Ten Commandments an example of the divine command theory; or can the Ten Commandments be defended as moral principles without reference to religion or to God?

5. Apply the Ten Commandments to a contemporary moral issue such as abortion, euthanasia, cloning, meat eating, or pornography. Do the Ten Commandments offer practical guidance in resolving these issues?

6. Compare and contrast the Sermon on the Mount with the Ten Commandments. Do they support and complement each other? Or, is Jesus offering a new set of moral guidelines for people? Relate your answer to the passage in Matthew 5:17–20.

7. Compare and contrast the moral teachings of the *Holy Bible* to those offered in the *Qu'ran* and in the *Bhagavad Gita*. To what extent do these religions share the same moral code? If they do share the same moral code, what does this suggest about the relation between morality and religion?

8. Is Jesus saying that we should be morally good so we will go to heaven? What is the connection between heaven and moral goodness? Are our actions genuinely moral if our primary motive in doing them is personal reward? Why do you behave morally?

9. What did Jesus mean when he called his disciples the "salt of the earth" and "the light of the world"? Relate your answer to the concept of moral and social reform. Are you a morally "salty" person? Use examples to illustrate your answer.

10. Jesus often spoke in parables. Do you think the teachings given in the Sermon on the Mount are meant to be taken literally? Is the Sermon on the Mount meant only for his disciples? Or did Jesus intend it as a universal moral code for everyone?

11. Does the Sermon on the Mount offer practical moral guidelines for everyday living? Use examples to illustrate your answer.

12. What does Jesus mean when he says that a sound tree cannot bear evil fruit? What are good fruits, morally speaking? Can we judge people by their actions? Do people of good will always do what is right?

13. What does Jesus mean when he says we cannot serve two masters? Does this command mean we should not save money for our education or our future?

14. What does Jesus mean when he says "Judge not, that you be not judged"? Is he telling us we should refrain from any sort of moral judgment? If so, did the people who did not try to stop the death of Kitty Genovese outside of her apartment house in New York City do the right thing by not passing judgment on her assailant? Were the abolitionists, who judged slavery to be wrong, immoral people?

15. What does Jesus mean when he says we must be perfect like God? How is God perfect? Is Jesus referring to moral perfection? If so, do you agree that we have an obligation to strive toward moral perfection? Relate your answer to Aristotle's view of human nature.

16. Are the moral guidelines given in the *Holy Bible* meant to apply only to Jews and Christians? Or are they meant to be universally binding on everyone? Support your position.

Lippman Bodoff

God Tests Abraham, Abraham Tests God

The *Akedah*—the biblical story of Abraham's willingness to obey God's command to sacrifice his son Isaac—has been used as an example of the divine command theory. Abraham's righteousness, according to divine command theorists, stemmed from his unquestioning obedience to the will of God.

Jewish scholar Lippman Bodoff offers another explanation. He interprets the story of Abraham and Isaac as a conflict between blind obedience (divine command theory) and moral choice (natural law theory). Rather than expecting blind obedience, Bodoff argues that while God was testing Abraham, Abraham was also testing this new god to see if He was worthy of worship. A god who was worthy of worship would not allow Abraham to kill his son because this was against the moral law. In the end, both Abraham and God passed the test.

CRITICAL THINKING QUESTIONS

1. What, according to Bodoff, is the traditional interpretation of the story of Abraham and Isaac?
2. Why did God want to test Abraham?
3. Did God pass Abraham's test?
4. Did Abraham pass God's test?
5. Did Abraham always have faith in God's justice and righteousness?
6. Why did the incident strengthen Abraham's faith in God as well as his moral courage?

In Jewish tradition, the Torah has 70—that is, many—facets. Its interpretations are inexhaustible. I would like to suggest a new interpretation of the *Akedah,* the binding of Isaac (Genesis 22), a story that has received as much "interpretation" as any in the Hebrew Bible.

[In the] . . . story of *Akedah* . . . God commands Abraham to slaughter his beloved son Isaac as a sacrifice to God. As Abraham is about to sacrifice the boy on the altar, an angel calls out to him to stop "because now I see that you are a

---

"God Tests Abraham, Abraham Tests God," *Bible Review* (October 1993), pp. 53–56, 62. Some notes have been omitted.

God-fearing person and you would not withhold your son . . . from me" (Genesis 22:12).

In the traditional understanding of this story, God never intended Abraham to slaughter Isaac, because it was wrong—as we know from the beginning of the story, which speaks of God "testing" Abraham, and from the end of the story, when Abraham is told to desist. Abraham, on the other hand, out of fear of God, was willing to violate God's moral law in faithfulness to God's command. Abraham passed the test.

The message of the *Akedah* is quite plainly that God does not want even his most God-fearing adherents to go so far as to murder in his name or even at his command. Indeed, the angel orders Abraham "not to do anything to [the boy]." Implicitly, we are being told, God will never ask for this kind of proof of loyalty or fear of God again. He only asked it of Abraham, the first forefather of the Jewish people, to demonstrate Abraham's boundless fear of God.

Because Abraham is praised for being prepared to do what we may not do, and because God, the source of all morality, asked Abraham to do what no moral person before or since should ever contemplate, the *Akedah* has remained one of the most difficult texts to understand, justify and transmit to new generations.

I believe there is a countermessage in the text that exists in parallel with its traditional meaning, a simultaneous and necessary conceptual theological balance to the awesome mystery and the daunting problems of the traditional interpretation.

I believe that God was testing Abraham to see if he would remain loyal to God's moral law, but Abraham—who could not know this—was simultaneously testing God to see what kind of covenant and religion he, Abraham, was being asked to join.

After all, it was Abraham who found God, not the other way around. According to the midrash,* "Until Abraham arrived, God reigned only over the heavens." It was Abraham who "crowned" him God on earth, the God of man. In these circumstances, Abraham not surprisingly had certain moral expectations—and perhaps even requirements—of the all-powerful God of the ordered universe, whose tradition as a God who abhorred violence and all immorality he had received and studied, and in whose name he was about to establish a new world religion.

In testing God, as it were, Abraham was, ultimately, testing himself. I have found God, he seems to be saying, and my tradition and experience have revealed him and made him known to me as an all-powerful, all-knowing, just and compassionate God. But I need to be sure that this is the God to which I truly wish to dedicate myself and my progeny and my followers for all time. If the God I have found demands the same kind of immorality that I saw in my father's pagan society, I must be mistaken. I must look further. To obey such a God is not a moral advance at all. To paraphrase our sages, Better observance without God than God without observance.

---

*The midrash is a genre of rabbinic literature that includes homilies as well as commentaries on specific books of the Bible.

In short, Abraham wanted to see if God would stop him.

One may well ask, if this were the case, why didn't Abraham challenge God at the outset, when first commanded to sacrifice Isaac. Abraham had earlier done just that when God had told him of his plan to destroy Sodom and Gomorrah (Genesis 18:20–32).* We cannot justify Abraham's refusal to at least protest God's command that he kill Isaac on the grounds that prophets must *silently* obey whenever consulted or commanded by God. The opposite is true when God's justice or compassion, and the morality of His commands, is at issue.

There is an alternative strategy, however—stalling for time. I do not believe Abraham ever intended to kill Isaac. He was obviously terribly concerned that God had commanded him to do so. However, those who seek simultaneously to obey their superiors—whom they admire, respect and sometimes fear—*and* give their superiors a chance to change their minds about what seems to be an unwise or immoral idea, rarely challenge the idea head on. They stretch things out.

The matter may be compared to a father who asks his son to violate the Sabbath in some way. The child does not know whether his father is testing his obedience to the law—which requires him to resist his father and observe the Sabbath commandments—or whether his father is testing his love (and fear) of his parent. The child can protest immediately, perhaps thereby showing disrespect and causing the parent anguish, or the child can make the necessary preparations to do what the parent has requested, seeming to go along, hoping that when the actual time comes the parent will never let the child take the last step.

This is precisely what the texts tells us that Abraham did. He did not rush—he stalled! He broke up the task that he was given into numerous tasks, or steps, and at each one he stopped, waiting to see whether "the Boss" had reconsidered. It was never Abraham's intention to kill his son, and God never indicated whether he wanted Abraham to kill Isaac, or whether he wanted Abraham to refuse to do so. Given Abraham's moral purity, we may reasonably conclude that if, at the very end, God had not rescinded his command for Isaac's death, Abraham would have rejected the command, chosen the moral course of not committing murder and saved his son—and then been forced to reexamine the prospects of his new religion, and the belief and faith on which it rested. Abraham was waiting for God to say: "Don't do it." . . .

The point of the text is quite clear. At each step Abraham is waiting for God to evidence a change of mind, to withdraw his command. When that is not forthcoming, Abraham takes the next step, and puts the Almighty to the next test—as it were—always showing obedience, always *giving God the opportunity* to make the moral statement that God does not want man to murder or to commit other

---

*This is in contrast to Noah, whom our sages criticize for not speaking up when God announced his plan to destroy the world by the Flood. Moses, too, was told about God's plan to destroy the Jewish people and start a new nation from Moses' progeny, after the sin of the golden calf (Exodus 32: 1–14), and he is praised by our sages because he objected. In Jewish tradition, a prophet's conscientious objection to a divine plan or order is praiseworthy; in Jewish law, a prophet may only follow divine commands to violate God's law if his purpose is to protect the law. . . .

immoral acts in God's name. And, at the very end, when Abraham takes the last step before he would be forced by his conscience to stop and challenge God's command, the angelic order to stop finally comes.

Those who argue that Abraham intended to kill Isaac before being stopped, cannot prove it from the *Akedah*, because Abraham never agreed to kill his son, and never had to. Had he done so, and said "I still believe in God," we would have had proof. We would also have had a religion to which few, perhaps none of us, could subscribe, because such a religion would never have endured.*

. . .

Abraham did not want God's moral law against murder to be affirmed merely as a divine response to a human plea, as occurred at Sodom, or to be proclaimed merely as a response to human arguments about God's mercy, justice and righteousness. To achieve this, Abraham had to have an enduring, unshakable faith in God's justice and righteousness, a faith that allowed him to proceed with the *Akedah, not* with the steadfast, zealous intent to kill Issac, but with the steadfast, serene faith that God, *without the need for human pleading,* would ultimately pronounce for all, and for all time, the prohibition against murder—even for God's glory and in God's name.

The *Akedah* is a morality tale of Abraham's staunch defense of God's moral law against any temptation—even God's command—to violate it. It establishes Judaism's unique insight among ancient religions, cults and cultures about the dangers of having human beings submit to the orders of individuals who claim unique access to the wishes of "the gods," or of any god.

The corrective is a religion based on a covenant between God and *all* of the people, in a revealed text to which *all* have access and which *all* can master. No person or elite can misguide the people down paths of immorality in the name of a supernatural power.

God was testing Abraham to see if he would remain faithful to his revealed moral law even when divinely commanded to violate it, in order fully and finally to expunge the belief and practice of child sacrifice or any murder (ostensibly) in God's name or for God's benefit. Abraham never intended to kill Isaac but, with faith in God's morality, Abraham was waiting for God to say, "Stop, don't do it, I didn't mean it," just as God was waiting for Abraham to say, "I won't do it."

In his determination not to kill Isaac, and his willingness to go forward with God's command until ordered to stop, Abraham passed the twin tests of the *Akedah,* the tests of the strongest moral courage and the purest religious faith.

DISCUSSION QUESTIONS

1. How does Bodoff's interpretation of the *Akedah* differ from the traditional interpretation and that of the divine command theorists? Whose interpretation is strongest?

---

*According to the midrash, Abraham's apparent obedience to God's command caused Sarah's death and Isaac's alienation from him forever after. Although Abraham and Isaac ascend Moriah together, the Torah emphasizes that Abraham "returned to his servants" alone (Genesis 22:19); Abraham and Isaac settle in different places and never speak to each other again.

2. What support does Bodoff offer for his interpretation? Are you convinced by his argument?
3. What was more important to Abraham—the moral law or obeying God's command? Why did God have to pass a test before Abraham would obey Him?
4. Why did Abraham have doubts about God's justice and righteousness? Do you agree with Bodoff that it is possible for God to be unjust? Support your answer.
5. Why does Bodoff say that Abraham showed moral courage? Is there a distinction between moral courage and religious faith? If so, how do they differ?

Plato

Euthyphro

Although Socrates (c. 469–399 B.C.E.) is honored as the Father of Western philosophy, he never wrote anything himself. What we know of Socrates and his philosophy comes mainly from the writings of his renowned student Plato (427–347 B.C.E.).

In ancient Greek philosophy, philosophical questions arose out of ordinary experience. In this Platonic dialogue, Euthyphro is on the way to court to bring a charge against his father when he runs into Socrates, who is awaiting trial on charges of impiety. Their conversation touches on the perennial question of whether the Good is good because God loves it or whether God loves the Good because it is good. In other words, is an action moral because the *Bible, Qu'ran, Bhagavad Gita,* or another holy book says it is? Or does the religion merely reinforce what people already know to be moral?

In the early days of Athens many people looked to religious sanctions in deciding what was moral. "Piety" in this dialogue, therefore, is used in a much broader sense to include what is righteous or moral. Euthyphro claims to have the correct definition of piety or morality. This leads Socrates to seek a clearer definition of piety. In cross-examining Euthyphro, Socrates brings out the contradictions in Euthyphro's position.

CRITICAL THINKING QUESTIONS

1. Why is Socrates surprised when Euthyphro tells him he is bringing charges against his father? Would it have made a difference to Socrates if the man being charged was a stranger instead of his father?

2. How does Euthyphro defend his bringing charges against his father?

3. Why is Socrates not satisfied when Euthyphro defines piety as what is dear to the gods?

4. What does Socrates mean when he speaks of the one form presented by all actions that are called pious? How does Euthyphro respond when Socrates asks him to define this form? Why is this response also unsatisfactory to Socrates?

5. Does Euthyphro use the term *piety* in a logically consistently manner throughout his argument? Identify some of the different definitions used by Euthyphro.

Euthyphro in *The Dialogues of Plato*, vol. 2, B. Jowett, translation. New York: Macmillan Publishing Co., 1892.

6. Why does Socrates keep pushing Euthyphro to explain what piety means? Is Socrates genuinely interested in finding a definition or is he just being difficult?

7. Which does Socrates believe to be more fundamental—religion or morality?

Socrates: And what is your suit, Euthyphro? are you the pursuer or the defendant?

Euthyphro: I am the pursuer.

Socrates: Of whom?

Euthyphro: You will think me mad when I tell you.

Socrates: Why, has the fugitive wings?

Euthyphro: Nay, he is not very volatile at his time of life.

Socrates: Who is he?

Euthyphro: My father.

Socrates: Your father! my good man?

Euthyphro: Yes.

Socrates: And of what is he accused?

Euthyphro: Of murder, Socrates.

Socrates: By the powers, Euthyphro! how little does the common herd know of the nature of right and truth. A man must be an extraordinary man, and have made great strides in wisdom, before he could have seen his way to bring such an action.

Euthyphro: Indeed, Socrates, he must.

Socrates: I suppose that the man whom your father murdered was one of your relatives—clearly he was; for if he had been a stranger you would never have thought of prosecuting him.

Euthyphro: I am amused, Socrates, at your making a distinction between one who is a relation and one who is not a relation; for surely the pollution is the same in either case, if you knowingly associate with the murderer when you ought to clear yourself and him by proceeding against him. The real question is whether the murdered man has been justly slain. If justly, then your duty is to let the matter alone; but if unjustly, then even if the murderer lives under the same roof with you and eats at the same table, proceed against him. Now the man who is dead was a poor dependent of mine who worked for us as a field labourer on our farm in Naxos, and one day in a fit of drunken passion he got into a quarrel with one of our domestic servants and slew him. My father bound him hand and foot and threw him into a ditch, and then sent to Athens to ask of a diviner what he should do with him. Meanwhile he never attended to him and took no care about him, for he regarded him as a murderer; and thought that no great harm would be done even if he did die. Now this was just what happened. For such was the effect of cold and hunger and chains upon him, that before the messenger returned from the diviner, he was dead. And my father and family are angry with me for taking the part of the murderer and prosecuting my father. They say that he did not kill him, and that if he did, the dead man was but a murderer, and I ought not to take any notice, for that a son is impious who prosecutes a father. Which shows, Socrates, how little they know what the gods think about piety and impiety.

Socrates: Good heavens, Euthyphro! and is your knowledge of religion and of things pious and impious so very exact, that, supposing the circumstances to be as you state them, you are not afraid lest you too may be doing an impious thing in bringing an action against your father?

Euthyphro: The best of Euthyphro, and that which distinguishes him, Socrates, from other men, is his exact knowledge of all such matters. What should I be good for without it?

Socrates: Rare friend! I think that I cannot do better than be your disciple. Then before the trial with Meletus comes on I shall challenge him, and say that I have always had a great interest in religious questions, and now, as he charges me with rash imaginations and innovations in religion, I have become your disciple. You, Meletus, as I shall say to him, acknowledge Euthyphro to be a great theologian, and sound in his opinions; and if you approve of him you ought to approve of me, and not have me into court; but if you disapprove, you should begin by indicting him who is my teacher, and who will be the ruin, not of the young, but of the old; that is to say, of myself whom he instructs, and of his old father whom he admonishes and chastises. And if Meletus refuses to listen to me, but will go on, and will not shift the indictment from me to you, I cannot do better than repeat this challenge in the court.

Euthyphro: Yes, indeed, Socrates; and if he attempts to indict me I am mistaken if I do not find a flaw in him; the court shall have a great deal more to say to him than to me.

Socrates: And I, my dear friend, knowing this, am desirous of becoming your disciple. For I observe that no one appears to notice you—not even this Meletus; but his sharp eyes have found me out at once, and he has indicted me for impiety. And therefore, I adjure you to tell me the nature of piety and impiety, which you said that you knew so well, and of murder, and of other offences against the gods. What are they? Is not piety in every action always the same? and impiety, again—is it not always the opposite of piety, and also the same with itself, having, as impiety, one notion which includes whatever is impious?

Euthyphro: To be sure, Socrates.

Socrates: And what is piety, and what is impiety?

Euthyphro: Piety is doing as I am doing; that is to say, prosecuting any one who is guilty of murder, sacrilege, or of any similar crime—whether he be your father or mother, or whoever he may be—that makes no difference; and not to prosecute them is impiety. And please to consider, Socrates, what a notable proof I will give you of the truth of my words, a proof which I have already given to others:—of the principle, I mean, that the impious, whoever he may be, ought not to go unpunished. For do not men regard Zeus as the best and most righteous of the gods?—and yet they admit that he bound his father (Cronos) because he wickedly devoured his sons, and that he too had punished his own father (Uranus) for a similar reason, in a nameless manner. And yet when I proceed against my father, they are angry with me. So inconsistent are they in their way of talking when the gods are concerned, and when I am concerned.

Socrates: May not this be the reason, Euthyphro, why I am charged with impiety—that I cannot away with these stories about the gods? and therefore I suppose that people think me wrong. But, as you who are well informed about them approve of them, I cannot do better than assent to your superior wisdom. What else can I say, confessing as I do, that I know nothing about them? Tell me, for the love of Zeus, whether you really believe that they are true.

Euthyphro: Yes, Socrates; and things more wonderful still, of which the world is in ignorance.

Socrates: And do you really believe that the gods fought with one another, and had dire quarrels, battles, and the like, as the poets say, and as you may see represented in the works of great artists? The temples are full of them; and notably the robe of Athene, which is carried up to the Acropolis at the great Panathenaea, is embroidered with them. Are all these tales of the gods true, Euthyphro?

Euthyphro: Yes, Socrates; and, as I was saying, I can tell you, if you would like to hear them, many other things about the gods which would quite amaze you.

Socrates: I dare say; and you shall tell me them at some other time when I have leisure. But just at present I would rather hear from you a more precise answer, which you have not as yet given, my friend, to the question, What is "piety"? When asked, you only replied, Doing as you do, charging your father with murder.

Euthyphro: And what I said was true, Socrates.

Socrates: No doubt, Euthyphro; but you would admit that there are many other pious acts?

Euthyphro: There are.

Socrates: Remember that I did not ask you to give me two or three examples of piety, but to explain the general idea which makes all pious things to be pious. Do you not recollect that there was one idea which made the impious impious, and the pious pious?

Euthyphro: I remember.

Socrates: Tell me what is the nature of this idea, and then I shall have a standard to which I may look, and by which I may measure actions, whether yours or those of any one else, and then I shall be able to say that such and such an action is pious, such another impious.

Euthyphro: I will tell you, if you like.

Socrates: I should very much like.

Euthyphro: Piety, then, is that which is dear to the gods, and impiety is that which is not dear to them.

Socrates: Very good, Euthyphro; you have now given me the sort of answer which I wanted. But whether what you say is true or not I cannot as yet tell, although I make no doubt that you will prove the truth of your words.

Euthyphro: Of course.

Socrates: Come, then, and let us examine what we are saying. That thing or person which is dear to the gods is pious, and that thing or person which is hateful to the gods is impious, these two being the extreme opposites of one another. Was not that said?

Euthyphro: It was.

Socrates: And well said?

Euthyphro: Yes, Socrates, I thought so; it was certainly said.

Socrates: And further, Euthyphro, the gods were admitted to have enmities and hatreds and differences?

Euthyphro: Yes, that was also said.

Socrates: And what sort of difference creates enmity and anger? Suppose, for example, that you and I, my good friend, differ about a number; do differences of this sort make us enemies and set us at variance with one another? Do we not go at once to arithmetic, and put an end to them by a sum?

Euthyphro: True.

Socrates: Or suppose that we differ about magnitudes, do we not quickly end the difference by measuring?

Euthyphro: Very true.

Socrates: And we end a controversy about heavy and light by resorting to a weighing machine?

Euthyphro: To be sure.

Socrates: But what differences are there which cannot be thus decided, and which therefore make us angry and set us at enmity with one another? I dare say the answer does not occur to you at the moment, and therefore I will suggest that these enmities arise when the matters of difference are the just and unjust, good and evil, honourable and dishonourable. Are not these the points about which men differ, and about which when we are unable satisfactorily to decide our differences, you and I and all of us quarrel, when we do quarrel?

Euthyphro: Yes, Socrates, the nature of the differences about which we quarrel is such as you describe.

Socrates: And the quarrels of the gods, noble Euthyphro, when they occur, are of a like nature?

Euthyphro: Certainly they are.

Socrates: They have differences of opinion, as you say, about good and evil, just and unjust, honourable and dishonourable: there would have been no quarrels among them, if there had been no such differences—would there now?

Euthyphro: You are quite right.

Socrates: Does not every man love that which he deems noble and just and good, and hate the opposite of them?

Euthyphro: Very true.

Socrates: But, as you say, people regard the same things, some as just and others as unjust—about these they dispute; and so there arise wars and fightings among them.

Euthyphro: Very true.

Socrates: Then the same things are hated by the gods and loved by the gods, and are both hateful and dear to them?

Euthyphro: True.

Socrates: And upon this view the same things, Euthyphro, will be pious and also impious?

Euthyphro: So I should suppose.

Socrates: Then, my friend, I remark with surprise that you have not answered the question which I asked. For I certainly did not ask you to tell me what action is both pious and impious: but now it would seem that what is loved by the gods is also hated by them. And therefore, Euthyphro, in thus chastising your father you may very likely be doing what is agreeable to Zeus but disagreeable to Cronos or Uranus, and what is acceptable to Hephaestus but unacceptable to Herè, and there may be other gods who have similar differences of opinion.

Euthyphro: But I believe, Socrates, that all the gods would be agreed as to the propriety of punishing a murderer: there would be no difference of opinion about that.

Socrates: Well, but speaking of men, Euthyphro, did you ever hear any one arguing that a murderer or any sort of evil-doer ought to be let off?

Euthyphro: I should rather say that these are the questions which they are always arguing, especially in courts of law: they commit all sorts of crimes, and there is nothing which they will not do or say in their own defence.

Socrates: But do they admit their guilt, Euthyphro, and yet say that they ought not to be punished?

Euthyphro: No; they do not.

Socrates: Then there are some things which they do not venture to say and do: for they do not venture to argue that the guilty are to be unpunished, but they deny their guilt, do they not?

Euthyphro: Yes.

Socrates: Then they do not argue that the evil-doer should not be punished, but they argue about the fact of who the evil-doer is, and what he did and when?

Euthyphro: True.

Socrates: And the gods are in the same case, if as you assert they quarrel about just and unjust, and some of them say while others deny that injustice is done among them. For surely neither God nor man will ever venture to say that the doer of injustice is not to be punished?

Euthyphro: That is true, Socrates, in the main.

Socrates: But they join issue about the particulars—gods and men alike; and, if they dispute at all, they dispute about some act which is called in question, and which by some is affirmed to be just, by others to be unjust. Is not that true?

Euthyphro: Quite true.

Socrates: Well then, my dear friend Euthyphro, do tell me, for my better instruction and information, what proof have you that in the opinion of all the gods a servant who is guilty of murder, and is put in chains by the master of the dead man, and dies because he is put in chains before he who bound him can learn from the interpreters of the gods what he ought to do with him, dies unjustly; and that on behalf of such an one a son ought to proceed against his father and accuse him of murder. How would you show that all the gods absolutely agree in approving of his act? Prove to me that they do, and I will applaud your wisdom as long as I live.

Euthyphro: It will be a difficult task; but I could make the matter very clear indeed to you.

Socrates: I understand; you mean to say that I am not so quick of apprehension as the judges: for to them you will be sure to prove that the act is unjust, and hateful to the gods.

Euthyphro: Yes indeed, Socrates; at least if they will listen to me.

Socrates: But they will be sure to listen if they find that you are a good speaker. There was a notion that came into my mind while you were speaking; I said to myself: "Well, and what if Euthyphro does prove to me that all the gods regarded the death of the serf as unjust, how do I know anything more of the nature of piety and impiety? for granting that this action may be hateful to the gods, still piety and impiety are not adequately defined by these distinctions, for that which is hateful to the gods has been shown to be also pleasing and dear to them." And therefore, Euthyphro, I do not ask you to prove this; I will suppose, if you like, that all the gods condemn and abominate such an action. But I will amend the definition so far as to say that what all the gods hate is impious, and what they love pious or holy; and what some of them love and others hate is both or neither. Shall this be our definition of piety and impiety?

Euthyphro: Why not, Socrates?

Socrates: Why not! certainly, as far as I am concerned, Euthyphro, there is no reason why not. But whether this admission will greatly assist you in the task of instructing me as you promised, is a matter for you to consider.

Euthyphro: Yes, I should say that what all the gods love is pious and holy, and the opposite which they all hate, impious.

Socrates: Ought we to enquire into the truth of this, Euthyphro, or simply to accept the mere statement on our own authority and that of others? What do you say?

Euthyphro: We should enquire; and I believe that the statement will stand the test of enquiry.

Socrates: We shall know better, my good friend, in a little while. The point which I should first wish to understand is whether the pious or holy is beloved by the gods because it is holy, or holy because it is beloved of the gods.

Euthyphro: I do not understand your meaning, Socrates.

Socrates: I will endeavour to explain: we speak of carrying and we speak of being carried, of leading and being led, seeing and being seen. You know that in all such cases there is a difference, and you know also in what the difference lies?

Euthyphro: I think that I understand.

Socrates: And is not that which is beloved distinct from that which loves?

Euthyphro: Certainly.

Socrates: Well; and now tell me, is that which is carried in this state of carrying because it is carried, or for some other reason?

Euthyphro: No; that is the reason.

Socrates: And the same is true of what is led and of what is seen?

Euthyphro: True.

Socrates: And a thing is not seen because it is visible, but conversely, visible because it is seen; nor is a thing led because it is in the state of being led, or carried because it is in the state of being carried, but the converse of this. And now I think, Euthyphro, that my meaning will be intelligible; and my meaning is, that any state of action or passion implies previous action or passion. It does not become because it is becoming, but it is in a state of becoming because it becomes; neither does it suffer because it is in a state of suffering, but it is in a state of suffering because it suffers. Do you not agree?

Euthyphro: Yes.

Socrates: Is not that which is loved in some state either of becoming or suffering?

Euthyphro: Yes.

Socrates: And the same holds as in the previous instances; the state of being loved follows the act of being loved, and not the act the state.

Euthyphro: Certainly.

Socrates: And what do you say of piety, Euthyphro: is not piety, according to your definition, loved by all the gods?

Euthyphro: Yes.

Socrates: Because it is pious or holy, or for some other reason?

Euthyphro: No, that is the reason.

Socrates: It is loved because it is holy, not holy because it is loved?

Euthyphro: Yes.

Socrates: And that which is dear to the gods is loved by them, and is in a state to be loved of them because it is loved of them?

Euthyphro: Certainly.

Socrates: Then that which is dear to the gods, Euthyphro, is not holy, nor is that which is holy loved of God, as you affirm; but they are two different things.

Euthyphro: How do you mean, Socrates?

Socrates: I mean to say that the holy has been acknowledged by us to be loved of God because it is holy, not to be holy because it is loved.

Euthyphro: Yes.

Socrates: But that which is dear to the gods is dear to them because it is loved by them, not loved by them because it is dear to them.

Euthyphro: True.

Socrates: But, friend Euthyphro, if that which is holy is the same with that which is dear to God, and is loved because it is holy, then that which is dear to God would have been loved as being dear to God; but if that which is dear to God is dear to him because loved by him, then that which is holy would have been holy because loved by him. But now you see that the reverse is the case, and that they are quite different from one another. For one (θεοφιλὲς) is of a kind to be loved because it is loved, and the other (ὅσιον) is loved because it is of a kind to be loved. Thus you appear to me, Euthyphro, when I ask you what is the essence of holiness, to offer an attribute only, and not the essence—the attribute of being loved by all the gods. But you still refuse to explain to me the nature of holiness. And therefore, if you please, I will ask you not to hide your treasure, but to tell me once more what holiness or piety really is, whether dear to the gods or not (for that is a matter about which we will not quarrel); and what is impiety?

Euthyphro: I really do not know, Socrates, how to express what I mean. For somehow or other our arguments, on whatever ground we rest them, seem to turn around and walk away from us.

. . .

Socrates: Then we must begin again and ask, What is piety? That is an enquiry which I shall never be weary of pursuing as far as in me lies; and I entreat you not to scorn me, but to apply your mind to the utmost, and tell me the truth. For, if any man knows, you are he; and therefore I must detain you, like Proteus, until you tell. If you had not certainly known the nature of piety and impiety, I am confident that you would never, on behalf of a serf, have charged your aged father with murder. You would not have run such a risk of doing wrong in the sight of the gods, and you would have had too much respect for the opinions of men. I am sure, therefore, that you know the nature of piety and impiety. Speak out then, my dear Euthyphro, and do not hide your knowledge.

Euthyphro: Another time, Socrates; for I am in a hurry, and must go now.

Socrates: Alas! my companion, and will you leave me in despair? I was hoping that you would instruct me in the nature of piety and impiety; and then I might have cleared myself of Meletus and his indictment. I would have told him that I had been enlightened by Euthyphro, and had given up rash innovations and speculations, in which I indulged only through ignorance, and that now I am about to lead a better life.

DISCUSSION QUESTIONS

1. Show how Euthyphro's definition of the term *piety* changes throughout the course of his argument. What are Socrates' objections to each of these definitions?
2. Why does Socrates reject religion as the source of morality? Are you convinced by his argument? Support your position.
3. Can a person's moral beliefs and religious beliefs come into conflict? If so, how can the conflict be resolved? Illustrate your answer with examples.
4. Socrates often uses irony and feigned humility to break through peoples' resistance and to flatter them into clarifying their position. This gives Socrates the opportunity to point out the weaknesses and inconsistencies in his opponents' thinking. Identify passages where Socrates successfully uses this method with Euthyphro.
5. How would Socrates most likely respond to Bodoff's interpretation of the story of Abraham and Isaac?

Thomas Aquinas

The Summa Theologica

Thomas Aquinas (c.1225–1274) is the most important Christian philosopher and scholar of the medieval period. Aquinas's natural law theory has become incorporated into the ethics of the Catholic Church.

In his *Summa Theologica,* Aquinas seeks to merge the philosophy of Aristotle ("the philosopher") with Christian theology. The following excerpts from his great work discuss the various types of laws. Aquinas then goes on to explore the effects of these laws, and, in particular, natural or moral law, on making people good.

CRITICAL THINKING QUESTIONS

1. What, according to Aquinas, do all people seek and what do all people avoid?
2. In what does our ultimate happiness consist? When will we enjoy this happiness?
3. What does Aquinas mean by "natural law"? What is the connection between natural law and morality?
4. Why did God create natural law?
5. How is natural law related to eternal law?
6. What is human law? How is natural law related to human law?
7. Is natural law the same for all people?
8. Why does the application of natural law change over time?

Question 91

OF THE VARIOUS KINDS OF LAW

We must now consider the various kinds of law: under which head there are six points of inquiry: (1) Whether there is an eternal law? (2) Whether there is a natural law? (3) Whether there is a human law? (4) Whether there is a Divine law? (5) Whether there is one Divine law, or several? (6) Whether there is a law of sin?

"Natural Law," *The Summa Theologica,* Vol. II, translated by the Fathers of the English Dominican Province (Westminster, MD: Christian Classic, 1911), QQ. 90–108.

FIRST ARTICLE

Whether There Is an Eternal Law?

. . . A law is nothing else but a dictate of practical reason emanating from the ruler who governs a perfect community. Now it is evident, granted that the world is ruled by Divine Providence, as was stated in the First Part (Q. 22, AA. 1, 2), that the whole community of the universe is governed by Divine Reason. Wherefore the very Idea of the government of things in God the Ruler of the universe, has the nature of a law. And since the Divine Reason's conception of things is not subject to time but is eternal, according to Prov. viii. 23, therefore it is that this kind of law must be called eternal. . . .

. . . It is evident that all things partake somewhat of the eternal law, in so far as, namely, from its being imprinted on them, they derive their respective inclinations to their proper acts and ends. Now among all others, the rational creature is subject to Divine providence in the most excellent way, in so far as it partakes of a share of providence, by being provident both for itself and for others. Wherefore it has a share of the Eternal Reason, whereby it has a natural inclination to its proper act and end: and this participation of the eternal law in the rational creature is called the natural law. Hence the Psalmist after saying (Ps. iv. 6): *Offer up the sacrifice of justice,* as though someone asked what the works of justice are, adds: *Many say, Who showeth us good things?* in answer to which question he says: *The light of Thy countenance, O Lord, is signed upon us:* thus implying that the light of natural reason, whereby we discern what is good and what is evil, which is the function of the natural law, is nothing else than an imprint on us of the Divine light. It is therefore evident that the natural law is nothing else than the rational creature's participation of the eternal law. . . .

THIRD ARTICLE

Whether There Is a Human Law?

. . . A law is a dictate of the practical reason. Now it is to be observed that the same procedure takes place in the practical and in the speculative reason: for each proceeds from principles to conclusions, as stated above (*ibid.*). Accordingly we conclude that just as, in the speculative reason, from naturally known indemonstrable principles, we draw the conclusions of the various sciences, the knowledge of which is not imparted to us by nature, but acquired by the efforts of reason, so too it is from the precepts of the natural law, as from general and indemonstrable principles, that the human reason needs to proceed to the more particular determination of certain matters. These particular determinations, devised by human reason, are called human laws, provided the other essential conditions of law be observed, as stated above (Q. 90, AA. 2, 3, 4). Wherefore Tully says in his *Rhetoric (De Invent. Rhet.* ii) that *justice has its source in nature; thence certain things came into custom by reason of their utility; afterwards these things which emanated from nature and were approved by custom, were sanctioned by fear and reverence for the law.* . . .

. . . Human reason is not, of itself, the rule of things: but the principles impressed on it by nature, are general rules and measures of all things relating to human conduct, whereof the natural reason is the rule and measure, although it is not the measure of things that are from nature. . . .

Question 92

OF THE EFFECTS OF LAW

We must now consider the effects of law; under which head there are two points of inquiry: (1) Whether an effect of law is to make men good? (2) Whether the effects of law are to command, to forbid, to permit, and to punish, as the Jurist states?

FIRST ARTICLE

Whether an Effect of Law Is to Make Men Good?

. . . A law is nothing else than a dictate of reason in the ruler by whom his subjects are governed. Now the virtue of any subordinate thing consists in its being well subordinated to that by which it is regulated: thus we see that the virtue of the irascible and concupiscible faculties consists in their being obedient to reason; and accordingly *the virtue of every subject consists in his being well subjected to his ruler,* as the Philosopher [Aristotle] says (*Polit.* i). But every law aims at being obeyed by those who are subject to it. Consequently it is evident that the proper effect of law is to lead its subjects to their proper virtue: and since virtue is *that which makes its subject good,* it follows that the proper effect of law is to make those to whom it is given, good, either simply or in some particular respect. . . .

. . . Virtue is twofold, as explained above (Q. 63, A. 2), viz., acquired and infused. Now the fact of being accustomed to an action contributes to both, but in different ways; for it causes the acquired virtue; while it disposes to infused virtue, and preserves and fosters it when it already exists. And since law is given for the purpose of directing human acts; as far as human acts conduce to virtue, so far does law make men good. Wherefore the Philosopher says in the second book of the *Politics* (*Ethic.* ii) that *lawgivers make men good by habituating them to good works.*

. . . It is not always through perfect goodness of virtue that one obeys the law, but sometimes it is through fear of punishment, and sometimes from the mere dictates of reason, which is a beginning of virtue, as stated above (Q. 63, A. 1).

. . . The goodness of any part is considered in comparison with the whole; hence Augustine says (*Conf.* iii) that *unseemly is the part that harmonizes not with the whole.* Since then every man is a part of the state, it is impossible that a man be good, unless he be well proportionate to the common good: nor can the whole be well consistent unless its parts be proportionate to it. Consequently the common good of the state cannot flourish, unless the citizens be virtuous, at least those whose business it is to govern. But it is enough for the good of the community, that the other citizens be so far virtuous that they obey the commands of their rulers. Hence the Philosopher says (*Polit.* iii. 2) that *the virtue of a sovereign is the same as that of a good man, but the virtue of any common citizen is not the same as that of a good man.*

. . . A tyrannical law, through not being according to reason, is not a law, absolutely speaking, but rather a perversion of law; and yet in so far as it is something in the nature of a law, it aims at the citizens' being good. For all it has in the nature of a law consists in its being an ordinance made by a superior to his subjects, and aims at being obeyed by them, which is to make them good, not simply, but with respect to that particular government. . . .

Question 94

OF THE NATURAL LAW

We must now consider the natural law; concerning which there are six points of inquiry: (1) What is the natural law? (2) What are the precepts of the natural law? (3) Whether all acts of virtue are prescribed by the natural law? (4) Whether the natural law is the same in all? (5) Whether it is changeable? (6) Whether it can be abolished from the heart of man?

FIRST ARTICLE

Whether the Natural Law Is a Habit?

. . . A thing may be called a habit in two ways. First, properly and essentially: and thus the natural law is not a habit. For it has been stated above (Q. 90, A. 1 *ad* 2) that the natural law is something appointed by reason, just as a proposition is a work of reason. Now that which a man does is not the same as that whereby he does it: for he makes a becoming speech by the habit of grammar. Since then a habit is that by which we act, a law cannot be a habit properly and essentially. . . .

SECOND ARTICLE

Whether the Natural Law Contains Several Precepts, or One Only?

. . . The precepts of the natural law in man stand in relation to practical matters, as the first principles to matters of demonstration. But there are several first indemonstrable principles. Therefore there are also several precepts of the natural law.

. . . the precepts of the natural law are to the practical reason, what the first principles of demonstrations are to the speculative reason; because both are self-evident principles. Now a thing is said to be self-evident in two ways: first, in itself; secondly, in relation to us. Any proposition is said to be self-evident in itself, if its predicate is contained in the notion of the subject: although, to one who knows not the definition of the subject, it happens that such a proposition is not self-evident. For instance, this proposition, *Man is a rational being,* is, in its very nature, self-evident, since who says *man,* says *a rational being:* . . . But some propositions are self-evident only to the wise, who understand the meaning of the terms of such propositions: thus to one who understands that an angel is not a body, it is self-evident that an angel is not circumscriptively in a place: but this is not evident to the unlearned, for they cannot grasp it.

Now a certain order is to be found in those things that are apprehended universally. For that which, before aught else, falls under apprehension, is *being,* the notion of which is included in all things whatsoever a man apprehends. Wherefore the first indemonstrable principle is that *the same thing cannot be affirmed and denied at the same time,* which is based on the notion of *being* and *not-being:* and on this principle all others are based, as is stated in *Metaph.* iv, text. 9. Now as *being* is the first thing that falls under the apprehension simply, so *good* is the first thing that falls under the apprehension of the practical reason, which is directed to action: since every agent acts for an end under the aspect of good. Consequently the first principle in the practical reason is one founded on the notion of good, viz., that *good is that which all things seek after.* Hence this is the first precept of law, that *good is to be done and pursued, and evil is to be avoided.* All other precepts of the natural law are based upon this: so that whatever the practical reason naturally apprehends as man's good (or evil) belongs to the precepts of the natural law as something to be done or avoided.

Since, however, good has the nature of an end, and evil, the nature of a contrary, hence it is that all those things to which man has a natural inclination, are naturally apprehended by reason as being good, and consequently as objects of pursuit, and their contraries as evil, and objects of avoidance. Wherefore according to the order of natural inclinations, is the order of the precepts of the natural law. Because in man there is first of all an inclination to good in accordance with the nature which he has in common with all substances: inasmuch as every substance seeks the preservation of its own being, according to its nature: and by reason of this inclination, whatever is a means of preserving human life, and of warding off its obstacles, belongs to the natural law. Secondly, there is in man an inclination to things that pertain to him more specially, according to that nature which he has in common with other animals: and in virtue of this inclination, those things are said to belong to the natural law, *which nature has taught to all animals,* such as sexual intercourse, education of offspring and so forth. Thirdly, there is in man an inclination to good, according to the nature of his reason, which nature is proper to him: thus man has a natural inclination to know the truth about God, and to live in society: and in this respect, whatever pertains to this inclination belongs to the natural law; for instance, to shun ignorance, to avoid offending those among whom one has to live, and other such things regarding the above inclination. . . .

THIRD ARTICLE

Whether All Acts of Virtue Are Prescribed by the Natural Law?

. . . We may speak of virtuous acts in two ways: first, under the aspect of virtuous; secondly, as such and such acts considered in their proper species. If then we speak of acts of virtue, considered as virtuous, thus all virtuous acts belong to the natural law. . . . To the natural law belongs everything to which a man is inclined according to his nature. Now each thing is inclined naturally to an operation that is suitable to it according to its form: thus fire is inclined to give heat. Wherefore, since the rational soul is the proper form of man, there is in every man a natural inclination to act according to reason: and this is to act according to virtue. Consequently, considered thus, all acts of virtue are prescribed by the natural law: since each one's reason naturally dictates to him to act virtuously. But if we speak of virtuous acts, considered in themselves, i.e., in their proper species, thus not all virtuous acts are prescribed by the natural law: for many things are done virtuously, to which nature does not incline at first; but which, through the inquiry of reason, have been found by men to be conducive to well-living. . . .

FOURTH ARTICLE

Whether the Natural Law Is the Same in All Men?

. . . To the natural law belongs those things to which a man is inclined naturally: and among these it is proper to man to be inclined to act according to reason. Now the process of reason is from the common to the proper, as stated in *Phys*. i. The speculative reason, however, is differently situated in this matter, from the practical reason. For, since the speculative reason is busied chiefly with necessary things, which cannot be otherwise than they are, its proper conclusions, like the universal principles, contain the truth without fail. The practical reason, on the other hand, is busied with contingent matters, about which human actions are concerned: and consequently, although there is necessity in the general principles, the more we descend to matters of detail, the more frequently we encounter defects. Accordingly then in speculative matters truth is the same in all men, both as to principles and as to conclusions: although the truth is not known to all as regards the conclusions, but only as regards the principles which are called common notions. . . .

It is therefore evident that, as regards the general principles whether of speculative or of practical reason, truth or rectitude is the same for all, and is equally known by all. As to the proper conclusions of the speculative reason, the truth is the same for all, but is not equally known to all: thus it is true for all that the three angles of a triangle are together equal to two right angles, although it is not known to all. But as to the proper conclusions of the practical reason, neither is the truth or rectitude the same for all, nor, where it is the same, is it equally known by all. Thus it is right and true for all to act according to reason. . . .

Consequently we must say that the natural law, as to general principles, is the same for all, both as to rectitude and as to knowledge. But as to certain matters of detail, which are conclusions, as it were, of those general principles, it is the same for all in the majority of cases, both as to rectitude and as to knowledge; and yet in some few cases it may fail, both as to rectitude, by reason of certain obstacles (just as natures subject to generation and corruption fail in some few cases on account of some obstacle), and as to knowledge, since in some the reason is perverted by passion, or evil habit, or an evil disposition of nature; . . .

DISCUSSION QUESTIONS

1. Do you agree with Aquinas that all rational beings seek the good and shun evil? How about the people who were involved in the Nazi Holocaust and the slave trade? Were they seeking the good?
2. Compare and contrast Aquinas's concept of human nature with Aristotle's.
3. How is Aquinas using the term *natural?* Is natural simply that which is most prevalent among humans? What is an example of a natural law?
4. Do natural law ethics, as described by Aquinas, offer practical and clear guidelines for determining which beliefs and actions are moral and which are immoral? Use specific examples to illustrate your answer.
5. Discuss whether Aquinas's natural law ethics are consistent with the moral teaching from the *Holy Bible.*
6. How might Aquinas respond to Bodoff's interpretation of the story of Abraham and Isaac? Is Bodoff's interpretation consistent with natural law theory?
7. Aquinas states that natural law is teleological. By this he means that natural law is grounded in a specific view about the purpose or goal of the natural order. The moral or natural law is our human way of participating in and actively working toward that vision. Because the natural order is dynamic, the application of the general principles of natural law may change over time as we move toward God's vision for us. For example, some Catholic ethicists argue that the ban on artificial birth control is no longer required by natural law. Do you agree? How might Aquinas respond? Support your answer.
8. Aquinas argues that the moral law was created by God as part of His plan for the universe. However, other natural law ethicists, such as Aristotle, argue that God is not necessary for the existence of natural law. Discuss the two positions regarding the origin of natural law. Is God necessary for morality? Or can natural law exist without God?

Friedrich Nietzsche

Beyond Good and Evil *and* The Joyful Wisdom

German existentialist Friedrich Nietzsche (1844–1900) is often accused of being antimorality. However, it was not morality per se that Nietzsche opposed but the Western bourgeois (middle-class) Christian ethic, which he contemptuously referred to as "slave morality." To Nietzsche, the truly virtuous person, what he called the "noble man" or overman, was not meek and self-sacrificing but exercised the "will to power."

Nietzsche believed that the current "slave morality" promoted by Christianity is not part of the teachings of Jesus of Nazareth. Indeed, Nietzsche apparently admired Jesus as an example of an overman. Nietzsche also believed that "the last Christian died on the cross" and that modern Christian morality bears little resemblance to that promoted by Jesus of Nazareth.

CRITICAL THINKING QUESTIONS

1. Who, according to the madman, killed God?
2. Why did the madman declare "I come too early"?
3. What is Nietzsche's opinion of the aristocracy?
4. What, according to Nietzsche, is the primary purpose of society?
5. What is the difference between the slave morality and the master morality? Which does Nietzsche think is preferable?
6. What is the relation between slave morality and religion?
7. How does Nietzsche define the "noble man"? How does the noble man view those who subscribe to slave morality?
8. What did Nietzsche mean by the "will to power"?
9. What is the difference between vanity and true pride?

Master and Slave Morality

The Madman.—Have you ever heard of the madman who on a bright morning lighted a lantern and ran to the market-place calling out unceasingly: "I seek God! I seek God!"—As there were many people standing about who did not

"Religions and 'Slave Morality'," from *Beyond Good and Evil* and *The Joyful Wisdom*, in *The Complete Works of Nietzsche*, edited by Oscar Levy, Vols. 10 and 11 (T.N. Foulis, 1910). 1 line for publisher tk.

believe in God, he caused a great deal of amusement. Why! is he lost? said one. Has he strayed away like a child? said another. Or does he keep himself hidden? Is he afraid of us? Has he taken a sea-voyage? Has he emigrated?—the people cried out laughingly, all in a hubbub. The insane man jumped into their midst and transfixed them with his glances. "Where is God gone?" he called out. "I mean to tell you! *We have killed him,*—you and I! We are all his murderers! But how have we done it? How were we able to drink up the sea? Who gave us the sponge to wipe away the whole horizon? What did we do when we loosened this earth from its sun? Whither does it now move? Whither do we move? Away from all suns? Do we not dash on unceasingly? Backwards, sideways, forewards, in all directions? Is there still an above and below? Do we not stray, as through infinite nothingness? Does not empty space breathe upon us? Has it not become colder? Does not night come on continually, darker and darker? Shall we not have to light lanterns in the morning? Do we not hear the noise of the grave-diggers who are burying God? Do we not smell the divine putrefaction?—for even Gods putrefy! God is dead! God remains dead! And we have killed him! How shall we console ourselves, the most murderous of all murderers? The holiest and the mightiest that the world has hitherto possessed, has bled to death under our knife,—who will wipe the blood from us? With what water could we cleanse ourselves? What lustrums, what sacred games shall we have to devise? Is not the magnitude of this deed too great for us? Shall we not ourselves have to become Gods, merely to seem worthy of it? There never was a greater event,—and on account of it, all who are born after us belong to a higher history than any history hitherto!"—Here the madman was silent and looked again at his hearers; they also were silent and looked at him in surprise. At last he threw his lantern on the ground, so that it broke in pieces and was extinguished. "I come too early," he then said, "I am not yet at the right time. This prodigious event is still on its way, and is travelling,—it has not yet reached men's ears. Lightning and thunder need time, the light of the stars needs time, deeds need time, even after they are done, to be seen and heard. This deed is as yet further from them than the furthest star,—*and yet they have done it!*"—It is further stated that the madman made his way into different churches on the same day, and there intoned his *Requiem aeternam deo.* When led out and called to account, he always gave the reply: "What are these churches now, if they are not the tombs and monuments of God?"— . . .

WHAT IS NOBLE?

Every elevation of the type "man," has hitherto been the work of an aristocratic society and so it will always be—a society believing in a long scale of gradations of rank and differences of worth among human beings, and requiring slavery in some form or other. . . .

Corruption—as the indication that anarchy threatens to break out among the instincts, and that the foundation of the emotions, called "life," is convulsed—is something radically different according to the organisation in which it manifests itself. When, for instance, an aristocracy like that of France at the beginning of the Revolution, flung away its privileges with sublime disgust and sacrificed itself to an excess of its moral sentiments, it was corruption:—it was really only the closing act of the corruption which had existed for centuries, by virtue of which that aristocracy had abdicated step by step its lordly prerogatives and lowered itself to a *function* of royalty (in the end even to its decoration and parade-dress). The essential thing, however, in a good and healthy aristocracy is that it should *not* regard itself as a function either of the kingship or the commonwealth, but as the *significance* and highest justification thereof—that it should therefore accept with a good conscience the sacrifice of a legion of individuals, who, *for its sake,* must be suppressed and reduced to imperfect men, to slaves and instruments. Its fundamental belief must be precisely that society is *not* allowed to exist for its own sake, but only as a foundation and scaffolding, by means of which a select class of beings may be able to elevate themselves to their higher duties, and in general to a higher *existence:* like those sun-seeking climbing plants in Java—they are called *Sipo Matador,*—which encircle an oak so long and so often with their arms, until at last, high above it, but supported by it, they can unfold their tops in the open light, and exhibit their happiness.

To refrain mutually from injury, from violence, from exploitation, and put one's will on a par with that of others: this may result in a certain rough sense in good conduct among individuals when the necessary conditions are given (namely, the actual similarity of the individuals in amount of force and degree of worth, and their co-relation within one organisation). As soon, however, as one wished to take this principle more generally, and if possible even as *the fundamental principle of society,* it would immediately disclose what it really is—namely, a Will to the *denial* of life, a principle of dissolution and decay. Here one must think profoundly to the very basis and resist all sentimental weakness: life itself is *essentially* appropriation, injury, conquest of the strange and weak, suppression, severity, obtrusion of peculiar forms, incorporation, and at the least, putting it mildest, exploitation;—but why should one for ever use precisely these words on which for ages a disparaging purpose has been stamped? Even the organisation within which, as was previously supposed, the individuals treat each other as equal—it takes place in every healthy aristocracy—must itself, if it be a living and not a dying organisation, do all that towards other bodies, which the individuals within it refrain from doing to each other: it will have to be the incarnated Will to Power, it will endeavour to grow, to gain ground, attract to itself and acquire ascendency—not owing to any morality or immorality, but because it *lives,* and because life *is* precisely Will to Power. On no point, however, is the ordinary consciousness of Europeans more unwilling to be corrected than on this matter; people now rave everywhere, even under the guise of science, about coming conditions of society in which "the exploiting character" is to be absent:—that sounds to my ears as if they promised to invent a mode of life which should refrain from all organic functions. "Exploitation" does not belong to a depraved, or imperfect and primitive society: it belongs to the *nature* of the living being as a primary organic function; it is a consequence of the intrinsic Will to Power, which is precisely the Will to Life.—Granting that as a theory this is a novelty—as a reality it is the *fundamental fact* of all history: let us be so far honest towards ourselves!

In a tour through the many finer and coarser moralities which have hitherto prevailed or still prevail on the earth, I found certain traits recurring regularly together, and connected with one another, until finally two primary types revealed themselves to me, and a radical distinction was brought to light. There is *master-morality* and *slave-morality*;—I would at once add, however, that in all higher and mixed civilisations, there are also attempts at the reconciliation of the two moralities; but one finds still oftener the confusion and mutual misunderstanding of them, indeed, sometimes their close juxtaposition—even in the same man, within one soul. The distinctions of moral values have either originated in a ruling caste, pleasantly conscious of being different from the ruled—or among the ruled class, the slaves and dependents of all sorts. In the first case, when it is the rulers who determine the conception "good," it is the exalted, proud disposition which is regarded as the distinguishing feature, and that which determines the order of rank. The noble type of man separates from himself the beings in whom the opposite of this exalted, proud disposition displays itself: he despises them. Let it at once be noted that in this first kind of morality the antithesis "good" and "bad" means practically the same as "noble" and "despicable";— the antithesis "good" and "*evil*" is of a different origin. The cowardly, the timid, the insignificant, and those thinking merely of narrow utility are despised; moreover, also, the distrustful, with their constrained glances, the self-abasing, the dog-like kind of men who let themselves be abused, the mendicant flatterers, and above all the liars:—it is a fundamental belief of all aristocrats that the common people are untruthful. "We truthful ones"—the nobility in ancient Greece called themselves. It is obvious that everywhere the designations of moral value were at first applied to *men,* and were only derivatively and at a later period applied to *actions;* it is a gross mistake, therefore, when historians of morals start with questions like, "Why have sympathetic actions been praised?" The noble type of man regards *himself* as a determiner of values; he does not require to be approved of; he passes the judgment: "What is injurious to me is injurious in itself"; he knows that it is he himself only who confers honour on things; he is a *creator of values.* He honours whatever he recognises in himself: such morality is self-glorification. In the foreground there is the feeling of plenitude, of power, which seeks to overflow, the happiness of high tension, the consciousness of a wealth which would fain give and bestow:—the noble man also helps the unfortunate, but not—or scarcely—out of pity, but rather from an impulse generated by the super-abundance of power. The noble man honours in himself the powerful one, him also who has power over himself, who knows how to speak and how to keep silence, who takes pleasure in subjecting himself to severity and hardness, and has reverence for all that is severe and hard. "Wotan placed a hard heart in my breast," says an old Scandinavian Saga: it is thus rightly expressed from the soul of a proud Viking. Such a type of man is even proud of *not* being made for sympathy; the hero of the Saga therefore adds warningly: "He who has not a hard heart when young, will never have one." The noble and brave who think thus are the furthest removed from the morality which sees precisely in sympathy, or in acting for the good of others, or in *désintéressement,* the characteristic of the moral; faith in oneself, pride in oneself, a radical enmity and irony towards "selflessness," belong as definitely to noble morality, as do a careless scorn and precaution in presence of sympathy and the "warm heart."—It is the powerful who *know* how to honour, it is their art, their domain for invention. The profound reverence for age and for tradition—all law rests on this double reverence,—the belief and prejudice in favour of ancestors and unfavourable to newcomers, is typical in the morality of the powerful; and if, reversely, men of "modern ideas" believe almost instinctively in "progress" and the "future," and are more and more lacking in respect for old age, the ignoble origin of these "ideas" has complacently betrayed itself thereby. A morality of the ruling class, however, is more especially foreign and irritating to present-day taste in the sternness of its principle that one has duties only to one's equals; that one may act towards beings of a lower rank, towards all that is foreign, just as seems good to one, or "as the heart desires," and in any case "beyond good and evil": it is here that sympathy and similar sentiments can have a place. The ability and obligation to exercise prolonged gratitude and prolonged revenge—both only within the circle of equals,—artfulness in retaliation, *raffinement* of the idea in friendship, a certain necessity to have enemies (as outlets for the emotions of envy, quarrelsomeness, arrogance—in fact, in order to be a good *friend*): all these are typical characteristics of the noble morality, which, as has been pointed out, is not the morality of "modern ideas," and is therefore at present difficult to realise and also to unearth and disclose.—It is otherwise with the second type of morality, *slave-morality*. Supposing that the abused, the oppressed, the suffering, the unemancipated, the weary, and those uncertain of themselves, should moralise, what will be the common element in their moral estimates? Probably a pessimistic suspicion with regard to the entire situation of man will find expression, perhaps a condemnation of man, together with his situation. The slave has an unfavourable eye for the virtues of the powerful; he has a scepticism and distrust, a *refinement* of distrust of everything "good" that is there honoured—he would fain persuade himself that the very happiness there is not genuine. On the other hand, *those* qualities which serve to alleviate the existence of sufferers are brought into prominence and flooded with light; it is here that sympathy, the kind, helping hand, the warm heart, patience, diligence, humility, and friendliness attain to honour; for here these are the most useful qualities, and almost the only means of supporting the burden of existence. Slave-morality is essentially the morality of utility. Here is the seat of the origin of the famous antithesis "good" and "evil":—power and dangerousness are assumed to reside in the evil, a certain dreadfulness, subtlety, and strength, which do not admit of being despised. According to slave-morality, therefore, the "evil" man arouses fear; according to master-morality, it is precisely the "good" man who arouses fear and seeks to arouse it, while the bad man is regarded as the despicable being. The contrast attains its maximum when, in accordance with the logical consequences of slave-morality, a shade of depreciation—it may be slight and well-intentioned—at last attaches itself to the "good" man of this morality; because, according to the servile mode of thought, the good man must in any case be the *safe* man: he is good-natured, easily deceived, perhaps a little stupid, *un bonhomme*. Everywhere that slave-morality gains the ascendency, language shows a tendency to approximate the significations of the words "good" and "stupid."—A last fundamental difference: the desire for *freedom*, the instinct for happiness and the refinements of the feeling of liberty belong as necessarily to slave-morals and morality, as artifice and enthusiasm in reverence and devotion are the regular symptoms of an aristocratic mode of thinking and estimating. . . .

Vanity is one of the things which are perhaps most difficult for a noble man to understand: he will be tempted to deny it, where another kind of man thinks he sees it self-evidently. The problem for him is to represent to his mind beings who seek to arouse a good opinion of themselves which they themselves do not possess—and consequently also do not "deserve,"—and who yet *believe* in this good opinion afterwards. This seems to him on the one hand such bad taste and so self-disrespectful, and on the other hand so grotesquely unreasonable, that he would like to consider vanity an exception, and is doubtful about it in most cases when it is spoken of. He will say, for instance: "I may be mistaken about my value, and on the other hand may nevertheless demand that my value should be acknowledged by others precisely as I rate it:—that, however, is not vanity (but self-conceit, or, in most cases, that which is called 'humility,' and also 'modesty')." Or he will even say: "For many reasons I can delight in the good opinion of others, perhaps because I love and honour them, and rejoice in all their joys, perhaps also because their good opinion endorses and strengthens my belief in my own good opinion, perhaps because the good opinion of others, even in cases where I do not share it, is useful to me, or gives promise of usefulness:—all this, however, is not vanity." The man of noble character must first bring it home forcibly to his mind, especially with the aid of history, that, from time immemorial, in all social strata in any way dependent, the ordinary man *was* only that which he *passed for*:—not being at all accustomed to fix values, he did not assign even to himself any other value than that which his master assigned to him (it is the peculiar *right of masters* to create values). It may be looked upon as the result of an extraordinary atavism, that the ordinary man, even at present, is still always *waiting* for an opinion about himself, and then instinctively submitting himself to it; yet by no means only to a "good" opinion, but also to a bad and unjust one (think, for instance, of the greater part of the self-appreciations and self-depreciations which believing women learn from their confessors, and which in general the believing Christian learns from his Church). In fact, conformably to the slow rise of the democratic social order (and its cause, the blending of the blood of masters and slaves), the originally noble and rare impulse of the masters to assign a value to themselves and to "think well" of themselves, will now be more and more encouraged and extended; but it has at all times an older, ampler, and more radically ingrained propensity opposed to it—and in the phenomenon of "vanity" this older propensity overmasters the younger. The vain person rejoices over *every* good opinion which he hears about himself (quite apart from the point of view of its usefulness, and equally regardless of its truth or falsehood), just as he suffers from every bad opinion: for he subjects himself to both, he *feels* himself subjected to both, by that oldest instinct of subjection which breaks forth in him.—It is "the slave" in the vain man's blood, the remains of the slave's craftiness—and how much of the "slave" is still left in woman, for instance!—which seeks to *seduce* to good opinions of itself; it is the slave, too, who immediately afterwards falls prostrate himself before these opinion, as though he had not called them forth.—And to repeat it again: vanity is an atavism.

DISCUSSION QUESTIONS

1. What does the Nietzsche mean when he says we have killed God? Does he mean this literally? What do you think the term *God* stands for in the story of the madman? What or who does the madman represent? Discuss the nature of the relation between the death of God, religion, and the demise of morality.

2. Is the exploitation and domination of the weak by the strong a "fundamental fact of history," as Nietzsche claims? If so, does this morally justify the exploitation and domination? Support your answer.

3. Why does Nietzsche think the democratic principle of human equality is based on the "denial of life"? How does religion, in his view, support the democratic ideal? Are you satisfied with Nietzsche's argument? What does he offer as an alternative? Do you agree with him?

4. What does Nietzsche mean when he accuses bourgeois Christianity of advocating a slave morality? In what ways, according to Nietzsche, does this morality compromise our freedom? Why, according to Nietzsche, does religion encourage people to accept a slave morality instead of a master morality? Are you satisfied with the support Nietzsche offers for his position?

5. Do you agree with Nietzsche that Christian slave morality has turned morality upside-down (transvaluation), making vices into virtues and virtues into vices? Use specific examples to support your answer.

6. Discuss how the "will to power" differs from the "will to the denial of life." Does Nietzsche's distinction between these two concepts provide helpful moral guidelines for your life? Explain using specific examples.

7. Nietzsche has been accused of being an ethical subjectivist. Is this criticism justified? Does freedom for Nietzsche mean the same thing as simply going with one's opinions without concern for others? Who determines what is moral for the noble man?

8. Is slave morality implicit in the teachings of Jesus? Or did it come later in the development of Christianity? If so, why? Discuss Nietzsche's concept of the noble man in light of Jesus's moral teachings, especially the Sermon on the Mount.

9. Nietzsche believes that Christian morality involves a sacrifice of our autonomy. Do you agree? Is organized religion detrimental to morality by requiring us to be slavish? Or does religion make it easier for a person to be moral? Support your answer.

10. Nietzsche has been accused of inspiring Nazism. Is there anything in the reading selection that supports this accusation? Is there anything in the reading that suggests that this accusation is unfair?

Kai Nielsen

Religious Ethics Versus Humanistic Ethics

One of the persistent questions in moral philosophy is whether there would be any reason to be moral if God did not exist. University of Calgary philosopher Kai Nielsen (b. 1926) explores this question in his article "Religious Ethics Versus Humanistic Ethics." After examining some of the weaknesses of Aquinas's natural law theory, Nielsen goes on to analyze the divine command theory as defended by Protestant theologian Emil Brunner. Both theories, Nielsen argues, are logically inconsistent. Morality, he concludes, does not need either God or religion. Instead, humanistic ethics offers a better alternative than religious ethics.

CRITICAL THINKING QUESTIONS

1. Why does Nielsen claim that Aquinas goes beyond an empirical theory about morality?

2. Why, according to Nielsen, are Aquinas's assumptions about the *summum bonum* theological rather than empirical in nature?

3. On what grounds does Nielsen challenge Aquinas's claim that moral laws are self-evident to rational humans?

4. How does Nielsen's position on our essential human nature differ from Aquinas's?

5. Why does Nielsen accuse the Catholic natural law theologians of being inconsistent in their application of natural law theory?

6. What is Emil Brunner's theory regarding the relation between morality and religion? How does it differ from Aquinas's natural law theory?

7. What role, according to Brunner, do universal moral principles play in morality?

8. What, according to Brunner, should be our motive for doing the good?

9. On what grounds does Nielsen dismiss Brunner's divine command theory as logically inconsistent?

10. Why does Nielsen claim that the statement "God is good" is a tautology?

"Religious Ethics Versus Humanistic Ethics," in *Philosophy and Atheism: In Defense of Atheism* (Amherst, NY: Prometheus Books, 1985). Notes have been omitted.

11. Why, according to Nielsen, do some people feel a need to believe in God? Does Nielsen think that believing in God is good for humans?

II

Thomas Aquinas argues that all men have at least the potential ability to attain objective knowledge of good and evil. Moral knowledge, for him, did not rest on Divine revelation nor need we simply assume on *faith* that the ordinances of God are good. Aquinas would have us believe that we all have at least the capacity to know that there are certain fundamental things we should avoid and certain fundamental things we should seek.

If we will only note and then dwell on our most basic inclinations and the inclinations—the strivings and avoidings—of our fellow men, we will come to know what is good. This argument is almost like an argument that some anthropologists are inclined to make. The good is somehow the normal. We can discover what it is by noting what normal human beings strive for and avoid.

Good is thus an objective concept and it is somehow in the very nature of things. But it is not in physical nature that one finds what is good. As the Neo-Thomist philosopher, Father C. B. Daly, puts it, "Catholic moralists . . . do not pronounce morally right whatever nature does; do not equate statistical averages of subhuman physical events with the moral good." The good, the moral law that we can at least simply apprehend, is to be discovered in our own human natures. As "physico-spiritual" beings we find the rule of right within.

If we stopped at just this empirical strand in Aquinas's thinking—a strand that Jacques Maritain likes to stress when he is talking about relativism—Aquinas's theory would be a variety of ethical naturalism and his theory would be beset with the standard difficulties facing any ethical naturalism. "X is good" does not mean "I approve of X," "My culture approves of X," "People generally seek X," "Men desire X," or "Normal men seek X," for people may desire, approve of, or seek something that is bad. . . . We do *not eo ipso* establish that something is good by discovering that I or others approve of it, like it, desire it, strive for it, seek it and the like. A cross-cultural examination of what people desire is no doubt very important to a full understanding of what is good and what ends are worth seeking, but it is not enough to establish what ends are good or what ought to be. Even when people desire something after careful reflection it does not follow that what they so desire is desirable. They might in various different ways be mistaken about what they desire or their moral thinking might in some way be defective. If we stress only this empirical strand of natural law morality we will encounter all of the traditional difficulties connected with ethical naturalism.

III

Aquinas's theory, it must be noted, is not simply an empirical theory. It has a metaphysical-theological strand as well. . . . we can only properly understand Aquinas's conception of the natural moral law if we place it against his doctrine of man as a creature of God in a rational, purposive universe. . . . All men, whether they know it or not, are, Aquinas believes, seeking union with God. The *summum bonum* is in God's very essence. In this life we can not know what this essence is, but God, in His mercy, enables us in this life to understand *something* of His goodness. All lesser goods derive their goodness from God. Without God life could have no meaning or value, for in a Godless world nothing could, on Aquinas's view, be genuinely good. God tells us what is good by giving us laws. Laws, for Aquinas, are "ordinances of reason" promulgated "for the common good, by him who has care of the community." There are rational precepts that are given to us to guide our conduct by authoritatively telling us what to do. . . .

IV

I am fully aware of the long and varied history of the natural moral law; and, I understand very well the strong ideological support that natural law conceptions have provided for the morally perplexed from the Greeks until the present, but as emotionally comforting as these conceptions are they do not constitute an adequate foundation for morality. I shall limit myself here to four general criticisms of the Thomistic conception of the natural moral law.

1. We are told that natural moral laws are self-evident, absolute, rational laws. They are certain and can be known without any doubt at all to be true. This sounds very reassuring for it promises to give us the kind of objective knowledge of good and evil that we very much desire. But there is here no genuine surcease from our perplexities about an objective justification of moral beliefs. . . . Since the natural laws are only *self-evident in themselves* and not necessarily self-evident to us, what could it *mean* to say that they are certain and that we can justifiably claim to be certain of them? For such a certain knowledge of good and evil, we require moral principles that can be seen to be self-evident to us or natural moral laws of whose truths we can be certain. But since natural moral laws are only self-evident in themselves (assuming we know what that means) and since it is God's reason and not man's that is the source of the moral law, we poor mortals can have no rational certitude that the precepts claimed to be natural laws are really natural laws. . . .

2. We find out what man *ought* to be, natural theorists claim, by finding out what are the specific rational ways in which he is to conform to the Eternal Law, by finding out what man is, by discovering man's *essential nature*. (They claim these things come to the same thing.) As one natural law moralist put it, "Moral-

ity is man's knowledge that he ought to become what he is; that he ought to become a man by conduct becoming to a man." In order to know how men should live and die we must understand man's essential nature.

But to this it can be objected that from the point of view of science man has *no* essential human nature. Men are not artifacts with an assigned function. It is both linguistically odd and cosmologically question-begging to ask what men are for—assuming by this very question that they are Divine artifacts rather than persons in their own right. . . .

3. The first principle of the natural moral law ["Good is to be done and gone after and evil is to be avoided."] is a tautology (if you will, a truism) and is thus not a substantive moral proposition. It is compatible with a completely relativistic view of morals, for it does not tell us *what* is good or *what* is evil but it only makes explicit what is already implicit in the use of the words "good" and "evil," namely, that if something is good it is, everything else being equal, to be sought and if it is evil it is, everything else being equal, to be avoided. But it does not and cannot tell us *what* is to be sought and *what* is to be avoided.

To discover this we must turn to the substantive secondary precepts of the natural moral law. But some of these run afoul of the facts concerning moral relativity, for some of them are not always even assented to, much less are they always accepted as self-evident by all people. . . . What actually happens is that those moral beliefs that are incompatible with Catholic doctrine, and as a result are called corrupt and sinful, are simply arbitrarily labelled as "unnatural" and "abnormal." . . .

If in defense of such natural law conceptions, it is replied: "We do not claim that all people and all cultures always acknowledge these laws, but the crucial thing is that most of them do," we make another egregious error, for, if we argue in this way, we have now presupposed that moral issues can be settled by statistics or by some cross-cultural Gallup Poll. But Aquinas would surely not wish to say that moral issues are "vote issues." As Father Daly puts it, "Catholic moralists . . . do not equate moral right with statistical averages." To argue that what most people value is valuable is to assume rather simple democratic standards and by assuming them we again have a standard that is (a) *not* self-evident and (b) *independent* of the natural law. To avoid ethical relativism the natural law theorist must incorporate into his theory moral conceptions that are not based on the natural moral law and are questionable in their own right.

4. . . . To discover what our natural inclinations are is simply to discover a fact about ourselves; to discover what purposes we have is simply to discover another fact about ourselves, but that we ought to have these inclinations or purposes or that it is desirable that we have them does not follow from statements asserting that people have such and such inclinations or purposes. These statements can very well be true but no moral or normative conclusions follow from them.

V

. . . Smerdyakov is wrong. The choice is not between nihilism or God.

I view morality as a practical (i.e., action-guiding, attitude-molding, rule-governed activity, whose central function it is to adjudicate the conflicting desires and interests of everyone involved in some human conflict in an impartial and fair manner. In morality we are most fundamentally concerned with the reasoned pursuit of what is in everyone's best interest. How do we decide what is in anyone's best interest? . . . In talking about a person's best interests we are talking about her most extensive welfare and well-being and in talking about the best interests of everyone we are talking about the most extensive welfare or well-being possible for all in a given situation. . . .

In morality we are concerned with the practical tasks of guiding conduct and altering behavior in such a way as to harmonize conflicting desires and interests so as to maximize to the greatest extent possible the welfare and well-being of each person involved. . . .

Using this general conception of the function of morality, we can make appraisals of many practical moral issues. The natural law moralist can do this as well. But using my theoretical framework, I can do it more reasonably and with greater objectivity and internal consistency than can advocates of the natural moral law.

. . .

VII . . .

The distinguished Protestant theologian Emil Brunner argues that we cannot discover any sound abstract principles of right action or good conduct under which we could subsume particular moral statements that concretely direct us to do this or that. *Genuine human good is found only in the unconditional, unquestioned obedience of man to God.* Human conduct is good—that is, we are doing what we ought to be doing—when God Himself acts in it, through the Holy Spirit.

The religious person's obedience is not, Brunner would have us understand, obedience to a law or a principle "but only to the free sovereign will of God." The will of God cannot be summed up under any principle. We do not know what God is or what love is by apprehending a principle. We do not even understand these conceptions unless, quite concretely—existentially if you will—"we learn to know God in His action, in faith." All ethical thought and moral understanding is rooted in an existential knowledge of God; and "really good Christian conduct" needs to have the whole of the Revealed existential Christian knowledge of God behind it. This *Deus Absconditus*, this God that we should love and fear, is manifested solely in His Revelation. . . .

Since we cannot rely on abstract principles, we can never, as the natural law tradition claims, know beforehand what God requires. Rather, God commands, and whatever it is He commands, we must obey. Therein lies our sole good, for "The Good is simply what God wills that we should do on the basis of a principle of love." It is indeed true that God wills our true happiness; but *He* wills it, and He wills it in such a way that no one else knows what His will is. . . .

Yet, Brunner argues, "God's will is expressed by His sanctions, by His rewards and punishments." God holds the keys to the Kingdom. Like Pascal, Brunner believes that man is lost, damned, without God but blest with Him.

> God alone gives life: to be with Him is life, to resist Him is ruin. It is impossible to exist apart from God; it is impossible to be neutral towards Him. He who is not for Him is against Him. God's Command means eternal life and good means nothing else than this. He is Love. But His will is utterly serious; it is the will of the Lord of Life and Death. Anyone who—finally—resists Him, will only dash himself to pieces against the rock of His Being. This is the holiness of the love of God. As the divine love cannot be separated from His gift of life, so the Holiness of God cannot be separated from His judicial wrath, the denial and destruction of life. To have a share in the will of God, in the sense of union with His will, means salvation; to resist Him spells utter disaster.

Many people, including Kantians, have complained that a morally good man (as distinct from a man who is only a man of good morals) does what is good because it is good, not because of what he will get out of it or because he will be damned or punished if he fails to act. The truly moral man, Kant argues, requires no such sanctions, no such pricks to his own intent. To require them is a perversion of moral endeavor. It is—in the Kantian phrase—to make morality heteronomous. We ought instead to do the good simply for the sake of the good.

Brunner rejects this Kantian approach. He argues that such a critique of the morality of Divine Commands fails to realize "that the Good is done for the sake of the Good when it is done for the sake of God, in obedience to the Divine Command."

VIII

We have here, starkly contrasting with the traditional Thomistic conception of the natural moral law, a powerful and classical expression of the morality of Divine Commands, a conception of morality that has been a very central one in the Protestant tradition.

To start to look at it critically, let us first ask again this ancient question: "Is something good because God wills it or commands it or does God command it because it is good?" Let us consider the alternatives we can take here. If we say God commands it because it is good, this implies that something can be good *independently* of God. Why? Because "God commands it *because* it is good" implies that God apprehends it to be good and then tells us to do it. But if God does this then it is at least *logically* possible for us to see or in some way know or come to appreciate that it is good without God's telling us to do it or informing us that it is good.

This last point needs explanation and justification. The above clearly implies that good is not a creation of God but it is rather something apprehended by God or known by God. If this is so, it is *in some way* there to be apprehended or known and thus it is logically possible for us to apprehend it or know it without knowing anything of God. Furthermore, since God apprehends it to be good, since it does not become good simply because he wills it or commands it, it is not unreasonable to believe that there can be this goodness even in a Godless world. Translated into the concrete, this means that it would be correct to assert that even in a world without God, killing little children just for the fun of it is wrong and caring for them is good. . . .

Suppose we say instead—as Brunner surely would—that an action or attitude is right or good simply because God *wills* it or *commands* it. Its goodness arises from Divine *fiat*. *God makes something good simply by commanding it.* (That, of course, is the course a consistent Divine Command theorist should take.)

Can *anything* be good or become good simply by being commanded or willed? Can a fiat, command or ban create goodness or moral obligation? I do not think so. But again I need to justify my thinking that it cannot. As a first step in seeing that it cannot, consider two ordinary, mundane examples of ordering or commanding.

Suppose you are in a course and the professor tells you "You must get a loose leaf notebook for this class." His commanding it, his telling you to do it, does not *eo ipso* make it something you *ought* to do or even make doing it good, though it might, given your circumstance, make it a prudent thing to do. But, whether or not it is prudent for you to do it, given his position of authority, and your dependence on him, it is, if there are no reasons for getting that particular type of notebook or any notebook at all, other than those consequent on his telling you to do it, all the same a perfectly arbitrary injunction on his part and not something that could properly be said to be good. Commanding it does not make it either good or obligatory. . . .

To this it will surely be replied: "It is true that these moral concepts cannot be identified with any old commands but *Divine* commands make all the difference. It is *God's* willing it, *God's* telling us to do it, that makes it good."

It is indeed true that, for the believer at least, it's being *God* who commands it, who wills it, that makes all the difference. This is so because believers assume that God is good. But now, it should be asked, *how* does the believer *know*, or indeed *does* he know, that God is good, except by what is in the end his own quite fallible moral judgment that God is good? Must he not appeal to his own considered judgments, his own moral sense here? Is there any escaping that?

It would seem not. To know that God is good we must see or come to appreciate that His acts, His revelation, His commands, are good and it is through the majesty and the goodness of His Revelation revealed in the Scriptures that we come to understand that God is good, that God supposedly is the ultimate criterion for all our moral actions and attitudes. But this, of course, rests on our own capacity to make moral assessments. It presupposes our own ability to make moral judgments and to recognize or appreciate the difference between right and wrong. . . .

We can see from the very structure of this argumentation that we must use our own moral insight to decide whether God's acts are good. We finally must judge the moral quality of the revelation; or, more accurately and less misleadingly, it is finally by what is no doubt fallible human insight that we must judge whether what *purports* to be Revelation is *indeed* Revelation. We must finally use our own moral understanding, if we are ever to know that God is good or, again more accurately, that there is a reality of such goodness that we should call in reality "God." Fallible or not, our own moral understanding is *logical* prior to our religious understanding. . . .

. . . But let us assume, what it is reasonable to assume, namely, that in some way "God is good," "God is the Perfect Good" are tautologies or "truths of reason," it still remains true that we can only come to know that anything is good or evil through our own moral insight. Let us see how this is so. First it is important to see that "God is good" is not an identity statement, e.g., "God" is not equivalent to "good." . . . we still must independently understand what is meant by "Good" and the criterion of goodness remains *independent* of God. . . .

But is not "God is the Perfect Good" an identity statement? Do not "God" and "the Perfect Good" refer to and/or mean the same thing? The meaning of both of these terms is so very indefinite that it is hard to be sure, but it is plain enough that a believer cannot question "God is the Perfect Good." But granting that, we still must have a criterion for good that is independent of religion, that is independent of a belief in God, for clearly we could not judge anything to be *perfectly* good, until we could judge that it was good and we have already seen that our criterion for goodness must be independent of God. . . .

If this be arrogance, it is inescapable, for it is built into the logic of our language about God. We cannot base our morality on our conception of God. Rather, our ability to have the concept of God we do have presupposes a reasonably sophisticated, and independent, moral understanding on our part. Brunner, and the whole Divine Command tradition, has the matter topsy-turvy.

. . . I have shown that in a purely logical sense moral notions cannot rest on the doctrinal cosmic claims of religion. In fact quite the reverse is the case, namely, that only if a man has a religiously independent concept of good and evil can he even have the Judeo-Christian-Islamic conception of Deity. In this very fundamental sense, it is not morality that rests on religion but religion that rests on morality. . . .

Some defenders of the faith will grant that there is indeed such a fundamental independence of ethical belief from religious belief, though very few, if any, would accept my last argument about the dependence of religious belief on human moral understanding. They could accept my basic claim and still argue that to develop a *fully human* and *adequate normative* ethic one must make it a religious ethic. Here in the arguments, for and against, the intellectual reliability of religious claims will become relevant.

The claim that such a religious apologist wishes to make is that only with a God-centered morality could we get a morality that would be adequate, that would go beyond the relativities and formalisms of a nonreligious ethic. Only a God-centered and perhaps only a Christ-centered morality could meet our most persistent moral demands. Human beings have certain desires and needs; they experience loneliness and despair; they create certain "images of excellence"; they seek happiness and love. . . . Unless we can picture ourselves as creations of such a loving Sovereign, and really convince ourselves of the truth of our picture, our deepest moral expectations will be frustrated.

No purely secular ethic can offer such a hope to us, a hope that is perhaps built on an illusion, but still a hope that is worth the full risk of faith. Whatever the rationality of such a faith, our very human nature makes us long for such assurances. Without it our lives will be without significance, without moral sense; morality finds its psychologically realistic foundation in certain human purposes, but human life without God will be devoid of all purpose or at least devoid of everything but trivial purposes. Thus without a belief in God, there could be no humanly satisfying morality. Secular humanism is in reality inhuman.

It is true that a secular morality can offer no hope for a blissful immortality; it is also true that secular morality does not provide for a protecting, living Father or some overarching Purpose to Life. But we have to balance this against the fact that these religious concepts are myths. We human beings are helpless, utterly dependent creatures for years and years. Because of this there develops in us a deep psychological need for an all-protecting Father or, depending on what culture we are in, some other cosmic assurances. It is natural enough for human beings to thirst for such security, but there is not the slightest reason to think that there is such security. That we have *feelings* of dependence does not mean that there is something on which we can depend. That we have such needs most certainly does not give us any reason at all to think that there is such a Supermundane prop for our feelings of dependence. . . .

. . . We do not need a God to *give* meaning to our lives by making us for His Sovereign Purpose and thereby arguably robbing us of our freedom. We, by our deliberate acts and commitments, give meaning to our own lives. Here man has the "dreadful freedom" that gives him human dignity; freedom will indeed bring him anxiety, but he will be the *rider* and not the *ridden,* and by being able to choose, he can seek out and sometimes realize the things he most deeply prizes and admires, and thus his life can take on a significance. A life lived without purpose is indeed a most dreadful life, but we do not need God or the gods to give purpose to our lives.

There are believers who would say that these purely human purposes, forged in freedom and anguish, are not sufficient to meet our deepest moral needs. Man needs very much to see himself as a creature with a Purpose in a Divinely Ordered Universe. He needs to find some cosmic significance for his ideals and commitments; he wants the protection and the certainty of having a function. As the Grand Inquisitor realized, some religionists argue, this is even more desirable than his freedom. He wants and needs to live and be guided by the utterly Sovereign Will of God. If that entails a sacrifice of his autonomy, so be it. . . .

DISCUSSION QUESTIONS

1. How can we know that God is good? Is it possible for God to do evil or to command us to do evil? How does Nielsen answer this question?
2. Do you think Nielsen's critique of Catholic natural law theory is well grounded? How might Aquinas respond to Nielsen's criticisms of his theory?
3. Nielsen accuses the Catholic Church of being arbitrary at times and even resorting to cultural relativism, in deciding which beliefs and actions it labels as "unnatural" or "sinful." Is Nielsen justified in making this accusation? On what grounds can a natural law theorist decide which acts are unnatural and which are not? Does being unnatural necessarily entail being immoral?
4. Why does Nielsen conclude that "we cannot base our morality on our conception of God"? Do you agree with Nielsen's argument on this point? Support your position.
5. Can an atheist live a moral life? How does Nielsen answer this question? Are you satisfied with his answer?
6. Make a list of the premises Nielsen uses to support his conclusion that humanistic ethics are better than religious ethics. Are you convinced by his argument? Support your position.
7. Compare and contrast Nielsen's and Nietzsche's moral philosophies. Discuss whether Nielsen would agree with Nietzsche's "noble man" as our moral ideal.
8. Does a belief in God actually hinder us in living the moral life? Like Nietzsche, Nielsen believes that religious ethics compromise our autonomy. The need to believe in God for meaning in our life, they claim, entails a sacrifice of our autonomy. Do you agree with Nielsen and Nietzsche? In what ways might a belief in God involve a sacrifice of your autonomy? What are the implications of this on your ability to make good moral decisions?

Chapter Applications

1. Mass Suicide at Heaven's Gate

On March 22, 1997, thirty-nine members of Heaven's Gate—a California cult—left their earthly bodies and ascended to a "Higher Level." According to them, the physical body is merely an earthbound vessel for the soul. Do, the "sainted one" and the leader of the cult, had recently heard of plans to move to a "Higher Level" from his companion Ti, a nurse who died in 1985 and communicated with Do from this "Higher Level." Although Do was not sure of the exact nature of the plan, he talked to his followers about "leaving their vehicles" soon but only by their own choice.

The command finally came to exodus this earth and join a spaceship in the tail of the Hale-Bopp comet, which was passing earth. The mass suicide of the members took place in stages, with those who chose to go last helping the others administer poison.

Richard Ford, also known as Rio DiAngelo, was one of the followers who chose to remain behind in his earthbound body as—in his words—"an instrument of clarification." DiAngelo told reporters that shortly before the mass suicide he recalled a "sense of urgency" about becoming "nonhuman." Their deaths were "not suicide," he explained, "because their souls live on at a Higher Level."[1]

Discussion Questions

1. What is the definition of religion? Is Heaven's Gate a religion or a cult? Discuss whether the moral commands of cults are worthy of the same respect as are religious moral codes.

2. Was the mass suicide morally justified under the divine command theory? What is the relation between theological beliefs and morality? Does acting on sincerely held religious beliefs morally justify our actions? Discuss how one might go about verifying whether the instruction to commit suicide was, in fact, a command from a "Higher Level."

3. Compare and contrast the biblical narrative of Abraham and Isaac with the Heaven's Gate incident. Discuss whether the followers of Heaven's Gate, like Abraham, showed moral courage and faith in responding to the higher call.

4. Would it have made any difference morally if the cult members had been coerced into committing suicide? Discuss whether the divine command theory morally justifies coercing other people or taking their lives against their will, as happened in the 1978 mass suicide and massacre involving the People's Temple sect in Jonestown, Guyana.

5. In his book *Thought Contagion*, Aaron Lynch equates the Heaven's Gate mass suicide with an Ebola virus, which has the potential to infect and kill others. "Let's say 100 million people were exposed to Heaven's Gate meme

as a result of the suicide," Lynch writes. "If one in a million of those people contracted the meme, the suicides would have yielded 100 new infections."[2] With the turning of the millennium, this scenario is even more likely, he argues. How might divine command theorists respond to the criticism that their actions are immoral because they harm more than just themselves?

2. Suzie Valdez: "Doing God's Work"

Every morning Suzie Valdez and her two assistants make hundreds of sandwiches with food donated from a local market in El Paso, Texas. After loading the boxes of sandwiches into her run-down van, they head across the border into Mexico. Their first stop is the huge garbage dump outside Ciudad Juarez, where scores of people—adults and children—forage each day for food and other necessities. Here at the edge of this bleak landscape Valdez, affectionately known as "the Queen of the Dump," and her assistants pass out sandwiches and clothing to the people.

What motivates Valdez to dedicate her life, at great expense to herself and her children, to the welfare of those less fortunate? Valdez believes that God is working through her. Inspired by the message of God's love, Valdez founded the Christ for Mexico Missions in 1963 to serve the poor of Mexico. She has a deep belief that "God will provide, God will take care of me." A woman of tremendous energy and moral conviction, Valdez believes that without her faith in God, she would not have been able to accomplish so much.

When asked if giving up her home and material security to minister to the poor was an act of moral courage, Valdez replied, "Well, I guess it did take courage, but at the same time inside of me I didn't know how I was doing it or why, but I know the Holy Spirit was leading me."[3]

Discussion Questions

1. In their study of moral exemplars, psychologists Anne Colby and William Damon found that although many of the exemplars they interviewed were nonreligious, "All those who spoke of the importance of love in their work were deeply religious." Colby and Damon also found that religious people were less likely to become embittered by adversity and contempt from others and more likely to feel grateful for the opportunity to serve others. "Since service to others helps one find one's own inner spirituality," they write, "one is grateful to the other for the opportunity to serve."[4] Do you agree with Colby and Damon?

2. Do you agree that religious faith can make it easier for a person to behave morally? How might Kai Nielsen respond to this question? To what extent is Valdez acting as an autonomous moral agent? Does religious faith necessarily compromise our moral autonomy, as Nielsen claims? Support your answer.

3. Friedrich Nietzsche believed that organized religion is detrimental to morality. Discuss whether Nietzsche would regard Valdez's actions in helping the poor of Ciudad Juarez as an example of slave morality.

4. Martin Luther King, Jr., like Suzie Valdez, claims that it was his religious faith that gave him the strength to lead the civil rights movement. Compare and contrast their lives with those of other people you consider to be moral exemplars.

3. Cloning: Are We Playing God?

On February 25, 1997, Ian Wilmut of the Rolin Institute in Scotland stunned the world with his announcement that he had successfully cloned an adult mammal. The cloning of an adult sheep has raised serious moral as well as religious issues. A Time/CNN poll taken shortly after Wilmut's announcement found that 74 percent of the people living in the United States agreed with the statement that "it is against God's will to clone human beings."[5]

Most religious ethicists regard human life as sacred and belonging to God. In 1993 Pope John Paul II condemned the cloning experiments at George Washington University, arguing that the sex act is the only theologically permissible way to procreate. At a meeting two years later, 187 religious leaders in the United States voted overwhelmingly against genetic manipulation, stating that "we believe that humans and animals are creations of God, not humans."[6]

The Lepkowskis disagree that cloning is against God's will. A musical prodigy and a straight A student in physics at the University of Chicago, Teresa Lepkowski was left with massive brain damage after an automobile accident. According to her doctors, she would probably live only another few days. Her parents gave researchers permission to clone Teresa because they felt this would give her the chance she deserved in life.

The Smiths also want to have their daughter cloned. Four-year-old Abigail is suffering from cancer and needs a bone marrow donor. The cancer has also damaged other organs. The ideal donor would be a clone—a baby created with the sole purpose of harvesting her organs for Abigail. The Smiths believe that because the technology to use cloning to cure diseases is based on reason, it is consistent with God's natural law.

Discussion Questions

1. Do you believe that cloning is against God's will? Or do you agree with the Lepkowskis and the Smiths? On what grounds can we determine God's will regarding cloning and reproduction?

2. According to John Paris, a bioethicist at Boston College, "Choosing personal characteristics as if they were options on a car is an invitation to misadventure." What do you think he means by this? We choose our mates on the basis of their desirable personal characteristics. How does this differ morally from choosing the personal characteristics we want in our children through cloning?

3. In Ira Levin's 1976 book *The Boys from Brazil,* an ex-Nazi clones a generation of Hitler youth from the cells of Hitler. Discuss the moral implications of the possibility of using cloning technology to mass produce a particular type of human.

4. If we could clone people such as Gandhi, Jesus, and Buddha, would we have a moral obligation to do so? Isn't it better to bring another Teresa Lepkowski into the world instead of a baby with unknown genetic qualities? Are there any moral problems in wanting to have a perfect child? After all, didn't Jesus say that we must be perfect like God?

5. Discuss whether it is morally acceptable to use human beings as a means only, as in the case of Abigail's clone. On the other hand, is it morally acceptable to allow Abigail to die when there is a way of saving her life?

6. Nigel Cameron of the Center for Bioethics and Human Dignity argues that "Part of our notion of human dignity is that we are different. Cloning humans diminishes the dignity of all of us."[7] Do you agree that human dignity requires being different? In what ways, if any, does being an identical twin, or having a child who is a clone of ourselves, diminish our dignity?

4. Christian Ethics and War

Perhaps at no time in our history was there more public opposition to war than during the American Revolution. The Quakers—also known as the Society of Friends—were steadfastly opposed to the use of military force in the independence effort. Founder George Fox urged his followers to live "in the virtue of that life and power that took away the occasion of all wars." Those who participated in the war effort were expelled from the Society.

Job Scott, a Quaker minister, refused to take the oath of allegiance to the revolutionary effort or to pay taxes to finance the war. Like Fox, Scott believed that war, in all its forms, is contrary to the Christian principles of "love your enemy" and "no rendering evil for evil." Even the Old Testament principle of "An eye for an eye and a tooth for a tooth," he argued, does not work in war because the retaliation against the aggressor almost always ends up exceeding the offense and injuring innocent parties.[8]

As a result of their religious beliefs many of the Quakers were flogged, hanged, or tarred and feathered. Others were thrown into jail or forced to flee the country. Although Quakers are no long disowned by the Society of Friends if they participate in war, many Quakers resisted the draft during World War I and II and the Vietnam War. Others currently engage in war tax resistance—refusing to pay their federal income tax. Like their colonial counterparts, some have been jailed as a consequence of their religious beliefs, and others have had their property confiscated by the government for nonpayment of taxes.

Discussion Questions

1. Like Gandhi, the Quakers believe that their religious teachings require pacifism. However, many Hindus reject Gandhi's interpretation of the *Bhagavad Gita,* and not all Christians believe that war is incompatible with biblical teachings. According to Aquinas, defensive wars that abide by certain codes of conduct—such as avoiding killing civilians—may be justified under natural law theory. When there are two conflicting interpretations of Christian

ethics, as with the permissibility of war, how are we to decide which is the correct interpretation of scripture?

2. Can a government keep law and order and, at the same time, respect all religious beliefs? Discuss how conflicts between the law and a person's religious beliefs regarding what is moral should be resolved. To what extent is the motive for refusing to pay taxes morally relevant? What if the war tax refuser was a member of an anti-American militia rather than a pacifist?

3. Following the end of the Vietnam War in 1973, people who deserted or avoided the draft by defecting to Canada were granted amnesty by Presidents Nixon, Ford, and Carter. President Ford, however, offered clemency only to those who were willing to do public service. Discuss the morality of the amnesty program.

5. Refusing Medical Treatment

Christian Scientists believe that reality consists solely of the mind. Illnesses, therefore, are really mental in origin, and prayer is the proper anecdote to suffering. For Christian Scientists, seeking medical care runs contrary to their faith. To place their faith in both prayer and in medicine is hypocrisy and, as such, it is believed, greatly diminishes the power of prayer.

In 1990 the health of Colin Newmark, the 3-year-old son of Christian Scientists, began to rapidly deteriorate. His parents reluctantly took him to a nearby hospital. Diagnostic tests indicated that Colin suffered from an intestinal blockage. His parents agreed to surgery to remove the blockage because they considered the procedure to be purely mechanical rather than medical.

A pathological report on tissue taken during the surgery revealed that Colin was suffering from non-Hodgkin's lymphoma. The doctors in charge of the case recommended chemotherapy and radiation therapy. Without medical intervention Colin would probably die within eight months. On the other hand, the therapy, which gave Colin a 40 percent chance of survival, would be painful and debilitating to Colin and could result in kidney failure, immunological and neurological problems, and sterility.

The Newmarks refused treatment and attempted to have Colin removed from the hospital into the care of a Christian Science practitioner. The hospital in turn sued for custody of Colin so they could treat him. The Delaware Supreme Court ruled in favor of the parents.[9]

Discussion Questions

1. The U.S. medical establishment opposes the legal right of Christian Scientists to refuse medical care, especially when physicians perceive it as threatening the health and fundamental rights of children. The American Academy of Pediatrics is working to remove the religious exemptions from states' child abuse and neglect laws.[10] Should members of the medical community be given exclusive authority over matters of physical health? Should they be

allowed to impose their values at the expense of religious values about spiritual health?

2. People in the United States have a legal right to forgo life-sustaining medical treatment. Should this right include the right of Christian Science parents to refuse medical treatment for their dying children? Would the chemotherapy and radiation therapy in Colin's case fall under life-sustaining treatment or under curative treatment? Support your answer.

3. Do parents have a right to impose their religious values on their children, as in the Newmark case? If so, are there any limits on what parents may impose on their children in the name of religion? Support your answer.

4. The conflict between medical professionals and Christian Scientists is not just one between cultural and religious values. Physicians claim that it is also a violation of their professional duty to allow a person to suffer when the suffering can be prevented by medical treatment. How should this conflict be resolved when it arises? What would you have done had you been Colin Newmark's attending physician?

5. Are there limits to the exercise of religious freedom? How should religious freedom and respect for pluralism be balanced against overall community cohesiveness?

6. How should we go about resolving a conflict between cultural and religious values? Are there universal moral values that transcend both culture and religion that we can appeal to in resolving these conflicts? If so, what are some of these values? Answer using the above case study.

NOTES

[1] Mark Miller, "Secrets of the Cult," *Newsweek,* April 14, 1997, pp. 28–37.

[2] Geoffrey Cowley, "Viruses of the Mind: How Odd Ideas Survive," *Newsweek,* April 14, 1997, p. 14.

[3] See "Suzie Valdez: 'Queen of the Dump'," in Anne Colby and William Damon, *Some Do Care: Contemporary Lives of Moral Commitment* (New York: The Free Press, 1992), p. 45.

[4] Ibid, p. 279.

[5] Jeffrey Kluger, "Will We Follow the Sheep?" *Time,* March 10, 1997, p. 66.

[6] Kenneth L. Woodward, "Thou Shalt Not Patent," *Newsweek,* May 29, 1995, p. 68.

[7] Jeffrey Kluger, "Will We Follow the Sheep?" *Time,* March 10, 1997, p. 66.

[8] Job Scott, "War Is Inconsistent with the Doctrine and Example of Jesus Christ," c. 1782, in Angie O'Gorman, *The Universe Bends Toward Justice: A Reader on Christian Nonviolence in the U.S.* (Philadelphia: New Society Publishers, 1990).

[9] *Newmark v. Williams* 588 A 2d 1108 (Del. 1991).

[10] Paula A. Monopoli, "Allocating the Costs of Parental Free Exercise: Striking a New Balance Between Sincere Religious Belief and a Child's Right to Medical Treatment," *Pepperdine Law Review* 18 (1991): 331.

CHAPTER FOUR

Beyond Relativism
Conscience and Moral Development

*Because [college] students generally have not yet internalized the principles neces-
sary to make ethical judgments, they substitute personal and subjective criteria.
This makes it appear as though they lack character. A more accurate description is
that they are in the process of developing it.*

Gregory Blimling, "Developing Character in College Students" [1]

The purpose of ethics education is not to tell us what our moral values ought to
be. Most of us already know what is right and wrong—at least in principle. The
problem comes in living what we know and in applying this general moral
knowledge to particular contexts. If we agree with philosophers such as Aristotle
that one of the primary reasons for studying ethics is to make us better people,
then an examination of our moral development must be part of that process.
According to researchers on moral development, we can advance our moral
growth by learning about the psychological mechanisms that underlie it.

Until the 1970s psychology was dominated by behaviorism. Both behaviorists
and cultural relativists claimed that moral behavior was simply the result of cultural conditioning. The Vietnam War protest and the civil rights movement gave
rise to dissatisfaction with cultural relativism.

Harvard psychologist Lawrence Kohlberg's ideas about moral development
became popular in the wake of these two movements. Kohlberg rejected all forms
of ethical relativism. According to him and other developmental theorists, there
are innate cognitive structures that are fundamental to all humans. Although the
specific content of moral codes may vary from culture to culture, this difference is
only surface deep. The conceptual structures from which these specific codes are
formulated are universal.

One of the assumptions underlying developmental theories, in both philosophy and psychology, is that humans have an innate desire to grow and fulfill their
potential. Developmental theorists also claim that people who live up to their
potential and lead good lives will be happier, experience greater inner peace and
harmony, and be more satisfied with their moral decisions.

In the first selection from *The Moral Sense*, James Q. Wilson presents a case
for the existence of an innate moral sense in humans. This selection also contains

brief introductions to some of the other theories that will be covered in later readings in this section.

In the next selection from *The Philosophy of Moral Development,* Lawrence Kohlberg argues for a developmental, or stage, approach to moral development. His theory, as we already noted, has had a tremendous influence on current thinking about moral development and ethics education.

Carol Gilligan, in the selection from her book *In a Different Voice,* argues that Kohlberg's theory of moral development does not offer an adequate explanation of how women make moral decisions. She offers another explanation of the process of women's moral decision making.

In her article "The Meshing of Care and Justice," Virginia Held looks for a wider framework that encompasses both Kohlberg's justice perspective and Gilligan's care perspective. Although she thinks both perspectives are important, she concludes that the care perspective is more overarching.

The selection on Huck's conscience from Mark Twain's *The Adventures of Huckleberry Finn* focuses on Huck's decision of whether or not to rescue his friend Jim, a runaway slave. This selection points out some of the inadequacies of the types of moral reasoning found at the earlier stages of moral development.

The final selection, "We Are All Related," is from Eagle Man's book *Mother Earth Spirituality: Native American Paths to Healing Ourselves and Our World.* His essay raises the question of whether we have to set our ideals higher.

NOTE

[1] Gregory Blimling, "Developing Character in College Students," NASPA Journal, Summer 1990, 27 (4): 286.

James Q. Wilson

The Moral Sense

James Q. Wilson is a professor of management and public policy at UCLA. In his studies of how public policy is formulated, Wilson noticed that there is a paradox involved in the way we currently think about morality. Although we publicly adhere to ethical subjectivism, with its denial that there are objective moral standards, in actual practice we continue to employ moral standards in making moral judgments. Why is this? In the following selection from his book *The Moral Sense*, Wilson analyzes the findings of philosophers and psychologists regarding the possibility of an innate moral sense.

CRITICAL THINKING QUESTIONS

1. How does Adam Smith define *sympathy?* Does Adam Smith think that pity or compassion is always an appropriate response to others' distress? What is the source of human moral sentiments according to Adam Smith?

2. What is the role of imagination in morality?

3. What, according to Wilson, is the relation between sympathy and moral judgment?

4. What motivates us to pass moral judgment on ourselves as well as on others?

5. What, according to Wilson, is the conscience? What are the origins of conscience? How does conscience motivate us to behave morally?

6. What does Wilson think of Freud's explanation of the conscience?

7. What is a psychopath? How do lie detectors work? Why don't they work on psychopaths? In what ways is a psychopath deficient in a moral sense?

8. What findings from child psychologists does Wilson use to support his theory that the moral sense is based on an innate disposition to be moral?

9. How do the findings of developmental psychologists support Wilson's theory about a moral sense?

10. According to Wilson, what is the primary problem with both Kant's and Kohlberg's theories about moral reasoning?

The Moral Sense (New York: The Free Press, 1993), pp. 31–35, 102–109, 130–131, 179, 190–193. Notes have been omitted.

SYMPATHY AS A STANDARD

Before he became the preeminent economist of all time, Adam Smith was the pre-eminent moral philosopher of his time, and his attempt to explain moral sentiments was founded on the near-universal human attribute of sympathy. How ever man may be supposed, Smith wrote, "there are evidently some principles in his nature, which interest him in the fortune of others, and render their happiness necessary to him, though he derives nothing from it except the pleasure of seeing it." One such principle is "pity or compassion, the emotion which we feel for the misery of others, when we either see it, or are made to conceive it in a very lively manner."

This statement is often taken to mean that Smith believed that we have, or ought to have, a tendency to help others—that is, to be benevolent. That is almost correct, but not quite. Smith did not mean that we always feel so much distress at the plight of others that we feel obliged to alleviate it; were that the case, it would behoove us to perform endless and probably futile acts of benevolence. Indeed, were pity our chief motive, we would all soon be either paupers or busybodies. What he said was a bit more complicated: sympathy, defined as the capacity for and inclination to imagine the feelings of others, is a source—to Smith, *the* source—of human moral sentiments.

We have a natural desire to be admired by others; to be admired by them, we must please them. Since our happiness depends somewhat on the goodwill of our fellows, we naturally seek to understand what may please or offend them. To do this we seek to enter into the minds and feelings of others, and we are aware that others try to grasp our own thoughts and feelings. We cannot, of course, know what others feel, and so we must imagine it. Our powers of imagination are very strong; they can be aroused not only by the plight of a friend but by the flickering lights and shadows on a motion picture screen, so that we are reduced to tears by the sight of a fictitious boy looking in vain for an equally fictitious dog.

But we do not simply share the feelings we imagine others to have; we also judge them. More particularly, we judge whether the actions and feelings of another person are proportionate. A rich boy distraught at the loss of a penny arouses not sympathy but derision; a boy indifferent to the loss of a loving dog arouses not sympathy but disdain. We approve of the conduct and character of another person if, when we imagine ourselves in his position, our feelings correspond to those that we think motivate him.

This sounds more complicated than it is. Suppose we see someone reacting angrily to being overcharged. We ordinarily do nothing, but we judge the other person's reactions. If we think they are appropriate, we say to ourselves something like this: "I know just how he felt! I wouldn't have paid that bill either!" If we think his reaction was too extreme, we judge differently: "He's overreacting; there's no need to get carried away." In neither case have we done anything, but that does not mean we lack sympathy. Sympathy—our sense of another's feelings and of their appropriateness given the circumstances—is the basis of our judgment. More bluntly, to sympathize *is* to judge.

Sometimes another person's situation may prompt our action. He may be injured, or he may be injuring another. How we behave will depend in part on our assessment of his motives: If he is injured, was he blameless? If he is harming another, is it for good reason? There will be, of course, many other factors that determine whether we act, some of which we shall examine later on. But even when we do not act, we judge. We say to ourselves: "He has only himself to blame," or "He shouldn't hit that child." Even when we judge but do not act we express—and thereby reaffirm—a standard of moral character.

As we grow from childhood to adulthood, we increasingly judge ourselves as we judge others. We do so at first because we imagine what others must think of our motives when they see us acting in a certain way. Since we want to be admired, we want to conform, within reason, to the expectations of others. But at some point a remarkable transformation occurs in how we judge ourselves. We desire not only to be praised, but to be praiseworthy. As Adam Smith put it, "man naturally desires, not only to be loved, but to be lovely." Thus we are often embarrassed when we are praised without deserving the praise.

Just how this transformation occurs is not well understood. Smith believed it arose out of our desire to be like those we most admire. When we emulate a parent, a friend, a popular hero, or even a fictional character, we become acutely aware of the difference between merely pretending to be excellent and really being so. Up to a point we can fake honesty, courage, or generosity; but we know the difference between *really* being honest, brave, or generous and just going through the motions in order to impress other people. Smith said that at this point we are beginning to listen to the voice of an impartial spectator located within our breast; in modern terms, we begin to hear the voice of our conscience. At first we judge others; we then begin to judge ourselves as we think others judge us; finally we judge ourselves as an impartial, disinterested third party might. The importance of this last step can hardly be exaggerated, because the "man within the breast," unlike some other person, *knows* our real motives. We can fool our friends, but not ourselves.

Not that we don't try, of course. We rationalize our actions, suppress self-awareness, and drown out the whisper of conscience with impulsive actions and synthetic exuberance. But in our calmer moments, or perhaps when our lack of self-command has led to tragic consequences, we reflect bitterly on how wrong it was—and not merely how inconvenient—to have allowed our actions to be governed by the wrong motives. And even in our daily lives, there will be innumerable cases of our obeying rules, resisting temptations, and doing the honorable thing for no other reason than that we instinctively act that way and reflexively feel guilty when we don't. . . .

Insofar as they arise out of sympathy, then, our moral sentiments originate in our natural sociability. Because we like the company and desire the approval of others, we adjust our actions to conform to others' expectations. If that were the end of the matter, we might properly conclude that morality is little more than a popularity contest. But that is not the whole story. Our natural sociability leads us not only to act so as to please others but also to judge how others act toward us; and in judging them we learn to judge ourselves. We want the approval of others, but—to a degree that cannot be explained by immediate self-interest—we also want to deserve that approval. And insofar as we want to deserve it from others, we also want to deserve it from ourselves. In other words, we desire not only respect but self-respect.

SYMPATHY AS A MOTIVE

If sympathy merely shaped our judgments, it would be important, but it acquires even greater significance to the extent that it governs our actions. Since the 1960s, psychologists and other scholars have explored in considerable detail the circumstances under which and the degree to which feelings of sympathy lead to benevolent or altruistic actions. Their conclusions are these: Sympathy is not an idle sentiment; on the contrary, it often—but not always—leads to benevolence. A person who feels distress at the plight of another is more likely to help than is one who does not, though specific aspects of the situation and of the person will influence his response.

Psychologists debate whether feeling distress at the plight of another means that the sympathetic person "really wants" to help the distressed person or whether the former gets some psychic benefit (such as avoiding shame or relieving stress) from helping the latter. Though this may seem like the worst sort of academic hair-splitting, in fact it is a significant issue. Suppose that you confront a person who has collapsed on a bus. You feel distressed. If your distress is truly sympathetic, your only course of action is to help the person, unless, of course, someone else helps him first. But if all that you want to do is to relieve your sense of distress, you can get off the bus at the next stop. Out of sight, out of mind.

Some people will help, some will get off the bus, and some will do one or the other depending on the situation. Most of the evidence obtained from laboratory experiments suggests that people feeling distress prefer helping to running away. Some of the research done on the street (involving staged scenes of distress) suggests that many people will move away. This should not be surprising; if sympathy always or even usually led to benevolence, we would not regard benevolent action as so praiseworthy. We praise only motives that have defeated self-interest; we reserve our greatest praise for those motives that have the greatest difficulty in overcoming self-interest.

When people donate blood, offer help to a collapsed stranger, assist motorists trapped in a car, intervene to stop a crime in progress, or rescue Jews whom the Nazis want to send to a death camp, they are acting benevolently. That benevolence can have many motives, ranging from a desire to impress onlookers to sympathy for the victim. . . .

Knowing the advantages of having a reputation for honesty, narrowly self-interested people may try to acquire one, but it is not as easy as it seems. A person may be fooled by a chance encounter, but during a continuing relationship he will usually form an accurate assessment of another person's character. For people to be impressed by your honesty, you must either be honest all of the time (in which case you will have to stop taking selfish advantage of the many opportunities for cheating, and so you might as well stop being greedy altogether), or you will have to be honest in some very conspicuous, highly dramatic fashion, such as telling the truth even when it costs a lot of money to do so. As the economist Robert Frank puts it in his excellent analysis of how we signal a reputation to others, people will accept your behavior as a sign of honesty or duty only when it would be costly to fake it. If it is very costly to fake it, you can't fake it; the reputation you then earn for honesty or duty corresponds exactly to reality. You *are* dutiful.

The uneasy relationship between conscience and sociability helps explain why our sense of duty is often evoked by events that anger us. We are often aroused to act, not by our warm sympathy for the plight of a victim or our calm deliberation over what justice requires, but by our rage at somebody who seems to be "getting away with something," that is, conspicuously violating, even flouting, some obligation.

Thirty-two people who had gone to the aid of crime victims in California were studied to find out why they intervened even though they did not know the victim, often acted alone, and in almost every case suffered an injury, sometimes a serious one. These Good Samaritans stopped beatings, broke up robberies, and challenged bullies. One got a broken jaw for his trouble; another was cut by a shattered bottle. Not surprisingly, almost all the Samaritans were relatively young men who were bigger and heavier than most men their age. More surprisingly, they were not especially idealistic, and they did not speak much of their sympathy for the victims. Most acted reflexively, without deliberation. What seemed to distinguish them from similar men who did not intervene was that they were quick to anger and temperamentally aggressive. When someone flagrantly and unjustifiably violates the social compact, all of us are angered to some degree; these men let their anger impel them to risky action. Conscience, in short, is not entirely a calm sentiment; it both restrains our self-interest and unleashes our indignation.

This is evident in the portrait Samuel and Pearl Oliner have painted of the gentiles who rescued Jews during World War II. As we saw in the chapter on sympathy, many of the rescuers were led to act by a face-to-face confrontation with a victim. Empathy—fellow feeling—was their chief motive. But some of the helpers, roughly a tenth, did not feel sympathy for the victims so much as they experienced anger at their oppressors; their motive was principle, animated by rage. Their relations with those they aided were more impersonal than those of their empathic colleagues. They did not wait to meet a Jew before acting; they began acting by looking for Jews to help. Suzanne, for example, helped several hundred Jews. She was not part of any organized group, did not seek out the company of others in order to win their esteem or support, and did not get involved in the lives of those whom she helped. On a psychological test she scored well below the average in empathy but well above it on a scale of social responsibility. Because she held strong views about right and wrong, she was ready to sacrifice some sociability in favor of affirming her principles. Among her friends she was disputatious; as she later put it, "we argued about everything." Her conscience made it hard for her either to ignore injustice or cultivate popularity.

A reader eager to reduce all human motivation to self-interest narrowly conceived may interpret what the Good Samaritans or the Holocaust rescuers did as efforts at reputation building, but taking this view so stretches the concept of self-interest as to deprive it of any meaning. Expressing genuine indignation at an injustice and acting to set matters right at considerable cost to ourselves are not merely ways by which we signal to others our sense of duty; they are ways by which we live.

THE ORIGINS OF CONSCIENCE

For about a century, the study of conscience has been chiefly the province of Freudians. In their view, the conscience is the superego, formed out of the child's strong identification with a parent; more particularly, the superego is, in Freud's words, "the heir of the Oedipus complex." Every boy secretly lusts after his mother and, as a consequence, sees his father as a powerful rival. Because he cannot have his mother or overcome his father, he represses his erotic love for the former and his anger with the latter. These repressed feelings persist in his subconscious, reappearing occasionally in the form of dreams and neuroses, but at the conscious level they are replaced by a set of rules—the superego—that control his impulses. His conscience has been formed.

The word that dominates Freud's account of the conscience is "repression" (*Unterdrückung*). The superego represses the boy's Oedipus complex and his natural and innate aggressiveness, obliging him to renounce revenge against his father. "Men are not gentle creatures who want to be loved," Freud wrote; they are, on the contrary, instinctively aggressive. Although he is not clear on this, Freud implies that people with the strongest conscience are the most repressed: they are driven by a "cruel" superego that they come to "fear." The resulting sense of guilt can, in the extreme case, cause illness or even crime. Many who have accepted Freud's theory have drawn from the idea of repression and the more unattractive features of its stronger forms the view that repression, with its connotation of victimization, is bad and ought to be overcome. Though Freud may not have intended it, Freudianism has made conscience suspect.

The continued popularity of this view is in sharp contrast to its scientific implausibility. . . .

A book-length review of studies that tested the scientific validity of Freud's theories, written by scholars who were by no means hostile to his ideas, concluded, with respect to the formation of the superego, that whatever oedipal conflict a boy may experience, it is not resolved because his fear of his father leads him to identify with that awesome figure. On the contrary, boys are more likely to develop a masculine personality and acquire strong moral standards when they have a loving and nurturant rather than a threatening or fear-inspiring father.

There is another, much more straightforward account of the origins of conscience. Conscience, like sympathy, fairness, and self-control, arises not out of repressed lust and rage but out of our innate desire for attachment, and thus it acquires its strongest development when those attachments are the strongest. People with the strongest conscience will not be those with the most powerfully repressed aggressiveness but those with the most powerfully developed affiliation. That conclusion is consistent with the evidence that undermines the Freudian oedipal theory: attachment, not fear, is associated with later moral development. Just as we are predisposed to develop a good ear for the voices of others as they judge our actions, so also are we disposed to develop one for that inner voice by which we judge our own actions. When we disappoint other people by acting immorally, we feel shame; when we disappoint ourselves by failing to honor an obligation, we feel guilt. Since the sanctions that others can impose on us are more numerous and, in most cases, more powerful than those we impose on ourselves, we ordinarily fear shame more than guilt. . . .

The machines popularly called lie detectors are devices that measure the operation of the heart, lungs, and sweat glands. The machines can't, of course, distinguish between a lie and the truth; that is why their operators prefer to call them polygraphs. But they can measure changes in our autonomic nervous system. Without getting into the debate over whether these measured changes are good indicators of a person's truthfulness, it is worth noting that most people do undergo involuntary bodily reactions when they tell a lie. If there were no such thing as a conscience, that would not occur. Everybody would be able to defeat the lie detector every time.

Some people can beat it all the time. That is because they have no involuntary reactions to lying; they are psychopaths. A psychopath is not a lunatic suffering from disabling delusions or an obviously neurotic person displaying phobias and anxieties; rather, he or she is an outwardly normal person with an apparently logical mind who happens to be an emotional cipher. Hiding behind what Hervey Cleckley called "the mask of sanity," the psychopath is the extreme case of the nonsocial personality, someone for whom the ordinary emotions of life have no meaning. Psychopaths lie without compunction, injure without remorse, and cheat with little fear of detection. Wholly self-centered and unaware of the emotional needs of others, they are, in the fullest sense of the term, unsocial. They can mimic feelings without experiencing them. If man were simply the pure calculator that some economists and game theories imagine, this is what he would be.

Much of what we know about conscience has been learned by studying those who have none, that is, by investigating psychopaths. In general, psychopaths are hard to condition. When most people hear a tone that is then followed by a painful electric shock, they quickly learn to associate the tone with the shock. Their apprehension can be gauged by measuring changes in the rate at which their skin conducts electricity. Robert Hare found that ordinary people became very apprehensive after just a few experiences with the tone-shock sequence, but psychopaths became far less apprehensive. . . .

Accompanying this inability to internalize anxieties is the psychopath's difficulty in entering imaginatively into the emotional state of someone else. A test measuring role-taking ability developed by Harrison Gough can predict with some accuracy who will and will not become a serious delinquent, independently of a person's social class. In addition, psychopaths are often thrill seekers, not simply because they discount the bad things that may happen to them if they take risks, but because they are underaroused: that is, their emotional void leaves them bored and restless. Knowing little of true feelings, they cannot rely on their own feelings to supply them with much satisfaction, and so they seek it out from dangerous activities, wild parties, and an agitated quest for excitement.

By turning these findings upside down we can depict the features of men and women that dispose us to acquire a conscience. We are fully social beings: we have genuine emotions and can sense the emotional state of others. We are not so greatly in need of excitement that we are inclined to treat others as objects designed for our amusement. We judge others and expect to be judged by them. In time we acquire the disposition to judge our own behavior through the eyes of a disinterested spectator, what Adam Smith called "the man within the breast." We acquire this internal spectator from others; eager to earn praise and avoid blame, we adjust our actions accordingly. To a degree that varies among individuals, but to some degree in almost all of us, we develop a visceral reaction to the actions that we contemplate, experiencing internally and automatically the prospect of praise or blame, whether or not it will actually occur. Of special importance is fear: our memory of unpleasant consequences begins to arouse our apprehension even when no consequences may occur. In this way our conscience is shaped. The stronger the conscience the more distant and uncertain the prospects that it will illuminate.

A sense of duty—a strong conscience—is not the product of repressed feelings of lust or rage directed at parents, but of precisely the opposite. Compared to bystanders, the gentiles who rescued Jews out of a sense of duty were particularly close to their parents. Suzanne described her family as emotionally "very close," as did Louisa, another highly principled rescuer. Both women recalled growing up in families that combined love with an emphasis on accepting personal responsibility and taking one's obligations seriously. But it would be a mistake to suppose that these women were taking great risks simply to please their parents. On the contrary; they had so internalized their principles that Suzanne did not tell her parents what she intended to do until after she had begun, and Louisa ignored her mother's urgings that she take care of her own children rather than run risks on behalf of someone else's.

The case of Suzanne and Louisa has much in common with accounts of social activists. Campus radicals and civil rights leaders during the 1960s were hardly in rebellion against their parents: they were taking parental values seriously, behaving in ways that were consistent with, albeit often more extreme than, what they had learned at home. In time journalistic talk of a "generation gap" was replaced with a far more accurate account of radical students following in the footsteps of radical parents, earning for themselves the label "red-diaper babies." We now know that conservative activists are quite similar to their leftist counterparts in at least this regard: for both groups, a politics of principle represents a continuation of, not a break with, parental attitudes. This is true not only in the United States but around the world. After analyzing the opinions of university students in eleven nations in 1969–70, Otto Klineberg was stuck by the fact that "so many students express a feeling of closeness to their parents rather than conflict."

Of course, the motives for public action will usually be more complex than those for private beliefs. When people are watching, a sense of principled obligation may be reinforced by (and in some cases play second fiddle to) a desire for power or status, a desire that can only be realized when the right opportunity presents itself. Social movements often founder on a struggle for influence among rival leaders or are corrupted by one leader's inability to distinguish between his followers' duty to a cause and their duty to him. In speaking of activists, it is important to distinguish the sense of duty (which leads people to act on principles) from the love of power (which leads them to manipulate principles).

. . .

LANGUAGE AND MORALITY

. . . What is striking about the newer findings of child psychologists is that the emergence of a moral sense occurs before the child has acquired much in the way of a language. The rudiments of moral action—a regard for the well-being of others and anxiety at having failed to perform according to a standard—are present well before anything like moral reasoning could occur. If mankind were not by nature social, if morality had to be written on a blank slate wholly by means of instruction, then it would not emerge until well after language had been acquired so that concepts could be understood, and by that time it would probably be too late. If the child's mind were truly a blank slate, it would probably remain, at least with respect to important matters, blank forever.

Indeed, the acquisition of language itself, rather than a necessary precursor of moral action, is itself a manifestation of the natural sociability of mankind. . . .

This view of how a moral sense emerges was stated with utmost clarity by Charles Darwin a century before developmental psychologists began to gather data that confirmed it. The third chapter of *The Descent of Man* is about the moral sense, and the key passage is this: "Any animal whatever, endowed with well-marked social instincts, would inevitably acquire a moral sense or conscience, as soon as its intellectual powers had become as well-developed, or nearly as well-developed, as in man."* . . .

Before Darwin, Adam Smith had attempted to base the moral sentiments on sympathy. While he agreed with Smith's view up to a point, Darwin saw that sympathy was not the sole foundation of moral conduct. For one thing, there are certain moral impulses, such as fairness and duty, the exercise of which does not

---

*Darwin, 1871:71–72. On the same page, Darwin chides John Stuart Mill and others for saying that moral feelings are entirely learned during each individual's lifetime. Since social feelings are instinctive in lower animals, "why should they not be so in man?" And since moral feelings arise out of social instincts, the notion that the former are solely the product of learning is "at least extremely improbable" (71, note 5).

depend on feeling compassion for others. For another, sympathy is aroused far more powerfully by a beloved person than by a passing stranger; while this explains why moral actions begin in familial settings and extend at first to family members, it does not explain how people come to assign value to the well-being of people they scarcely know or have never met or why people will often do their duty toward someone whose unpleasant manner elicits in us no sympathy whatsoever.

GENDER, TEMPERAMENT, AND MORAL SENSES*

. . .

Early childhood experiences interacting with innate temperamental differences may create a disposition to give greater emphasis to one or the other of the several moral senses. One person may be more inclined to emphasize justice, fairness, and duty, another to stress sympathy, care, and helping. If Harvard's Carol Gilligan and her colleagues are correct, the former emphasis is more characteristic of men, the latter of women. For example, when people are asked to describe moral dilemmas that they have faced or that they encounter in Aesop's fables, boys overwhelmingly do so in terms of justice (honoring contracts, making a fair division, or respecting rights) while girls are more likely to do so in terms of care (helping people in need, resolving conflict). . . .

. . . Under every experimental condition, women take less of the reward for themselves than do men, and they do so regardless of whether the partners with whom they are sharing are male or female. This does not mean that women are less greedy than men, but rather that they seem to apply somewhat different principles to the allocation process.

When a woman has performed better than her partner in some common task, she tends to split the reward equally; when a man has performed better than his partner, he divides the reward equitably (that is, in proportion to the value of each person's contributions). Men also give more to female partners than they do to male ones, whereas women do not allow the sex of their partner to influence their allocation decisions.

These findings hold true under one important condition: the participants expect to have further interactions with their partners. When they don't—when they perform a task with somebody they never expect to meet again—men and women allocate rewards in the same way. It is the prospect of future involvement that leads women to reduce the share they give themselves even when they are entitled to more. The clear implication is that women assign a higher value to ongoing relationships than do men. . . .

Though some students of child development suggest that individuals move through various stages of moral reasoning, with the highest stage being the one at

*I am acutely aware of the risks I run in writing of gender differences. On no topic is it easier to produce misunderstandings or arouse resentments. To some, any talk of differences implies a claim about rights. It does not. People can be equal without being the same.

which the individual applies universal principles of justice to moral dilemmas, this claim, in my view, assigns too much importance to how a person formulates justifications for his moral inclinations and too little to the inclinations themselves. (I also am a bit suspicious of any theory that says that the highest moral stage is one in which people talk like college professors.) Ranking moral stages from low to high does not capture the reality of many moral problems, which often involve choosing which of several moral sentiments ought to govern one's action. For these reasons, the theory that men and women differ in the kinds of moral sentiments they emphasize cannot be tested by measuring what stage each gender is in; much less can the worth of a man's moral sentiments be compared to that of a woman's by noting where each stands in the presumed hierarchy of moral stages. To say that the two sexes differ is not the same thing as saying that morality defined as justice and fairness is superior to morality defined as benevolence and caring. Everyone applies various combinations of principles and feelings to the management of moral problems. Sometimes principle and feeling coincide, and so no difficulty arises; indeed, in these circumstances we act reflexively, without having engaged in moral reasoning at all. Sometimes they diverge; and then, if we are calm and self-aware, we struggle to reconcile the competing dispositions. . . .

Whether the gender differences in moral sentiments that Gilligan observes in the United States will be found in East Asian (or other) cultures remains to be seen. But the problem of male socialization is, I think, the same everywhere; cultures differ not in whether they must cope with it, but how and with what success.

The Universal Aspiration

The most remarkable change in the moral history of mankind has been the rise—and occasionally the application—of the view that all people, and not just one's own kind, are entitled to fair treatment. Americans are so familiar with the passage in the Declaration of Independence asserting that "all men are created equal" that they forget how astonishing and, in a sense, unnatural that claim is. Of course, their actions often speak louder than their words. For Americans, as for peoples everywhere, morality governs our actions toward others in much the same way that gravity governs the motions of the planets: its strength is in inverse proportion to the square of the distance between them.

Children are intuitive moralists, but the range of their moral judgments is limited by the circumstances in which they are formed. Children feel sympathy for many playmates but not for all; they often feel obliged to act fairly toward others they know but less often to those whom they do not know. A difference in age of as little as one year or in location of as little as a hundred yards can mark the boundaries of their sense of obligation: a nine-year-old boy may regard an eight-year-old as unworthy of anything save condescension, and a group playing a game in front of one house may view a group in front of another house with suspicion or even hostility.

Older children may be even less tolerant than younger ones. Teenage boys living in one neighborhood often view those from another as rivals in games and as challengers for territory. Teenage girls define their friendship networks by standards of dress and demeanor that, however obscure to outsiders, are well understood and rigidly enforced by insiders. The minor cruelties that many adolescents practice on one another—by teasing, bullying, and social ostracism—reduce many young people to tearful despair over matters that, to adults, seem trivial.

Lest we adults think that these childlike prejudices disappear with age, we should remember the countless places where one group of adults has systematically reduced another to servitude and the numberless centuries during which men have used torture and merciless warfare to impose on others religious convictions that to someone from Mars would differ only in esoteric and irrelevant detail from the beliefs of the victims. Even people who fancy themselves too moral and cosmopolitan to practice slavery or religious persecution would do well to recall how wary they are when they encounter people who differ in race, accent, dress, or political outlook. Mankind has a moral sense, but much of the time its reach is short and its effect uncertain.

As I have attempted to show, the human proclivities and social experiences that give rise to our moral sense tend to make that sense operate in small groups more than in large ones, to say nothing of embracing mankind as a whole. Our natural sociability is reinforced by attachment to familiar others, and so we tend to value the familiar over the strange, the immediate over the distant; in common with most species, we are by nature locals, not cosmopolitans. To the extent that this is true, some observers argue that we are not, in any fundamental sense, moral at all; true morality, in their view, consists of having allegiance to and acting on the basis of principles of universal applicability. In his influential theory of moral development, Lawrence Kohlberg argued that people, as they grow up, move from lower stages of moral thinking (for example, breaking a rule is bad if you are punished for it) through higher stages (for example, you have a duty to obey rules even if you are not punished for breaking them) toward the highest stage, that of universal ethical principles (for example, the Golden Rule). In his version of the highest stage, Kohlberg was following in the footsteps of Immanuel Kant, to whom moral obligation had to rest on pure reason and in particular on the degree to which the maxim of one's action could be made a universal principle. In Kant's famous example, breaking a promise can never be moral, no matter how beneficial to the person who breaks it, because promise breaking, if made a universal rule, would be self-defeating: no one would ever accept a promise if it were known in advance that all promises could be broken whenever it was to the advantage of the maker.

The problem with Kant's example and with Kohlberg's stages is that they presuppose general agreement as to what constitutes the relevant universe within which a rule is to operate. It is not at all self-defeating to reformulate Kant's principle as follows: I, a white, Christian male living in a village in southern Lebanon, must always keep promises I make to others in my village, since it would be contradictory and self-defeating to will a rule that promises need not be kept, but I have no obligation to keep them to people living outside my universe, that is, to people in other villages, especially if they are Muslims, heathens, or women. They will cheat me at every opportunity and so I am free to cheat them; indeed, their readiness to cheat me shows that they are less than human and deserve no more respect than what I might give a goat. So long as my experience were consistent with this view—so long, that is, as I saw nothing self-contradictory in honoring promises to villagers and ignoring promises to strangers—I would be entitled to think of strangers as so defective in reason as to be undeserving of respect. My universe would be the village.

But mankind is not devoid of moral sense if most of its members treat villagers better than strangers and family better than nonkin. On the contrary; unless people are disposed to favor the familiar face to the strange one, their natural sociability would not become a moral sense at all. What is remarkable—indeed, what constitutes the most astonishing thing about the moral development of humanity—has been the slow, uneven, but more or less steady expansion of the idea that the moral sense ought to govern a wide range—perhaps, indeed, the whole range—of human interactions. Our universe has been enlarged.

DISCUSSION QUESTIONS

1. Both Adam Smith and James Q. Wilson draw a distinction between sympathy as a moral sentiment that is always present when we see another person in distress and sympathy as the source of human moral sentiments. Why is it important to make this distinction? What are some of the practical implications of both views of sympathy?

2. In our culture we often draw a sharp line between sentiment and reason. Why does Wilson disagree with this division? Discuss this question in light of Wilson's statement that to sympathize *is* to judge. Do you agree with Wilson? Use examples from your own life to support your answer.

3. Does Wilson offer convincing evidence that the moral sense in young children is innate rather than the result of the family and cultural influences? Are your moral values the same as your parents'? If not, on what grounds did you reject some of your family's moral values?

4. Do you agree with Wilson that morality arises out of our natural sociability? Is an action moral if the motive is to win the approval of others? To what extent do your actions stem from a desire to be liked or to belong?

5. What does Wilson mean when he refers to the uneasy relationship between conscience and sociability? Why is sociability alone not always sufficient in motivating us to act morally? Relate your answer to the Kitty Genovese case.

6. Why does Wilson find Freud's theory of the origins of the conscience scientifically implausible? Discuss Wilson's argument against the Freudian theory of the superego. Does your sense of moral duty stem from repressed feelings of lust or rage at your parents, as Freud claims? Or do you find Wilson's argument regarding the origin of the sense of moral duty more convincing? Support your position.

7. Wilson points out that the study of psychopaths can help us learn more about the moral sense. A psychopath is the quintessential ethical subjectivist. Psychopaths not only do not recognize the existence of universal moral standards, but their actions are consistent with this belief. What would life be like if everyone was really a psychopath?

8. Wilson argues that our moral sense becomes more developed as we get older. In what ways or directions does it develop, according to Wilson? What changes have you noticed in your own moral development over your lifetime?

Lawrence Kohlberg

The Philosophy of Moral Development

Educator and psychologist Lawrence Kohlberg (1927–1987) was director of the Harvard University Center for Moral Development and Education. Like Allan Bloom, Kohlberg was concerned with the problems of ethical relativism in teaching ethics. At the same time he was also opposed to the value indoctrination approach in which moral norms are simply imposed on students.

As a psychologist, Kohlberg was primarily influenced by the child psychologist Jean Piaget. Philosophically, Kohlberg was strongly influenced by such moral philosophers as Socrates, Immanuel Kant, and John Rawls—all philosophers whose works, Kohlberg believed, exemplified a high stage of moral reasoning. In the following selection Kohlberg discusses his six-stage theory of moral development. He then applies this theory to moral education. Kohlberg's contributions to the psychological study of morality have had a major impact on ethics education.

CRITICAL THINKING QUESTIONS

1. How did Kohlberg collect the data that was used for formulating his stage theory?
2. Why does Kohlberg reject cultural relativism?
3. What are the six stages of moral development? What are the three main levels of moral development?
4. Does all our moral reasoning, in Kohlberg's view, come from the same stage?
5. Why does Kohlberg claim that the higher (later) stages are preferable to lower stages?
6. Is moral development, according to Kohlberg, related to one's culture or religion?
7. What are some of the suggestions Kohlberg makes for incorporating developmental theory into ethics education?

The Philosophy of Moral Development (San Francisco: Harper & Row, 1981), pp. 16–28.

My own work on morality started from Piaget's notions of stages and Piaget's notion that the child was a philosopher. Inspired by Jean Piaget's (1948) pioneering effort to apply a structural approach to moral development, I have gradually elaborated over the years a typological scheme describing general stages of moral thought that can be defined independently of the specific content of particular moral decisions or actions. We studied seventy-five American boys from early adolescence on. These youths were continually presented with hypothetical moral dilemmas, all deliberately philosophical, some found in medieval works of casuistry. On the basis of their reasoning about these dilemmas at a given age, we constructed the typology of definite and universal levels of development in moral thought.

The typology contains three distinct levels of moral thinking, and within each of these levels are two related stages. These levels and stages may be considered separate moral philosophies, distinct views of the social-moral world.

We can speak of the children as having their own morality or series of moralities. Adults seldom listen to children's moralizing. If children throw back a few adult clichés and behave themselves, most parents—and many anthropologists and psychologists as well—think that the children have adopted or internalized the appropriate parental standards.

Actually, as soon as we talk with children about morality we find that they have many ways of making judgments that are not "internalized" from the outside and do not come in any direct and obvious way from parents, teachers, or even peers.

The preconventional level is the first of three levels of moral thinking; the second level is conventional; and the third is postconventional or autonomous. Although preconventional children are often "well behaved" and responsive to cultural labels of good and bad, they interpret these labels in terms of their physical consequences (punishment, reward, exchange of favors) or in terms of the physical power of those who enunciate the rules and labels of good and bad.

This level is usually occupied by children aged four to ten, a fact well known to sensitive observers of children. The capacity of "properly behaved" children of this age to engage in cruel behavior when there are holes in the power structure is sometimes noted as tragic (*Lord of the Flies* and *High Wind in Jamaica*), sometimes as comic (Lucy in *Peanuts*).

The second or conventional level also can be described as *conformist*—but that is perhaps too smug a term. Maintaining the expectations and rules of the individual's family, group, or nation is perceived as valuable in its own right. There is a concern not only with conforming to the individual's social order but in maintaining, supporting, and justifying this order.

The posconventional level is characterized by a major thrust toward autonomous moral principles that have validity and application apart from authority of the groups or people who hold them and apart from the individual's identification with those people or groups.

Within each of these three levels, there are two discernible stages. The following paragraphs explain the dual moral stages of each level just described.

DEFINITION OF MORAL STAGES

Preconventional Level

At this level, the child is responsive to cultural rules and labels of good and bad, right or wrong, but interprets these labels in terms of either the physical or the hedonistic consequences of action (punishment, reward, exchange of favors) or in terms of the physical power of those who enunciate the rules and labels. The level is divided into the following two stages:

Stage 1. The Punishment and Obedience Orientation

The physical consequences of action determine its goodness or badness regardless of the human meaning or value of these consequences. Avoidance of punishment and unquestioning deference to power are valued in their own right.

Stage 2. The Instrumental Relativist Orientation

Right action consists of that which instrumentally satisfies one's needs and occasionally the needs of others. Human relations are viewed in terms like those of the marketplace. Elements of fairness, reciprocity, and equal sharing are present, but they are always interpreted in a physical, pragmatic way. Reciprocity is a matter of "You scratch my back and I'll scratch yours."

Conventional Level

At this level, maintaining the expectations of the individual's family, group, or nation is perceived as valuable in its own right, regardless of immediate and obvious consequences. The attitude is not only one of conformity to personal expectations and social order, but of loyalty to it, of actively maintaining, supporting, and justifying the order and of identifying with the people or group involved in it. At this level, there are the following two stages:

Stage 3. The Interpersonal Concordance or "Good Boy–Nice Girl" Orientation

Good behavior is that which pleases or helps others and is approved by them. There is much conformity to stereotypical images of what is majority or "natural" behavior. Behavior is frequently judged by intention—the judgment "he means well" becomes important for the first time. One earns approval by being "nice."

Stage 4. Society Maintaining Orientation

There is an orientation toward authority, fixed rules, and the maintenance of the social order. Right behavior consists of doing one's duty, showing respect for authority, and maintaining the given social order for its own sake.

Postconventional, Autonomous, or Principled Level

At this level, there is a clear effort to define moral values and principles that have validity and application apart from the authority of the groups or people holding these principles and apart for the individual's own identification with these groups. This level again has two stages:

Stage 5. The Social Contract Orientation

Right action tends to be defined in terms of general individual rights and in terms of standards that have been critically examined and agreed on by the whole society. There is a clear awareness of the relativism of personal values and opinions and a corresponding emphasis on procedural rules for reaching consensus. Aside from what is constitutionally and democratically agreed on, the right is a matter of personal "values" and "opinion." The result is a emphasis on the "legal point of view," but with an emphasis on the possibility of changing law in terms of rational considerations of social utility (rather than freezing it in terms of Stage 4 "law and order"). Outside the legal realm, free agreement and contract are the binding elements of obligation. This is the "official" morality of the American government and Constitution.

Stage 6. The Universal Ethical Principle Orientation

Right is defined by the decision of conscience in accord with self-chosen ethical principles appealing to logical comprehensiveness, universality, and consistency. These principles are abstract and ethical (the Golden Rule, the categorical imperative); they are not concrete moral rules such as the Ten Commandments. At heart, these are universal principles of justice, of the reciprocity and equality of human rights, and of respect for the dignity of human beings as individuals.

To understand what these stages mean concretely, let us look at them with regard to two of twenty-five basic moral concepts or aspects used to form the dilemmas we used in our research. One such aspect, for instance, is "motive given for rule obedience or moral action." In this instance, the six stages look like this:

1. Obey rules to avoid punishment.
2. Conform to obtain rewards, have favors returned, as so on.
3. Conform to avoid disapproval and dislike by others.
4. Conform to avoid censure by legitimate authorities and resultant guilt.
5. Conform to maintain the respect of the impartial spectator judging in terms of community welfare.
6. Conform to avoid self-condemnation.

In another of these twenty-five moral aspects, the value of human life, the six stages can be defined thus:

1. The value of human life is confused with the value of physical objects and is based on the social status or physical attributes of the possessor.

2. The value of human life is seen as instrumental to the satisfaction of the needs of its possessor or of other people.

3. The value of human life is based on the empathy and affection of family members and others toward its possessor.

4. Life is conceived as sacred in terms of its place in a categorical moral or religious order of rights and duties.

5. Life is valued both in terms of its relation to community welfare and in terms of life being a universal human right.

6. Human life is sacred—a universal human value of respect for the individual.

I have called this scheme a *typology*. This is because about 67 percent of most people's thinking is at a single stage, regardless of the moral dilemma involved. We call our types *stages* because they seem to represent an invariant developmental sequence. "True" stages come one at a time and always in the same order.

In our stages, all movement is forward in sequence and does not skip steps. Children may move through these stages at varying speeds, of course, and may be found half in and half out of a particular stage. Individuals may stop at any given stage and at any age, but if they continue to move, they must move in accord with these steps. Moral reasoning of the conventional kind or Stages 3–4, never occurs before the preconventional Stage 1 and Stage 2 thought has taken place. No adult in Stage 4 has gone through Stage 5, but all Stage 5 adults have gone through Stage 4.

Although the evidence is not complete, my study strongly suggests that moral change fits the stage pattern just described.

As a single example of our findings of stage sequence, take the progress of two boys on the aspect "the value of human life." . . .

Let us take . . . Richard, to show us sequential movement through the remaining three steps. At age thirteen, Richard said about the mercy killing "If she requests it, it's really up to her. She is in such terrible pain, just the same as people are always putting animals out of their pain," and in general showed a mixture of Stage 2 and Stage 3 responses concerning the value of life. At sixteen, he said, "I don't know. In one way, it's murder, it's not right or privilege of man to decide who shall live and who should die. God put life into everybody on earth and you're taking away something from that person that came directly from God, and you're destroying something that is very sacred, it's in a way part of God and it's almost destroying a part of God when you kill a person. There's something of God in everyone."

Here Richard clearly displays a Stage 4 concept of life as sacred in terms of its place in a categorical moral or religious order. The value of human life is universal; it is true for all humans. It still, however, depends on something else—on respect for God and God's authority; it is not an autonomous human value. Presumably if God told Richard to murder, as God commanded Abraham to murder Isaac, he would do so.

At age twenty, Richard said to the same question, "There are more and more people in the medical profession who think it is a hardship on everyone, the person, the family, when you know they are going to die. When a person is kept alive by an artificial lung or kidney, it's more like being a vegetable than being a human. If it's her own choice, I think there are certain rights and privileges that go along with being a human being. I am a human being, and I have certain desires for life, and I think everybody else does too. You have a world of which you are the center, and everybody else does too, and in that sense we're all equal."

Richard's response is clearly Stage 5, in that the value of life is defined in terms of equal and universal human rights in a context of relativity ("You have a world of which you are the center, and in that sense we're all equal") and of concern for utility or welfare consequences.

At twenty-four, Richard says, "A human life, whoever it is, takes precedence over any other moral or legal value. A human life has inherent value whether or not it is valued by a particular individual. The worth of the individual human being is central where the principles of justice and love are normative for all human relationships."

This young man is at Stage 6 in seeing the value of human life as absolute in representing a universal and equal respect for the human as an individual. He has moved step by step through a sequence culminating in a definition of human life as centrally valuable rather than derived from or dependent on social or divine authority. . . .

In summary, the nature of our sequence in not significantly affected by widely varying social, cultural, or religious conditions. The only thing that is affected is the rate at which individuals progress through this sequence.

Why should there be such a universal invariant sequence of development? In answering this question, we need first to analyze these developing social concepts in terms of their internal logical structure. At each stage, the same basic moral concept or aspect is defined, but at each higher stage this definition is more differentiated, more integrated, and more general or universal. When one's concept of human life moves from Stage 1 to Stage 2, the value of life becomes more differentiated from the value of property, more integrated (the value of life enters an organizational hierarchy where it is "higher" than property so that one steals property in order to save life), and more universalized (the life of any sentient being is valuable regardless of status or property). The same advance is true at each stage in the hierarchy. Each step of development, then, is a better cognitive organization than the one before it, one that takes account of everything present in the previous stage but making new distinctions and organizes them into a more comprehensive or more equilibrated structure. The fact that this is the case has been demonstrated by a series of studies indicating that children and adolescents comprehend all stages up to their own, but not more than one stage beyond their own. . . . And, importantly, they prefer this next stage.

Moral thought, then, seems to behave like all other kinds of thought. Progress through the moral levels and stages is characterized by increasing differentiation and increasing integration, and hence is the same kind of progress that scientific theory represents. Like acceptable scientific theory—or like any theory or structure of knowledge—moral thought may be considered partially to generate its own data as it goes along, or at least to expand so as to contain in a balanced, self-consistent way a wider and wider experiential field. The raw data in the case of our ethical philosophies may be considered as conflicts between roles, or values, or as the social order in which people live.

The social worlds of all people seem to contain the same basic structures. All the societies we have studied have the same basic institutions—family, economy, law, government. In addition, however, all societies are alike because they are societies—systems of defined complementary roles. In order to play a social role in the family, school, or society, children must implicitly take the role of others toward themselves and toward others in the group. These role-taking tendencies form the basis of all social institutions. They represent various patternings of shared or complementary expectations. . . .

The way to stimulate stage growth is to pose real or hypothetical dilemmas to students in such a way as to arouse disagreement and uncertainty as to what is right. The teacher's primary role is to present such dilemmas and to ask Socratic questions that arouse student reasoning and focus student listening on one another's reasons.

I noted research by Rest (1973) showing that students prefer the highest stage of reasoning they comprehend but that they do not comprehend more than one stage above their own. As a result, assimilation of reasoning occurs primarily when it is the next stage up from the student's level. Developmental moral discussion thus arouses cognitive-moral conflict and exposes students to reasoning by other students at the next stage above their own.

Using this approach, Blatt and Kohlberg (1975) were able to stimulate one-third of experimental classes of students to advance one stage in a time period in which control classes remained unchanged in moral stage. One year later, the experimental classes retained their relative advance over the control classes.

The developmental approach, first experimentally elaborated by Blatt, is one that any thoughtful classroom teacher may practice. Unlike values clarification, its assumptions are not relativistic but, rather, are based on universal goals and principles. It asks the student for reasons, on the assumption that some reasons are more adequate than others.

The approach differs from indoctrinative approaches because it tries to move student's thinking in a direction that is natural for the student rather than moving the student in the direction of accepting the teacher's moral assumptions. It avoids preaching or didacticism linked to the teacher's authority.

As I have characterized developmental moral education, it is neither an indoctrinative or relativistic classroom discussion process. When we shift from a curriculum of moral discussion to the "hidden curriculum" of the classroom, a further set of philosophic and educational issues are raised. In my opinion, the resolution of these problems rests on creating a democratic classroom in which issues of fairness are settled by discussion and a democratic vote. These issues are discussed in Volume III and presuppose the concepts of justice developed in this volume.

DISCUSSION QUESTIONS

1. Examine the evidence Kohlberg uses to support his claim that moral development is similar in all cultures. Is the evidence compelling? Are his premises purely descriptive, or does he make certain prescriptive judgments (about what ought to be) in coming up with his theory?
2. Does Kohlberg's theory disprove ethical relativism? Discuss how a cultural relativist such as Ruth Benedict might explain Kohlberg's findings.
3. What answer does Kohlberg give to the question: Why bother to work on my moral development? Are you satisfied with his answer?
4. How might Kohlberg respond to Wilson's criticism that Kohlberg's stage theory incorrectly "presupposes general agreement as to what constitutes the relevant universe within which a rule is to operate"? Discuss whether this criticism of Kohlberg's theory is justified.
5. According to Kohlberg, different cultures encourage people to remain at different stages of moral development. Discuss some of the forces in our culture—including the college experience—that discourage people from developing past the conventional stage of moral development.
6. Kohlberg has been accused of ignoring women's experience in formulating his theory. Do you agree? Is his model of moral reasoning appropriate for both men and women? What are some examples of women's experience in making moral decisions that are neglected by Kohlberg?
7. Is Kohlberg's theory practical? Discuss ways in which Kohlberg's theory offers practical guidance for ethics education, both in the classroom and in your personal life.

Carol Gilligan

In a Different Voice

Carol Gilligan (b. 1936) is a professor of education at Harvard University. She argues that Kohlberg's emphasis on autonomy, rationality, and justice is biased toward men's thinking. Because both philosophers and psychologists have neglected to take into account women's perspectives, the impression has been created that women are morally deficient compared to men.

In the following selection from *In a Different Voice,* Gilligan examines women's ways of making moral decisions. She concludes that by viewing women in the context of their life cycle and relationships we can come up with a theory of moral development that is richer and more encompassing.

CRITICAL THINKING QUESTIONS

1. Why does Gilligan say that traditional descriptions of moral development, such as that used by Kohlberg, are biased against women? What examples does she use to support her position?

2. Why does this bias against women exist in Western culture?

3. What was Freud's view of women's moral development? Does Gilligan agree with Freud?

4. Does Gilligan accept Kohlberg's stages of moral development as appropriate for describing women's moral development?

5. Why does Gilligan regard the "male ethic" as inadequate?

6. What, according to Gilligan, are some of the differences in the ways in which men and women handle moral dilemmas?

7. What are the particular strengths of women, according to Gilligan, in making moral decisions?

Woman's Place in Man's Life Cycle

In the second act of *The Cherry Orchard,* Lopahin, a young merchant, describes his life of hard work and success. Failing to convince Madame Ranevskaya to cut down the cherry orchard to save her estate, he will go on in the next act to buy it himself. He is the self-made man who, in purchasing the estate where his father and grandfather were slaves, seeks to eradicate the "awkward, unhappy life" of

In a Different Voice (Cambridge, MA: Harvard University Press, 1982), pp. 5–8, 18–21, 23, 128–129, 173–174. Notes have been omitted.

the past, replacing the cherry orchard with summer cottages where coming generations "will see a new life." In elaborating this developmental vision, he reveals the image of man that underlies and supports his activity: "At times when I can't go to sleep, I think: Lord, thou gavest us immense forests, unbounded fields and the widest horizons, and living in the midst of them we should indeed be giants" —at which point, Madame Ranevskaya interrupts him, saying, "You feel the need for giants—They are good only in fairy tales, anywhere else they only frighten us."

Conceptions of the human life cycle represent attempts to order and make coherent the unfolding experiences and perceptions, the changing wishes and realities of everyday life. But the nature of such conceptions depends in part on the position of the observer. The brief excerpt from Chekhov's play suggests that when the observer is a woman, the perspective may be of a different sort. Different judgments of the image of man as giant imply different ideas about human development, different ways of imagining the human condition, different notions of what is of value in life.

At a time when efforts are being made to eradicate discrimination between the sexes in the search for social equality and justice, the differences between the sexes are being rediscovered in the social sciences. This discovery occurs when theories formerly considered to be sexually neutral in their scientific objectivity are found instead to reflect a consistent observational and evaluative bias. Then the presumed neutrality of science, like that of language itself, gives way to the recognition that the categories of knowledge are human constructions. The fascination with point of view that has informed the fiction of the twentieth century and the corresponding recognition of the relativity of judgment infuse our scientific understanding as well when we begin to notice how accustomed we have become to seeing life through men's eyes. . . .

. . . It all goes back, of course, to Adam and Eve—a story which shows, among other things, that if you make a woman out of a man, you are bound to get into trouble. In the life cycle, as in the Garden of Eden, the woman has been the deviant.

The penchant of developmental theorists to project a masculine image, and one that appears frightening to women, goes back at least to Freud . . . , who built his theory of psychosexual development around the experiences of the male child that culminate in the Oedipus complex. In the 1920s, Freud struggled to resolve the contradictions posed for his theory by the differences in female anatomy and the different configuration of the young girl's early family relationships. After trying to fit women into his masculine conception, seeing them as envying that which they missed, he came instead to acknowledge, in the strength and persistence of women's pre-Oedipal attachments to their mothers, a developmental difference. He considered this difference in women's development to be responsible for what he saw as women's developmental failure.

Having tied the formation of the superego or conscience to castration anxiety, Freud considered women to be deprived by nature of the impetus for a clear-cut Oedipal resolution. Consequently, women's superego—the heir to the Oedipus complex—was compromised: it was never "so inexorable, so impersonal, so independent of its emotional origins as we require it to be in men." From this observation of difference, that "for women the level of what is ethically normal is different from what it is in men," Freud concluded that women "show less sense of justice than men, that they are less ready to submit to the great exigencies of life, that they are more often influenced in their judgements by feelings of affection or hostility"....

Thus a problem in theory became cast as a problem in women's development, and the problem in women's development was located in their experience of relationships. Nancy Chodorow . . . , attempting to account for "the reproduction within each generation of certain general and nearly universal differences that characterize masculine and feminine personality and roles," attributes these differences between the sexes not to anatomy but rather to "the fact that women, universally, are largely responsible for early child care." Because this early social environment differs for and is experienced differently by male and female children, basic sex differences recur in personality development. As a result, "in any given society, feminine personality comes to define itself in relation and connection to other people more than masculine personality does" . . . .

In her analysis, Chodorow relies primarily on Robert Stoller's studies which indicate that gender identity, the unchanging core of personality formation, is "with rare exception firmly and irreversibly established for both sexes by the time a child is around three." Given that for both sexes the primary caretaker in the first three years of life is typically female, the interpersonal dynamics of gender identity formation are different for boys and girls. Female identity formation takes place in a context of ongoing relationship since "mothers tend to experience their daughters as more like, and continuous with, themselves." Correspondingly, girls, in identifying themselves as female, experience themselves as like their mothers, thus fusing the experience of attachment with the process of identity formation. In contrast, "mothers experience their sons as a male opposite," and boys, in defining themselves as masculine, separate their mothers from themselves, thus curtailing "their primary love and sense of empathic tie." Consequently, male development entails a "more emphatic individuation and a more defensive firming of experienced ego boundaries." For boys, but not girls, "issues of differentiation have become intertwined with sexual issues" . . . .

Writing against the masculine bias of psychoanalytic theory, Chodorow argues that the existence of sex differences in the early experiences of individuation and relationship "does not mean that women have 'weaker' ego boundaries than men or are more prone to psychosis." It means instead that "girls emerge from this period with a basis for 'empathy' built into their primary definition of self in a way that boys do not." Chodorow thus replaces Freud's negative and derivative description of female psychology with a positive and direct account of her own: "Girls emerge with a stronger basis for experiencing another's needs or feelings as one's own (or of thinking that one is so experiencing another's needs and feelings). Furthermore, girls do not define themselves in terms of the denial of preoedipal relational modes to the same extent as do boys. Therefore, regression to these modes tends not to feel as much a basic threat to their ego. From very early, then, because they are parented by a person of the same gender . . . girls come to experience themselves as less differentiated than boys, as more continuous with and related to the external object-world, and as differently oriented to their inner object-world as well" . . . .

Consequently, relationships, and particularly issues of dependency, are experienced differently by women and men. Of boys and men, separation and individuation are critically tied to gender identity since separation from the mother is essential for the development of masculinity. For girls and women, issues of femininity or feminine identity do not depend on the achievement of separation from the mother or on the progress of individuation. Since masculinity is defined through separation while femininity is defined through attachment, male gender identity is threatened by intimacy while female gender identity is threatened by separation. Thus males tend to have difficulty with relationships, while females tend to have problems with individuation. The quality of embeddedness in social interaction and personal relationships that characterizes women's lives in contrast to men's, however, becomes not only a descriptive difference but also a developmental liability when the milestones of childhood and adolescent development in the psychological literature are markers of increasing separation. Women's failure to separate then becomes by definition a failure to develop. . . .

The criticism that Freud makes of women's sense of justice, seeing it as compromised in its refusal of blind impartiality, reappears not only in the work of Piaget but also in that of Kohlberg. While in Piaget's account . . . of the moral judgment of the child, girls are an aside, a curiosity to whom he devotes four brief entries in an index that omits "boys" altogether because "the child" is assumed to be male, in the research from which Kohlberg derives his theory, females simply do not exist. Kohlberg's . . . six stages that describe the development of moral judgment from childhood to adulthood are based empirically on a study of eighty-four boys whose development Kohlberg has followed for a period of over twenty years. Although Kohlberg claims universality for his stage sequence, those groups not included in his original sample rarely reach his higher stages. . . . Prominent among those who thus appear to be deficient in moral development when measured by Kohlberg's scale are women, whose judgments seem to exemplify the third stage of his six-stage sequence. At this stage morality is conceived in interpersonal terms and goodness is equated with helping and pleasing others. This conception of goodness is considered by Kohlberg and Kramer . . . to be functional in the lives of mature women insofar as their lives take place in the home. Kohlberg and Kramer imply that only if women enter the traditional arena of male activity will they recognize the inadequacy of this moral perspective and progress like men toward higher stages where relationships are subordinated to rules (stage four) and rules to universal principles of justice (stages five and six).

Yet herein lies a paradox, for the very traits that traditionally have defined the "goodness" of women, their care for and sensitivity to the needs of others, are those that mark them as deficient in moral development. In this version of moral development, however, the conception of maturity is derived from the study of men's lives and reflects the importance of individuation in their development. Piaget . . . , challenging the common impression that a developmental theory is built like a pyramid from its base in infancy, points out that a conception of development instead hangs from its vertex of maturity, the point toward which progress is traced. Thus, a change in the definition of maturity does not simply alter the description of the highest stage but recasts the understanding of development, changing the entire account.

When one begins with the study of women and derives developmental constructs from their lives, the outline of a moral conception different from that described by Freud, Piaget, or Kohlberg begins to emerge and informs a different description of development. In this conception, the moral problem arises from conflicting responsibilities rather than from competing rights and requires for its resolution a mode of thinking that is contextual and narrative rather than formal and abstract. This conception of morality as concerned with the activity of care centers moral development around the understanding of responsibility and relationships, just as the conception of morality as fairness ties moral development to the understanding of rights and rules.

This different construction of the moral problem by women may be seen as the critical reason for their failure to develop within the constraints of Kolhberg's system. Regarding all constructions of responsibility as evidence of a conventional moral understanding, Kohlberg defines the highest stages of moral development as deriving from a reflective understanding of human rights. That the morality of rights differs from the morality of responsibility in its emphasis on separation rather than connection, in its consideration of the individual rather than the relationship as primary, is illustrated by two responses to interview questions about the nature of morality. The first comes from a twenty-five-year-old man, one of the participants in Kohlberg's study:

> [*What does the word morality mean to you?*] Nobody in the world knows the answer. I think it is recognizing the right of the individual, the rights of other individuals, not interfering with those rights. Act as fairly as you would have them treat you. I think it is basically to preserve the human being's right to existence. I think that is the most important. Secondly, the human being's right to do as he pleases, again without interfering with somebody else's rights.
>
> [*How have your views on morality changed since the last interview?*] I think I am more aware of an individual's rights now. I used to be looking at it strictly from my point of view, just for me. Now I think I am more aware of what the individual has a right to.

Kohlberg . . . cites this man's response as illustrative of the principled conception of human rights that exemplifies his fifth and sixth stages. Commenting on the response, Kohlberg says: "Moving to a perspective outside of that of his society, he identifies morality with justice (fairness, rights, the Golden Rule), with recognition of the rights of others as these are defined naturally or intrinsically. The human's being right to do as he pleases without interfering with somebody else's rights is a formula defining rights prior to social legislation" . . . .

The second response comes form a woman who participated in the rights and responsibilities study. She also was twenty-five and, at the time, a third-year law student:

[*Is there really some correct solution to moral problems, or is everybody's opinion equally right?*] No, I don't think everybody's opinion is equally right. I think that in some situations there may be opinions that are equally valid, and one could conscientiously adopt one of several courses of action. But there are other situations in which I think there are right and wrong answers, that sort of inhere in the nature of existence, of all individuals here who need to live with each other to live. We need to depend on each other, and hopefully it is not only a physical need but a need of fulfillment in ourselves, that a person's life is enriched by cooperating with other people and striving to live in harmony with everybody else, and to that end, there are right and wrong, there are things which promote that end and that move away from it, and in that way it is possible to choose in certain cases among different courses of action that obviously promote or harm that goal.

[*Is there a time in the past when you would have thought about these things differently?*] Oh, yeah, I think that I went through a time when I thought that things were pretty relative, that I can't tell you what to do and you can't tell me what to do, because you've got your conscience and I've got mine.

[*When was that?*] When I was in high school. I guess that it just sort of dawned on me that my own ideas changed, and because my own judgment changed, I felt I couldn't judge another person's judgment. But now I think even when it is only the person himself who is going to be affected, I say it is wrong to the extent it doesn't cohere with what I know about human nature and what I know about you, and just from what I think is true about the operation of the universe, I could say I think you are making a mistake.

[*What led you to change, do you think?*] Just seeing more of life, just recognizing that there are an awful lot of things that are common among people. There are certain things that you come to learn promote a better life and better relationships and more personal fulfillment than other things that in general tend to do the opposite, and the things that promote these things, you would call morally right.

This response also represents a personal reconstruction of morality following a period of questioning and doubt, but the reconstruction of moral understanding is based not on the primacy and universality of individual rights, but rather on what she describes as a "very strong sense of being responsible to the world." Within this construction, the moral dilemma changes from how to exercise one's rights without interfering with the rights of others to how "to lead a moral life which includes obligations to myself and my family and people in general." The problem then becomes one of limiting responsibilities without abandoning moral concern. When asked to describe herself, this woman says that she values "having other people that I am tied to, and also having people that I am responsible to. I have a very strong sense of being responsible to the world, that I can't just live for my enjoyment, but just the fact of being in the world gives me an obligation to do what I can to make the world a better place to live in, no matter how small a scale that may be on." Thus while Kohlberg's subject worries about people interfering with each other's rights, this woman worries about "the possibility of omission, of your not helping others when you could help them."

The issue that this woman raises is addressed by Jane Loevinger's fifth "autonomous" stage of ego development, where autonomy, placed in a context of relationships, is defined as modulating an excessive sense of responsibility through the recognition that other people have responsibility for their own destiny. The autonomous stage in Loevinger's account . . . witnesses a relinquishing of moral dichotomies and their replacement with "a feeling for the complexity and multi-faceted character of real people and real situations" . . . . Whereas the rights conception of morality that informs Kohlberg's principled level (stages five and six) is geared to arriving at an objectively fair or just resolution to moral dilemmas upon which all rational persons could agree, the responsibility conception focuses instead on the limitations of any particular resolution and describes the conflicts that remain.

Thus it becomes clear why a morality of rights and noninterference may appear frightening to women in its potential justification of indifference and unconcern. At the same time, it becomes clear why, from a male perspective, a morality of responsibility appears inconclusive and diffuse, given its insistent contextual relativism. Women's moral judgments thus elucidate the pattern observed in the description of the developmental differences between the sexes, but they also provide an alternative conception of maturity by which these differences can be assessed and their implications traced. The psychology of women that has consistently been described as distinctive in its greater orientation toward relationships and interdependence implies a more contextual mode of judgment and a different moral understanding: Given the differences in women's conceptions of self and morality, women bring to the life cycle a different point of view and order human experience in terms of different priorities. . . .

The elusive mystery of women's development lies in its recognition of the continuing importance of attachment in the human life cycle. Woman's place in man's life cycle is to protect this recognition while the developmental litany intones the celebration of separation, autonomy, individuation, and natural rights. The myth of Persephone speaks directly to the distortion in this view by reminding us that narcissism leads to death, that the fertility of the earth is in some mysterious way tied to the continuation of the mother-daughter relationship, and that the life cycle itself arises from an alternation between the world of women and that of men. Only when life-cycle theorists divide their attention and begin to live with women as they have lived with men will their vision encompass the experience of both sexes and their theories become correspondingly more fertile.

Women's Rights and Women's Judgment

When in the summer of 1848 Elizabeth Cady Stanton and Lucretia Mott convened a conference at Seneca Falls, New York, to consider "the social, civil and religious condition and rights of women," they presented for adoption a Declaration of Sentiments, modeled on the Declaration of Independence. The issue was simple, and the analogy made their point clear: women are entitled to the rights deemed natural and inalienable by men. The Seneca Falls Conference was spurred by the exclusion of Stanton and Mott, along with other female delegates, from participation in the World Anti-Slavery Convention held in London in 1840. Outraged by their relegation to the balconies to observe the proceedings in which they had come to take part, these women claimed for themselves in 1848 only what they had attempted eight years previously to claim for others, the rights of citizenship in a professedly democratic state. Anchoring this claim in the premise of equality and drawing on the notions of social contract and natural rights, the Seneca Falls Declaration argues no special consideration for women but simply holds "these truths to be self-evident: that all men and women are created equal; that they are endowed by their Creator with certain inalienable rights; that among these are life, liberty, and the pursuit of happiness."

But the claim to rights on the part of women had from the beginning brought them onto a seeming opposition with virtue, an opposition challenged by Mary Wollstonecraft in 1792. In "A Vindication of the Rights of Woman," she argues that liberty, rather than leading to license, is "the mother of virtue," since enslavement causes not only abjectness and despair but also guile and deceit. Wollstonecraft's "arrogance" in daring "to exert my own reason" and challenge "the mistaken notions that enslave my sex" was subsequently matched by Stanton's boldness in telling a reporter to "put it down in capital letters: SELF-DEVELOPMENT IS A HIGHER DUTY THAN SELF-SACRIFICE. The thing which most retards and militates against women's self-development is self-sacrifice." Countering the accusation of selfishness, the cardinal sin in the ladder of feminine virtue that reached toward an ideal of perfect devotion and self-abnegation, in relation not only to God but to men, these early proponents of women's rights equated self-sacrifice with slavery and asserted that the development of women, like that of men, would serve to promote the general good.

As in claiming rights women claimed responsibility for themselves, so in exercising their reason they began to address issues of responsibility in social relationships. This exercise of reason and the attempt of women to exert control over conditions affecting their lives led, in the latter half of the nineteenth century, to various movements for social reform, ranging from the social purity movements for temperance and public health to the more radical movements for free love and birth control. All of these movements joined in support of suffrage, as women, claiming their intelligence and, to varying degrees, their sexuality as party of their human nature, sought through the vote to include their voices in the shaping of history and to change prevailing practices that were damaging to present and future generations. While the disappointment of suffrage is recorded in the failure of many women to vote and the tendency of others in voting only to second their husbands' opinions, the twentieth century has in fact witnessed the legitimation of many of the rights the early feminists sought. . . .

Visions of Maturity

. . .

Among the most pressing items on the agenda for research on adult development is the need to delineate *in women's own terms* the experience of their adult life. My own work in that direction indicates that the inclusion of women's experience brings to developmental understanding a new perspective on relationships that changes the basic constructs of interpretation. The concept of identity expands to include the experience of interconnection. The moral domain is similarly enlarged by the inclusion of responsibility and care in relationships. And the underlying epistemology correspondingly shifts from the Greek ideal of knowledge as a correspondence between mind and form to the Biblical conception of knowing as a process of human relationship.

Given the evidence of different perspectives in the representation of adulthood by women and men, there is a need for research that elucidates the effects of these differences in marriage, family, and work relationships. My research suggests that men and women may speak different languages that they assume are the same, using similar words to encode disparate experiences of self and social relationships. Because these languages share an overlapping moral vocabulary, they contain a propensity for systematic mistranslation, creating misunderstandings which impede communication and limit the potential for cooperation and care in relationships. At the same time, however, these languages articulate with one another in critical ways. Just as the language of responsibilities provides a web-like imagery of relationships to replace a hierarchical ordering that dissolves with the coming of equality, so the language of rights underlines the importance of including in the network of care not only the other but also the self.

As we have listened for centuries to the voices of men and the theories of development that their experience informs, so we have come more recently to notice not only the silence of women but the difficulty in hearing what they say when they speak. Yet in the different voice of women lies the truth of an ethic of care, the tie between relationship and responsibility, and the origins of aggression in the failure of connection. The failure to see the different reality of women's lives and to hear the differences in their voices stems in part from the assumption that there is a single mode of social experience and interpretation. By positing instead two different modes we arrive at a more complex rendition of human experience which sees the truth of separation and attachment in the lives of women and men and recognizes how these truths are carried by different modes of language and thought.

To understand how the tension between responsibilities and rights sustains the dialectic of human development is to see the integrity of two disparate modes of experience that are in the end connected. While an ethic of justice proceeds from the premise of equality—that everyone should be treated the same— an ethic of care rests on the premise of nonviolence—that no one should be hurt. In the representation of maturity, both perspectives converge in the realization that just as inequality adversely affects both parties in an unequal relationship, so too violence is destructive for everyone involved. This dialogue between fairness and care not only provides a better understanding of relations between the sexes but also gives rise to a more comprehensive portrayal of adult work and family relationships.

As Freud and Piaget call our attention to the differences in children's feelings and thought, enabling us to respond to children with greater care and respect, so a recognition of the differences in women's experience and understanding expands our vision of maturity and points to the contextual nature of developmental truths. Through this expansion in perspective, we can begin to envision how a marriage between adult development as it is currently portrayed and women's development as it begins to be seen could lead to a changed understanding of human development and a more generative view of human life.

DISCUSSION QUESTIONS

1. Do you agree with Gilligan that relationships and caring are more important to women, whereas issues of rights and justice are more important to men? Compare and contrast Gilligan's and Kohlberg's stages of moral development. Does Gilligan offer a better alternative? Support your answer.

2. Would Gilligan find Wilson's description of the moral sense more acceptable than Kohlberg's? Does Wilson do a better job at taking into account women's ways of thinking about moral issues? Support your answer.

3. According to Gilligan and Nancy Chodorow, males and females experience childhood and adolescence differently. Do you agree? Use examples from your own experience to support your answer. Are these differences evident at the college level? How have these different experiences affected, and how do they continue to affect, your own moral development?

4. Is it true, as Gilligan claims, that our culture sees interdependence and inability to separate from our parents as a failure of development? Do you agree with Gilligan that interdependence can be good? To what extent does your current relationship with your family influence your moral development?

5. Discuss, in light of Gilligan's theory of moral development, the statement by Elizabeth Cady Stanton that "self-development is a higher duty than self-sacrifice." To what extent and why does our culture encourage self-sacrifice as a virtue in women? Is it also encouraged as a virtue for men?

6. Discuss whether Friedrich Nietzsche would agree or disagree with Gilligan's claim that women should strive to move beyond a morality based on self-sacrifice. Is what Nietzsche calls slave morality simply a stage in our moral development? Would Gilligan agree with Nietzsche's master morality as the highest stage of moral development? Support your answer.

7. How might Rousseau and Wollstonecraft respectively respond to Gilligan's claim that moral development is different for men and women?

8. Recent studies have shown that the differences between men's and women's moral reasoning is not as dramatic as Gilligan first thought. Studies have also found that most people, although tending to favor one perspective over the other, draw from both perspectives. Which of the two perspectives, the justice or care perspective, do you tend to favor in making moral decisions? Illustrate your answer with specific examples.

9. Discuss ways in which Gilligan's findings might be incorporated into ethics education in colleges.

Virginia Held

The Meshing of Care and Justice

Philosopher Virginia Held (b. 1929) is affiliated with the City University of New York. In her article "The Meshing of Care and Justice," Held discusses the respective roles of the justice and care perspectives in real-life moral contexts. Unlike Carol Gilligan, who in her later work came to see the care and justice perspectives as equally valid, Held argues that the care perspective provides a wider moral framework.

CRITICAL THINKING QUESTIONS

1. Why does Held regard as unsatisfactory the traditional division of justice as belonging to the public sphere and care as belonging to the private sphere?

2. What are some of the examples Held uses to support her position that justice is also important in the private sphere and care in the public sphere?

3. Does Held agree with Gilligan's position regarding the equal validity of the care and justice perspectives?

4. What role does justice play in morality?

5. Why does Held argue that the care perspective provides a wider moral framework than the justice perspective?

Feminist understandings of justice and care have by now made clear, in my view, that these are different values, reflecting different ways of interpreting moral problems and of expressing moral concern. And feminist discussion has also made clear that neither can be dispensed with: both are highly important for morality. Not all feminists agree, by any means, but this is how I see the debates of the last decade on these issues. . . .

What remains to be worked out, as I see it, is how justice and care and their related concerns fit together. How does the framework that structures justice, equality, rights, and liberty mesh with the network that delineates care, relatedness, and trust? Or are they incompatible views we must, at least at a given time and in a given context, choose between?

"The Meshing of Care and Justice," *Hypatia*, Spring 1995, 10 (2): 128–132. Notes have been omitted.

One clearly unsatisfactory possibility is to think that justice is a value appropriate to the public sphere of the political, while care belongs to the private domains of family and friends and charitable organizations. Feminist analyses have shown how faulty are traditional divisions between the personal and the political, but even if we use cleaned-up versions of these concepts, we can see how unsatisfactory it is to assign justice to public life and care to private, although I myself in earlier work may have failed to say enough along these lines. . . . I have argued that we need different moral approaches for different domains, and have tried to map out which are suitable for which domains. And there is an initial plausibility, certainly, in thinking of justice as a primary value in the domain of law, and care as a primary value in the domain of the family. But more needs to be said.

Justice is badly needed in the family as well as in the state: in a more equitable division of labor between women and men in the household, in the protection of vulnerable family members from domestic violence and abuse, in recognizing the rights of family members to respect for their individuality. In the practice of caring for children or the elderly, justice requires us to avoid paternalistic and materialistic domination.

At the same time, we can see that care is badly needed in the public domain. Welfare programs are an intrinsic part of what contemporary states provide, and no feminist should fail to acknowledge the social responsibilities they reflect, however poorly. The nightwatchman state is not a feminist goal. Almost all feminists recognize that there should be much more social and public concern for providing care than there now is in the United States, although it should be provided in appropriate and empowering ways very different from the current system of welfare. There should be greatly increased public concern for child care, education, and health care, infused with the values of care.

Caretaking is needed by everyone when they are children, ill, or very old, and it is needed by some most of their lives. Assuring that care is available to those who need it should be a central political concern, not one imagined to be a solely private responsibility of families and charities. Providing care has always fallen disproportionately to women and minorities, who do the bulk of unpaid or badly paid actual work of caring for those needing it. But in addition to a fairer division of responsibilities for care, the care made available through the institutions of the welfare state needs to be strengthened as well as reformed. Care and justice, then, cannot be allocated to the separate spheres of the private and the public. But they are different, and they are not always compatible.

Consider the category of "welfare" in its narrower sense rather than what is referred to by the term "welfare state." One way of thinking about the issues surrounding welfare and recommending action would be from a perspective of justice, equality, and rights. We could then recognize welfare as something to which each person is entitled by right under conditions of need. Welfare rights would be recognized as basic rights guaranteeing persons the resources needed to live. Against the traditional liberal view that freedom is negative only, we would recognize the positive rights of persons to what they need to act freely. And persons in need would be seen as entitled to the means to live, not as undeserving suppliants for private or public charity. An interpretation of such rights within the framework of justice would then be likely to yield monetary payments such as social security checks and unemployment insurance supplemented by other such payments for those in need. For many competent persons whose only major problem is a lack of money or a temporary lack of employment, such arrangements would seem recommended, and would be preferable to an array of social workers who are expected to practice care but who, whether because of paternalistic tendencies or bureaucratic constraints, often threaten the autonomy of persons in need.

Many persons, however, are not competent, autonomous, and only temporarily unemployed. Due to deficiencies of care at earlier stages or in various areas of their lives, their needs are complex and persistent. Inadequately cared for as children, at home, in school, and elsewhere, or inadequately provided with work and earning experience, they have grown up with more serious problems than a lack of money, or they suffer from illness or disability. In such cases care itself is needed. It should be addressed to specific persons and their needs. Dealing with these needs requires other specific persons to provide actual care and caring labor, not a machine turning out equal payments to all in a given category. The care should be sensitive and flexible, allowing for the interaction of care provider and care receiver in such a way that the care receiver is empowered to develop toward needing less care when such a decrease is part of a process of growth or training or recovery. When the care needed will be lasting, practices should evolve that preclude the provision of care from becoming dominating, and the receiving of care from becoming humiliating.

Whether we employ the perspectives of justice or care will affect how we interpret the moral problems involved and what we recommend as institutional policies or individual actions. We might try to combine care and justice into a recommendation concerning welfare that each person is entitled to the care needed for appropriate development, but such a recommendation will remain an abstract and empty formulation until we deal with just the kinds of very different policies and practices I've tried to outline.

If we try to see justice and care as alternative interpretations that we can apply to the same moral problem, as I think Carol Gilligan recommends, we can try to think of care and justice as different but equally valid. But we are still left with the question of which interpretation to apply when we act, or which to appeal to when we draw our recommendations. If we are merely describing the problem and possible interpretations of it, as in alternative literary accounts of it, we could maintain both of these alternative moral frameworks and not have to choose between them. But if policy decisions must be made about the problem, we will sometimes have to choose between these interpretations. If we use the analogy Gilligan suggests, should we see the figure as a duck or a rabbit? Moral theory should provide guidance for choice about actions and policies, and the problem of choosing between the interpretive frameworks of justice and care often persists after we have clarified both frameworks.

When the concerns of justice and care conflict, how should we try to reconcile these values? Does either have priority? Many philosophers have supposed that justice is the primary value of political institutions, but the example concerning welfare that I have been discussing is one from an important function of the modern state, and it did not yield the clear priority of justice over care. To suppose that the "justice system" of courts and law enforcement is the primary function of the contemporary state is surely unhelpful; to what extent it should or should not be would be among the very questions to be addressed by an adequately integrated ethic.

One possibility I have considered in the past is that justice deals with moral minimums, a floor of moral requirements beneath which we should not sink as we avoid the injustices of assault and disrespect. In contrast, care deals with what is above and beyond the floor of duty. Caring well for children, for instance, involves much more than honoring their rights to not be abused or deprived of adequate food; good care brings joy and laughter. But as a solution to our problem, I am coming to think that this is not clear. Perhaps one can have ever more justice in the sense of more and more understanding of rights, equality, and respect. And certainly there are minimums of care that *must* be provided for persons to live, though excellent care will far exceed them.

Another possible metaphor is that justice and rights set more or less absolute bounds or moral constraints within which we pursue our various visions of the good life, which would for almost everyone include the development of caring relationships. But this metaphor collapses for many of the same reasons as does that of justice as a floor of moral minimums. For instance, if there is anything that sets near absolute constraints on our pursuit of anything, including justice, it is responding to the needs of our children for basic care.

I now think—somewhat tentatively—that care is the wider framework into which justice should be fitted. Care seems to me the most basic moral value. As a practice, empirically described, we can say that without care we cannot have life at all. All human beings require a great deal of care in their early years, and most of us need and want caring relationships throughout our lives. As a value, care indicates what many practices ought to involve. When, for instance, necessities are provided without the relational human caring children need, children do not develop well, if at all. And when, in society, individuals treat each other with only the respect that justice requires, the social fabric of trust and concern can be missing or disappearing.

Though justice is surely a most important moral value, much life has gone on without it, and much of that life has been moderately good. There has, for instance, been little justice within the family, but much care; so we can have care without justice. Without care, however, there would be no persons to respect, either in the public system of rights—even if it could be just—or in the family. But care is not simply causally primary, it is more inclusive as a value. Within a network of caring, we can and should demand justice, but justice should not then push care to the margins, imagining justice's political embodiment as the model of morality, which is, I think, what has been done.

From a perspective of care, persons are relational and interdependent, not the individualistic autonomous agents of the perspective of justice and rights. This relational view is the better view of human beings, of persons engaged in developing human morality. We can decide to treat persons *as* individuals, to be the bearers of rights, for the sake of constructing just political and other institutions. But we should not forget the reality and the morality this view obscures. Persons *are* relational and interdependent. We can and should value autonomy, but it must be developed and sustained within a framework of relations of trust.

At the levels of global society and of our own communities, we should develop frameworks of caring about and for one another as human beings. These will of course be different from caring about and for the human beings who are members of our families or who are friends. We should care for one another as persons in need of a habitable environment with a sufficient absence of violence and with sufficient provision of care for human life to flourish. We need to acknowledge the moral values of the practices and family ties underlying the caring labor on which human life has always depended, and we need to consider how the best of these values can be better realized. Within a recognized framework of care we should see persons as having rights and as deserving justice, most assuredly. But we should embed this picture, I think, in the wider tapestry of human care.

Of course, in these short remarks, I cannot elaborate or fill in this tapestry. What I am trying to do is to suggest the directions in which I think we should be heading as we explore these issues of feminist morality.

DISCUSSION QUESTIONS

1. Held argues that the care perspective provides a wider moral framework into which "justice should be fitted." Carol Gilligan, on the other hand, came to believe that the care and justice perspectives are equally valid. Which of the two, Gilligan or Held, presents the strongest argument? Support your position.

2. Why does Held think that we need to give greater weight to the justice perspective in dealing with family issues? To what extent would paying more attention to issues of justice and rights help improve the status of children, women, and the elderly in our families? Use specific examples to illustrate your answer.

3. What evidence does Held use to support her argument that the care perspective is at least as important as the justice perspective in forming public policy? Do you agree with Held? How would public policy analyst Wilson most likely respond to Held's thesis?

4. Select a particular public policy issue such as welfare, same-sex marriages, or health care. Discuss it in light of the two perspectives. How helpful is each perspective in coming up with a public policy?

5. Why does Held argue that we need to further develop the care perspective at the level of global ethics? Do you agree with her?

6. Discuss the ethical teachings from the *Bhagavad Gita,* the *Bible,* and/or the *Qu'ran* in light of the care and justice perspectives. Do any of these teachings emphasize one perspective over another? To what extent do they successfully integrate the two perspectives? Use examples to support your answer.

Mark Twain

The Adventures of Huckleberry Finn

Author and lecturer Mark Twain (1835–1910) grew up around the Mississippi River at a time when the morality of slavery was beginning to be openly questioned. In *The Adventures of Huckleberry Finn,* Huck struggles between his sympathy for Jim, a runaway slave, and the official morality that does not recognize slaves as persons. In his struggle, Huck looks to his conscience for guidance.

The selection included here opens shortly after Huck and Jim have just made their escape from two shysters who were up to no good. Huck gets back to his raft and finds that Jim isn't there. Meanwhile a boy comes by and tells Huck that a runaway slave has just been captured a few miles down the river. The runaway slave matches Jim's description. This gets Huck to thinking about whether he should try to rescue Jim or whether he should turn him in to the authorities.

This selection is an excellent example of how the care and the justice perspectives are not mutually exclusive; rather, they work together in helping us make real-life moral decisions.

Critical Thinking Questions

1. What is the moral dilemma facing Huck?
2. Which passages show Huck using moral reasoning at the preconventional and conventional stages of moral reasoning? Why does he find this reasoning inadequate?
3. Which passages show Huck using postconventional moral reasoning?
4. Does Huck's religion help him in making his final decision?
5. Why did Huck tear up the letter to Miss Watson?
6. What did Huck mean when he said, after tearing up the letter, "All right, then, I'll *go* to hell"?

. . . I went to the raft, and set down in the wigwam to think. But I couldn't come to nothing. I thought till I wore my head sore, but I couldn't see no way out of the trouble. After all this long journey, and after all we'd done for them scoundrels, here it was all come to nothing, everything all busted up and ruined,

---

The Adventures of Huckleberry Finn (New York: Harper & Brothers, 1896).

because they could have the heart to serve Jim such a trick as that, and make him a slave again all his life, and amongst strangers, too, for forty dirty dollars.

Once I said to myself it would be a thousand times better for Jim to be a slave at home where his family was, as long as he'd *got* to be a slave, and so I'd better write a letter to Tom Sawyer and tell him to tell Miss Watson where he was. But I soon give up that notion for two things: she'd be mad and disgusted at his rascality and ungratefulness for leaving her, and so she'd sell him straight down the river again; and if she didn't, everybody naturally despises an ungrateful nigger, and they'd make Jim feel it all the time; and so he'd feel ornery and disgraced. And then think of *me!* It would get all around that Huck Finn helped a nigger to get his freedom; and if I was ever to see anybody from that town again I'd be ready to get down and lick his boots for shame. That's just the way: a person does a low-down thing, and then he don't want to take no consequences of it. Thinks as long as he can hide, it ain't no disgrace. That was my fix exactly. The more I studied about this the more my conscience went to grinding me, and the more wicked and low-down and ornery I got to feeling. And at last, when it hit me all of a sudden that here was the plain hand of Providence slapping me in the face and letting me know my wickedness was being watched all the time from up there in heaven, whilst I was stealing a poor old woman's nigger that hadn't ever done me no harm, and now was showing me there's One that's always on the lookout, and ain't a-going to allow no such miserable doings to go only just so fur and no further, I most dropped in my tracks I was so scared. Well, I tried the best I could to kinder soften it up somehow for myself by saying I was brung up wicked, and so I warn't so much to blame; but something inside of me kept saying, "There was the Sunday-school, you could a gone to it; and if you'd a done it they'd a learnt you there that people that acts as I'd been acting about that nigger goes to everlasting fire."

It made me shiver. And I about made up my mind to pray, and see if I couldn't try to quit being the kind of a boy I was and be better. So I kneeled down. But the words wouldn't come. Why wouldn't they? It warn't no use to try and hide it from Him. Nor from *me,* neither. I knowed very well why they wouldn't come. It was because my heart warn't right; it was because I warn't square; it was because I was playing double. I was letting *on* to give up sin, but away inside of me I was holding on to the biggest one of all. I was trying to make my mouth *say* I would do the right thing and the clean thing, and go and write to that nigger's owner and tell where he was; but deep down in me I knowed it was a lie, and He knowed it. You can't pray a lie—I found that out.

So I was full of trouble, full as I could be; and didn't know what to do. At last I had an idea; and I says, I'll go and write the letter—and *then* see if I can pray. Why, it was astonishing, the way I felt as light as a feather right straight off, and my troubles all gone. So I got a piece of paper and a pencil, all glad and excited, and set down and wrote:

Miss Watson, your runaway nigger Jim is down here two mile below Pikesville and Mr. Phelps has got him and he will give him up for the reward if you send.

                                                              HUCK FINN.

I felt good and all washed clean of sin for the first time I had ever felt so in my life, and I knowed I could pray now. But I didn't do it straight off, but laid the paper down and set there thinking—thinking how good it was all this happened so, and how near I come to being lost and going to hell. And went on thinking. And got to thinking over our trip down the river; and I see Jim before me all the time: in the day and in the night-time, sometimes moonlight, sometimes storms, and we a-floating along, talking and singing and laughing. But somehow I couldn't seem to strike no places to harden me against him, but only the other kind. I'd see him standing my watch on top of his'n, 'stead of calling me, so I could go on sleeping; and see him how glad he was when I come back out of the fog; and when I come to him again in the swamp, up there where the feud was; and such-like times; and would always call me honey, and pet me, and do every-thing he could think of for me, and how good he always was; and at last I struck the time I saved him by telling the men we had small-pox aboard, and he was so grateful, and said I was the best friend old Jim ever had in the world, and the *only* one he's got now; and then I happened to look around and see that paper.

It was a close place. I took it up, and held it in my hand. It was a-trembling, because I'd got to decide, forever, betwixt two things, and I knowed it. I studied a minute, sort of holding my breath, and then says to myself:

"All right, then, I'll *go* to hell"—and tore it up.

It was awful thoughts and awful words, but they was said. And I let them stay said; and never thought no more about reforming. I shoved the whole thing out of my head, and said I would take up wickedness again, which was in my line, being brung up to it, and the other warn't. And for a starter I would go to work and steal Jim out of slavery again; and if I could think up anything worse, I would do that, too; because as long as I was in, and in for good, I might as well go the whole hog. . . .

DISCUSSION QUESTIONS

1. What level of moral reasoning is Huck using when he first begins thinking about turn-ing in Jim? What level is Huck using when he makes his final decision? Discuss your answers using both Kohlberg's and Gilligan's stages.
2. Does Huck have a "moral sense?" Or is his morality simply the result of cultural con-ditioning? Use specific examples to illustrate your answer.
3. Why does Huck come to reject cultural relativism as a source of moral guidance? What, in the end, does Huck see as the source of morality?
4. Identify passages in this selection that illustrate Kohlberg's justice perspective and Gilligan's care perspective. Discuss how the two perspectives work together to help Huck make his final decision.
5. Identify the logical fallacies Huck uses in trying to come to a decision about whether to turn in Jim. Show how Huck recognized and rejected fallacies in his reasoning.

Eagle Man

We Are All Related

As we develop morally, our sense of moral community tends to become broader. Western philosophers and psychologists generally interpret the higher stages of moral development in terms of universal respect for all humans. However, many Native American and Eastern philosophers regard respect for the earth and all living beings, not just humans, as the goal of moral development.

Eagle Man, also known as Ed McGaa, is an Oglala Sioux writer and lawyer. He believes that all Native Americans share the same philosophy of life. In his excerpt from "We Are All Related," he looks to traditional Native American values for an ethic that is compatible with the survival of all living beings and the environment.

CRITICAL THINKING QUESTIONS

1. Why does Eagle Man think that we have to change our way of thinking about the world?
2. How is our way of thinking about the world reflected in our language?
3. What does Eagle Man mean by "respect for Mother Earth"? Why does Mother Earth deserve our respect?
4. Why does Eagle Man think that the traditional way of living of the American Indian is morally preferable to the current lifestyle of most Americans?
5. What are the four commandments of the Great Spirit?
6. Does Eagle Man think that these commandments are intended only for Native Americans? Or does he regard them as universal moral principles that are binding on everyone?

The plight of the non-Indian world is that it has lost respect for Mother Earth, from whom and where we all come.

We all start out in this world as tiny seeds—no different from our animal brothers and sisters, the deer, the bear, the buffalo, or the trees, the flowers, the

---

"We Are All Related," from Ed McGaa, *Mother Earth Spirituality: Native American Paths to Healing Ourselves and Our World* (San Francisco: Harper & Row, 1990), pp. 203–209.

winged people. Every particle of our bodies comes from the good things Mother Earth has put forth. Mother Earth is our real mother, because every bit of us truly comes from her, and daily she takes care of us.

The tiny seed takes on the minerals and the waters of Mother Earth. It is fueled by *Wiyo,* the sun, and given a spirit by *Wakan Tanka.*

This morning at breakfast we took from Mother Earth to live, as we have done every day of our lives. But did we thank her for giving us the means to live? The old Indian did. When he drove his horse in close to a buffalo running at full speed across the prairie, he drew his bow-string back and said as he did so, "Forgive me, brother, but my people must live." After he butchered the buffalo, he took the skull and faced it toward the setting sun as a thanksgiving and an acknowledgment that all things come from Mother Earth. He brought the meat back to camp and gave it first to the old, the widowed, and the weak. For thousands of years great herds thrived across the continent because the Indian never took more than he needed. Today, the buffalo is gone.

You say *ecology.* We think the words *Mother Earth* have a deeper meaning. If we wish to survive, we must respect her. It is very late, but there is still time to revive and discover the old American Indian value of respect for Mother Earth. She is very beautiful, and already she is showing us signs that she may punish us for not respecting her. Also, we must remember she has been placed in this universe by the one who is the All Powerful, the Great Spirit Above, or *Wakan Tanka*—God. But a few years ago, there lived on the North American continent people, the American Indians, who knew a respect and value system that enabled them to live on their native grounds without having to migrate, in contrast to the white brothers and sisters who migrated by the thousands from their homelands because they had developed a value system different from that of the American Indian. There is no place now to which we can migrate, which means we can no longer ignore the red man's value system.

Carbon-dating techniques say that the American Indian has lived on the North American continent for thousands upon thousands of years. If we did migrate, it was because of a natural phenomenon—a glacier. We did not migrate because of a social system, value system, and spiritual system that neglected its responsibility to the land and all living things. We Indian people say we were always here.

We, the American Indian, had a way of living that enabled us to live within the great, complete beauty that only the natural environment can provide. The Indian tribes had a common value system and a commonality of religion, without religious animosity, that preserved that great beauty that the two-leggeds definitely need. Our four commandments from the Great Spirit are: (1) respect for Mother Earth, (2) respect for the Great Spirit, (3) respect for our fellow man and woman, and (4) respect for individual freedom (provided that individual freedom does not threaten the tribe or the people or Mother Earth).

We who respect the great vision of Black Elk see the four sacred colors as red, yellow, black, and white. They stand for the four directions—red for the east, yellow for the south, black for the west, and white for the north.

From the east comes the rising sun and new knowledge from a new day.

From the south will come the warming south winds that will cause our Mother to bring forth the good foods and grasses so that we may live.

To the west where the sun goes down, the day will end, and we will sleep; and we will hold our spirit ceremonies at night, from where we will communicate with the spirit world beyond. The sacred color of the west is black; it stands for the deep intellect that we will receive from the spirit ceremonies. From the west come the life-giving rains.

From the north will come the white winter snow that will cleanse Mother Earth and put her to sleep, so that she may rest and store up energy to provide the beauty and bounty of springtime. We will prepare for aging by learning to create, through our arts and crafts, during the long winter season. Truth, honesty, strength, endurance, and courage also are represented by the white of the north. Truth and honesty in our relationships bring forth harmony.

All good things come from these sacred directions. These sacred directions, or four sacred colors, also stand for the four races of humanity: red, yellow, black, and white. We cannot be a prejudiced people, because all men and women are brothers and sisters and because we all have the same mother—Mother Earth. One who is prejudiced, who hates another because of that person's color, hates what the Great Spirit has put here. Such a one hates that which is holy and will be punished, even during this lifetime, as humanity will be punished for violating Mother Earth. Worse, one's conscience will follow into the spirit world, where it will be discovered that all beings are equal. This is what we Indian people believe.

We, the Indian people, also believe that the Great Spirit placed many people throughout this planet: red, yellow, black, and white. What about the brown people? The brown people evolved from the sacred colors coming together. Look at our Mother Earth. She, too, is brown because the four directions have come together. After the Great Spirit, *Wakan Tanka,* placed them in their respective areas, the *Wakan Tanka* appeared to each people in a different manner and taught them ways so that they might live in harmony and true beauty. Some men, some tribes, some nations have still retained the teachings of the Great Spirit. Others have not. Unfortunately, many good and peaceful religions have been assailed by narrow-minded zealots. Our religious beliefs and our traditional Indian people have suffered the stereotype that we are pagans, savages, or heathens; but we do not believe that only one religion controls the way to the spirit world that lies beyond. We believe that *Wakan Tanka* loves all of its children equally, although the Great Spirit must be disturbed at times with those children who have destroyed proven value systems that practiced sharing and generosity and kept Mother Earth viable down through time. We kept Mother Earth viable because we did not sell her or our spirituality!

Brothers and sisters, we must go back to some of the old ways if we are going to truly save our Mother Earth and bring back the natural beauty that every person seriously needs, especially in this day of vanishing species, vanishing rain forests, overpopulation, poisoned waters, acid rain, a thinning ozone layer, drought, rising temperatures, and weapons of complete annihilation.

Weapons of complete annihilation? Yes, that is how far the obsession with war has taken us. These weapons are not only hydraheaded; they are hydroheaded as well, meaning that they are the ultimate in hydrogen bomb destruction. We will have to divert our obsessions with defense and wasteful, all-life-ending weapons of war to reviving our environment. If such weapons are ever fired, we will wind up destroying ourselves. The Armageddon of war is something that we have all been very close to and exposed to daily. However, ever since that day in August when people gathered in fields and cities all across the planet to beseech for peace and harmony, it appears that we are seeing some positives steps toward solving this horror. *Maybe some day two-leggeds will read this book and missiles will no longer be pointed at them.*

The quest for peace can be more efficiently pursued through communication and knowledge than by stealth and unending superior weaponry. If the nations of the world scale back their budgets for weaponry, we will have wealth to spend to solve our serious environmental problems. Our home planet is under attack. It is not an imagined problem. This calamity is upon us now. We are in a real war with the polluting, violating blue man of Black Elk's vision.

Chief Sitting Bull advised us to take the best of the white man's ways and to take the best of the old Indian ways. He also said, "When you find something that is bad, or turns out bad, drop it and leave it alone."

The fomenting of fear and hatred is something that has turned out very badly. This can continue no longer; it is a governmental luxury maintained in order to support pork-barrel appropriations to the Department of Defense, with its admirals and generals who have substituted their patriotism for a defense contractor paycheck after retirement. War has become a business for profit. In the last two wars, we frontline warriors—mostly poor whites and minoritiess—were never allowed to win our wars, which were endlessly prolonged by the politicians and profiteers, who had their warrior-aged sons hidden safely away or who used their powers, bordering on treason, to keep their offspring out of danger. The wrong was that the patriotic American or the poor had to be the replacement. The way to end wars in this day and age is to do like the Indian: put the chiefs and their sons on the front lines.

Sitting Bull answered a relative, "Go ahead and follow the white man's road and do whatever the [Indian] agent tells you. But I cannot so easily give up my old ways and Indian habits; they are too deeply ingrained in me."

My friends, I will never cease to be an Indian. I will never cease respecting the old Indian values, especially our four cardinal commandments and our values of generosity and sharing. It is true that many who came to our shores brought a great amount of good to this world. Modern medicine, transportation, communication, and food production are but a few of the great achievements that we should all appreciate. But it is also true that too many of those who migrated to North America became so greedy and excessively materialistic that great harm has been caused. We have seen good ways and bad ways. The good way of the non-Indian way I am going to keep. The very fact that we can hold peace-seeking communication and that world leaders meet and communicate for peace shows the wisdom of the brothers and sisters of this time. By all means, good technology should not be curtailed, but care must be taken lest our water, air, and earth become irreparably harmed. The good ways I will always respect and support. But, my brothers and sisters, I say we must give up this obsession with excess consumption and materialism, especially when it causes the harming of the skies surrounding our Mother and the pollution of the waters upon her. *She is beginning to warn us!*

Keep those material goods that you need to exist, but be a more sharing and generous person. You will find that you can do with less. Replace this empty lifestyle of hollow impressing of the shallow ones with active participation for your Mother Earth. At least then, when you depart into the spirit world, you can look back with pride and fulfillment. Other spirit beings will gather around you, other spirits of your own higher consciousness will gather around you and share your satisfaction with you. The eternal satisfaction of knowing you did not overuse your Mother Earth and that you were here to protect her will be a powerful satisfaction when you reach the spirit world.

Indian people do not like to say that the Great Mystery is exactly this or exactly that, but we do know there is a spirit world that lies beyond. We are allowed to know that through our ceremonies. We know that we will go into a much higher plane beyond. We know nothing of hell-fire and eternal damnation from some kind of unloving power that placed us here as little children. None of that has ever been shown to us in our powerful ceremonies, conducted by kind, considerate, proven, and very nonmaterialistic leaders. We do know that everything the Great Mystery makes is in the form of a circle. Our Mother Earth is a very large, powerful circle.

Therefore, we conclude that our life does not end. A part of it is within that great eternal circle. If there is a hell, then our concept of hell would be an eternal knowing that one violated or took and robbed from Mother Earth and caused this suffering that is being bestowed upon the generations unborn. This then, if it were to be imprinted upon one's eternal conscience, this would surely be a terrible, spiritual, mental hell. Worse, to have harmed and hurt one's innocent fellow beings, and be unable to alter (or conceal) the harmful actions would also be a great hell. Truth in the spirit world will not be concealed, nor will it be for sale. Lastly, we must realize that the generations unborn will also come into the spirit world. Let us be the ones that they wish to thank and congratulate, rather than eternally scorn.

While we are shedding our overabundant possessions, and linking up with those of like minds, and advancing spiritual and environmental appreciation, we should develop a respect for the aged and for family-centered traditions, even those who are single warriors, fighting for the revitalization of our Mother on a lone, solitary, but vital front. We should have more respect for an extended family, which extends beyond a son or a daughter, goes beyond to grandparents and aunts and uncles, goes beyond to brothers, sisters, aunts, and uncles that we have adopted or made as relatives—and further beyond, to the animal or plant world as our brothers and sisters, to Mother Earth and Father Sky and then above to *Wakan Tanka*, the *Unci/Tankashilah,* the Grandparent of us all. When we pray directly to the Great Spirit, we say *Unci* (Grandmother) or *Tankashilah* (Grandfather) because we are so family-minded that we think of the Great Power above as a grandparent, and we are the grandchildren. Of course, this is so because every particle of our being is from Mother Earth, and our energy and life force are fueled by Father Sky. This is a vital part of the great, deep feeling and spiritual psychology that we have as Indian people. It is why we preserved and respected our ecological environment for such a long period. *Mitakuye oyasin!* We are all related!

In conclusion, our survival is dependent on the realization that Mother Earth is a truly holy being, that all things in this world are holy and must not be violated, and that we must share and be generous with one another. You may call this thought by whatever fancy words you wish—psychology, theology, sociology, or philosophy—but you must think of Mother Earth as a living being. Think of your fellow men and women as holy people who were put here by the Great Spirit. Think of being related to all things! With this philosophy in mind as we go on with our environmental ecology efforts, our search for spirituality, and our quest for peace, we will be far more successful when we truly understand the Indians' respect for Mother Earth.

DISCUSSION QUESTIONS

1. What does Eagle Man mean when he says that the words *Mother Earth* have "a deeper meaning" than the word *ecology*? Discuss ways in which language marginalizes certain beings. How can our choice of words reflect moral respect or lack of respect for certain beings? Use specific examples to illustrate your answer.
2. Is Eagle Man's concept of moral maturity compatible with Kohlberg's? Does it go beyond Kohlberg's, or does it offer a completely different concept of moral development?
3. Compare and contrast the moral philosophy of Eagle Man with traditional Western philosophies, such as Aquinas's natural law theory, which maintain that humans are above and separate from nature. Which philosophy do you find most satisfactory?
4. Does Eagle Man's philosophy offer practical guidelines for making everyday moral decisions? What are some of the implications of Eagle Man's philosophy for your own life and lifestyle?
5. Our moral beliefs have a strong influence on our actual behavior. Do you agree with Eagle Man that we have to change the way we think about Mother Earth if we as humans are going to survive? What recommendations might Eagle Man make for teaching ethics in college?

Chapter Applications

1. "Monster" Kody Scott

At the age of 11 "Monster" Kody Scott was recruited into the Crips, a notorious South Central Los Angeles gang. His brutality earned him the nickname "Monster." As a gang member, Scott's motto was "*My neighborhood,* right or wrong." "Death, or fear of death," he later wrote, "became my constant companion. But still my dedication, my patriotism, was strong."[1]

At the age of 19, while in prison, Scott attended a Muslim service where he met Muhammad Abdullah who taught Scott that he was a member of a moral community beyond that of his gang or neighborhood. Scott later wrote regarding his friendship with Muhammad: "My consciousness about the larger enemy was being raised bit by bit. . . . Muhammad and I kept in contact, and he sent me a lot of literature, mostly Islamic but always Afrocentric. The banging mentality [. . . killin' and not caring, and dying without fear . . . love for your set and hate for the enemy . . .] was still uppermost in my mind. . . . But questions of right and wrong now came to my mind immediately after every action I took. Muhammad had made a tremendous difference in my life that was barely noticeable then, but cannot be overlooked today."[2]

It took several years for Scott to develop to the point where, according to him, Muhammad's teachings really made sense. Scott changed his name to Sanyika Shakur, published an autobiography of his life, and began taking an interest in political issues and the problem of racism. He was released from Pelican Bay State Prison in September 1995.

Since then, Shakur has served a short sentence for a parole violation. The LAPD who arrested him on the violation found him on the porch of a South Central Los Angeles house, signing autographs for a crowd of admirers. According to the police, Shakur was "cooperative and unintimidating"—a surprising change from the "Monster" Kody Scott they had known.[3] Shakur is currently working on a second book.

Discussion Questions

1. What most likely was Shakur's stage of moral development prior to meeting Muhammad Abdullah? How did Muhammad's moral reasoning differ from Shakur's?

2. Discuss how Shakur's life as a gang member illustrates some of the problems in an ethical relativist's moral reasoning.

3. What are some of the factors that made Shakur reassess his level of moral reasoning? How important is having a positive role model who challenges our thinking in enhancing moral development?

4. How can we know if a person who previously exhibited a lower level of moral reasoning has changed? If you were Shakur's parole officer, what sort of questions might you ask him or what sort of evidence would you want to determine if his change is genuine?

5. Can criminals be rehabilitated or reformed? If so, is jail the best way to reform criminals, or does jail impede moral development? Support your answer.

2. *Gandhi: Moral Saint*

Born in India in 1869, Mohandas Gandhi showed a high degree of moral sensitivity and interest in issues of right and wrong, taking on the role of peacekeeper when playing games with other children. At the age of 13 his parents arranged a marriage to Kasturba, a girl his own age.

During his college years in England, Gandhi had the usual aspirations. George Orwell writes: "There was a time . . . when [Gandhi] wore a top hat, took dancing lessons, studied French and Latin, went up the Eiffel Tower, and even tried to learn the violin—all this was the idea of assimilating European civilization as thoroughly as possible."[4]

In 1893 Gandhi went to South Africa to practice law. Here he immediately ran into discrimination because of his Indian heritage. It was only because of this, and rather unwillingly, that Gandhi changed his views and developed civil disobedience as a political and moral strategy. When he returned to India twenty-one years later, Gandhi became a nationalist leader and an opponent of British imperialism and the rigid Hindu caste system.

Gandhi believed that "To love humanity as a whole, one cannot give one's preference to any individual person."[5] To achieve this, Gandhi abstained from sexual intercourse and close friendships. His refusal to give preference to his family or to have sexual relations with his wife became a cause of stress within his family. Gandhi also abstained from meat, spices, alcohol, and tobacco. He believed that it was better to let someone die than to eat meat. On three different occasions, he refused an animal-based medical treatment for ailing members of his family. On the other hand, Gandhi's unflinching commitment to justice and his nonviolent leadership led to substantial improvements in civil rights and to the eventual independence of India from British rule in 1947.

Discussion Questions

1. Both Gilligan and Kohlberg point out that movement from one stage of moral reasoning to the next is generally preceded by cognitive or social dissonance. Discuss the events that led to Gandhi's transition from a conventional moral reasoner to a postconventional moral reasoner.

2. Is Gandhi's moral reasoning more justice oriented or more care oriented? Support your answer.

3. George Orwell once wrote that sainthood is "a thing that human beings must avoid." Is moral perfection or sainthood a noble goal? Is it possible to seek

moral perfection and still remain humane? Does humanity require that we show preferential treatment toward our family and friends? Can this favoritism be reconciled with moral perfection?

4. Orwell argues that Gandhi's vegetarianism, although perhaps noble, was inhumane when carried to the point where he would stick to his moral principles at the expense of his family's health. Is it possible to be too principled? Support your answer. Discuss how Lawrence Kohlberg and Virginia Held might each respond to this question.

3. The Subservient Wife

In Amy Tan's novel *The Joy Luck Club*, Rose Hsu Jordan was the perfect wife. She sacrificed her dreams of a career and habitually deferred to her husband Ted's wishes. "Over the years," Rose explains, "Ted decided where we went on vacation. He decided what new furniture we should buy. . . . We used to discuss some of these matters, but we both knew the question would boil down to my saying, 'Ted, you decide.' After a while, there were no more discussions. Ted simply decided."

After taking stock of his life following a crisis at work, Ted finds he is no longer satisfied with a wife who does not think for herself. He asks Rose to share in the family decisions. "I thought about things, the pros and the cons," Rose recalls. "But in the end I would be so confused, because I never believed there was any one right answer, yet there were many wrong ones. So whenever I said, 'You decide,' or 'I don't care,' or 'Either way is fine with me,' Ted would say in his impatient voice, 'No *you* decide.' 'You can't have it both ways, none of the responsibility, none of the blame."

When Ted asks Rose for a divorce, she is stunned. She tried "to listen to her heart, to make the right decision." But it had been so long since she had made an important decision for herself that she didn't even know what her options were. "My mother once told me why I was so confused all the time," she recalls. "She said I was without wood. Born without wood so that I listened to too many people. . . . But by the time she told me this, it was too late."[6]

Discussion Questions

1. Gilligan claims that our culture does not encourage the transition from conventional moral reasoning (cultural relativism) to moral maturity. The identification of good women with self-sacrifice and deference to others' wishes can be destructive to women's self-esteem as well as to their ability to be in genuine caring relationships. Do you agree?

2. Is servility ever a virtue? Is it morally acceptable to abdicate responsibility for our lives to another person? Is servility morally acceptable if the servile person enjoys habitually putting the needs of others before her or his own and if the dominant person also enjoys being in control? Support your answer.

3. Discuss the meaning of the statement that Rose was confused because she was "born without wood." What does this mean? Would Mencius and Wilson agree?

4. Do people have an obligation to work on their moral development? If so, what is the source of this obligation?

5. Is it immoral to simply accept another person's servile or self-destructive behavior (such as alcoholism) in a relationship? Do we have a moral obligation to expect better from others? What if they refuse to change? What should Ted have done when Rose refused to or seemed unable to change?

6. What advice might Nietzsche have for Rose? Create a conversation between the two.

4. The Moral Context of College Football

In 1995 Lawrence Phillips, a player for the University of Nebraska football team, broke into an apartment, beat up his former girlfriend, and dragged her down three flights of stairs.[7] As punishment, Phillips was ordered to pay his victim's uninsured medical expenses and repairs to the apartment, attend counseling sessions on anger control, and perform community service. Phillips was reinstated on the team after only a one-month suspension. "Lawrence needs football as a structure for his life," Husker's coach Tom Osborne explained.[8] Football, apparently, was Phillip's only community.

However, L. Gregory Jones, author of *Embodying Forgiveness,* suggests that football may not provide the moral context Phillips needs. The fellowship of athletes, Jones points out, did not prevent Phillips from assaulting his former girlfriend. In fact, his privileged status as a football star regarding his light punishment may even have reinforced his abusive attitude toward women.

Research supports Jones's position. Studies show that participation and interest in high-contact sports, such as boxing and football, is associated with greater tendencies to engage in aggression, including sexual assault,[9] as well as immature egocentric moral reasoning. This is because athletes are encouraged to focus on their own goals, or those of their team, to the relative neglect of concern for the well-being of others.[10] The low level of moral reasoning reinforced by contact sports can also spill over into everyday moral reasoning. Studies have found an increase in violence in college dormitories on football weekends and Super Bowl Sundays.

Discussion Questions

1. Do we have a moral obligation to avoid or remove ourselves from situations, such as participating in or attending football games, that may tend to inhibit moral growth? Support your answer.

2. Although contact sports may inhibit some people's moral development, others seem to be able to separate their behavior in sports and in the real world. For example, former heavyweight boxing champion Larry Holmes once said that before he enters the ring "I have to change, I have to leave the goodness

out and bring all the bad in, like Dr. Jekyll and Mr. Hyde."[11] Would it be fair if athletes like Holmes, even though they may be in the minority, were deprived of the opportunity to engage in contact sports because some players and fans are unable to separate sports and real life?

3. Jones points out that college athletes often get little more than a slap on the wrist when they engage in violent behavior off the field. Is this the case at your college? Discuss ways in which violence on campus might be handled so as to promote offenders' moral development rather than reinforce lower levels of moral reasoning.

4. More women are getting involved in contact sports. In 1994 there were only 295 young women playing high school varsity football in the United States; by the end of 1996, this figure had climbed to 791.[12] Is this a desirable trend? Support your answer.

5. Devise a campus policy regarding contact sports. Discuss ways in which the sports programs and athletic events might be structured so as to counteract some of the negative effects of contact sports and to promote moral development.

5. The Jilted Boyfriend: "My Low Self-Esteem Made Me Do It"

John Anthony Diaz and Kimberlee Brown met in August 1991 at the Mill Hill Club, a nightclub on Cape Cod. After ten months Brown broke off the relationship. In 1993 Brown became engaged to someone else. On the day of her bridal shower Diaz went to the Brown house in a jealous rage. He hid behind a tree until he thought he saw Kimberlee approaching. Diaz then jumped out and shot 25-year-old Dawn Brown, Kimberlee's look-alike sister. Dawn died six hours later of a gunshot wound to the face.

After three years on the lam, Diaz was captured in Guyana after someone saw him on the television show *Unsolved Mysteries.* In his defense at his trial for the murder of Dawn Brown, Diaz argued that his judgment was impaired by the self-loathing he felt when Kimberlee and her family rejected him. Diaz believes he was rejected because he is black. "I hated my skin color," he said. "It was something so minor, but it was major in society's eyes. I couldn't control anything any more. I was always by myself, depressed, in my own world, always in my room."[13]

Discussion Questions

1. Discuss Diaz's level of moral development in light of his behavior and his attempted justification of his behavior.

2. Studies show that jealousy is more likely to occur in people who have low self-esteem.[14] Discuss the relationship between Diaz's self-loathing, cultural norms, and his level of moral development.

3. To what extent do you, like Diaz, depend on feedback from others to define your self-worth? Do we have a moral obligation to develop good self-esteem and a strong, independent sense of self-worth?

4. Studies have found that jealousy is most prevalent in people who accept traditional cultural values regarding sex roles.[15] Jealousy, on the other hand, is least likely to occur in postconventional moral reasoners.[16] Using examples to illustrate your answer, discuss ways in which conventional morality condones, and even romanticizes, jealous behavior in a relationship.

5. Research shows that jealousy can lead to violence such as abuse, suicide, self-destructive behaviors, and even murder.[17] Discuss why this so in light of the above findings about jealousy, self-esteem, and moral maturity.

6. Why do you think a person at the postconventional stage of moral development is less likely to become jealous? Are people at the postconventional stage of moral development better equipped to resolve moral conflicts in their relationships? Use this case study as well as examples from your own experience to illustrate your answer.

6. *Prozac: Enhancing Morality Through Drugs*

Although the role of drugs—such as alcohol, heroin, and cocaine—in lowering inhibitions against immoral behavior is widely acknowledged,[18] there is considerable resistance to the similar idea that certain drugs may actually enhance moral behavior. This resistance is based mainly on the prevalent belief in Western philosophy that there is an autonomous, rational self that operates independently of the body.

Depressed people can become self-occupied almost to the point of seeming sociopathic in their indifference to the consequences of their actions for others. In these cases, treatment with a drug such as Prozac[19] can, according to Peter Kramer, author of *Listening to Prozac*, "turn a morally unattractive person into an admirable one."[20] Prozac, however, may also be accompanied by a feeling of "the numbing of moral sensibility."[21]

Phillip, an undergraduate, was undergoing psychotherapy because of the humiliation he had received from his parents. Initially Phillip resisted the use of medication. As his depression became more severe, however, Phillip agreed to try Prozac. Although he felt better on the Prozac, he also hated it. He felt phony. Why? Because he had been robbed of his disdain, resentment, and rage without having to first work through it.[22]

Prozac is not only used by people who feel depressed or overwhelmed by the challenges of life. Many use it as a means of self-transformation. According to Kramer, using Prozac can increase a person's autonomy and life choices by "lend[ing] people courage and allow[ing] them to choose life's ordinary risky undertakings."[23]

Discussion Questions

1. James Q. Wilson argues that morality arises out of our natural sociability. In cases where our natural sociability is deficient or suppressed by neurosis, would it be morally acceptable, or perhaps even morally obligatory, to use drugs to enhance it?

2. Is it morally admirable to use drugs in our quest to become better people? If we can find a shortcut to self-realization and moral maturity, shouldn't we take it?

3. The use of mood-altering drugs such as Prozac has been criticized as masking our true personality or our essence, as well as freeing us from having to struggle with reality. Do you agree? What is meant by "our essence," or "reality"?

4. Prozac use is more prevalent among women. However, unlike valium, which made women more compliant, Prozac is described as the feminist drug because it seems to transform people into assertive, self-confident, high achievers and social adepts. Given this, would it be morally desirable for servile women such as Rose (see Application 3, "The Subservient Wife") to take Prozac? Is the assertiveness and self-confidence of women on Prozac morally equivalent to that of women who are at the postconventional stage of moral reasoning? Support your answer.

5. Is unhappiness or depression necessarily an indication of a moral failing? Discuss your answer in light of Phillip's experience.

6. Discuss the following statement by Peter Kramer:

> Working with Prozac has heightened my awareness of the extent to which compulsion is a basis for moral actions. Is it a sound basis? Surely one could make the case that what is compelled is inherently amoral; what characterizes moral action is choice. Still, in addressing this effect of Prozac [tempering compulsive behavior], we face the least irrational, most cogent aspect of pharmacological Calvinism: perhaps diminishing pain can dull the soul.[24]

NOTES

[1] Sanyika Shakur ("Monster" Kody Scott), *Monster: The Autobiography of an L.A. Gang Member* (New York: Atlantic Monthly Press, 1993), p. 60.

[2] Ibid., p. 232.

[3] "Roxane Farmanfarmaian, "Author Signing: Police Keep Away," *Publishers Weekly,* June 3, 1997.

[4] George Orwell, "Reflections on Gandhi," in *Shooting an Elephant and Other Essays* (New York: Harcourt Brace Jovanovich, Inc., 1949).

[5] Ibid.

[6] Amy Tan, *The Joy Luck Club* (New York: Ivy Books), p. 213.

[7] Kenneth L. Woodward, "To Abuse Is Human, to Repent Is Rare," *Newsweek,* November 6, 1995, p. 78.

[8] Ibid.

[9] Brenda Jo Light Bredemeier & David Lyle Light Shields, "Applied Ethics and Moral Reasoning in Sport," in James R. Rest & Darcia Narvaez (eds.), *Moral Development in the Professions* (pp. 173–187) (Hillsdale, NJ: Lawrence Erlbaum, 1994).

[10] Ibid., p. 177.

[11] Ibid.

[12] Cynthia Wang, "The Guy Thing," *People Weekly,* December 23, 1996, p. 67.

[13] "Jilted Lover Charged with Murdering Wrong Sister," *The Good Five Cent Cigar,* April 11, 1997, p. 4.

[14] Anthony R. Palisi, "Romantic Jealousy and Self-Esteem," *Family Letter* (Springfield, NJ: National Academy of Counselors and Family Therapists), 12(1–2), 1992.

[15] Gary Hanson, "Reactions to Hypothetical, Jealousy Producing Events," *Family Relations,* October 1982, 31(4): 513–518; and Eugene W. Mathes & Donna J. Deuger, "Jealousy and Moral Maturity," Paper presented at the annual meeting of the Midwestern Psychological Association (Chicago, May 2–4, 1985).

[16] Ibid.

[17] Anthony R. Palisi, "Romantic Jealousy and Self-Esteem," *Family Letter* (Springfield, NJ: National Academy of Counselors and Family Therapists), 12 (1–2), 1992.

[18] "Drugs and Crimes Are Closely Connected. The Majority of Prison Inmates Are Serving Time for Drug Related Crimes." See Ted Gup, "Drugs and Crime," *Cosmopolitan,* July 1996, p. 180.

[19] Prozac has enjoyed the greatest popularity of any psychotherapeutic drug in history. By 1993, seven years after the drug first appeared on the market, 8 million people were using or had used Prozac. See Peter D. Kramer, *Listening to Prozac* (New York: Viking, 1993), p. xix.

[20] Ibid., p. 294.

[21] Ibid., p. 291.

[22] Ibid.

[23] Ibid., p. 258.

[24] Ibid.

CHAPTER FIVE

Ethical Egoism

Whatever road I take, the guiding star is within me; the guiding star and the lode-stone which point the way. They point in but one direction. They point to me.

Ayn Rand, *The Anthem*

Like ethical subjectivism, ethical egoism focuses on the individual. Ethical egoism differs from ethical subjectivism, however, in that it is concerned not just with what a person may feel is right but with what *is in a person's rational self-interest*. What we may feel is right for us is not always the same as what is in our self-interest. For example, there are times when we may have to forgo our immediate desires for the sake of fulfilling our long-term interests.

Although ethical egoism emphasizes autonomy over social concerns, seeking our own interests does not necessarily entail ignoring the interests of others. What the ethical egoists are opposed to is putting other people's interests *before* our own. There are times, however, when our rational self-interests are best advanced by allowing or even helping others to pursue their interests.

The first reading in this section is from Plato's *Republic*. In this selection, Glaucon tries to convince Socrates that ethical egoism is the best description of morality. Glaucon argues that if people were not restrained by concerns of what others would think of them or by fear of punishment, they would pursue their own self-interests.

In the second selection sociobiologist Edward O. Wilson makes the case that humans, like other animals, are genetically programmed to act in ways that further their self-interests. Even altruism, Wilson claims, is fundamentally selfish because it increases our chances to pass on our genes to future generations.

The third selection is from Ayn Rand's best-selling novel *The Fountainhead*. In this book, Rand defends rational ethical egoism and laissez-faire capitalism that, she argues, are grounded in ethical egoism.

Mary Midgley, in the selection from her book *Can't We Make Moral Judgements?* offers a critique of Rand's ethical egoism. In particular, Midgley argues that Rand's ethical egoism is inconsistent and has implications that most of us would be unwilling to accept.

Although some moral theories, such as egoism, are unsuccessful when taken on their own, they provide valuable insights into key aspects of morality. In the final reading, "The Wisdom of the Egoist: The Moral and Political Implications of Valuing the Self," Jean Hampton argues that egoism, although it cannot stand on its own as a moral theory, is an important component of other moral theories such as deontology, utilitarianism, rights ethics, and virtue ethics.

Plato

The Republic

Plato's *Republic* is one of the most important books in Western philosophy. This great work discusses not only theoretical concepts such as justice and the nature of knowledge, but also covers areas of practical concern such as marriage, politics, and education. Although written by Plato, scholars believe that *The Republic* reflects, in part, the thinking of Plato's teacher Socrates.

In the following selection, Glaucon, Glaucon's brother Adeimantus, and Socrates engage in a debate over whether humans are naturally just. To illustrate his point that people are basically selfish, Glaucon tells the story of a shepherd named Gyges. Gyges finds a ring that makes him invisible when he turns it. Delighted with his discovery, Gyges takes advantage of his invisibility to take what he wants from others. Glaucon then tries to convince Socrates that everyone would behave like Gyges if they knew they could get away with it. This leads to a discussion of the more basic question of what justice is.

CRITICAL THINKING QUESTIONS

1. What is Glaucon's view of human nature?
2. How does Glaucon define justice?
3. What, according to Glaucon, motivates people to act justly?
4. What evidence do Glaucon and Adeimantus use to show that the unjust often flourish while the just live lives of misery?
5. Is Adeimantus convinced by the argument supporting ethical egoism?

With these words I was thinking that I had made an end of the discussion; but the end, in truth, proved to be only a beginning. For Glaucon, who is always the most pugnacious of men, was dissatisfied at Thrasymachus' retirement; he wanted to have the battle out. So he said to me: Socrates, do you wish really to persuade us, or only to seem to have persuaded us, that to be just is always better than to be unjust?

I should wish really to persuade you, I replied, if I could.

. . .

"Gyges' Ring" from *The Republic,* translated by Benjamin Jowett (New York: Collier, 1901). Notes have been omitted.

. . . If you please, then, I will revive the argument of Thrasymachus. And first I will speak of the nature and origin of justice according to the common view of them. Secondly, I will show that all men who practise justice do so against their will, of necessity, but not as a good. And thirdly, I will argue that there is reason in this view, for the life of the unjust is after all better far than the life of the just —if what they say is true, Socrates, since I myself am not of their opinion. But still I acknowledge that I am perplexed when I hear the voices of Thrasymachus and myriads of others dinning in my ears; and, on the other hand, I have never yet heard the superiority of justice to injustice maintained by any one in a satisfactory way. I want to hear justice praised in respect of itself; then I shall be satisfied, and you are the person from whom I think that I am most likely to hear this; and therefore I will praise the unjust life to the utmost of my power, and my manner of speaking will indicate the manner in which I desire to hear you too praising justice and censuring injustice. Will you say whether you approve of my proposal?

Indeed I do; nor can I imagine any theme about which a man of sense would oftener wish to converse.

I am delighted, he replied, to hear you say so, and shall begin by speaking, as I proposed, of the nature and origin of justice.

They say that to do injustice is, by nature, good; to suffer injustice, evil; but that the evil is greater than the good. And so when men have both done and suffered injustice and have had experience of both, not being able to avoid the one and obtain the other, they think that they had better agree among themselves to have neither; hence there arise laws and mutual covenants; and that which is ordained by law is termed by them lawful and just. This they affirm to be the origin and nature of justice;—it is a mean or compromise, between the best of all, which is to do injustice and not be punished, and the worst of all, which is to suffer injustice without the power of retaliation; and justice, being at a middle point between the two, is tolerated not as a good, but as the lesser evil, and honoured by reason of the inability of men to do injustice. For no man who is worthy to be called a man would ever submit to such an agreement if he were able to resist; he would be mad if he did. Such is the received account, Socrates, of the nature and origin of justice.

Now that those who practise justice do so involuntarily and because they have not the power to be unjust will best appear if we imagine something of this kind: having given both to the just and the unjust power to do what they will, let us watch and see whither desire will lead them; then we shall discover in the very act the just and unjust man to be proceeding along the same road, following their interest, which all natures deem to be their good, and are only diverted into the path of justice by the force of law. The liberty which we are supposing may be most completely given to them in the form of such a power as is said to have been possessed by Gyges, the ancestor of Croesus the Lydian. According to the tradition, Gyges was a shepherd in the service of the king of Lydia; there was a great storm, and an earthquake made an opening in the earth at the place where he was feeding his flock. Amazed at the sight, he descended into the opening, where, among other marvels, he beheld a hollow brazen horse, having doors, at which he stooping and looking in saw a dead body of stature, as appeared to him, more than human, and having nothing on but a gold ring; this he took from the finger of the dead and reascended. Now the shepherds met together, according to custom, that they might send their monthly report about the flocks to the king; into their assembly he came having the ring on his finger, and as he was sitting among them he chanced to turn the collet of the ring inside his hand, when instantly he became invisible to the rest of the company and they began to speak to him as if he were no longer present. He was astonished at this, and again touching the ring he turned the collet outwards and reappeared; he made several trials of the ring, and always with the same result—when he turned the collet inwards he became invisible, when outwards he reappeared. Whereupon he contrived to be chosen one of the messengers who were sent to the court; where as soon as he arrived he seduced the queen, and with her help conspired against the king and slew him, and took the kingdom. Suppose now that there were two such magic rings, and the just put on one of them and the unjust the other; no man can be imagined to be of such an iron nature that he would stand fast in justice. No man would keep his hands off what was not his own when he could safely take what he liked out of the market, or go into houses and lie with any one at his pleasure, or kill or release from prison whom he would, and in all respects be like a god among men. Then the actions of the just would be as the actions of the unjust; they would both come at last to the same point. And this we may truly affirm to be a great proof that a man is just, not willingly or because he thinks that justice is any good to him individually, but of necessity, for wherever any one thinks that he can safely be unjust, there he is unjust. For all men believe in their hearts that injustice is far more profitable to the individual than justice, and he who argues as I have been supposing, will say that they are right. If you could imagine any one obtaining this power of becoming invisible, and never doing any wrong or touching what was another's, he would be thought by the lookers-on to be a most wretched idiot, although they would praise him to one another's faces, and keep up appearances with one another from a fear that they too might suffer injustice. Enough of this.

Now, if we are to form a real judgement of the life of the just and unjust, we must isolate them; there is no other way; and how is the isolation to be effected? I answer: Let the unjust man be entirely unjust, and the just man entirely just; nothing is to be taken away from either of them, and both are to be perfectly furnished for the work of their respective lives. First, let the unjust be like other distinguished masters of craft; like the skillful pilot or physician, who knows intuitively his own powers and keeps within their limits, and who, if he fails at any point, is able to recover himself. So let the unjust make his unjust attempts in the right way, and lie hidden if he means to be great in his injustice: (he who is found out is nobody:) for the highest reach of injustice is, to be deemed just when you are not. Therefore I say that in the perfectly unjust man we must assume the most perfect injustice; there is to be no deduction, but we must allow him, while doing the most unjust acts, to have acquired the greatest reputation for justice. If he have taken a false step he must be able to recover himself; he must be one who can speak with effect, if any of his deeds come to light, and who can force his way where force is required by his courage and strength, and command of money and friends. And at his side let us place the just man in his nobleness and simplicity, wishing, as Aeschylus says, to be and not to seem good. There must be no seeming, for if he seem to be just he will be honoured and rewarded, and then we shall not know whether he is just for the sake of justice or for the sake of honours and rewards; therefore, let him be clothed in justice only, and have no other covering; and he must be imagined in a state of life the opposite to the former. Let him be the best of men, and let him be thought the worst; then he will have been put to the proof; and we shall see whether he will be affected by the fear of infamy and its consequences. And let him continue thus to the hour of death; being just and seeming to be unjust. When both have reached the uttermost extreme, the one of justice and the other of injustice, let judgement be given which of them is the happier of the two.

Heavens! my dear Glaucon, I said, how energetically you polish them up for the decision, first one and then the other, as if they were two statues.

I do my best, he said. And now that we know what they are like there is no difficulty in tracing out the sort of life which awaits either of them. This I will proceed to describe; but as you may think the description a little too coarse, I ask you to suppose, Socrates, that the words which follow are not mine.—Let me put them into the mouths of the eulogists of injustice: They will tell you that the just man who is thought unjust will be scourged, racked, bound—will have his eyes burnt out; and, at last, after suffering every kind of evil, he will be impaled: Then he will understand that he ought to seem only, and not to be, just; the word of Aeschylus may be more truly spoken of the unjust than of the just. For the unjust is pursuing a reality; he does not live with a view to appearances—he wants to be really unjust and not to seem only:—

> His mind has a soil deep and fertile,
> Out of which spring his prudent counsels.

In the first place, he is thought just, and therefore bears rule in the city; he can marry whom he will, and give in marriage to whom he will; also he can trade and deal where he likes, and always to his own advantage, because he has no misgivings about injustice; and at every contest, whether in public or private, he gets the better of his antagonists, and gains at their expense, and is rich, and out of his gains he can benefit his friends, and harm his enemies; moreover, he can offer sacrifices, and dedicate gifts to the gods abundantly and magnificently, and can honour the gods or any man whom he wants to honour in a far better style than the just, and therefore he is likely to be dearer than they are to the gods. And thus, Socrates, gods and men are said to unite in making the life of the unjust better than the life of the just.

I was going to say something in answer to Glaucon, when Adeimantus, his brother, interposed: Socrates, he said, you do not suppose that there is nothing more to be urged?

. . .

. . . But let me add something more: There is another side to Glaucon's argument about the praise and censure of justice and injustice, which is equally required in order to bring out what I believe to be his meaning. Parents and tutors are always telling their sons and their wards that they are to be just; but why? not for the sake of justice, but for the sake of character and reputation; in the hope of obtaining for him who is reputed just some of those offices, marriages, and the like which Glaucon has enumerated among the advantages accruing to the unjust from the reputation of justice. More, however, is made of appearances by this class of persons than by the others; for they throw in the good opinion of the gods, and will tell you of a shower of benefits which the heavens, as they say, rain upon the pious; . . . Some extend their rewards yet further; the posterity, as they say, of the faithful and just shall survive to the third and fourth generation. This is the style in which they praise justice. But about the wicked there is another strain; they bury them in a slough in Hades, and make them carry water in a sieve; also while they are yet living they bring them to infamy, and inflict upon them the punishments which Glaucon described as the portion of the just who are reputed to be unjust; nothing else does their invention supply. Such is their manner of praising the one and censuring the other.

Once more, Socrates, I will ask you to consider another way of speaking about justice and injustice, which is not confined to the poets, but is found in prose writers. The universal voice of mankind is always declaring that justice and virtue are honourable, but grievous and toilsome; and that the pleasures of vice and injustice are easy of attainment, and are only censured by law and opinion. They say also that honesty is for the most part less profitable than dishonesty; and they are quite ready to call wicked men happy, and to honour them both in public and private when they are rich or in any other way influential, while they despise and overlook those who may be weak and poor, even though acknowledging them to be better than the others. But most extraordinary of all is their mode of speaking about virtue and the gods: they say that the gods apportion calamity and misery to many good men, and good and happiness to the wicked. . . .

He proceeded: And now when the young hear all this said about virtue and vice, and the way in which gods and men regard them, how are their minds likely to be affected, my dear Socrates,—those of them, I mean, who are quick-witted, and, like bees on the wing, light on every flower, and from all that they hear are prone to draw conclusions as to what manner of persons they should be and in what way they should walk if they would make the best of life? Probably the youth will say to himself in the words of Pindar—

> *Can I by justice or by crooked ways of deceit ascend a loftier tower which may be a fortress to me all my days?*

For what men say is that, if I am really just and am not also thought just, profit there is none, but the pain and loss on the other hand are unmistakeable. But if, though unjust, I acquire the reputation of justice, a heavenly life is promised to me. Since then, as philosophers prove, appearance tyrannizes over truth and is lord of happiness, to appearance I must devote myself. . . . With a view to concealment we will establish secret brotherhoods and political clubs. And there are professors of rhetoric who teach the art of persuading courts and assemblies; and so, partly by persuasion and partly by force, I shall make unlawful gains and not be punished. Still I hear a voice saying that the gods cannot be deceived, neither can they be compelled. But what if there are no gods? or suppose them to have no care of human things—why in either case should we mind about concealment? And even if there are gods, and they do care about us, yet we know of them only from tradition and the genealogies of the poets; and these are the very persons who say that they may be influenced and turned by "sacrifices and soothing entreaties and by offerings." Let us be consistent then, and believe both or neither. If the poets speak truly, why then we had better be unjust, and offer of the fruits of injustice; for if we are just, although we may escape the vengeance of heaven, we shall lose the gains of injustice; but, if we are unjust, we shall keep the gains, and by our sinning and praying, and praying and sinning, the gods will be propitiated, and we shall not be punished. "But there is a world below in which either we or our posterity will suffer for our unjust deeds." Yes, my friend, will be the reflection, but there are mysteries and atoning deities, and these have great power. That is what mighty cities declare; and the children of the gods, who were their poets and prophets, bear a like testimony.

On what principle, then, shall we any longer choose justice rather than the worst injustice? when, if we only unite the latter with a deceitful regard to appearances, we shall fare to our mind both with gods and men, in life and after death, as the most numerous and the highest authorities tell us. Knowing all this, Socrates, how can a man who has any superiority of mind or person or rank or wealth, be willing to honour justice; or indeed to refrain from laughing when he hears justice praised?

. . .

. . . I speak in this vehement manner, as I must frankly confess to you, because I want to hear from you the opposite side; and I would ask you to show not only the superiority which justice has over injustice, but what effect they have on the possessor of them which makes the one to be a good and the other an evil to him. . . . Let others praise justice and censure injustice, magnifying the rewards and honours of the one and abusing the other; that is a manner of arguing which, coming from them, I am ready to tolerate, but from you who have spent your whole life in the consideration of this question, unless I hear the contrary from your own lips, I expect something better. And therefore, I say, not only prove to us that justice is better than injustice, but show what they either of them do to the possessor of them, which makes the one to be a good and the other an evil, whether seen or unseen by gods and men.

I had always admired the genius of Glaucon and Adeimantus, but on hearing these words I was quite delighted, . . . for there is something truly divine in being able to argue as you have done for the superiority of injustice, and remaining unconvinced by your own arguments. And I do believe that you are not convinced—this I infer from your general character, for had I judged only from your speeches I should have mistrusted you. . . .

DISCUSSION QUESTIONS

1. Does ethical egoism, as defended by Glaucon, provide a correct picture of human nature?
2. If you could be invisible at will, would you behave as Gyges did? If not, why not?

3. Do people act morally only to avoid punishment or public censure? Does empirical evidence support Glaucon's claim that people are basically selfish? Illustrate your answer with specific examples.
4. Is the possibility of heaven and hell the only reason why we should behave justly? What other reasons does Adeimantus explore for being just?
5. How would developmental psychologists such as Carol Gilligan and Lawrence Kohlberg respond to Glaucon's claim that people are basically selfish? Would they agree that this is true of all people or only some people?
6. Do our actions speak louder than our words? What did Socrates mean when he said that he not only was unconvinced by Adeimantus's argument but inferred that Adeimantus was not convinced either?
7. On what grounds might you argue that justice is preferable to injustice, even if we can get away with and benefit from injustice? Are you satisfied with this response to Glaucon's argument that justice is simply a means to an end? Support your position.

Edward O. Wilson

On Human Nature

Harvard zoologist Edward O. Wilson (b. 1929) is one of the leading advocates of sociobiology. Sociobiology is the study of the evolution of animal
social behavior. According to sociobiologists, natural selection applies to
behavior in the same way it applies to physical evolution. Human social
behavior, like that of other social animals, is primarily oriented toward the
propagation of the species. This goal is achieved through inborn cooperative
behavior, which sociobiologists call *biological altruism*. Even though altruism appears to be self-sacrificing, it is in reality based in selfishness.

CRITICAL THINKING QUESTIONS

1. What does Wilson mean by altruism? What are some examples
   of altruistic behavior?
2. Does Wilson consider altruism to be a transcendent moral quality found only in humans? What is the source of altruism?
3. In what other animals do we find examples of altruistic suicide
   comparable to that in humans? Does Wilson conclude from this
   that humans and these other animals think alike?
4. How does Wilson explain the persistence of altruistic genes
   when selfishness seems to be better adapted for passing on
   genes? Does Wilson reject the Darwinian theory of natural
   selection?
5. How, according to Wilson, does altruism advance our own self-
   interests in kin selection?
6. Why does Wilson claim that compassion is ultimately self-
   serving?
7. What is the distinction between soft-core and hard-core altruism?
8. Why does Wilson say that soft-core altruism is ultimately selfish?
9. What does Wilson think of sainthood?
10. How does Wilson use Kohlberg's stage theory of moral develop-
    ment to support his theory?
11. What, according to Wilson, is the ultimate function of morality?

On Human Nature (Cambridge, MA: Harvard University Press, 1978), pp. 149–167.

Altruism

"The blood of martyrs is the seed of the church." With that chilling dictum the third-century theologian Tertullian confessed the fundamental flaw of human altruism, an intimation that the purpose of sacrifice is to raise one human group over another. Generosity without hope of reciprocation is the rarest and most cherished of human behaviors, subtle and difficult to define, distributed in a highly selective pattern, surrounded by ritual and circumstance, and honored by medallions and emotional orations. We sanctify true altruism in order to reward it and thus to make it less than true, and by that means to promote its recurrence in others. Human altruism, in short, is riddled to its foundations with the expected mammalian ambivalence.

As mammals would be and ants would not, we are fascinated by the extreme forms of self-sacrifice. In the First and Second World Wars, Korea, and Vietnam, a large percentage of Congressional Medals of Honor were awarded to men who threw themselves on top of grenades to shield comrades, aided the rescue of others from battle sites at the cost of certain death to themselves, or made other extraordinary decisions that led to the same fatal end. Such altruistic suicide is the ultimate act of courage and emphatically deserves the country's highest honor. But it is still a great puzzle. What could possibly go on in the minds of these men in the moment of desperation? . . .

The annihilating mixture of reason and passion, which has been described often in first-hand accounts of the battlefield, is only the extreme phenomenon that lies beyond the innumerable smaller impulses of courage and generosity that bind societies together. One is tempted to leave the matter there, to accept the purest elements of altruism as simply the better side of human nature. Perhaps, to put the best possible construction on the matter, conscious altruism is a transcendental quality that distinguishes human beings from animals. But scientists are not accustomed to declaring any phenomenon off limits, and it is precisely through the deeper analysis of altruism that sociobiology seems best prepared at this time to make a novel contribution.

. . .

In spite of a fair abundance of such examples among vertebrates, it is only in the lower animals, and in the social insects particularly, that we encounter altruistic suicide comparable to man's. Many members of ant, bee, and wasp colonies are ready to defend their nests with insane charges against intruders. This is the reason that people move with circumspection around honeybee hives and yellow-jacket burrows, but can afford to relax near the nests of solitary species such as sweat bees and mud daubers.

. . .

Sharing the capacity for extreme sacrifice does not mean that the human mind and the "mind" of an insect (if such exists) work alike. But it does mean that the impulse need not be ruled divine or otherwise transcendental, and we are justified in seeking a more conventional biological explanation. A basic problem immediately arises in connection with such an explanation: fallen heroes do not have children. If self-sacrifice results in fewer descendants, the genes that allow heroes to be created can be expected to disappear gradually from the population. A narrow interpretation of Darwinian natural selection would predict this outcome: because people governed by selfish genes must prevail over those with altruistic genes, there should also be a tendency over many generations for selfish genes to increase in prevalence and for a population to become ever less capable of responding altruistically.

How then does altruism persist? In the case of social insects, there is no doubt at all. Natural selection has been broadened to include kin selection. The self-sacrificing termite soldier protects the rest of its colony, including the queen and king, its parents. As a result, the soldier's more fertile brothers and sisters flourish, and through them the altruistic genes are multiplied by a greater production of nephews and nieces.

It is natural, then, to ask whether through kin selection the capacity for altruism has also evolved in human beings. In other words, do the emotions we feel, which in exceptional individuals may climax in total self-sacrifice, stem ultimately from hereditary units that were implanted by the favoring of relatives during a period of hundreds or thousands of generations? This explanation gains some strength from the circumstance that during most of mankind's history the predominant social unit was the immediate family and a tight network of other close relatives. Such exceptional cohesion, combined with detailed kin classifications made possible by high intelligence, might explain why kin selection has been more forceful in human beings than in monkeys and other mammals.

To anticipate a common objection raised by many social scientists and others, let me grant at once that the form and intensity of altruistic acts are to a large extent culturally determined. Human social evolution is obviously more cultural than genetic. The point is that the underlying emotion, powerfully manifested in virtually all human societies, is what is considered to evolve through genes. The sociobiological hypothesis does not therefore account for differences among societies, but it can explain why human beings differ from other mammals and why, in one narrow aspect, they more closely resemble social insects.

The evolutionary theory of human altruism is greatly complicated by the ultimately self-serving quality of most forms of that altruism. No sustained form of human altruism is explicitly and totally self-annihilating. Lives of the most towering heroism are paid out in the expectation of great reward, not the least of which is a belief in personal immortality. . . .

Compassion is selective and often ultimately self-serving. Hinduism permits lavish preoccupation with the self and close relatives but does not encourage compassion for unrelated individuals or, least of all, outcastes. A central goal of Nibbanic Buddhism is preserving the individual through altruism. The devotee earns points toward a better personal life by performing generous acts and offsets bad acts with meritorious ones. While embracing the concept of universal compassion, both Buddhist and Christian countries have found it expedient to wage aggressive wars, many of which they justify in the name of religion.

Compassion is flexible and eminently adaptable to political reality; that is to say it conforms to the best interests of self, family, and allies of the moment. The Palestinian refugees have received the sympathy of the world and have been the beneficiaries of rage among the Arab nations. But little is said about the Arabs killed by King Hussein or those who live in Arab countries with fewer civil rights and under far worse material conditions than the displaced people of the West Bank. When Bangladesh began its move toward independence in 1971, the President of Pakistan unleashed the Punjabi army in a campaign of terror that ultimately cost the lives of a million Bengalis and drove 9.8 million others into exile. In this war more Moslem people were killed or driven from their homes than make up the entire populations of Syria and Jordan. Yet not a single Arab state, conservative or radical, supported the Bangladesh struggle for independence. Most denounced the Bengalis while proclaiming Islamic solidarity with West Pakistan.

To understand this strange selectivity and resolve the puzzle of human altruism we must distinguish two basic forms of cooperative behavior. The altruistic impulse can be irrational and unilaterally directed at others; the bestower expresses no desire for equal return and performs no unconscious actions leading to the same end. I have called this form of behavior "hard-core" altruism, a set of responses relatively unaffected by social reward or punishment beyond childhood. Where such behavior exists, it is likely to have evolved through kin selection or natural selection operating on entire, competing family or tribal units. We would expect hard-core altruism to serve the altruist's closest relatives and to decline steeply in frequency and intensity as relationship becomes more distant. "Soft-core" altruism, in contrast, is ultimately selfish. The "altruist" expects reciprocation from society for himself or his closest relatives. His good behavior is calculating, often in a wholly conscious way, and his maneuvers are orchestrated by the excruciatingly intricate sanctions and demands of society. The capacity for soft-core altruism can be expected to have evolved primarily by selection of individuals and to be deeply influenced by the vagaries of cultural evolution. Its psychological vehicles are lying, pretense, and deceit, including self-deceit, because the actor is most convincing who believes that his performance is real.

. . .

. . . in human beings soft-core altruism has been carried to elaborate extremes. Reciprocation among distantly related or unrelated individuals is the key to human society. The perfection of the social contract has broken the ancient vertebrate constraints imposed by rigid kin selection. Through the convention of reciprocation, combined with a flexible, endlessly productive language and a genius for verbal classification, human beings fashion long-remembered agreements upon which cultures and civilizations can be built.

Yet the question remains: Is there a foundation of hard-core altruism beneath all of this contractual superstructure? The conception is reminiscent of David Hume's striking conjecture that reason is the slave of the passions. So we ask, to what biological end are the contracts made, and just how stubborn is nepotism?

The distinction is important because pure, hard-core altruism based on kin selection is the enemy of civilization. If human beings are to a large extent guided by programmed learning rules and canalized emotional development to favor their own relatives and tribe, only a limited amount of global harmony is possible. International cooperation will approach an upper limit, from which it will be knocked down by the perturbations of war and economic struggle, canceling each upward surge based on pure reason. The imperatives of blood and territory will be the passions to which reason is slave. One can imagine genius continuing to serve biological ends even after it has disclosed and fully explained the evolutionary roots of unreason.

My own estimate of the relative proportions of hard-core and soft-core altruism in human behavior is optimistic. Human beings appear to be sufficiently selfish and calculating to be capable of indefinitely greater harmony and social homeostasis. This statement is not self-contradictory. True selfishness, if obedient to the other constraints of mammalian biology, is the key to a more nearly perfect social contract.

My optimism is based on evidence concerning the nature of tribalism and ethnicity. If altruism were rigidly unilateral, kin and ethnic ties would be maintained with commensurate tenacity. The lines of allegiance, being difficult or impossible to break, would become progressively tangled until cultural change was halted in their snarl. Under such circumstances the preservation of social units of intermediate size, the extended family and the tribe, would be paramount. We should see it working at the conspicuous expense of individual welfare on the one side and of national interest on the other.

In order to understand this idea more clearly, return with me for a moment to the basic theory of evolution. Imagine a spectrum of self-serving behavior. At one extreme only the individual is meant to benefit, then the nuclear family, next the extended family (including cousins, grandparents, and others who might play a role in kin selection), then the band, the tribe, chiefdoms, and finally, at the other extreme, the highest sociopolitical units. Which units along this spectrum are most favored by the innate predispositions of human social behavior? To reach an answer we can look at natural selection from another perspective: those units subjected to the most intense natural selection, those that reproduce and die most frequently and in concert with the demands of the environment, will be the ones protected by the innate behavior of individual organisms belonging to them. In sharks natural selection occurs overwhelmingly at the individual level; all behavior is self-centered and exquisitely appropriate to the welfare of one shark and its immediate offspring. In the Portuguese man-of-war and other siphonophore jellyfish that consist of great masses of highly coordinated individuals, the unit of selection is almost exclusively the colony. The individual organism, a zooid reduced and compacted into the gelatinous mass, counts for very little. Some members of the colony lack stomachs, others lack nervous systems, most never reproduce, and almost all can be shed and regenerated. Honeybees, termites, and other social insects are only slightly less colony-centered.

Human beings obviously occupy a position on the spectrum somewhere between the two extremes, but exactly where? The evidence suggests to me that human beings are well over toward the individual end of the spectrum. We are not in the position of sharks, or selfish monkeys and apes, but we are closer to them than we are to honeybees in this single parameter. Individual behavior, including seemingly altruistic acts bestowed on tribe and nation, are directed, sometimes very circuitously, toward the Darwinian advantage of the solitary human being and his closest relatives. The most elaborate forms of social organization, despite their outward appearance, serve ultimately as the vehicles of individual welfare. Human altruism appears to be substantially hard-core when directed at closest relatives, although still to a much lesser degree than in the case of the social insects and the colonial invertebrates. The remainder of our altruism is essentially soft. The predicted result is a melange of ambivalence, deceit, and guilt that continuously troubles the individual mind.

The same intuitive conclusion has been drawn independently by the biologist Robert L. Trivers and in less technical terms by the social psychologist Donald T. Campbell, who has been responsible for a renaissance of interest in the scientific study of human altruism and moral behavior. And in reviewing a large body of additional information from sociology, Milton M. Gordon has generalized that "man defending the honor or welfare of his ethnic group is man defending himself."

The primacy of egocentrism over race has been most clearly revealed by the behavior of ethnic groups placed under varying conditions of stress. For example, Sephardic Jews from Jamaica who emigrate to England or America may, according to personal circumstances, remain fully Jewish by joining the Jews of the host society, or may abandon their ethnic ties promptly, marry gentiles, and blend into the host culture. Puerto Ricans who migrate back and forth between San Juan and New York are even more versatile. A black Puerto Rican behaves as a member of the black minority in Puerto Rico and as a member of the Puerto Rican minority in New York. If given the opportunity to use affirmative action in New York he may emphasize his blackness. But in personal relationships with whites he is likely to minimize the color of his skin by references to his Spanish language and Latin culture. And like Sephardic Jews, many of the better educated Puerto Ricans sever their ethnic ties and quickly penetrate the mainland culture.

. . .

Sainthood is not so much the hypertrophy of human altruism as its ossification. It is cheerfully subordinate to the biological imperatives above which it is supposed to rise. The true humanization of altruism, in the sense of adding wisdom and insight to the social contract, can come only through a deeper scientific examination of morality. Lawrence Kohlberg, an educational psychologist, has traced what he believes to be six sequential stages of ethical reasoning through which each person progresses as part of his normal mental development. The child moves from an unquestioning dependence on external rules and controls to an increasingly sophisticated set of internalized standards, . . .

. . . Depending on intelligence and training, individuals can stop at any rung on the ladder. Most attain stages four or five. By stage four they are at approximately the level of morality reached by baboon and chimpanzee troops. At stage five, when the ethical reference becomes partly contractual and legalistic, they incorporate the morality on which I believe most of human social revolution has been based. To the extent that this interpretation is correct, the ontogeny of moral development is likely to have been genetically assimilated and is now part of the automatically guided process of mental development. Individuals are steered by learning rules and relatively inflexible emotional responses to progress through stage five. Some are diverted by extraordinary events at critical junctures. Sociopaths do exist. But the great majority of people reach stages four or five and are thus prepared to exist harmoniously—in Pleistocene hunter-gatherer camps.

Since we no longer live as small bands of hunter-gatherers, stage six is the most nearly nonbiological and hence susceptible to the greatest amount of hypertrophy. The individual selects principles against which the group and the law are judged. Precepts chosen by intuition based on emotion are primarily biological in origin and are likely to do no more than reinforce the primitive social arrangements. Such a morality is unconsciously shaped to give new rationalizations for the consecration of the group, the proselytizing role of altruism, and the defense of territory.

But to the extent that principles are chosen by knowledge and reason remote from biology, they can at least in theory be non-Darwinian. This leads us ineluctably back to the second great spiritual dilemma. The philosophical question of interest that it generates is the following: Can the cultural evolution of higher ethical values gain a direction and momentum of its own and completely replace genetic evolution? I think not. The genes hold culture on a leash. The leash is very long, but inevitably values will be constrained in accordance with their effects on the human gene pool. The brain is a product of evolution. Human behavior—like the deepest capacities for emotional response which drive and guide it—is the circuitous technique by which human genetic material has been and will be kept intact. Morality has no other demonstrable ultimate function.

DISCUSSION QUESTIONS

1. Is altruism a moral virtue if it is genetically programmed into us? Can traits, such as altruism and compassion, be virtues if they ultimately benefit us?
2. Compare and contrast Edward O. Wilson's view of human nature with Glaucon's in *The Republic*. Is the egoism supported by Glaucon the same egoism that Wilson argues advances the human species?
3. Wilson argues that humans are basically egocentric. What support does he give for this? How, according to Wilson, can we be both altruistic and egocentric? Do you agree with Wilson? Support your answer.
4. Compare and contrast Edward Wilson's description of moral behavior in terms of sociobiology with James Wilson's concept of the innate origin of moral sense.
5. Research has shown that people, in fact, are more attracted to potential mates who are altruistic. Does this finding support Edward O. Wilson's theory that altruistic people are basically self-interested?
6. What does Wilson mean when he says that "sainthood is not so much the hypertrophy of human altruism as its ossification"? Would Nietzsche agree with the statement? Support your answer.
7. Discuss Wilson's statement that "the genes hold culture on a leash." How would Ruth Benedict respond to this statement?
8. If altruism is genetically programmed into different species, does this mean that other animals, such as chimpanzees, birds, and ants, are moral beings like humans? Support your answer. How would Edward O. Wilson answer this question?
9. Does sociobiology support Herbert Spencer's theory that humanity evolves culturally over time from the ignorant savage cultures to the intelligent and morally civilized Christians?

Ayn Rand

The Fountainhead

The current popularity of ethical egoism has been fueled by the work of American novelist, screenwriter, and philosopher Ayn Rand (1905–1982). Like Edward O. Wilson, Rand maintains that we value that which helps us survive. What helps us survive is what is in our self-interest. However, Rand interprets self-interest much more individualistically. Disillusioned with the demoralizing effects on people of collectivism and Soviet communism, Rand concludes that ethical egoism, as exemplified in laissez-faire capitalism, is the only philosophy compatible with respect for the integrity and the reality of the individual human. Rand is especially critical of altruistic moralities that call for self-sacrifice. She believes that the best life is one that is consistent with the principles of rational egoism—a life exemplified by that of architect Howard Roark, the hero in her novel *The Fountainhead*.

Rand's purpose in writing *The Fountainhead* was to present an example of an ideal man (Howard Roark), his values, motives, and destiny. In the novel, Rand uses Roark to express her views on moral philosophy. In this selection Roark is giving a speech in front of a courtroom in which he defends his action in dynamiting a housing project he had designed.

CRITICAL THINKING QUESTIONS

1. Why was the crowd hostile toward Roark? How, according to Rand, do people generally respond to new ideas and visions?

2. What, according to Rand, usually motivates creators and people of vision?

3. How does Rand define the word *truth?*

4. What faculty does Rand claim is key for human survival? How does she use this claim to support her theory of ethical egoism?

5. What is the relation of humans to nature?

6. What is a "second-hander"? Why does Rand believe that second-handers are immoral?

7. What have people been taught to think is the highest virtue? Why does Rand think this virtue is, in fact, immoral?

8. How does Rand's ethical egoism differ from egotism?

The Fountainhead (Philadelphia: The Blakiston Company, 1943), pp. 736–742.

9. What is the most moral and proper type of relationship between people?

10. What, according to Rand, is our first right?

11. What is the relation between the common good and tyranny?

12. What, in Rand's view, is the true goal of civilization?

Roark stood before them as each man stands in the innocence of his own mind. But Roark stood like that before a hostile crowd—and they knew suddenly that no hatred was possible to him. For the flash of an instant, they grasped the manner of his consciousness. Each asked himself: do I need anyone's approval?—does it matter?—am I tied? And for that instant, each man was free—free enough to feel benevolence for every other man in the room.

It was only a moment; the moment of silence when Roark was about to speak.

"Thousands of years ago, the first man discovered how to make fire. He was probably burned at the stake he had taught his brothers to light. He was considered an evildoer who had dealt with a demon mankind dreaded. But thereafter men had fire to keep them warm, to cook their food, to light their caves. He had left them a gift they had not conceived and he had lifted darkness off the earth. Centuries later, the first man invented the wheel. He was probably torn on the rack he had taught his brothers to build. He was considered a transgressor who ventured into forbidden territory. But thereafter, men could travel past any horizon. He had left them a gift they had not conceived and he had opened the roads of the world.

"That man, the unsubmissive and first, stands in the opening chapter of every legend mankind has recorded about its beginning. Prometheus was chained to a rock and torn by vultures—because he had stolen the fire of the gods. Adam was condemned to suffer—because he had eaten the fruit of the tree of knowledge. Whatever the legend, somewhere in the shadows of its memory mankind knew that its glory began with one and that that one paid for his courage.

"Throughout the centuries there were men who took first steps down new roads armed with nothing but their own vision. Their goals differed, but they all had this in common: that the step was first, the road new, the vision unborrowed, and the response they received—hatred. The great creators—the thinkers, the artists, the scientists, the inventors—stood alone against the men of their time. Every great new thought was opposed. Every great new invention was denounced. The first motor was considered foolish. The airplane was considered impossible. The power loom was considered vicious. Anesthesia was considered sinful. But the men of unborrowed vision went ahead. They fought, they suffered and they paid. But they won.

"No creator was prompted by a desire to serve his brothers, for his brothers rejected the gift he offered and that gift destroyed the slothful routine of their lives. His truth was his only motive. His own truth, and his own work to achieve it in his own way. A symphony, a book, an engine, a philosophy, an airplane or a building—that was his goal and his life. Not those who heard, read, operated, believed, flew or inhabited the thing he had created. The creation, not its users. The creation, not the benefits others derived from it. The creation which gave form to his truth. He held his truth above all things and against all men.

"His vision, his strength, his courage came from his own spirit. A man's spirit, however, is his self. That entity which is his consciousness. To think, to feel, to judge, to act are functions of the ego.

"The creators were not selfless. It is the whole secret of their power—that it was self-sufficient, self-motivated, self-generated. A first cause, a fount of energy, a life force, a Prime Mover. The creator served nothing and no one. He had lived for himself.

"And only by living for himself was he able to achieve the things which are the glory of mankind. Such is the nature of achievement.

"Man cannot survive except through his mind. He comes on earth unarmed. His brain is his only weapon. Animals obtain food by force. Man has no claws, no fangs, no horns, no great strength of muscle. He must plant his food or hunt it. To plant, he needs a process of thought. To hunt, he needs weapons, and to make weapons—a process of thought. From this simplest necessity to the highest religious abstraction, from the wheel to the skyscraper, everything we are and everything we have comes from a single attribute of man—the function of his reasoning mind.

"But the mind is an attribute of the individual. There is no such thing as a collective brain. There is no such thing as a collective thought. An agreement reached by a group of men is only a compromise or an average drawn upon many individual thoughts. It is a secondary consequence. The primary act—the process of reason—must be performed by each man alone. We can divide a meal among many men. We cannot digest it in a collective stomach. No man can use his lungs to breathe for another man. No man can use his brain to think for another. All the functions of body and spirit are private. They cannot be shared or transferred. . . .

"Nothing is given to man on earth. Everything he needs has to be produced. And here man faces his basic alternative: he can survive in only one of two ways —by the independent work of his own mind or as a parasite fed by the minds of others. The creator originates. The parasite borrows. The creator faces nature alone. The parasite faces nature through an intermediary.

"The creator's concern is the conquest of nature. The parasite's concern is the conquest of men.

"The creator lives for his work. He needs no other men. His primary goal is within himself. The parasite lives second-hand. He needs others. Others become his prime motive.

"The basic need of the creator is independence. The reasoning mind cannot work under any form of compulsion. It cannot be curbed, sacrificed or subordinated to any consideration whatsoever. It demands total independence in function and in motive. To a creator, all relations with men are secondary.

"The basic need of the second-hander is to secure his ties with men in order to be fed. He places relations first. He declares that man exists in order to serve others. He preaches altruism.

"Altruism is the doctrine which demands that man live for others and place others above self.

"No man can live for another. He cannot share his spirit just as he cannot share his body. But the second-hander has used altruism as a weapon of exploitation and reversed the base of mankind's moral principles. Men have been taught every precept that destroys the creator. Men have been taught dependence as a virtue.

"The man who attempts to live for others is a dependent. He is a parasite in motive and makes parasites of those he serves. The relationship produces nothing but mutual corruption. It is impossible in concept. The nearest approach to it in reality—the man who lives to serve others—is the slave. If physical slavery is repulsive, how much more repulsive is the concept of servility of the spirit? The conquered slave has a vestige of honor. He has the merit of having resisted and of considering his condition evil. But the man who enslaves himself voluntarily in the name of love is the basest of creatures. He degrades the dignity of man and he degrades the conception of love. But this is the essence of altruism.

"Men have been taught that the highest virtue is not to achieve, but to give. Yet one cannot give that which has not been created. Creation comes before distribution—or there will be nothing to distribute. The need of the creator comes before the need of any possible beneficiary. Yet we are taught to admire the second-hander who dispenses gifts he has not produced above the man who made the gifts possible. We praise an act of charity. We shrug at an act of achievement.

"Men have been taught that their first concern is to relieve the suffering of others. But suffering is a disease. Should one come upon it, one tries to give relief and assistance. To make that the highest test of virtue is to make suffering the most important part of life. Then man must wish to see others suffer—in order that he may be virtuous. Such is the nature of altruism. The creator is not concerned with disease, but with life. Yet the work of the creators has eliminated one form of disease after another, in man's body and spirit, and brought more relief from suffering than any altruist could ever conceive.

"Men have been taught that it is a virtue to agree with others. But the creator is the man who disagrees. Men have been taught that it is a virtue to swim with the current. But the creator is the man who goes against the current. Men have been taught that it is a virtue to stand together. But the creator is the man who stands alone.

"Men have been taught that the ego is the synonym of evil, and selflessness the ideal of virtue. But the creator is the egotist in the absolute sense, and the selfless man is the one who does not think, feel, judge or act. These are functions of the self.

"Here the basic reversal is most deadly. The issue has been perverted and man has been left no alternative—and no freedom. As poles of good and evil, he was offered two conceptions: egotism and altruism. Egotism was held to mean the sacrifice of others to self. Altruism—the sacrifice of self to others. This tied man irrevocably to other men and left him nothing but a choice of pain: his own pain borne for the sake of others or pain inflicted upon others for the sake of self. When it was added that man must find joy in self-immolation, the trap was closed. Man was forced to accept masochism as his ideal—under threat that sadism was his only alternative. This was the greatest fraud ever perpetrated on mankind.

"This was the device by which dependence and suffering were perpetuated as fundamentals of life.

"The choice is not self-sacrifice or domination. The choice is independence or dependence. The code of the creator or the code of the second-hander. This is the basic issue. It rests upon the alternative of life or death. The code of the creator is built on the needs of the reasoning mind which allows man to survive. The code of the second-hander is built on the needs of a mind incapable of survival. All that which proceeds from man's independent ego is good. All that which proceeds from man's dependence upon men is evil.

"The egotist in the absolute sense is not the man who sacrifices others. He is the man who stands above the need of using others in any manner. He does not function through them. He is not concerned with them in any primary matter. Not in his aim, not in his motive, not in his thinking, not in his desires, not in the source of his energy. He does not exist for any other man—and he asks no other man to exist for him. This is the only form of brotherhood and mutual respect possible between men.

"Degrees of ability vary, but the basic principle remains the same: the degree of a man's independence, initiative and personal love for his work determines his talent as a worker and his worth as a man. Independence is the only gauge of human virtue and value. What a man is and makes of himself; not what he has or hasn't done for others. There is no substitute for personal dignity. There is no standard of personal dignity except independence.

"In all proper relationships there is no sacrifice of anyone to anyone. An architect needs clients, but he does not subordinate his work to their wishes. They need him, but they do not order a house just to give him a commission. Men exchange their work by free, mutual consent to mutual advantage when their personal interests agree and they both desire the exchange. If they do not desire it, they are not forced to deal with each other. They seek further. This is the only possible form of relationship between equals. Anything else is a relation of slave to master, or victim to executioner.

"No work is ever done collectively, by a majority decision. Every creative job is achieved under the guidance of a single individual thought. An architect requires a great many men to erect his building. But he does not ask them to vote on his design. They work together by free agreement and each is free in his proper function. An architect uses steel, glass, concrete, produced by others. But the materials remain just so much steel, glass and concrete until he touches them. What he does with them is his individual product and his individual property. This is the only pattern for proper co-operation among men.

"The first right on earth is the right of the ego. Man's first duty is to himself. His moral law is never to place his prime goal within the persons of others. His moral obligation is to do what he wishes, provided his wish does not depend *primarily* upon other men. This includes the whole sphere of his creative faculty, his thinking, his work. But it does not include the sphere of the gangster, the altruist and the dictator.

"A man thinks and works alone. A man cannot rob, exploit or rule—alone. Robbery, exploitation and ruling presuppose victims. They imply dependence. They are the province of the second-hander.

"Rulers of men are not egotists. They create nothing. They exist entirely through the persons of others. Their goal is in their subjects, in the activity of enslaving. They are as dependent as the beggar, the social worker and the bandit. The form of dependence does not matter.

"But men were taught to regard second-handers—tyrants, emperors, dictators —as exponents of egotism. By this fraud they were made to destroy the ego, themselves and others. The purpose of the fraud was to destroy the creators. Or to harness them. Which is a synonym.

"From the beginning of history, the two antagonists have stood face to face: the creator and the second-hander. When the first creator invented the wheel, the first second-hander responded. He invented altruism.

"The creator—denied, opposed, persecuted, exploited—went on, moved forward and carried all humanity along on his energy. The second-hander contributed nothing to the process except the impediments. The contest has another name: the individual against the collective.

"The 'common good' of a collective—a race, a class, a state—was the claim and justification of every tyranny ever established over men. Every major horror of history was committed in the name of an altruistic motive. Has any act of selfishness ever equaled the carnage perpetrated by disciples of altruism? Does the fault lie in men's hypocrisy or in the nature of the principle? The most dreadful butchers were the most sincere. They believed in the perfect society reached through the guillotine and the firing squad. Nobody questioned their right to murder since they were murdering for an altruistic purpose. It was accepted that man must be sacrificed for other men. Actors change, but the course of the tragedy remains the same. A humanitarian who starts with declarations of love for mankind and ends with a sea of blood. It goes on and will go on so long as men believe that an action is good if it is unselfish. That permits the altruist to act and forces his victims to bear it. The leaders of collectivist movements ask nothing for themselves. But observe the results.

"The only good which men can do to one another and the only statement of their proper relationship is—Hands off!

"Now observe the results of a society built on the principle of individualism. This, our country The noblest country in the history of men. The country of greatest achievement, greatest prosperity, greatest freedom. This country was not based on selfless service, sacrifice, renunciation or any precept of altruism. It was based on a man's right to the pursuit of happiness. His own happiness. Not anyone else's. A private, personal, selfish motive. Look at the results. Look into your own conscience.

"It is an ancient conflict. Men have come close to the truth, but it was destroyed each time and one civilization fell after another. Civilization is the progress toward a society of privacy. The savage's whole existence is public, ruled by the laws of his tribe. Civilization is the process of setting man free from men.

"Now, in our age, collectivism, the rule of the second-hander and second-rater, the ancient monster, has broken loose and is running amuck. It has brought men to a level of intellectual indecency never equaled on earth. It has reached a scale of horror without precedent. It has poisoned every mind. It has swallowed most of Europe. It is engulfing our country. . . .

DISCUSSION QUESTIONS

1. Does Rand do an adequate job in defining her key terms such as *creator, truth,* and *achievement?* Does she use these terms in a consistent manner?
2. Do you agree with Rand's assertion that "no creator was prompted by a desire to serve his brothers"? Does she offer sufficient evidence to support this claim?
3. Do you agree with Rand that people of vision are usually motivated by truth rather than a desire to serve others? Support your answer with examples.
4. Rand argues that laissez-faire capitalism is the most moral economic system. Why does she make this claim? Do you agree with her? Support your answer.
5. What does Rand mean when she says that "the only good which men can do to one another and the only statement of their proper relationship is—Hands off!"? Does this mean that we should not perform community service or provide welfare and Social Security benefits?
6. Why, according to Rand, is the United States morally off course right now? What is her solution? Would our society be a better place if everyone were an ethical egoist like Howard Roark? Support your answer.
7. To what extent is Rand's philosophy based on her perspective of the American way? Is her philosophy appropriate for people from all cultures or is it culturally relative? How might a cultural relativist such as Ruth Benedict respond to Roark's speech?
8. Is Rand's depiction of what is rational and what is in our self-interest any better than that presented to us by Glaucon in the story of Gyges's ring? Why should we be independent if we can get ahead by stealing someone else's ideas or property? Why should we be just if we can get away with being unjust? Why should we work if we can enjoy our days laying in the sun? How do you think Howard Roark would respond if he found Gyges's ring?
9. Do sociobiologist E. O. Wilson's views support Rand's claim that ethical egoism is the best moral theory and the one that is most in harmony with our human nature?
10. What are some of the implications of Rand's ethical egoism for economic and social policy in the United States and the international market? Use specific examples to support your answer. Are these implications of her theory morally acceptable?

Mary Midgley

Can't We Make Moral Judgements?

English philosopher Mary Midgley (b. 1919) is a staunch opponent of both ethical relativism and ethical egoism. Midgley is also well known outside academic circles as an author, newspaper columnist, and activist in environmental and animal protection groups.

In her book *Can't We Make Moral Judgements?* Midgley questions the currently fashionable view that objective moral judgments are no longer needed or useful. In the following selection, Midgley offers a searing critique of Rand's philosophy of ethical egoism as portrayed in *The Fountainhead*.

CRITICAL THINKING QUESTIONS

1. How does Midgley describe Rand's philosophy?
2. Midgley says that Rand divides the human race into three groups. What are these three groups?
3. What is Midgley's opinion of Rand's book? Does she admire Roark?
4. Why does Midgley claim that Rand is inconsistent when Rand tells people to follow the "guiding star" within them?
5. What does Midgley mean when she says that *The Fountainhead* has a "strong civic slant"?
6. Why does Midgley compare Rand's philosophy with Spencer's Social Darwinism? How are they similar?

THE AMERICAN PREDICAMENT, AYN RAND

Here is a less familiar name, but ideas no less influential. Ayn Rand is a contemporary American prophet of extreme egoistic individualism. In her novels the human race appears divided into three groups. The first group, containing nearly everybody, is a mass of worthless, contented sheep known as "second-handers." They never for a moment think for themselves, and scarcely know that it would be possible to do so, but when other people do it, they respond with terrified

Can't We Make Moral Judgements? (New York: St. Martin's Press, 1993), pp. 119–123.

resentment and persecute the innovators. The second group, which is tiny, contains people who do sometimes think for themselves. They are aware that the life going on around them is a senseless, unchosen existence, and they would like to introduce something better. But they cannot do this because they are not themselves original enough to provide something different. They react to this frustration either with fatalistic despair, or by perversely joining with the vulgar herd to resist and persecute the vanishingly small number of geniuses in the third group —partly from envy, partly from a sense that even this form of action is better than doing nothing. Those in the third group are terribly few, perhaps "a dozen men, down the ages." They are the genuinely creative, original people, able not only to think but to act on their own initiative. But of course, as things are, they are doomed to attract almost universal hatred, and they do the human race a service entirely against its will.

Ayn Rand's best-selling novel, *The Fountainhead,* published in 1947, is an idealised account of the architectural career of Frank Lloyd Wright. Its villains are traditional architects and their supporters, who insist on continuing their servile imitation of earlier styles and fiercely reject the modern buildings of the hero, Howard Roark. The novel is an extreme instance of the romantic cult of the lonely genius. It is also, incidentally, a splendid example of that almost religious exaltation of modernity . . . .

The reason for taking Ayn Rand seriously is not that she invented these ideas. Paradoxically, there is very little that is original here; the ideas are widespread and have many sources. There is surely a great deal of Nietzsche in them, notably from the crowd-hating Nietzsche. . . . What is interesting about Ayn Rand is that she crystallises this cluster of ideas, brings them together so determinedly and expresses them so forcefully. This fact has made her quite an influential writer. *The Fountainhead* is virtually the only book that Allan Bloom sometimes heard cited, by the American students he questioned, as having had an important influence on their lives. (In general, books mean little to them.) The book is still in print and has been frequently republished, both in the US and in Britain.

Much of *The Fountainhead* is an unremarkable social satire—sharp, often effective, and often very funny—directed against the second-handers. The peculiar thing about the book is not what it satirises but what it accepts—its naivety about the honoured groups at the top. As so often happens, a satire is betrayed by the satirist's weakness for some supposed exceptions to the general condemnation—in this case, those taken to be real individuals. The alleged strugglers after integrity are a most unconvincing bunch, and Roark himself is simply a comic-book hero, a featureless, standard he-man, a mere incarnation of virility. Much of the time, fortunately, he is strong and silent, but occasionally he makes speeches. Notably, he makes one to the jury who are trying him for dynamiting some buildings he had designed, but which other architects had inexcusably altered. Having made the expected points about artistic integrity, Roark by no means falls strongly silent, but delivers a six-page lecture on the principles of individualism. (This, rather surprisingly, persuades the jury to acquit him.) . . .

MORAL OR NO MORAL?

What is being said here? Once again, there is a fatal clash of aims. The ideal of a world where nobody ever listens to anybody else is at war with an irresistible desire on the writer's part to be listened to while preaching that ideal, and to shape it so that other people use their freedom in the correct way.

If the ideal of the fragmented, non-listening world prevails, we get subjectivism. In that case, each person generates and lives by a separate and wholly private morality. One of the quotations (from another novel) . . . does seem to call for that approach; "Whatever road I take, the guiding star is within me; the guiding star and the lodestone which point the way." But this passage then goes on, "They point to me."

This is not only a strange and unhelpful thing for a guiding star or a lodestone to do, it is also unmistakably a piece of positive moralising. If anybody else thinks that their guiding stars and lodestones point them rather towards helping others, Ayn Rand is there to tell them that they are mistaken.

In *The Fountainhead,* this positive moralising is clearly the path chosen. There is no attempt to silence positive morality in order to avoid influencing people's individual judgements. What the book calls for is not so much independence in judgement as extreme independence in life; self-sufficiency. To call for that—especially with such passion—clearly assumes the right to influence other people's judgement. The book has a strong civic slant, it wants to change society; it is full of confident criticism both of individual lives lived in mutual, co-operative dependence and of the kind of society that is taken to be built from such lives. In fact, it is full of very sharp criticism of the vulgarity, hypocrisy and pretentiousness that the author detects in contemporary American society.

There is, therefore, something very odd and jarring about the last paragraph that I have quoted, where Roark suddenly decides to celebrate his country, not just grudgingly, as slightly less bad than others, but quite uncritically, in the spirit of a flag-waving presidential candidate.

BELIEVING IN THE SURVIVAL OF THE FITTEST

What has come crashing in here is Social Darwinism—the extra element that distinguishes most English-speaking individualism today sharply from its continental forerunners. The myth that glorifies commercial freedom by viewing it as part of a huge, self-justifying cosmic evolutionary process, and exalts it as the model for all social life, was brought to America by Herbert Spencer in the 1880s. It has little to do with Darwin, and nothing at all to do with serious biology. It has always been centrally a metaphysical way of justifying economic policies, using some selected biological stories as its persuasive myth. Spencer was its main progenitor, though it has sources further back, such as Adam Smith. But Spencer, being extremely ignorant of biology, mistakenly supposed that he could support it from Darwin's biological theories, and the idea has stuck. This quasi-evolutionary view had such a success in the United States that for a long time Spencer's work outsold, in that country, those of every other philosopher.

It is essentially a public and political myth, confidently recommending a particular way of running society. This means that the kind of individualism associated with it is quite different from Nietzsche's kind, which was anarchic, antipolitical and disillusioned with all institutions. It is equally different from Sartre's, which existed to provide a channel of alienation from one particular existing system. After the war, Sartre was always looking for better systems, and was for a long time drawn to Marxism. But he continued to see a great deal of difficulty in bringing his individualism to terms with any political forms. Ayn Rand, by contrast, seems in passages like these to see no difficulty at all in fitting her (officially very demanding) ideas of personal freedom into the framework of that very corporate thing, modern Western-style plutocracy. And there are many other people in the West today who don't seem to find this difficult either.

DISCUSSION QUESTIONS

1. Is Midgley's critique of Rand's philosophy justified? What arguments does Midgley use to support her position? How might Rand respond to some of her criticisms?
2. Midgley notes that, according to Allan Bloom, college students sometimes cite *The Fountainhead* as the only book that has an important influence on their lives. How does Midgley interpret this fondness of college students for *The Fountainhead?* Is Midgley fair in her assessment of students' motives for liking the novel?
3. Is the "civic slant" in Rand's book consistent, according to Midgley, with Rand's philosophy of rational egoism? Is Rand just engaged in "positive moralizing" for the American way of life?
4. In what ways, if any, is Rand's philosophy really based on cultural relativism instead of ethical egoism?

Jean Hampton

The Wisdom of the Egoist: The Moral and Political Implications of Valuing the Self

Jean Hampton was a philosophy professor at the University of Arizona. In her article, "The Wisdom of the Egoist: The Moral and Political Implications of Valuing the Self," Hampton explores the contributions of ethical egoism to a satisfactory account of morality. Although Hampton stops short of concluding that egoism is a comprehensive moral theory, she does maintain that an adequate moral theory must take egoism into account. In particular, Hampton argues that a healthy sense of self-worth is an important tool in fighting political and social oppression.

CRITICAL THINKING QUESTIONS

1. What, according to Hampton, is the traditional understanding of morality?

2. What is the difference between self-honor and self-worship?

3. What is self-worth, and why does Hampton think it is important? Why are moral theories that ignore the primacy of self-worth, such as principle-based theories, inadequate?

4. How do political and social forces affect our ability to carry out our interests?

5. What are some of the theories or attitudes regarding self-worth?

6. In what ways are Dorothea, Mr. Casaubon, and Rosamond, in George Eliot's *Middlemarch,* egoists?

7. Why does Hampton argue that a correct moral theory must be personal?

8. What, according to Hampton, are some of the weaknesses of the egoist's point of view? What are some of the strengths of the egoist's point of view to a correct moral theory?

"The Wisdom of the Egoist: The Moral and Political Implications of Valuing the Self," *Social Philosophy and Policy,* Winter 1997, 14 (1): 21–51. Some notes have been omitted.

I. INTRODUCTION

There is a traditional understanding of what morality is, an understanding that most contemporary moral philosophers take for granted. This understanding is not itself a theory, but rather an account of the phenomenon of morality, to which these philosophers have thought any theory of the phenomenon must conform if it is to be considered successful as either an explanation or a justification of our moral life. According to this account, there are three prominent features that, together, characterize the moral:

First, moral action and moral regard are taken to be other-regarding. While some philosophers have identified a certain kind of self-respect as part of morality, in general morality has been thought to involve duties to others, requiring that they be treated with respect. Self-interest is generally taken to be outside the province of the moral.

Second, morality is supposed to be highly authoritative. In any contest between reasons derived from morality and other sorts of reasons, particularly demands of self-interest, the moral reasons are thought to be almost always the rightful winner (albeit often not the de facto winner). The idea that morality should be accorded such authority has been criticized in recent years by philosophers who accept the idea that morality is largely other-regarding in nature, and who are concerned that individuals will be stifled in their self-pursuits by an overdemanding moral sense. Note that these attacks on the authority of morality presuppose acceptance of the idea that it is largely or exclusively other-regarding in nature.

Third, morality is supposed to be "impersonal" in two senses. First, its content is supposed to be impersonal: whereas we care for our friends or our family because we love things about them that are personal and distinctive to them, our moral attitudes toward people are supposed to be disengaged from the contingencies of their personalities, and responsive to something about them (e.g., their reason) that is common to all human beings. Second, this responsiveness is supposed to be impersonal in the sense that it is motivated by morality itself: that is, the moral worth of our actions is supposed to arise from the fact that we do them "for the sake of" duty, and not for the sake of some interest or affection we have that just happens to accord with moral demands.

In this essay, I will be attacking the first and third tenets, claiming that morality involves considerable self-interested concern, and is much more particular and personal in both content and motivation than it is standardly thought to be. . . .

II. THE POLITICAL ASPECTS OF OUR SELF-CONCERN

One way to see how self-concern is part of the realm of the moral is to appreciate the extent to which unjust political structures can affect human beings such that they are disabled from pursuing their self-interest effectively. Consider the following quotation from a novel by Zora Neale Hurston, in which a dying African-American mother speaks to her daughter:

"Stop cryin', Isie, you can't hear what Ahm sayin', 'member tuh git all de educa-tion you kin. Dat's de onliest way you kin keep out from under people's feet. You always strain tuh be de bell cow, never be de tail uh nothin'. Do de best you kin, honey, 'cause neither yo' paw nor dese older chillun is goin' tuh be bothered too much wid you, but you goin' tuh git 'long. Mark mah words, You got de spunk, but mah po' li'l' sandy-haired chile goin' suffer uh lot 'fo' she git tuh de place she kin 'fend fuh herself. And Isie, honey, stop cryin' and lissen tuh me. Don't you love nobody better'n you do yo'self. Do, you'll be dying befo' yo' time is out. And Isie, uh person kin be killed 'thout being struck uh blow." *

This mother appreciates the extent to which her daughter's future ability to fend for herself, pursue her own interests, and have ambitions that she effectively achieves, is directly linked to the extent to which she believes in her own worth —that is, the extent to which she thinks she is someone who matters, whose tal-ents are real, whose interests are important to satisfy, whose ideas and ambi-tions are something that others should take seriously. This mother knows, however, that once she has died, her daughter's sense of her own worth as a per-son will be imperiled in the environment in which she is growing up. As the youngest female in a family that doesn't take females to be the equals of males, and as a member of an oppressed group in her society, the child will be sent mes-sage after message telling her that she doesn't matter, that her educational and occupational horizons are limited, that her concerns, her views, and her words should not be taken seriously. Hence, the mother tries from her deathbed to bestow upon the child the courage to resist the denigrating messages that she is sure to receive.

. . .

Contrast this passage with a discussion by John Stuart Mill in *The Subjection of Women,* describing how certain boys in his society are raised to think about themselves in relation to women:

> [H]ow early the notion of his inherent superiority to a girl arises in his mind; how
> it grows with his growth and strengthens with his strength; how it is inoculated by
> one schoolboy upon another; how early the youth thinks himself superior to his
> mother, owing her perhaps forbearance, but no real respect; and how sublime and
> sultan-like a sense of superiority he feels, above all, over the woman he honours by
> admitting her to a partnership of his life.†

Particularly insofar as Mill had middle-class and upper-class British men in mind when he wrote this passage, he is portraying the kind of self-conception held by human beings who occupy a high place in the hierarchy of their society. A bit

---

*Zora Neale Hurston, *Jonah's Gourd Vine* (1934; reprint, London: Virago, 1987), pp. 206–207.

†John Stuart Mill, *The Subjection of Women,* ed. Susan Moller Okin (Indianapolis: Hackett, 1988), p. 87.

later, Mill refers to these people as enjoying not self-love—which is what Isie's mother wants her to strive for—but rather "self-worship":

> It is an exact parallel to the feeling of a hereditary king that he is excellent above others by being born a king, or a noble by being born a noble. . . . The self-worship of the monarch, or of the feudal superior, is matched by the self-worship of the male.[*]

Reared to believe in their own superiority, Mill says, these males receive training in "arrogance and overbearingness."[†]

. . . Henceforth I will call the regard that Isie's mother wants her to have "self-honor" and the regard that Mill's boys are taught "self-worship." The term "pride" can refer to either self-honor or self-worship. Criticisms of "prideful-ness" commonly found, for example, in Christian religious literature are appropriate, in my view, as criticisms of self-worship, but never of self-honor. As I will explain more fully below, this is, in part, because self-honor is a way to fight against the lack of self-regard which threatens Isie, and which I will henceforth call "self-denigration."

Each of these attitudes reflects the view one takes about one's own value and how that value is related to the value of others. What actions one takes, what aims one develops, what ambitions one believes one is allowed to have, all depend upon the kind of worth one is prepared to accord oneself and others. If Isie thinks she is too unimportant for a certain career, she will not pursue it; if she thinks that her race or gender makes her too "low" or "the wrong sort of person" for certain kinds of interests, she will not develop them. Even if she refuses to believe these messages, the rest of her society may contain enough people who accept them to make it virtually impossible for her to get access to what she needs in order to pursue activities thought inappropriate for "her kind." (For example, in my mother's high school in the 1940s, girls were not allowed to take physics; for much of this century, African Americans were effectively prohibited from pursuing many careers in the United States.) Indeed, merely being poor can be taken as reflective of a person's importance in societies where worth tracks wealth, so that the fact that a person such as Isie comes from the "wrong side of the tracks" (where this fact may be manifested in her accent, her clothes, or her level of education) can be thought, by her or by others in society, to preclude her from pursuing certain kinds of occupations or from getting into certain kinds of colleges. People on the receiving end of messages branding them as "low" in value are in danger of learning to accept being the "tail of the herd."

. . .

. . . Social and political forces can indirectly affect what interests we have and our sense of the importance of these interests, by playing a part in constructing

---

[*]*Ibid.,* pp. 87–88.
[†]*Ibid.,* p. 88.

our sense of our own worth. This construction can work by relying on certain intrinsic features we have (e.g., our race, our gender), so that we think: because I'm a female, I'm not worth all that much; or because I'm white, I'm very important. Or that construction can work by defining the worth of roles, to which certain kinds of people are steered (e.g., I'm only a mother, and hence I'm not as important as that lawyer over there). The kind of self-worth you believe that you have can affect any or all of the following:

1. the kind and extent of the talents you believe you have, or are supposed to have;

2. the kind of interests and desires you have, or believe you are supposed to have, and the extent to which you believe these interests or desires should be taken into account in any practical calculation about how to allocate resources or define policies for a group of which you are a member;

3. the kind of treatment you believe you can demand from others;

4. the extent to which you believe your views, ideas, and beliefs count in any theoretical reflection or in any discussion with other people;

5. the kind of ambition(s) you have, and the extent to which you believe you are entitled to have it (that is, believe this ambition is appropriate for one such as you).

However, the construction of your sense of your own worth is not entirely a social and political product—indeed, that is why the mother in Hurston's story is speaking in such an impassioned way to her daughter. Each of us has to choose the kind of worth we wish to accord ourselves, and the kind of worth we are willing to fight to have others accord us. The social and political pressures against the worth we would accord ourselves can be considerable, so that maintaining a belief in that worth can require significant inner strength. That fact does not make the choice impossible, and in my view, does not remove responsibility from those who "give in" and accept a conception of worth that is too low (any more than the social pressure that encourages self-worship in certain classes of men exculpates them from responsibility for the denigrating attitudes they take toward women and the arrogance they assume for themselves). However, I shall leave such issues of responsibility aside for now.

In any case, the implications of one's sense of self-worth are enormous. So what is self-worth? What is the right conception of worth? How should a social and political environment affect children such that they get the right sense of worth? And what does talk of worth have to do with *morality?*

III. THEORIES OF WORTH

When I speak of the notion of self-worth, I do not mean the (currently trendy) concept of self-esteem. To the extent that I can figure out what self-esteem is supposed to be, it is either pride in accomplishment, or else some kind of "feel-good-about-myself" sentiment that we are supposed to promote in ourselves and others (especially our children) so that we and they will be happy.

But the notion of self-worth need have nothing to do with personal effort and is not a kind of feeling. It is defined by a theory of human worth, a theory that sets out, among other things, what the criteria of worth are, such that each of us can evaluate our own worth. . . .

Different attitudes toward the self are generated by the theory of worth one accepts. Mill's boys, who are reared to self-worship, accept a hierarchical theory of worth that places them at or near the top, and places women well below them. Isie's mother worries that Isie will come to regard herself with self-denigration by accepting her society's view that, because of her race and gender, her value is well below that of others of a different race or gender. Both Mill and Isie's mother are implicitly pushing an egalitarian theory of worth, one that defines the nature of the self-honor which they wish all of us to accord ourselves, and which they believe many in their society are wrong to reject.

It is important to recognize the hold that inegalitarian theories of worth have exercised over people, if we are to understand the history of oppression and injustice. Consider Harper Lee's portrayal of the inegalitarian structure of the American South during the 1930s in her book *To Kill a Mockingbird*. In one passage, twelve-year-old Jem attempts to explain to his eight-year-old sister Scout the facts about value in their society:

> There are four kinds of folks in the world. There's the ordinary kind like us and the
> neighbors, there's the kind like the Cunninghams out in the woods, the kind like
> the Ewells down at the dump, and the Negroes.*

Scout struggles to figure out where she will fit in this hierarchy given that she will be a woman some day in a town where women are supposed to be "ladies" and are thereby precluded from a variety of jobs and positions. She also knows that Jem's ranking cannot be complete, because it leaves some people out: "What about the Chinese, and the Cajuns down yonder in Baldwin County?" she asks her brother. And in the end, she rejects her brother's assessment of the facts about value, in part because of her acceptance of her father's egalitarian point of view, and in part because of her own experiences. She insists, "Naw, Jem, I think there's just one kind of folks. Folks."† The collusion between the inegalitarian ranking accepted by most folks in this society and the egalitarian ranking endorsed by Scout and her father (and a few other people in their county) is the central theme of the novel. Harper Lee, who comes down clearly on the side of the truth of the egalitarian theory, is nonetheless concerned to show how the popularity of the false hierarchical theory has profound implications for nearly all the social and political institutions of Maycomb County, including its criminal justice system, its employment practices, its educational system, and its religious life.

---

*Harper Lee, *To Kill a Mockingbird* (Philadelphia: J. B. Lippincott, 1960), p. 239.
†*Ibid.*, p. 240.

. . .

As these examples show, one reason it is important to recognize the reality of inegalitarian theories of worth is in order to explain certain aspects of the nature of oppression. When people oppress other people, they generally take their mastery to be *rightful* and legitimate. Hence, they work from a theory of relative value which justifies their advantages and their control over people whom they regard as their inferiors, and which defines the sorts of behavior appropriate to both the oppressors and the oppressed.

. . .

But how do we know that *any* egalitarian theory is right? From where do theories of worth, and their attendant theories of rightful treatment, come? Are they basic, or are they derived from some more fundamental moral law?

IV. THE PRIMACY OF THE IDEA OF WORTH

Generations of readers of Kant have puzzled over which of the first two formulations of his Moral Law is the better and more fundamental characterization of the foundations of morality. The first formulation asks us to test our courses of action, implementing them only if we could "will" a world in which everyone pursued that course of action for the purpose for which we want to pursue it. As Kant puts it, this version of the Moral Law says: "Act only on that maxim through which you can at the same time will that it should become a universal law." The second formulation works rather differently. Kant states it as: "Act in such a way that you always treat humanity, whether in your own person or in the person of any other, never simply as a means, but always at the same time as an end." Note that this formulation works by establishing that human beings are "ends" in themselves, and calls upon us to accord them certain treatment by virtue of their standing as "ends."

Whether or not these two formulations generate the same set of permissions and prohibitions, they are nonetheless different by virtue of the way they ground those permissions and prohibitions. The first formulation represents morality as arising from a kind of reasoning procedure, from which it follows that human beings have a certain kind of equal standing. In contrast, the second formulation represents morality as arising from the fact that human beings have a certain kind of equal standing, from which it follows that we must reason a certain way prior to determining how we should act. Thus, both formulations involve a theory of human worth and a theory of rightful treatment, but the first formulation derives the first theory (i.e., the theory of human worth) from the second (i.e., the theory of rightful treatment, which, in turn, is itself defined via a reasoning procedure), whereas the second formulation takes the theory of human worth to be more basic, so that specific moral reasoning procedures and policies dictating rightful treatment are derived from it.

It is not only Kant's theory that admits of these two theoretical interpretive alternatives. Mill's remarks above show the extent to which utilitarianism can be understood to be based on a theory of worth, rather than on a principle from which that theory of worth is derived. If it is principle-based, utilitarianism grounds its moral recommendations in the principle of utility, whose recommendations define a theory of moral treatment which we can take to express a certain kind of egalitarian theory of worth. On this interpretation, that theory of worth (as well as the recommendations for treatment) can be considered correct only because the principle of utility is the correct foundation for all action. . . . On this view, the principle of utility simply expresses the equality of human value, while taking a certain stand on the way that value can be aggregated.

Which kind of interpretation of these two moral theories is better, the principle-dependent kind, or the worth-dependent kind?

The standard way of interpreting both sorts of theories is principle-dependent. Somehow contemporary moral thinkers have taken it as obvious that moral behavior is commanded fundamentally by some sort of principle or abstract norm. If the principle or norm directs our attention to the consequences of actions, the theory is called consequentialist; if the principle or norm directs our attention to the "rightness" or "wrongness" of the actions themselves, considered apart from their consequences, the theory is called deontological.

Michael Stocker argues, however, that principle-based moral theories portray moral action in a way that is divorced from the nature of the actual moral motives people have, producing a kind of "schizophrenia" with respect to moral reasons and moral motives in those who believe contemporary moral theories. Whether the theory is consequentialist or deontological, what such a theory values, says Stocker, is something abstract and impersonal—e.g., some principle, or moral law, or duty—from which we are supposed to act. Yet he notes that real moral action seems motivated not by austere moral principles but by concern for the person or persons who will be affected by the moral action: . . . It is as if, says Stocker, such theories are "devoid of all people." In contrast, he notes that an egoistic theory at least recognizes the value and the appeal of *one* person, namely, the self. The egoist welcomes certain actions or events not merely because he takes them to be good, but more fundamentally because he takes them to be good *for him*—the one person he values.

. . .

V. EGOISM

In order to understand what the egoist values with respect to himself, we need some portraits of egoists to work from. There are a number of such portraits in George Eliot's *Middlemarch,** in which egoism, and its attendant evils, is a central theme.

Two of the major characters in the novel are Dorothea and her first husband, Mr. Casaubon. While Dorothea eventually escapes the egoistic point of view, poor Casaubon never does, retreating more and more into a kind of prison of

---

*George Eliot, *Middlemarch* (1871), ed. W. J. Harvey (Hardmondsworth: Penguin, 1965); all page references to this work will be given parenthetically in the text.

egoistic loneliness as he ages. Happy with his own dreams of his brilliant scholar-ship, and frightened of the possibility of outsiders who may well have different views of that scholarship, he hides in his study, particularly from Dorothea, his observant new wife, who rather too quickly divines the sterility of his work. Eliot presents us with a sympathetic but unyieldingly critical analysis of his egoism. Lest we judge him too harshly, however, she continually invites us to compare ourselves with him: "Mr Casaubon, too, was the centre of his own world; if he was liable to think that others were providentially made for him . . . this trait is not quite alien to us, and, like the other mendicant hopes of mortals, claims some of our pity" (p. 111). And: "Mr Casaubon had an intense consciousness within him, and was spiritually a-hungered like the rest of us" (p. 312). For this man, who insisted he was not to be disturbed in his library or in his own thoughts, and who could not tolerate criticism or the evaluations of others, being married was a difficult and frightening experience, because it meant that another person, with another point of view unlike—and sometimes opposed to—his own, was contin-ually foisted upon him.

A different kind of egoist is presented in the person of Rosamond Lydgate, who is even more taken with herself than Casaubon is taken with himself, know-ing few of his fears, and displaying even more "hunger" for her own way. In one amusing passage, she displays her remarkable self-centeredness by evaluating everyone *else* she knows as selfish.

> [She complained of the] disagreeable people who only thought of themselves, and did not mind how annoying they were to her. Even her father was unkind, and might have done more for them. In fact there was but one person in Rosamond's world whom she did not regard as blameworthy, and that was the graceful creature with blond plaits and with little hands crossed before her, who had never expressed herself unbecomingly, and had always acted for the best—the best being what she best liked. (p. 716)

Rosamond's self-centered perspective is in many respects matched by that of her husband, Dr. Lydgate, whose other-regarding profession belies a selfish ambi-tiousness and contempt for women that leads him into a disastrous marriage with Rosamond: "Poor Lydgate! Or shall I say, Poor Rosamond! Each lived in a world of which the other knew nothing" (p. 195).

What is it that Casaubon, Rosamond, and Lydgate have in common that makes them egoists? It is not, as in the account of egoism suggested by some philosophers, that they have a solipsistic point of view. Each of them is very much aware that there are other people in the world: for example, Casaubon fears these potentially critical centers of subjectivity, and Rosamond is a very social creature, who needs and thrives on the company of others. However, both per-ceive other people as "providentially made" for them (and both curse their bad luck if these other people behave in a way that hurts their interests). As Eliot puts it, each of them is at the center of his or her own world, which means that each takes himself or herself to be the only person who matters to any significant degree. Hence, each of them views other people as deriving what value they have from the fact that they are useful in some way to the one person—namely, him-

or herself—who really matters. Lydgate is valued by Rosamond as a pleasant, handsome companion and source of money and social status; Dorothea is valued by Casaubon only to the extent that she is a pleasing, uncritical, and nonjudgmental helpmate at the margins of his world.

These egoists are not without their virtues. Even horrible Rosamond is impressive in the power of her will. . . . Rosamond's self-assertion is something we are meant to admire; it is something that the main heroine of the book, Dorothea, has to learn.

Dorothea has to learn it because, unlike Rosamond, Dorothea is intent on not being selfish, which she initially thinks means that she must sublimate her will to others. Dorothea learns, however, that selfishness and self-assertion are not the same, and that the latter can be not only admirable but even required in the selfless person. Dorothea's interest in devoting herself to others comes perilously close at various times in the novel to servility and loss of self. Professing "the necessity of some individuals to hold fast to their personal view of the nature of things" (p. 96), she eventually learns to stand up to the bullying commands of Casaubon, finally telling him: "Do you not see now that I could not submit my soul to yours, by working hopelessly at what I have no belief in?" (p. 583). This resolve is something that comes hard for Dorothea, whose fervent belief that she needs to help others—particularly her husband—tends to cripple her ability to stand up for herself. Eliot's message, however, is that the healthy soul is capable of self-assertion—albeit for the right cause. In a letter, Eliot once wrote:

> The martyr at the stake seeks its gratification [i.e., the gratification of ego] as much as the court sycophant, the difference lying in the comparative dignity and beauty of the two egos. People absurdly talk of self-denial—why there is none in Virtue to a being of moral excellence—the greatest torture to such a soul would be to run counter to the dictates of conscience . . .*

Thus, Eliot's cure for the egoist is not to give up asserting herself, and not to engage in self-denial. Her cure is to get the egoist to take up a new cause.

But what is the nature of this better cause? The novel suggests that it has to do with letting other people into one's world such that their points of view, their desires, their welfare, their ideas, *matter*. Dorothea's growth toward moral maturity is instructive. At first she is filled with a romantic vision of helping other people, leading her to marry Casaubon, whom she believes is striving for truth and wisdom. What she discovers in her marriage is that helping other people is *hard*, in part because seeing them as they really are, and not as one might wish to see them, is hard. . . . Dorothea learns that helping even one person is a mighty struggle, because it is hard to get the yearnings and feelings and being of even one person into one's sight; and this is because it is hard not to be preoccupied with one's own yearnings and feelings and being, insofar as one's own person seems so much more important than others. *Middlemarch* is, in part, a novel about the

---

*George Eliot, letter to Maria Lewis dated February 18, 1842, in *The George Eliot Letters*, ed. Gordon S. Haight (New Haven, CT: Yale University Press, 1954), vol. 1, p. 127.

struggles of being married, a state in which two people have to learn to admit another's point of view into their lives. Both Rosamond and Casaubon are so absorbed in themselves that they struggle to get any glimmer of the perspective and interests of their partners (although Casaubon's kind words in the passage above, and Rosamond's one act of kindness toward Lydgate late in the novel, suggest that each might not be completely ignorant of his or her spouse's point of view). Dorothea learns more, appreciating that true service to others requires not self-denial but rather what might be called a "roving sympathy" toward others, a sympathy which may not generate agreement or unity or harmony, but which enables one partner to honor and understand the other, and which presupposes, to a considerable extent, one partner's sense of the other as *mattering*.

All of this provides interesting lessons for us moral theorists; for what Dorothea learns is quite unlike the kind of lesson that a contemporary moral philosopher would preach to her.

VI. A PERSONAL MORAL THEORY

The first lesson Dorothea learns is that moral regard is strikingly *personal* rather than impersonal. There is a marvelous line in which Eliot describes Dorothea's progress in her view of her troubled husband: "[S]he seemed to be looking along the one track where duty becomes tenderness" (p. 400). Dorothea learns to act not from grand principle, but from concern for *him*. She comes to understand his difficulties, his needs, his point of view, so that her behavior comes to reflect not just *her* needs, beliefs, and interests, but also his—although not necessarily in a way that he likes or wants. Learning to admit another—as that person really is—into one's view of the world often does not produce saccharine harmony or untroubled unity, particularly if the other person hungers after something harmful for himself or others. Once Dorothea understands Casaubon, she is empowered to resist his selfish bullying; but she is also empowered to feel compassion toward him, in a way that genuinely does him some good (far more good than her youthful romantic visions could provide him).

. . .

Here is a vision of the impersonal, commanding, authoritative, awful Moral Law about which we contemporary moral philosophers have theorized. In a way, it is a "scientific" view of morality, in that morality is presented as directing us—controlling us—via a moral law governing our will, analogous to the way in which scientific laws direct, control, and govern matter—with the exception, of course, that we can flout the moral law but not the laws of nature.

In *Middlemarch*, however, where duty shades into tenderness for the most successful characters, the lesson is different. Morality certainly calls, but it has a personal face. It is not duty, but Casaubon himself, to which Dorothea finally responds. It is not duty, but the viewpoints, aspirations, and desires of Lydgate, that Rosamond determinedly keeps at bay. Marriage turns out to be a kind of moral test for these characters, in which the close proximity of another person challenges them to learn either to admit the other as an equal into their own world, or else to fashion an egoistic sphere of movement, such that they can still dream their own dreams about themselves despite living with another.

. . .

The second lesson *Middlemarch* teaches us through its portrait of egoism is the importance of retaining the self in the moral point of view. Dorothea's story warns us about the danger of too little ego, too little self-assertiveness, and the risks of annihilating oneself if one gives oneself too thoroughly to others. If the center of your world only includes others, then you yourself are lost. Hence, the moral person must retain the self-assertiveness, the self-enjoyment, and the self-definition of the egoist, but expand the "cause" for which she acts to include the interests, needs, and beliefs of others as well as her own. Again, Rosamond teaches us something here. Whereas Dorothea's life is in danger of being joyless and dour, Rosamond has fun. She sings, she rides, she converses with friends while Dorothea frets in monastic dress about how to serve others. Whereas Dorothea decides to give up horseback riding because she concludes it is unfair to have such enjoyment given the plight of the poor in the countryside through which she rides, Rosamond enjoys a good gallop in the country. We are meant, I believe, to judge both of them as making a mistake, albeit in different directions. Rosamond eventually has a miscarriage because she rides while she is pregnant—a telling indication of the extent to which she puts her own desires first. On the other hand, Dorothea's gray life (which reflects, in part, the strictures of a sexist society that gives her very little opportunity to spend it in pursuit of something fine) makes us anxious and exasperated. Were she not so sweet and well-meaning, we would find her tedious.

Thus, the second lesson of the novel (which I suspect George Eliot herself may have had great difficulty learning) is that morality should not be understood as some impersonal law whose "inevitable fate" is destined to kill us off with its relentless other-regarding commands.

In the rest of this essay, I will consider how both of these lessons can be incorporated into a successful theory of our moral life.

VII. ACTING FOR THE SAKE OF THE SELF

What do egoists like Rosamond and Casaubon teach us? They do *not* teach us that we should all like ourselves. This is, in part, because not all egoists do like themselves. Many egoists (like Casaubon) are dissatisfied with who they are, often working relentlessly to remedy what they regard as their deficiencies (think of self-absorbed dieters, or discontented business executives who continually go to self-improvement classes). What marks someone as an egoist, then, is not an attitude of approval or adoration toward herself (an egoist needn't be a narcissist). More importantly, we are sometimes right not to like ourselves, particularly when we have attitudes or character traits basic to our personalities that are morally disreputable, and thus worth condemning. Such dislike can even be valuable, if it instigates a decision to try to change for the better.

Nor do egoists teach us the correct theory of value. Egoism is generated by an extreme form of a hierarchical theory of value: whereas the males in Mill's world accept a hierarchical theory of worth that puts all males (or at least all males of a certain class) at the top of the ladder of value, the egoist puts only himself at the top, regarding other people as (to use Eliot's phrase regarding Casaubon) "providentially made for him." Moreover, as the character of Casaubon illustrates, deep dissatisfaction with some or all of his traits can coexist in the egoist with the view that he matters far more than any other. One might also speculate about the extent to which an egoist's view of his value feeds off a conception of others as mere servants of his interests, such that his sense of his own high worth is dependent on his view of others as radically lower than him. (Compare the way in which, in Hegel's master/slave dialectic, the master derives his higher value from his perception of the slave's vastly lower value.)

Finally, we cannot learn from egoists any sound lessons about what really counts as good for oneself, or what will be truly self-advancing. People such as Rosamond or Casaubon have little idea what the good really is, in part because, like all people who leave out the well-being of others from their view of the world, they are invariably going to miss important components of the good life. (At the end of *Middlemarch* it is striking that the person who achieves the most happiness and personal satisfaction is Dorothea.)

However, we can learn from egoists what I will call the correct "object of concern" of moral behavior. While egoists have the wrong theory of human worth, and hence the wrong understanding of self-worth, they are nonetheless correct in thinking that what it is important to be concerned about is the *self*. Of course, they are concerned with only one self, and it is a self that they may not like, and may wish to improve, upbraid, punish, or even loathe. But what makes them egoists is that they act for the sake of that self, and not for the sake of some abstract principle, rule or object. As I shall now discuss, it is the idea of "acting for the sake of the self," rather than acting for the sake of a principle, that I take to be important for moral theory.

. . .

Now imagine a moral theory that accepts the egoist's view that the self is what has value, even while insisting that *every* self has value. On such a theory, egoists such as Rosamond are not wrong to value themselves, and are not wrong to think that the source of their value comes from their being selves; they are only wrong to value themselves exclusively. Many different religious and moral traditions recognize some formulation of the Golden Rule: i.e., love others as you love yourself. We can imagine an interpretation of that rule such that it expresses the attitude each of us should take toward others in the face of the reality of our own value. If "love" is defined here as the attitude of recognition of value, then the egoist stops too soon—the value he accords himself points toward the value he should be prepared to accord all other human beings because that which makes appropriate an attribution of value to himself is also what makes appropriate the same attitude toward others—namely, that they too are selves. On this view, then, the egoist's mistake is the hierarchical nature of his value-scheme, which drops others far below himself; but unlike people grandly planning to benefit "humanity" in the abstract, he is at least alive to the value of one human being, namely himself. Were he also alive to the value that all other persons possess, then he would begin to assume the moral point of view.

Recognizing the value of other selves does not necessarily mean liking them. A self that has worth may also be a self that is maddening, irritating, evil, disrespectful, ugly, or unfriendly—these characteristics do not detract from the fact that it is still valuable, so that certain kinds of treatments of it are precluded. Or to use Kantian language, the fact that the will of this self may be bad does not lessen the fact that the self is still an "end in itself."

Can we construct an argument that proves the egoist ought to value others besides herself? . . .

Suppose the egoist contends that there is something about herself that means that only she is valuable. This will not work, for two reasons. First, if this distinctive thing is some trait or characteristic, it will likely be found in at least one other person, so that this other will also have value, or perhaps have even more value than she has. Second, on such a view, the egoist would ultimately be valuable only because this trait is valuable, not because there is anything worthwhile about *her.* Suppose, then, that the egoist claims she is valuable by virtue of being the particular self that she is. But then, since everyone else is also a particular self, why wouldn't each other person be just as valuable as she is?

In the end, the egoist is hard-pressed to explain why she is warranted in according herself such overwhelming value. (Although, interestingly, most real egoists do not seem particularly worried about this. Do they take their overwhelming value to be obvious?) It is worth pressing this point: moral theorists have traditionally been challenged to explain why any of us should have regard for others, but what I take to be much harder, indeed impossible, to explain is why an egoist should be justified in according such extreme regard to herself. The absurdity of the egoist's hierarchy of value is at least one consideration relevant to constructing an argument for the plausibility of the moral point of view.

Using the egoist's idea that the self is the carrier of value, we can construct an alternative to the impersonal portrayal of Kantian morality suggested in the first formulation of the Moral Law. On a personalized interpretation of the Kantian theory (an interpretation hinted at in the second formulation of the Moral Law, which calls on us to treat human beings as ends in themselves), morality concerns the value of each individual understood as a self (for now, I mean each human individual, but we might extend the realm of the moral to include animals by arguing that a theory of morality also concerns their value, given the nature of their selves —a value that we may not think is the equal of humans, but which is considerable nonetheless). On this view, to speak of a person's value is not to speak of something that is contingent; nor is it to speak of something that is possessed in full by only some. In that sense, value is impersonal. On the other hand, doing something "for morality's sake" on this view comes down to doing it not because one is moved by some abstract moral principle or norm, but because one is moved by the value of *that self*—a value that engages us in a variety of ways, perhaps not only rationally but also emotionally. Thus, even if I dislike a person and eschew friendship with her, a certain sort of treatment of her is still mandated because of something about *her,* not because of some abstract moral principle. Moreover, on such a Kantian theory, this worth is also something which I have myself, and which I must respect in myself just as much as I must respect it in others.

. . .

Not only Kantian theory but also utilitarianism admits of a "personalized" version (which I have suggested may be the version animating Mill's moral theorizing). This version of utilitarianism agrees with the personalized Kantian theory of the equality of human value, but differs on the question of how our values can be aggregated. The fact that aggregation is possible allows us, according to the utilitarian, to calculate the answers to moral questions using the principle of utility, which, in this view, is not foundational but rather derived from a theory of how and why people are valuable. Henceforth, I will call the Kantian and utilitarian value-based theories "personalized" alternatives to the utilitarian and Kantian theories that Stocker criticizes.

VIII. SELF-INTEREST

The egoist teaches us a second lesson: that our own selves are valuable. This lesson has been taken by moral theorists to be blatantly obvious, but it is nonetheless not obvious to many people. Probably because most philosophers have, up until now, been males from relatively privileged social positions—a background that encourages people to think well of themselves—there has been virtually no recognition of how difficult it can be for some people to believe in their own worth. For a person like Isie in Hurston's novel (quoted in the beginning of Section II)—that is, a person who is subjected to social and political forces that attempt to construct her conception of her own worth so as to make her feel lower than others, thereby affecting her ability to accomplish certain tasks, acquire certain interests, or develop certain ambitions—maintaining a belief in one's self-worth can be hard. This shows that the content of a person's self-interested concerns is not part of the moral in any direct sense. But the ability of a person to be *appropriately* self-concerned, and to develop interests and objectives, is a moral matter. Our self-concerns are indirectly part of the moral to the extent that they reflect our sense of our self-worth, which *is* a moral matter. It is a moral matter at the personal level, requiring certain kinds of choices from us; but it is also a social and political matter, insofar as our sense of our self-worth can reflect powerful (and perhaps virtually inescapable) sociopolitical messages of inferiority or superiority, or messages about our "place" or proper role, that we may find difficult to resist or fight.

Can we accommodate these reflections by saying, in Kantian fashion, that each of us has duties not only to others but also to the self? Not completely. We can certainly speak of each of us having a duty to accord ourselves worth that is the equal of every other person's, entailing a duty to resist servility and a duty to develop self-respect. But doing things for oneself, e.g., giving oneself a gift, should not be a "duty," any more than giving a good friend a gift should be a duty. Kantian ethics has been criticized because it encourages, at least in certain forms, an impersonal portrayal of moral action that removes it from the emotional engagements that we want moral persons to have. But one should be able to enjoy one's gifts both to others and to oneself, whether those gifts be an extra round of golf, a trip to see a good friend, or a second topping on one's pizza. And one should not be ashamed to want a good education, or a good career, or a good time. I would argue, then, that an inability to feel joy when you give yourself a gift *is* a moral matter, just as an inability to enjoy gift-giving to others is a moral matter. . . .

If the value of the self and the values possessed by other selves are equal, then how is it that we should work out whose interests matter more when the interests of the self and the interests of others conflict? This is the subject matter of normative ethics: any normative theory needs to provide principles for adjudicating the conflicting interests of different people. It is an issue we face on a daily basis when we are worried only about the conflicting interests of people other than ourselves, for example, when deciding how to resolve the conflicting interests of our children, or our friends, or our employees. We have the same type of problem when we put ourselves into the equation: adjudicating competing interests—including situations when some of these interests are our own—requires a normative moral theory, which expresses a conception of how to weight the interests of equally valuable people.

Note that in the passage quoted at the start of Section II, Zora Neale Hurston presents one principle of such a normative theory: that is, "Never love others more than you love yourself"—which is not to say that you cannot love others as much as you do yourself, but only that you should never love them more. It is a principle that one does not find clearly stated in either the utilitarian or the Kantian tradition, although each can be interpreted so as to be consistent with it. I have argued elsewhere that something like this principle can be thought to animate a contractarian moral theory, and I have commended a certain kind of contractarian reasoning procedure as a way of adjudicating conflicting claims—even (indeed, especially) when some of those claims are your own. In any case, whether or not I am right about the structure that a good normative theory should have, my point here is that it must recognize and accommodate self-worth and the self-interest that worth mandates, lest it fail to acknowledge correctly the value that any acceptable moral theory should accord each of us.

IX. CONCLUSION

In order to investigate the source and nature of any value human beings are thought to have, we need to do meta-ethics. Whether our value is projected or constructed or discovered is not something that I can pursue further here. Certainly some kind of sound meta-ethical theory will be necessary to vindicate the intuition that human value is equal. Exactly *why* racists and sexists and egoists are wrong about who has value is something any good theory of morality should explain, and I have at least tried to offer some preliminary ruminations on this topic.

What I have been mainly concerned to argue in this essay, however, is that assumptions about human value form the heart of the moralities that actually animate people's views and actions in any society, that they are basic both to other-regard and self-regard, that they are fundamental to people's actual motives to do the right thing, and that a just society accepts a thesis of equal value whereas an unjust society accepts an inegalitarian theory of value that licenses the oppression of those at the bottom. I have also insisted that unless each of us takes responsibility for acknowledging value not only in others but also in ourselves, we will be in danger not only of harming others but also of harming ourselves. Or to use the language of Isie's mother, unless we honor our own worth, the self in each of us will die without being "struck a blow." Indeed, the sort of self-regard that I have called "self-honor" is, as she appreciated, a critical tool in the fight against sociopolitical oppression.

Finally, I have tried to show that an impersonal conception of morality is harmful to the moral cause: to see morality as some kind of unrelenting force of duty, which commands us as surely as the law of gravity, is the worst way we could try to sell the moral life to egoists such as Rosamond or Casaubon, who have a real fear that their selves and their points of view are at risk, and whose egoism may be in part a protection against the kind of loss of self that threatens "selfless" people such as Dorothea. A personalized view of morality protects, above all else, the agent to whom we are commending the moral life; for if that self can be a casualty of "duty," then why should we respect its commands or its authority over us? Why shouldn't it be hated, fought, rebelled against? Whatever morality is, it should not be construed as a force that is out to get us, but rather as a way of regarding human beings, ourselves included, that seeks to generate individual actions and social policies that will bring us a finer and richer world.

DISCUSSION QUESTIONS

1. Do you agree with Hampton that a successful moral theory must include "considerable self-interested concern"? What arguments does she use to support her position?
2. Discuss whether or not Hampton's description of human nature is consistent with E. O. Wilson's view of human nature.
3. What does Hampton mean when she refers to a trait as a vice or a virtue? Are self-denigration and self-worship both vices? Discuss how our attitude about our self-worth affects our ability to interact with others and to make satisfactory moral decisions.
4. Why does Hampton reject inegalitarian theories of worth? How is egoism partly a corrective to this?
5. Discuss Michael Stocker's statement that principle-based moral theories, such as Kantian deontology, produce a kind of schizophrenia.
6. Compare and contrast Rand's and Hampton's descriptions of an egoist. Discuss how Rand's ideal egoist—Howard Roark in her novel *The Fountainhead*—differs from Hampton's example of an egoist—Mr. Casaubon in George Eliot's *Middlemarch*. Which person, Rand or Hampton, presents the most accurate portrayal of an egoist? Support your answer.
7. Would Virginia Held agree with Hampton's argument that moral theory has to be more personal? Discuss how Held would most likely respond to Hampton's argument about the importance of self-concern in fighting unjust political structures.
8. Why does Hampton reject egoism as satisfactory moral theory? Do you agree with her? Discuss how Rand would most likely respond to Hampton's conclusion.

Chapter Applications

ᘒ

1. Battles in Toyland: Mattel Versus Hasbro

In February 1996, Hasbro refused an offer by Mattel, the nation's largest toy manufacturer, to buy it out. If Hasbro had been sold, 1,700 employees of Hasbro would have, in all likelihood, lost their jobs. Although the news of the refusal was greeted with exuberance by the employees of Hasbro and the people of Rhode Island where Hasbro is located, some of the shareholders were furious.

If the deal from Mattel had been accepted, shareholders in Hasbro would have been given stock in Mattel that could have been sold at a considerable profit.[1] They argued in their lawsuit against Hasbro that the company has a legal obligation to maximize the profit for the shareholders.

Discussion Questions

1. Were the shareholders morally justified in demanding that Hasbro sell out to Mattel? How would an ethical egoist such as Ayn Rand respond to the question? Do you agree with her?
2. Rand describes people who live off the productivity of others as second-handers. In the case of Hasbro, who are the second-handers—the shareholders or the employees? Support your answer.
3. Discuss the reaction of the different parties involved in light of E. O. Wilson's claim that altruistic people are basically self-interested.

2. Should the Tobacco Industry Be Regulated?

The tobacco industry is currently negotiating with the U.S. government to be granted immunity from lawsuits by people who die allegedly as a result of smoking. In exchange for immunity from future lawsuits, the tobacco giants are offering to put cigarettes out of sight behind store counters, cut back drastically on advertising, submit to regulation by the FDA, and put aside $300 billion to settle current lawsuits.

"The potential benefits to children and to the public health are historic, and they should be. The tobacco industry has a lot of wrongs to right," Massachusetts Attorney General Scott Harsharger commented.

Some people oppose making any concessions to the tobacco companies. They think it is unfair that the tobacco companies can negotiate their way out of future liability. Many public health officials want to see even tighter regulation on tobacco companies, including the extension of any new rules to foreign markets where the tobacco companies have lucrative markets.

Discussion Questions

1. Does the government have a right to interfere in private business? How might an ethical egoist such as Ayn Rand respond to this question? As a laissez-faire capitalist, would she be opposed to interference, even if the company were producing a harmful product such as cigarettes?

2. According to Ayn Rand, the only proper policy for relationships is "Hands off." However, is this policy always consistent with ethical egoism? Could Rand justify a hands off or laissez-faire policy regarding tobacco companies as in our best rational self-interests?

3. Tobacco companies are currently looking to foreign markets for growth. Would an ethical egoist approve of this trend? Does this trend lend support to Mary Midgley's argument that Rand's philosophy is simply a modern version of Social Darwinism?

4. Communitarians are opposed to ethical egoism and the presumption of individualism. They argue that our actions do not exist in isolation; rather, they affect others, making the separation of private business and government an impossible goal. Millions of dollars in public funds, as well as money from private insurance companies, have been expended for medical resources for people who have cancer from smoking. Does this justify government regulation of the tobacco industry?

5. People, including tobacco users, do not always act in their own best self-interests. Could a government ban on the production and consumption of tobacco products be morally justified using ethical egoism?

3. Corporate America and Volunteerism

With Washington cutting back on welfare and Social Security, nongovernment groups are expected to pick up the slack. In April 1997, retired General Colin Powell and Presidents Clinton, Bush, Carter, and Ford formally launched a campaign to encourage community service. About half of all Americans are already engaged in some sort of volunteer work. Powell's efforts, however, are primarily directed at getting corporations involved.

Corporate America is eager to pick up the welfare slack. Prozac, for example, gave $2 million to the World Health Organization for mental health awareness programs in Third World nations. Levi Strauss has been active in fighting the exploitation of child labor; Ben and Jerry's ice cream donates a portion of their proceeds to environmental causes; and American Express is involved in programs to relieve world hunger. Other companies, such as AT&T, are giving employees a paid day off to volunteer.

Volunteerism can be a win–win proposition for corporations. When IBM gives computers to struggling schools, or building companies donate supplies or workers for building low-cost housing, it's good advertising. "I don't think it's cynical to say businesses have a stake in enlightened self-interest," Harvard business professor Rosabeth Moss Kanter remarks. "When you can tap a real business motivation into corporate values and a desire for civic involvement, that's real power."[2]

Others argue that true philanthropy and altruism are aimed at human welfare, not profit. When a corporation links its products directly to a good cause for the sake of increasing company profits, that's a perversion of philanthropy. Alan Andreasen, marketing professor at Georgetown University, disagrees: "More than ever, non-profits need what many companies can offer; crucial new sources of revenue. But non-profits offer corporate partners a great deal in return: the opportunity to enhance their image—and increase the bottom line—by supporting a worthy cause."[3]

Discussion Questions

1. How realistic is the expectation that corporations and individuals will volunteer or donate money to charity purely out of unselfish concern for the welfare of humanity? Is altruism always linked to self-interest? Discuss how E. O. Wilson would respond to this question.

2. What is volunteerism? Discuss whether donating money and products fall under the rubric of volunteerism and altruism.

3. Discuss what Ayn Rand might think of increased corporate participation in charitable work and the downsizing of government participation in welfare programs. Would she see it as the United States going farther off course or getting back on course? Support your answer.

4. Are There Any Real Heroes?

Lucille, the poetry editor of a local newspaper, is considered by many to be a real hero.[4] One July afternoon while Lucille was working on a manuscript, she heard a scream outside her window. Although she is an elderly woman with a serious heart condition and braces on her back and legs, Lucille headed downstairs to come to the aid of the victim. After screaming and repeatedly hitting the rapist with her cane, the man finally loosened his grip on his victim. As he attempted to flee the scene of the crime, Lucille slammed his car door on his leg, thus preventing his escape. By this time, help had arrived and the rapist was arrested.

When author Kristen Monroe interviewed Lucille for her book on altruism, Monroe discovered that Lucille had a long history of heroic actions stemming from her work in the civil rights movement and in the army. Asked where she got her courage, Lucille replied: "It's really not a matter of courage. It's that you care enough about someone, about the human person, that you feel that you have to help no matter what."

Discussion Questions

1. Did Lucille's heroism stem from disinterested altruism or from rational self-interest? Is heroism out of altruism different from heroism out of self-interest? Are egoism and heroism incompatible? Discuss whether Lucille

would be any less of a hero if her actions were in her best rational self-interest. Support your answer.

2. Kristen Monroe rejects the egoist's explanation of the behavior of rescuers such as Lucille, who come to the aid of others even at the risk of their own lives. According to egoists, rescuers perform heroic deeds purely because of the benefits and fame it brings to them. However, in Monroe's study, rescuers, almost without exception, deny having received any material reward or having been motivated by any expectation of recognition, prestige, or gratitude. Rather than stemming from self-regard, their morality stems from a sense of affiliation and interdependence with other humans and a belief that we ought to respond to the concerns and cares of others. Discuss how E. O. Wilson and Ayn Rand might respond to Monroe's findings.

3. Lucille said that she "felt she had to help no matter what." Discuss how E. O. Wilson would probably interpret this statement. Would Wilson consider Lucille's behavior to be soft-core or hard-core altruism? Support your answer.

4. Can Lucille's behavior be adequately explained as an example of biological altruism? Support your answer. Even if her altruism can be explained using sociobiology, how can we be sure that this is the correct explanation of her behavior? What are some alternative explanations of her behavior? Which explanation do you find most satisfactory?

5. Would Jean Hampton regard Lucille as a virtuous person and a hero? Discuss Lucille's behavior in light of Hampton's concepts of self-worth and considered self-interest.

5. Academic Cheating

At Saratoga High School in northern California, as many as seventy juniors may have their scores on an advanced placement history exam tossed out because of cheating. According to test officials, one of the students got the answers to the exam from a friend who had taken the exam the day before in Singapore. The student then shared the answers with her classmates at a study session on the morning of the exam.

This is not the first case of mass cheating on standardized tests. In the fall of 1996, a three-year scam was uncovered that took advantage of the three-hour time difference between the east and west coasts.[5] For $6,000, students flew to Los Angeles to take the exams and were given a pencil with the answers to the graduate school entrance exams inscribed on it in a secret code.

Cheating, however, is not just for the rich. For just $10 students can purchase a copy of the best-seller *Cheating 101: The Benefits and Fundamentals of Earning the Easy A*. There is also a Web site called "The Cheating Page" that allows students to download term papers and information on how to cheat on tests. For those who want a more customized product, companies such as Research and Educational Associates, Ltd., will, for a fee, ghostwrite term papers, masters theses, and even doctoral dissertations.

Discussion Questions

1. Ghostwriter Larry Groeger maintains that cheating is not an ethical matter but simply "just the way the world works." "The real ethos of America," he explains, "is 'Anything you do is okay if you don't get caught.'"[6] Do you agree with Groeger? If so, does this morally justify cheating?

2. If you had Gyges's ring and could cheat without fear of getting caught, would you do so? Explain how you would morally justify your decision.

3. Studies show that cheating, as well as tolerance of cheating, is becoming far more prevalent in our high schools and colleges. At UC Berkeley, over 100 cases of academic cheating come before the student council in an average year. In a survey at Rutger's College, 67 percent of the students admitted to cheating in college.[7] Why do you think cheating is on the rise? Relate your answer to issues regarding moral education and moral development in college students.

4. Do we have a moral obligation to report others who cheat? If so, under what conditions? Discuss how you would have responded had you been at the study session where the student was sharing the answers to the exam or if you had been offered a pencil with the answers to the GRE encoded on it.

5. According to Ayn Rand, what helps us to survive is in our best self-interests. What did Rand mean by survive? If cheating helps us to get into a good school and even earn a doctorate degree, do we have a moral obligation to cheat? Or would Rand consider cheaters to be second-handers? Support your answer.

6. Many ethicists are opposed to cheating on the grounds that it compromises our integrity and weakens our character. Indeed, studies have found that students who are doing poorly in school and who have lower self-esteem are more likely to cheat. Rand also promoted integrity and honesty as being in our best self-interests. Why would acting with integrity be in our best rational self-interests? Is cheating inconsistent with integrity and self-respect?

NOTES

[1]Gregory Smith, "Four Stockholders Sue Hasbro for Damages," *Providence Journal,* February 3, 1996, p. A4.

[2]Mary Leonard, "Count Them In," *Boston Sunday Globe,* April 20, 1997, p. F1.

[3]Ibid., p. F5.

[4]The story of Lucille's heroism is told in Kristen W. Monroe, *The Heart of Altruism: Perceptions of a Common Humanity* (Princeton, NJ: Princeton University Press, 1996).

[5]Adam Rogers, "For $6000, You Get a Pencil with the Answers Included: Federal Agents Break up a Cheating Ring Charged with Beating Graduate Entrance Exams," *Newsweek,* November 11, 1996, p. 69.

[6]Richard S. Johnson, "Students Clamor for Ghosted Research Papers," *The National Observer,* October 30, 1971.

[7]Eileen Garred, "Schools for Scandal," *People Weekly,* May 13, 1991, p. 103.

CHAPTER SIX

Utilitarianism

Actions are right in proportion as they tend to promote happiness, wrong as they tend to produce the reverse of happiness.

John Stuart Mill, *Utilitarianism*

According to utilitarians, the morality of an action is determined solely by its consequences. Actions are right to the extent that they promote happiness for the greatest number and wrong to the extent that they promote unhappiness for the greatest number. Happiness is defined as pleasure and unhappiness as pain.

Unlike the ethical egoists, utilitarians believe that people are naturally sympathetic and concerned with promoting the happiness of others as well. This desire for happiness, they claim, is universal, and humans intuitively recognize it as the greatest good.

The first selection is from Mo Tzu's work, "Universal Love." Mo Tzu views morality pragmatically. The good society, he believes, can best be achieved not through passivity but by actively seeking and promoting the good of the many. Mo Tzu believes that we should try to promote what is beneficial and eliminate what is harmful.

In the second selection from *An Introduction to the Principles of Morals and Legislation*, Jeremy Bentham defends the position that the principle of utility is the basic principle of right conduct. He suggests seven circumstances that can be used in calculating the utility of an action or policy.

John Stuart Mill, in the selection from *Utilitarianism*, reformulates Bentham's strict utilitarianism so that it takes into account the quality as well as the quantity of pleasures.

In the next selection from *Animal Liberation,* Peter Singer discusses the implications of utilitarian theory for our treatment of nonhuman animals. He concludes that our exclusion of nonhuman animals from moral consideration cannot be justified.

In the final selection, Bernard Williams offers a critique of utilitarianism. He argues that utilitarianism does not take into account the importance of individual integrity.

Mo Tzu

Universal Love

Mo Tzu (c. 470–391 B.C.E.) lived in China during the period of the hundred philosophers (the late sixth to the early third centuries B.C.E.). This period in Eastern thought was paralleled by the golden age of Greek philosophy in the West. Mo Tzu was born the same year as Socrates and died nine years after the death of Confucius.

Mo Tzu (spelled "Motse" in the reading) was concerned primarily with social and political reform. The utilitarian philosophy of Mo Tzu developed as a challenge to the passivity of Confucianism and Taoism, both of which emphasize virtue over action. Unlike Confucius, Mo Tzu also believed that moral consideration should be applied equally and universally to all people. By using the standard of utility or universality, Mo Tzu believed, we can achieve a world of peace and harmony.

CRITICAL THINKING QUESTIONS

1. What, according to Mo Tzu, is the first thing a wise ruler needs to know?
2. What is the cause of disorder?
3. What does Mo Tzu mean by "universal love"?
4. What are the consequences of lack of universal love?
5. What are the consequences of universal love?
6. What is the purpose of the magnanimous or benevolent person?
7. What is the difference between partiality and universality?
8. How does Mo Tzu support his claim that universal love is practical?

UNIVERSAL LOVE (I)

The wise man who has charge of governing the empire should know the cause of disorder before he can put it in order. Unless he knows its cause, he cannot regulate it. It is similar to the problem of a physician who is attending a patient. He has to know the cause of the ailment before he can cure it. Unless he knows its

---

Universal Love, translated by Yi-Pao Mei (London: Arthur Probsthain, 1929).

cause he cannot cure it. How is the situation different for him who is to regulate disorder? He too has to know the cause of the disorder before he can regulate it. Unless he knows its cause he cannot regulate it. The wise man who has charge of governing the empire must, then, investigate the cause of disorder.

Suppose we try to locate the cause of disorder, we shall find it lies in the want of mutual love. What is called disorder is just the lack of filial piety on the part of the minister and the son towards the emperor and the father. As he loves himself and not his father the son benefits himself to the disadvantage of his father. As he loves himself and not his elder brother, the younger brother benefits himself to the disadvantage of his elder brother. As he loves himself and not his emperor, the minister benefits himself to the disadvantage of his emperor. And these are what is called disorder. When the father shows no affection to the son, when the elder brother shows no affection to the younger brother, and when the emperor shows no affection to the minister, on the other hand, it is also called disorder. When the father loves only himself and not the son, he benefits himself to the disadvantage of the son. When the elder brother loves only himself and not his younger brother, he benefits himself to the disadvantage of the younger brother. When the emperor loves only himself and not his minister, he benefits himself to the disadvantage of his minister, and the reason for all these is want of mutual love.

This is true even among thieves and robbers. As he loves only his own family and not other families, the thief steals from other families to profit his own family. As he loves only his own person and not others, the robber does violence to others to profit himself. And the reason for all this is want of love. This again is true in the mutual disturbance among the houses of the ministers and the mutual invasions among the states of the feudal lords. As he loves only his own house and not the others, the minister disturbs the other houses to profit his own. As he loves only his own state and not the others, the feudal lord attacks the other states to profit his own. These instances exhaust the confusion in the world. And when we look into the causes we find they all arise from want of mutual love.

Suppose everybody in the world loves universally, loving others as one's self. Will there yet be any unfilial individual? When every one regards his father, elder brother, and emperor as himself, whereto can he direct any unfilial feeling? Will there still be any unaffectionate individual? When every one regards his younger brother, son, and minister as himself, whereto can he direct any disaffection? Therefore there will not be any unfilial feeling or disaffection. Will there then be any thieves and robbers? When every one regards other families as his own family, who will steal? When every one regards other persons as his own person, who will rob? Therefore there will not be any thieves or robbers. Will there be mutual disturbance among the houses of the ministers and invasion among the states of the feudal lords? When every one regards the houses of others as one's own, who will be disturbing? When every one regards the states of others as one's own, who will invade? Therefore there will be neither disturbances among the houses of the ministers nor invasion among the states of the feudal lords.

If every one in the world will love universally; states not attacking one another; houses not disturbing one another; thieves and robbers becoming extinct; emperor and ministers, fathers and sons, all being affectionate and filial

—if all this comes to pass the world will be orderly. Therefore, how can the wise man who has charge of governing the empire fail to restrain hate and encourage love? So, when there is universal love in the world it will be orderly, and when there is mutual hate in the world it will be disorderly. This is why Motse insisted on persuading people to love others.

UNIVERSAL LOVE (II)

Motse said: The purpose of the magnanimous is to be found in procuring benefits for the world and eliminating its calamities.

But what are the benefits of the world and what its calamities?

Motse said: Mutual attacks among states, mutual usurpation among houses, mutual injuries among individuals; the lack of grace and loyalty between ruler and ruled, the lack of affection and filial piety between father and son, the lack of harmony between elder and younger brothers—these are the major calamities in the world.

But whence did these calamities arise, out of mutual love?

Motse said: They arise out of want of mutual love. At present feudal lords have learned only to love their own states and not those of others. Therefore they do not scruple about attacking other states. The heads of houses have learned only to love their own houses and not those of others. Therefore they do not scruple about usurping other houses. And individuals have learned only to love themselves and not others. Therefore they do not scruple about injuring others. When feudal lords do not love one another there will be war on the fields. When heads of houses do not love one another they will usurp one another's power. When individuals do not love one another they will injure one another. When ruler and ruled do not love one another they will not be gracious and loyal. When father and son do not love each other they will not be affectionate and filial. When elder and younger brothers do not love each other they will not be harmonious. When nobody in the world loves any other, naturally the strong will overpower the weak, the many will oppress the few, the wealthy will mock the poor, the honoured will disdain the humble, the cunning will deceive the simple. Therefore all the calamities, strifes, complaints, and hatred in the world have arisen out of want of mutual love. Therefore the benevolent disapproved of this want.

Now that there is disapproval, how can we have the condition altered?

Motse said it is to be altered by the way of universal love and mutual aid.

But what is the way of universal love and mutual aid?

Motse said: It is to regard the state of others as one's own, the houses of others as one's own, the persons of others as one's self. When feudal lords love one another there will be no more war; when heads of houses love one another there will be no more mutual usurpation; when individuals love one another there will be no more mutual injury. When ruler and ruled love each other they will be gracious and loyal; when father and son love each other they will be affectionate and filial; when elder and younger brothers love each other they will be harmonious.

When all the people in the world love one another, then the strong will not over-power the weak, the many will not oppress the few, the wealthy will not mock the poor, the honoured will not disdain the humble, and the cunning will not deceive the simple. And it is all due to mutual love that calamities, strifes, complaints, and hatred are prevented from arising. Therefore the benevolent exalt it.

But the gentlemen of the world would say: "So far so good. It is of course very excellent when love becomes universal. But it is only a difficult and distant ideal."

Motse said: This is simply because the gentlemen of the world do not recognize what is to the benefit of the world, or understand what is its calamity. Now, to besiege a city, to fight in the fields, or to achieve a name at the cost of death—these are what men find difficult. Yet when the superior encourages them, the multitude can do them. Besides, universal love and mutual aid is quite different from these. Whoever loves others is loved by others; whoever benefits others is benefited by others; whoever hates others is hated by others; whoever injures others is injured by others. Then, what difficulty is there with it (universal love)? Only, the ruler fails to embody it in his government and the ordinary man in his conduct.

. . .

Therefore Motse said: If the rulers sincerely desire the empire to be wealthy and dislike to have it poor, desire to have it orderly and dislike to have it chaotic, they should bring about universal love and mutual aid. This is the way of the sage-kings and the way to order for the world, and it should not be neglected.

UNIVERSAL LOVE (III)

Motse said: The purpose of the magnanimous lies in procuring benefits for the world and eliminating its calamities. Now among all the current calamities, which are the most important? The attack on the small states by the large ones, disturbances of the small houses by the large ones, oppression of the weak by the strong, misuse of the few by the many, deception of the simple by the cunning, disdain towards the humble by the honoured—these are the misfortunes in the empire. Again, the lack of grace on the part of the ruler, the lack of loyalty on the part of the ruled, the lack of affection on the part of the father, the lack of filial piety on the part of the son—these are further calamities in the empire. Also, the mutual injury and harm which the unscrupulous do to one another with weapons, poison, water, and fire is still another calamity in the empire.

When we come to think about the cause of all these calamities, how have they arisen? Have they arisen out of love of others and benefiting others? Of course we should say no. We should say they have arisen out of hate of others and injuring others. If we should classify one by one all those who hate others and injure others, should we find them to be universal in love or partial? Of course we should say they are partial. Now, since partiality against one another is the cause of the major calamities in the empire, then partiality is wrong.

Motse continued: Whoever criticizes others must have something to replace them. Criticism without suggestion is like trying to stop flood with flood and put out fire with fire. It will surely be without worth.

Motse said: Partiality is to be replaced by universality. But how is it that partiality can be replaced by universality? Now, when every one regards the states of others as he regards his own, who would attack the others' states? Others are regarded like self. When every one regards the capitals of others as he regards his own, who would seize the others' capitals? Others are regarded like self. When every one regards the houses of others as he regards his own, who would disturb the others' houses? Others are regarded like self. Now, when the states and cities do not attack and seize each other and when the clans and individuals do not disturb and harm one another—is this a calamity or a benefit to the world? Of course it is a benefit. When we come to think about the several benefits in regard to their cause, how have they arisen? Have they arisen out of hate of others and injuring others? Of course we should say no. We should say they have arisen out of love of others and benefiting others. If we should classify one by one all those who love others and benefit others, should we find them to be partial or universal? Of course we should say they are universal. Now, since universal love is the cause of the major benefits in the world, therefore Motse proclaims universal love is right.

And, as has already been said, the interest of the magnanimous lies in procuring benefits for the world and eliminating its calamities. Now that we have found out the consequences of universal love to be the major benefits of the world and the consequences of partiality to be the major calamities in the world; this is the reason why Motse said partiality is wrong and universality is right. When we try to develop and procure benefits for the world with universal love as our standard, then attentive ears and keen eyes will respond in service to one another, then limbs will be strengthened to work for one another, and those who know the Tao will untiringly instruct others. Thus the old and those who have neither wife nor children will have the support and supply to spend their old age with, and the young and weak and orphans will have the care and admonition to grow up in. When universal love is adopted as the standard, then such are the consequent benefits. It is incomprehensible, then, why people should object to universal love when they hear it.

Yet the objection is not all exhausted. It is asked: "It may be a good thing, but can it be of any use?"

Motse replied: If it were not useful then even I would disapprove of it. But how can there by anything that is good but not useful? Let us consider the matter from both sides. Suppose there are two men. Let one of them hold to partiality and the other to universality. Then the advocate of partiality would say to himself, how can I take care of my friend as I do of myself, how can I take care of his parents as my own? Therefore when he finds his friend hungry he would not feed him, and when he finds him cold he would not clothe him. In his illness he would not minister to him, and when he is dead he would not bury him. Such is the word and such is the deed of the advocate of partiality. The advocate of universality is quite unlike this both in word and in deed. He would say to himself, I have heard that to be a superior man one should take care of his friend as he does of himself, and take care of his friend's parents as his own. Therefore when he finds his friend hungry he would feed him, and when he finds him cold he would clothe him. In his sickness he would serve him, and when he is dead he would bury him. Such is the word and such is the deed of the advocate of universality. . . .

DISCUSSION QUESTIONS

1. Are humans capable of universal love? Do you agree with Mo Tzu that the feeling of universal love or unity with our fellow creatures is deeply rooted in our character? Would sociobiologist E. O. Wilson agree or disagree with Mo Tzu? Support your answer.
2. In our culture we often draw a sharp distinction between private life and public life. Mo Tzu, on the other hand, claims that we can only improve ourselves by improving society. How does Mo Tzu support this claim? Do you agree with Mo Tzu?
3. Mo Tzu says that it is wrong to criticize others unless we have an alternative to offer them. Do you agree? Is this advice consistent with his utilitarian philosophy? Use specific examples to support your answer.
4. Is partiality always wrong? What happens when loyalty to our family conflicts with loyalty to our society? Would Mo Tzu agree with Euthyphro's action in taking his father to court?
5. Is universal love an impossible norm? Is Mo Tzu's philosophy of universal love applicable in today's world? How might this principle be applied on an international level?
6. How might ethical egoist Ayn Rand respond to Mo Tzu's claim that the best way to assure mutual benefit is through universal love? Support your answer.

Jeremy Bentham

An Introduction to the Principles of Morals and Legislation

English jurist, philosopher, and social reformer Jeremy Bentham (1748–1832) was born more than a millennium after Mo Tzu. Like Mo Tzu, Bentham promoted utilitarianism as a tool of social reform. Bentham developed his theory of utilitarianism primarily in response to the flagrant injustices and exploitation of workers that marred the Industrial Revolution.

Bentham argued that the principle of utility should be applied in creating more equitable legislation. In his great work *An Introduction to the Principles of Morals and Legislation,* Bentham offers practical suggestions in the form of a utilitarian calculus for determining public policy and what legislation ought to be enacted.

CRITICAL THINKING QUESTIONS

1. What, according to Bentham, are the two sovereign masters that govern human behavior?

2. What is the principle of utility?

3. What does Bentham mean by "happiness"? What is the relation between happiness and pleasure?

4. What does Bentham mean by "right"?

5. How do the utilitarians determine who or what should be given moral consideration?

6. What is the relation between the interests of the community and the interests of the individual?

7. What, according to Bentham, are the roles, if any, of reason and sentiment in morality?

8. Why does Bentham claim that he does not have to offer proof for the principle of utility?

9. What are the principles that are adverse to that of utility?

10. What are the seven criteria or circumstances Bentham gives for determining the value of pleasure and pain? How do we use these criteria in calculating the utility of an action?

An Introduction to the Principles of Morals and Legislation (London: Clarendon Press, 1907). Some notes have been omitted.

Of the Principle of Utility

I. Nature has placed mankind under the governance of two sovereign masters, *pain* and *pleasure*. It is for them alone to point out what we ought to do, as well as to determine what we shall do. On the one hand the standard of right and wrong, on the other the chain of causes and effects, are fastened to their throne. They govern us in all we do, in all we say, in all we think: every effort we can make to throw off our subjection, will serve but to demonstrate and confirm it. In words a man may pretend to abjure their empire: but in reality he will remain subject to it all the while. The *principle of utility* recognises this subjection, and assumes it for the foundation of that system, the object of which is to rear the fabric of felicity by the hands of reason and of law. Systems which attempt to question it, deal in sounds instead of sense, in caprice instead of reason, in darkness instead of light.

But enough of metaphor and declamation: it is not by such means that moral science is to be improved.

II. The principle of utility is the foundation of the present work: it will be proper therefore at the outset to give an explicit and determinate account of what is meant by it. By the principle* of utility is meant that principle which approves or disapproves of every action whatsoever, according to the tendency which it appears to have to augment or diminish the happiness of the party whose interest is in question: or, what is the same thing in other words, to promote or to oppose that happiness. I say of every action whatsoever; and therefore not only of every action of a private individual, but of every measure of government.

III. By utility is meant that property in any object, whereby it tends to produce benefit, advantage, pleasure, good, or happiness, (all this in the present case comes to the same thing) or (what comes again to the same thing) to prevent the happening of mischief, pain, evil, or unhappiness to the party whose interest is considered: if that party be the community in general, then the happiness of the community: if a particular individual, then the happiness of that individual.

IV. The interest of the community is one of the most general expressions that can occur in the phraseology of morals: no wonder that the meaning of it is often lost. When it has a meaning, it is this. The community is a fictitious *body*, composed of the individual persons who are considered as constituting as it were its *members*. The interest of the community then is, what?—the sum of the interests of the several members who compose it.

V. It is in vain to talk of the interest of the community, without understanding what is the interest of the individual. A thing is said to promote the interest, or to be *for* the interest, of an individual, when it tends to add to the sum total of his

---

*The principle here in question may be taken for an act of the mind; a sentiment; a sentiment of approbation; a sentiment which, when applied to an action, approves of its utility, as that quality of it by which the measure of approbation or disapprobation bestowed upon it ought to be governed.

pleasures: or, what comes to the same thing, to diminish the sum total of his pains.

VI. An action then may be said to be conformable to the principle of utility, or, for shortness sake, to utility, (meaning with respect to the community at large) when the tendency it has to augment the happiness of the community is greater than any it has to diminish it.

VII. A measure of government (which is but a particular kind of action, performed by a particular person or persons) may be said to be conformable to or dictated by the principle of utility, when in like manner the tendency which it has to augment the happiness of the community is greater than any which it has to diminish it.

. . .

X. Of an action that is conformable to the principle of utility one may always say either that it is one that ought to be done, or at least that it is not one that ought not to be done. One may say also, that it is right it should be done; at least that it is not wrong it should be done: that it is a right action; at least that it is not a wrong action. When thus interpreted, the words *ought*, and *right* and *wrong*, and others of that stamp, have a meaning: when otherwise, they have none.

XI. Has the rectitude of this principle been ever formally contested? It should seem that it had, by those who have not known what they have been meaning. Is it susceptible of any direct proof? it should seem not: for that which is used to prove every thing else, cannot itself be proved: a chain of proofs must have their commencement somewhere. To give such proof is as impossible as it is needless.

XII. Not that there is or ever has been that human creature breathing, however stupid or perverse, who has not on many, perhaps on most occasions of his life, deferred to it. By the natural constitution of the human frame, on most occasions of their lives men in general embrace this principle, without thinking of it: if not for the ordering of their own actions, yet for the trying of their own actions, as well as of those of other men. There have been, at the same time, not many, perhaps, even of the most intelligent, who have been disposed to embrace it purely and without reserve. There are even few who have not taken some occasion or other to quarrel with it, either on account of their not understanding always how to apply it, or on account of some prejudice or other which they were afraid to examine into, or could not bear to part with. For such is the stuff that man is made of: in principle and in practice, in a right track and in a wrong one, the rarest of all human qualities is consistency.

XIII. When a man attempts to combat the principle of utility, it is with reasons drawn, without his being aware of it, from that very principle itself.* His

---

*"The principle of utility, (I have heard it said) is a dangerous principle: it is dangerous on certain occasions to consult it." This is as much as to say, what? that it is not consonant to utility, to consult utility: in short, that it is *not* consulting it, to consult it.

arguments, if they prove any thing, prove not that the principle is *wrong*, but that, according to the applications he supposes to be made of it, it is *misapplied*. Is it possible for a man to move the earth? Yes; but he must first find out another earth to stand upon. . . .

. . . Admitting any other principle than the principle of utility to be a right principle, a principle that it is right for a man to pursue; admitting (what is not true) that the word *right* can have a meaning without reference to utility, let him say whether there is any such thing as a *motive* that a man can have to pursue the dictates of it: if there is, let him say what that motive is, and how it is to be distinguished from those which enforce the dictates of utility: if not, then lastly let him say what it is this other principle can be good for?

Of Principles Adverse to That of Utility

I. If the principle of utility be a right principle to be governed by, and that in all cases, it follows from what has been just observed, that whatever principle differs from it in any case must necessarily be a wrong one. To prove any other principle, therefore, to be a wrong one, there needs no more than just to show it to be what it is, a principle of which the dictates are in some point or other different from those of the principle of utility: to state it is to confute it.

. . .

V. There are two classes of men of very different complexions, by whom the principle of asceticism appears to have been embraced; the one a set of moralists, the other a set of religionists. Different accordingly have been the motives which appear to have recommended it to the notice of these different parties. Hope, that is the prospect of pleasure, seems to have animated the former: hope, the aliment of philosophic pride: the hope of honour and reputation at the hands of men. Fear, that is the prospect of pain, the latter: fear, the offspring of superstitious fancy: the fear of future punishment at the hands of a splenetic and revengeful Deity. I say in this case fear: for of the invisible future, fear is more powerful than hope. These circumstances characterize the two different parties among the partizans of the principle of asceticism; the parties and their motives different, the principle the same.

Value of a Lot of Pleasure or Pain, How to Be Measured

I. Pleasures then, and the avoidance of pains, are the *ends* which the legislator has in view: it behoves him therefore to understand their *value*. Pleasures and pains are the *instruments* he has to work with: it behoves him therefore to understand their force, which is again, in other words, their value.

II. To a person considered *by himself,* the value of a pleasure or pain considered *by itself,* will be greater or less, according to the four following circumstances:*

1. Its *intensity.*
2. Its *duration.*
3. Its *certainty* or *uncertainty.*
4. Its *propinquity* or *remoteness.*

III. These are the circumstances which are to be considered in estimating a pleasure or a pain considered each of them by itself. But when the value of any pleasure or pain is considered for the purpose of estimating the tendency of any *act* by which it is produced, there are two other circumstances to be taken into the account; these are,

5. Its *fecundity,* or the chance it has of being followed by sensations of the *same* kind: that is, pleasures, if it be a pleasure: pains, if it be a pain.
6. Its *purity,* or the chance it has of *not* being followed by sensations of the *opposite* kind: that is, pains, if it be a pleasure: pleasures, if it be a pain.

These two last, however, are in strictness scarcely to be deemed properties of the pleasure or the pain itself; they are not, therefore, in strictness to be taken into the account of the value of that pleasure or that pain. They are in strictness to be deemed properties only of the act, or other event, by which such pleasure or pain has been produced; and accordingly are only to be taken into the account of the tendency of such act or such event.

IV. To a *number* of persons, with reference to each of whom the value of a pleasure or a pain is considered, it will be greater or less, according to seven circumstances: to wit, the six preceding ones; *viz.*

1. Its *intensity.*
2. Its *duration.*
3. Its *certainty* or *uncertainty.*
4. Its *propinquity* or *remoteness.*
5. Its *fecundity.*
6. Its *purity.*

And one other; to wit:

7. Its *extent;* that is, the number of persons to whom it *extends;* or (in other words) who are affected by it.

---

*These circumstances have since been denominated *elements* or *dimensions of value* in a pleasure or a pain.

V. To take an exact account then of the general tendency of any act, by which the interests of a community are affected, proceed as follows. Begin with any one person of those whose interests seem most immediately to be affected by it: and take an account,

1. Of the value of each distinguishable *pleasure* which appears to be produced by it in the *first* instance.

2. Of the value of each *pain* which appears to be produced by it in the *first* instance.

3. Of the value of each pleasure which appears to be produced by it *after* the first. This constitutes the *fecundity* of the first *pleasure* and the *impurity* of the first *pain.*

4. Of the value of each *pain* which appears to be produced by it after the first. This constitutes the *fecundity* of the first *pain,* and the *impurity* of the first pleasure.

5. Sum up all of the values of all the *pleasures* on the one side, and those of all the pains on the other. The balance, if it be on the side of pleasure, will give the *good* tendency of the act upon the whole, with respect to the interests of that *individual* person; if on the side of pain, the *bad* tendency of it upon the whole.

6. Take an account of the *number* of persons whose interests appear to be concerned; and repeat the above process with respect to each. *Sum up* the numbers expressive of the degrees of *good* tendency, which the act has, with respect to each individual, in regard to whom the tendency of it is *good* upon the whole: do this again with respect to each individual, in regard to whom the tendency of it is *good* upon the whole: do this again with respect to each individual, in regard to whom the tendency of it is *bad* upon the whole. Take the *balance;* which, if on the side of *pleasure,* will give the general *good tendency* of the act, with respect to the total number or community of individuals concerned; if on the side of pain, the general *evil tendency,* with respect to the same community.

VI. It is not to be expected that this process should be strictly pursued previously to every moral judgment, or to every legislative or judicial operation. It may, however, be always kept in view: and as near as the process actually pursued on these occasions approaches to it, so near will such process approach to the character of an exact one. . . .

DISCUSSION QUESTIONS

1. Are you satisfied with Bentham's definition of happiness? Is happiness, as Bentham defines it, the only thing that people value? Support your answer.

2. Do you agree with Bentham that the principle of utility is the only principle needed for creating good legislation and public policy? Choose an issue—such as mandatory AIDS testing for college students or physician-assisted suicide—and come up with a

policy using Bentham's utilitarian calculus. Is the utilitarian calculus helpful? Are you satisfied with your policy?

3. Compare and contrast Mo Tzu's principle of universal love with Bentham's principle of utility.

4. Are all pleasures equal in value, as Bentham claims? Or are some pleasures higher or better than others? How might Social Darwinist Herbert Spencer respond to this question?

5. Why, according to Bentham, do some people call the principle of utility a dangerous principle? Does Bentham do a satisfactory job in responding to this objection?

6. Bentham claims that there is no such thing as any sort of motive that is in itself bad. Do you agree with Bentham? Are our motives or intentions irrelevant in determining the morality of an action? Discuss your answer in light of your own experience.

7. Discuss whether Bentham is saying that we ought to judge each specific act in light of its consequences, or whether we should follow the rule that in general brings about the greatest happiness for the greatest number. What are the different implications of these two interpretations of utilitarianism?

8. Bentham developed the principle of utility primarily to be used in formulating public policy and legislation. However, does the principle of utility provide practical guidelines for making moral decisions in our personal lives? Does the principle of utility require that we always put the interests of the community over our own personal interests? Support your answer.

John Stuart Mill

Utilitarianism, Liberty, and Representative Government

Bentham's influence, both on a personal and an intellectual level, on John Stuart Mill's (1806–1873) philosophy can hardly be overestimated. Educated at home by his father James Mill, with the help of Bentham, Mill was trained to carry on the utilitarian tradition. When Mill was about 20, he had a breakdown and sank into a deep depression that lasted for about two years. During this time, he began to question some of the tenets of Bentham's utilitarian theory.

Like Bentham, Mill was interested in legislation and social reform. However, whereas Bentham was concerned only with the overall consequences of our actions, Mill believed that certain consequences or pleasures should count more than others.

CRITICAL THINKING QUESTIONS

1. What, according to Mill, are the only things that the principle of utility regards as desirable moral ends? Does Mill agree?
2. Does Mill regard the pleasures of humans and beasts as morally equivalent?
3. Which pleasures does Mill regard as superior?
4. What method does Mill use for determining which pleasures are higher?
5. Whose interests should be taken into account in determining the utility of an action?

What Utilitarianism Is

A passing remark is all that needs be given to the ignorant blunder of supposing that those who stand up for utility as the test of right and wrong, use the term in that restricted and merely colloquial sense in which utility is opposed to pleasure. An apology is due to the philosophical opponents of utilitarianism, for even the momentary appearance of confounding them with any one capable of so absurd a misconception; which is the more extraordinary, inasmuch as the contrary

Utilitarianism (London: J. M. Dent & Sons, Ltd., 1910). Notes have been omitted.

accusation, of referring everything to pleasure, and that too in its grossest form, is another of the common charges against utilitarianism: and, as has been pointedly remarked by an able writer, the same sort of persons, and often the very same persons, denounce the theory "as impracticably dry when the word utility precedes the word pleasure, and as too practicably voluptuous when the word pleasure precedes the word utility." Those who know anything about the matter are aware that every writer, from Epicurus to Bentham, who maintained the theory of utility, meant by it, not something to be contradistinguished from pleasure, but pleasure itself, together with exemption from pain; and instead of opposing the useful to the agreeable or the ornamental, have always declared that the useful means these, among other things. Yet the common herd, including the herd of writers, not only in newspapers and periodicals, but in books of weight and pretension, are perpetually falling into this shallow mistake. Having caught up the word utilitarian, while knowing nothing whatever about it but its sound, they habitually express by it the rejection, or the neglect, of pleasure in some of its forms; of beauty, of ornament, or of amusement. Nor is the term thus ignorantly misapplied solely in disparagement, but occasionally in compliment; as though it implied superiority to frivolity and the mere pleasures of the moment. And this perverted use is the only one in which the word is popularly known, and the one from which the new generation are acquiring their sole notion of its meaning. Those who introduced the word, but who had for many years discontinued it as a distinctive appellation, may well feel themselves called upon to resume it, if by doing so they can hope to contribute anything towards rescuing it from this utter degradation.

The creed which accepts as the foundation of morals, Utility, or the Greatest Happiness Principle, holds that actions are right in proportion as they tend to promote happiness, wrong as they tend to produce the reverse of happiness. By happiness is intended pleasure, and the absence of pain; by unhappiness, pain, and the privation of pleasure. To give a clear view of the moral standard set up by the theory, much more requires to be said; in particular, what things it includes in the ideas of pain and pleasure; and to what extent this is left an open question. But these supplementary explanations do not affect the theory of life on which this theory of morality is grounded—namely, that pleasure, and freedom from pain, are the only things desirable as ends; and that all desirable things (which are as numerous in the utilitarian as in any other scheme) are desirable either for the pleasure inherent in themselves, or as means to the promotion of pleasure and the prevention of pain.

Now, such a theory of life excites in many minds, and among them in some of the most estimable in feeling and purpose, inveterate dislike. To suppose that life has (as they express it) no higher end than pleasure—no better and nobler object of desire and pursuit—they designate as utterly mean and grovelling; as a doctrine worthy only of swine, to whom the followers of Epicurus were, at a very early period, contemptuously likened; and modern holders of the doctrine are occasionally made the subject of equally polite comparisons by its German, French, and English assailants.

When thus attacked, the Epicureans have always answered, that it is not they, but their accusers, who represent human nature in a degrading light; since the accusation supposes human beings to be capable of no pleasures except those of which swine are capable. If this supposition were true, the charge could not be gainsaid, but would then be no longer an imputation; for if the sources of pleasure were precisely the same to human beings and to swine, the rule of life which is good enough for the one would be good enough for the other. The comparison of the Epicurean life to that of beasts is felt as degrading, precisely because a beast's pleasures do not satisfy a human being's conceptions of happiness. Human beings have faculties more elevated than the animal appetites, and when once made conscious of them, do not regard anything as happiness which does not include their gratification. I do not, indeed, consider the Epicureans to have been by any means faultless in drawing out their scheme of consequences from the utilitarian principle. To do this in any sufficient manner, many Stoic, as well as Christian elements require to be included. But there is no known Epicurean theory of life which does not assign to the pleasures of the intellect, of the feelings and imagination, and of the moral sentiments, a much higher value as pleasures than to those of mere sensation. It must be admitted, however, that utilitarian writers in general have placed the superiority of mental over bodily pleasures chiefly in the greater permanency, safety, uncostliness, etc., of the former—that is, in their circumstantial advantages rather than in their intrinsic nature. And on all these points utilitarians have fully proved their case; but they might have taken the other, and, as it may be called, higher ground, with entire consistency. It is quite compatible with the principle of utility to recognise the fact, that some *kinds* of pleasure are more desirable and more valuable than others. It would be absurd that while, in estimating all other things, quality is considered as well as quantity, the estimation of pleasures should be supposed to depend on quantity alone.

If I am asked, what I mean by difference of quality in pleasures, or what makes one pleasure more valuable than another, merely as a pleasure, except its being greater in amount, there is but one possible answer. Of two pleasures, if there be one to which all or almost all who have experience of both give a decided preference, irrespective of any feeling of moral obligation to prefer it, that is the more desirable pleasure. If one of the two is, by those who are competently acquainted with both, placed so far above the other that they prefer it, even though knowing it to be attended with a greater amount of discontent, and would not resign it for any quantity of the other pleasure which their nature is capable of, we are justified in ascribing to the preferred enjoyment a superiority in quality, so far outweighing quantity as to render it, in comparison, of small account.

Now it is an unquestionable fact that those who are equally acquainted with, and equally capable of appreciating and enjoying, both, do give a most marked preference to the manner of existence which employs their higher faculties. Few human creatures would consent to be changed into any of the lower animals, for a promise of the fullest allowance of a beast's pleasures; no intelligent human being would consent to be a fool, no instructed person would be an ignoramus, no person of feeling and conscience would be selfish and base, even though they should be persuaded that the fool, the dunce, or the rascal is better satisfied with his lot than they are with theirs. They would not resign what they possess more than he for the most complete satisfaction of all the desires which they have in common with him. If they ever fancy they would, it is only in cases of unhappiness so extreme, that to escape from it they would exchange their lot for almost any other, however undesirable in their own eyes. A being of higher faculties requires more to make him happy, is capable probably of more acute suffering, and certainly accessible to it at more points, than one of an inferior type; but in spite of these liabilities, he can never really wish to sink into what he feels to be a lower grade of existence. We may give what explanation we please of this unwillingness; we may attribute it to pride, a name which is given indiscriminately to some of the most and to some of the least estimable feelings of which mankind are capable: we may refer it to the love of liberty and personal independence, an appeal to which was with the Stoics one of the most effective means for the inculcation of it; to the love of power, or to the love of excitement, both of which do really enter into and contribute to it: but its most appropriate appellation is a sense of dignity, which all human beings possess in one form or other, and in some, though by no means in exact, proportion to their higher faculties, and which is so essential a part of the happiness of those in whom it is strong, that nothing which conflicts with it could be, otherwise than momentarily, an object of desire to them. Whoever supposes that this preference takes place at a sacrifice of happiness—that the superior being, in anything like equal circumstances, is not happier than the inferior—confounds the two very different ideas, of happiness, and content. It is undisputable that the being whose capacities of enjoyment are low, has the greatest chance of having them fully satisfied; and a highly endowed being will always feel that any happiness which he can look for, as the world is constituted, is imperfect. But he can learn to bear its imperfections, if they are at all bearable; and they will not make him envy the being who is indeed unconscious of the imperfections, but only because he feels not at all the good which those imperfections qualify. It is better to be a human being dissatisfied than a pig satisfied; better to be Socrates dissatisfied than a fool satisfied. And if the fool, or the pig, are of a different opinion, it is because they only know their own side of the question. The other party to the comparison knows both sides.

It may be objected, that many who are capable of the higher pleasures, occasionally, under the influence of temptation, postpone them to the lower. But this is quite compatible with a full appreciation of the intrinsic superiority of the higher. Men often, from infirmity of character, make their election for the nearer good, though they know it to be the less valuable; and this no less when the choice is between two bodily pleasures, than when it is between bodily and mental. They pursue sensual indulgences to the injury of health, though perfectly aware that health is the greater good. It may be further objected, that many who begin with youthful enthusiasm for everything noble, as they advance in years sink into indolence and selfishness. But I do not believe that those who undergo this very common change, voluntarily choose the lower description of pleasures in preference to the higher. I believe that before they devote themselves exclusively to the one, they have already become incapable of the other. . . .

From this verdict of the only competent judges, I apprehend there can be no appeal. On a question which is the best worth having of two pleasures, or which of two modes of existence is the most grateful to the feelings, apart from its moral attributes and from its consequences, the judgment of those who are qualified by knowledge of both, or, if they differ, that of the majority among them, must be admitted as final. And there needs be the less hesitation to accept this judgment respecting the quality of pleasures, since there is no other tribunal to be referred to even on the question of quantity. What means are there of determining which is the acutest of two pains, or the intensest of two pleasurable sensations, except the general suffrage of those who are familiar with both? Neither pains nor pleasures are homogeneous, and pain is always heterogeneous with pleasure. What is there to decide whether a particular pleasure is worth purchasing at the cost of a particular pain, except the feelings and judgment of the experienced? When, therefore, those feelings and judgment declare the pleasures derived from the higher faculties to be preferable *in kind,* apart from the question of intensity, to those of which the animal nature, disjoined from the higher faculties, is susceptible, they are entitled on this subject to the same regard.

I have dwelt on this point, as being a necessary part of a perfectly just conception of Utility or Happiness, considered as the directive rule of human conduct. But it is by no means an indispensable condition to the acceptance of the utilitarian standard; for that standard is not the agent's own greatest happiness, but the greatest amount of happiness altogether; and if it may possibly be doubted whether a noble character is always the happier for its nobleness, there can be no doubt that it makes other people happier, and that the world in general is immensely a gainer by it. Utilitarianism, therefore, could only attain its end by the general cultivation of nobleness of character, even if each individual were only benefited by the nobleness of others, and his own, so far as happiness is concerned, were a sheer deduction from the benefit. But the bare enunciation of such an absurdity as this last, renders refutation superfluous.

According to the Greatest Happiness Principle, as above explained, the ultimate end, with reference to and for the sake of which all other things are desirable (whether we are considering our own good or that of other people), is an existence exempt as far as possible from pain, and as rich as possible in enjoyments, both in point of quantity and quality; the test of quality, and the rule for measuring it against quantity, being the preference felt by those who in their opportunities of experience, to which must be added their habits of self-consciousness and self-observation, are best furnished with the means of comparison. This, being, according to the utilitarian opinion, the end of human action, is necessarily also the standard of morality; which may accordingly be defined, the rules and precepts for human conduct, by the observance of which an existence such as has been described might be, to the greatest extent possible, secured to all mankind; and not to them only, but, so far as the nature of things admits, to the whole sentient creation.

. . .

I must again repeat, what the assailants of utilitarianism seldom have the justice to acknowledge, that the happiness which forms the utilitarian standard of what is right in conduct, is not the agent's own happiness, but that of all concerned. As between his own happiness and that of others, utilitarianism requires him to be as strictly impartial as a disinterested and benevolent spectator. In the golden rule of Jesus of Nazareth, we read the complete spirit of the ethics of utility. To do as you would be done by, and to love your neighbour as yourself, constitute the ideal perfection of utilitarian morality. As the means of making the nearest approach to this ideal, utility would enjoin, first, that laws and social arrangements should place the happiness, or (as speaking practically it may be called) the interest, of every individual, as nearly as possible in harmony with the interest of the whole; and secondly, that education and opinion, which have so vast a power over human character, should so use that power as to establish in the mind of every individual an indissoluble association between his own happiness and the good of the whole; especially between his own happiness and the practice of such modes of conduct, negative and positive, as regard for the universal happiness prescribes; so that not only he may be unable to conceive the possibility of happiness to himself, consistently with conduct opposed to the general good, but also that a direct impulse to promote the general good may be in every individual one of the habitual motives of action, and the sentiments connected therewith may fill a large and prominent place in every human being's sentient existence. If the impugners of the utilitarian morality represented it to their own minds in this its true character, I know not what recommendation possessed by any other morality they could possibly affirm to be wanting to it; what more beautiful or more exalted developments of human nature any other ethical system can be supposed to foster, or what springs of action, not accessible to the utilitarian, such systems rely on for giving effect to their mandates. . . .

DISCUSSION QUESTIONS

1. How does Mill's concept of pleasure differ from Bentham's? Which definition is most useful? How might Bentham respond to Mill's claim that some pleasures are more valuable than others?

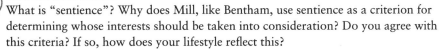

2. What is "sentience"? Why does Mill, like Bentham, use sentience as a criterion for determining whose interests should be taken into consideration? Do you agree with this criteria? If so, how does your lifestyle reflect this?

3. Do you agree with Mill that the life of an unhappy human is preferable to that of a satisfied pig? On what grounds does Mill make such an assertion? Is this distinction between the different pleasures justified? If so, on what basis?

4. Is Mill's notion that we should take into consideration the quality as well as the quantity of pleasure consistent with the principle of utility?

5. What are some of the implications of utilitarian theory for the treatment of nonhuman animals? How would Mill and Bentham each weigh the interests of nonhuman animals against human interests? Which one of them would give more weight to the interests of nonhuman animals? What might each of them conclude about the morality of meat eating or using nonhuman animals in cosmetic and medical experiments? Are there times when we would be justified in using nonconsenting humans in medical experiments?

6. Mill's brand of utilitarianism has been used to justify colonialism and the imposition of higher pleasures of the mind on primitive people. Is this really an implication of Mill's theory? Support your answer.

7. Compare Mo Tzu's concept of the happiness of the greatest number with the utilitarian theories of Bentham and Mill. In what ways, if any, do their philosophies reflect cultural differences in the application of the principle of utility? In what ways might the different versions of utilitarian theory be used to enrich one another?

Peter Singer

Animal Liberation

Australian philosopher Peter Singer (b. 1946) is Director of the Centre for Human Bioethics at Monash University in Melbourne. He is also actively involved in the animal liberation movement.

In his book *Animal Liberation,* Singer applies the principle of utility to the animal liberation movement. Singer argues that utilitarian theory requires that the interests of all sentient beings be given equal consideration. The principle of utility requires not only that we oppose human suffering; we must also take a stand against the tremendous suffering that humans inflict on nonhuman animals.

CRITICAL THINKING QUESTIONS

1. What is the principle of equality?
2. What is a "speciesist"? What does Peter Singer mean when he says most humans are speciesists? Why does Peter Singer consider speciesism to be morally wrong?
3. On what grounds does Singer argue that both racism and speciesism violate the principle of equality?
4. Does the principle of equality require that we treat other animals exactly the same as we treat humans?
5. What criteria does Singer suggest we use in order to avoid being speciesists?
6. What kind of lives, according to Singer, have more value than others?

All Animals Are Equal . . .

or why the ethical principle on which human equality rests
requires us to extend equal consideration to animals too

"Animal Liberation" may sound more like a parody of other liberation movements than a serious objective. The idea of "The Rights of Animals" actually was once used to parody the case for women's rights. When Mary Wollstonecraft, a forerunner of today's feminists, published her *Vindication of the Rights of*

Animal Liberation, 2nd ed. (New York: Random House, 1990), pp. 5–20. Notes have been omitted.

Woman in 1792, her views were widely regarded as absurd, and before long an anonymous publication appeared entitled *A Vindication of the Rights of Brutes.* The author of this satirical work (now known to have been Thomas Taylor, a distinguished Cambridge philosopher) tried to refute Mary Wollstonecraft's arguments by showing that they could be carried one stage further. If the argument for equality was sound when applied to women, why should it not be applied to dogs, cats, and horses? The reasoning seemed to hold for these "brutes" too; yet to hold that brutes had rights was manifestly absurd. Therefore the reasoning by which this conclusion had been reached must be unsound, and if unsound when applied to brutes, it must also be unsound when applied to women, since the very same arguments had been used in each case.

. . .

. . . *The principle of the equality of human beings is not a description of an alleged actual equality among humans: it is a prescription of how we should treat human beings.*

Jeremy Bentham, the founder of the reforming utilitarian school of moral philosophy, incorporated the essential basis of moral equality into his system of ethics by means of the formula: "Each to count for one and none for more than one." In other words, the interests of every being affected by an action are to be taken into account and given the same weight as the like interests of any other being. A later utilitarian, Henry Sidgwick, put the point in this way: "The good of any one individual is of no more importance, from the point of view (if I may say so) of the Universe, than the good of any other." More recently the leading figures in contemporary moral philosophy have shown a great deal of agreement in specifying as a fundamental presupposition of their moral theories some similar requirement that works to give everyone's interests equal consideration—although these writers generally cannot agree on how this requirement is best formulated.

It is an implication of this principle of equality that our concern for others and our readiness to consider their interests ought not to depend on what they are like or on what abilities they may possess. Precisely what our concern or consideration requires us to do may vary according to the characteristics of those affected by what we do: concern for the well-being of children growing up in America would require that we teach them to read; concern for the well-being of pigs may require no more than that we leave them with other pigs in a place where there is adequate food and room to run freely. But the basic element—the taking into account of the interests of the being, whatever those interests may be —must, according to the principle of equality, be extended to all beings, black or white, masculine or feminine, human or nonhuman.

. . .

. . . Speciesism—the word is not an attractive one, but I can think of no better term—is a prejudice or attitude of bias in favor of the interests of members of one's own species and against those of members of other species. It should be obvious that the fundamental objections to racism and sexism made by Thomas Jefferson and Sojourner Truth apply equally to speciesism. If possessing a higher degree of intelligence does not entitle one human to use another for his or her own ends, how can it entitle humans to exploit nonhumans for the same purpose?

Many philosophers and other writers have proposed the principle of equal consideration of interests, in some form or other, as a basic moral principle; but not many of them have recognized that this principle applies to members of other species as well as to our own. Jeremy Bentham was one of the few who did realize this. In a forward-looking passage written at a time when black slaves had been freed by the French but in the British dominions were still being treated in the way we now treat animals, Bentham wrote:

> The day *may* come when the rest of the animal creation may acquire those rights which never could have been withholden from them but by the hand of tyranny. The French have already discovered that the blackness of the skin is no reason why a human being should be abandoned without redress to the caprice of a tormentor. It may one day come to be recognized that the number of the legs, the villosity of the skin, or the termination of the *os sacrum* are reasons equally insufficient for abandoning a sensitive being to the same fate. What else is it that should trace the insuperable line? Is it the faculty of reason, or perhaps the faculty of discourse? But a full-grown horse or dog is beyond comparison a more rational, as well as a more conversable animal, than an infant of a day or a week or even a month, old. But suppose they were otherwise, what would it avail? The question is not, Can they *reason?* nor Can they *talk?* but, Can they *suffer?*

In this passage Bentham points to the capacity for suffering as the vital characteristic that gives a being the right to equal consideration. The capacity for suffering—or more strictly, for suffering and/or enjoyment or happiness—is not just another characteristic like the capacity for language or higher mathematics. Bentham is not saying that those who try to mark "the insuperable line" that determines whether the interests of a being should be considered happen to have chosen the wrong characteristic. By saying that we must consider the interests of all beings with the capacity for suffering or enjoyment Bentham does not arbitrarily exclude from consideration any interests at all—as those who draw the line with reference to the possession of reason or language do. The capacity for suffering and enjoyment is *a prerequisite for having interests at all,* a condition that must be satisfied before we can speak of interests in a meaningful way. . . .

Racists violate the principle of equality by giving greater weight to the interests of members of their own race when there is a clash between their interests and the interests of those of another race. Sexists violate the principle of equality by favoring the interests of their own sex. Similarly, speciesists allow the interests of their own species to override the greater interests of members of other species. The pattern is identical in each case.

Most human beings are speciesists. . . . ordinary human beings—not a few exceptionally cruel or heartless humans, but the overwhelming majority of humans—take an active part in, acquiesce in, and allow their taxes to pay for practices that require the sacrifice of the most important interests of members of other species in order to promote the most trivial interests of our own species.

. . .

Although, . . . the view that animals are automata was proposed by the seventeenth-century French philosopher René Descartes, to most people, then and now, it is obvious that if, for example, we stick a sharp knife into the stomach of an unanesthetized dog, the dog will feel pain. That this is so is assumed by the laws in most civilized countries that prohibit wanton cruelty to animals. . . .

Do animals other than humans feel pain? How do we know? Well, how do we know if anyone, human or nonhuman, feels pain? We know that we ourselves can feel pain. We know this from the direct experience of pain that we have when, for instance, somebody presses a lighted cigarette against the back of our hand. But how do we know that anyone else feels pain? We cannot directly experience anyone else's pain, whether that "anyone" is our best friend or a stray dog. Pain is a state of consciousness, a "mental event," and as such it can never be observed. Behavior like writhing, screaming, or drawing one's hand away from a lighted cigarette is not pain itself; nor are the recordings a neurologist might make of activity within the brain observations of pain itself. Pain is something that we feel, and we can only infer that others are feeling it from various external indications.

In theory, we *could* always be mistaken when we assume that other human beings feel pain. It is conceivable that one of our close friends is really a cleverly constructed robot, controlled by a brilliant scientist so as to give all the signs of feeling pain, but really no more sensitive than any other machine. We can never know, with absolute certainty, that this is not the case. But while this might present a puzzle for philosophers, none of us has the slightest real doubt that our close friends feel pain just as we do. This is an inference, but a perfectly reasonable one, based on observations of their behavior in situations in which we would feel pain, and on the fact that we have every reason to assume that our friends are beings like us, with nervous systems like ours that can be assumed to function as ours do and to produce similar feelings in similar circumstances.

If it is justifiable to assume that other human beings feel pain as we do, is there any reason why a similar inference should be unjustifiable in the case of other animals?

Nearly all the external signs that lead us to infer pain in other humans can be seen in other species, especially the species most closely related to us—the species of mammals and birds. The behavioral signs include writhing, facial contortions, moaning, yelping or other forms of calling, attempts to avoid the source of pain, appearance of fear at the prospect of its repetition, and so on. In addition, we know that these animals have nervous systems very like ours, which respond physiologically as ours do when the animal is in circumstances in which we would feel pain: an initial rise of blood pressure, dilated pupils, perspiration, an increased pulse rate, and, if the stimulus continues, a fall in blood pressure. Although human beings have a more developed cerebral cortex than other animals, this part of the brain is concerned with thinking functions rather than with basic impulses, emotions, and feelings. These impulses, emotions, and feelings are located in the diencephalon, which is well developed in many other species of animals, especially mammals and birds.

We also know that the nervous systems of other animals were not artificially constructed—as a robot might be artificially constructed—to mimic the pain behavior of humans. The nervous systems of animals evolved as our own did, and in fact the evolutionary history of human beings and other animals, especially mammals, did not diverge until the central features of our nervous systems were already in existence. A capacity to feel pain obviously enhances a species' prospects of survival, since it causes members of the species to avoid sources of injury. It is surely unreasonable to suppose that nervous systems that are virtually identical physiologically, have a common origin and a common evolutionary function, and result in similar forms of behavior in similar circumstances should actually operate in an entirely different manner on the level of subjective feelings.

. . .

It may be objected that comparisons of the sufferings of different species are impossible to make and that for this reason when the interests of animals and humans clash the principle of equality gives no guidance. It is probably true that comparisons of suffering between members of different species cannot be made precisely, but precision is not essential. Even if we were to prevent the infliction of suffering on animals only when it is quite certain that the interests of humans will not be affected to anything like the extent that animals are affected, we would be forced to make radical changes in our treatment of animals that would involve our diet, the farming methods we use, experimental procedures in many fields of science, our approach to wildlife and to hunting, trapping and the wearing of furs, and areas of entertainment like circuses, rodeos, and zoos. As a result, a vast amount of suffering would be avoided.

So far I have said a lot about inflicting suffering on animals, but nothing about killing them. This omission has been deliberate. The application of the principle of equality to the infliction of suffering is, in theory at least, fairly straightforward. Pain and suffering are in themselves bad and should be prevented or minimized, irrespective of the race, sex, or species of the being that suffers. How bad a pain is depends on how intense it is and how long it lasts, but pains of the same intensity and duration are equally bad, whether felt by humans or animals.

The wrongness of killing a being is more complicated. I have kept, and shall continue to keep, the question of killing in the background because in the present state of human tyranny over other species the more simple, straightforward principle of equal consideration of pain or pleasure is a sufficient basis for identifying and protesting against all the major abuses of animals that human beings practice. Nevertheless, it is necessary to say something about killing.

Just as most human beings are speciesists in their readiness to cause pain to animals when they would not cause a similar pain to humans for the same reason, so most human beings are speciesists in their readiness to kill other animals when they would not kill human beings. . . .

This does not mean that to avoid speciesism we must hold that it is as wrong to kill a dog as it is to kill a human being in full possession of his or her faculties. The only position that is irredeemably speciesist is the one that tries to make the boundary of the right to life run exactly parallel to the boundary of our own species. Those who hold the sanctity of life view do this, because while distinguishing sharply between human beings and other animals they allow no distinctions to be made within our own species, objecting to the killing of the severely retarded and the hopelessly senile as strongly as they object to the killing of normal adults.

To avoid speciesism we must allow that beings who are similar in all relevant respects have a similar right to life—and mere membership in our own biological species cannot be a morally relevant criterion for this right. Within these limits we could still hold, for instance, that it is worse to kill a normal adult human, with a capacity for self-awareness and the ability to plan for the future and have meaningful relations with others, than it is to kill a mouse, which presumably does not share all of these characteristics; or we might appeal to the close family and other personal ties that humans have but mice do not have to the same degree; or we might think that it is the consequences for other humans, who will be put in fear for their own lives, that makes the crucial difference; or we might think it is some combination of these factors, or other factors altogether.

Whatever criteria we choose, however, we will have to admit that they do not follow precisely the boundary of our own species. We may legitimately hold that there are some features of certain beings that make their lives more valuable than those of other beings; but there will surely be some nonhuman animals whose lives, by any standards, are more valuable than the lives of some humans. A chimpanzee, dog, or pig, for instance, will have a higher degree of self-awareness and a greater capacity for meaningful relations with others than a severely retarded infant or someone in a state of advanced senility. So if we base the right to life on these characteristics we must grant these animals a right to life as good as, or better than, such retarded or senile humans.

This argument cuts both ways. It could be taken as showing that chimpanzees, dogs, and pigs, along with some other species, have a right to life and we commit a grave moral offense whenever we kill them, even when they are old and suffering and our intention is to put them out of their misery. Alternatively one could take the argument as showing that the severely retarded and hopelessly senile have no right to life and may be killed for quite trivial reasons, as we now kill animals.

Since the main concern of this book is with ethical questions having to do with animals and not with the morality of euthanasia I shall not attempt to settle this issue finally. I think it is reasonably clear, though, that while both of the positions just described avoid speciesism, neither is satisfactory. What we need is some middle position that would avoid speciesism but would not make the lives of the retarded and senile as cheap as the lives of pigs and dogs now are, or make the lives of pigs and dogs so sacrosanct that we think it wrong to put them out of hopeless misery. What we must do is bring nonhuman animals within our sphere of moral concern and cease to treat their lives as expendable for whatever trivial purposes we may have. At the same time, once we realize that the fact that a being is a member of our own species is not in itself enough to make it always wrong to kill that being, we may come to reconsider our policy of preserving human lives at all costs, even when there is no prospect of a meaningful life or of existence without terrible pain.

I conclude, then, that a rejection of speciesism does not imply that all lives are of equal worth. While self-awareness, the capacity to think ahead and have hopes and aspirations for the future, the capacity for meaningful relations with others and so on are not relevant to the question of inflicting pain—since pain is pain, whatever other capacities, beyond the capacity to feel pain, the being may have—these capacities are relevant to the question of taking life. It is not arbitrary to hold that the life of a self-aware being, capable of abstract thought, of planning for the future, of complex acts of communication, and so on, is more valuable than the life of a being without these capacities. . . .

DISCUSSION QUESTIONS

1. Compare and contrast Singer's understanding of utilitarianism to the theories of Bentham or Mill.
2. Do you agree with Singer that most humans are speciesists? If you are a speciesist, on what grounds do you morally justify it? In what way does your lifestyle contribute to the unnecessary suffering of the members of other species?
3. Do you agree with Singer that speciesism is morally akin to racism and sexism? Support your answer.
4. Should the principle of equality extend to all sentient beings? If not, on what grounds can you justify excluding other animals? Do you agree with Singer that morality requires that we extend the same moral consideration to all sentient beings, whether they are human or nonhuman, who are similar in all relevant respects? If not, how can you justify showing partiality to a human who is on a par intellectually with a non-human animal?
5. Apply Singer's utilitarian theory to the use of nonhuman animals in medical experiments. Would it be morally preferable to use humans instead of nonhuman animals in some cases? Or should the use of all sentient beings be forbidden?
6. Is Singer being consistent when he argues that not all lives are of equal value? Is he being a speciesist when he says that "the life of a self-aware being, capable of abstract thought, of planning for the future, of complex acts of communication, and so on," is more valuable than the life of a being without these capacities? Are there times when the life of a nonhuman animal is more valuable than that of a human?
7. Is some degree of speciesism unavoidable and perhaps even morally desirable? How might sociobiologist E. O. Wilson respond to this question?

Bernard Williams

A Critique of Utilitarianism

In the last selection for this chapter, British philosopher Bernard Williams (b. 1929) rejects utilitarianism on the grounds that it sometimes requires us to do something that we intuitively know is wrong. He also points out that utilitarianism is inconsistent in its neglect of integrity. Williams presents two case studies to illustrate some of the problems with utilitarianism.

CRITICAL THINKING QUESTIONS

1. What particular feature or features of utilitarian theory does Williams find most objectionable?
2. What does Williams mean by "integrity"? What is the relation, according to Williams, between an understanding of integrity and an understanding of happiness?
3. What is negative responsibility?
4. Why is George facing a moral dilemma? What moral values are in conflict?
5. Why is Jim facing a moral dilemma? What moral values are in conflict?
6. Why does Williams claim that utilitarians are being inconsistent when they ignore integrity?

This essay is concerned with utilitarianism, and in so far as it goes into consequentialism in general, this is only in order to suggest that some undesirable features of utilitarianism follow from its general consequentialist structure. Others follow more specifically from the nature of its concern with happiness. I shall say something about that, and about the relations between direct and indirect forms of utilitarianism. I shall consider the uneasy relations of utilitarianism to certain other values which people . . . might consider to have something seriously to do with human life. One value which has caused particular discomfort to utilitarianism is *justice*. . . . but I shall be more concerned with something rather different, *integrity*. I shall try to show . . . that utilitarianism cannot hope to make sense, at any serious level, of integrity. It cannot do that for the very basic reason that it can

"A Critique of Utilitarianism," from *Utilitarianism: For and Against,* J. J. C. Smart & Bernard Williams, eds. (Cambridge, England: University Press, 1973). Notes have been omitted.

make only the most superficial sense of human desire and action at all; and hence only very poor sense of what was supposed to be its own specialty, happiness. . . .

NEGATIVE RESPONSIBILITY: AND TWO EXAMPLES

. . . It is because consequentialism attaches value ultimately to states of affairs, and its concern is with what states of affairs the world contains, that it essentially involves the notion of *negative responsibility:* that if I am ever responsible for anything, then I must be just as much responsible for things that I allow or fail to prevent, as I am for things that I myself, in the more everyday restricted sense, bring about. Those things also must enter my deliberations, as a responsible moral agent, on the same footing. What matters is what states of affairs the world contains, and so what matters with respect to a given action is what comes about if it is done, and what comes about if it is not done, and those are questions not intrinsically affected by the nature of the causal linkage, in particular by whether the outcome is partly produced by other agents.

The strong doctrine of negative responsibility flows directly from consequentialism's assignment of ultimate value to states of affairs. Looked at from another point of view, it can be seen also as a special application of something that is favoured in many moral outlooks not themselves consequentialist—something which, indeed, some thinkers have been disposed to regard as the essence of morality itself: a principle of impartiality. Such a principle will claim that there can be no relevant difference from a moral point of view which consists just in the fact, not further explicable in general terms, that benefits or harms accrue to one person rather than to another—"it's me" can never in itself be a morally comprehensible reason. This principle, familiar with regard to the reception of harms and benefits, we can see consequentialism as extending to their production: from the moral point of view, there is no comprehensible difference which consists just in my bringing about a certain outcome rather than someone else's producing it. That the doctrine of negative responsibility represents in this way the extreme of impartiality, and abstracts from the identity of the agent, leaving just a locus of causal intervention in the world—that fact is not merely a surface paradox. It helps to explain why consequentialism can seem to some to express a more serious attitude than non-consequentialist views, why part of its appeal is to a certain kind of high-mindedness. Indeed, that is part of what is wrong with it.

For a lot of the time so far we have been operating at an exceedingly abstract level. This has been necessary in order to get clearer in general terms about the differences between consequentialist and other outlooks, an aim which is important if we want to know what features of them lead to what results for our thought. Now, however, let us look more concretely at two examples, to see what utilitarianism might say about them, what we might say about utilitarianism and, most importantly of all, what would be implied by certain ways of thinking about the situations. The examples are inevitably schematized, and they are open to the objection that they beg as many questions as they illuminate. There are two ways in particular in which examples in moral philosophy tend to beg important questions. One is that, as presented, they arbitrarily cut off and restrict the range of alternative courses of action—this objection might particularly be made against the first of my two examples. The second is that they inevitably present one with the situation as a going concern, and cut off questions about how the agent got into it, and correspondingly about moral considerations which might flow from that: this objection might perhaps specially arise with regard to the second of my two situations. These difficulties, however, just have to be accepted, and if anyone finds these examples cripplingly defective in this sort of respect, then he must in his own thought rework them in richer and less question-begging form. If he feels that no presentation of any imagined situation can ever be other than misleading in morality, and that there can never be any substitute for the concrete experienced complexity of actual moral situations, then this discussion, with him, must certainly grind to a halt: but then one may legitimately wonder whether every discussion with him about conduct will not grind to a halt, including any discussion about the actual situations, since discussion about how one would think and feel about situations somewhat different from the actual (that is to say, situations to that extent imaginary) plays an important role in discussion of the actual.

(1) George, who has just taken his Ph.D. in chemistry, finds it extremely difficult to get a job. He is not very robust in health, which cuts down the number of jobs he might be able to do satisfactorily. His wife has to go out to work to keep them, which itself causes a great deal of strain, since they have small children and there are severe problems about looking after them. The results of all this, especially on the children, are damaging. An older chemist, who knows about this situation, says that he can get George a decently paid job in a certain laboratory, which pursues research into chemical and biological warfare. George says that he cannot accept this, since he is opposed to chemical and biological warfare. The older man replies that he is not too keen on it himself, come to that, but after all George's refusal is not going to make the job or the laboratory go away; what is more, he happens to know that if George refuses the job, it will certainly go to a contemporary of George's who is not inhibited by any such scruples and is likely if appointed to push along the research with greater zeal than George would. Indeed, it is not merely concern for George and his family, but (to speak frankly and in confidence) some alarm about this other man's excess of zeal, which has led the older man to offer to use his influence to get George the job . . . George's wife, to whom he is deeply attached, has views (the details of which need not concern us) from which it follows that at least there is nothing particularly wrong with research into CBW. What should he do?

(2) Jim finds himself in the central square of a small South American town. Tied up against the wall are a row of twenty Indians, most terrified, a few defiant, in front of them several armed men in uniform. A heavy man in a sweat-stained khaki shirt turns out to be the captain in charge and, after a good deal of questioning of Jim which establishes that he got there by accident while on a botanical expedition, explains that the Indians are a random group of the inhabitants who, after recent acts of protest against the government, are just about to be

killed to remind other possible protestors of the advantages of not protesting. However, since Jim is an honoured visitor from another land, the captain is happy to offer him a guest's privilege of killing one of the Indians himself. If Jim accepts, then as a special mark of the occasion, the other Indians will be let off. Of course, if Jim refuses, then there is no special occasion, and Pedro here will do what he was about to do when Jim arrived, and kill them all. Jim, with some desperate recollection of schoolboy fiction, wonders whether if he got hold of a gun, he could hold the captain, Pedro and the rest of the soldiers to threat, but it is quite clear from the set-up that nothing of that kind is going to work: any attempt at that sort of thing will mean that all the Indians will be killed, and himself. The men against the wall, and the other villagers, understand the situation, and are obviously begging him to accept. What should he do?

To these dilemmas, it seems to me that utilitarianism replies, in the first case, that George should accept the job, and in the second, that Jim should kill the Indian. Not only does utilitarianism give these answers but, if the situations are essentially as described and there are no further special factors, it regards them, it seems to me, as *obviously* the right answers. But many of us would certainly wonder whether, in (1), that could possibly be the right answer at all; and in the case of (2), even one who came to think that perhaps that was the answer, might well wonder whether it was obviously the answer. Nor is it just a question of the rightness or obviousness of these answers. It is also a question of what sort of considerations come into finding the answer. A feature of utilitarianism is that it cuts out a kind of consideration which for some others makes a difference to what they feel about such cases: a consideration involving the idea, as we might first and very simply put it, that each of us is specially responsible for what *he* does, rather than for what other people do. This is an idea closely connected with the value of integrity. It is often suspected that utilitarianism, at least in its direct forms, makes integrity as a value more or less unintelligible. I shall try to show that this suspicion is correct. Of course, even if that is correct, it would not necessarily follow that we should reject utilitarianism; perhaps, as utilitarians sometimes suggest, we should just forget about integrity, in favour of such things as a concern for the general good. However, if I am right, we cannot merely do that, since the reason why utilitarianism cannot understand integrity is that it cannot coherently describe the relations between a man's projects and his actions. . . .

DISCUSSION QUESTIONS

1. Williams argues that utilitarianism implies that we are not only responsible for what we do but also for our failure to prevent pain to others. Should we be held responsible for not taking action to prevent or alleviate pain? Relate your answer to the case of Kitty Genovese.
2. Do you agree with Williams that a utilitarian would advise George to take the job? How does Williams come to this conclusion? What would you do if you were in a similar situation? Explain why. How might an ethical egoist such as Ayn Rand advise George about taking the job?

3. What would you do if you were in Jim's position? Was your decision based solely on concerns about the consequences of your action? What other factors entered into your decision?

4. Is Williams defining utility too narrowly? How might Mo Tzu respond to Williams interpretation of utilitarianism? How might Mo Tzu have responded had he been in Jim's position or in George's position? Would Mo Tzu consider killing a person or taking a job that involves making weapons actions to be consistent with universal love?

5. Williams claims that "utilitarianism cannot hope to make sense, at any serious level, of integrity." Is this charge justified?

6. Is putting concern for our integrity over a concern for the general good and the well-being of others morally justified or is it merely vanity? How would a utilitarian respond to this question? Why is Williams dissatisfied with this answer?

7. Apply the seven criteria in Bentham's utilitarian calculus to Jim's case. Can utilitarianism be used to justify Jim's refusal to kill one of the Indians? Shouldn't we, for example, also consider the long-range psychological effects on Jim of having killed a person? What other consequences should be taken into consideration?

Chapter Applications

1. Four Men in a Life Boat

In 1884 the private yacht Mignonette set sail from England on its way to Sydney, Australia. There were four persons aboard the yacht: Dudley the captain, Stephens the mate, Brooks the seaman, and Parker the 17-year-old cabin boy and apprentice seaman. The yacht went down in the South Atlantic and the crew put off in a 13-foot lifeboat.

They drifted for twenty days, during which they had no water except rainwater and no food for the last eight days. They had no way of getting food (fish or plants) from the ocean. By the twentieth day, the men were facing starvation. It seemed clear that they might not even last the day unless they could find some food.

Parker had become delirious from drinking sea water. The others had tried to stop him at first, but after days without food they were too weak to hold him back.

"Our only hope of survival is to sacrifice one of us," Captain Dudley murmured. His lips were so parched by exposure and dehydration that it was painful to speak.

The long silence that followed was broken only by the occasional incoherent ramblings of Parker and the monotonous lapping of the water on the side of the lifeboat.

Finally Stephens spoke up, "Yes, if we don't, we will all die."

Brooks raised himself up on one arm. "No, it's wrong," he protested weakly. "It is better that we all die together than commit murder."

Captain Dudley looked over at Stephens, who nodded his assent. Captain Dudley then killed Parker. The three men fed on the body of the boy for the next five days, when they were finally rescued. According to their rescuers, it is unlikely any of them would have survived if they had not had something to eat.

Discussion Questions

1. Did Dudley do the right thing by killing Parker? Support your answer. Discuss the extent to which your answer was based on utilitarian considerations and the extent to which it was based on nonutilitarian considerations. Which considerations were most morally compelling in making your decision?

2. Use Bentham's utilitarian calculus to come up with a solution that maximizes pleasure and minimizes pain. Remember to take into account all seven criteria in formulating your solution. Are you satisfied with the results of your calculus? Explain.

3. Is killing someone for food in a case such as this consistent with Mo Tzu's principle of universal love? Support your answer. If not, what solution might Mo Tzu have suggested had he been in the lifeboat?

4. Would a cultural relativist have approved of what the captain did? Discuss how a cultural relativist might make a decision in a case such as this.

5. Bernard criticizes utilitarianism as not taking sufficient account of individual integrity. To what extent is the situation in the lifeboat similar to that faced by Jim in the selection from Williams? Was Brooks more morally culpable because he fed on the body of Parker even though he had protested that it was wrong to kill him?

2. Why Not Murder?

In his novel *Crime and Punishment* Feodor Dostoevski (1821–1881) explores the mind and motivations of a well-intentioned murderer named Raskolnikov. The following scene from the novel is set in a tea house where Raskolnikov, a poor student, is musing over whether or not he should murder a wealthy and miserly old woman, Alyona Ivanovna. Raskolnikov's intentions in murdering her seem noble enough. By killing the old woman he can redistribute her wealth, thus correcting the injustice of her having so much money while others who need it go without.

While he is pondering this question, he overhears a conversation between another student and a young officer. This conversation, by a wild coincidence, is about the very same topic.

"Of course [Alyona] does not deserve to live," remarks the officer, "but there it is, it's nature."

"Oh, well, brother, but we have to correct and direct nature, and, but for that, we should drown in a sea of prejudice." . . .

"You are talking and speechifying away, but tell me, would you kill the old woman yourself?"

"Of course not! I was only arguing the justice of it. . . . It's nothing to do with me."

"But I think," [the officer responds], "if you would not do it yourself, there's no justice about it."

Discussion Questions

1. Which person, the student or the officer, presents the strongest argument? Do we have a moral obligation to "correct and direct nature," even if it means killing someone? Support your answer.

2. Did the student have a moral obligation to kill Ivanovna? Do we have a moral obligation to act in a way that maximizes happiness for the greatest number even if it brings great pain to one person? Does the principle of utility require that we kill people whose lives bring about more pain than pleasure? How about people who are a burden to society, such as people who are severely mentally retarded or comatose, through no fault of their own?

3. Imagine that Raskolnikov had come to you first and told you of his plan to murder Ivanovna. He then asks you if you think he is doing the right thing. How would you reply? How would Mo Tzu have replied? How would Bentham have replied? Which answer is most satisfactory?

3. Medical Experiments on Humans

Infectious hepatitis is a disease that can leave a person seriously ill for several weeks with symptoms such as nausea, fever, jaundice, abdominal pain, and general malaise. Permanent liver damage may also occur. Death, however, is rare. Infectious hepatitis has its highest frequency among young people living together in close quarters, such as college dormitories and other institutional settings.

The Willowbrook State School in New York City, which houses mentally retarded children between the ages of 5 and 15, had periodic outbreaks of infectious hepatitis in the early to mid-1900s. By 1950, most newly admitted children contracted the disease within the first twelve months of residency.

In 1956, in order to learn more about the disease, Drs. Saul Krugman and Joan Giles of the New York University School of Medicine decided to conduct a long-range study of the disease at Willowbrook. With the permission of the children's parents or guardians, a group of newly admitted children were intentionally infected with the disease and then carefully observed. The researchers hoped to use the information gained from the experiment to prevent future outbreaks of infectious hepatitis.

Krugman and Giles justified the study as being in the best interests of the children. "It was inevitable that the susceptible children would become infected in the institution," they wrote.[1] They also argued that the children would benefit because the studies would be carried out in isolation facilities where the children would be protected from other infectious diseases that were prevalent in the institution.

Discussion Questions

1. Was this experiment morally justified? Which moral considerations did you use in making your decision? How important were consequences in your decision? Would a utilitarian agree with your decision?

2. Apply Bentham's utilitarian calculus to this experiment. Are you satisfied with the results? Explain.

3. This experiment was carried out in the 1950s. At the time there were no laws in the United States regulating the use of human subjects in medical experiments. The study had also been reviewed and approved by the New York State Department of Mental Health, as well as other agencies. Would this information make a difference to a utilitarian? Would this information be morally relevant to a cultural relativist?

4. The children used in this experiment had a low cognitive ability—lower in some cases than many nonhuman animals that are currently used in medical experiments. Is this fact morally relevant? Discuss the respective positions that John Stuart Mill and Peter Singer each might take regarding the morality of this experiment.

5. Do parents have the right to permit their children to be used in non-therapeutic medical experiments? Could a utilitarian argue that these parents actually had a moral obligation, based on the principle of utility, to permit their children to be used in this experiment? Support your answer.

4. Television and the "Mean World Syndrome"

In 1977 Ronny Zamora, a 15-year-old, shot and killed his 82-year-old neighbor. Zamora's lawyer entered a "not guilty" plea, arguing that Zamora had become habituated to violence until he could no longer tell right from wrong. "If you judge Ronny Zamora guilty," his lawyer stated, "television would be an accessory."[2]

There is a large body of evidence suggesting a strong link between television viewing and aggression. According to Reed Hundt, Chairman of the Federal Communications Commission, "there are substantial risks of harmful effects from viewing violence throughout the television environment."[3]

Studies show that Americans, on average, spend about one-third of their free time watching television. A 1992 study in the *Journal of the American Medical Association*, found that the average child in the United States will have watched 40,000 murders and 200,000 acts of violence by age 18. Brandon Centerwald of the University of Washington hypothesizes that the sharp increase in murder rates in the United States beginning in 1955 is the result of viewing television.

In addition to fueling violence, studies show that the more violence people watch on television, the more they feel threatened by violence in their own lives —a situation that has been labeled the "Mean World Syndrome." Women and members of minority groups are most likely to grow up feeling they are vulnerable because television shows disproportionately portray them as victims of violence. "For every white male victim of violence there are 17 white females . . . and 22 minority females . . . . Villains are disproportionately male, lower-class, young and Latino or foreign."[4]

Discussion Questions

1. Was Ronny Zamora morally responsible for killing his neighbor? Were the television networks accessories in the murder, as his lawyer claimed? Discuss how a utilitarian judge would most likely have ruled in this case.

2. Does the correlation between television viewing and violence justify limiting the pleasure many people receive from watching violent programs on television? If so, should programming be regulated for adults as well as for children? Use the utilitarian calculus to formulate a social policy for the regulation of television.

3. John Stuart Mill argues that security and a safe environment are "the most indispensable of all necessaries [for happiness] after physical nutriment."[5] Should television producers be prohibited from showing programs that portray repeated violence against women and members of minority groups? Is censorship an infringement on producers' freedom of speech and artistic license? How should freedom of speech be balanced against the harmful effects of television?

4. To what extent does television viewing influence your behavior? Do you agree that television has made people meaner, as well as less secure? Support your answer using examples from your own experience.

5. Using the principle of utility, discuss whether television viewing ought to be restricted on your campus.

5. AIDS Testing

By 1995 AIDS (acquired immune deficiency syndrome) had surpassed injuries and accidents as the leading killer of Americans from age 25 to 44,[6] and was the sixth leading cause of death among 15–24-year-olds.[7] The Centers for Disease Control estimates that in 1990 there were 10,000 to 35,000 college students in the United States who were HIV positive,[8] meaning they are infected with the AIDS virus. Most students who are HIV positive are not aware of their status until the first symptoms of AIDS are diagnosed.

In 1993 Montana State University-Northern adopted the following policy for dealing with AIDS on campus:

- The Student Health Director . . . will collect and disseminate relevant AIDS information to the campus community.
- The Student Health Service will offer anonymous AIDS counseling and testing.[9]

It was also decided, as recommended by the American College Health Association, that the university would not "engage in mandatory testing of employees or students . . . [nor] disclose the identity of students or employees who have AIDS or the AIDS virus, except as authorized by law or as recommended by the relevant guidelines of the American College Health Association."[10]

Discussion Questions

1. Do people who engage in high-risk behavior have a social responsibility to get tested and to provide the names of previous contacts should the test results be positive? If so, should they be punished if they knowingly infect another person?[11] Or do we have a right not to know or divulge our HIV status? Support your answer.

2. Some people, such as Dr. Bernard Rabinowitz, disagree with allowing AIDS testing to be voluntary, as it is at the Montana State University. Rabinowitz argues that the overriding moral obligation when there is an epidemic is the protection of the uninfected. This has not been the case with the AIDS epidemic where, Rabinowitz writes, "we had endorsed the first legally protected epidemic in medical history. . . . with AIDS the right to secrecy of a tiny minority were deemed ethically more important than the right of the huge uninfected majority."[12] Discuss whether utilitarians would be more likely to agree with the policy at Montana State University or more likely to prefer a mandatory testing policy?

3. Federal and state governments are now paying about 40 percent of AIDS-related medical expenses, amounting to several billion dollars a year. Discuss whether financial cost provides a justification for coercing people, or at least people at high risk for AIDS, into being tested or into notifying partners.

4. During the 1990s AIDS has spread faster among intravenous drug users than among any other population. Some countries provide addicts with free sterile needles in order to reduce the rate of infection. Using the utilitarian calculus, discuss the pros and cons of your campus or state instituting a free sterile needle policy.

5. A bill requiring mandatory AIDS testing for all pregnant women is currently under consideration by Congress. This proposed bill would help prevent the spread of AIDS to newborns, because prompt treatment of an HIV-infected mother can prevent transfer of the virus to the fetus.[13] Should all pregnant women be required to undergo HIV testing? Support your answer.

6. Dr. Kevorkian and the Assisted Suicide of Judith Curren

On August 15, 1996, Judith Curren, a 42-year-old mother of two young daughters, committed suicide with the assistance of Dr. Jack Kevorkian. Unlike most of Kevorkian's clients, Curren was not terminally ill. However, she was suffering from depression, chronic fatigue syndrome, and fibromyalgia—a benign inflammation of fibromuscular tissue.

Curren's husband, psychiatrist Franklin Curren, who was present at his wife's death, was a strong supporter of physician-assisted suicide and his wife's choice to end her life.[14] Kevorkian was surprised when he read a press release a few days later stating that Dr. Curren had been charged with assaulting his wife just three weeks earlier. This was not the first domestic assault charge that had been brought against Curren by his wife.[15]

When questioned about the role that domestic violence may have played in her decision to end her life, Kevorkian replied that he had asked the Currens if there had been any trouble in the family and that they had said no. "You can't know what goes on domestically," Kevorkian added in defense of his action.

Discussion Questions

1. Judith Curren was not terminally ill at the time of her death. Should assisted suicide be extended to anyone who wishes to end their life? Support your answer. Discuss how you would respond if someone you knew asked you to assist in their suicide because he or she was depressed and/or suffering from a chronic illness.

2. Was the assisted suicide of Judith Curren consistent with Mo Tzu's principle of universal love? Discuss how Mo Tzu might have responded had Curren come to him with a request for assisted suicide.

3. Some opponents of euthanasia argue that many people consider euthanasia because they lack adequate pain control medication or medical insurance to seek proper treatment and care, or because they feel they have become a burden to their friends and family and that the world would be better off without them. The hospice movement, for example, is based on the belief that we should provide terminally ill people with better palliative care so that they can live their last days in relative comfort, rather than granting wider legal access to euthanasia.[16] Compare and contrast the utility of the two policies.

4. The American Medical Association is opposed to euthanasia. If assisted suicide is legal, they argue, it may become a duty to die when our burden on society outweighs the benefits. How would a utilitarian respond to this criticism?

5. There are about 250,000 terminally ill Americans annually. Treatment in an intensive care unit can cost $1,000 a day or more.[17] Could the financial burden on the family and on society justify euthanasia of terminally ill people, with or without their consent? Discuss how a utilitarian might compare the utility of death with the utility of money.

6. John Stuart Mill argues that security and a safe environment are "the most indispensable of all necessaries after physical nutriment."[18] Would allowing physicians to assist in the suicide of their terminally ill patients damage this sense of security and safety in a physician–patient relationship? Or would it expand the freedom of the dying patient to choose his or her destiny? Support your answer.

NOTES

[1] Case from Ronald Munson, *Intervention and Reflection: Basic Issues in Medial Ethics,* 4th ed. (Belmont, CA: Wadsworth, 1992), pp. 312–314.

[2] Scott Stossel, "The Man Who Counts the Killings," *The Atlantic Monthly,* May 1997, p. 86.

[3] Ibid., p. 89.

[4] Ibid., p. 91.

[5] John Stuart Mill, "Utilitarianism," in *Utilitarianism,* ed. Mary Warnock (New York: Meridian Books, 1962), p. 308.

[6] "AIDS Is Leading Killer of Americans from Age 25 to 44," *Jet,* February 20, 1995, p. 22.

[7] "The Growing Specter of AIDS in the Young," *Medical Update,* March 1994, 17 (9): 3

[8] "College HIV Rate Holds Steady, but Risk of Exposure Remains High," *AIDS Alert,* November 1994, 9 (11): 153–156.

[9] This policy is in accordance with Montana Statute 50-16 part 10, AIDS Prevention Act.

[10] "1003.3 Aids," http://www.nmclites.edu/policy/1003_3nm.htm. Also see American College Health Association, "General Statement on Institutional Response to AIDS" (November 1988).

[11] In a 1988 study almost 25 percent of sexually active people said that if they tested positive for the AIDS virus, they would not inform casual sexual partners of their status. Study cited in Ronald Munson, *Intervention and Reflections: Basic Issues in Medical Ethics,* 4th ed. (Belmont, CA: Wadsworth, 1992), p. 220.

[12] Bernard Rabinowitz, "The Great Hijack," *British Medical Journal,* September 28, 1996, 313 (7060): 826.

[13] Julie Rovner, "HIV Tests for Babies to be Mandatory in USA," *Lancet,* May 11, 1996.

[14] "Kevorkian Charged in Assisting 3 Suicides," *Patriot Ledger* (Quincy, MA), November 1, 1996, p. 11.

[15] Doreen Iudica Vigue, "The Top 10 Local News Stories of 1996," *Boston Globe,* January 1, 1997, p. B1.

[16] Donna White, "Death on Trial," *U.S. News & World Report,* April 25, 1994, pp. 31–41.

[17] Ibid., p. 34.

[18] John Stuart Mill, "Utilitarianism," in *Utilitarianism,* ed. Mary Warnock (New York: Meridian Books, 1962), p. 308.

CHAPTER SEVEN

Deontology

Act only on that maxim through which you can at the same time will that it should become a universal law.

Immanuel Kant, *Fundamental Principles of the Metaphysic of Ethics*

Deontologists regard moral duty as the basis of morality. These moral duties are universally binding on all people, and take priority over other duties such as legal obligations.

Moral duty requires acting out of the right intentions. Because our intentions are so important in deontology, the cultivation of self-respect is one of our most important moral duties. Persons with self-respect can be counted on to do their duty in the face of temptations.

Deontology is one of the most popular moral theories. There are strong strands of deontology in many Western philosophies, as well as in Confucian and Hindu philosophy.

In the first reading from *Fundamental Principles of the Metaphysic of Ethics,* Immanuel Kant argues that moral duty is imposed on us by reason. Only reason, he claims, can provide a sound foundation for morality.

Deontology in Western philosophy is often identified with Kant's moral theory. However, there are many other versions of duty-based ethics. In the second reading from *The Analects of Confucius,* the writer argues that respect for duty is essential to a stable and harmonious social order.

In her book *Lying,* Sissela Bok applies deontological theory to the issue of lying. She asks, "Are lies always wrong?"

William David Ross, in a selection from *The Right and the Good,* argues that moral duties need not be absolute, as Kant claimed. Instead moral duties are *prima facie*. A *prima facie* duty is one that is morally binding unless it conflicts with a more pressing moral duty.

In the last selection from *A Theory of Justice,* John Rawls focuses on the duty of justice. Rawls regards justice as the most important social duty.

Immanuel Kant

Fundamental Principles of the Metaphysic of Ethics

German philosopher Immanuel Kant (1724–1804) was one of the great modern philosophers. Kant's first major work in the field of philosophy was not published until he was in his late 50s. According to his friends and colleagues, Kant was a truly moral person who lived what he taught. During his later years, people came from all over to consult him on a variety of moral issues.

Kant believed that most people *know* what is right. The problem comes in *doing* what is right. In his *Fundamental Principles of the Metaphysic of Ethics,* Kant attempted to provide a foundation for ethics that would explain why we ought to act morally.

CRITICAL THINKING QUESTIONS

1. What, according to Kant, is the only thing that is good without qualification? Why is it good without qualification?
2. What does Kant mean by a Good Will?
3. According to Kant, what is the relation between the will and reason?
4. How does Kant define *duty?*
5. What does Kant mean when he says we should promote happiness out of a sense of duty rather than out of inclinations or feelings?
6. Does our duty in any particular situation depend on the consequences or effects of our actions?
7. What is the source of all our moral conceptions?
8. What is an imperative? What are the two types of imperatives?
9. Which imperative, according to Kant, is concerned with morality?
10. What are the two versions of the categorical imperative?
11. Why does Kant claim that humans exist as ends in themselves?
12. Why, according to Kant, is suicide immoral?
13. What does Kant mean when he says that the autonomy of the will is the supreme principle of morality?

Fundamental Principles of the Metaphysic of Ethics, translated by Thomas Kingsmill Abbott (London: Longmans, Green and Co., Ltd., 1873), pp. 30–39, 44–59, and 71. Some notes have been omitted.

Nothing can possibly be conceived in the world, or even out of it, which can be called good without qualification, except a Good Will. Intelligence, wit, judgment, and the other *talents* of the mind, however they may be named, or courage, resolution, perseverance, as qualities of temperament, are undoubtedly good and desirable in many respects; but these gifts of nature may also become extremely bad and mischievous if the will which is to make use of them, and which, therefore, constitutes what is called *character,* is not good. It is the same with the *gifts of fortune.* Power, riches, honour, even health, and the general well-being and contentment with one's condition which is called *happiness,* inspire pride, and often presumption, if there is not a good will to correct the influence of these on the mind, and with this also to rectify the whole principle of acting, and adapt it to its end.

. . .

A good will is good not because of what it performs or effects, not by its aptness for the attainment of some proposed end, but simply by virtue of the volition, that is, it is good in itself, and considered by itself is to be esteemed much higher than all that can be brought about by it in favour of any inclination, nay, even of the sum total of all inclinations. Even if it should happen that, owing to special disfavour of fortune, or the niggardly provision of a step-motherly nature, this will should wholly lack power to accomplish its purpose, if with its greatest efforts it should yet achieve nothing, and there should remain only the good will (not, to be sure, a mere wish, but the summoning of all means in our power), then, like a jewel, it would still shine by its own light, as a thing which has its whole value in itself. Its usefulness or fruitlessness can neither add to nor take away anything from this value. . . .

To be beneficent when we can is a duty; and besides this, there are many minds so sympathetically constituted that, without any other motive of vanity or self-interest, they find a pleasure in spreading joy around them, and can take delight in the satisfaction of others so far as it is their own work. But I maintain that in such a case an action of this kind, however proper, however amiable it may be, has nevertheless no true moral worth, but is on a level with other inclinations, *e.g.* the inclination to honour, which, if it is happily directed to that which is in fact of public utility and accordant with duty, and consequently honourable, deserves praise and encouragement, but not esteem. For the maxim lacks the moral import, namely, that such actions be done *from duty,* not from inclination. Put the case that the mind of that philanthropist were clouded by sorrow of his own extinguishing all sympathy with the lot of others, and that while he still has the power to benefit others in distress, he is not touched by their trouble because he is absorbed with his own; and now suppose that he tears himself out of this dead insensibility, and performs the action without any inclination to it, but simply from duty, then first has his action its genuine moral worth. Further still; if nature has put little sympathy in the heart of this or that man; if he, supposed to be an upright man, is by temperament cold and indifferent to the sufferings of others, perhaps because in respect of his own he is provided with the special gift of patience and fortitude, and supposes, or even requires, that others should have the same—and such a man would certainly not be the meanest product of nature

—but if nature had not specially framed him for a philanthropist, would he not still find in himself a source from whence to give himself a far higher worth than that of a good-natured temperament could be? Unquestionably. It is just in this that the moral worth of the character is brought out which is incomparably the highest of all, namely, that he is beneficent, not from inclination, but from duty.

To secure one's own happiness is a duty, at least indirectly; for discontent with one's condition, under a pressure of many anxieties and amidst unsatisfied wants, might easily become a great *temptation to transgression of duty*. But here again, without looking to duty, all men have already the strongest and most intimate inclination to happiness, because it is just in this idea that all inclinations are combined in one total. But the precept of happiness is often of such a sort that it greatly interferes with some inclinations, and yet a man cannot form any definite and certain conception of the sum of satisfaction of all of them which is called happiness. It is not then to be wondered at that a single inclination, definite both as to what it promises and as to the time within which it can be gratified, is often able to overcome such a fluctuating idea, and that a gouty patient, for instance, can choose to enjoy what he likes, and to suffer what he may, since, according to his calculation, on this occasion at least, he has [only] not sacrificed the enjoyment of the present moment to a possibly mistaken expectation of a happiness which is supposed to be found in health. But even in this case, if the general desire for happiness did not influence his will, and supposing that in his particular case health was not a necessary element in this calculation, there yet remains in this, as in all other cases, this law, namely, that he should promote his happiness not from inclination but from duty, and by this would his conduct first acquire true moral worth.

It is in this manner, undoubtedly, that we are to understand those passages of Scripture also in which we are commanded to love our neighbour, even our enemy. For love, as an affection, cannot be commanded, but beneficence for duty's sake may; even though we are not impelled to it by any inclination—nay, are even repelled by a natural and unconquerable aversion. The is *practical* love, and not *pathological*—a love which is seated in the will, and not in the propensions of sense—in principles of action and not of tender sympathy; and it is this love alone which can be commanded.

The second* proposition is. That an action done from duty derives its moral worth, *not from the purpose* which is to be attained by it, but from the maxim by which it is determined, and therefore does not depend on the realization of the object of the action, but merely on the *principle of volition* by which the action has taken place, without regard to any object of desire. It is clear from what precedes that the purposes which we may have in view in our actions, or their effects regarded as ends and springs of the will, cannot give to actions any unconditional or moral worth. In what, then, can their worth lie, if it is not to consist in the will and in reference to its expected effect? It cannot lie anywhere but in the *principle of the will* without regard to the ends which can be attained by the action. For

---

*[The first proposition was that, to have moral worth, an action must be done from duty.]

the will stands between its *à priori* principle, which is formal, and its *à posteriori* spring, which is material, as between two roads, and as it must be determined by something, it follows that it must be determined by the formal principle of volition when an action is done from duty, in which case every material principle has been withdrawn from it.

The third proposition, which is a consequence of the two preceding, I would express thus: *Duty is the necessity of acting from respect for the law.* I may have *inclination* for an object as the effect of my proposed action, but I cannot have *respect* for it, just for this reason, that it is an effect and not an energy of will. . . .

Thus the moral worth of an action does not lie in the effect expected from it, nor in any principle of action which requires to borrow its motive from this expected effect. For all these effects—agreeableness of one's condition, and even the promotion of the happiness of others—could have been also brought about by other causes, so that for this there would have been no need of the will of a rational being; whereas it is in this alone that the supreme and unconditional good can be found. The pre-eminent good which we call moral can therefore consist in nothing else than *the conception of law* in itself, *which certainly is only possible in a rational being,* in so far as this conception, and not the expected effect, determines the will. This is a good which is already present in the person who acts accordingly, and we have not to wait for it to appear first in the result.

But what sort of law can that be, the conception of which must determine the will, even without paying any regard to the effect expected from it, in order that this will may be called good absolutely and without qualification? As I have deprived the will of every impulse which could arise to it from obedience to any law, there remains nothing but the universal conformity of its actions to law in general, which alone is to serve the will as a principle, *i.e.* I am never to act otherwise than so *that I could also will that my maxim should become a universal law.* Here now, it is the simple conformity to law in general, without assuming any particular law applicable to certain actions, that serves the will as its principle, and must so serve it, if duty is not to be a vain delusion and a chimerical notion. The common reason of men in its practical judgments perfectly coincides with this, and always has in view the principle here suggested. Let the question be, for example: May I when in distress make a promise with the intention not to keep it? I readily distinguish here between the two significations which the question may have: Whether it is prudent, or whether it is right, to make a false promise. The former may undoubtedly often be the case. I see clearly indeed that it is not enough to extricate myself from a present difficulty by means of this subterfuge, but it must be well considered whether there may not hereafter spring from this lie much greater inconvenience than that from which I now free myself, and as, with all my supposed *cunning,* the consequences cannot be so easily foreseen but that credit once lost may be much more injurious to me than any mischief which I seek to avoid at present, it should be considered whether it would not be more *prudent* to act herein according to a universal maxim, and to make it a habit to promise nothing except with the intention of keeping it. But it is soon clear to me that such a maxim will still only be based on the fear of consequences. Now it is a wholly different thing to be truthful from duty, and to be so from apprehension of injurious consequences. In the first case, the very notion of the action already implies a law for me; in the second case, I must first look about elsewhere to see what results may be combined with it which would affect myself. For to deviate from the principle of duty is beyond all doubt wicked; but to be unfaithful to my maxim of prudence may often be very advantageous to me, although to abide by it is certainly safer. The shortest way, however, and an unerring one, to discover the answer to this question whether a lying promise is consistent with duty, is to ask myself, Should I be content that my maxim (to extricate myself from difficulty by a false promise) should hold good as a universal law, for myself as well as for others? and should I be able to say to myself, "Every one may make a deceitful promise when he finds himself in a difficulty from which he cannot otherwise extricate himself"? Then I presently become aware that while I can will the lie, I can by no means will that lying should be a universal law. For with such a law there would be no promises at all, since it would be in vain to allege my intention in regard to my future actions to those who would not believe this allegation, or if they over-hastily did so would pay me back in my own coin. Hence my maxim, as soon as it should be made a universal law, would necessarily destroy itself.

I do not, therefore, need any far-reaching penetration to discern what I have to do in order that my will may be morally good. Inexperienced in the course of the world, incapable of being prepared for all its contingencies, I only ask myself: Canst thou also will that thy maxim should be a universal law? If not, then it must be rejected, and that not because of a disadvantage accruing from it to myself or even to others, but because it cannot enter as a principle into a possible universal legislation, and reason extorts from me immediate respect for such legislation. I do not indeed as yet *discern* on what this respect is based (this the philosopher may inquire), but at least I understand this, that it is an estimation of the worth which far outweighs all worth of what is recommended by inclination, and that the necessity of acting from *pure* respect for the practical law is what constitutes duty, to which every other motive must give place, because it is the condition of a will being good *in itself*, and the worth of such a will is above everything.

. . .

From what has been said, it is clear that all moral conceptions have their seat and origin completely *à priori* in the reason, and that, moreover, in the commonest reason just as truly as in that which is in the highest degree speculative; that they cannot be obtained by abstraction from any empirical, and therefore merely contingent knowledge; that it is just this purity of their origin that makes them worthy to serve as our supreme practical principle, and that just in proportion as we add anything empirical, we detract from their genuine influence, and from the absolute value of actions; that it is not only of the greatest necessity, in a purely speculative point of view, but is also of the greatest practical importance to derive these notions and laws from pure reason, to present them pure and unmixed, and even to determine the compass of this practical or pure rational knowledge, *i.e.* to determine the whole faculty of pure practical reason; and, in doing so, we must not make its principles dependent on the particular nature of human reason, though in speculative philosophy this may be permitted, or may even at times be necessary; but since moral laws ought to hold good for every rational creature, we must derive them from the general concept of a rational being. In this way, although for its *application* to man morality has need of anthropology, yet, in the first instance, we must treat it independently as pure philosophy, *i.e.* as metaphysic, complete in itself (a thing which in such distinct branches of science is easily done); knowing well that unless we are in possession of this, it would not only be vain to determine the moral element of duty in right actions for purposes of speculative criticism, but it would be impossible to base morals on their genuine principles, even for common practical purposes, especially of moral instruction, so as to produce pure moral dispositions, and to engraft them on men's minds to the promotion of the greatest possible good in the world.

. . .

Everything in nature works according to laws. Rational beings alone have the faculty of acting according *to the conception* of laws, that is according to principles, *i.e.* have a *will*. Since the deduction of actions from principles requires *reason,* the will is nothing but practical reason. If reason infallibly determines the will, then the actions of such a being which are recognised as objectively necessary are subjectively necessary also, *i.e.* the will is a faculty to choose *that only* which reason independent on inclination recognises as practically necessary, *i.e.* as good. But if reason of itself does not sufficiently determine the will, if the latter is subject also to subjective conditions (particular impulses) which do not always coincide with the objective conditions; in a word, if the will does not *in itself* completely accord with reason (which is actually the case with men), then the actions which objectively are recognised as necessary are subjectively contingent, and the determination of such a will according to objective laws is *obligation,* that is to say, the relation of the objective laws to a will that is not thoroughly good is conceived as the determination of the will of a rational being by principles of reason, but which the will from its nature does not of necessity follow.

The conception of an objective principle, in so far as it is obligatory for a will, is called a command (of reason), and the formula of the command is called an Imperative.

All imperatives are expressed by the word *ought* [or *shall*], and thereby indicate the relation of an objective law of reason to a will, which from its subjective constitution is not necessarily determined by it (an obligation). They say that something would be good to do or to forbear, but they say it to a will which does not always do a thing because it is conceived to be good to do it. . . .

Now all *imperatives* command either *hypothetically* or *categorically.* The former represent the practical necessity of a possible action as means to something else that is willed (or at least which one might possibly will). The categorical imperative would be that which represented an action as necessary of itself without reference to another end, *i.e.* as objectively necessary.

Since every practical law represents a possible action as good, and on this account, for a subject who is practically determinable by reason, necessary, all imperatives are formulæ determining an action which is necessary according to the principle of a will good in some respects. If now the action is good only as a means *to something else,* then the imperative is *hypothetical;* if it is conceived as good *in itself* and consequently as being necessarily the principle of a will which of itself conforms to reason, then it is *categorical.*

Thus the imperative declares what action possible by me would be good, and presents the practical rule in relation to a will which does not forthwith perform an action simply because it is good, whether because the subject does not always know that it is good, or because, even if it know this, yet its maxims might be opposed to the objective principles of practical reason.

Accordingly the hypothetical imperative only says that the action is good for some purpose, *possible* or *actual.* In the first case it is a Problematical, in the second an Assertorial practical principle. The categorical imperative which declares an action to be objectively necessary in itself without reference to any purpose, *i.e.* without any other end, is valid as a (practical) Apodictic principle.

. . .

Finally, there is an imperative which commands a certain conduct immediately, without having as its condition any other purpose to be attained by it. This imperative is Categorical. It concerns not the matter of the action, or its intended result, but its form and the principle of which it is itself a result; and what is essentially good in it consists in the mental disposition, let the consequence be what it may. This imperative may be called that of Morality.

. . .

We shall therefore have to investigate *à priori* the possibility of a categorical imperative, as we have not in this case the advantage of its reality being given in experience, so that [the elucidation of] its possibility should be requisite only for its explanation, not for its establishment. In the meantime it may be discerned beforehand that the categorical imperative alone has the purport of a practical law: all the rest may indeed be called *principles* of the will but not laws, since whatever is only necessary for the attainment of some arbitrary purpose may be considered as in itself contingent, and we can at any time be free from the precept if we give up the purpose: on the contrary, the unconditional command leaves the will no liberty to choose the opposite; consequently it alone carries with it that necessity which we require in a law.

Secondly, in the case of this categorical imperative or law of morality, the difficulty (of discerning its possibility) is a very profound one. It is an *à priori* synthetical practical proposition;* and as there is so much difficulty in discerning the possibility of speculative propositions of this kind, it may readily be supposed that the difficulty will be no less with the practical.

In this problem we will first inquire whether the mere conception of a categorical imperative may not perhaps supply us also with the formula of it, containing

---

*I connect the act with the will without presupposing any condition resulting from any inclination, but *à priori,* and therefore necessarily (though only objectively, *i.e.* assuming the idea of a reason possessing full power over all subjective motives). This is accordingly a practical proposition which does not deduce the willing of an action by mere analysis from another already presupposed (for we have not such a perfect will), but connects it immediately with the conception of the will of a rational being, as something not contained in it.

the proposition which alone can be a categorical imperative; for even if we know the tenor of such an absolute command, yet how it is possible will require further special and laborious study, which we postpone to the last section.

When I conceive a hypothetical imperative in general I do not know beforehand what it will contain until I am given the condition. But when I conceive a categorical imperative I know at once what it contains. For as the imperative contains besides the law only the necessity that the maxims* shall conform to this law, while the law contains no conditions restricting it, there remains nothing but the general statement that the maxim of the action should conform to a universal law, and it is this conformity alone that the imperative properly represents as necessary.

There is therefore but one categorical imperative, namely this: *Act only on that maxim whereby thou canst at the same time will that it should become a universal law.*

Now if all imperatives of duty can be deduced from this one imperative as from their principle, then, although it should remain undecided whether what is called duty is not merely a vain notion, yet at least we shall be able to show what we understand by it and what this notion means.

Since the universality of the law according to which effects are produced constitutes what is properly called *nature* in the most general sense (as to form), that is, the existence of things so far as it is determined by general laws, the imperative of duty may be expressed thus: *Act as if the maxim of thy action were to become by thy will a Universal Law of Nature. . . .*

1. A man reduced to despair by a series of misfortunes feels wearied of life, but is still so far in possession of his reason that he can ask himself whether it would not be contrary to his duty to himself to take his own life. Now he inquires whether the maxim of his action could become a universal law of nature. His maxim is: From self-love I adopt it as a principle to shorten my life when its longer duration is likely to bring more evil than satisfaction. It is asked then simply whether this principle founded on self-love can become a universal law of nature. Now we see at once that a system of nature of which it should be a law to destroy life by means of the very feeling whose special nature it is to impel to the improvement of life would contradict itself, and therefore could not exist as a system of nature; hence that maxim cannot possibly exist as a universal law of nature, and consequently would be wholly inconsistent with the supreme principle of all duty.

2. Another finds himself forced by necessity to borrow money. He knows that he will not be able to repay it, but sees also that nothing will be lent to him,

---

*A MAXIM is a subjective principle of action, and must be distinguished from the *objective principle,* namely, practical law. The former contains the practical rule set by reason according to the conditions of the subject (often its ignorance or its inclinations), so that it is the principle on which the subject *acts;* but the law is the objective principle valid for every rational being, and is the principle on which it *ought to act,* that is, an imperative.

unless he promises stoutly to repay it in a definite time. He desires to make this promise, but he has still so much conscience as to ask himself: Is it not unlawful and inconsistent with duty to get out of a difficulty in this way? Suppose however that he resolves to do so, then the maxim of his action would be expressed thus: When I think myself in want of money, I will borrow money and promise to repay it, although I know that I never can do so. Now this principle of self-love or of one's own advantage may perhaps be consistent with my whole future welfare; but the question now is, is it right? I change then the suggestion of self-love into a universal law, and state the question thus: How would it be if my maxim were a universal law? Then I see at once that it could never hold as a universal law of nature but would necessarily contradict itself. For supposing it to be a universal law that everyone when he thinks himself in a difficulty should be able to promise whatever he pleases, with the purpose of not keeping his promise, the promise itself would become impossible, as well as the end that one might have in view in it, since no one would consider that anything was promised to him, but would ridicule all such statements as vain pretences.

3. A third finds in himself a talent which with the help of some culture might make him a useful man in many respects. But he finds himself in comfortable circumstances, and prefers to indulge in pleasure rather than to take pains in enlarging and improving his happy natural capacities. He asks, however, whether his maxim of neglect of his natural gifts, besides agreeing with his inclination to indulgence, agrees also with what is called duty. He sees then that a system of nature could indeed subsist with such a universal law although men (like the South Sea islanders) should let their talents rust, and resolve to devote their lives merely to idleness, amusement, and propagation of their species—in a word, to enjoyment; but he cannot possibly *will* that this should be a universal law of nature, or be implanted in us as such by a natural instinct. For, as a rational being, he necessarily wills that his faculties be developed, since they serve him, and have been given him, for all sorts of possible purposes.

. . .

We have thus established at least this much, that if duty is a conception which is to have any import and real legislative authority for our actions, it can only be expressed in categorical, and not at all in hypothetical imperatives. We have also, which is of great importance, exhibited clearly and definitely for every practical application the content of the categorical imperative, which must contain the principle of all duty if there is such a thing at all. We have not yet, however, advanced so far as to prove *à priori* that there actually is such an imperative, that there is a practical law which commands absolutely of itself, and without any other impulse, and that the following of this law is duty.

. . .

If then there is a supreme practical principle or, in respect of the human will, a categorical imperative, it must be one which, being drawn from the conception of that which is necessarily an end for every one because it is *an end in itself,* constitutes an *objective* principle of will, and can therefore serve as a universal practical law. The foundation of this principle is: *rational nature exists as an end in itself.* Man necessarily conceives his own existence as being so: so far then this is a *subjective* principle of human actions. But every other rational being regards its existence similarly, just on the same rational principle that holds for me:* so that it is at the same time an objective principle, from which as a supreme practical law all laws of the will must be capable of being deduced. Accordingly the practical imperative will be as follows: *So act as to treat humanity, whether in thine own person or in that of any other, in every case as an end withal, never as means only.* We will now inquire whether this can be practically carried out.

To abide by the previous examples:

Firstly, under the head of necessary duty to oneself: He who contemplates suicide should ask himself whether his action can be consistent with the idea of humanity *as an end in itself.* If he destroys himself in order to escape from painful circumstances, he uses a person merely as a *mean* to maintain a tolerable condition up to the end of life. But a man is not a thing, that is to say, something which can be used merely as means, but must in all his actions be always considered as an end in himself. I cannot, therefore, dispose in any way of a man in my own person so as to mutilate him, to damage or kill him. (It belongs to ethics proper to define this principle more precisely so as to avoid all misunderstanding, *e.g.* as to the amputation of the limbs in order to preserve myself; as to exposing my life to danger with a view to preserve it, &c. This question is therefore omitted here.)

Secondly, as regards necessary duties, or those of strict obligation, towards others; he who is thinking of making a lying promise to others will see at once that he would be using another man *merely as a mean,* without the latter containing at the same time the end in himself. For he whom I propose by such a promise to use for my own purposes cannot possibly assent to my mode of acting towards him, and therefore cannot himself contain the end of this action. This violation of the principle of humanity in other men is more obvious if we take in examples of attacks on the freedom and property of others. For then it is clear that he who transgresses the rights of men, intends to use the person of others merely as means, without considering that as rational beings they ought always to be esteemed also as ends, that is, as beings who must be capable of containing in themselves the end of the very same action. . . .

. . . Hence follows the third practical principle of the will, which is the ultimate condition of its harmony with the universal practical reason, viz.: the idea of *the will of every rational being as a universally legislative will.*

On this principle all maxims are rejected which are inconsistent with the will being itself universal legislator. Thus the will is not subject simply to the law, but so subject that it must be regarded *as itself giving the law,* and on this ground only, subject to the law (of which it can regard itself as the author). . . .

---

*This proposition is here stated as a postulate. The grounds of it will be found in the concluding section.

DISCUSSION QUESTIONS

1. Why does Kant reject utilitarianism? Compare and contrast Kant's concept of duty with the utilitarian's concept of duty as maximizing pleasure and minimizing pain.
2. What motivates a person of good will? To what extent are you a person of good will? Use examples to support your answer.
3. Why does Kant argue that only reason, and not empirical data and feelings, can provide a sound foundation for morality? Do you agree with Kant? How would Ayn Rand respond to Kant's claim? How would Ruth Benedict respond to Kant's claim?
4. In saying that persons are lawmakers unto themselves, is Kant claiming that morality is different for everyone? Compare and contrast Kant's concept of the autonomy of the will with ethical subjectivism.
5. Discuss whether it is desirable, or even possible, for people to make moral judgments independently of their particular circumstances. How might Carol Gilligan respond to this question?
6. Why does Kant claim that only rational beings have "absolute" worth? What does it mean to be a rational being? Are you satisfied with Kant's definition of rationality?
7. Do you agree with Kant that we can treat nonrational beings as means only? Would Kant's categorical imperative allow us to discriminate against nonrational humans? Support your position.
8. Do you agree with Kant that reason provides the foundation of morality? Why or why not? Would all rational people agree with the categorical imperative?
9. Does Kant's categorical imperative offer sufficient guidance for making real-life moral decisions? Use specific examples to illustrate your answer.
10. Some people think that our private life is outside the realm of morality. Kant disagrees. He claims that as a person we have to respect ourselves as well. On what grounds does he support this claim? Do you believe we have a duty to respect ourselves as well as others? If so, do you treat yourself with proper self-respect? How does self-respect, or lack of it, affect your treatment of other people?
11. Kant claims that, because the categorical imperative is grounded in reason, there will never be a conflict between our moral duties. Do you agree? Is it logically necessary, as Kant claims, that all moral imperatives be categorical? If not, does Kant's categorical imperative offer sufficient guidance for making real-life moral decisions when there appears to be a conflict among moral obligations?
12. Is Kantian deontology better than utilitarianism for dealing with issues that involve personal integrity? What might a Kantian have done had he or she been in the same situation as Jim or George in Bernard Williams's "Critique of Utilitarianism"?

Translated by Arthur Waley

The Analects of Confucius

Confucius (551 B.C.E.–479 B.C.E.) is one of the most highly revered philosophers in China. Mostly self-educated, he began the tradition of wandering scholars in China. With his pupils, Confucius traveled from province to province, teaching the rulers about the importance of their duty to humanity. The *Analects* are generally attributed to Confucius. However, they were also probably compiled from the sayings of his disciples.

Confucian ethics is a combination of deontology and virtue ethics. Although the Confucian notion of "Way" has been given a supernatural connotation by some Western thinkers, for Confucius it meant "the duties of man to man."* We learn about our duties, according to Confucians, by following the Way of the ancients. To follow the Way is to live a principled and virtuous life. Like Kant, Confucius believed that we should do our duty because it is the right thing to do. However, unlike Kantian deontology, Confucius emphasized communitarian values over individual autonomy.

CRITICAL THINKING QUESTIONS

1. What, according to Confucians, is the source of goodness in children?
2. What is a young person's first duty?
3. What do Confucians mean by moral force?
4. According to Confucians, in what ways do we change as we get older?
5. What is the relation between goodness and action?
6. Does moral force reside in the individual alone?
7. What are the four virtues of the true gentleman?
8. Can a truly good person also be unhappy?
9. What is meant by "piling up moral force"? How does it differ from "deciding when in two minds"?

The Confucian Analects, translated by Arthur Waley (New York: Macmillan, 1939), Book I: 2–4, 6, 8; Book II: 1, 3–4; Book IV: 1–7, 25; Book V: 15; Book IX: 24, 28; Book XII: 2, 10; Book XVI: 10. Some notes have been omitted.

The Analects of Confucius, translated by Arthur Waley (New York: Macmillan, 1939), p. 31.

Book I

. . .

2. . . . Master Yu said, Those who in private life behave well towards their parents and elder brothers, in public life seldom show a disposition to resist the authority of their superiors. And as for such men starting a revolution, no instance of it has ever occurred. It is upon the trunk* that a gentleman works. When that is firmly set up, the Way grows. And surely proper behaviour towards parents and elder brothers is the trunk of Goodness?

3. The Master said, "Clever talk and a pretentious manner" are seldom found in the Good.

4. Master Tsêng said, Every day I examine myself on these three points: in acting on behalf of others, have I always been loyal to their interests? In intercourse with my friends, have I always been true to my word? Have I failed to repeat the precepts that have been handed down to me?

. . .

6. The Master said, A young man's duty is to behave well to his parents at home and to his elders abroad, to be cautious in giving promises and punctual in keeping them, to have kindly feelings towards everyone, but seek the intimacy of the Good. If, when all that is done, he has any energy to spare, then let him study the polite arts.†

. . .

8. The Master said, If a gentleman is frivolous,‡ he will lose the respect of his inferiors and lack firm ground upon which to build up his education. First and foremost he must learn to be faithful to his superiors, to keep promises, to refuse the friendship of all who are not like him.§ And if he finds he has made a mistake, then he must not be afraid of admitting the fact and amending his ways. . . .

Book II

1. The Master said, He who rules by moral force (*tê*) is like the pole-star, which remains in its place while all the lesser stars do homage to it.

. . .

---

*i.e. upon what is fundamental, as opposed to "the twigs," i.e. small arts and accomplishments, which the gentleman leaves to his inferiors.

†i.e. learn to recite the *Songs,* practise archery, deportment, and the like.

‡i.e. irresponsible and unreliable in his dealings with others.

§i.e. of those who still reckon in terms of "profit and loss," and have not taken *jên* (Goodness) as their standard.

3. The Master said, Govern the people by regulations, keep order among them by chastisements, and they will flee from you, and lose all self-respect. Govern them by moral force, keep order among them by ritual and they will keep their self-respect and come to you of their own accord.

4. The Master said, At fifteen I set my heart upon learning. At thirty, I had planted my feet firm upon the ground. At forty, I no longer suffered from perplexities. At fifty, I knew what were the biddings of Heaven. At sixty, I heard them with docile ear. At seventy, I could follow the dictates of my own heart; for what I desired no longer overstepped the boundaries of right. . . .

Book IV

1. The Master said, It is Goodness that gives to a neighbourhood its beauty. One who is free to choose, yet does not prefer to dwell among the Good—how can he be accorded the name of wise?

2. The Master said, Without Goodness a man

Cannot for long endure adversity,

Cannot for long enjoy prosperity.

The Good Man rests content with Goodness; he that is merely wise pursues Goodness in the belief that it pays to do so.

3, 4. Of the adage "Only a Good Man knows how to like people, knows how to dislike them," the Master said, He whose heart is in the smallest degree set upon Goodness will dislike no one.

5. Wealth and rank are what every man desires; but if they can only be retained to the detriment of the Way he professes, he must relinquish them. Poverty and obscurity are what every man detests; but if they can only be avoided to the detriment of the Way he professes, he must accept them. The gentleman who ever parts company with Goodness does not fulfil that name. Never for a moment does a gentleman quit the way of Goodness. He is never so harried but that he cleaves to this; never so tottering but that he cleaves to this.

6. The Master said, I for my part have never yet seen one who really cared for Goodness, nor one who really abhorred wickedness. One who really cared for Goodness would never let any other consideration come first. One who abhorred wickedness would be so constantly doing Good that wickedness would never have a chance to get at him. Has anyone ever managed to do Good with his whole might even as long as the space of a single day? I think not. Yet I for my part have never seen anyone give up such an attempt because he had not the *strength* to go on. It may well have happened, but I for my part have never seen it.

7. The Master said, Every man's faults belong to a set. If one looks out for faults it is only as a means of recognizing Goodness.

. . .

25. The Master said, Moral force (*tê*) never dwells in solitude; it will always bring neighbours.*

. . .

Book V

. . .

15. Of Tzu-ch'an† the Master said that in him were to be found four of the virtues that belong to the Way of the true gentleman. In his private conduct he was courteous, in serving his master he was punctilious, in providing for the needs of the people he have them even more than their due; in exacting service from the people, he was just. . . .

Book IX

. . .

24. The Master said, First and foremost, be faithful to your superiors, keep all promises, refuse the friendship of all who are not like you; and if you have made a mistake, do not be afraid of admitting the fact and amending your ways.

. . .

28. The Master said, he that is really Good can never be unhappy. He that is really wise can never be perplexed. He that is really brave is never afraid.‡

Book XII

. . .

2. Jan Jung asked about Goodness. The Master said, Behave when away from home as though you were in the presence of an important guest. Deal with the common people as though you were officiating at an important sacrifice. Do not do to others what you would not like yourself. Then there will be no feelings of opposition to you, whether it is the affairs of a State that you are handling or the affairs of a Family.

Jan Yung said, I know that I am not clever; but this is a saying that, with your permission, I shall try to put into practice.

. . .

---

*Whenever one individual or one country substitutes *tê* for physical compulsion, other individuals or other countries inevitably follow suit.

†Minister in the Chêng State; died 522 B.C.

‡Goodness, wisdom and courage are the Three Ways of the true gentleman. . . . Confucius always ranks courage below wisdom and wisdom below Goodness. . . .

10. Tzu-chang asked what was meant by "piling up moral force" and "deciding when in two minds." The Master said, "by piling up moral force" is meant taking loyalty and good faith as one's guiding principles, and migrating to places where right prevails.* Again, to love a thing means wanting it to live, to hate a thing means wanting it to perish. But suppose I want something to live and at the same time want it to perish; that is "being in two minds."

> Not for her wealth, oh no!
> But merely for a change.

Book XVI

. . .

10. Master K'ung said, The gentleman has nine cares. In seeing he is careful to see clearly, in hearing he is careful to hear distinctly, in his looks he is careful to be kindly; in his manner to be respectful, in his words to be loyal, in his work to be diligent. When in doubt he is careful to ask for information; when angry he has a care for the consequences, and when he sees a chance of gain, he thinks carefully whether the pursuit of it would be consonant with the Right. . . .

DISCUSSION QUESTIONS

1. Compare and contrast Kant's categorical imperative with the Confucian notion of moral force.
2. Do you agree with the Confucians that fulfilling our filial duty is the source or trunk of goodness? What does it mean to respect our parents and elders? To what extent has your relationship with your family made you more, or less, likely to put moral duty above other concerns? Use specific examples to illustrate your answer.
3. Are the Confucians claiming that the tradition of the ancients is the only source of moral knowledge and duty? In what ways does this differ from cultural relativism?
4. Compare and contrast Mo Tzu's utilitarian ethics with the duty-based ethics of Confucianism. Which moral philosophy do you think provides the best guidelines for making effective moral decisions in our everyday lives? Support your answer.
5. Make a list of some of the duties set out in the *Analects*. Discuss whether or not these duties meet the standards of universality set forth in Kant's categorical imperative.
6. Like Lawrence Kohlberg and Carol Gilligan, Confucians regard moral development as a dynamic process that is ongoing throughout one's life. How would Confucians most likely respond to Kohlberg's and Gilligan's stage theory of moral development?
7. Discuss whether in your life you are "piling up moral force" or are of "two minds." Do you find, as Confucians claim, that happiness is associated with "piling up moral force"? Illustrate your answer with specific examples.

---

* "If right prevails in a country, then serve it; if right does not prevail, then seek service elsewhere."

Sissela Bok

Lying: Moral Choice in Public and Private Life

Swedish born philosopher, writer, and educator Sissela Bok (b. 1934) is primarily interested in the application of moral theory to real-life issues such as euthanasia, lying, and war and peace. The daughter of two Nobel prize winners—Alva and Gunnar Myrdal—Bok is currently affiliated with the Harvard Center for Population and Development Studies.

According to Kant, we ought to always do our duty no matter what the consequences. This means that it is always wrong to lie, even to save someone's life. Although Bok agrees that in general we have a duty not to lie, she disagrees with Kant that lying is wrong under all circumstances. In this selection from her book *Lying,* Bok begins by comparing and contrasting the notions of truthfulness and lying.

Critical Thinking Questions

1. Do we have a duty to always tell the truth?
2. How does Bok define the term *lying?* What is the relation between deception and lying?
3. What, according to Bok, are the two forms of deliberate assault on human beings? Why does Bok regard lying as a type of assaults?
4. According to Bok, what would society be like if there were no moral prohibition on lying?
5. Why is seeing lying from the perspective of those who are deceived important to Bok?
6. What are some of the excuses liars use to justify their lies?
7. Why, according to Bok, does lying also harm the liar?
8. Why does Kant say that lying is always wrong? Why does Bok disagree with Kant?
9. What is the principle of veracity?
10. What is the principle of publicity?

Lying: Moral Choice in Public and Private Life (New York: Vintage Books, 1978), pp. 4–6, 14–27. Notes have been omitted.

I
Is the "Whole Truth" Attainable?

. . .

THE "WHOLE TRUTH"

Is it not naïve to set forth on a general exploration of lying and truth-telling? Some will argue that the task is impossible. Life is too complex, they will say, and societies too diverse. How can one compare the bargaining in an Eastern bazaar, the white lies of everyday life, the lie for national defense, and that to spare a dying child? Is it not arrogant and myopic to conceive of doing so?

And even if these variations could somehow be encompassed, the argument continues, how can we ever attain the truth about any complex matter . . . or even a single circumstance? How can one, in fact, do full justice to the words used in court: "The truth, the whole truth, and nothing but the truth"?

These words mock our clumsy efforts to remember and convey our experiences. The "whole truth" has seemed so obviously unattainable to some as to cause them to despair of human communication in general. They see so many barriers to prevent us from obtaining truthful knowledge, let alone communicating it; so many pitfalls in conveying what we mean.

How can a physician, for example, tell the "whole truth" to a patient about a set of symptoms and their causes and likely effects? He certainly does not know all there is to know himself. Even all he does know that might have a bearing—incomplete, erroneous, and tentative though it be—could not be conveyed in less than weeks or even months. Add to these difficulties the awareness that everything in life and experience connects, that all is a "seamless web" so that nothing can be said without qualifications and elaborations in infinite regress, and a sense of lassitude begins to steal over even the most intrepid.

This book is intended as a reply to such arguments. The whole truth *is* out of reach. But this fact has very little to do with our choices about whether to lie or to speak honestly, about what to say and what to hold back. . . .

TRUTH AND TRUTHFULNESS

In all such speculation, there is great risk of a conceptual muddle, of not seeing the crucial differences between two domains: the *moral* domain of intended truthfulness and deception, and the much vaster domain of truth and falsity in general. The moral question of whether you are lying or not is not *settled* by establishing the truth or falsity of what you say. In order to settle this question, we must know whether you *intend your statement to mislead*. . . .

DEFINING INTENTIONAL DECEPTION AND LYING

When we undertake to deceive others intentionally, we communicate messages meant to mislead them, meant to make them believe what we ourselves do not believe. We can do so through gesture, through disguise, by means of action or inaction, even through silence. Which of these innumerable deceptive messages are also lies? I shall define as a lie any intentionally deceptive message which is *stated*. Such statements are most often made verbally or in writing, but can of course also be conveyed via smoke signals, Morse code, sign language, and the like. Deception, then, is the larger category, and lying forms part of it.* . . .

II
Truthfulness, Deceit, and Trust

LYING AND CHOICE

Deceit and violence—these are the two forms of deliberate assault on human beings. Both can coerce people into acting against their will. Most harm that can befall victims through violence can come to them also through deceit. But deceit controls more subtly, for it works on belief as well as action. Even Othello, whom few would have dared to try to subdue by force, could be brought to destroy himself and Desdemona through falsehood.

The knowledge of this coercive element in deception, and of our vulnerability to it, underlies our sense of the *centrality* of truthfulness. Of course, deception—again like violence—can be used also in self-defense, even for sheer survival. Its use can also be quite trivial, as in white lies. Yet its potential for coercion and for destruction is such that society could scarcely function without some degree of truthfulness in speech and action.†

Imagine a society, no matter how ideal in other respects, where word and gesture could never be counted upon. Questions asked, answers given, information exchanged—all would be worthless. Were all statements randomly truthful or deceptive, action and choice would be undermined from the outset. There must be a minimal degree of trust in communication for language and action to be more than stabs in the dark. This is why some level of truthfulness has always been seen as essential to human society, no matter how deficient the observance

---

*It is perfectly possible to define "lie" so that it is identical with "deception." This is how expressions like "living a lie" can be interpreted. For the purposes of this book, however, it is best to stay with the primary distinction between deceptive *statements*—lies—and all the other forms of deception.

†But truthful statements, though they are not meant to deceive, can, of course, themselves be coercive and destructive; they can be used as weapons, to wound and do violence.

of other moral principles. Even the devils themselves, as Samuel Johnson said, do not lie to one another, since the society of Hell could not subsist without truth any more than others.

A society, then, whose members were unable to distinguish truthful messages from deceptive ones, would collapse. But even before such a general collapse, individual choice and survival would be imperiled. The search for food and shelter could depend on no expectations from others. A warning that a well was poisoned or a plea for help in an accident would come to be ignored unless independent confirmation could be found.

All our choices depend on our estimates of what is the case; these estimates must in turn often rely on information from others. Lies distort this information and therefore our situation as we perceive it, as well as our choices. A lie, in Hartmann's words, "injures the deceived person in his life; it leads him astray."

To the extent that knowledge gives power, to that extent do lies affect the distribution of power; they add to that of the liar, and diminish that of the deceived, altering his choices at different levels. A lie, first, may misinform, so as to obscure some *objective,* something the deceived person wanted to do or obtain. It may make the objective seem unattainable or no longer desirable. It may even create a new one, as when Iago deceived Othello into wanting to kill Desdemona.

Lies may also eliminate or obscure relevant *alternatives,* as when a traveler is falsely told a bridge has collapsed. At times, lies foster the belief that there are more alternatives than is really the case; at other times, a lie may lead to the unnecessary loss of confidence in the best alternative. Similarly, the estimates of *costs and benefits* of any action can be endlessly varied through successful deception. The immense toll of life and human welfare from the United States' intervention in Vietnam came at least in part from the deception (mingled with self-deception) by those who channeled overly optimistic information to the decision-makers.

Finally, the degree of *uncertainty* in how we look at our choices can be manipulated through deception. Deception can make a situation falsely uncertain as well as falsely certain. It can affect the objectives seen, the alternatives believed possible, the estimates made of risks and benefits. Such a manipulation of the dimension of certainty is one of the main ways to gain power over the choices of those deceived. And just as deception can initiate actions a person would otherwise never have chosen, so it can prevent action by obscuring the necessity for choice. This is the essence of camouflage and of the cover-up—the creation of apparent normality to avert suspicion.

Everyone depends on deception to get out of a scrape, to save face, to avoid hurting the feelings of others. Some use it much more consciously to manipulate and gain ascendancy. Yet all are intimately aware of the threat lies can pose, the suffering they can bring. This two-sided experience which we all share makes the singleness with which either side is advocated in action all the more puzzling. Why are such radically different evaluations given to the effects of deception, depending on whether the point of view is that of the liar or the one lied to?

THE PERSPECTIVE OF THE DECEIVED

Those who learn that they have been lied to in an important matter—say, the identity of their parents, the affection of their spouse, or the integrity of their government—are resentful, disappointed, and suspicious. They feel wronged; they are wary of new overtures. And they look back on their past beliefs and actions in the new light of the discovered lies. They see that they were manipulated, that the deceit made them unable to make choices for themselves according to the most adequate information available, unable to act as they would have wanted to act had they known all along.

. . .

Nor is this perspective restricted to those who are actually deceived in any given situation. Though only a single person may be deceived, many others may be harmed as a result. If a mayor is deceived about the need for new taxes, the entire city will bear the consequences. Accordingly, the perspective of the deceived is shared by all those who feel the consequences of a lie, whether or not they are themselves lied to. When, for instance, the American public and world opinion were falsely led to believe that bombing in Cambodia had not begun, the Cambodians themselves bore the heaviest consequences, though they can hardly be said to have been deceived about the bombing itself.

An interesting parallel between skepticism and determinism exists here. Just as skepticism denies the possibility of *knowledge,* so determinism denies the possibility of *freedom.* Yet both knowledge and freedom to act on it are required for reasonable choice. Such choice would be denied to someone genuinely convinced —to the very core of his being—of both skepticism and determinism. He would be cast about like a dry leaf in the wind. Few go so far. But more may adopt such views selectively, as when they need convenient excuses for lying. Lies, they may then claim, do not add to or subtract from the general misinformation or "unfreedom" of those lied to. Yet were they to adopt the perspective of the deceived, such excuses for lying to them would seem hollow indeed. Both skepticism and determinism have to be bracketed—set aside—if moral choice is to retain the significance for liars that we, as deceived, know it has in our lives.

Deception, then, can be coercive. When it succeeds, it can give power to the deceiver—power that all who suffer the consequences of lies would not wish to abdicate. From this perspective, it is clearly unreasonable to assert that people should be able to lie with impunity whenever they want to do so. It would be unreasonable, as well, to assert such a right even in the more restricted circumstances where the liars claim a good reason for lying. . . .

THE PERSPECTIVE OF THE LIAR

Those who adopt the perspective of would-be-liars, on the other hand, have different concerns. For them, the choice is often a difficult one. They may believe, with Machiavelli, that "great things" have been done by those who have "little regard for good faith." They may trust that they can make wise use of the power that lies bring. And they may have confidence in their own ability to distinguish the times when good reasons support their decision to lie.

Liars share with those they deceive the desire not to *be* deceived. As a result, their choice to lie is one which they would like to reserve for themselves while insisting that others be honest. They would prefer, in other words, a "free-rider" status, giving them the benefits of lying without the risks of being lied to. Some think of this free-rider status as for them alone. Others extend it to their friends, social groups or profession. This category of persons can be narrow or broad; but it does require as a necessary backdrop the ordinary assumptions about the honesty of most persons. The free rider trades upon being an exception, and could not exist in a world where everybody chose to exercise the same prerogatives.

At times, liars operate as if they believed that such a free-rider status is theirs and that it excuses them. At other times, on the contrary, it is the very fact that others *do* lie that excuses their deceptive stance in their own eyes. It is crucial to see the distinction between the freeloading liar and the liar whose deception is a strategy for survival in a corrupt society.*

All want to avoid being deceived by *others* as much as possible. But many would like to be able to weigh the advantages and disadvantages in a more nuanced way whenever they are themselves in the position of choosing whether or not to deceive. They may invoke special reasons to lie—such as the need to protect confidentiality or to spare someone's feelings. They are then much more willing, in particular, to exonerate a well-intentioned lie on their own part; dupes tend to be less sanguine about the good intentions of those who deceive them.

But in this benevolent self-evaluation by the liar of the lies he might tell, certain kinds of disadvantage and harm are almost always overlooked. Liars usually weigh only the immediate harm to others from the lie against the benefits they want to achieve. The flaw in such an outlook is that it ignores or underestimates two additional kinds of harm—the harm that lying does to the liars themselves and the harm done to the general level of trust and social cooperation. Both are cumulative; both are hard to reverse.

How is the liar affected by his own lies? The very fact that he *knows* he has lied, first of all, affects him. He may regard the lie as an inroad on his integrity; he certainly looks at those he has lied to with a new caution. And if they find out that he has lied, he knows that his credibility and the respect for his word have been damaged. . . .

. . . While no one lie always carries harm for the liar, then, there is *risk* of such harm in most.

These risks are increased by the fact that so few lies are solitary ones. It is easy, a wit observed, to tell a lie, but hard to tell only one. The first lie "must be thatched with another or it will rain through." More and more lies may come to be needed; the liar always has more mending to do. And the strains on him

---

*While different, the two are closely linked. If enough persons adopt the free-rider strategy for lying, the time will come when all will feel pressed to lie to survive.

become greater each time—many have noted that it takes an excellent memory to keep one's untruths in good repair and disentangled. The sheer energy the liar has to devote to shoring them up is energy the honest man can dispose of freely.

After the first lies, moreover, others can come more easily. Psychological barriers wear down; lies seem more necessary, less reprehensible; the ability to make moral distinctions can coarsen; the liar's perception of his chances of being caught may warp. These changes can affect his behavior in subtle ways; even if he is not found out he will then be less trusted than those of unquestioned honesty. And it is inevitable that more frequent lies *do* increase the chance that some will be discovered. At that time, even if the liar has no personal sense of loss of integrity* from his deceitful practices, he will surely regret the damage to his credibility which their discovery brings about. Paradoxically, once his word is no longer trusted, he will be left with greatly *decreased* power—even though a lie often does bring at least a short-term gain in power over those deceived.

Even if the liar cares little about the risks to others from his deception, therefore, all these risks to himself argue in favor of at least weighing any decision to lie quite seriously. . . .

THE PRINCIPLE OF VERACITY

The perspective of the deceived, then, reveals several reasons why lies are undesirable. Those who share it have cause to fear the effects of undiscovered lies on the choices of liars and dupes. They are all too aware of the impact of discovered and suspected lies on trust and social cooperation. And they consider not only the individual lie but the practice of which it forms a part, and the long-term results which it can have.

For these reasons, I believe that we must at the very least accept as an initial premise Aristotle's view that lying is "mean and culpable" and that truthful statements are preferable to lies in the absence of special considerations. This premise gives an initial negative weight to lies. It holds that they are not neutral from the point of view of our choices; that lying requires explanation, whereas truth ordinarily does not. It provides a counterbalance to the crude evaluation by liars of their own motives and of the consequences of their lies. And it places the burden of proof squarely on those who assume the liar's perspective.

This presumption against lying can also be stated so as to stress the positive worth of truthfulness or veracity. I would like, in the chapters to come, to refer to the "principle of veracity" as an expression of this initial imbalance in our weighing of truthfulness and lying.

---

*The word "integrity" comes from the same roots which have formed "intact" and "untouched." It is used especially often in relation to truthfulness and fair dealing and reflects, I believe, the view that by lying one hurts oneself. The notion of the self-destructive aspects of doing wrong is part of many traditions. See, for example, the *Book of Mencius:* "Every man has within himself these four beginnings [of humanity, righteousness, decorum, wisdom]. The man who considers himself incapable of exercising them is destroying himself." . . .

It is not necessarily a principle that overrides all others, nor even the one most frequently appealed to. Nor is it, obviously, sufficient by itself—witness the brutal but honest regime or the tormentor who prides himself on his frankness. Rather, trust in some degree of veracity functions as a *foundation* of relations among human beings; when this trust shatters or wears away, institutions collapse.*

Such a principle need not indicate that all lies should be ruled out by the initial negative weight given to them, nor does it even suggest what kinds of lies should be prohibited. But it does make at least one immediate limitation on lying: in any situation where a lie is a possible choice, one must first seek truthful alternatives. If lies and truthful statements appear to achieve the same result or appear to be as desirable to the person contemplating lying the lies should be ruled out. And only where a lie is a *last resort* can one even begin to consider whether or not it is morally justified. Mild as this initial stipulation sounds, it would, if taken seriously, eliminate a great many lies told out of carelessness or habit or unexamined good intentions. . . .

III

Never to Lie?

> By a lie a man throws away and, as it were, annihilates his dignity as a man.
> Immanuel Kant, *Doctrine of Virtue*

REJECTING ALL LIES

The simplest answer to the problems of lying, at least in principle, is to rule out all lies. Many theologians have chosen such a position; foremost among them is St. Augustine. He cut a clear swath through all the earlier opinions holding that some lies might be justified. He claimed that God forbids all lies and that liars therefore endanger their immortal souls. . . .

. . . [Kant's] views set forth the strongest arguments we have against all lying.

Kant takes issue, first, with the idea that any generous motive, any threat to life, could excuse a lie. He argues that:

> Truthfulness in statements which cannot be avoided is the formal duty of an individual to everyone, however great may be the disadvantage accruing to himself or to another.

---

*The function of the principle of veracity as a foundation is evident when we think of trust. I can have different kinds of trust: that you will treat me fairly, that you will have my interests at heart, that you will do me no harm. But if I do not trust your word, can I have genuine trust in the first three? If there is no confidence in the truthfulness of others, is there any way to assess their fairness, their intentions to help or to harm? How, then, can they be trusted? *Whatever* matters to human beings, trust is the atmosphere in which it thrives.

This is the absolutist position, prohibiting all lies, even those told for the best of purposes or to avoid the most horrible of fates. For someone holding such a position, to be called a liar was a mortal insult—perhaps cause even for legal action or a duel; to be *proved* a liar could lead to self-exile out of shame.

Kant's view, if correct, would eliminate any effort to distinguish among lies, since he rejects them all. He takes the duty of truthfulness to be an "unconditional duty which holds in all circumstances"; a lie, even if it does not wrong any particular individual, always harms mankind generally, "for it vitiates the source of law." It harms the liar himself, moreover, by destroying his human dignity and making him more worthless even than a mere thing.

Kant also rejects the way around Augustine's prohibition that consists in defining certain falsehoods as not being lies. He defines a lie as "merely an intentional untruthful declaration to another person" and dismisses the idea that we owe the duty of speaking the truth only to those who have a right to the truth. On the contrary, truthfulness is a duty which no circumstances can abrogate. Whatever else may be said about Kant's position, it seems to have the virtue of clarity and simplicity. Others may argue about when to lie, but he makes a clean sweep.

CONFLICT OF DUTY

But can we agree with Kant? His position has seemed too sweeping to nearly all his readers, even obsessive to some. For although veracity is undoubtedly an important duty, most assume that it leaves room for exceptions. It can clash with other duties, such as that of averting harm to innocent persons. Yet Kant holds that "a conflict of duties and obligations is inconceivable," that if one does one's duty, one will turn out to have had no conflicting obligations. It is this refusal to consider conflicts of duty which drives Kant into such inflexible positions.

Most have held the contrary view—that there are times when truthfulness causes or fails to avert such great harm that a lie is clearly justifiable. One such time is where a life is threatened and where a lie might avert the danger. The traditional testing case advanced against the absolutist position is that discussed by Kant himself, where a would-be murderer inquires whether "our friend who is pursued by him had taken refuge in our house." Should one lie in order to save one's friend? Or should one tell the truth?

. . .

Most others have argued that, in such cases, where innocent lives are at stake, lies are morally justified, if indeed they are lies in the first place. Kant believes that to lie is to annihilate one's human dignity; yet for these others, to reply honestly, and thereby betray one's friend, would in itself constitute a compromise of that dignity. In such an isolated case, they would argue, the costs of lying are small and those of telling the truth catastrophic.

Similarly, a captain of a ship transporting fugitives from Nazi Germany, if asked by a patrolling vessel whether there were any Jews on board would, for Kant's critics, have been justified in answering No. His duty to the fugitives, they claim, would then have conflicted with the duty to speak the truth and would have far outweighed it. In fact, in times of such crisis, those who share Kant's opposition to lying clearly put innocent persons at the mercy of wrongdoers.

Furthermore, force has been thought justifiable in all such cases of wrongful threat to life. If to use force in self-defense or in defending those at risk of murder is right, why then should a lie in self-defense be ruled out? Surely if force is allowed, a lie should be equally, perhaps at times more, permissible. Both words and force, . . . can be used coercively, so as to alter behavior. And even though we need the strongest protection against such coercion, there are times when it must be allowed. Kant's single-minded upholding of truthfulness above all else nullifies the use of falsehoods in self-defense. Can the principle of veracity reasonably be made to carry such a burden?

This burden would clearly create guilt for many: guilt at having allowed the killing of a fellow human rather than lie to a murderer. Kant attempts to assuage this guilt by arguing as follows: If one stays close to the truth, one cannot, strictly speaking, be responsible for the murderous acts another commits. The murderer will have to take the whole blame for his act. In speaking to him truthfully, one has done nothing blameworthy. If, on the other hand, one tells him a lie, Kant argues, one becomes responsible for all the bad consequences which might befall the victim and anyone else. One may, for instance, point the murderer in what one believes to be the wrong direction, only to discover with horror that that is exactly where the victim has gone to hide.

There is much truth in saying that one is responsible for what happens after one has done something wrong or questionable. But it is a very narrow view of responsibility which does not also take some blame for a disaster one could easily have averted, no matter how much others are also to blame. A world where it is improper even to tell a lie to a murderer pursuing an innocent victim is not a world that many would find safe to inhabit. . . .

VII

Justification

. . .

JUSTIFICATION AND PUBLICITY

How can we single out, then, justifiable lies from all those that their perpetrators regard as so highly excusable? Assume, as before, that we are dealing with clearcut lies, deliberate efforts to mislead. We can examine the alternatives confronting the liar, and the excuses he gives. Which excuses not only mitigate and extenuate, but remove moral blame? And if we accept the excuses for some lies, do we thereby merely remove blame from the liar retroactively? Or are we willing to allow those lies ahead of time under certain circumstances? Could we, finally, recommend a *practice* of telling such lies whenever those circumstances arise—whenever, for instance, an innocent life is otherwise threatened?

We have already seen how often the liar is caught in a distorting perspective; his efforts to answer questions of justification can then show a systematic bias. His appeals to principle may be hollow, his evaluation flimsy. The result is that he can arrive at diametrically opposed weighings of alternatives and reasons, depending upon what he puts into the weighing process in the first place.

Justification must involve more than such untested personal steps of reasoning. To justify is to defend as just, right, or proper, by providing adequate reasons. It means to hold up to some standard, such as a religious or legal or moral standard. Such justification requires an audience: it may be directed to God, or a court of law, or one's peers, or one's own conscience; but in ethics it is most appropriately aimed, not at any one individual or audience, but rather at "reasonable persons" in general.

. . .

Moral justification, therefore, cannot be exclusive or hidden; it has to be capable of being made public. In going beyond the purely private, it attempts to transcend also what is merely subjective. Wittgenstein pointed to these elements of justification in observing that "justification consists in appealing to something independent." Many moral philosophers have assumed that such an appeal is of the very essence in reasoning about moral choice. John Rawls has set it forth most explicitly, under the name of *publicity,* as a formal constraint on any moral principle worth considering. According to such a constraint, a moral principle must be capable of public statement and defense. A secret moral principle, or one which could be disclosed only to a sect or a guild, could not satisfy such a condition.

Such publicity is, I believe, crucial to the justification of all moral choice. But it is, perhaps, particularly indispensable to the justification of lies and other deceptive practices. For publicity is connected more directly to veracity than to other moral principles. In ethics, publicity without truthfulness is misleading and thus worthless. In addition, lies, inherently secretive, may call for submission to public justification more than openly performed problematic acts. Such acts are more likely to arouse controversy eventually, whereas lies, if they succeed, may never do so.

I would like to combine this concept of *publicity* with the view of justification in ethics as being *directed to reasonable persons,* in order to formulate a workable test for looking at concrete moral choice. It will be a test to weigh the various excuses advanced for disputed choices, and therefore for lies. Such a test counters the self-deception and bias inherent in the liar's perspective. It challenges privately held assumptions and hasty calculations. It requires clear and understandable formulation of the arguments used to defend the lie—arguments which might otherwise have remained inchoate or seemed intuitively right without ever being questioned. Its advantages, moreover, are cumulative: the objectivity and ability to shift perspectives gained in each appeal to publicity carry over to subsequent ones. Basically, it is through the exercise of such appeals and the debates that they engender that a more finely tuned moral sense will develop.

The test of publicity asks which lies, if any, would survive the appeal for justification to reasonable persons. It requires us to seek concrete and open performance of an exercise crucial to ethics: the Golden Rule, basic to so many religious and moral traditions.* We must share the perspective of those affected by our choices, and ask how we would react if the lies we are contemplating were told to us. We must, then, adopt the perspective not only of liars but of those lied to; and not only of particular persons but of all those affected by lies—the collective perspective of reasonable persons seen as potentially deceived. We must formulate the excuses and the moral arguments used to defend the lies and ask how they would stand up under the public scrutiny of these reasonable persons. . . .

DISCUSSION QUESTIONS

1. Some people confuse the moral imperative not to lie with a moral duty to always tell the truth. However, lying and not telling the whole truth can be very different. Neither Bok nor Kant meant that we always have to tell the whole truth. Why don't we have a duty to always tell the truth? Imagine a world, if possible, where everyone always told the whole truth.

2. What argument might Bok use to convince an ethical egoist that it is wrong to lie? Discuss whether Gyges, in the story of Gyges's ring in Plato's *Republic,* would be convinced by Bok's argument? Are you convinced by Bok's argument?

3. Explain how the development of moral sensitivity and empathy make us less likely to lie. Discuss an example from your life when you or someone else lied without first considering the effects of the lie from the perspective of the person being deceived. How did you or the other person justify the lie? Would the act of lying in this case have passed the test of publicity?

4. Discuss whether little white lies, which are intended to spare someone's feelings or to spare you embarrassment, are ever morally justified. Would Bok agree?

5. Bok allows lying only in rare cases in which there is a crisis, such as the case of the ship transporting fugitives from Nazi Germany. Kant, on the other hand, says that lying is always wrong. Discuss the relative merits of the two arguments.

6. Compare and contrast a utilitarian view of lying with Bok's analysis of the permissibility of lying. Are there cases when a utilitarian might allow lying when Bok would not? Use specific examples to support your answer.

---

*The Golden Rule has a very powerful negative form, as in the *Analects* of Confucius:
   Tzu Kung asked: "Is there any one word that can serve as a principle for the conduct of life?"
   Confucius said: "Perhaps . . . 'reciprocity': Do not do to others what you would not want others to do to you."
   See also Rabbi Hillel's saying: "What is hateful to you do not do to your neighbour; that is the whole Torah, while the rest is commentary thereof;" . . .

William David Ross

The Right and the Good

Scottish-born Sir W. D. Ross (1877–1971) is one of the most important moral philosophers of the twentieth century. In addition to teaching philosophy, Ross also served as vice chancellor of Oxford University.

   Like Kant, Ross regards duty as the foundation of morality. However, unlike Kant, who dismissed consequences as not being morally relevant, Ross incorporates some of the strengths of utilitarianism by suggesting that we have, among other duties, duties to promote good and avoid harm.

CRITICAL THINKING QUESTIONS

1. What is the difference between a duty of perfect obligation and a duty of imperfect obligation?
2. Why does Ross reject both the Kantian and the utilitarian explanation of duty?
3. What does Ross mean by a *prima facie* duty? Is a *prima facie* duty arbitrary?
4. What are the seven *prima facie* duties described by Ross?
5. What is the relation between the good and the right? Can the good ever be wrong?
6. According to Ross, what is the source of the moral order? How do we come to know what the general principles of duty are?
7. How does our judgment in particular situations differ from our judgment about the general principles of duty?
8. According to Ross, how should we go about making a moral judgment when two or more *prima facie* duties come into conflict?

There are two theories, each in its way simple, that offer a solution of such cases of conscience. One is the view of Kant, that there are certain duties of perfect obligation, such as those of fulfilling promises, of paying debts, of telling the truth, which admit of no exception whatever in favour of duties of imperfect obligation, such as that of relieving distress. The other is the view of, for instance, Professor Moore and Dr. Rashdall, that there is only the duty of producing good, and that all "conflicts of duties" should be resolved by asking "by which action

---

The Right and the Good (Oxford: Clarendon Press, 1930), pp. 18–33. Some notes have been omitted.

will most good be produced?" But it is more important that our theory fit the facts than that it be simple, and the account we have given above corresponds (it seems to me) better than either of the simpler theories with what we really think, viz. that normally promise-keeping, for example, should come before benevolence, but that when and only when the good to be produced by the benevolent act is very great and the promise comparatively trivial, the act of benevolence becomes our duty.

In fact the theory of "ideal utilitarianism," if I may for brevity refer so to the theory of Professor Moore, seems to simplify unduly our relations to our fellows. It says, in effect, that the only morally significant relation in which my neighbours stand to me is that of being possible beneficiaries by my action. They do stand in this relation to me, and this relation is morally significant. But they may also stand to me in the relation of promisee to promiser, of creditor to debtor, of wife to husband, of child to parent, of friend to friend, of fellow countryman to fellow countryman, and the like; and each of these relations is the foundation of a *prima facie* duty, which is more or less incumbent on me according to the circumstances of the case. When I am in a situation, as perhaps I always am, in which more than one of these *prima facie* duties is incumbent on me, what I have to do is to study the situation as fully as I can until I form the considered opinion (it is never more) that in the circumstances one of them is more incumbent than any other; then I am bound to think that to do this *prima facie* duty is my duty *sans phrase* in the situation.

I suggest "*prima facie* duty" or "conditional duty" as a brief way of referring to the characteristic (quite distinct from that of being a duty proper) which an act has, in virtue of being of a certain kind (e.g. the keeping of a promise), of being an act which would be a duty proper if it were not at the same time of another kind which is morally significant. Whether an act is a duty proper or actual duty depends on *all* the morally significant kinds it is an instance of. The phrase "*prima facie* duty" must be apologized for, since (1) it suggests that what we are speaking of is a certain kind of duty, whereas it is in fact not a duty, but something related in a special way to duty. Strictly speaking, we want not a phrase in which duty is qualified by an adjective, but a separate noun. (2) "*Prima*" *facie* suggests that one is speaking only of an appearance which a moral situation presents at first sight, and which may turn out to be illusory; whereas what I am speaking of is an objective fact involved in the nature of the situation, or more strictly in an element of its nature, though not, as duty proper does, arising from its *whole* nature. . . .

There is nothing arbitrary about these *prima facie* duties. Each rests on a definite circumstance which cannot seriously be held to be without moral significance. Of *prima facie* duties I suggest, without claiming completeness or finality for it, the following division.*

---

*I should make it plain at this stage that I am *assuming* the correctness of some of our main convictions as to *prima facie* duties, or, more strictly, am claiming that we *know* them to be true. To me it seems as self-evident as anything could be, that to make a promise, for instance, is to create a moral claim on us in someone else. Many readers will perhaps say that they do *not* know this to be true. If so, I certainly cannot prove it to them; I can only ask them to reflect again, in the hope that they will ultimately agree that they also know it to be true. The main moral convictions of the plain man seem to me to be, not opinions which it is for philosophy to prove or disprove, but knowledge from the

WHAT MAKES RIGHT ACTS RIGHT?

(1) Some duties rest on previous acts of my own. These duties seem to include two kinds, (*a*) those resting on a promise or what may fairly be called an implicit promise, such as the implicit undertaking not to tell lies which seems to be implied in the act of entering into conversation (at any rate by civilized men), or of writing books that purport to be history and not fiction. These may be called the duties of fidelity. (*b*) Those resting on a previous wrongful act. These may be called the duties of reparation. (2) Some rest on previous acts of other men, i.e. services done by them to me. These may be loosely described as the duties of gratitude. (3) Some rest on the fact or possibility of a distribution of pleasure or happiness (or of the means thereto) which is not in accordance with the merit of the persons concerned; in such cases there arises a duty to upset or prevent such a distribution. These are the duties of justice. (4) Some rest on the mere fact that there are other beings in the world whose condition we can make better in respect of virtue, or of intelligence, or of pleasure. These are the duties of beneficence. (5) Some rest on the fact that we can improve our own condition in respect of virtue or of intelligence. These are the duties of self-improvement. (6) I think that we should distinguish from (4) the duties that may be summed up under the title of "not injuring others." No doubt to injure others is incidentally to fail to do them good; but it seems to me clear that non-maleficence is apprehended as a duty distinct from that of beneficence, and as a duty of a more stringent character. It will be noticed that this alone among the types of duty has been stated in a negative way. An attempt might no doubt be made to state this duty, like the others, in a positive way. It might be said that it is really the duty to prevent ourselves from acting either from an inclination to harm others or from an inclination to seek our own pleasure, in doing which we should incidentally harm them. But on reflection it seems clear that the primary duty here is the duty not to harm others, this being a duty whether or not we have an inclination that if followed would lead to our harming them; and that when we have such an inclinaiton the primary duty not to harm others gives rise to a consequential duty to resist the inclination. The recognition of this duty of non-maleficence is the first step on the way to the recognition of the duty of beneficence; and that accounts for the prominence of the commands "thou shalt not kill," "thou shalt not commit adultery," "thou shalt not steal," "thou shalt not bear false witness," in so early a code as the Decalogue. But even when we have come to recognize the duty of beneficence, it appears to me that the duty of non-maleficence is recognized as a distinct one, and as *prima facie* more binding. We should not in general consider it justifiable to kill one person in order to keep another alive, or to steal from one in order to give alms to another.

The essential defect of the "ideal utilitarian" theory is that it ignores, or at least does not do full justice to, the highly personal character of duty. If the

---

start; and in my own case I seem to find little difficulty in distinguishing these essential convictions from other moral convictions which I also have, which are merely fallible opinions based on an imperfect study of the working for good or evil of certain institutions or types of action.

only duty is to produce the maximum of good, the question who is to have the good—whether it is myself, or my benefactor, or a person to whom I have made a promise to confer that good on him, or a mere fellow man to whom I stand in no such special relation—should make no difference to my having a duty to produce that good. But we are all in fact sure that it makes a vast difference. . . .

. . . In actual experience they [*prima facie* duties} are compounded together in highly complex ways. Thus, for example, the duty of obeying the laws of one's country arises partly (as Socrates contends in the *Crito*) from the duty of gratitude for the benefits one has received from it; partly from the implicit promise to obey which seems to be involved in permanent residence in a country whose laws we know we are *expected* to obey, and still more clearly involved when we ourselves invoke the protection of its laws (this is the truth underlying the doctrine of the social contract); and partly (if we are fortunate in our country) from the fact that its laws are potent instruments for the general good.

Or again, the sense of a general obligation to bring about (so far as we can) a just apportionment of happiness to merit is often greatly reinforced by the fact that many of the existing injustices are due to a social and economic system which we have, not indeed created, but taken part in and assented to; the duty of justice is then reinforced by the duty of reparation.

It is necessary to say something by way of clearing up the relation between *prima facie* duties and the actual or absolute duty to do one particular act in particular circumstances. If, as almost all moralists except Kant are agreed, and as most plain men think, it is sometimes right to tell a lie or to break a promise, it must be maintained that there is a difference between *prima facie* duty and actual or absolute duty. When we think ourselves justified in breaking, and indeed morally obliged to break, a promise in order to relieve someone's distress, we do not for a moment cease to recognize a *prima facie* duty to keep our promise, and this leads us to feel, not indeed shame or repentance, but certainly compunction, for behaving as we do; we recognize, further, that it is our duty to make up somehow to the promisee for the breaking of the promise. . . .

Something should be said of the relation between our apprehension of the *prima facie* rightness of certain types of act and our mental attitude towards particular acts. It is proper to use the word "apprehension" in the former case and not in the latter. That an act, *qua* fulfilling a promise, or *qua* effecting a just distribution of good, or *qua* returning services rendered, or *qua* promoting the good of others, or *qua* promoting the virtue or insight of the agent, is *prima facie* right, is self-evident; not in the sense that it is evident from the beginning of our lives, or as soon as we attend to the proposition for the first time, but in the sense that when we have reached sufficient mental maturity and have given sufficient attention to the proposition it is evident without any need of proof, or of evidence beyond itself. It is self-evident just as a mathematical axiom, or the validity of a form of inference, is evident. The moral order expressed in these propositions is just as much part of the fundamental nature of the universe (and, we may add, of any possible universe in which there were moral agents at all) as is the spatial or numerical structure expressed in the axioms of geometry or arithmetic. In our confidence that these propositions are true there is involved the same trust in our reason that is involved in our confidence in mathematics; and we should have no justification for trusting it in the latter sphere and distrusting it in the former. In both cases we are dealing with propositions that cannot be proved, but that just as certainly need no proof.

. . .

Our judgements about our actual duty in concrete situations have none of the certainty that attaches to our recognition of the general principles of duty. A statement is certain, i.e. is an expression of knowledge, only in one or other of two cases: when it is either self-evident, or a valid conclusion from self-evident premisses. And our judgements about our particular duties have neither of these characters. (1) They are not self-evident. Where a possible act is seen to have two characteristics, in virtue of one of which it is *prima facie* right, and in virtue of the other *prima facie* wrong, we are (I think) well aware that we are not certain whether we ought or ought not to do it; that whether we do it or not, we are taking a moral risk. We come in the long run, after consideration, to think one duty more pressing than the other, but we do not feel certain that it is so. And though we do not always recognize that a possible act has two such characteristics, and though there *may* be cases in which it has not, we are never certain that any particular possible act has not, and therefore never certain that it is right, nor certain that it is wrong. For, to go no further in the analysis, it is enough to point out that any particular act will in all probability in the course of time contribute to the bringing about of good or of evil for many human beings, and thus have a *prima facie* rightness or wrongness of which we know nothing. (2) Again, our judgements about our particular duties are not logical conclusions from self-evident premisses. The only possible premisses would be the general principles stating their *prima facie* rightness or wrongness *qua* having the different characteristics they do have; and even if we could (as we cannot) apprehend the extent to which an act will tend on the one hand, for example, to bring about advantages for our benefactors, and on the other hand to bring about disadvantages for fellow men who are not our benefactors, there is no principle by which we can draw the conclusion that it is on the whole right or on the whole wrong. In this respect the judgement as to the rightness of a particular act is just like the judgement as to the beauty of a particular natural object or work of art. A poem is, for instance, in respect of certain qualities beautiful and in respect of certain others not beautiful; and our judgement as to the degree of beauty it possesses on the whole is never reached by logical reasoning from the apprehension of its particular beauties or particular defects. Both in this and in the moral case we have more or less probable opinions which are not logically justified conclusions from the general principles that are recognized as self-evident.

. . .

The general principles of duty are obviously not self-evident from the beginning of our lives. How do they come to be so? The answer is, that they come to be self-evident to us just as mathematical axioms do. We find by experience that this couple of matches and that couple make four matches, that this couple of balls on a wire and that couple make four balls: and by reflection on these and similar discoveries we come to see that it is of the nature of two and two to make four. In a precisely similar way, we see the *prima facie* rightness of an act which would be the fulfilment of a particular promise, and of another which would be the fulfilment of another promise, and when we have reached sufficient maturity to think in general terms, we apprehend *prima facie* rightness to belong to the nature of any fulfilment of promise. What comes first in time is the apprehension of the self-evident *prima facie* rightness of an individual act of a particular type. From this we come by reflection to apprehend the self-evident general principle of *prima facie* duty. From this, too, perhaps along with the apprehension of the self-evident *prima facie* rightness of the same act in virtue of its having another characteristic as well, and perhaps in spite of the apprehension of its *prima facie* wrongness in virtue of its having some third characteristic, we come to believe something not self-evident at all, but an object of probable opinion, viz. that this particular act is (not *prima facie* but) actually right. . . .

DISCUSSION QUESTIONS

1. Does reason, as Kant argued, require that moral duties be absolute? Or does reason require that duties be *prima facie,* as Ross claims? Discuss the merits and weaknesses of each person's arguments.
2. Why does Ross regard utilitarian theory as inadequate? What evidence does he use to support his argument? Discuss ways in which the examples presented by Williams in "A Critique of Utilitarianism" support Ross's argument.
3. Would Ross be more supportive than Kant of Bok's argument regarding the permissibility of lying under certain circumstances? Discuss the *prima facie* duties involved in Bok's scenario of the ship carrying fugitives from Nazi Germany. Which *prima facie* duties are more compelling in this scenario? Support your answer.
4. Discuss whether Confucius would be more likely to agree with Ross's *prima facie* deontology or with Kantian deontology.
5. Do you agree with Ross that the moral order is a part of the fundamental nature of the universe? If so, how would Ross explain the presence of moral evil in the world?
6. Which of Ross's *prima facie* duties do you think is most important? Explain why.
7. Ross acknowledged that his list of *prima facie* duties may be incomplete. Can you think of any other *prima facie* moral duties? Defend your answer.

John Rawls

A Theory of Justice

In *A Theory of Justice,* Harvard philosopher and political theorist John
Rawls (b. 1921) offers an alternative to utilitarian social theory. Rawls's theory of justice is an example of social contract theory, a concept that has its
roots in classical Greek philosophy.

According to Rawls, justice is our most important social duty. This duty is
grounded in a social contract. Rawls also maintains that fairness is the fundamental concept in justice. This element of justice, he argues, is absent in strict
utilitarianism. In the following selection, Rawls comes up with two principles
of justice that, he believes, would be chosen by people in the "original position." The first principle relates to the assignment of rights and duties. The second principle governs the distribution of goods and economic opportunities.

CRITICAL THINKING QUESTIONS

1. How does Rawls define the term *society?*
2. What does Rawls mean by the "original contract"? What is the
   purpose of the original contract?
3. What is Rawls's view of human nature?
4. What is the "original position"? Why is impartiality important in
   the original position?
5. According to Rawls, what two principles of justice would be chosen by people in the original position?
6. Why does Rawls claim that both of these principles of justice are
   necessary in a well-ordered and just society?

Justice as Fairness

THE ROLE OF JUSTICE

Justice is the first virtue of social institutions, as truth is of systems of thought. A
theory however elegant and economical must be rejected or revised if it is untrue;
likewise laws and institutions no matter how efficient and well-arranged must be

A Theory of Justice (Cambridge, MA: Harvard University Press, 1971), pp. 4, 11–19, 60–65. Notes
have been omitted.

reformed or abolished if they are unjust. Each person possesses an inviolability founded on justice that even the welfare of society as a whole cannot override. . . .

. . . A society is a more or less self-sufficient association of persons who in their relations to one another recognize certain rules of conduct as binding and who for the most part act in accordance with them. Suppose further that these rules specify a system of cooperation designed to advance the good of those taking part in it. Then, although a society is a cooperative venture for mutual advantage, it is typically marked by a conflict as well as by an identity of interests. There is an identity of interests since social cooperation makes possible a better life for all than any would have if each were to live solely by his own efforts. There is a conflict of interests since persons are not indifferent as to how the greater benefits produced by their collaboration are distributed, for in order to pursue their ends they each prefer a larger to a lesser share. A set of principles is required for choosing among the various social arrangements which determine this division of advantages and for underwriting an agreement on the proper distributive shares. These principles are the principles of social justice: they provide a way of assigning rights and duties in the basic institutions of society and they define the appropriate distribution of the benefits and burdens of social cooperation.

. . .

In these preliminary remarks I have distinguished the concept of justice as meaning a proper balance between competing claims from a conception of justice as a set of related principles for identifying the relevant considerations which determine this balance. I have also characterized justice as but one part of a social ideal, although the theory I shall propose no doubt extends its everyday sense. This theory is not offered as a description of ordinary meanings but as an account of certain distributive principles for the basic structure of society. I assume that any reasonably complete ethical theory must include principles for this fundamental problem and that these principles, whatever they are, constitute its doctrine of justice. The concept of justice I take to be defined, then, by the role of its principles in assigning rights and duties and in defining the appropriate division of social advantages. A conception of justice is an interpretation of this role.

Now this approach may not seem to tally with tradition. I believe, though, that it does. The more specific sense that Aristotle gives to justice, and from which the most familiar formulations derive, is that of refraining for *pleonexia,* that is, from gaining some advantage for oneself by seizing what belongs to another, his property, his reward, his office, and the like, or by denying a person that which is due to him, the fulfillment of a promise, the repayment of a debt, the showing of proper respect, and so on. It is evident that this definition is framed to apply to actions, and persons are thought to be just insofar as they have, as one of the permanent elements of their character, a steady and effective desire to act justly. Aristotle's definition clearly presupposes, however, an account of what properly belongs to a person and of what is due to him. Now such entitlements are, I believe, very often derived from social institutions and the legitimate expectations to which they give rise. . . .

THE MAIN IDEA OF THE THEORY OF JUSTICE

My aim is to present a conception of justice which generalizes and carries to a high level of abstraction the familiar theory of the social contract as found, say, in Locke, Rousseau, and Kant. In order to do this we are not to think of the original contract as one to enter a particular society or to set up a particular form of government. Rather, the guiding idea is that the principles of justice for the basic structure of society are the object of the original agreement. They are the principles that free and rational persons concerned to further their own interests would accept in an initial position of equality as defining the fundamental terms of their association. These principles are to regulate all further agreements; they specify the kinds of social cooperation that can be entered into and the forms of government that can be established. This way of regarding the principles of justice I shall call justice as fairness.

Thus we are to imagine that those who engage in social cooperation choose together, in one joint act, the principles which are to assign basic rights and duties and to determine the division of social benefits. Men are to decide in advance how they are to regulate their claims against one another and what is to be the foundation charter of their society. Just as each person must decide by rational reflection what constitutes his good, that is, the system of ends which it is rational for him to pursue, so a group of persons must decide once and for all what is to count among them as just and unjust. The choice which rational men would make in this hypothetical situation of equal liberty, assuming for the present that this choice problem has a solution, determines the principles of justice.

In justice as fairness the original position of equality corresponds to the state of nature in the traditional theory of the social contract. This original position is not, of course, thought of as an actual historical state of affairs, much less as a primitive condition of culture. It is understood as a purely hypothetical situation characterized so as to lead to a certain conception of justice. Among the essential features of this situation is that no one knows his place in society, his class position or social status, nor does any one know his fortune in the distribution of natural assets and abilities, his intelligence, strength, and the like. I shall even assume that the parties do not know their conceptions of the good or their special psychological propensities. The principles of justice are chosen behind a veil of ignorance. This ensures that no one is advantaged or disadvantaged in the choice of principles by the outcome of natural chance or the contingency of social circumstances. Since all are similarly situated and no one is able to design principles to favor his particular condition, the principles of justice are the result of a fair agreement or bargain. For given the circumstances of the original position, the symmetry of everyone's relations to each other, this initial situation is fair between individuals as moral persons, that is, as rational beings with their own ends and capable, I shall assume, of a sense of justice. The original position is, one might say, the appropriate initial status quo, and thus the fundamental agreements reached in it are fair. This explains the propriety of the name "justice as fairness": it conveys the idea that the principles of justice are agreed to in an initial situation that is fair. The name does not mean that the concepts of justice and fairness are the same, any more than the phrase "poetry as metaphor" means that the concepts of poetry and metaphor are the same.

Justice as fairness begins, as I have said, with one of the most general of all choices which persons might make together, namely, with the choice of the first principles of a conception of justice which is to regulate all subsequent criticism and reform of institutions. Then, having chosen a conception of justice, we can suppose that they are to choose a constitution and a legislature to enact laws, and so on, all in accordance with the principles of justice initially agreed upon. Our social situation is just if it is such that by this sequence of hypothetical agreements we would have contracted into the general system of rules which defines it. Moreover, assuming that the original position does determine a set of principles (that is, that a particular conception of justice would be chosen), it will then be true that whenever social institutions satisfy these principles those engaged in them can say to one another that they are cooperating on terms to which they would agree if they were free and equal persons whose relations with respect to one another were fair. . . .

In working out the conception of justice as fairness one main task clearly is to determine which principles of justice would be chosen in the original position. To do this we must describe this situation in some detail and formulate with care the problem of choice which it presents. . . . It may be observed, however, that once the principles of justice are thought of as arising from an original agreement in a situation of equality, it is an open question whether the principle of utility would be acknowledged. Offhand it hardly seems likely that persons who view themselves as equals, entitled to press their claims upon one another, would agree to a principle which may require lesser life prospects for some simply for the sake of a greater sum of advantages enjoyed by others. Since each desires to protect his interests, his capacity to advance his conception of the good, no one has a reason to acquiesce in an enduring loss for himself in order to bring about a greater net balance of satisfaction. In the absence of strong and lasting benevolent impulses, a rational man would not accept a basic structure merely because it maximized the algebraic sum of advantages irrespective of its permanent effects on his own basic rights and interests. Thus it seems that the principle of utility is incompatible with the conception of social cooperation among equals for mutual advantage. It appears to be inconsistent with the idea of reciprocity implicit in the notion of a well-ordered society. Or, at any rate, so I shall argue.

I shall maintain instead that the persons in the initial situation would choose two rather different principles: the first requires equality in the assignment of basic rights and duties, while the second holds that social and economic inequalities, for example inequalities of wealth and authority, are just only if they result in compensating benefits for everyone, and in particular for the least advantaged members of society. These principles rule out justifying institutions on the grounds that the hardships of some are offset by a greater good in the aggregate. It may be expedient but it is not just that some should have less in order that others may prosper. But there is no injustice in the greater benefits earned by a few provided that the situation of persons not so fortunate is thereby improved. . . .

THE ORIGINAL POSITION

. . .

It seems reasonable to suppose that the parties in the original position are equal. That is, all have the same rights in the procedure for choosing principles; each can make proposals, submit reasons for their acceptance, and so on. Obviously the purpose of these conditions is to represent equality between human beings as moral persons, as creatures having a conception of their good and capable of a sense of justice. The basis of equality is taken to be similarity in these two respects. Systems of ends are not ranked in value; and each man is presumed to have the requisite ability to understand and to act upon whatever principles are adopted. Together with the veil of ignorance, these conditions define the principles of justice as those which rational persons concerned to advance their interests would consent to as equals when none are known to be advantaged or disadvantaged by social and natural contingencies.

There is, however, another side to justifying a particular description of the original position. This is to see if the principles which would be chosen match our considered convictions of justice or extend them in an acceptable way. We can note whether applying these principles would lead us to make the same judgments about the basic structure of society which we now make intuitively and in which we have the greatest confidence; or whether, in cases where our present judgments are in doubt and given with hesitation, these principles offer a resolution which we can affirm on reflection. There are questions which we feel sure must be answered in a certain way. For example, we are confident that religious intolerance and racial discrimination are unjust. We think that we have examined these things with care and have reached what we believe is an impartial judgment not likely to be distorted by an excessive attention to our own interests. . . .

TWO PRINCIPLES OF JUSTICE

I shall now state in a provisional form the two principles of justice that I believe would be chosen in the original position. In this section I wish to make only the most general comments, and therefore the first formulation of these principles is tentative. As we go on I shall run through several formulations and approximate step by step the final statement to be given much later. I believe that doing this allows the exposition to proceed in a natural way.

The first statement of the two principles reads as follows.

> First: each person is to have an equal right to the most extensive basic liberty compatible with a similar liberty for others.
>
> Second: social and economic inequalities are to be arranged so that they are both (a) reasonably expected to be to everyone's advantage, and (b) attached to positions and offices open to all.

. . .

By way of general comment, these principles primarily apply, as I have said, to the basic structure of society. They are to govern the assignment of rights and duties and to regulate the distribution of social and economic advantages. As their formulation suggests, these principles presuppose that the social structure can be divided into two more or less distinct parts, the first principle applying to the one, the second to the other. They distinguish between those aspects of the social system that define and secure the equal liberties of citizenship and those that specify and establish social and economic inequalities. The basic liberties of citizens are, roughly speaking, political liberty (the right to vote and to be eligible for public office) together with freedom of speech and assembly; liberty of conscience and freedom of thought; freedom of the person along with the right to hold (personal) property; and freedom from arbitrary arrest and seizure as defined by the concept of the rule of law. These liberties are all required to be equal by the first principle, since citizens of a just society are to have the same basic rights.

The second principle applies, in the first approximation, to the distribution of income and wealth and to the design of organizations that make use of differences in authority and responsibility, or chains of command. While the distribution of wealth and income need not be equal, it must be to everyone's advantage, and at the same time, positions of authority and offices of command must be accessible to all. One applies the second principle by holding positions open, and then, subject to this constraint, arranges social and economic inequalities so that everyone benefits.

These principles are to be arranged in a serial order with the first principle prior to the second. This ordering means that a departure from the institutions of equal liberty required by the first principle cannot be justified by, or compensated for, by greater social and economic advantages. The distribution of wealth and income, and the hierarchies of authority, must be consistent with both the liberties of equal citizenship and equality of opportunity.

It is clear that these principles are rather specific in their content, and their acceptance rests on certain assumptions that I must eventually try to explain and justify. A theory of justice depends upon a theory of society in ways that will become evident as we proceed. For the present, it should be observed that the two principles (and this holds for all formulations) are a special case of a more general conception of justice that can be expressed as follows.

> All social values—liberty and opportunity, income and wealth, and the bases of self-respect—are to be distributed equally unless an unequal distribution of any, or all, of these values is to everyone's advantage.

Injustice, then, is simply inequalities that are not to the benefit of all. Of course, this conception is extremely vague and requires interpretation.

. . .

The fact that the two principles apply to institutions has certain consequences. Several points illustrate this. First of all, the rights and liberties referred to by these principles are those which are defined by the public rules of the basic structure. Whether men are free is determined by the rights and duties established by the major institutions of society. Liberty is a certain pattern of social forms. The first principle simply requires that certain sorts of rules, those defining basic liberties, apply to everyone equally and that they allow the most extensive liberty compatible with a like liberty for all. The only reason for circumscribing the rights defining liberty and making men's freedom less extensive than it might otherwise be is that these equal rights as institutionally defined would interfere with one another.

Another thing to bear in mind is that when principles mention persons, or require that everyone gain from an inequality, the reference is to representative persons holding the various social positions, or offices, or whatever, established by the basic structure. Thus in applying the second principle I assume that it is possible to assign an expectation of well-being to representative individuals holding these positions. This expectation indicates their life prospects as viewed from their social station. In general, the expectations of representative persons depend upon the distribution of rights and duties throughout the basic structure. When this changes, expectations change. I assume, then, that expectations are connected: by raising the prospects of the representative man in one position we presumably increase or decrease the prospects of representative men in other positions. Since it applies to institutional forms, the second principle (or rather the first part of it) refers to the expectations of representative individuals. As I shall discuss below, neither principle applies to distributions of particular goods to particular individuals who may be identified by their proper names. The situation where someone is considering how to allocate certain commodities to needy persons who are known to him is not within the scope of the principles. They are meant to regulate basic institutional arrangements. We must not assume that there is much similarity from the standpoint of justice between an administrative allotment of goods to specific persons and the appropriate design of society. Our common sense intuitions for the former may be a poor guide to the latter.

Now the second principle insists that each person benefit from permissible inequalities in the basic structure. This means that it must be reasonable for each relevant representative man defined by this structure, when he views it as a going concern, to prefer his prospects with the inequality to his prospects without it. One is not allowed to justify differences in income or organizational powers on the ground that the disadvantages of those in one position are outweighed by the greater advantages of those in another. Much less can infringements of liberty be counterbalanced in this way. Applied to the basic structure, the principle of utility would have us maximize the sum of expectations of representative men (weighted by the number of persons they represent, on the classical view); and this would permit us to compensate for the losses of some by the gains of others. Instead, the two principles require that everyone benefit from economic and social inequalities. . . .

DISCUSSION QUESTIONS

1. Is Rawls's assumption about how people in the original position would respond justified? Are people by nature mutually self-interested, rational, and similar in needs and interests, as Rawls claims?

2. Would you have chosen the same two principles of justice if you were in the original position? Support your answer.

3. Is it possible for people to put themselves in Rawls's hypothetical original position? Can we be genuinely impartial? Would a person who lacks social privileges come to the same conclusion as Rawls did regarding the two principles of justice? To what extent, if at all, do you think Rawls's principles of justice are influenced by his American heritage and his social standing?

4. On what grounds does Rawls argue that justice does not require equality in social position? Are you convinced by Rawls's argument?

5. Are Rawls's two principles of justice adequate for designing social policy? How would Carol Gilligan and Virginia Held most likely respond to this question?

6. What does Rawls mean when he says that "each person is to have an equal right to the most extensive basic liberty compatible with a similar liberty for others"? Does this principle offer sufficient guidance for formulating social policy? For example, would Rawls's first principle of justice permit hate speech on campus? Would it permit two people in an already financially well-off family to hold full-time jobs when adults in other families in the area are unemployed? Would it permit imprisoning offenders, such as prostitutes or tax evaders, who are not a threat to other people's liberties?

7. Apply Rawls's second principle of justice to health care reform in the United States. Does this principle of justice, on its own, offer adequate guidelines for designing a more just medical care system?

8. Discuss how an ethical egoist such as Ayn Rand would most likely respond to Rawls's second principle of justice, which states that inequalities in wealth and position are just only when they can be reasonably expected to work to the advantage of those who are worse off. Would Rand agree with Rawls that people in the original position would choose this principle for their social contract?

Chapter Applications

1. A Nazi's Version of the Categorical Imperative

Adolf Eichmann sat sullenly in his bullet-proof glass witness box. He felt betrayed. During the police investigation Eichmann had protested that he had lived his whole life according to Kant's categorical imperative. He had done his duty, he told the police, according to the Kantian definition of duty. He had not just blindly obeyed orders, he had obeyed the law. Now he was being prosecuted for doing what was right.

Curious and perhaps outraged by Eichmann's reference to Kant's moral law, Judge Raveh questioned Eichmann further about the categorical imperative. To everyone's surprise Eichmann had indeed read Kant's *Critique of Practical Reason* and was able to give a reasonably accurate definition of the categorical imperative.

"I meant by my remark about Kant," Eichmann explained to the court, "that the principle of my will must always be such that it can become the principle of general laws."

Hannah Arendt in her book *Eichmann in Jerusalem*,[1] argues that Eichmann had not dismissed the categorical imperative when he became involved in the Final Solution but had distorted the notion of universality and self-legislation to mean "Act as if the principle of your actions were the same as that of the legislator or the law of the land."

Arendt refers to this distortion of the imperative as the version of Kant for the "little man." "Whatever Kant's role in the formation of 'the little man's' mentality in Germany may have been," Arendt writes, "there is not the slightest doubt that in one respect Eichmann did indeed follow Kant's precepts: a law was a law, there could be no exceptions."

Discussion Questions

1. In 1962 Eichmann was sentenced to death by an Israeli court for crimes against the Jewish people and humanity. Should law-abiding people be punished if they act out of good intentions? After all, Eichmann acted in a manner that was consistent with his conventional stage of moral development.

2. Relate Kant's concept of the good will to Eichmann's notion of acting out of good intentions.

3. Does an understanding of Kant's categorical imperative require that a person be at the postconventional stage of moral reasoning as defined by Lawrence Kohlberg? Is one of the implications of Kant's theory that the only truly rational beings are the 10 percent of people who are at the postconventional stage of moral reasoning?

2. The Milgram Experiment: The Use of Deception in Research

Yale social psychologist Stanley Milgram greatly admired Hannah Arendt's book *Eichmann in Jerusalem*. In the early 1960s, he recruited subjects for an experiment on obedience to determine if Americans would be as ready to blindly follow the orders of an authority figure as were the Nazis.

In his experiment, subjects were led to believe that they were delivering a series of increasingly painful electric shocks as part of a learning experiment on the effect of punishment on learning. When the subjects balked upon hearing the screams of pain of the learner, they were urged to continue by an experimenter in a white lab coat. In fact, the learner was an accomplice of the experimenter and was not actually receiving the shocks.

Despite the feigned protests of the learner, about two-thirds of the subjects obeyed the experimenter and continued delivering what they believed were potentially fatal electric shocks. The findings of this experiment yielded valuable information about human social behavior. They suggest that people can be persuaded to torture and perhaps even kill another person simply at the urging of an authority figure.

Each of the subjects was debriefed following the experiment. Nevertheless, several of the subjects suffered mental distress and had to seek counseling.

Discussion Questions

1. Sissela Bok argues that it is wrong to use lies in research in part because it gives the experimenter power over the subject, thereby undermining the subject's autonomy. Do you agree with Bok? Does the fact that the subjects were debriefed at the end of Milgram's experiment justify the lie in this case? Would this experiment pass Bok's principle of publicity? Support your answer.

2. In their article "Milgram, Method and Morality," Charles Pigden and Grant Gillet disagree with Bok's assessment of lying in the Milgram experiment. They counter Bok's objection by noting that the deception, and loss of autonomy, was only temporary. Furthermore, they argue, "far from 'disrespecting' his subjects Milgram enhanced their autonomy as rational agents." As a result of the experiment, Pigden and Gillet argue, the subjects' self-knowledge was increased. Although the knowledge that we may be capable of torturing another person may be painful, this does not mean it is harmful. Even painful self-knowledge, they argue, increases our autonomy by "open[ing] the way for soul-searching and reform."[2] Do you agree? Support your answer. Discuss whether Kant would agree with Pigden and Gillet's analysis of the morality of the Milgram experiment.

3. W. D. Ross argues that sometimes the right and the good do not coincide. Although not lying may be good, it may not always be right. Is this the case in the Milgram experiment? What are the *prima facie* duties in this experiment? Do the valuable insights about human behavior obtained from this experiment outweigh the immoral methods used in the experiment? How might a utilitarian answer this question?

4. Discuss whether the Milgram subjects were as morally blameworthy for their actions as people who, on their own, torture others with electric shocks.

5. Milgram was surprised to find out how willing people were to follow an authority figure. Discuss his finding in light of your own experience.

3. Selective Abortion

The Browns had talked about having a third child. However, they had put it off for several years, and now, with both of them in their 40s, it seemed too late. With her two daughters in high school and her husband semi-retired, Jayne Brown decided to return to college to complete her degree in business administration.

She had just started her first semester when she found out she was pregnant. The early months of the pregnancy were uneventful. However, because of her age, she underwent amniocentesis at 16 weeks to see if the fetus had any genetic disorders. The following week Dr. Lee called and told her "Congratulations. You're going to have a healthy daughter!"

Two weeks later Mrs. Brown called Dr. Lee back and asked if she would perform an abortion. Mrs. Brown explained that she already had two daughters, and although she would have continued the pregnancy had the fetus been a boy, she was not interested in having another daughter.

Her husband was opposed to the abortion. He stated that he did not care whether the child was a girl or a boy. Having a third child also would not pose a financial burden on the family because they had a large home and were financially secure. Furthermore, because he was retired and only working part-time out of the home, he was willing to do most of the child care.

Discussion Questions

1. Is Jayne Brown's decision morally justified? Discuss your answer in light of Ross's *prima facie* duties as well as both versions of Kant's categorical imperative.

2. Unlike Kantian deontology, Confucian deontology emphasizes communitarian and filial duties over individual duties. If Dr. Lee was a Confucian, what advice might she give to the Browns?

3. Although the primary reason for selective abortion in the United States is for genetic disorders, more and more women are using early prenatal diagnosis to determine the gender of their fetus.[3] Because the great majority of U.S. parents prefer to have sons as firstborn or only children, it is generally female fetuses that are aborted. In 1975 a survey of genetic counselors in the United States found that only 1 percent would perform prenatal diagnosis for sex selection. By 1988 this figure had climbed to 62 percent with the majority of geneticists giving as their primary reason "respect of women's autonomy."[4] Is prenatal diagnosis and abortion for sex selection morally justified on the grounds of autonomy? Support your answer.

4. Although most people in the United States disapprove of abortion for sex selection, many believe that abortion in the case of a genetic disorder is morally justified. Is this distinction morally relevant? Like women, people with disabilities are also discriminated against in our culture. Using Rawls's two principles of justice, come up with a social policy regarding selective abortion for both gender and birth disorders.

5. In parts of China and India abortion of female girls is relatively common. Does the fact that selective abortion is culturally acceptable in these areas and that daughters impose a greater hardship on families than sons justify the practice in these countries? Discuss how a deontologist would answer this question.

6. Is abortion ever morally justified? Support your answer.

4. The Alien Abduction

Imagine the following. A strange craft is found floating off the coast of Florida. Upon investigation it is found to be an elaborate research vessel. Survivors, who have been abandoned when the craft crashes, tell of their grisly experiences as research subjects. Apparently, an alien culture has been doing research on human subjects for at least the past fifty years. Human fetuses have also been removed and used as subjects in biomedical experiments involving genetic manipulation, organ transplants, and toxicity testing. Other hybrid humans have been bred as potential food sources for the aliens.

The human subjects aboard, most of whom are under the age of 9 with the exception of a handful who are being raised for breeding purposes, are housed in small pens that are clean and well supplied with food and water. The alien researchers also used an anesthesia or an amnesiac drug when performing experiments on the subjects. Most of the human subjects rescued from the craft have known no other home, and several of them protested vehemently when removed from the craft.

Without the results of their research on human subjects, it is almost certain that this planet would have been destroyed several decades ago. For example, the aliens developed telepathic techniques to interfere with the brain waves of terrorists and government leaders who are bent on using nuclear weapons and biological warfare.

The aliens apparently are a highly advanced, very intelligent life form who communicate by telepathy. As far as could be surmised, they do not understand human language. The aliens regard humans as a dangerous and irrational species and a much lower life form. They see no problem morally in using humans to benefit their own species. Indeed, they regard the use of human subjects in their research as a moral duty because it has done so much to benefit their own species and to preserve the earth.

Discussion Questions

1. If you could find a means to communicate with the aliens, what arguments might you use to convince them that it is immoral to use human subjects for experiments? Do more rational species, such as humans or aliens in the above scenario, have a moral right and perhaps even a duty to use members of lower species as a means of advancing themselves? Support your answer.

2. What does it mean to be rational? If you came upon an alien species, how would you go about determining if they were rational? To what extent would your findings determine how you would treat the members of that species?

3. Discuss how Kant might respond to the above scenario. Does the fact that adult subjects were given an amnesiac drug and returned to their homes in between experiments fulfill the requirements of the categorical imperative?

4. Because the human subjects who had lived all their lives on the craft wanted to remain on the craft, does that mean that their autonomy was not being compromised by the alien experimenters? Support your answer.

5. Affirmative Action: Cheryl J. Hopwood v. The State of Texas[5]

In 1992 Cheryl Hopwood's application to the University of Texas Law School was turned down despite the fact that she had better grades and LSAT scores than many of the minority students who were admitted. At the time, the University of Texas (UT) had a quota system that gave preferential treatment to both African Americans and Mexican Americans. Hopwood sued the State of Texas on the grounds that their policy violated the equal protection clause of the Fourteenth Amendment, which "prevent[ed] the States from purposefully discriminating between individuals on the basis of race."[6]

In ruling in favor of Hopwood, the federal circuit court stated that UT's admissions policy was discriminatory in that it treated minorities as a group rather than as individuals. Hopwood's victory against the State of Texas brought an end to affirmative action at UT and changed college admissions policies across the country.

The State of Texas appealed the ruling. The U.S. Supreme Court, however, rejected the appeal, agreeing with the circuit court's ruling that "the law school has presented no compelling justification under the Fourteenth Amendment or Supreme Court precedent that allows it to continue to elevate some races over others, even for the wholesome purposes of correcting perceived racial imbalance in the student body."[7]

Discussion Questions

1. In its ruling, the court acknowledged that Texas had a "long history of racially discriminatory practices in its primary and secondary schools," and that "remedial action is necessary" to correct past injustices against minority groups in the state.[8] The court also agreed that "obtaining the educational benefits that flow from a racially and ethnically diverse student body" is a desirable goal. Given the past history of discrimination in this country against certain groups of people, discuss ways in which this goal might be achieved without engaging in discriminatory practices.

2. Hopwood had been accepted at Princeton for undergraduate school but couldn't afford to attend. Instead, she worked her way through school at a community college, graduating with a 3.8 average. Is it fair that minorities who come from well-off families be given preferential treatment over white people, like Hopwood, who come from economically disadvantaged families? Support your answer.

3. Studies indicate that minority enrollment in law schools and college in general would drop significantly without affirmative action.[9] Does the promotion of diversity justify reverse discrimination? Discuss and answer in light of Ross's *prima facie* duties as well as Rawls's two principles of justice.

4. Compare and contrast the equal protection clause of the Fourteenth Amendment with Kant's categorical imperative. Discuss whether the affirmative action policy of UT violated Kant's categorical imperative.

5. Did Hopwood have a moral duty to protest her rejection by UT? If so, what is the source of this duty? Discuss how Kant and Confucius would have answered these questions.

6. Former Senator Bob Dole is opposed to affirmative action. "We ought to do away with preferences," he stated in a 1996 speech. "This is America. It ought to be based on merit." Discuss Dole's position.

7. Many colleges already extend preferences to athletes. Compare and contrast this policy with the affirmative action policy at UT.

For Wed in Class

6. The Death Penalty and the Oklahoma City Bomber

Shortly after 9:00 A.M. on April 19,1995, a fireball ripped through the plate-glass doors of the Oklahoma City Federal Building, collapsing all nine floors on the north side. One hundred sixty-eight people were killed, and 850 were injured by the explosion.

Patrolman Charlie Hanger was outside of town patrolling for speeders when he heard about the explosion on his police radio. About 10:34 A.M. Hanger stopped a car for having no license plates. When he approached the driver, Hanger noticed a semiautomatic pistol poking out of the driver's shoulder strap. Hanger arrested the driver for driving an unregistered car and carrying an unregistered handgun and took him to the Noble County Jail.

The driver, as it turned out, was 27-year-old Timothy McVeigh. In June 1997, McVeigh was found guilty of murder and conspiracy and sentenced to death for his role in the Oklahoma City bombing.

Discussion Questions

1. In 1976 the U.S. Supreme Court in *Gregg v. Georgia* reversed an earlier ruling that declared capital punishment unconstitutional because it was "cruel and unusual punishment." The 1976 ruling stated: "capital punishment may be the appropriate sanction in extreme cases is an expression of the communities' belief that certain crimes are themselves so grievous an affront to humanity that the only adequate response may be the penalty of death." Do you agree with the *Gregg v. Georgia* ruling? Discuss it in light of Ross's *prima facie* duties. Relate your answer to the McVeigh case.

2. In his *Philosophy of Law* Kant wrote: "The Penal Law is a Categorical Imperative; and woe to him who creeps though the serpent-windings of Utilitarianism to discover some advantage that may discharge him from the Justice of Punishment. . . . For if Justice and Righteousness perish, human life would no longer have any value in the world. . . . Whoever has committed murder must die." Do you agree with Kant? Is punishment—whether imprisonment or capital punishment—consistent with the categorical imperative?

3. Sister Helen Prejean, author of *Dead Man Walking,* argues that capital punishment is inconsistent with the intrinsic value of human life. "Nobody," she writes, "is disposable human waste. . . . Despite their terrible crimes, murderers are human beings and deserve to be treated with dignity."[10] Do you agree? Does morality require that people like McVeigh who treat others as "disposable human waste" be treated with dignity?

4. Mindful of how much hurt would be opened up by the victim testimonies, Judge Richard P. Matsch cautioned the jurors that "we are not here to seek

revenge on Timothy McVeigh."[11] What did Matsch mean by this? What is the difference between revenge and retribution?

5. Does having an instinct for retribution justify acting on that instinct? If so, are there other ways retribution may be satisfied in the McVeigh case?

6. McVeigh, a decorated Gulf War veteran, saw the U.S. government as an enemy force responsible for killing eighty Branch Davidians near Waco, Texas. Compare and contrast the morality of McVeigh's actions as a terrorist with those of the soldiers who bombed Baghdad during the Gulf War or the pilots who dropped the atomic bomb on Hiroshima. Should soldiers who kill civilians during wartime be held morally accountable for their actions?

7. French existentialist Albert Camus claimed that there is a moral contradiction in a policy, such as capital punishment, that imitates the violence it is claiming to hate.[12] Do you agree with Camus?

NOTES

[1]Hannah Arendt, *Eichmann in Jerusalem: A Report on the Banality of Evil* (London: Faber, 1963).

[2]Charles R. Pigden and Grant R. Gillet, "Milgram, Method and Morality," *Journal of Applied Philosophy* (1996), 13 (3): 244.

[3]G. Rhoads et al., "The Safety and Efficacy of Chorionic Villus Sampling for Early Prenatal Diagnosis of Cytogenetic Abnormalities," *New England Journal of Medicine* (1989), Vol. 320: 609–617.

[4]Dorothy Wertz and John Fletcher, "Ethics and Medical Genetics in the United States," *American Journal of Medical Genetics* (April 1988), Vol. 29: 323.

[5]*Cheryl J. Hopwood v. The State of Texas*, 78 F.3d 932 (5th Cir. 1996).

[6]Ibid., p. 939.

[7]Ibid., p. 934.

[8]Ibid., p. 939.

[9]Kim Strosnider, "Minority Law-School Enrollment Would Drop Without Affirmative Action, Study Finds," *Chronicle of Higher Education,* January 31, 1997, 43: A28.

[10]Helen Prejean, *Dead Man Walking* (New York: Random House, 1993), p. 122.

[11]Richard Serrano, "McVeigh's Sentencing Opens with Victims' Grief," *Providence Journal-Bulletin,* June 5, 1997, p. A13.

[12]Albert Camus, *Reflexions sur la Pein Capital* (Paris: Calmann-Levy, 1957), p. 199.

CHAPTER EIGHT

Rights Ethics

We hold these truths to be self-evident, that all men are created equal, that they are endowed by their Creator with certain inalienable Rights, that among these are Life, Liberty and the Pursuit of Happiness.

United States Declaration of Independence, July 4, 1776

Almost all moral philosophies, with the obvious exceptions of ethical subjectivism and emotivism, acknowledge the existence of moral rights. The concept of moral rights, however, has been most extensively explored within the context of Western enlightenment philosophy. Prior to the eighteenth century, the focus of moral theory was primarily on duty. The language of human rights in Western philosophy emerged mainly as a protest against the principle of absolute sovereignty and the divine right to rule. The French Declaration of the Rights of Man and the American Bill of Rights, both written in 1789, were expressions of the movement to extend rights to all people.

Although most moral philosophies recognize moral rights, there is disagreement about the source as well as the extent of the rights. Natural rights philosophers maintain that moral rights stem from our human nature. These rights, they claim, are self-evident and exist independently and prior to any duties we may have. Other ethicists believe that rights are derived from duties.

In the first selection from *Two Treatises of Civil Government*, John Locke argues that rights stem from our human nature. These rights, according to Locke, are self-evident.

Karl Marx disagrees with Locke that rights are natural and independent of duties. In the next selection from his essay "On the Jewish Question" Marx argues that rights can only exist within a cultural context.

Gustavo Gutierrez, in the selection from his book *The Power of the Poor in History*, agrees with the Marxist criticism of natural rights. Gutierrez argues that society has a duty to defend the rights of those who are most oppressed.

The fourth selection is from the United Nations's "Universal Declaration of Human Rights." This declaration was adopted by the United Nations following World War II.

Jeane Kirkpatrick, in the next selection from "Establishing a Viable Human Rights Policy," questions the purpose of the UN's "Universal Declaration of Human Rights" and the current proliferation of rights.

In the final selection of Chapter 8, *Rights, Justice, and the Bounds of Liberty,* Joel Feinberg explores the connection between rights and duties.

John Locke

Two Treatises of Civil Government

British philosopher John Locke (1632–1704) was born into a liberal Puritan family. Locke's family was also involved in political activism. His father, a country attorney, had fought on the Parliamentary side in the first rebellion against King Charles I.

John Locke's theory of natural rights emerged primarily as a protest against the idea of the divine rights of kings. A deeply religious man, Locke believed that God created the earth as a resource for humans. Locke's natural rights ethics had a profound effect on the founders of the United States, such as Thomas Jefferson. Locke maintained that our natural rights include life, liberty, and property. In the following selection from his *Two Treatises of Civil Government,* Locke defends our right to own property.

CRITICAL THINKING QUESTIONS

1. How does Locke define political power?
2. What is the state of nature? What rights do humans have in a state of nature?
3. What is the law of Nature?
4. On what grounds does Locke argue that civil government is preferable to a state of nature?
5. According to Locke, why do humans as a group have a right to the resources of the earth?
6. How do humans, as individuals, make these resources their property?
7. What, according to Locke, sets the limits on what we can claim as our property?
8. Will there be enough property for everyone?
9. What does Locke say makes the greatest contribution to the value of the things we enjoy?
10. What is Locke's view of the wilderness?
11. What freedoms do people enjoy in a state of nature?
12. What, according to Locke, is the purpose of money?
13. According to Locke, why do people come together to form a political society?

"Natural Rights," from *Two Treatises of Civil Government* (London: A & J Churchill, 1698). Notes have been omitted.

14. What is the chief purpose of political society and government?

3. Political power, . . . I take to be a right of making laws, with penalties of death, and consequently all less penalties for the regulating and preserving of property, and of employing the force of the community in the execution of such laws, and in the defence of the commonwealth from foreign injury, and all this only for the public good.

OF THE STATE OF NATURE

4. To understand political power aright, and derive it from its original, we must consider what estate all men are naturally in, and that is, a state of perfect freedom to order their actions, and dispose of their possessions and persons as they think fit, within the bounds of the law of Nature, without asking leave or depending upon the will of any other man.

A state also of equality, wherein all the power and jurisdiction is reciprocal, no one having more than another, there being nothing more evident than that creatures of the same species and rank, promiscuously born to all the same advantages of Nature, and the use of the same faculties, should also be equal one amongst another, without subordination or subjection, unless the lord and master of them all should, by any manifest declaration of his will, set one above another, and confer on him by an evident and clear appointment an undoubted right to dominion and sovereignty.

. . .

6. But though this be a state of liberty, yet it is not a state of license; though man in that state have an uncontrollable liberty to dispose of his person or possessions, yet he has not liberty to destroy himself, or so much as any creature in his possession, but where some nobler use than its bare preservation calls for it. The state of nature has a law of nature to govern it, which obliges everyone; and reason, which is that law, teaches all mankind who will but consult it, that, being all equal and independent, no one ought to harm another in his life, health, liberty, or possessions. For men being all the workmanship of one omnipotent and infinitely wise Maker—all the servants of one sovereign Master, sent into the world by His order, and about His business; they are His property, whose workmanship they are made to last during His, not one another's pleasure. And, being furnished with like faculties, sharing all in one community of Nature, there cannot be supposed any such subordination among us that may authorise us to destroy one another, as if we were made for one another's uses, as the inferior ranks of creatures are for ours. Every one as he is bound to preserve himself, and not to quit his station wilfully, so by the like reason, when his own preservation

comes not in competition, ought he as much as he can to preserve the rest of mankind, and not unless it be to do justice on an offender, take away or impair the life, or what tends to the preservation of the life, the liberty, health, limb, or goods of another.

7. And that all men may be restrained from invading others' rights, and from doing hurt to one another, and the law of Nature be observed, which willeth the peace and preservation of all mankind, the execution of the law of Nature is in that state put into every man's hands, whereby every one has a right to punish the transgressors of that law to such a degree as may hinder its violation. For the law of Nature would, as all other laws that concern men in this world, be in vain if there were nobody that in the state of Nature had a power to execute that law, and thereby preserve the innocent and restrain offenders; and if any one in the state of Nature may punish another for any evil he had done, every one may do so. For in that state of perfect equality, where naturally there is no superiority or jurisdiction of one over another, what any may do in prosecution of that law, every one must needs have a right to do.

8. And thus, in the state of Nature, one man comes by a power over another, but yet no absolute or arbitrary power to use a criminal, when he has got him in his hands, according to the passionate heats or boundless extravagancy of his own will, but only to retribute to him so far as calm reason and conscience dictate, what is proportionate to his transgression, which is so much as may serve for reparation and restraint. For these two are the only reasons why one man may lawfully do harm to another, which is that we call punishment. In transgressing the law of Nature, the offender declares himself to live by another rule than that of reason and common equity, which is that measure God has set to the actions of men for their mutual security, and so he becomes dangerous to mankind; . . .

10. Besides the crime which consists in violating the laws, and varying from the right rule of reason, whereby a man so far becomes degenerate, and declares himself to quit the principles of human nature and to be a noxious creature, there is commonly injury done, and some person or other, some other man, receives damage by his transgression; in which case, he who hath received any damage has (besides the right of punishment common to him, with other men) a particular right to seek reparation from him that hath done it. And any other person who finds it just may also join with him that is injured, and assist him in recovering from the offender so much as may make satisfaction for the harm he hath suffered.

11. From these two distinct rights (the one of punishing the crime, for restraint and preventing the like offence, which right of punishing is in everybody, the other of taking reparation, which belongs only to the injured party) comes it to pass that the magistrate, who by being magistrate hath the common right of punishing put into his hands, can often, where the public good demands not the execution of the law, remit the punishment of criminal offences by his own authority, but yet cannot remit the satisfaction due to any private man for

the damage he has received. That he who hath suffered the damage has a right to demand in his own name, and he alone can remit. The damnified person has this power of appropriating to himself the goods or service of the offender by right of self-preservation, as every man has a power to punish the crime to prevent its being committed again, by the right he has of preserving all mankind, and doing all reasonable things he can in order to that end. And thus it is that every man in the state of Nature has a power to kill a murderer, both to deter others from doing the like injury (which no reparation can compensate) by the example of the punishment that attends it from everybody, and also to secure men from the attempts of a criminal who, having renounced reason, the common rule and measure God hath given to mankind, hath, by the unjust violence and slaughter he hath committed upon one, declared war against all mankind, and therefore may be destroyed as a lion or a tiger, one of those wild savage beasts with whom men can have no society nor security. And upon this is grounded that great law of Nature, "Whoso sheddeth man's blood, by man shall his blood be shed." And Cain was so fully convinced that every one had a right to destroy such a criminal, that, after the murder of his brother, he cries out, "Every one that findeth me shall slay me," so plain was it writ in the hearts of all mankind.

. . .

13. To this strange doctrine—viz., That in the state of Nature every one has the executive power of the law of Nature—I doubt not but it will be objected that it is unreasonable for men to be judges in their own cases, that self-love will make men partial to themselves and their friends; and, on the other side, ill-nature, passion, and revenge will carry them too far in punishing others, and hence nothing but confusion and disorder will follow, and that therefore God hath certainly appointed government to restrain the partiality and violence of men. I easily grant that civil government is the proper remedy for the inconveniences of the state of Nature, which must certainly be great where men may be judges in their own case, since it is easy to be imagined that he who was so unjust as to do his brother an injury will scarce be so just as to condemn himself for it. But I shall desire those who make this objection to remember that absolute monarchs are but men; and if government is to be the remedy of those evils which necessarily follow from men being judges in their own cases, and the state of Nature is therefore not to be endured, I desire to know what kind of government that is, and how much better it is than the state of Nature, where one man commanding a multitude has the liberty to be judge in his own case, and may do to all his subjects whatever he pleases without the least question or control of those who execute his pleasure? and in whatsoever he doth, whether led by reason, mistake, or passion, must be submitted to? which men in the state of Nature are not bound to do one to another. And if he that judges, judges amiss in his own or any other case, he is answerable for it to the rest of mankind.

14. It is often asked as a mighty objection, where are, or ever were, there any men in such a state of Nature? To which it may suffice as an answer at present, that since all princes and rulers of "independent" governments all through the

world are in a state of Nature, it is plain the world never was, nor never will be, without numbers of men in that state. I have named all governors of "independent" communities, whether they are, or are not, in league with others; for it is not every compact that puts an end to the state of Nature between men, but only this one of agreeing together mutually to enter into one community, and make one body politic; other promises and compacts men may make one with another, and yet still be in the state of Nature. The promises and bargains for truck, etc., between the two men in Soldania, in or between a Swiss and an Indian, in the woods of America, are binding to them, though they are perfectly in a state of Nature in reference to one another for truth, and keeping of faith belongs to men as men, and not as members of society.

15. To those that say there were never any men in the state of Nature, I will not only oppose the authority of the judicious Hooker . . . , where he says, "the laws which have been hitherto mentioned"—*i.e.,* the laws of Nature—"do bind men absolutely, even as they are men, although they have never any settled fellowship, never any solemn agreement amongst themselves what to do or not to do; but for as much as we are not by ourselves sufficient to furnish ourselves with competent store of things needful for such a life as our Nature doth desire, a life fit for the dignity of man, therefore to supply those defects and imperfections which are in us, as living single and solely by ourselves, we are naturally induced to seek communion and fellowship with others; this was the cause of men uniting themselves as first in politic societies." But I, moreover, affirm that all men are naturally in that state, and remain so till, by their own consents, they make themselves members of some politic society, and I doubt not, in the sequel of this discourse, to make it very clear. . . .

OF PROPERTY

24. Whether we consider natural reason, which tells us that men, being once born, have a right to their preservation, and consequently to meat and drink and such other things as Nature affords for their subsistence, or "revelation," which gives us an account of those grants God made of the world to Adam, and to Noah and his sons, it is very clear that God, as King David says (Psalm cxv. 16), "has given the earth to the children of men," given it to mankind in common. But, this being supposed, it seems to some a very great difficulty how any one should ever come to have a property in anything, I will not content myself to answer, that, if it be difficult to make out "property" upon a supposition that God gave the world to Adam and his posterity in common, it is impossible that any man but one universal monarch should have any "property" upon a supposition that God gave the world to Adam and his heirs in succession, exclusive of all the rest of his posterity; but I shall endeavour to show how men might come to have a property in several parts of that which God gave to mankind in common, and that without any express compact of all the commoners.

25. God, who hath given the world to men in common, hath also given them reason to make use of it to the best advantage of life and convenience. The earth and all that is therein is given to men for the support and comfort of their being. And though all the fruits it naturally produces, and beasts it feeds, belong to mankind in common, as they are produced by the spontaneous hand of Nature, and nobody has originally a private dominion exclusive of the rest of mankind in any of them, as they are thus in their natural state, yet being given for the use of men, there must of necessity be a means to appropriate them some way or other before they can be of any use, or at all beneficial, to any particular men. . . .

26. Though the earth and all inferior creatures be common to all men, yet every man has a "property" in his own "person." This nobody has any right to but himself. The "labour" of his body and the "work" of his hands, we may say, are properly his. Whatsoever, then, he removes out of the state that Nature hath provided and left it in, he hath mixed his labour with it, and joined to it something that is his own, and thereby makes it his property. It being by him removed from the common state Nature placed it in, it hath by this labour something annexed to it that excludes the common right of other men. For this "labour" being the unquestionable property of the labourer, no man but he can have a right to what that is once joined to, at least where there is enough, and as good left in common for others.

27. He that is nourished by the acorns he picked up under an oak, or the apples he gathered from the trees in the wood, has certainly appropriated them to himself. Nobody can deny but the nourishment is his. I ask, then, when did they begin to be his? when he digested? or when he ate? or when he boiled? or when he brought them home? or when he picked them up? And it is plain, if the first gathering made them not his, nothing else could. That labour put a distinction between them and common. That added something to them more than Nature, the common mother of all, had done, and so they became his private right. And will any one say he had no right to those acorns or apples he thus appropriated because he had not the consent of all mankind to make them his? Was it a robbery thus to assume to himself what belonged to all in common? If such a consent as that was necessary, man had starved, notwithstanding the plenty God had given him. We see in commons, which remain so by compact, that it is the taking any part of what is common, and removing it out of the state Nature leaves it in, which begins the property, without which the common is of no use. And the taking of this or that part does not depend on the express consent of all the commoners. Thus, the grass my horse has bit, the turfs my servant has cut, and the ore I have digged in any place, where I have a right to them in common with others, become my property without the assignation or consent of anybody. The labour that was mine, removing them out of that common state they were in, hath fixed my property in them.

. . .

30. It will, perhaps, be objected to this, that if gathering the acorns or other fruits of the earth, etc., makes a right to them, then any one may engross as much as he will. To which I answer, Not so. The same law of Nature that does by this means give us property, does also bound that property too. "God has given us all things richly." Is the voice of reason confirmed by inspiration? But how far has He given it us—"to enjoy"? As much as any one can make use of to any advantage of life before it spoils, so much he may by his labour fix a property in. Whatever is beyond this is more than his share, and belongs to others. Nothing was made by God for man to spoil or destroy. And thus considering the plenty of natural provisions there was a long time in the world, and the few spenders, and to how small a part of that provision the industry of one man could extend itself and engross it to the prejudice of others, especially keeping within the bounds set by reason of what might serve for his use, there could be then little room for quarrels or contentions about property so established.

31. But the chief matter of property being now not the fruits of the earth and the beasts that subsist on it, but the earth itself, as that which takes in and carries with it all the rest, I think it is plain that property in that too is acquired as the former. As much land as a man tills, plants, improves, cultivates, and can use the product of, so much is his property. . . .

33. God gave the world to men in common, but since He gave it them for their benefit and the greatest conveniences of life they were capable to draw from it, it cannot be supposed He meant it should always remain common and uncultivated. He gave it to the use of the industrious and rational (and labour was to be his title to it); not to the proportion, and such as he might appropriate to himself without injury to anybody in the first ages of the world, when men were more in danger to be lost, by wandering from their company, in the then vast wilderness of the earth than to be straitened for want of room to plant in.

36. The same measure may be allowed still, without prejudice to anybody, full as the world seems. For, supposing a man or family, in the state they were at first, peopling of the world by the children of Adam or Noah, let him plant in some inland vacant places of America. We shall find that the possessions he could make himself, upon the measures we have given, would not be very large, nor, even to this day, prejudice the rest of mankind or give them reason to complain or think themselves injured by this man's encroachment, though the race of men have now spread themselves to all the corners of the world, and do infinitely exceed the small number was at the beginning. Nay, the extent of ground is of so little value without labour that I have heard it affirmed that in Spain itself a man may be permitted to plough, sow, and reap, without being disturbed, upon land he has no other title to, but only his making use of it. But, on the contrary, the inhabitants think themselves beholden to him who, by his industry on neglected, and consequently waste land, has increased the stock of corn, which they wanted. But be this as it will, which I lay no stress on, this I dare boldly affirm, that the same rule of propriety—viz., that every man should have as much as he could make use of, would hold still in the world, without straitening anybody, since there is land

enough in the world to suffice double the inhabitants, had not the invention of money, and the tacit agreement of men to put a value on it, introduced (by consent) larger possessions and a right to them; which, how it has done, I shall by and by show more at large.

. . .

45. Thus labour, in the beginning, gave a right of property, wherever any one was pleased to employ it, upon what was common, which remained a long while, the far greater part, and is yet more than mankind makes use of. Men at first, for the most part, contented themselves with what unassisted Nature offered to their necessities; and though afterwards, in some parts of the world, where the increase of people and stock, with the use of money, had made land scarce, and so of some value, the several communities settled the bounds of their distinct territories, and, by laws, within themselves, regulated the properties of the private men of their society, and so, by compact and agreement, settled the property which labour and industry began. And the leagues that have been made between several states and kingdoms, either expressly or tacitly disowning all claim and right to the land in the other's possession, have, by common consent, given up their pretences to their natural common right, which originally they had to those countries; and so have, by positive agreement, settled a property amongst themselves, in distinct parts of the world; yet there are still great tracts of ground to be found, which the inhabitants thereof, not having joined with the rest of mankind in the consent of the use of their common money, lie waste, and are more than the people who dwell on it, do, or can make use of, and so still lie in common; though this can scarce happen amongst that part of mankind that have consented to the use of money.

46. The greatest part of things really useful to the life of man, and such as the necessity of subsisting made the first commoners of the world look after—as it doth the Americans now—are generally things of short duration, such as—if they are not consumed by use—will decay and perish of themselves. Gold, silver, and diamonds are things that fancy or agreement hath put the value on, more than real use and the necessary support of life. Now of those good things which Nature hath provided in common, every one hath a right (as hath been said) to as much as he could use, and had a property in all he could effect with his labour; all that his industry could extend to, to alter from the state Nature had put it in, was his. He that gathered a hundred bushels of acorns or apples had thereby a property in them; they were his goods as soon as gathered. He was only to look that he used them before they spoiled, else he took more than his share, and robbed others. And, indeed, it was a foolish thing, as well as dishonest, to hoard up more than he could make use of. If he gave away a part to anybody else, so that it perished not uselessly in his possession, these he also made use of. And if he also bartered away plums that would have rotted in a week, for nuts that would last good for his eating a whole year, he did no injury; he wasted not the common stock; destroyed no part of the portion of goods that belonged to others, so long as nothing perished uselessly in his hands. Again, if he would

give his nuts for a piece of metal, pleased with its colour, or exchange his sheep for shells, or wool for a sparkling pebble or a diamond, and keep those by him all his life, he invaded not the right of others; he might heap up as much of these durable things as he pleased; the exceeding of the bounds of his just property not lying in the largeness of his possession, but the perishing of anything uselessly in it.

47. And thus came in the use of money; some lasting thing that men might keep without spoiling, and that, by mutual consent, men would take in exchange for the truly useful but perishable supports of life.

48. And as different degrees of industry were apt to give men possessions in different proportions, so this invention of money gave them the opportunity to continue and enlarge them. . . .

51. And thus, I think, it is very easy to conceive, without any difficulty, how labour could at first begin a title of property in the common things of Nature, and how the spending it upon our uses bounded it; so that there could then be no reason of quarrelling about title, nor any doubt about the largeness of possession it gave. Right and conveniency went together. For as a man had a right to all he could employ his labour upon, so he had no temptation to labour for more than he could make use of. This left no room for controversy about the title, nor for encroachment on the right of others. What portion a man carved to himself was easily seen; and it was useless, as well as dishonest, to carve himself too much, or take more than he needed.

. . .

OF THE BEGINNING OF POLITICAL SOCIETIES

95. Men being, as has been said, by nature all free, equal, and independent, no one can be put out of this estate and subjected to the political power of another without his own consent, which is done by agreeing with other men, to join and unite into a community for their comfortable, safe, and peaceable living, one amongst another, in a secure enjoyment of their properties, and a greater security against any that are not of it. This any number of men may do, because it injures not the freedom of the rest; they are left, as they were, in the liberty of the state of Nature. When any number of men have so consented to make one community or government, they are thereby presently incorporated, and make one body politic, wherein the majority have a right to act and conclude the rest.

96. For, when any number of men have, by the consent of every individual, made a community, they have thereby made that community one body, with a power to act as one body, which is only by the will and determination of the majority. For that which acts any community, being only the consent of the individuals of it, and it being one body, must move one way, it is necessary the body should move that way whither the greater force carries it, which is the consent of

the majority, or else it is impossible it should act or continue one body, one community, which the consent of every individual that united into it agreed that it should; and so every one is bound by that consent to be concluded by the majority. And therefore we see that in assemblies empowered to act by positive laws where no number is set by that positive law which empowers them, the act of the majority passes for the act of the whole, and of course determines as having, by the law of Nature and reason, the power of the whole.

97. And thus every man, by consenting with others to make one body politic under one government, puts himself under an obligation to every one of that society to submit to the determination of the majority, and to be concluded by it; or else this original compact, whereby he with others incorporates into one society, would signify nothing, and be no compact if he be left free and under no other ties than he was in before in the state of Nature. For what appearance would there be of any compact? What new engagement if he were no farther tied by any decrees of the society than he himself thought fit and did actually consent to? This would be still as great a liberty as he himself had before his compact, or any one else in the state of Nature, who may submit himself and consent to any acts of it if he thinks fit.

. . .

99. Whosoever, therefore, out of a state of Nature unite into a community, must be understood to give up all the power necessary to the ends for which they unite into society to the majority of the community, unless they expressly agreed in any number greater than the majority. And this is done by barely agreeing to unite into one political society, which is all the compact that is, or needs be, between the individuals that enter into or make up a commonwealth. And thus, that which begins and actually constitutes any political society is nothing but the consent of any number of freemen capable of majority, to unite and incorporate into such a society. And this is that, and that only, which did or could give beginning to any lawful government in the world. . . .

DISCUSSION QUESTIONS

1. Do you agree with Locke that people can exist outside of civil society in a "state of nature"? Support your answer.
2. Do you agree with Locke that there is a "law of Nature" that gives individuals living in a state of nature the right to punish transgressors? Does the lack of an international government mean that nations are living in a state of nature? Discuss whether this justifies the use of war against nations that, for example, violate our property rights.
3. Do you agree with Locke's assumption that God gave the earth to humans to use as their resource? What evidence does Locke use to support this premise? Are you satisfied with his argument? Can his theory of natural human rights stand without this assumption? Even if we do accept Locke's premise, does this logically imply that humans have a moral right to exploit the environment as they wish?
4. Natural rights ethicists claim that human equality is self-evident. What does this mean? What are the implications of this statement for public policy?

5. Discuss how animal liberationist Peter Singer might respond to Locke's claim that only humans have moral rights. Can Locke justify extending rights only to humans, or is Locke being a speciesist by extending rights only to humans?

6. Ralph Waldo Emerson once said that "people say law but they mean wealth." In the United States 90 percent of the resources are owned by 10 percent of the people. Compare and contrast the capitalist system of property ownership, as supported by Ayn Rand, with Locke's philosophy. Use specific examples to illustrate your answer.

7. How would Locke most likely respond to the current environmental rights movement? Imagine a conversation between Locke and Eagle Man.

8. Do you agree with Locke that the primary purpose of government is the protection of people's property? Is the protection of people's property sufficient to ensure that people's rights will be respected? Support your answer.

9. Is Locke's natural rights ethics, especially as it affects the ownership of property, practical in today's world? Are there enough resources for everyone?

Karl Marx

The Jewish Question

German philosopher and social reformer Karl Marx (1818–1883) was one
of the most outspoken critics of the Lockean concept of natural rights. He
argued that the concept of natural rights, and in particular Locke's natural
right to own property, supports an economic system that permits the increasing accumulation of property and wealth in the hands of a few people. An
advocate of socialism, Marx argued that true equality and freedom entails
communal rather than private ownership of property.

In the following excerpt from his essay "The Jewish Question," Marx
defends a concept of rights based on cooperation and the needs of those
within the community. The essay was written, in part, in response to a question by philosopher Bruno Bauer in which Bauer equated economics with
Judaism.

CRITICAL THINKING QUESTIONS

1. What does Marx mean by the rights of citizens? According to
   Marx, is there a distinction between the natural rights of man and
   the rights of citizens?

2. Why does Marx object to the concept of rights set forth in the
   1793 "Declaration of the Rights of Man and of the Citizen"?

3. What, according to Marx, is the practical application of the right
   to liberty?

4. Why does Marx argue that the right to security is the assurance of
   egoism?

5. What is Marx's view of the human nature?

. . . Let us consider for a moment the so-called rights of man; let us examine them
in their most authentic form, that which they have among those who *discovered*
them, the North Americans and the French! These rights of man are, in part,
political rights, which can only be exercised if one is a member of a community.
Their content is *participation* in the *community* life, in the *political* life of the
community, the life of the state. They fall in the category of *political liberty,* of
civil rights, which as we have seen do not at all presuppose the consistent and

---

"The Jewish Question," in *Karl Marx, Early Writings,* Tom Bottomore, trans. (New York: McGraw-
Hill, 1963), pp. 23–31. Notes have been omitted.

positive abolition of religion; nor consequently, of Judaism. It remains to consider the other part, namely the *rights of man* as distinct from the *rights of the citizen.*

Among them is to be found the freedom of conscience, the right to practise a chosen religion. The *privilege of faith* is expressly recognized, either as a *right of man* or as a consequence of a right of man, namely liberty. *Declaration of the Rights of Man and of the Citizen,* 1791, Article 10: "No one is to be disturbed on account of his opinions, even religious opinions." There is guaranteed, as one of the rights of man, "the liberty of every man to practise the *religion* to which he adheres." . . .

A distinction is made between the rights of man and the rights of the citizen. Who is this *man* distinct from the *citizen?* No one but the *member of civil society.* Why is the member of civil society called "man," simply man, and why are his rights called the "rights of man"? How is this fact to be explained? By the relation between the political state and civil society, and by the nature of political emancipation.

Let us notice first of all that the so-called *rights of man,* as distinct from the *rights of the citizen,* are simply the rights of a *member of civil society,* that is, of egoistic man, of man separated from other men and from the community. The most radical constitution, that of 1793, says: *Declaration of the Rights of Man and of the Citizen:* Article 2. "These rights, etc. (the natural and imprescriptible rights) are: *equality, liberty, security, property.*

What constitutes liberty?

Article 6. "Liberty is the power which man has to do everything which does not harm the rights of others."

Liberty is, therefore, the right to do everything which does not harm others. The limits within which each individual can act without harming others are determined by law, just as the boundary between two fields is marked by a stake. It is a question of the liberty of man regarded as an isolated monad, withdrawn into himself. . . .

The practical application of the right of liberty is the right of private property. What constitutes the right of private property?

Article 16 (Constitution of 1793). "The right of *property* is that which belongs to every citizen of enjoying and disposing *as he will* of his goods and revenues, of the fruits of his work and industry."

The right of property is, therefore, the right to enjoy one's fortune and to dispose of it as one will; without regard for other men and independently of society. It is the right of self-interest. This individual liberty, and its application, form the basis of civil society. It leads every man to see in other men, not the *realization,* but rather the *limitation* of his own liberty. It declares above all the right "to enjoy and to dispose *as one will,* one's goods and revenues, the fruits of one's work and industry."

There remain the other rights of man, equality and security.

The term "equality" has here no political significance. It is only the equal right to liberty as defined above; namely that every man is equally regarded as a self-sufficient monad. The Constitution of 1795 defines the concept of liberty in this sense.

Article 5 (*Constitution* of 1795). "Equality consists in the fact that the law is the same for all, whether it protects or punishes."

And security?

Article 8 (*Constitution* of 1793). "Security consists in the protection afforded by society to each of its members for the preservation of his person, his rights, and his property."

Security is the supreme social concept of civil society; the concept of the police. The whole society exists only in order to guarantee for each of its members the preservation of his person, his rights and his property. It is in this sense that Hegel calls civil society "the state of need and of reason."

The concept of security is not enough to raise civil society above its egoism. Security is, rather, the *assurance* of its egoism.

None of the supposed rights of man, therefore, go beyond the egoistic man, man as he is, as a member of civil society; that is, an individual separated from the community, withdrawn into himself, wholly preoccupied with his private interest and acting in accordance with his private caprice. Man is far from being considered, in the rights of man, as a species-being; on the contrary, species-life itself—society—appears as a system which is external to the individual and as a limitation of his original independence. The only bond between men is natural necessity, need and private interest, the preservation of their property and their egoistic persons.

It is difficult enough to understand that a nation which has just begun to liberate itself, to tear down all the barriers between different sections of the people and to establish a political community, should solemnly proclaim (*Declaration* of 1791) the rights of the egoistic man, separated from his fellow men and from the community, and should renew this proclamation at a moment when only the most heroic devotion can save the nation (and is, therefore, urgently called for), and when the sacrifice of all the interests of civil society is in question and egoism should be punished as a crime. (*Declaration of the Rights of Man, etc.* 1793). The matter becomes still more incomprehensible when we observe that the political liberators reduce citizenship, the *political community,* to a mere *means* for preserving these so-called rights of man; and consequently, that the citizen is declared to be the servant of egoistic "man," that the sphere in which man functions as a species-being is degraded to a level below the sphere where he functions as a partial being, and finally that it is man as a bourgeois and not man as a citizen who is considered the *true* and *authentic* man. . . .

But the liberty of egoistic man, and the recognition of this liberty, is rather the recognition of the *frenzied* movement of the cultural and material elements which form the content of his life.

Thus man was not liberated from religion; he received religious liberty. He was not liberated from property; he received the liberty to own property. He was not liberated from the egoism of business; he received the liberty to engage in business.

The *formation of the political state,* and the dissolution of civil society into independent *individuals* whose relations are regulated by *law,* as the relations between men in the corporations and guilds were regulated by *privilege,* are accomplished by *one and the same act.* Man as a member of civil society—*non-political* man—necessarily appears as the *natural* man. The rights of man appear as natural rights because *conscious* activity is concentrated upon political *action.* *Egoistic* man is the *passive, given* result of the dissolution of society, an object of *direct apprehension* and consequently a *natural* object. The *political revolution* dissolves civil society into its elements without *revolutionizing* these elements themselves or subjecting them to criticism. This revolution regards civil society, the sphere of human needs, labour, private interests and civil law, as the *basis of its own existence,* as a self-subsistent *precondition,* and thus as its *natural basis.* Finally, man as a member of civil society is identified with *authentic man,* man as distinct from citizen, because he is man in his sensuous, individual and *immediate* existence, whereas *political* man is only abstract, artificial man, man as an *allegorical, moral* person. Thus man as he really is, is seen only in the form of *egoistic* man, and man in his *true* nature only in the form of the *abstract citizen.* . . .

Human emancipation will only be complete when the real, individual man has absorbed into himself the abstract citizen; when as an individual man, in his everyday life, in his work, and in his relationships, he has become a *species-being;* and when he has recognized and organized his own powers *(forces propres)* as *social* powers so that he no longer separates this social power from himself as *political* power.

DISCUSSION QUESTIONS

1. Discuss Marx's argument that the natural right to property renders the term *equality* politically meaningless.
2. Do you agree with Marx that natural rights ethics isolates people and encourages egoism rather than community? Has this happened in the United States? Is an emphasis on individualism rather than community necessarily bad? How might Marx respond to this last question?
3. Marx argues that natural rights ethics is not only unjust but reduces citizens to a "mere means for preserving the so-called rights of man." Do you agree with Marx? Discuss whether the Lockean notion of a natural right to property violates Kant's categorical imperative.
4. According to Marx, humans are basically cooperative rather than egoists. Compare and contrast Marx's view of human nature with Locke's. Which person makes the most convincing argument?
5. Does the right to property, as part of our social contract, meet the criteria laid out in Rawls's two principles of justice? Which type of economic system—one based on collective ownership of property or one based on a capitalist notion of private ownership —would a person in Rawls's original position be most likely to choose? Support your answer.
6. Ethical egoist Ayn Rand, an avid opponent of Marxism, supported the concept of natural rights. How might she respond to some of Marx's criticisms of natural rights ethics?

Gustavo Gutierrez

The Power of the Poor in History

Peruvian liberation ethicist and theologian Gustavo Gutierrez (b. 1928) agrees with Marx's criticism of natural rights ethics. After attending Roman Catholic theological school in Europe, he returned to Peru to work with the poor of Lima. His moral philosophy was formulated in the context of the poverty of Latin America.

In the selection from his book, *The Power of the Poor in History,* Gutierrez argues that natural rights ethics has been used as a justification by capitalists for the takeover of lands and the exploitation of the working poor in Latin America. He proposes an alternative: a biblically based concept of rights that, he believes, is more just and consistent with respect for human dignity. Rather than rights being based on the ability to assert one's power, Gutierrez like Marx, argues that rights also stem from need.

Critical Thinking Questions

1. According to Gutierrez, what is the primary cause of poverty in Latin America today?

2. What are the rights of the poor?

3. Why does Gutierrez argue that acceptance of the claim that all people are equal can make us blind to oppression?

4. What does Gutierrez mean by the right to liberation? According to him, what is the foundation of this right?

5. According to Gutierrez, why do the people in power persecute the poor for exercising their right to liberation? What does Gutierrez mean when he says the poor have "the right to exist and to think"?

6. What is the connection between the right to liberation and liberation praxis?

A NEW FORM OF DOMINATION

As I have been insisting so strongly, the situation of captivity in which the peoples of Latin America find themselves today has its roots in history long gone by. This situation of ours is an ongoing one. I likewise emphasize the maturation, despite

The Power of the Poor in History (Maryknoll, NY: Orbis Books, 1979), pp. 83–102. Notes have been omitted.

appearances, of the popular movement. But I am by no means denying that new forms of oppression exist in our region of the world today. I appreciate that our polemical tack may have given a wrong impression.

My purpose in taking this approach has been to recall the deep-rooted character of this exploitive situation and to point out that this is the reason why the popular classes raised the banner of liberation some years ago, not because they thought their deliverance was at hand. They called for liberation because they had become conscious of oppression. This may seem evident, but it apparently bears repeating today.

However, important and significant changes have taken place in the interim. To ignore them would be to become mired in the past. We would be condemning ourselves to historical sterility and ineffectiveness. In the light of what has been said before, we are now in a position to make a more correct evaluation of the new forms of oppression in Latin America. Now what is new in them will disconcert us no longer. Our experience will come to our aid, and we shall be able to confront "new" forms of oppression without committing the errors of the past.

The qualitative difference in this new state of affairs will be better perceived if we view these changes as the response made by the prevailing system not only to its own internal contradictions but to the popular movements of years past as well. Indeed, these movements flooded the dominant classes with the fear that they might lose their privileges, perhaps for the first time in the history of our nations. And fear never creates; it petrifies.

Internationalization of Capitalism

International capitalism has passed through various stages of development over the past several decades. Each stage has had a different meaning for the people of Latin America.

The aftermath of World War II witnessed a consistently high rate of growth in the capitalist economies. This expansive thrust even led a number of economists and politicians to envision the possibility of transcending the economic crises so characteristic of capitalism.

This period of continuous growth of capitalism produced the remarkable phenomenon of the transnational industrial conglomerates. In search of ever greater profit, companies in industrially developed countries now engineered a groundswell of productive capital to Europe and the Third World. First they transferred manufacturing facilities from the United States to the European Common Market. Then, on a more restricted scale, the United States, Europe, and Japan set up plants in underdeveloped countries that could offer suitable economic advantages—especially, as far as Latin America was concerned, in Mexico, Brazil, and Argentina. The majority of the countries of the Third World, however, representing the lowest step on the now complete international capitalist staircase, saw no substantial changes in the traditional form of their participation in the international order. The accelerating pace of industrialization took no root there, and these countries, making up the bulk of the Third World, were found useful only for high production at low wages through the exploitation of the labor force. The rare instances of "export platforms," such as Singapore and Hong Kong, do not alter the general situation in this respect.

During these years of the "big boom," of international capitalism, the proliferation of the transnationals gave rise to an ever more important trade network among them, but of such a nature that the term "trade" is used in a very attenuated sense: it should imply a minimum of autonomy on the part of the contractual parties. In fact, however, the assigned cost and market value of a product floated free of its real cost and value, and world capital became extremely liquid. Now the methods of "decapitalizing" the poor countries became even more sophisticated, and their effectiveness in exploiting labor and producing hunger was greatly improved.

At the same time, as part and parcel of this same process, financial resources themselves came to be concentrated in ever fewer and fewer capitalist enterprises, to the accompaniment of a diversification of the areas serving as intermediaries in the decapitalization of poor countries.

Next, technological capabilities were concentrated in the United States, the emergence of economies such as those of Japan or Germany notwithstanding. This concentration of technological power, and its appropriation by a small group of countries, was owing in no small measure to the development of the arms industry to which these economies are devoted. Thus the power to master nature through technology was cruelly achieved by the development of the power to destroy humanity.

Finally, the control by the United States of a huge proportion of the world's food surplus completed the hexagon of concentration of economic, financial, military, technological, commercial, and alimentary power in a small clutch of countries, headed by the United States.

This process of growth and restructuring within the capitalist economic order has scarcely signaled progress for the nations of Latin America, especially where the masses of the people are concerned. The distance between the poor countries and the rich ones in our capitalist world is widening, as numerous studies by international agencies have shown. The upsurge of capitalism, and the situation of the poor, in recent decades has demonstrated once again that capitalist development is of its very nature detrimental to the masses, as the naked exploitation now endured by the poor nations of the world all too abundantly attests.

But around 1970, the unbroken capitalist advance and its seeming security began to teeter and sway. A number of different researchers are currently engaged in a study of the origins, depth, and foreseeable duration of the international capitalist crisis. Their studies concur in exonerating the oil-producing countries for the crisis in international capitalism, in spite of efforts to spread the impression that it was they who were responsible and thus discourage the formation of cartels by producers of other raw materials.

Instead, it would seem, the international capitalist crisis is a result of the industrial decline of economic leaders such as the United States (as, earlier, of the United Kingdom), with a consequent weakening of the dollar. These findings suggest that the current crisis may be a long one. It will very likely last until new industrial technology can increase profitability, and until stable political and economic relationships among the capitalist nations will allow for a reliable international monetary standard.

In the meantime, until all these problems can somehow be resolved, international capital copes with the problem of profitably applying substantive technological improvements, and thus achieving a fiscal stability that will encourage long-term investment, by brutally devaluing the contribution of the world labor force. Only thus, it is thought, can profit be increased in the short run. Thus wage earners in the underdeveloped countries, in addition to their traditional prostration, now bear the burden of the sacrifices and deprivation demanded by this "interim" approach to stemming the tide of the new crisis.

The outlook for the poor is dismal, then, whether the capitalist system prospers or languishes. In either case the function of underdeveloped economies is to provide more capital, either to enhance an already flourishing foreign economy or to collaborate in the solution of its problems.

Changes in the international economic order, begun in decades past and seemingly immune from crisis thus far, entail no diminution whatever of the level of dependency of our Latin American countries. On the contrary, they diversify and deepen it. Accordingly, the apostles of compromise have abandoned their half-hearted longings for viable nationalisms, and now unashamedly throw themselves into the arms of transnational capital. The hypocritical mask of "negotiation" fails to disguise the capitulation. Thus any hopes for national liberation slip from the hands of the other social strata into the laps of the exploited classes alone. . . .

The Rights of the Poor

All this makes for a complicated and explosive setting for the presence and voice of the church in Latin America. The coming of age of the popular masses' political awareness over the last decade, the growing involvement of Christian groups in the liberation process, and the fact that repression has begun to strike the official church to a degree hitherto unknown, coupled with the brutality shown by repressive regimes during these same years, have moved bishops' conferences and other church groups to undertake a vigorous defense of human rights. At times, the church's voice has been the only one to be raised against the crushing of human liberties. Thus the church has helped bring this nefarious situation to the attention of the world, with the effect that its scope has been reduced.

At the same time, a structural analysis better suited to Latin American reality has led certain Christians to speak of the "rights of the poor" and to interpret the defense of human rights under this new formality. The adjustment is not merely a matter of words. This alternative language represents a critical approach to the laissez-faire, liberal doctrine to the effect that our society enjoys an equality that in fact does not exist. This new formulation likewise seeks constantly to remind us of what is really at stake in the defense of human rights: the misery and spoliation of the poorest of the poor, the conflictive character of Latin American life and society, and the biblical roots of the defense of the poor.

One of the traps that may yet ensnare the church in Latin America will be a facile, naive acquiescence in the "restricted democracy" mentioned above. Certain liberties and individual rights could be formally restored, but the profound social and economic inequality that undermines them would be left intact. The church's denunciation of violations of human rights will quickly become a hollow cry if church officials rest content with the beginnings of a "democracy" that is only for the middle class and actually only enhances the flexibility with which the prevailing system exercises its domination over the popular masses.

Only from within the poor classes of Latin American society will it be possible to grasp the true meaning of the biblical cry for the defense of human rights. Only thus will it be clear that, for the church, this task is an expression of the proclamation of the gospel in Latin America today. . . .

PERSECUTED IN THE CAUSE OF RIGHT

The hand of the dominator reaches out ruthlessly to castigate any protest on the part of the oppressed, any attempt at altering a social order that routinely manufactures a poor class. One of the significant facts of Latin American life in recent years is the open, brutal repression that has struck down groups and persons explicitly calling themselves Christian, including many who exercise official responsibilities in the institutional church.

These realities, already in the making ten years ago, today are commonplace. They are painful but unmistakable evidence, full of promise, that our Christian community is moving ever closer to the poor of Latin America, that we have actually begun to experience the lot of the poor. These Christians—these farmhands, laborers, priests, bishops, university students, nuns—are not jailed, tortured, and murdered for their "religious ideas" but for their social praxis—their evangelization. They are persecuted because, believing as they do in a God of liberation, they denounce injustice done to the poor, and become involved in the lives and the struggles of the poor. They are struck down because they try to rethink their faith from a viewpoint of solidarity with the liberation of the oppressed. Frequently they are persecuted by governments themselves claiming to be Christians, regimes that loudly announce that their efforts "in defense of Western Christian civilization" certify them as champions of the faith and protectors of the church. This monstrous lie has been denounced by many representatives of the church. But many others embrace it, and this is a scandal. . . .

THE RIGHT TO EXIST AND TO THINK

All genuine theology has its point of departure in the life of faith. Faith, after all, is what leads us to become disciples of Christ, and theology is about discipleship. Discipleship is not simply listening to a teaching. Before all else, discipleship is the following of Christ. Discipleship means making his practice our practice.

In the first part of this chapter we considered the deeply human and Christian meaning of the "temporal life and increase of the poor." That is, we considered the meaning of the physical life of the poor, the area in which, precisely, the poor are despoiled and have their most elemental rights violated. For there is a dialectic between the life of faith and the life of the body, between faith in the resurrection and our temporal death. In this dialectic the theology of liberation represents *the right of the poor to think*.

What do we mean by the right of the poor to think? We mean the right to express—to plumb, comprehend, come to appreciate, and then insist upon—that other right that an oppressive system denies them: the right to a human life.

Hence it will be appropriate to consider the points of breach and continuity between the theology of liberation and other theologies past and present. What will be the same, and what will be different, about a theology whose point of departure is the life of faith on the "underside of history"?

At the same time, we shall be coming to an appreciation of the meaning and potentialities of theological reflection as the right of an exploited and believing people that struggles to throw off the shackles of oppression that drag it to the dust to speak up and tell us about its faith and its hope. . . .

Elements of an Authentic Response

And so we return to our questions. I shall not pretend to exhaust their depth and scope, but shall only make certain observations, along the lines alluded to above.

Even the poor have the right to think. The right to think is a corollary of the human right to be, and to assert the right to think is only to assert the right to exist. "Blacks assert that they exist," begins a famous text of black theology published by black church leaders in the United States.

This kind of language could be somewhat shocking. But it is altogether justified. The right to be, to exist, is the first demand of those whom James H. Cone, the principal representative of black liberation theology, calls the victims of history. Of course, recognition of blacks' existence is sure to be subversive, hence disquieting for the dominating classes.

The right to engage in theological reflection is part of the right of an exploited Christian people to think. The faith of the poor in the God of their deliverance seeks, from its own exigencies, to understand itself. This is the classic Anselmian *fides quaerens intellectum*. Christians have the right to think through their faith in the Lord, to think out the experience of their own liberation. They have the right to reclaim their faith—a faith that is continually diverted away from their experience of being poor—in order to turn it into an ideological exposé of the situation of domination that makes and keeps them poor. They have the right to repossess the Bible, and thus prevent the private proprietors of this world's goods from being the private proprietors of the word of the Lord as well.

This is what I meant when, some years ago, I spoke about a social appropriation of the gospel. The social appropriation of the gospel is a reading of the gospel in solidarity with the struggles of the poor. It is a militant reading of the Bible. The interpretation that the poor give their life situation opens a rich vein for the understanding of the gift of God's kingdom. A point of departure in that life situation will enable the theologian to take into account the data of modern scientific exegesis and give it a new, radical dimension.

In this perspective, the theological endeavor, from a point of departure in (and through the actual agency of) the exploited, pertains to their right to liberation. We dare not forget that all reflection is a way of exercising power in history. It is only one way, of course, but it is a real way. It makes a real contribution to the transformation of history—to the destruction of the system of oppression and the construction of a just and humane society. Reflection on the faith as lived in this struggle is a necessary condition for the proclamation of the living God from a pulpit in the midst of the poor.

This is the reason why certain Christian communities committed to the liberation process have, for some time now, been attempting to develop an elaboration of the faith out of their own experience—an elaboration of which they themselves are the primary historical subject. Similar theological undertakings have arisen among the black descendants of slaves in the United States, in the cruel context of racial discrimination in South Africa, and in the midst of the oppression suffered in certain Asian countries (the Philippines and Korea, for instance). The same thing is occurring among women in today's society—especially women who, as members of the popular classes, are doubly exploited, marginalized, and degraded.

We are seeing only the beginnings. But these beginnings already show a way of taking account of the hope of the Lord that is present at the very heart of the historical praxis of liberation. For the first time in many centuries, the confluence of these various currents is producing an effort of reflection on the faith outside the classic centers of theological production. The international conferences of the Ecumenical Association of Third World Theologians are a case in point. They are examples of reflection springing up from the "underside of history."

To renounce thinking, as some persons seem to advise us, is to give ground. To give up thinking would be to betray the vitality of the faith of a people struggling for its liberation. It would mean creating a vacuum that would promptly be filled by reflection representing other categories, other concerns and interests.

In view of all these considerations, I hold that theology should be looked upon as an expression of the right to think on the part of the "wretched of the earth." . . .

DISCUSSION QUESTIONS

1. To what extent is the problem of poverty in Latin America today an outcome of the influence of Locke's natural rights ethics—particularly the natural right to own property—on the thinking of business owners in the United States?

2. Why does Gutierrez claim that the poor have special rights? Do you agree with Gutierrez? If the poor do have special rights, discuss how this might be reflected in a public policy regarding welfare reform in this country.

3. Both Locke and Gutierrez claim to have derived their concept of rights from biblical scripture; yet both came up with very different concepts of rights. Which person do you think presents the strongest argument? Support your answer.

4. Is Gutierrez's rights ethics consistent with the philosophy of the UN's "Universal Declaration of Human Rights"? Which articles from the Declaration might Gutierrez use to support his argument?

The Universal Declaration of Human Rights

"The Universal Declaration of Human Rights" was adopted by the United Nations in 1948, following World War II, as "a common standard of achievement for all peoples and all nations." The Declaration delineates both liberty rights and welfare rights.

Articles 3 through 21 are liberty rights. Liberty rights are those that entail the right to be left alone to pursue our own legitimate interests—that is, those interests that don't violate other people's similar and equal rights. The natural rights ethics of John Locke focuses on liberty rights, as does the U.S. Bill of Rights.

Articles 22 to 28 cover welfare rights. Welfare rights entail the right to receive certain social goods such as education, housing, medical care, and police and fire protection. These rights are emphasized more by the community-based rights ethics of Marx and Gutierrez.

Critical Thinking Questions

1. What, according to the Declaration, is the foundation of freedom, justice, and peace in the world?

2. What concept of human nature does the United Nations adopt? What does the Declaration mean by the phrase "the full development of the human personality"?

3. Why are rights outlined in Articles 3 to 21 generally referred to as liberty rights? In what sense are these rights liberty rights?

4. What welfare rights are being protected in Articles 22 to 28?

Preamble

Whereas recognition of the inherent dignity and of the equal and inalienable rights of all members of the human family is the foundation of freedom, justice and peace in the world,

Whereas disregard and contempt for human rights have resulted in barbarous acts which have outraged the conscience of mankind, and the advent of a world in which human beings shall enjoy freedom of speech and belief and freedom

---

United Nations, "The Universal Declaration of Human Rights" (1948).

from fear and want has been proclaimed as the highest aspiration of the common people,

Whereas it is essential, if man is not to be compelled to have recourse, as a last resort, to rebellion against tyranny and oppression, that human rights should be protected by the rule of law,

Whereas it is essential to promote the development of friendly relations between nations,

Whereas the peoples of the United Nations have in the Charter reaffirmed their faith in fundamental human rights, in the dignity and worth of the human person and in the equal rights of men and women and have determined to promote social progress and better standards of life in larger freedom,

Whereas Member States have pledged themselves to achieve, in cooperation with the United Nations, the promotion of universal respect for and observance of human rights and fundamental freedoms,

Whereas a common understanding of these rights and freedoms is of the greatest importance for the full realization of this pledge,

Now, therefore,

The General Assembly,

Proclaims this Universal Declaration of Human Rights as a common standard of achievement for all peoples and all nations, to the end that every individual and every organ of society, keeping this Declaration constantly in mind, shall strive by teaching and education to promote respect for these rights and freedoms and by progressive measures, national and international, to secure their universal and effective recognition and observance, both among the peoples of Member States themselves and among the peoples of territories under their jurisdiction.

Article 1

All human beings are born free and equal in dignity and rights. They are endowed with reason and conscience and should act towards one another in a spirit of brotherhood.

Article 2

Everyone is entitled to all the rights and freedoms set forth in this Declaration, without distinction of any kind, such as race, colour, sex, language, religion, political or other opinion, national or social origin, property, birth or other status.

Furthermore, no distinction shall be made on the basis of the political, jurisdictional or international status of the country or territory to which a person belongs, whether it be independent, trust, non-self-governing or under any other limitation of sovereignty.

Article 3

Everyone has the right to life, liberty and security of person.

Article 4

No one shall be held in slavery or servitude; slavery and the slave trade shall be prohibited in all their forms.

Article 5

No one shall be subjected to torture or to cruel, inhuman or degrading treatment or punishment.

Article 6

Everyone has the right to recognition everywhere as a person before the law.

Article 7

All are equal before the law and are entitled without any discrimination to equal protection of the law. All are entitled to equal protection against any discrimination in violation of this Declaration and against any incitement to such discrimination.

Article 8

Everyone has the right to an effective remedy by the competent national tribunals for acts violating the fundamental rights granted him by the constitution or by law.

Article 9

No one shall be subjected to arbitrary arrest, detention or exile.

Article 10

Everyone is entitled in full equality to a fair and public hearing by an independent and impartial tribunal, in the determination of his rights and obligations and of any criminal charge against him.

Article 11

1. Everyone charged with a penal offence has the right to be presumed innocent until proved guilty according to law in a public trial at which he has had all the guarantees necessary for his defence.
2. No one shall be held guilty of any penal offence on account of any act or omission which did not constitute a penal offence, under national or international law, at the time when it was committed. Nor shall a heavier

penalty be imposed than the one that was applicable at the time the penal offence was committed.

Article 12

No one shall be subjected to arbitrary interference with his privacy, family, home or correspondence, nor to attacks upon his honour and reputation. Everyone has the right to the protection of the law against such interference or attacks.

Article 13

1. Everyone has the right to freedom of movement and residence within the borders of each State.
2. Everyone has the right to leave any country, including his own, and to return to his country.

Article 14

1. Everyone has the right to seek and to enjoy in other countries asylum from persecution.
2. This right may not be invoked in the case of prosecutions genuinely arising from non-political crimes or from acts contrary to the purposes and principles of the United Nations.

Article 15

1. Everyone has the right to a nationality.
2. No one shall be arbitrarily deprived of his nationality nor denied the right to change his nationality.

Article 16

1. Men and women of full age, without any limitation due to race, nationality or religion, have the right to marry and to found a family. They are entitled to equal rights as to marriage, during marriage and at its dissolution.
2. Marriage shall be entered into only with the free and full consent of the intending spouses.
3. The family is the natural and fundamental group unit of society and is entitled to protection by society and the State.

Article 17

1. Everyone has the right to own property alone as well as in association with others.
2. No one shall be arbitrarily deprived of his property.

Article 18

Everyone has the right to freedom of thought, conscience and religion; this right includes freedom to change his religion or belief, and freedom, either alone or in community with others and in public or private, to manifest his religion or belief in teaching, practice, worship and observance.

Article 19

Everyone has the right to freedom of opinion and expression; this right includes freedom to hold opinions without interference and to seek, receive and impart information and ideas through any media and regardless of frontiers.

Article 20

1. Everyone has the right to freedom of peaceful assembly and association.
2. No one may be compelled to belong to an association.

Article 21

1. Everyone has the right to take part in the government of his country, directly or through freely chosen representatives.
2. Everyone has the right to equal access to public service in his country.
3. The will of the people shall be the basis of the authority of government; this will shall be expressed in periodic and genuine elections which shall be by universal and equal suffrage and shall be held by secret vote or by equivalent free voting procedures.

Article 22

Everyone, as a member of society, has the right to social security and is entitled to realization, through national effort and international co-operation and in accordance with the organization and resources of each State, of the economic, social and cultural rights indispensable for his dignity and the free development of his personality.

Article 23

1. Everyone has the right to work, to free choice of employment, to just and favourable conditions of work and to protection against unemployment.
2. Everyone, without any discrimination, has the right to equal pay for equal work.
3. Everyone who works has the right to just and favourable remuneration ensuring for himself and his family an existence worthy of human dignity, and supplemented, if necessary, by other means of social protection.

4. Everyone has the right to form and to join trade unions for the protection of his interests.

Article 24

Everyone has the right to rest and leisure, including reasonable limitation of working hours and periodic holidays with pay.

Article 25

1. Everyone has the right to a standard of living adequate for the health and well-being of himself and of his family, including food, clothing, housing and medical care and necessary social services, and the right to security in the event of unemployment, sickness, disability, widowhood, old age or other lack of livelihood in circumstances beyond his control.

2. Motherhood and childhood are entitled to special care and assistance. All children, whether born in or out of wedlock, shall enjoy the same social protection.

Article 26

1. Everyone has the right to education. Education shall be free, at least in the elementary and fundamental stages. Elementary education shall be compulsory. Technical and professional education shall be made generally available and higher education shall be equally accessible to all on the basis of merit.

2. Education shall be directed to the full development of the human personality and to the strengthening of respect for human rights and fundamental freedoms. It shall promote understanding, tolerance and friendship among all nations, racial or religious groups, and shall further the activities of the United Nations for the maintenance of peace.

3. Parents have a prior right to choose the kind of education that shall be given to their children.

Article 27

1. Everyone has the right freely to participate in the cultural life of the community, to enjoy the arts and to share in scientific advancement and its benefits.

2. Everyone has the right to the protection of the moral and material interests resulting from any scientific, literary or artistic production of which he is the author.

Article 28

Everyone is entitled to a social and international order in which the rights and freedoms set forth in this Declaration can be fully realized.

Article 29

1. Everyone has duties to the community in which alone the free and full development of his personality is possible.

2. In the exercise of his rights and freedoms, everyone shall be subject only to such limitations as are determined by law solely for the purpose of securing due recognition and respect for the rights and freedoms of others and of meeting the just requirements of morality, public order and the general welfare in a democratic society.

3. These rights and freedoms may in no case be exercised contrary to the purposes and principles of the United Nations.

Article 30

Nothing in this Declaration may be interpreted as implying for any State, group or person any right to engage in any activity or to perform any act aimed at the destruction of any of the rights and freedoms set forth herein.

DISCUSSION QUESTIONS

1. Do you agree with Article 1? Is it true that all humans are endowed with reason and conscience? Is our possession of rights dependent on our ability to reason and make moral decisions? What about people who lack a conscience (for instance, psychopaths) or who are not rational? Do they still have rights?

2. Is the distinction between liberty rights and welfare rights clear-cut? To what extent do liberty rights and welfare rights overlap? Use examples from the Declaration to illustrate your answer.

3. Discuss how John Locke and Karl Marx might each react to the UN Declaration. What changes, if any, might Locke and Marx each want to make?

4. Rights, according to deontologists, stem from duty. Do you agree? Which of the rights listed in the Declaration might be seen as stemming from the *prima facie* duties, as described by Ross?

5. To what extent does the U.S. government respect all the rights listed in the Declaration? Which rights, if any, do we lack? Are these primarily liberty rights or welfare rights? If we lack certain rights, does this mean we are an unjust nation? Does the United Nations have the right, or even the duty, to compel offending nations to extend these rights to all people? If so, what is the source of this right or duty?

6. Do these articles provide practical guidelines for creating public policy? For example, does Article 23 imply that the government should guarantee you a job upon graduation? Does Article 26 imply that we have a right to expect to be fully developed humans upon graduation from college?

Jeane Kirkpatrick

Establishing a Viable Human Rights Policy

Jeane Kirkpatrick (b. 1926) taught political science at Georgetown University. Between 1981 and 1985, she served as ambassador to the United Nations under President Ronald Reagan. The following selection, "Establishing a Viable Human Rights Policy," is from a paper she presented in 1981 at a human rights conference.

A political conservative, Kirkpatrick argues that the rhetoric of rights has gotten out of hand. She compares the practice of issuing endless declarations of human rights to a "letter to Santa Claus." She points out that when people lack the ability to assert these ideal rights or to fulfill their goals in life, they complain that someone or some government must be depriving them of their rights. Kirkpatrick argues that having an interest in achieving some goal is not the same as having a right to that goal.

Critical Thinking Questions

1. What, according to Kirkpatrick, is the distinction between ideas and institutions? What is the relevance of this distinction for translating rights into reality?

2. Why is it important to Kirkpatrick that we distinguish between rhetoric and politics?

3. According to Kirkpatrick, what is the distinction between rights and goals? Why has failure to observe this distinction led to a proliferation of rights?

4. What does Kirkpatrick think of the UN's "Universal Declaration of Human Rights"?

5. What is the difference between an intention and a consequence? Does Kirkpatrick agree with the focus of political purists on intentions?

6. What, according to Kirkpatrick, is the distinction between personal and political morality? What is the role of each in forming human rights policies?

7. What does Kirkpatrick argue should form the basis of an adequate human rights policy?

"Establishing a Viable Human Rights Policy," *World Affairs* (Winter 1980–81): 323–334.

TOWARD A MORE ADEQUATE CONCEPTION OF HUMAN RIGHTS

. . . Although debate about the existential and cognitive status of human rights has occupied philosophical giants in past centuries, recent discussions could profit from renewed and systematic attention to some fundamental distinctions. Four of these seem to me crucial. They are:

first distinction: between ideas and institutions;

second distinction: between rights and goals;

third distinction: between intentions and consequences;

fourth distinction: between morals and politics.

Ideas and Institutions

There are several important reasons that, in thinking about "rights" (as about all other plans for social systems), it is important to bear in mind the differences between ideas and institutions. Ideas are the product of the mind. They are abstractions which may have no empirical referents. Anything is possible in the domain of abstract reason that does not violate analytical canons which are themselves the products of mind. Robert Owen, for example, proposed "a world convention to emancipate the human race from ignorance, poverty, division, sin, and misery." In our times we propose declarations and laws to attempt to hold other nations responsible for the disappearance of some of these evils to which Owens referred.

Since the world has not arrived at Hegel's promised end where the rational becomes the real and the real rational, there exists no experience with the realization of abstract ideas in society. Many ideas can probably never be realized. Not everything that can be conceived can be created. One can, for example, conceive a unicorn, describe it, destroy whole forests in a determined effort to find one, and still fail. Ideas are readily brought into being and are readily manipulable by their creators. They are susceptible to being changed merely because a decision is made to change them. Their relationship to context is therefore also manipulable—subject to being held constant or altered depending on the decision of their creators.

But institutions have very different characteristics. Institutions are stabilized patterns of human behavior. They involve millions, they rest on *expectations* shaped by experience—or they rest on habit and internalized values and beliefs—or on coercion.

These internalized expectations become inextricably bound up with identity. They are extremely resistant to change. Since institutions exist not in the mind of philosophers but in the habits and beliefs of actual people, they can be brought into existence only as people are persuaded or coerced into conforming their thoughts, preferences, and behavior to the necessary patterns. History and recent experience indicate that some kinds of goals and plans cannot finally be implemented, no matter how much persuasion or coercion is employed. Moreover, in the absence of experience there is no way to accurately estimate the feasibility, the costs, even the concrete desirability of an idea or ideal.

Therefore, though rights are easy to claim, they are extremely difficult to translate into reality. In actual societies, unlike in definitions, political principles do not exist in isolation; they interact and the effort at maximization begins at some point to undermine some other value. Frequently the relations among values are themselves embedded in tradition and habit, and profoundly resistant to alteration.

Burke focused on the distinction between ideas and institutions. He said, therefore, of the French Revolution:

> I should therefore suspend my congratulations on the liberty of France until I was informed as to how it had been combined with government, with public force, with discipline, with obedience of armies, with the collection and effectiveness of a well distributed revenue, with morality and religion, with solidity and property, with peace and order, with civil and social manners. All these are good things, too. Without them liberty is of no benefit whilst it lasts and is not likely long to continue.

The failure to distinguish between the domains of rhetoric and politics is the essence of *rationalism*—which encourages us to believe anything that can be conceived can be realized. Rationalism not only encourages utopianism, utopianism is a form of rationalism. It shares the characteristic features including a disregard of the experience, the concrete probability, in favor of the affirmation of rationality, abstraction, and possibility.

Applied to human rights and foreign policy, disregard of the distinction between ideas and institutions leads to an expectation that declarations of rights have existential status—and constitute valid, practical programs of action.

Rights and Goals

The second distinction I want to emphasize is that between rights and goals. In our times, "rights" proliferate at the rhetorical level, with extraordinary speed. To the rights to life, liberty, and security of person have been added the rights to nationality, to privacy, to equal rights in marriage, to education, to culture, to the full development of personality, to self-determination, to self-government, to adequate standards of living.

The United Nations Universal Declaration of Human Rights claims as a universal every political, economic, social right yet conceived. . . .

Recently, in Geneva, the United Nations Commission on Human Rights affirmed a "right to development" which carries its own concomitant list of "rights" including the right to a new economic order, peace, and an end to the arms race.

Such declarations of human "rights" take on the character of "a letter to Santa Claus"—as Orwin and Prangle noted. They can multiply indefinitely because "no clear standard informs them, and no great reflection produced them." For every goal toward which human beings have worked, there is in our time a "right."

Neither nature, experience, nor probability informs these lists of "entitlements," which are subject to no constraints except those of the mind and appetite of their authors. The fact that such "entitlements" may be without possibility of realization does not mean they are without consequences.

The consequence of treating goals as rights is grossly misleading about how goals are achieved in real life. "Rights" are vested in persons; "goals" are achieved by the efforts of persons. The language of rights subtly vests the responsibility in some other. When the belief that one has a right to development coincides with facts of primitive technology, hierarchy, and dictatorship, the tendency to blame someone is almost overwhelming. If the people of the world do not fully enjoy their economic rights it must be because some *one*—some monopoly capitalist, some Zionist, some man—is depriving them of their rightful due.

Utopian expectations concerning the human condition are compounded then by a vague sense that Utopia is one's due; that citizenship in a perfect society is a reasonable expectation for real persons in real societies.

Intentions and Consequences

The third distinction with special relevance to human rights and foreign policy is the distinction between intentions and consequences.

In political philosophy as in ethics there are theories that emphasize motives and those that emphasize consequences.

Preoccupation with motives is a well-known characteristic of a breed of political purist that has multiplied in our times. The distinguishing characteristic of this breed is emphasis on internal criteria, on what one believes and feels is right. Doing what one "knows" is right then becomes more important than producing desired results.

In human rights and foreign policy this position leads to an overweaning concern with purity of intentions. When the morality of the motive is more important than the consequences, we are less concerned about creating new traditionalist tyranny than by the morality of our own intentions, and the principal function of a purist policy of human rights is to make us feel good about ourselves.

Personal and Political Morality

The fourth distinction important to thinking about human rights and foreign policy is that between personal and political morality. Where personal morality derives from the characteristics of single individuals and depends on the cultivation of personal virtues such as faith, hope, charity, and discipline, political morality depends on the structured *interactions* of persons—depends, that is, on institutions.

Justice, democracy, liberty are all the products of arrangements of offices and distributions of power. These arrangements and distributions embodied in *constitutions* produce *political* goods by respecting and harmonizing the diverse parts of a political community. The political goods—democracy, due process, protection of "rights" to free speech, assembly—are, as Plato, Aristotle, and the

American founding fathers understood, the consequences of wisely structured constitutions.

Rights, then, are embodied in institutions—not rhetoric. They are the consequences of prudential judgments, not good motives. They are always complex and rest on patterns of social life, not on individual virtues.

The consequence of trying to base a human rights policy on private virtue is failure. Where institutions are not constructed on the basis of human proclivities and habits, failure is the inevitable result.

TOWARD A MORE SUCCESSFUL HUMAN RIGHTS POLICY

Human rights can be, should be, must be, will be, taken into account by U.S. foreign policy, but we have had enough of rationalism and purism, of private virtues and public vices.

It is my hope that in its approach to human rights, the Reagan administration will take the "cure of history," which is nothing more or less than the cure of reality. If we take the cure of history, we will discover much about the very essence of freedom and the very essence of human rights. We will discover, for example, that the freedom of the American people was based not on the marvelous and inspiring slogans of Thomas Paine but on the careful web of restraint and permission and interests and traditions which was woven by our founding fathers into the Constitution and explained in the Federalist Papers—and rooted, of course, ultimately in our rights as Englishmen. We will find the freedoms of modern France are built not on the slogans of the French Revolution but on the long, arduous struggles of the French people to give reality to those slogans, a reality that exists in the constitutional structures and in the conventions and the institutions of French society.

An adequate human rights policy will also have a realistic conception of the relationships among force, freedom, morality, and power, because history teaches us too that in the real world force may be necessary to reinforce freedom; and today American power is necessary to protect and expand the frontiers of freedom in our time.

We think that by trying less we can produce more. Time, of course, will tell.

DISCUSSION QUESTIONS

1. What does Kirkpatrick mean when she says that the assumption that rights are natural has contributed to the current proliferation of rights? Why does Kirkpatrick regard this as a problem?
2. Do you agree with Kirkpatrick's criticism of the current proliferation of rights declarations? How are we to determine when the claim to a particular right is a reasonable expectation and when it is more like writing a letter to Santa Claus? Discuss whether Fitzpatrick would regard Gutierrez's right to liberation as just another letter to Santa Claus.

3. Discuss whether the UN's "Universal Declaration of Human Rights" is impractical, as Kirkpatrick suggests. Which articles of the Declaration would you delete, if you could? Justify your answer.

4. Kirkpatrick claims that the confusion of our interest in certain goals with rights leads to dissatisfaction with one's lifestyle and government. Do you agree? If so, is dissatisfaction necessarily morally problematic? Discuss how civil rights leader Martin Luther King, Jr., might respond to Kirkpatrick's argument.

5. Do you agree with Kirkpatrick's separation of personal and political morality? Are all rights politically based? Can we have rights that are not embodied in institutions? How might Confucius respond to Kirkpatrick's separation of the two types of morality?

6. Kirkpatrick argues that "in the real world force may be necessary to protect and expand the frontiers of freedom in our time." How should we respond to human rights violations in other countries? Do countries such as the United States have a right to force freedom on other countries, as Kirkpatrick claims? How would cultural relativist Ruth Benedict respond to this question?

Joel Feinberg

Rights, Justice, and the Bounds of Liberty

Joel Feinberg (b. 1926) is an American analytical philosopher with an interest in social and political philosophy as well as the philosophy of law. Feinberg is currently a professor of philosophy at the University of Arizona.

In the following selection, Feinberg looks at the correlation between rights and duties, such as commitment (fidelity), reparation, and gratitude. He then goes on to discuss the concept of a right as a claim or entitlement. Feinberg also draws a distinction between negative rights and duties and positive rights and duties.

CRITICAL THINKING QUESTIONS

1. What is the relation between a duty and a right? Which duties, according to Feinberg, have correlative rights?
2. What are the different classes of duties described by Feinberg and what are their correlative rights?
3. What does Feinberg mean when he allies the idea of duty with that of coercion? In what ways are duties coercive whereas rights are not?
4. What does Feinberg mean by a "claimant"? What does it mean to claim that we have a right to something?
5. What distinction does Feinberg make between negative and positive rights?
6. Which rights does Feinberg acknowledge as being valid moral claims?

Among the questions that still divide philosophers who are concerned with problems about rights are (1) whether, or to what extent, rights and duties are logically correlative, and (2) whether it is theoretically illuminating generally, and in particular, whether in considering question (1) it is strategically useful, to treat rights as *claims.* Although question (1) is in a familiar sense a logical question (Do statements of duties *entail* statements of other people's rights, and do statements of rights *entail* statements of other people's duties?), this paper is more a

---

"Duties, Rights, and Claims," in *Rights, Justice, and the Bounds of Liberty* (Princeton, NJ: Princeton University Press, 1980). Some notes have been omitted.

descriptive or impressionistic study than a formalistic one. Part I consists of an examination of the many kinds of normative relations called "duty" with the aim of distinguishing those that are clearly correlated with other people's rights from those that apparently are not. The second part of the paper shifts the focus to rights and argues that there is at least one kind of talk about rights-as-claims that is neither reducible to, nor in any clear logical relation with, talk about duties. The word "claim" of course is ambiguous. Claims *to* (I shall argue) are not always expressible as claims *against,* and "having a claim to . . ." and "making claim to . . ." are different sorts of things from "claiming that. . . ." The paper concludes, however, that each of the ideas capable of being expressed by the word "claim" is essential either to the understanding or the just appreciation of rights.

I. DUTIES AND RIGHTS

Which of the various kinds of duty are necessarily correlated with the rights of other people? Consider first the relation between a debtor and his creditor. Indebtedness is the clearest example of one person *owing* something to another; and owing, in turn, is a perspicuous model for the interpretation of that treacherous little preposition "to" as it occurs in the phrase "obligation *to* someone." Now it is unquestionably true that when one party *owes* something to another, the latter has a *right* to what he is owed. The debtor's obligation is his creditor's right seen from a different vantage point. A *duty of indebtedness,* moreover, entails a right of a very specific kind, called, in the jargon of jurisprudence, a positive *in personam* right, that is, a right against one specific person requiring him to perform a "positive act," not a mere omission.

A second class of duties, being based on promises, is also more properly called "obligations," but we can call them (other) *duties of commitment.* In discussing these, we must not be misled by the preposition "to." When a debtor owes money to a creditor, he can be said to have an obligation *to* the creditor; but the preposition here is ambiguous and obscures the distinction between two different offices the creditor occupies. On the one hand he is the one to whom the obligation is *owed,* and the one therefore who can claim it as his due. On the other hand, he is the intended beneficiary of his debtor's promised act. This dual role is also played sometimes by persons owed other kinds of duties of commitment. If Abel promises Baker to meet him at a certain time, or to shine his shoes, or favorably review his book, then Baker is both claimant and intended beneficiary of Abel's duty. There may, of course, be others who stand to gain, if only indirectly, from Abel's discharge of his obligation, but in most cases these so-called "third party beneficiaries" will profit in merely picayune and remote ways.

Sometimes, however, there is a separation of offices, and the intended direct beneficiary is not the promisee, but instead some third party designated by the promisee. This class of transactions can be further subdivided: In some cases, only the promisee is the claimant, or right-holder, while in other cases, both the promisee and the third-party beneficiary have rights to the promisor's performance. If Abel promises Baker to look after Baker's dog Fido, then Fido is the direct beneficiary of the promised services, while Baker himself, and probably only Baker, is the claimant. On the other hand, if Baker designates his wife or mother (or dog?) as beneficiary on his life insurance policy, then *both* Baker as promisee and the designated beneficiary can be said to have a right that the benefit-payment go to the beneficiary. (Even after Baker is dead, it can be said that the insurance company *owes it to him* to pay the beneficiary.)

. . .

In all of these cases, the important relation for our present purposes is that between promisor and *claimant,* whether the latter be promisee, or beneficiary, or both. This relation is another proper and familiar case of owing, although it is already one step removed from what we might call the "paradigm case" of indebtedness. Duties of commitment, like the standard cases of owing, are obviously correlated with other people's *in personam* rights. The claimant has a right *in personam* against the promisor to either a positive performance, as in the case of feeding Fido, or else a forebearance, as when I promise to waive my right to keep you off my land, giving you thereby a claim to my noninterference, that is, a negative *in personam* right.

Similar remarks can be made about a third class of duties, the *duties of reparation.* When your loss is "my fault," that is, when it was caused by my negligence, recklessness, impulsiveness, carelessness, dishonesty, malevolence, or the like, then I have a duty to you to repair the harm or otherwise make good the loss. I "owe" reparation to you in much the same manner as I would owe you the return of something I borrowed or took from you without your permission. My duty, in these examples, is to return to you what is really your own, or where this is impossible, something of equivalent value; and your correlative right is a claim *in personam* to my positive services.

A fourth class of duties also permits talk of "owing" something to someone, although we are now at least two steps away from the example of indebtedness. "Mr. Churchill feels that he owes this legacy to the world," said a 1964 advertisement for a set of recordings by Winston Churchill of public and private speeches, letters, and reminiscences. Presumably, Sir Winston did not feel that he must simply return what he had borrowed or keep some sort of promise, express or implied. I suspect rather that he felt a duty to give to the world something that it needs, but which he, at age 90, no longer had reason to keep his exclusive possession. I propose to call this, and other more worldly examples of the duty abundance owes to need, *duties of need-fulfillment.* Such duties clearly give rise to positive *in personam* rights, often in many claimants.

A fifth class of duties is related to gratitude, but had better be called *duties of reciprocation,* since gratitude, a feeling, is a less appropriate subject for duty than reciprocation, which is, after all, action. There are, moreover, other confusions commonly infecting the idea of a "duty of gratitude." Many writers speak of duties of gratitude as if they were special instances, or perhaps informal analogues, of duties of indebtedness. But gratitude, I submit, feels nothing at all like indebtedness. When a person under no duty to me does me a service or helps me out of a jam, from what I imagine to be benevolent motives, my feelings of gratitude toward him bears no important resemblance to the feeling I have toward a merchant who ships me ordered goods before I pay for them. The cause of the widespread confusion of gratitude with moral indebtedness, I suspect, is a disposition, allegedly characteristic of but certainly not peculiar to the Japanese, to feel some loss of status when helped by others, and some consequent resentment of the benefactor under the respectable mask of "gratitude." We feel impelled to pay back a benefactor sometimes because we feel that his benefaction has made him "one up" and we want to get even.

The expression "duty of reciprocation" is better used for a different kind of case: My benefactor once freely offered me his services when I needed them. There was, on that occasion, nothing for me to do in return but express my deepest gratitude to him. (How alien to gratitude any sort of *payment* would have been!) But now circumstances have arisen in which he needs help, and I am in a position to help him. Surely, I *owe* him my services now, and he would be entitled to resent my failure to come through. In short, he has a right to my help now, and I have a correlative duty to proffer it to him. Like the other examples, the right in this case is *in personam* and typically positive.

I think I have now enumerated the main classes of duties that permit talk of one person owing something to another. Of course, there may be a very wide sense of "owe" in which it goes with all talk of duty, perhaps as a kind of synonym for the feeling of requirement or "must do" that goes with all duty. But still in respect to the remaining classes of duties, while one must do something, this is not because he *owes* it to someone to do it.

The sixth kind of duty is typified by the duty we all have to stay off a landowner's property. I don't think we would naturally speak of this duty as something "owed" to the landowner, although I admit the law doesn't hesitate to speak that way. In acknowledging a duty not to interfere with another's property, we show our respect for his interest in the exclusive possession and control of it. Such duties of noninterference with the person or (prototypically) the property of another, I propose to call *duties of respect*. This use of the word "respect" is not the only one, but it is, I think, a familiar one. Webster's dictionary puts it thus, ". . . to esteem; value; hence to refrain from obtruding upon or interfering with; as to respect a person's privacy."

The rights correlative with duties of respect are typically negative, that is, rights to other people's abstentions, forebearances, or noninterference, and unlike the rights discussed in our earlier examples, they are what lawyers call *in rem* rather than *in personam* rights. An *in rem* right holds, not against one specific namable person or persons but rather, in the legal phrase, against the world at large. In saying that "the whole world" has a duty to stay off my land, all I can mean, of course, is that any person in a position to enter my property has a duty to stay out. That implies that even General De Gaulle, if I wished to keep him out, would have to stop at my gate. My right *in rem*, in imposing on others a duty of respect, is itself no respecter of persons.

Are all *in rem* rights negative? There is no denying that negative *in rem* rights, modeled after the proprietary right and then extended to cover personal interests as well, have had an enormous influence on political thought, especially in America. They dominated lists of "natural rights," for example, in various eighteenth-century manifestos. Still there are positive *in rem* rights too, whose importance has come to be appreciated anew only in recent decades. Consider, for example, the duty of care that every citizen is said to owe to any and every person in a position to be injured by his negligence. I have this duty to some degree even to the uninvited trespasser on my land. Or consider the duty (not equally recognized in our law) that every citizen has to come to the aid of accident victims. These unfortunates have a right to be assisted that holds against every or any person in a position to help. I propose to call such positive *in rem* rights, *rights of community membership*, because it is their recognition, more than anything else, that molds a society into a cohesive community.

An eighth class of duties, which I shall call *duties of status*, is perhaps the original from which many of the others derive. In the Middle Ages, a "duty" was something *due* a feudal lord, in virtue of his role and its status in the social system, from one of his inferiors, a vassal or a serf, in virtue of *his* status. A person, in being born into his relatively fixed position in the social order, was at the same time born into the duties that went with, and indeed defined, that position. One's duty was conceived as a kind of payment of one's proper share to the general economy of interests, and of course there were different shares to be exacted from different ranks and stations. Doing one's duty might be paying in crops or live-stock, or performing assigned tasks at periodic intervals, or for the higher ranks contributing troops, horses, and weapons. Very likely these payments were made in a spirit similar to that in which club members pay their dues, especially in a club whose rules prescribe different types of payment for different types of members.

It was difficult, in a rigidly hierarchical society, to know *to whom* one's duty was owed, for payments were generally from lower rank to higher, with the occupant of the higher rank always capable of exacting payment, if necessary, by force. With the decline of feudalism, however, it became increasingly difficult to find a specific claimant for every status duty. Offices and roles, of course, still survived, and carried with them their attached duties, but there was no longer a single clear line of direction in which they were owed, or single source of sanctions for their enforcement. To be sure, later when contract came to supplant status as a primary principle of social organization, one could in theory come to think of the duties of one's job as derived from the "employment contract" and therefore *owed as obligations* to the boss, as promisee. This was seldom, however, a convincing myth. Employment contracts were often unfairly bargained, and by the time conditions improved in that respect, the employer was so vast and impersonal he could hardly be conceived as the claimant of a personal obligation. Hence, duties of status have come less and less to be thought of as *owed* to anyone.

The concept of a duty, however, has by no means completely forgotten its past. It still preserves its ancestral connection with offices, stations, and jobs; it is still bound up, however remotely, with the idea of coercion, and it still commonly suggests the idea of a fair share of burdens, imposed on one as a levy, for the promotion of socially shared interests. In group undertakings, it is often said that "if only everybody pitches in and does his *share*, the job will be done." The share we are thereby exhorted to contribute is, of course, the very same as our duty, and it will be greater for the rich than the poor and lesser for the weak than the strong.

Does it still make sense to ask *to whom* one's duty or status is owed? Perhaps, but we can no longer always expect a simple answer mentioning some specific person, such as "one's feudal lord," or "one's employer." To whom does the left tackle on a football team owe his assigned duty to block the player opposing him? In a case like this it is odd to say that the duty is owed to anyone but "the team." And similarly we often hear of status-duties owed "to the company," or "to the university," or "to one's country." And in still other cases, for example the duty of a janitor to sweep the corridors, it might plausibly be urged that the duty is owed to *no one at all,* although it is no less a duty for that.

Perhaps the most important feature of our talk about duties I have only mentioned up to now, and that is the alliance of the idea of duty with the idea of coercion. A duty, whatever else it be, is something *required* of one. That is to say first of all that a duty, like an obligation, is something that *obliges.* It is something we conceive of as *imposed* upon our inclinations, something we must do *whether we want to or not.* Second, a requirement is, in a perfectly good sense, a *liability,* something *we must do or else* "face the consequences" (punishment, firing, guilt feelings). When the coercive element common to duties and obligations is in clear focus, it is likely to seem so centrally important as to dim the various differences between the two conceptions, as when the lawbooks, for example, speak interchangeably of imposing duties and obligations. Moreover, both terms, "duty" and "obligation," have developed extended senses in which *only* the coercive feature is essential, as when we speak, for example, of an action, fitting perhaps as a "gesture," or symbolic expression of feeling, as a duty when it seems to have a "compelling" appropriateness. "Duty" and "obligation" both tend now to be used for any action we feel we must (for whatever reason) do.

Duties of compelling appropriateness are perhaps only duties in an extended sense, but still there is no harm in labeling them and including them in our catalogue. The class probably includes such philosophically puzzling specimens as "duties of perfection," "duties of self-sacrifice," "duties of love," "duties of vicarious gratitude," and so on. It is clear, I think, that people who feel that they have duties of this kind do not feel them as owed to anyone.

In speaking of a duty as a liability, we should take care to distinguish it from another kind of liability, also imposed by roles and jobs, namely those that have come to be called *responsibilities.* A responsibility, like a duty, is both a burden and a liability; but unlike a duty it carries considerable discretion (sometimes called "authority") along with it. A goal is assigned and the means of achieving it are left to the independent judgment of the responsible party. Moreover, the liability to unwanted consequences in the case of a responsibility tends to be "stricter" than in the case of a mere duty. That a man tried his best is more likely to be accepted as an excuse for failure to perform one's duty than for failure to fulfill one's responsibility. Indeed, the more discretion allowed in the responsibility assignment, the stricter the liability for failure is likely to be. In general, the closer the resemblance of a task assignment to the purely nondiscretionary cases, where for example, the officer's command "Fire!" imposes the duty to pull the trigger, or where the annual dues notice imposes the duty to pay, the more likely we are to characterize it as a duty, and the less likely to call it a responsibility. A "duty to obey" makes sense; but there could be no such thing as a "responsibility to obey."

This leads us to our final class of duties, the *duties of obedience*. The medieval lord was, in relation to his serf's duty, both beneficiary, claimant, and enforcing authority. In the complication of social roles that followed the collapse of feudalism, the separation of these three offices became common. In particular, the man who can, in some institutions, command the performance of duty from us, and back up his command with sanctions, is not always the same as the person, if there is one, to whom that duty is *owed*. It appears then to be a quite different sense of the preposition "to" in which we have duties *to* a commanding authority. And yet we commonly enough hear talk of "owing obedience" to parents, police officers, and bosses, and these authorities speak readily enough of having a claim to our obedience. Does an authority then have a *right* to be obeyed by his inferiors?

A traffic cop blows his whistle, points and shouts "Stop!" This, of course, imposes a (legal) duty on a motorist to stop. Still it is not true that the policeman can claim the motorist's stopping as *his* due or that the motorist owes it to *him* to stop. Perhaps the policeman has an *official* right, derived from his status *qua* policeman, rather than a *personal* right, that the motorist stop. I suspect, however, that this is simply a roundabout way of saying that the policeman's office confers on him the authority to command motorists to stop, which of course is beyond question, yet does nothing to settle the further question whether authorities can be said to have a right that persons do as they command. In any case, many duties of obedience are "owed" to impersonal authority like "the law," or a painted stop sign. Here it is especially difficult to find an assignable person who can claim another's stopping as his due. Some duties of obedience, then, seem to entail no correlative rights; and if my suspicion is correct, none of them do. For if the preposition "to" in the phrase "duty (of obedience) to one's superior" means the same as it does in the expression "answerable to so-and-so for his failure," and I suspect that this is so, then the authority to whom one "owes" obedience is not a *claimant* in the manner of (say) a creditor, but rather simply the one who may properly command performance of duty and apply sanctions in case of failure. The little preposition "to" then is triply ambiguous when used with "duty." One can have a duty *to* his claimant, *to* (or toward) a mere beneficiary, and be liable for failure *to* an authority; but it is only the claimant who can properly be said to have a right to one's performance.

In summary, duties of indebtedness, commitment, reparation, need-fulfillment, and reciprocation are necessarily correlated with other people's *in personam* rights. Duties of respect and community membership are necessarily correlated with other people's *in rem* rights, negative in the case of duties of respect, positive in the case of duties of community membership. Finally, duties of status, duties of

obedience, and duties of compelling appropriateness are not necessarily correlated with other people's rights.

II. RIGHTS AS CLAIMS TO . . .

Having described the various kinds of duties that *are* correlated with rights, have
we thereby done all that is necessary to elucidate the concept of a right? Many
writers seem to think so. I am inclined, however, to agree with Richard Wasserstrom that we have not until we have said something further about rights as
claims. It will not help to attempt a formal definition of rights in terms of claims,
for the idea of a right is already included in that of a claim, and we would fall
into a circle. Nevertheless, certain facts about rights, more easily, if not solely,
expressible in the language of claims and claiming, are necessary to a full understanding of what rights are and why they are so vitally important.

There may at first sight be grounds for holding that claims are always *against*
someone, and therefore necessarily correlated with the duties of those against
whom they hold; but there is a sense of "claim," closely related to "need," in
which this is not always so. Imagine a hungry, sickly, fatherless infant, one of a
dozen children of a desperately impoverished and illiterate mother in a squalid
Mexican slum. Doesn't this child have a *claim* to be fed, to be given medical care,
to be taught to read? Can't we know this before we have any idea where correlative duties lie? Won't we still believe it even if we despair of finding anyone whose
duty it is to provide these things? Indeed, if we do finally *assign* the duty to someone, I suspect we would do so because there *is* this prior claim, looking, so to
speak, for a duty to go with it.

In our time it is commonplace to speak of *needs* as "constituting claims."
William James thought that every interest is a kind of claim against the world
and that the validity of an interest *qua* claim lies "in its mere existence as a matter of fact." This probably goes too far. We don't think of every desire or even
every need as a claim, but important needs are another matter. They "cry out,"
we say, for satisfaction. (Note the etymological connection of "claim" with
"clamor.") And when they cry no proper name but only their own need, we
speak of their claims "against the world"; but this is but a rhetorical way of saying "claim against no one at all." (Or perhaps a "claim against the world" is like
an explosion in the desert—there is no one to hear it, but were anyone to get
close to it what a commotion he would hear, and what an impact he would feel!
So it is perhaps with my little Mexican urchin. Perhaps her claim is like a "permanent possibility of sensation," real enough, though no one comes within its
range. Still note what one does hear, if he is not morally deaf, when he comes
close enough: He hears a *crying need,* a claim *to* . . . that is so strong it may be
felt as a claim *against.* . . .)

The right to education, like other positive *in rem* rights peculiar to twentieth-
century manifestos, has caused much confusion and dissension, partly because

theorists, in their eagerness to provide schematic translations for all rights in terms of other people's duties, have simply overlooked the sense of "right" uppermost in the minds of manifesto writers. Professor Brandt, for instance, says of "my having a right to an education" that it "implies roughly that each individual in my community has an obligation to do what he can [in another formulation Brandt says "to cooperate substantially"] in view of his opportunities and capacities and other obligations, to secure and maintain a system in which I and persons in my position are provided with an opportunity for education." But surely there is a familiar sense of "right" that requires more than that others try, or "do what they can" (considering of course how *busy* they all are) or "cooperate substantially." My right in this sense is *to* the education (there is that preposition again in still a fourth sense) and not simply to other people's dutiful efforts. More likely my right in this case (if I have one) entails not simply a duty to try but a responsibility to succeed; but even this doesn't do the whole job of translation, for there is a *must have* here not wholly translatable into any number of *must do's*.*

III. CLAIMING THAT ONE HAS A RIGHT

I wish finally to emphasize the importance of the verb "to claim," not to the analysis of a right, but to an understanding of why rights are, in Wasserstrom's phrase, such "valuable commodities." To claim that one has a right (or for that matter that one has any of the other things one might claim—knowledge, ability, whatever) is to *assert* in such a manner as to demand or insist that what is asserted be *recognized*. It is my contention that for every right there is a further right to claim, in appropriate circumstances, that one has that right. Why is the right to demand recognition of one's rights so important? The reason, I think, is that if one begged, pleaded, or prayed for recognition merely, at best one would receive a kind of beneficent treatment easily confused with the acknowledgment of rights, but in fact altogether foreign and deadly to it.

There are in general two quite distinct kinds of moral transaction. On the one hand there are gifts and services and favors motivated by love or pity or mercy and for which gratitude is the sole fitting response. On the other hand there are dutiful actions and omissions called for by the rights of other people. These can be demanded, claimed, insisted upon, without embarrassment or shame. When not forthcoming, the appropriate reaction is indignation; and when duly done there is no place for gratitude, an expression of which would suggest that it is not

---

*No doubt this is an extended sense of "right." I insist only that it is a proper and important one. Note that there are parallel extended senses of "claim" and "demand" both in quite general circulation. Webster's gives as its fourth sense of "demand," for example, "to call for or require as necessary or useful; to be in urgent need of, as in the phrase 'the case demands care.'" It is in this sense, *at the very least,* that children require education, sickness calls for medicine, and hunger demands food.

simply one's own or one's due that one was given.* Both kinds of transaction are important, and any world with one but not the other would—in Wasserstrom's phrase—be "morally impoverished." A world without loving favors would be cold and dangerous; a world full of kindness, but without universal rights, would be one in which self-respect would be rare and difficult. Too much gratitude is a very bad thing, leading donors to be complacent and hypocritical, and doing worse harm still to the recipients. If the rugged individualist who boasts in his blindness that he owes nothing to any man is no moral paragon, neither is he who feels gratitude for everything, for that is a kind of self-abasement; and from men who respect not their own interests nor feel even their most basic needs as claims, little good, and probably considerable mischief, can be anticipated.

DISCUSSION QUESTIONS

1. Does Feinberg consider duties to be absolute or *prima facie*? To what extent do the duties discussed by Feinberg match the *prima facie* duties listed by Ross? Are there any duties listed by Feinberg that Ross omitted from his list? Discuss whether Ross would agree that most of these duties have corresponding rights.
2. Feinberg believes that natural rights are essential for ensuring respect for human dignity and for ensuring that people are able to take responsibility for their lives. Do you agree?
3. Would Feinberg concur with the rights listed in the "Universal Declaration of Human Rights"? Discuss which duties are associated with each of the rights listed in the Declaration.
4. Discuss how Feinberg might respond to Gutierrez's statement that liberation is one of the fundamental rights.
5. Are there instances when one person's claiming a right unduly restricts the life choices of others? For example, do people have a duty to stay off other people's private property in societies where the ownership of property is concentrated in the hands of a few people? Discuss how Locke, Marx, and Gutierrez, respectively, would each be most likely respond to these question.
6. Would Kant agree with Feinberg that duties are, by their nature, coercive? Support your answer.
7. Do people have a right to an education? How does Feinberg answer this question? Do you agree with his answer? Would Jeane Kirkpatrick agree with Feinberg regarding the existence of a right to education?
8. Why, according to Feinberg, is a concept of universal moral rights essential in an adequate moral theory? What would the world be like without rights?

---

*The obverse of this point is worth noting too. Gratitude often *is* the appropriate response to a person's deliberate *failure* to press for his rights. I quote from a perceptive editorial in *The New Yorker* (June 3, 1961, p. 23): ". . . Conceivably it is in the national interest to persuade Negro leaders to set a slower pace, but the argument is one that does not permit a high moral tone. One can hardly, with justice, inform a Negro that he has a duty as a citizen to refrain from sharing in the rights of citizenship. We can imagine asking it, under special circumstances, but only as the immense favor that it would be, rather than as the obligation it certainly is not."

Chapter Applications

1. *Property Rights and the Yanomami Indians of the Amazon Rain Forests*

Increased mining and logging in the Amazon rain forests of Brazil and Venezuela have resulted in poverty as well as epidemics among the indigenous population. In addition, more than 70 percent of the indigenous population do not own title to the land on which they live, leaving them vulnerable to outside developers.

On November 15, 1991, Brazilian President Fernando Collor de Mello signed a decree legally protecting 36,000 square miles of the Amazon rain forest for the Yanomami Indians. Environmental Defense Fund scientist Dr. Stephen Schwartzman applauded the president's action: "Brazil has shown the world that it is a responsible global citizen, and that 'development at any price' no longer wins all arguments. When will the U.S. be able to say as much?"[1]

However, the decree did not end the Yanomami's troubles. Miners and other developers protested the decree. On August 15, 1993, about fifty Yanomami men, women, and children were massacred by gold miners with machetes.[2]

On April 22, 1994, the Yanomami and other members of the Union of Indian Nations (UIN) drafted a statement to the Brazilian authorities in which they expressed concern both about the survival of the Indian culture in Brazil and the denial of the fundamental rights of Indians. Their concerns went mostly unheeded. The following year, 400 Amazon Indians were forcibly evacuated from their lands in order to clear the way for a hydroelectric dam.

Groups of Yanomami are currently traveling around the world, visiting universities and churches as well as governmental and environmental agencies, trying to gain support for their cause.

Discussion Questions

1. Do the Yanomami Indians have a moral right to the land they now occupy? Discuss how Locke might answer this question. Would Locke have answered differently if the Yanomami were involved in developing the land rather than living off the land?

2. Is the fact that most of the Yanomami do not legally own the land morally relevant? Support your answer.

3. Do you agree with Schwartzman that the United States values "development at any price"? Is this a good policy?

4. Gustavo Gutierrez argues that society has a duty to defend the rights of those who are most oppressed. Would Gutierrez consider the Yanomami to be an oppressed people with a "right to liberation"? What policy might he suggest regarding the rights of the Yanomami Indians?

5. Discuss the concerns and rights of the Yanomami Indians in light of the "Universal Declaration of Human Rights."

6. How might Jeane Kirkpatrick respond if a group of Yanomami Indians approached her with their concerns? Discuss whether the rights they are demanding are based on reasonable expectations or if they are more like writing a letter to Santa Claus.

7. One of the primary reasons the rain forests are being cleared is to raise beef cattle for the U.S. market. If the Yanomami Indians have a right to their land, does this create a duty for you to stop eating beef?

2. *Campus Speech Codes:* **Doe v. University of Michigan**

In recent years several campuses in the United States have created speech codes. One of the most restrictive of these codes was at the University of Michigan. Their policy forbid all conduct that "stigmatizes or victimizes" students on the basis of "race, ethnicity, religion, sex and sexual orientation."[3] The University of Michigan code was created to cut down on the increasing frequency of racist, sexist, and other forms of "hate" speech. According to the court records:

> On January 27, 1987, unknown persons distributed a flier declaring "open season" on blacks which it referred to as "saucer lips, porch monkeys, and jigaboos." On February 4, 1987, a student disc jockey at an on-campus radio station allowed racist jokes to be broadcast. At a demonstration protesting these incidents, a Ku Klux Klan uniform was displayed from a dormitory window.[4]

Fearful that he would be charged as being sexist under the new speech code, a suit was brought against the university by a psychology teaching assistant who wanted to discuss the mental differences between men and women and how this difference might influence their career choices. Known only as John Doe, he argued that the speech code violated his First Amendment right to freedom of speech.

History Professor C. Vann Woodward supported Doe. Woodward noted:

> It simply seems unnatural to make a fuss about the rights of a speaker who offends the moral or political convictions passionately held by a majority. The far more natural impulse is to stop the nonsense, shut it up, punish it—anything but defend it. But to give rein to that inclination would be to make the majority the arbiters of truth for all. Furthermore, it would put the universities into the business of censorship.[5]

John Doe won his suit against the University of Michigan. The federal district court concluded that although it was "sympathetic to the University's obligation to ensure equal educational opportunities for all of its students, such efforts must not be at the expense of free speech."

Discussion Questions

1. Freedom of speech is highly valued in our society. However, are there any moral limits to the freedom of speech? Discuss the nature of these limits.

2. Do we have a right not to be offended? How might Jeane Kirkpatrick respond to this question?

3. How should *offensive* be defined? If there is a right not to be offended, how do we know when we have trampled on this right? Is there an objective criterion or should we rely on people's subjective feelings? If students claim that they feel offended by, let's say, the use of "he" rather than "he or she" in a textbook, is that sufficient to create a duty in the professor not to use that text? Support your answer.

4. Discuss how you could redraft the University of Michigan's speech code so that it did not infringe on the freedom of speech of students and faculty.

3. Vigilante Justice

For years the residents of the Dictionary Hill area of Spring Hills, California, had been terrorized by 48-year-old John Harper, Jr., with his reckless driving, threats, rock throwing, and running their cars off the road. He would often aim his car at pedestrians, including children, and other cars as though he was going to hit them.

The neighbors had repeatedly called the police to try to get them to put Harper in jail or to stop his threatening behavior. But the system had failed to protect them. In fact, Harper had only received a probationary sentence for intentionally ramming into a woman's car. When Harper, just hours later and smug in his victory, told one of his neighbors, retired Navy Commander Danny Palm, that "you and your family are as good as dead," Palm snapped. He shot an unarmed Harper thirteen times with a .45-caliber pistol as Harper sat in his car after returning to Dictionary Hill.

For the killing, Palm was sentenced to six years for manslaughter and another four years for a firearms conviction. During Palm's trial, Judge Mudd, who presided over the case, stated that "occasionally in the real world victims bring about their own death. The victim [Harper] set the wheels in motion for his own death but it was not a legal killing or a justifiable killing."[6]

Although Palm's neighbors felt the sentence was too harsh, Harper's relatives protested Mudd's decision, arguing that Palm was a cold-blooded murderer who did not have the right to be their son's "judge, jury and executioner."[7]

Discussion Questions

1. According to John Locke, people living in a state of nature, without a social contract or the benefit of civil government, have a right to punish transgressors. What if there is civil government but it is ineffective in protecting the people? If the social contract breaks down, or a person perceives it to be so, does the right to punish the transgressor once again revert to the victims?

2. Is vigilante justice ever morally justified in the United States? Discuss the issue of vigilante justice in light of the above case.

3. When, if ever, is it morally permissible to kill another person? Although Palm's killing Harper wasn't legal, was it morally justified?

4. Should Palm be punished for killing Harper? What purpose, if any, would punishment serve in this case? Discuss how you would have ruled had you been the judge in the murder trial.

4. Forcing the Homeless into Shelters

An estimated 50,000 homeless people live in New York City alone. Four years ago, 59-year-old Nellie Smith had lost her job as a nurse as a result of downsizing. A few months later her husband abandoned her, leaving her with no means of support. Her two children, a daughter in college and her lawyer son, wanted nothing to do with her. Smith was evicted from her apartment, and for the past three years she has been living on the streets of New York. Smith avoided shelters because she was afraid of having her few remaining possessions stolen while she slept.

In January, Mayor Koch ordered the police to remove homeless people from the streets on severely cold nights and place them in hospitals or shelters. Smith refused to go. The police handcuffed her, strapped her to a stretcher, and took her to a hospital for a psychiatric evaluation. After three days, she was released and allowed to return to the streets.

"Anyone who refused to go into a shelter when it is this cold out must be mentally ill," one of the police officers said in defense of his action. "It's the duty of the state to look out for the welfare of its citizens. We did what was best for her."

Nancy Potter, a social worker who runs a program for the homeless, agreed with the officers' decision. She cited the example of a homeless woman living in a cardboard box who had died of hypothermia while city officials were trying to get a court order to place her in a shelter. "We have been seeing people," Potter told a reporter, "die with their rights on."[8]

The New York Civil Liberties Union countered that although a small percentage of the homeless may be mentally disturbed, this does not justify an across-the-board rule forcing them into shelters. "Many are competent," argued William Levin, one of their staff lawyers, "and have devised ways to cope with the cold."

"The real civil liberties issue here is not the one raised by those very few who are being taken to the hospitals against their will," Levin added. "It's the ever-increasing number of people who have no safe and decent place to sleep at night."

Discussion Questions

1. Do we have a right to engage in activities that might lead to our death? Who has the right to make the decision that we are no longer competent to act in our best interests? Does the state have a moral obligation to act on our behalf when we are endangering ourselves?

2. Some people argue that the term *mentally ill* often means "inconvenient." How should we decide who is mentally competent and who is merely regarded by some as a nuisance? Is it fair to assume that people who are mentally ill cannot or should not be allowed to make decisions about their lives, such as sleeping in the streets when it is very cold?

3. Do people have a welfare right to decent housing even if they can't afford to pay for it? On the other hand, do people have a right to the use of property produced by someone else's labor? Discuss how Marx and Locke would each respond to these questions. What public policy might each philosopher suggest for dealing with homelessness?

4. Most philosophers, such as Kant, Confucius, and Feinberg, maintain that rights are based on other people's duties. Does Smith have a right to expect her adult children to care for her? Are her children being remiss in their duty? How might each of these philosophers respond to these questions? Discuss the answer in light of your own family.

5. *The Nest Egg That Went to the Birds: When Environment and Human Rights Conflict*

When 74-year-old Margaret Rector of Austin, Texas, tried to sell a 15-acre parcel of land that she had purchased in 1973 to raise funds for her retirement, she discovered that the land was home to two species of rare birds that were protected by the Endangered Species Act. The land, which had been ideal for development, was now almost worthless on the market. To make matters worse, Rector still had to pay property taxes on the land.

"At present," the disappointed Rector says, "I'd say there are hundreds of families in the 33 counties around Austin who, like me, are unable to sell land that may be set aside for a habitat."[9] Rector and her neighbors are only a few of many angry property owners in the United States whose land has been impacted in the name of conservation of the environment.

There are currently more than 450 local organizations across the country that are fighting the takeover of private lands, as well the restriction of grazing and lumbering on public lands by environmental protection groups. These organizations have a sympathetic ally in the U.S. Supreme Court. In 1992, for example, the Court ruled in favor of the owner of two South Carolina beachfront lots and against the coastal council which wanted to restrict development in the area in order to prevent beach erosion.

Rector agrees with the Supreme Court's position regarding the protection of private property rights. Although she says that she's 100 percent in favor of environmental conservation, she is "disturbed that protecting the environment has, for many, come to mean Federal control. I'm convinced that it is the private landowners who have kept the land beautiful. They are perfectly capable of protecting the environment."[10]

Discussion Questions

1. Locke assumed that the environment and other species existed solely to serve human needs. Discuss how this assumption is reflected in our Constitution. Can this assumption be morally justified in the modern world, or should our Constitution and laws regarding private ownership be revamped to take into consideration the rights of nonhumans and the environment?

2. Do nonhuman animals and the environment have rights? If so, what is the source and nature of these rights? Do nonhuman animals and the environment have rights independently of humans, or do they only have rights to the extent that humans benefit from environmental and wildlife conservation? Support your answer.

3. Do you agree with Rector that private landowners are "perfectly capable of protecting the environment"? Use the above case study and other relevant examples to illustrate your answer.

4. Discuss the solution a non-Western philosopher such as Eagle Man (Chapter 4) might suggest to resolve the conflict between personal property rights and the rights of nonhumans and the environment. Compare and contrast Eagle Man's solution with that of Lockean rights ethicists.

6. Gays in the Military: "Don't Ask, Don't Tell"

The U.S. policy on homosexuals in the military is summed up in the 1993 statement "Don't ask, don't tell."[11] Under this policy, applicants will not be asked about their sexual orientation. However, they can be discharged for homosexual conduct.[12]

As a protest against this policy, several colleges—including MIT and Yale University—have demanded that the Reserve Officer Training Corps (ROTC) be banned from their campuses until the military changes its policy. It is discriminatory, they argue, to have different standards for homosexuals and for heterosexuals. In response, Congress in February 1996 passed the ROTC Campus Access Act, which cut off all Department of Defense funding to campuses that banned ROTC.[13]

The Young American's Foundation, which actively worked to get the act passed, applauds this move by Congress. They claim that banning ROTC on campuses unfairly discriminates against ROTC cadets and denies students the right to participate in ROTC programs on their campuses.[14] The ban also discriminates against poorer students because ROTC has historically assisted economically disadvantaged students in attending college.

Discussion Questions

1. Discuss the arguments for and against banning ROTC. What and whose rights are at stake? How might this conflict of rights be resolved? Was the ban the best way to oppose the "don't ask, don't tell" policy? What would you have done if you were the president of MIT or Yale?

2. Although the U.S. Constitution does not recognize it as a legal right, the freedom to be open about our sexual orientation may still be a moral right. Is the freedom to be open about sexual orientation essential for ensuring self-respect and a sense of dignity? How might Joel Feinberg answer this question?

3. In *Meinhold v. US Department of Defense,* the Court upheld the Navy's action in discharging Keith Meinhold after he stated on television, "Yes, I am gay." The Court ruled that openly declaring one's sexual orientation demonstrates "a concrete, fixed, or expressed desire to commit homosexual acts despite their being prohibited."[15] Opponents of the decision argued that it is irrational to assume that because a person is open about their homosexuality that they will engage in homosexual actions while in the military.[16] Do you agree? Why is it important in a moral argument that arguments be based on rational premises? Use the arguments in the above court case to illustrate your answer.

4. Some natural law ethicists argue that homosexuality is immoral because it is abnormal, unnatural, and perverse. Do you agree? What is the relationship, if any, between an action being natural or normal and an action being morally acceptable?

5. Some argue that allowing gays in the military infringes on the privacy rights of heterosexuals, especially when it comes to housing. Women are housed in separate quarters because they have a right not to have their bodies looked at in a sexual manner by men. Do heterosexual men and women, likewise, have a right not to be looked at in a sexual manner by homosexuals? Does a right to privacy necessarily preclude allowing gay people in the military?

NOTES

[1]Statement of the Environmental Defense Fund, November 21, 1991.

[2]August 28, 1993, Interpress Third World News Agency.

[3]*Doe v. University of Michigan,* 721 F. Supp. 852 (E. D. Mich. 1989).

[4]*Doe v. University of Michigan,* 721 F. Supp. 852 (E. D. Mich. 1989).

[5]*The New York Times,* October 15, 1986, p. A27.

[6]Tony Perry, "Charge Reduced in Bully's Death Courts," *Los Angeles Times,* April 18, 1997.

[7]Ibid.

[8]David Margolick, "Weighing the Risks and Rights of Homelessness," *The New York Times,* December 8, 1985.

[9]John H. Ingersoll, "A Delicate Balance: Can Doing What's Right for the Environment Threaten Our Personal Property Rights?" *Country Living,* February 1995, p. 84.

[10]Ibid.

[11]10 USCA s. 654(b).

[12]See "Don't Ask, Don't Tell": Homosexuals and the Military," *Congressional Digest,* November 1996, 75(11): 262.

[13]"MIT Tries a New Approach in the Battle over ROTC," *The Chronicle of Higher Education,* May 31, 1996, 42(38): A23(1).

[14]"Foundation, ROTC Students Defeat Campus Leftists," *Liberatus,* 17(2), March/April 1996.

[15]*Meinhold v. US Department of Defense,* 34 F 3d 1469 at 1479 (9th Cir. 1994).

[16]For more on legal cases involving the sexual orientation and the military, see Robert Wintemute, *Sexual Orientation and Human Rights* (Oxford, England: Clarendon Press, 1995), pp. 78–83.

CHAPTER NINE

Virtue Ethics

Virtue in a man will be the disposition which (a) makes him a good man, and (b) enables him to perform his function well.

Aristotle, *Nicomachean Ethics*

In recent years there has been a reaction against moral theories that focus on duty at the expense of character development. Virtue ethics emphasizes *right being* over *right action*. According to virtue ethicists, our character—or the sort of person we are—is more important than the rules or principles we follow.

This is not to say that actions are unimportant. One of the hallmarks of virtuous people is that they give us an example to follow. However, although virtue involves right actions, it cannot be reduced to right actions. Being virtuous also involves the cultivation of the good will. A person who is virtuous acts from good intentions.

Virtue ethics is not an alternative to ethical theories that stress right conduct, such as utilitarianism and deontological theories. Rather, virtue ethics and theories of right action complement each other. Almost all moral theories contain a strand of virtue ethics. Even utilitarianism, the most action-oriented theory, maintains that it is important to cultivate a virtuous character because people who are virtuous are more likely to act in ways that benefit themselves and others, and to refrain from harming themselves and others.

The ancient Greek ethicists, like most Eastern ethicists, focused primarily on virtue and character, rather than on duty and principles. In the first reading, from the *Nicomachean Ethics*, Aristotle discusses the nature of virtue as well as how people become more virtuous. Like Confucius, Aristotle argues that virtue usually entails finding the mean.

Confucian ethics also emphasizes virtue (*jen*). The selections from Confucius's *Doctrine of the Mean* are similar in many respects to Aristotle's teachings on virtue.

The Buddhist lifestyle involves an attitude of compassion for all living beings, not just humans or rational beings. P. Don Premasiri argues that the moral discipline contained in the Buddhist Noble Eightfold Path offers guidance for being virtuous in contemporary society. In his essay "The Relevance of the Noble

Eightfold Path to Contemporary Society," Premasiri describes a way of living based on the Buddhist concept of virtue.

The selections from *The Instruction of Ptahhotep,* a list of moral maxims from ancient Egypt, illustrates the universality of the concept of virtue.

In the next selection from *An Enquiry Concerning the Principles of Morals,* David Hume explores the roles of reason and sentiment in morality and virtue. Unlike Aristotle and Confucius, he concludes that virtue is based on sentiment rather than reason.

The sixth selection is from Nel Noddings's book, *Caring: A Feminine Approach to Ethics and Moral Education.* Like Hume, Noddings emphasizes moral sentiment over reason.

The final selection is from Alasdair MacIntyre's book *After Virtue.* In this selection, MacIntyre urges the reader to return to a concept of human nature that is based on virtue rather than duty.

Aristotle

Nicomachean Ethics

Aristotle (384–322 B.C.E.) has had a profound influence on Western philosophers. Aristotle believed that living the good life—a life of virtue—is our most important activity as humans. The purpose of studying ethics is to become good. Aristotle believed that humans are so constituted as to be able to know and understand the world. Language, he thought, embodies certain intuitions about the world.

Aristotle takes as his starting point the assumption that no one can be completely wrong. From here he searches for the grain of truth in people's views about morality and the world by subjecting these views to rigorous analysis. In the following selection from his *Nicomachean Ethics,* Aristotle begins by asking how we use the term "good." He then goes on to explore the relationship between the good and happiness. In asking these questions, Aristotle ponders the nature of humans. He then attempts to define more clearly what he means by a moral virtue and to explain how people can become more virtuous. (Comments in italic are made by the translator, J. A. K. Thomson.)

CRITICAL THINKING QUESTIONS

1. How does Aristotle go about analyzing the term *good?*
2. How does Aristotle define *happiness* or *eudaenomia?* Is *eudaenomia* a feeling, or is it a more wholistic concept?
3. What is the connection between virtue and happiness?
4. What is Aristotle's view of human nature? What does Aristotle mean by the function of humans?
5. What is the source of morality?
6. What is virtue? What are the two kinds of virtue?
7. What does Aristotle mean by habituation? What does habituation have to do with becoming virtuous?
8. Is performing just acts, in Aristotle's view, sufficient for being a morally good person?
9. What does Aristotle mean when he says that the agent "must 'will' his action and will it for its own sake"?
10. What sort of disposition does a virtuous person have?

Nicomachean Ethics, from *The Ethics of Aristotle* translated by J. A. K. Thomson (Baltimore: Penguin Books, 1953), pp. 25–26; 28–31; 35–39; 55–59; 61–67. Some notes have been omitted.

11. Are virtues and vices feelings? According to Aristotle, what is the difference between a feeling and a disposition? Should a person, according to Aristotle, be held morally responsible for how he or she feels?

12. What is excellence? According to Aristotle, how is excellence related to our function as humans? What is the relation between virtue and excellence?

13. What does Aristotle mean when he says that "goodness is the quality that hits the mean"? Is virtue always a matter of hitting the mean?

14. What are some examples of moral virtues?

15. What does Aristotle mean by an excess or deficiency when it comes to virtue? What are some examples of vices that are excesses or deficiencies?

Book One

Aristotle begins, in a way characteristic of his method, with a generalization which, if accepted, will lead to a more exact account of his subject. It is a generalization which is fundamental to his philosophy and in his own mind there is no doubt about the truth of it. Yet he is not at this point asserting its truth. He is content to state a position which he has found reason to hold. It may be defined in some such words as these. The good is that at which all things aim. *If we are to understand this, we must form to ourselves a clear notion of what is meant by an aim or, in more technical language, an "end." The first chapter of the* Ethics *is concerned with making the notion clear.*

CHAPTER I

It is thought that every activity, artistic or scientific, in fact every deliberate action or pursuit, has for its object the attainment of some good. We may therefore assent to the view which has been expressed that "the good" is "that at which all things aim."* Since modes of action involving the practised hand and the instructed brain are numerous, the number of their ends is proportionately large. For instance, the end of medical science is health; of military science, victory; of economic science, wealth. All skills of that kind which come under a single "faculty"—a skill in making bridles or any other part of a horse's gear comes under

---

*It is of course obvious that to a certain extent they do not all aim at the same thing, for in some cases the end will be an activity, in others the product which goes beyond the actual activity. In the arts which aim at results of this kind the results or products are intrinsically superior to the activities.

the faculty or art of horsemanship, whole horsemanship itself and every branch of military practice comes under the art of war, and in like manner other arts and techniques are subordinate to yet others—in all these the ends of the master arts are to be preferred to those of the subordinate skills, for it is the former that provide the motive for pursuing the latter.

CHAPTER II

Now if there is an end which as moral agents we seek for its own sake, and which is the cause of our seeking all the other ends—if we are not to go on choosing one act for the sake of another, thus landing ourselves in an infinite progression with the result that desire will be frustrated and ineffectual—it is clear that this must be the good, that is the absolutely good. May we not then argue from this that a knowledge of the good is a great advantage to us in the conduct of our lives? Are we not more likely to hit the mark if we have a target? If this be true, we must do our best to get at least a rough idea of what the good really is, and which of the sciences, pure or applied, is concerned with the business of achieving it. . . .

Let us resume our consideration of what is the end of political science. For want of a better word we call it "Happiness." People are agreed on the word but not on its meaning.

CHAPTER IV

To resume. Since every activity involving some acquired skill or some moral decision aims at some good, what do we take to be the end of politics—what is the supreme good attainable in our actions? Well, so far as the name goes there is pretty general agreement. "It is happiness," say both intellectuals and the unsophisticated, meaning by "happiness" living well or faring well. But when it comes to saying in what happiness consists, opinions differ and the account given by the generality of mankind is not at all like that given by the philosophers. The masses take it to be something plain and tangible, like pleasure or money or social standing. Some maintain that it is one of these, some that it is another, and the same man will change his opinion about it more than once. When he has caught an illness he will say that it is health, and when he is hard up he will say that it is money. Conscious that they are out of their depths in such discussions, most people are impressed by anyone who pontificates and says something that is over their heads. Now it would no doubt be a waste of time to examine all these opinions; enough if we consider those which are most in evidence or have something to be said for them. Among these we shall have to discuss the view held by some that, over and above particular goods like those I have just mentioned, there is another which is good in itself and the cause of whatever goodness there is in all these others. . . .

A man's way of life may afford a clue to his genuine views upon the nature of happiness. It is therefore worth our while to glance at the different types of life.

CHAPTER V

... There is a general assumption that the manner of a man's life is a clue to what he on reflection regards as the good—in other words happiness. Persons of low tastes (always in the majority) hold that it is pleasure. Accordingly they ask for nothing better than the sort of life which consists in having a good time. (I have in mind the three well-known types of life—that just mentioned, that of the man of affairs, that of the philosophic student.) The utter vulgarity of the herd of men comes out in their preference for the sort of existence a cow leads. Their view would hardly get a respectful hearing, were it not that those who occupy great positions sympathize with a monster of sensuality like Sardanapalus. The gentleman, however, and the man of affairs identify the good with honour, which may fairly be described as the end which men pursue in political or public life. Yet honour is surely too superficial a thing to be the good we are seeking. Honour depends more on those who confer than on him who receives it, and we cannot but feel that the good is something personal and almost inseparable from its possessor. Again, why do men seek honour? Surely in order to confirm the favourable opinion they have formed of themselves. It is at all events by intelligent men who know them personally that they seek to be honoured. And for what? For their moral qualities. The inference is clear; public men prefer virtue to honour. It might therefore seem reasonable to suppose that virtue rather than honour is the end pursued in the life of the public servant. But clearly even virtue cannot be quite the end. It is possible, most people think, to possess virtue while you are asleep, to possess it without acting under its influence during any portion of one's life. Besides, the virtuous man may meet with the most atrocious luck or ill-treatment; and nobody, who was not arguing for argument's sake, would maintain that a man with an existence of that sort was "happy." The third type of life is the "contemplative," and this we shall discuss later.

As for the life of the business man, it does not give him much freedom of action. Besides, wealth obviously is not the good we seek, for the sole purpose it serves is to provide the means of getting something else. So far as that goes, the ends we have already mentioned would have a better title to be considered the good, for they are desired on their own account. But in fact even their claim must be disallowed. We may say that they have furnished the ground for many arguments, and leave the matter at that. . . .

> What then is the good? If it is what all men in the last resort aim at, it must be happiness. And that for two reasons: (1) happiness is everything it needs to be, (2) it has everything it needs to have.

CHAPTER VII

From this digression we may return to the good which is the object of our search. What is it? The question must be asked because good seems to vary with the art or pursuit in which it appears. It is one thing in medicine and another in strategy, and so in the other branches of human skill. We must enquire, then, what is the good which is the end common to all of them. Shall we say it is that for the sake of which everything else is done? In medicine this is health, in military science victory, in architecture a building, and so on—different ends in different arts; every consciously directed activity has an end for the sake of which everything that it does is done. This end may be described as its good. Consequently, if there be some one thing which is the end of all things consciously done, this will be the doable good; or, if there be more than one end, then it will be all of these. Thus the ground on which our argument proceeds is shifted, but the conclusion arrived at is the same.

I must try, however, to make my meaning clearer.

In our actions we aim at more ends than one—that seems to be certain—but, since we choose some (wealth, for example, or flutes and tools or instruments generally) as means to something else, it is clear that not all of them are ends in the full sense of the word, whereas the good, that is the supreme good, is surely such an end. Assuming then that there is some one thing which alone is an end beyond which there are no further ends, we may call *that* the good of which we are in search. If there be more than one such final end, the good will be that end which has the highest degree of finality. An object pursued for its own sake possesses a higher degree of finality than one pursued with an eye to something else. A corollary to that is that a thing which is never chosen as a means to some remoter object has a higher degree of finality than things which are chosen both as ends in themselves and as means to such ends. We may conclude, then, that something which is always chosen for its own sake and never for the sake of something else is without qualification a final end.

Now happiness more than anything else appears to be just such an end, for we always choose it for its own sake and never for the sake of some other thing. It is different with honour, pleasure, intelligence and good qualities generally. We choose them indeed for their own sake in the sense that we should be glad to have them irrespective of any advantage which might accrue from them. But we also choose them for the sake of our happiness in the belief that they will be instrumental in promoting that. On the other hand nobody chooses happiness as a means of achieving them or anything else whatsoever than just happiness.

The same conclusion would seem to follow from another consideration. It is a generally accepted view that the final good is self-sufficient. By "self-sufficient" is meant not what is sufficient of oneself living the life of a solitary but includes parents, wife and children, friends and fellow-citizens in general. For man is a social animal. A self-sufficient thing, then, we take to be one which on its own footing tends to make life desirable and lacking in nothing. And we regard happiness as such a thing. Add to this that we regard it as the most desirable of all things without having it counted in with some other desirable thing. For, if such an addition were possible, clearly we should regard it as more desirable when even the smallest advantage was added to it. For the result would be an increase in the number of advantages, and the larger sum of advantages is preferable to the smaller.

Happiness then, the end to which all our conscious acts are directed, is found to be something final and self-sufficient.

But we desire a clearer definition of happiness. The way to this may be prepared by a discussion of what is meant by the "function" of a man.

But no doubt people will say, "To call happiness the highest good is a truism. We want a more distinct account of what it is." We might arrive at this if we could grasp what is meant by the "function" of a human being. If we take a flautist or a sculptor or any craftsman—in fact any class of men at all who have some special job or profession—we find that his special talent and excellence comes out in that job, and this is his function. The same thing will be true of man simply as man—that is of course if "man" does have a function. But is it likely that joiners and shoemakers have certain functions or specialized activities, while man as such has none but has been left by Nature a functionless being? Seeing that eye and hand and foot and every one of our members has some obvious function, must we not believe that in like manner a human being has a function over and above these particular functions? Then what exactly is it? The mere act of living is not peculiar to man—we find it even in the vegetable kingdom—and what we are looking for is something peculiar to him. We must therefore exclude from our definition the life that manifests itself in mere nurture and growth. A step higher should come the life that is confined to experiencing sensations. But that we see is shared by horses, cows and the brute creation as a whole. We are left, then, with a life concerning which we can make two statements. First, it belongs to the rational part of man. Secondly, it finds expression in actions. The rational part may be either active or passive: passive in so far as it follows the dictates of reason, active in so far as it possesses and exercises the power of reasoning. A similar distinction can be drawn within the rational life; that is to say, the reasonable element in it may be active or passive. Let us take it that what we are concerned with here is the reasoning power in action, for it will be generally allowed that when we speak of "reasoning" we really mean *exercising* our reasoning faculties. (This seems the more correct use of the word.) Now let us assume for the moment the truth of the following propositions. (*a*) The function of a man is the exercise of his noncorporeal faculties or "soul" in accordance with, or at least not divorced from, a rational principle. (*b*) The function of an individual and of a *good* individual in the same class—a harp player, for example, and a good harp player, and so through the classes—is generically the same, except that we must add superiority in accomplishment to the function, the function of the harp player being merely to play on the harp, while the function of the good harp player is to play on it well. (*c*) The function of man is a certain form of life, namely an activity of the soul exercised in combination with a rational principle or reasonable ground of action. (*d*) The function of a good man is to exert such activity well. (*e*) A function is performed well when performed in accordance with the excellence proper to it.—If these assumptions are granted, we conclude that the good for man is "an activity of soul in accordance with goodness" or (on the supposition that there may be more than one form of goodness) "in accordance with the best and most complete form of goodness."

Happiness is more than momentary bliss.

There is another condition of happiness; it cannot be achieved in less than a complete lifetime. One swallow does not make a summer; neither does one fine day. And one day, or indeed any brief period of felicity, does not make a man entirely and perfectly happy. . . .

Book Two

This book is the first of a series (II–V) dealing with the moral virtues. But first we have to ask what moral virtue or goodness is. It is a confirmed disposition to act rightly, the disposition being itself formed by a continuous series of right actions.

CHAPTER I

Virtue, then, is of two kinds, intellectual and moral. Of these the intellectual is in the main indebted to teaching for its production and growth, and this calls for time and experience. Moral goodness, on the other hand, is the child of habit, from which it has got its very name, ethics being derived from *ethos*, "habit," by a slight alteration in the quantity of the *e*. This is an indication that none of the moral virtues is implanted in us by nature, since nothing that nature creates can be taught by habit to change the direction of its development. For instance a stone, the natural tendency of which is to fall down, could never, however often you threw it up in the air, be trained to go in that direction. No more can you train fire to burn downwards. Nothing in fact, if the law of its being is to behave in one way, can be habituated to behave in another. The moral virtues, then, are produced in us neither *by* Nature nor *against* Nature. Nature, indeed, prepares in us the ground for their reception, but their complete formation is the product of habit.

Consider again these powers or faculties with which Nature endows us. We acquire the ability to use them before we do use them. The senses provide us with a good illustration of this truth. We have not acquired the sense of sight from repeated acts of seeing, or the sense of hearing from repeated acts of hearing. It is the other way round. We had these senses before we used them, we did not acquire them as a result of using them. But the moral virtues we do acquire by first exercising them. The same is true of the arts and crafts in general. The craftsman has to learn how to make things, but he learns in the process of making them. So men become builders by building, harp players by playing the harp. By a similar process we become just by performing just actions, temperate by performing temperate actions, brave by performing brave actions. Look at what happens in political societies—it confirms our view. We find legislators seeking to make good men of their fellows by making good behaviour habitual with them. That is the aim of every lawgiver, and when he is unable to carry it out effectively, he is a failure; nay, success or failure in this is what makes the difference between a good constitution and a bad.

Again, the creation and the destruction of any virtue are effected by identical causes and identical means; and this may be said, too, of every art. It is as a result of playing the harp that harpers become good or bad in their art. The same is true of builders and all other craftsmen. Men will become good builders as a result of building well, and bad builders as a result of building badly. Otherwise what would be the use of having anyone to teach a trade? Craftsmen would all be born either good or bad. Now this holds also of the virtues. It is in the course of our dealings with our fellow-men that we become just or unjust. It is our behaviour in a crisis and our habitual reactions to danger that make us brave or cowardly, as it may be. So with our desires and passions. Some men are made temperate and gentle, others profligate and passionate, the former by conducting themselves in one way, the latter by conducting themselves in another, in situations in which their feelings are involved. We may sum it all up in the generalization, "Like activities produce like dispositions." This makes it our duty to see that our activities have the right character, since the differences of quality in them are repeated in the dispositions that follow in their train. So it is a matter of real importance whether our early education confirms us in one set of habits or another. It would be nearer the truth to say that it makes a very great difference indeed, in fact all the difference in the world.

If, then, everything depends upon the way in which we act, clearly it is incumbent on us to enquire what this way is, never forgetting that we must not look for the precision attainable in the exact sciences.

CHAPTER II

Since the branch of philosophy on which we are at present engaged differs from the others in not being a subject of merely intellectual interest—I mean we are not concerned to know what goodness essentially is, but how we are to become good men, for this alone gives the study its practical value—we must apply our minds to the solution of the problems of conduct. For, as I remarked, it is our actions that determine our dispositions.

. . .

After this reminder Aristotle proceeds to lay down a proposition or generalization which is cardinal in his system of ethics. Excess or deficiency in his actions impairs the moral quality of the agent.

Let us begin with the following observation. It is in the nature of moral qualities that they can be destroyed by deficiency on the one hand and excess on the other. We can see this in the instances of bodily health and strength. Physical strength is destroyed by too much and also by too little exercise. Similarly health is ruined by eating and drinking either too much or too little, while it is produced, increased and preserved by taking the right quantity of drink and victuals. Well, it is the same with temperance, courage, and the other virtues. The man who shuns and fears everything and can stand up to nothing becomes a coward. The man who is afraid of nothing at all, but marches up to every danger, becomes foolhardy. In the same way the man who indulges in every pleasure without refraining from a single one becomes incontinent. If, on the other hand, a man behaves like the Boor in comedy and turns his back on every pleasure, he will find his sensibilities becoming blunted. So also temperance and courage are destroyed both by excess and deficiency, and they are kept alive by observance of the mean.

Our virtues are employed in the same kinds of action as established them.

Let us go back to our statement that the virtues are produced and fostered as a result, and by the agency, of actions of the same quality as effect their destruction. It is also true that after the virtues have been formed they find expression in actions of that kind. We may see this in a concrete instance—bodily strength. It results from taking plenty of nourishment and going in for hard training, and it is the strong man who is best fitted to cope with such conditions. So with the virtues. It is by refraining from pleasures that we become temperate, and it is when we have become temperate that we are most able to abstain from pleasures. Or take courage. It is by habituating ourselves to make light of alarming situations and to confront them that we become brave, and it is when we have become brave that we shall be most able to face an alarming situation.

There is one way of discovering whether we are in full possession of a virtue or not. We possess it if we feel pleasure in its exercise; indeed, it is just with pleasures and pains that virtue is concerned.

CHAPTER III

We may use the pleasure (or pain) that accompanies the exercise of our dispositions as an index of how far they have established themselves. A man is temperate who abstaining from bodily pleasures finds this abstinence pleasant; if he finds it irksome, he is intemperate. Again, it is the man who encounters danger gladly, or at least without painful sensations, who is brave; the man who has these sensations is a coward. In a word, moral virtue has to do with pains and pleasures. . . .

Aristotle now meets an obvious objection: How can a man perform (say) just actions unless he is already just?

CHAPTER IV

A difficulty, however, may be raised as to what we mean when we say that we must perform just actions if we are to become just, and temperate actions if we are to be temperate. It may be argued that, if I do what is just and temperate, I am just and temperate already, exactly as, if I spell words or play music correctly, I must already be literate or musical. This I take to be a false analogy, even in the arts. It is possible to spell a word right by accident or because some-body tips you the answer. But you will be a scholar only if your spelling is done as a scholar does it, that is thanks to the scholarship in your own mind. Nor will the suggested analogy with the arts bear scrutiny. A work of art is good or bad in itself—let it possess a certain quality, and that is all we ask of it. But vir-tuous actions are not done in a virtuous—a just or temperate—way merely because *they* have the appropriate quality. The *doer* must be in a certain frame of mind when he does them. Three conditions are involved. (1) The agent must act in full consciousness of what he is doing. (2) He must "will" his action, and will it for its own sake. (3) The act must proceed from a fixed and unchange-able disposition. Now these requirements, if we except mere knowledge, are not counted among the necessary qualifications of an artist. For the acquisition of virtue, on the other hand, knowledge is of little or no value, but the other requirements are of immense, of sovran, importance, since it is the repeated performance of just and temperate actions that produces virtue. Actions, to be sure, are *called* just and temperate when they are such as a just or temperate man would do. But the doer is just or temperate not because he does such things but when he does them in the way of just and temperate persons. It is therefore quite fair to say that a man becomes just by the performance of just, and temperate by the performance of temperate, actions; nor is there the small-est likelihood of a man's becoming good by any other course of conduct. It is not, however, a popular line to take, most men preferring theory to practice under the impression that arguing about morals proves them to be philoso-phers, and that in this way they will turn out to be fine characters. Herein they resemble invalids, who listen carefully to all the doctor says but do not carry out a single one of his orders. The bodies of such people will never respond to treatment—nor will the souls of such "philosophers."

> It is now time to produce a formal definition of virtue. In the Aristotelean system this means stating its genus and differentia—that is to say, the class of things to which it belongs and the point or points which distinguish it from other members of the class.

CHAPTER V

We now come to the formal definition of virtue. Note first, however, that the human soul is conditioned in three ways. It may have (1) feelings, (2) capacities, (3) dispositions; so virtue must be one of these three. By "feelings" I mean desire, anger, fear, daring, envy, gratification, friendliness, hatred, longing, jealousy, pity and in general all states of mind that are attended by pleasure or pain. By "capac-ities" I mean those faculties in virtue of which we may be described as capable of the feelings in question—anger, for instance, or pain, or pity. By "dispositions" I mean states of mind in virtue of which we are well or ill disposed in respect of the feelings concerned. We have, for instance, a bad disposition where angry feelings are concerned if we are disposed to become excessively or insufficiently angry, and a good disposition in this respect if we consistently feel the due amount of anger, which comes between these extremes. So with the other feelings.

Now, neither the virtues nor the vices are feelings. We are not spoken of as good or bad in respect of our feelings but of our virtues and vices. Neither are we praised or blamed for the way we feel. A man is not praised for being frightened or angry, nor is he blamed just for being angry; it is for being angry in a particular way. But we *are* praised and blamed for our virtues and vices. Again, feeling angry or frightened is something we can't help, but our virtues are in a manner expressions of our will; at any rate there is an element of will in their formation. Finally, we are said to be "moved" when our feelings are affected, but when it is a question of moral goodness or badness we are not said to be "moved" but to be "disposed" in a particular way. A similar line of reasoning will prove that the virtues and vices are not capacities either. We are not spoken of as good or bad, nor are we praised or blamed, merely because we are *capable* of feeling. Again, what capacities we have, we have by nature; but it is not nature that makes us good or bad. . . . So, if the virtues are neither feelings nor capacities, it remains that they must be dispositions. . . .

> We have now to state the "differentia" of virtue. Virtue is a disposition; but how are we to distinguish it from other dispositions? We may say that it is such a disposition as enables the good man to perform his function well. And he performs it well when he avoids the extremes and chooses the mean in actions and feelings.

CHAPTER VI

It is not, however, enough to give this account of the *genus* of virtue—that it is a disposition; we must describe its *species*. Let us begin, then, with this proposition. Excellence of whatever kind affects that of which it is the excellence in two ways. (1) It produces a good state in it. (2) It enables it to perform its function well. Take eyesight. The goodness of your eye is not only that which makes your eye good, it is also that which makes it function well. Or take the case of a horse. The goodness of a horse makes him a good horse, but it also makes him good at running, carrying a rider and facing the enemy. Our proposition, then, seems to be true, and it enables us to say that virtue in a man will be the disposition which (*a*) makes him a good man, (*b*) enables him to perform his function well. We have already touched on this point, but more light will be thrown upon it if we consider what is the specific nature of virtue. . . .

Every form, then, of applied knowledge, when it performs its function well, looks to the mean and works to the standard set by that. It is because people feel this that they apply the *cliché,* "You couldn't add anything to it or take anything from it" to an artistic masterpiece, the implication being that too much and too little alike destroy perfection, while the mean preserves it. Now if this be so, and if it be true, as we say, that good craftsmen work to the standard of the mean, then, since goodness like nature is more exact and of a higher character than any art, it follows that goodness is the quality that hits the mean. By "goodness" I mean goodness of moral character, since it is moral goodness that deals with feelings and actions, and it is in them that we find excess, deficiency and a mean. It is possible, for example, to experience fear, boldness, desire, anger, pity, and pleasures and pains generally, too much or too little or to the right amount. If we feel them too much or too little, we are wrong. But to have these feelings at the right times on the right occasions towards the right people for the right motive and in the right way is to have them in the right measure, that is somewhere between the extremes; and this is what characterizes goodness. The same may be said of the mean and extremes in actions. Now it is in the field of actions and feelings that goodness operates; in them we find excess, deficiency and, between them, the mean, the first two being wrong, the mean right and praised as such.* Goodness, then, is a mean condition in the sense that it aims at and hits the mean.

Consider, too, that it is possible to go wrong in more ways than one. (In Pythagorean terminology evil is a form of the Unlimited, good of the Limited.) But there is only one way of being right. That is why going wrong is easy, and going right difficult; it is easy to miss the bull's eye and difficult to hit it. Here, then, is another explanation of why the too much and the too little are connected with evil and the mean with good. As the poet says,

> Goodness is one, evil is multiform.

We are now in a position to state our definition of virtue with more precision. Observe that the kind of virtue meant here is moral, not intellectual, and that Aristotle must not be taken as saying that the kind of virtue which he regards as the highest and truest is any sort of mean.

We may now define virtue as a disposition of the soul in which, when it has to choose among actions and feelings, it observes the mean relative to us, this being determined by such a rule or principle as would take shape in the mind of a man of sense or practical wisdom. We call it a mean condition as lying between two forms of badness, one being excess and the other deficiency; and also for this reason, that, whereas badness either falls short of or exceeds the right measure in feelings and actions, virtue discovers the mean and deliberately chooses it. Thus, looked at from the point of view of its essence as embodied in its definition, virtue no doubt is a mean; judged by the standard of what is right and best, it is an extreme.

Aristotle enters a caution. Though we have said that virtue observes the mean in actions and passions, we do not say this of all acts and all feelings. Some are essentially evil and, when these are involved, our rule of applying the mean cannot be brought into operation.

But choice of a mean is not possible in every action or every feeling. The very names of some have an immediate connotation of evil. Such are malice, shamelessness, envy among feelings, and among actions adultery, theft, murder. All these and more like them have a bad name as being evil in themselves; it is not

---

*Being right or successful and being praised are both indicative of excellence.

merely the excess or deficiency of them that we censure. In their case, then, it is impossible to act rightly; whatever we do is wrong. Nor do circumstances make any difference in the rightness or wrongness of them. When a man commits adultery there is no point in asking whether it is with the right woman or at the right time or in the right way, for to do anything like that is simply wrong. It would amount to claiming that there is a mean and excess and defect in unjust or cowardly or intemperate actions. If such a thing were possible, we should find ourselves with a mean quantity of excess, a mean of deficiency, an excess of excess and a deficiency of deficiency. But just as in temperance and justice there can be no mean or excess or deficiency, because the mean in a sense *is* an extreme, so there can be no mean or excess or deficiency in those vicious actions—however done, they are wrong. Putting the matter into general language, we may say that there is no mean in the extremes, and no extreme in the mean, to be observed by anybody. . . .

DISCUSSION QUESTIONS

1. Do you agree with Aristotle that every act and inquiry aims at some good (goal)? Is there really a single end toward which all human behavior is directed? Discuss this question in light of your own experience as well as modern findings regarding human behavior.
2. Are you satisfied with Aristotle's analysis of human nature and the function of humans? Do all humans have the same function, as he claims? Support your answer.
3. How does Aristotle justify the distinction he makes between humans and nonhuman animals? Are you satisfied with his argument?
4. Is Aristotle's definition of *happiness* or *eudaenomia* consistent with your notion of happiness? If not, in what ways do the definitions differ? Can we experience *eudaenomia* and not know it? Why, according to Aristotle, can't children and non-human animals experience *eudaenomia*?
5. Is reason essential for a virtuous character, as Aristotle claims? Does the good life necessarily have to be a rationally ordered life? Support your answer.
6. What evidence is there for Aristotle's division of the soul or psyche into two parts? How does Aristotle justify this division? Is this division a useful distinction or is it problematic?
7. Do you agree with Aristotle that the main purpose of ethics education is to help us become good or virtuous people? Should this be the primary goal for a college ethics course? If so, how should the ethics class be structured to reflect this goal?
8. What is the difference between Aristotle's moral philosophy and cultural relativism? Is habituation the same as cultural conditioning? Discuss how Aristotle's concept of the function of a human differs from that of cultural relativist Ruth Benedict.
9. Is Aristotle a consequentialist like the utilitarians? What, according to the utilitarians and Aristotle, respectively, is the relation between performing just acts and being a just person?
10. Do you agree with Aristotle that moral virtues are the result of habituation rather than being innate? Would James Q. Wilson and Mencius agree? Is it easier for some people to become virtuous? Support your answers.

11. According to Aristotle, living the good life entails working at being a more virtuous person. We can't just say "I am who I am—take me as I am." In what ways do you try to become more virtuous?

12. What is your strongest virtue? Is this virtue an example of a mean between excess and deficit? Explain.

13. Can altruism be a vice? Discuss sociobiologist E. O. Wilson's concept of altruism in light of Aristotle's doctrine of the mean.

14. Compare and contrast Aristotle's idea of the unity of virtue with Jesus's teaching that we shall know people by their fruits (Matthew 7:16).

Confucius

The Doctrine of the Mean

The Doctrine of the Mean is found in Eastern as well as in Western philosophies. According to this doctrine, virtue, in general, entails moderation or seeking the middle path. The most thorough explanation of the Doctrine of the Mean, however, is found in the philosophies of Aristotle and Confucius. For Confucius, the mean is what is consistent with harmony and equilibrium or the Way (*Tao*).

Confucius (551 B.C.E.–479 B.C.E.), as we noted earlier, is one of the foremost Chinese philosophers. The virtuous or superior person, according to Confucius, puts duty first.

CRITICAL THINKING QUESTIONS

1. What does Confucius mean by a state of harmony or equilibrium?
2. What, according to Confucius, is the Doctrine of the Mean?
3. What is the relation between harmony and seeking the mean?
4. What is the source of the Doctrine of the Mean?
5. What does Confucius mean by "the superior man"?
6. What is the principle of reciprocity?
7. How does Confucius describe the virtue of benevolence?
8. What are the five duties of universal obligation and what are the virtues associated with these duties?
9. Are virtues, according to Confucius, relative to the individual or to culture? Or, are they universally binding?
10. Why is sincerity important? What is the connection between sincerity and self-completion?

The Doctrine of the Mean, in *The Chinese Classics,* translated by James Legge (Shanghai: The Chinese Book Company, 1891).

CHAPTER I

. . .

4. While there are no stirrings of pleasure, anger, sorrow, or joy, the mind may be said to be in the state of *equilibrium*. When those feelings have been stirred, and they act in their due degree, there ensues what may be called the state of *harmony*. This *equilibrium* is the great root *from which grow all the human actings* in the world, and this *harmony* is the universal path *which they all should pursue.*

5. Let the states of equilibrium and harmony exist in perfection, and a happy order will prevail throughout heaven and earth, and all things will be nourished and flourish.

CHAPTER II

1. Chung-nî said, "The superior man *embodies* the course of the Mean; the mean man acts contrary to the course of the Mean.

2. "The superior man's embodying the course of the Mean is because he is a superior man, and so always maintains the Mean. The mean man's acting contrary to the course of the Mean is because he is a mean man, and has no caution."

CHAPTER III

The Master said, "Perfect is the virtue which is according to the Mean! Rare have they long been among the people, who could practice it!"

CHAPTER IV

1. The Master said, "I know how it is that the path *of the Mean* is not walked in:—The knowing go beyond it, and the stupid do not come up to it. I know how it is that the path of the Mean is not understood:—The men of talents and virtue go beyond it, and the worthless do not come up to it.

2. "There is no body but eats and drinks. But they are few who can distinguish flavors."

. . .

CHAPTER VI

The Master said, "There was Shun:—He indeed was greatly wise! Shun loved to question *others,* and to study their words, though they might be shallow. He concealed what was bad *in them,* and displayed what was good. He took hold of their two extremes, *determined* the Mean, and employed it in *his government* of the people. It was by this that he was Shun!"

. . .

CHAPTER VIII

The Master said, "This was the manner of Hûi:—he made choice of the Mean, and whenever he got hold of what was good, he clasped it firmly, as if wearing it on his breast, and did not lose it."

. . .

CHAPTER X

1. Tsze-lû asked about energy.
2. The Master said, "Do you mean the energy of the South, the energy of the North, or the energy which you should cultivate yourself?
3. "To show forbearance and gentleness in teaching others; and not to revenge unreasonable conduct:—this is the energy of southern regions, and the good man makes it his study.
4. "To lie under arms; and meet death without regret:—this is the energy of northern regions, and the forceful make it their study.
5. "Therefore, the superior man cultivates *a friendly* harmony, without being weak.—How firm is he in his energy! He stands erect in the middle, without inclining to either side.—How firm is he in his energy! When good principles prevail in the government of his country, he does not change from what he was in retirement.—How firm is he in his energy! When bad principles prevail in the country, he maintains his course to death without changing.—How firm is he in his energy!"

. . .

CHAPTER XIII

. . .

3. "When one cultivates to the utmost the principles of his nature, and exercises them on the principle of reciprocity, he is not far from the path. What you do not like when done to yourself, do not do to others.

. . .

5. The Master said, "In archery we have something like the way of the superior man. When the archer misses the center of the target, he turns around and seeks for the cause of his failure in himself."

. . .

CHAPTER XX

. . .

5. "Benevolence is *the characteristic element of* humanity, and the great exercise of it is in loving relatives. Righteousness is *the accordance of actions with what is* right, and the great exercise of it is in honoring the worthy. The decreasing measures of the love due to relatives, and the steps in the honor due to the worthy, are produced by *the principle of* propriety.

6. "When those in inferior situations do not possess the confidence of their superiors, they cannot retain the government of the people.

. . .

8. "The duties of universal obligation are five, and the virtues wherewith they are practiced are three. The duties are those between sovereign and minister, between father and son, between husband and wife, between elder brother and younger, and those belonging to the intercourse of friends. Those five are the duties of universal obligation. Knowledge, magnanimity, and energy, these three, are the virtues universally binding. And the means by which they carry *the duties* into practice is singleness.

9. "Some are born with the knowledge *of those duties;* some know them by study; and some acquire the knowledge after a painful feeling of their ignorance. But the knowledge being possessed, it comes to the same thing. Some practice them with a natural ease; some from a desire for their advantages; and some by strenuous effort. But the achievement being made, it comes to the same thing."

. . .

18. "Sincerity is the way of Heaven. The attainment of sincerity is the way of men. He who possesses sincerity is he who, without an effort, hits what is

right, and apprehends, without the exercise of thought;—he is the sage who naturally and easily embodies the *right* way. He who attains to sincerity is he who chooses what is good, and firmly holds it fast.

19. "To this attainment there are requisite the extensive study of what is good, accurate inquiry about it, careful reflection on it, the clear discrimination of it, and the earnest practice of it.

. . .

CHAPTER XXI

When we have intelligence resulting from sincerity, this condition is to be ascribed to nature; when we have sincerity resulting from intelligence, this condition is to be ascribed to instruction. But given the sincerity, and there shall be the intelligence; given the intelligence, and there shall be the sincerity.

. . .

CHAPTER XXV

1. Sincerity is that whereby self-completion is effected, and *its* way is that by which man must direct himself.

2. Sincerity is the end and beginning of things; without sincerity there would be nothing. On this account, the superior man regards the attainment of sincerity as the most excellent thing.

3. The possessor of sincerity does not merely accomplish the self-completion of himself. With this quality he completes *other men and* things *also.* The completing himself *shows his* perfect virtue. The completing *other men and* things *shows his* knowledge. *Both these are* virtues belonging to the nature, and *this is* the way by which a union is effected of the external and internal. Therefore, whenever he—*the entirely sincere man*—employs them,—*that is, these virtues,*—*their action will be* right.

. . .

CHAPTER XXVII

. . .

5. Hence it is said, "Only by perfect virtue can the perfect path, in all its courses, be made a fact."

6. Therefore, the superior man honors his virtuous nature, and maintains constant inquiry and study, seeking to carry it out to its breadth and greatness, so as to omit none of the more exquisite and minute points which it embraces, and to raise it to its greatest height and brilliancy, so as to pursue the course of the Mean. He cherishes his old knowledge, and is continually acquiring new. He exerts an honest, generous earnestness, in the esteem and practice of all propriety.

DISCUSSION QUESTIONS

1. According to Confucius, which is most important in the achievement of harmony and virtue—reason or sentiment? Support your answer. Would Aristotle agree with Confucius?
2. Compare and contrast Confucius's Doctrine of the Mean with Aristotle's.
3. Discuss how, according to Confucius, we become more virtuous people. Compare and contrast this with Aristotle's concept of habituation.
4. Does Confucius argue that it is easier for some people to achieve virtue than others? Explain.
5. Compare Confucius's principle of reciprocity—"What you do not like when done to yourself, do not do to others"—to Kant's categorical imperative and the biblical Golden Rule. How does the Doctrine of the Mean help us to live by this principle?
6. Compare and contrast Confucius's use of the term *benevolence* with the utilitarian notion of benevolence as acting in ways that tend to maximize pleasure for the greatest number.
7. Why, according to Confucius, should we seek to become more virtuous people? What does Confucius mean when he says that "sincerity is that whereby self-completion is effected"? How does this reflect his views about the nature of man and society? Do you agree with Confucius?

P. Don Premasiri

The Relevance of the Noble Eightfold Path to Contemporary Society

Buddhist moral philosopher P. Don Premasiri is a philosophy professor at the University of Peradeniya in Sri Lanka. Like Aristotle and Confucius, Premasiri denounces the extremes of excessive indulgence and self-mortification or denial. For Buddha, the path of liberation—the life of virtue and inner tranquility—entails taking the Middle Path, also known as the Noble Path or the Eightfold Path. This Path involves not only caring about other humans but avoiding harm to all living beings.

CRITICAL THINKING QUESTIONS

1. What is the Middle or Noble Eightfold Path?
2. What was the source of Buddha's teaching about the Middle Path?
3. What, according to Buddhists, is the source of immorality in society? How is this illustrated in contemporary society?
4. What is the greatest moral virtue in Buddhism? Why is it the greatest virtue? What are the fruits of this virtue?
5. What does Buddha mean by "right views"? What are some of the "wrong" views? Why does Buddha reject these views?
6. What is the moral law of *kamma*? How does it assist us in leading a virtuous life?
7. What is the role of free will and determinism in Buddhist virtue ethics?
8. What is the importance of reason and the mental life in Buddhist moral philosophy?
9. What does right speech entail? What does right action entail?
10. What does Buddha mean by "right livelihood"?
11. What are the last three steps of the Eightfold Path? Why are these steps important in achieving moral growth?

"The Relevance of the Noble Eightfold Path to Contemporary Society," in Charles Wei-hsun Fu and Sandra A. Wawrytko, eds., *Buddhist Ethics and Modern Society* (New York: Greenwood Press, 1991), pp. 134–139. Notes have been omitted.

The Buddha characterized his path of liberation as the Middle Way in the context of the two principal ways of life known to him at that time. One way of life, as described by the Buddha in his first sermon, was the life of excessive indulgence in sense pleasures (*kāmasukhallikānuyoga*). The other was the life of self-mortification (*attakilamathānuyoga*). These were judged by the Buddha to be two extremes, while the Middle Path was presented as the fourth Noble Truth of his teaching. The prescribed way for the attainment of the Buddhist goal is the cessation of misery (*dukkhanirodha*) and the attainment of perfect peace, tranquility, and happiness (*Nibbāna*).

Those who study the Buddhist doctrine, as well as professed Buddhists, have often focused attention on claims about the efficacy of the path to bring about the cessation of the miseries of the individual. But there is another important aspect to this path which has not been dealt with, although it is implicit in the Buddha's teaching. Buddhism traces the miseries of the individual to spiritual deficiency, implying that an individual's deficiency in spirituality not only causes suffering for the individual, but also creates suffering for others. It is in terms of this aspect of the Buddha's teaching that we can see its contemporary relevance. To evaluate the contemporary relevance of the Buddha's Noble Path, it is important to examine the nature of the present human condition.

THE CONTEMPORARY HUMAN CONDITION

In many respects the present age cannot be compared with Buddha's time. Today, human beings have made enormous progress in scientific knowledge. They have increased their knowledge about the nature of their own physical existence and the nature of their physical environment. With this increased theoretical knowledge, their technological capabilities to control and manipulate the physical environment have increased correspondingly. There is no doubt that we are making rapid and ongoing progress in the areas of scientific knowledge and technological skill. However, reflection on another aspect of our contemporary situation makes it evident that no corresponding progress has been achieved in practical wisdom. All the progress humanity has made appears to be endangered by the very technological skills that humans have achieved. We live in an age in which the evils that humans inflict on others have reached unparalleled extremes of barbarism. The horrendous sufferings inflicted on human beings inhabiting this planet by fellow human beings, with their advanced scientific and technological skills, far exceed the sufferings brought about by natural disasters.

According to Buddhism, society can never be totally free of immorality and the resulting tensions and conflicts, for the predominant factors that generally govern human behavior, untutored by spiritual nurture and impelled purely by the baser instincts of human nature, are greed, hatred, and confusion. Buddhism considers these three psychological dispositions to be the roots of evil and human misery. Scientific progress has not made it possible for humanity to overcome these roots. Consequently, we are placed in a more precarious predicament when the discoveries and inventions based on our own intelligence threaten us with destruction.

Since the end of the Second World War, more than one hundred major wars have been fought in more than sixty countries and territories, while more than sixteen million people have perished. More civilians have been victimized by these wars than soldiers. The frequency of such wars also has increased over the years. Killing and violence are advocated, and sometimes materially supported, as a means to achieve the religious, ethnic, or political interests of factional groups. Each party to a conflict rationalizes the moral justification of violence on the basis of its own ends. Although most of these conflicts occur in the developing world, in most cases the major powers are involved either directly or indirectly.

Nations of the world are sharply divided both internationally and intranationally on the basis of political ideology and other narrow identities. While millions of people die throughout the world of starvation, and millions more are deprived of proper shelter and health care, technological skills and other material resources are increasingly diverted not to find ways and means of helping people to live, but to bring about their death and destruction. The International Labor Organization has estimated that with a 10 per cent reduction in world military expenditure, it would be possible to meet the basic needs of the developing countries in terms of food, health, and education. Technological progress has been utilized to feed human greed, with no limits set for human wants and patterns of consumption. Ecologists and environmental scientists foresee devastating effects from modern technology on the natural environment, as is now becoming apparent.

Associated with the above trends is a growth of other types of social evils, such as the spread of alcoholism and drug addiction. The younger generation, who have moved away from traditional religious values, appears to be seeking a new kind of salvation in the hallucinatory and escapist experiences evoked by alcohol and psychedelic drugs. This has resulted in a dulling of reason and intellect and a debilitation of sound judgment, contributing further to the growing trends of violence, insanity, and irresponsible behavior. . . .

Today, morality is often believed to belong to the sphere of the nonrational. This has given rise to an intellectual climate in which morality is seen as devoid of a rational foundation. It came to be believed that no universally acceptable standards of morality could be rationally discovered. Consequently, the possibility of moral knowledge and moral truth has been denied.

THE NOBLE EIGHTFOLD PATH
IN A CONTEMPORARY CONTEXT

Buddhism does not subscribe to this view. It believes that what is indispensable in the life of humanity is moral wisdom. Those who lack moral wisdom are said to be stupid and deluded (*mando, momuho*). Each step in the Noble Eightfold Path of the Buddha is characterized morally and evaluatively as "right" (*sammā*). This path is the quintessence of Buddhist morality, and its importance to Buddhism lies in the fact that it is one of the earliest formulations of the Buddhist way of life, and is accepted by all Buddhist schools of thought as an authentic formulation of the Buddha's original doctrine. This path of practical wisdom is described by the Buddha as producing vision (*cakkhukaraṇi*) and understanding (*ñāṇakaraṇi*), conducive to the attainment of higher knowledge (*abhiññā*), enlightenment (*sambodhi*), and peace or tranquility (*nibbāna*). In other words, it produces self-transforming knowledge leading to the eradication of immoral traits (*āsavakkhayañāṇa*), emancipating knowledge and insight (*vimuttiñāṇadassana*). When we think of the present human predicament in the context of our global community, the Buddha's Noble Eightfold Path appears to be more relevant today than at any other time in human history.

Buddhist teaching aims at overcoming human suffering in all its manifestations. Suffering occurs in the form of individual psychological problems and conflicts, often as a consequence of social problems and conflicts, such as unjust social and political institutions, social upheavals, and wars. According to the Buddhist assessment, the source of all such maladies is the corruption of the human mind, as rooted in ignorance and confusion. Social harmony, peace, and justice depend largely on the moral development of the individual members constituting a society. Where this is lacking, we enter the vicious circle of morally degenerate individuals and a corrupt social order. Moral progress must reduce the intensity of the roots of evil. Our contemporary situation amply testifies to the fact that, although we have progressed in material science and technology, there has been no improvement, but rather a regression, in the moral sphere. Technological skill devoid of moral consciousness leads only to more effective expressions of cruelty and viciousness.

Buddhism is primarily a practical philosophy, a way of life. It ignores abstract metaphysical theories and dogmas, and focuses on the immediate need to alleviate human misery. According to the Buddhist view, this suffering is largely the creation of the human mind. The Eightfold Path is the practical means for the elimination of misery caused by human moral depravity.

Right Views

Right views (*sammā diṭṭhi*) is the first step of the Noble Path, and there is an important reason why. It brings into focus the need for a wholesome ideological orientation or worldview, as a prerequisite for anyone who embarks on the search for the meaning of life and wishes to make intelligent choices regarding the way one ought to conduct oneself. However, the Buddhist notion of right views does not imply a dogmatic clinging to an ideological position. Attachment to a view (*diṭṭhi rāga*) is as much a hindrance to moral progress as attachment to a material thing. The Buddha cautioned his disciples against converting his teachings into a dogma. Dogmatic clinging to an ideology can create conflicts not only among those with a diversity of aims and interests, but also among those whose aims and interests are the same. Fanaticism and intolerance often result from the delusion that, "this alone is the truth and everything else is false" (*idam eva saccam mogham aññam*), causing people to commit atrocities in the name of "truth." This applies to any ideological commitment—religious, moral, or political.

. . . In the ideological sphere of conflicting views, Buddhism advocates rational persuasion for the resolution of disagreements. Any other approach will result, not in the resolution of problems, but in the brutalization of humanity. Hence, while cautioning people against taking ideology as incontrovertible dogma, Buddhism holds that a wholesome ideology should be the basis for the transformation not only of individuals, but of social organizations and institutions as well.

Human behavior usually is associated with a particular worldview, the value of which can be judged in terms of its consequences for the behavior of the person who holds it. The Buddha mentions two opposing worldviews dominant in his time. One was the doctrine of eternalism (*sassatavāda*), according to which there is an enduring entity that forms the essence of the individual. . . . The Buddha considered the belief that there is an enduring element of one's personality (*sakkāya-diṭṭhi*) as a root cause of evil that has to be eliminated. Buddhism traces egoism, selfishness, and lack of compassion to the notion of a permanent ego that erects a barrier between the self and the not self. During the Buddha's day, the practice of self-mortification and ascetic penance was a consequence of holding such metaphysical views of the nature of the self. The practice persists in our time in a different form. There are other dogmas, some bound up with metaphysical assumptions, for the sake of which people fanatically lay down their lives and call upon others to sacrifice themselves.

The other extreme rejected by Buddhism as an unhealthy, false view (*micchā-diṭṭhi*) is the doctrine of annihilationism (*ucchedavāda*). This has greater relevance to the contemporary social context, since it is the worldview promoted by material science. Undoubtedly, the adoption of certain methodological principles has made it possible for science to develop an area of human knowledge of great benefit to us. But scientists are not merely specialists, but generalists, and have a tendency to make absolute claims for the epistemological foundations of the natural sciences. They fail to realize that phenomena exist in the universe that cannot be explained by a materialistic methodology. Materialist assumptions engender a disregard for life after death, a view described by the Buddha as annihilationism. Annihilationism denies survival of the individual after death. According to Buddhism, this view leads to a lack of moral responsibility during a person's present life, and promotes an extremely materialistic and sensualist approach to life.

In contrast, Buddhism believes in personal survival after death, while the moral law of *kamma* is conducive to moral restraint. The materialist worldview is for Buddhism a life devoid of moral, spiritual, or religious concerns (*abrahmacariyāvāsa*). In the age of science it is felt that scientific humanism, which is essentially the adoption of a utilitarian norm coupled with the conviction that individual existence is limited to this life, is sufficient to guide human behavior. There is good reason to question this based on modern day experience. The Buddhist position is that human beings can be motivated to lead a moral life only if they can be urged to act on enlightened self-interest, especially in the initial stages

of their spiritual development. The belief in *kamma* and rebirth, and the prudential concept of merit (*puñña*) serves an important role in the moral life of the
Buddhist. The combination of *kamma* and *puñña* helps people resist the temptation to act on motives of greed and immediate material gain. . . .

. . . The Buddhist position recognizes the primacy of moral initiative in breaking the vicious circle of human suffering, whether viewed at the level of the individual or of society. Social and political institutions need the participation of
individuals performing a variety of roles to function effectively. Although valid
criticisms of institutional structures can be made from moral and other points of
view, the role that individual moral initiative and spiritual development play in
the effective functioning of institutions cannot be denied. To believe otherwise is
to uphold a kind of materialistic determinism that contradicts human experience.
Many organizational structures that appear very coherent at the level of theory
fail miserably when concretely implemented. Such failure occurs due to the lack
of a moral and spiritual basis in those persons on whom the effective functioning
of the theory depends.

Right Thought, Right Speech, and Right Action

Buddhism recognizes three modes in which evil dispositions are expressed in
behavioral terms: physical, verbal, and mental acts. Three steps of the Noble
Path, right thought (*sammā sankappa*), right speech (*sammā vācā*), and right
action (*sammā kammanta*), are specifically meant to prevent these evils. Buddhism attaches great significance to our mental life. Moral progress becomes possible only when a person acquires the ability to bring the mental processes under
the direction of the will. . . .

Methods and schemes of moral development recommended by Buddhism
appear to be based on an understanding of the mutual relationship between overt
behavior and psychological dispositions. Moral evil is believed to operate at the
dispositional level of the mind in the form of dormant and subconscious tendencies (*anusaya*). Such dispositional traits, deep-rooted in our psychological constitution, are believed to find expression in overt behavior in certain situations, and
these are themselves the products of certain repeated patterns of overt behavior.
Every verbal and bodily act creates a disposition toward repetition, thus contributing to the formation of a general pattern of behavior. Recognizing this fact,
Buddhism emphasizes the importance of cultivating right speech and right action.
Right speech consists first of avoiding false speech (*musā-vāda*), while cultivating
truthfulness and trustworthiness. Second, it involves avoiding slanderous speech
(*pisuṇāvācā*) intent on causing dissension among people, and cultivating speech
that heals divisiveness and strengthens the bonds of those already united in bonds
of friendship. Third, it involves the avoidance of harsh speech (*pharusāvacā*) and
the cultivation of pleasant speech. Fourth, it involves abstention from frivolous
or vain talk (*samphappalāpa*) and the cultivation of meaningful, purposeful, useful, and timely speech.

In right action (*sammā kammanta*), one is expected to abstain from injury to
life, from violence and acts of terrorism, laying aside all weapons that cause

injury to living beings. It also involves the positive cultivation of a mind filled with love and compassion, leading to compassionate action. Abstention from theft, fraudulent behavior, dishonesty, and abstention from sexual misconduct or the wrongful gratification of sensuous desires are also aspects of right action. *Sammā vācā* and *sammā kammanta* aim at the conscious and willed transformation of behavior patterns expressed through bodily and verbal action to hinder the continued feeding and nourishment of evil dispositions.

Right Livelihood

Another step in the noble Path that has considerable contemporary relevance is right livelihood (*sammā ājiva*). E. F. Schumacher asserts that the inclusion of right livelihood in the Buddhist Eightfold Path implies a Buddhist economics. He further argues that the Buddhist way of life conceived under right livelihood has great relevance for the contemporary human condition. In the life of the *bhikkhu, sammā ājiva* stands for the perfect purity of livelihood, devoted entirely to the pursuit of the ideal of sainthood (*arahatta*). At the level of the ordinary layperson, *sammā ājiva* draws attention to the necessity of adopting a morally acceptable means of livelihood and avoiding occupations that might be materially productive but morally reprehensible. These occupations include trading in weapons (*satthāvaṇijjā*), living beings (*sattavanijja*), flesh (*mamsavanijjā*), intoxicants or drugs (*majjavaṇijjā*) and poisons (*visavaṇijjā*). Almost all these forms of trade are practiced today on a global scale purely to satisfy commercial interests, without regard for their harmful social consequences. Most destructive of all is the trade in military weapons and addictive drugs. Commercial interests associated with excessive greed hinder responsible people from taking effective measures to prevent the miseries resulting from these social menaces. We have already reached the age of biological warfare, the most dangerous stage of trading in weapons and poisons. The Buddha's concept of *sammā ājiva* seems to be of greater relevance to this technological age than in the Buddha's own time.

Right Effort, Right Mindfulness, and Right Contemplation

The sixth step, right effort (*sammāvāyāma*) recommends initiative and effort to prevent the growth of evil dispositions, cultivate healthy attitudes, and stabilize the wholesome dispositions of character already acquired. The moral agent constantly experiences inner conflict when choosing between what is considered to be the right thing to do and what passions, emotions, instincts, and inclinations prompt us to do. Right effort is considered to be the most effective means of overcoming those natural impulses. As pointed out in our discussion of *sammā diṭṭhi,* right effort is possible only if one does not to resign oneself to external causes due to a false belief in fatalism or strict determination.

The seventh step, right mindfulness (*sammāsati*), stands for watchfulness over the overall functioning of one's personality, both mental and physical. Such alertness checks the excitement of evil tendencies. This type of mindfulness needs to be systematically cultivated, for the nature of the mind is to act recklessly on the promptings of passion and hatred.

The eighth step of the path, right contemplation (*sammā samādhi*), stands for the clear and composed mind that is a prerequisite for the understanding that leads to moral perfection. Right contemplation is no doubt much needed by contemporary humanity; we are constantly bombarded by a dizzying variety of sensuous stimuli from our material environment, driving us to the brink of insanity. Those who have had the unsettling experience of sensory overload and excessive sensuous gratification suffer subsequent spells of boredom and depression, leading them to seek solace in psychedelic drugs that promise temporary states of altered consciousness, rapture, or mental ecstasy. Unfortunately, they are forms of false contemplation (*micchā samādhi*), in sharp contrast to the *sammā samādhi* advocated by Buddhism for the attainment of emancipating or self-transforming wisdom.

According to the Buddhist teaching, an unsettled mind is the result of the operation of mental hindrances (*nivaraṇa*). A person who suffers from mental disturbances created by the *nivaraṇa* cannot have a clear vision, and consequently cannot act with understanding. Most human suffering, of which human volition itself is the cause, springs from the actions of people whose minds are confused. Confused minds seem to be operative at all levels of contemporary society, from the topmost levels of decision-making to the lowest levels in the social hierarchy. In Buddhist theory, moral corruption or moral growth tends to flow from higher levels of the social hierarchy to the lower levels. It is imperative that we entrust the guidance of the destinies of the world to individuals who have cultivated the kind of right contemplation that Buddhism prescribes in its Noble Path if we are to avert the global annihilation that ominously looms before us.

CONCLUSION

. . .

The Middle Path of the Buddha shows a way of attaining happiness by realizing the enormous spiritual potential of humanity. The search for happiness in material terms leaves humanity eternally empty, like a bottomless vessel into which things are continuously thrown. By exploring the inner sources of joy, the riches of the deeper spiritual potential of humanity, that vessel can be finally sealed. The way of life recommended in the Buddha's Middle Path advocates neither the extreme of asceticism nor that of austerity (*attakilamathānuyoaga*). Poverty is not to be valued nor is wealth to be devalued. The fault lies in the mental attitudes of greed, attachment, and egotism. To remedy these ills, humanity requires, above all else, spiritual discipline, as provided by the Noble Eightfold Path.

DISCUSSION QUESTIONS

1. Do you agree with Premasiri that contemporary society is on the wrong path? Support your answer.
2. Compare and contrast the Buddhist concept of the Middle Path with Aristotle's and Confucius's Doctrine of the Mean.

3. Premasiri argues that "the belief that morality belongs to the sphere of the non-rational" is one of the primary reasons for the prevalence of social evils today. What does Premasiri mean by this? Do you agree with him? Relate your answer to the popularity of ethical relativism in our culture.

4. What does Premasiri mean by "moral wisdom"? What does the term mean to you? Discuss whether Aristotle would agree with Premasiri that moral wisdom is one of the most important virtues.

5. Why, according to Premasiri, are egoism and a right or virtuous world view incompatible? Discuss how a Buddhist would respond to Ayn Rand's claim that egoism is the correct moral philosophy.

6. Do you agree with Premasiri that the moral law of *kamma* assists people in being virtuous? Are we being truly virtuous if our motive is to enhance our spiritual development or, in Christianity, to go to heaven?

7. In the United States, we tend to separate our private lives and our public lives. Would a Buddhist agree with this distinction? Discuss whether it is morally acceptable to think slanderous thoughts about others as long as we don't articulate these thoughts or act on them.

8. Why is the "right livelihood" important in leading a virtuous life? Do you agree with Premasiri that we ought to engage only in those occupations that do not cause harm to ourselves or other living beings? Discuss the extent to which the notion of right livelihood is important in your career choice.

The Instruction of Ptahhotep

Is virtue relative to culture? Although there is little doubt that philosophers and people in general disagree about which virtues are most important, most people around the world do agree on what a virtue is and what a vice is. No one, for example, regards cruelty as a virtue or honesty as a vice.

The following selection is from the ancient Egyptian writing, *The Instruction of the Ptahhotep*. The Vizier Ptahhotep was the mayor of a city during the Fifth Dynasty. This work, which is probably more than 3,000 years old, contains thirty-seven maxims that focus on the moral virtues. These virtues are universal and to be practiced by all people. The *ka* in Egyptian literature is roughly translated as "vitality" or the "vital force."

CRITICAL THINKING QUESTIONS

1. How, according to the Ptahhotep, does a virtuous person respond to a dispute?
2. How should we treat our family and friends?
3. Why is greed a vice and generosity a virtue?
4. What sort of disposition does a virtuous person have?

. . .

4. If you meet a disputant in action,
    A poor man, not your equal,
    Do not attack him because he is weak,
    Let him alone, he will confute himself.
    Do not answer him to relieve your heart,
    Do not vent yourself against your opponent,
    Wretched is he who injures a poor man,
    One will wish to do what you desire,
    You will beat him through the magistrates' reproof.

. . .

8. If you are a man of trust,
    Sent by one great man to another,

"The Instruction of Ptahhotep," in Miriam Lichtheim, *Ancient Egyptian Literature: A Book of Readings, Volume I: The Old and Middle Kingdoms* (Berkeley: University of California Press, 1973).

Adhere to the nature of him who sent you,
Give his message as he said it.
Guard against reviling speech,
Which embroils one great with another;
Keep to the truth, don't exceed it,
But an outburst should not be repeated.
Do not malign anyone,
Great or small, the ka abhors it.

. . .

19. If you want a perfect conduct,
     To be free from every evil,
     Guard against the vice of greed:
     A grievous sickness without cure,
     There is no treatment for it.
     It embroils fathers, mothers,
     And the brothers of the mother,
     It parts wife from husband;
     It is a compound of all evils,
     A bundle of all hateful things.
     That man endures whose rule is rightness,
     Who walks a straight line;
     He will make a will by it,
     The greedy has no tomb.

20. Do not be greedy in the division,
     Do not covet more than your share;
     Do not be greedy toward your kin,
     The mild has a greater claim than the harsh.
     Poor is he who shuns his kin,
     He is deprived of [interchange].
     Even a little of what is craved
     Turns a quarreler into an amiable man.

. . .

34. Be generous as long as you live,
     What leaves the storehouse does not return;
     It is the food to be shared which is coveted,
     One whose belly is empty is an accuser;
     One deprived becomes an opponent,
     Don't have him for a neighbor.
     Kindness is a man's memorial
     For the years after the function.

35. Know your helpers, then you prosper,
     Don't be mean toward your friends,
     They are one's watered field,
     And greater than one's riches,
     For what belongs to one belongs to another.

> *The character of a son-of-man is profit to him;*
> *Good nature is a memorial.*

36. *Punish firmly, chastise soundly,*
    Then repression of crime becomes an example;
    Punishment except for crime
    Turns the complainer into an enemy.

DISCUSSION QUESTIONS

1. Make a list of the virtues mentioned in the reading. Do you agree with the Ptahhotep that these virtues are universally binding? Or, are the virtues extolled by the Ptahhotep culturally relative?
2. Compare and contrast them to the virtues mentioned by Aristotle and Confucius. Are there any instances when what one person considers to be a virtue the other(s) consider it to be a vice?
3. Compare and contrast the concept of the *ka* in Egyptian literature to the Western concept of the good will or the conscience.
4. Do the moral maxims of the Ptahhotep offer practical guidance for modern living? Support your answer.
5. Compare and contrast the moral maxims of the Ptahhotep with those found in the readings from the *Bible*, *Qu'ran* and *Bhagavad Gita*.

David Hume

An Enquiry Concerning the Principles of Morals

Scottish philosopher David Hume (1711–1776) disagreed with the traditional view of virtue that emphasizes reason over sentiment. In the following selection, Hume examines whether reason or sentiment provides the general foundation of morals. He then goes on to discuss which virtues are the most important.

Hume died shortly after hearing that the American colonies had declared their independence—a move he enthusiastically endorsed.

CRITICAL THINKING QUESTIONS

1. According to Hume, what is the general foundation of morals?
2. What does Hume say is the role of reason in morality?
3. What is the relation between reason and passion in morality?
4. What argument does Hume offer against reason being the ultimate source of morality?
5. What is the goal of all moral speculation?
6. According to Hume, what moves us to take moral actions?
7. What are the two great social virtues?
8. What is the purpose of justice?
9. What does Hume mean by a "moral sense"?

OF THE GENERAL PRINCIPLES OF MORALS

133   Disputes with men, pertinaciously obstinate in their principles, are, of all others, the most irksome; except, perhaps, those with persons, entirely disingenuous, who really do not believe the opinions they defend, but engage in the controversy, from affectation, from a spirit of opposition, or

An Enquiry Concerning the Principles of Morals, reprinted from the 1777 edition (La Salle, IL: The Open Court Publishing Co., 1946), pp. 1–9.

from a desire of showing wit and ingenuity, superior to the rest of mankind. The same blind adherence to their own arguments is to be expected in both; the same contempt of their antagonists; and the same passionate vehemence, in inforcing sophistry and falsehood. And as reasoning is not the source, whence either disputant derives his tenets; it is in vain to expect, that any logic, which speaks not to the affections, will ever engage him to embrace sounder principles.

Those who have denied the reality of moral distinctions, may be ranked among the disingenuous disputants; nor is it conceivable, that any human creature could ever seriously believe, that all characters and actions were alike entitled to the affection and regard of everyone. The difference, which nature has placed between one man and another, is so wide, and this difference is still so much farther widened, by education, example, and habit, that, where the opposite extremes come at once under our apprehension, there is no scepticism so scrupulous, and scarce any assurance so determined, as absolutely to deny all distinction between them. Let a man's insensibility be ever so great, he must often be touched with the images of Right and Wrong; and let his prejudices be ever so obstinate, he must observe, that others are susceptible of like impressions. The only way, therefore, of converting an antagonist of this kind, is to leave him to himself. For, finding that nobody keeps up the controversy with him, it is probable he will, at last, of himself, from mere weariness, come over to the side of common sense and reason.

134   There has been a controversy started of late, much better worth examination, concerning the general foundation of Morals; whether they be derived from Reason, or from Sentiment; whether we attain the knowledge of them by a chain of argument and induction, or by an immediate feeling and finer internal sense; whether, like all sound judgement of truth and falsehood, they should be the same to every rational intelligent being; or whether, like the perception of beauty and deformity, they be founded entirely on the particular fabric and constitution of the human species.

The ancient philosophers, though they often affirm, that virtue is nothing but conformity to reason, yet, in general, seem to consider morals as deriving their existence from taste and sentiment. On the other hand, our modern enquirers, though they also talk much of the beauty of virtue, and deformity of vice, yet have commonly endeavoured to account for these distinctions by metaphysical reasonings, and by deductions from the most abstract principles of the understanding. Such confusion reigned in these subjects, that an opposition of the greatest consequence could prevail between one system and another, and even in the parts of almost each individual system; and yet nobody, till very lately, was ever sensible of it. The elegant Lord Shaftesbury, who first gave occasion to remark this distinction, and who, in general, adhered to the principles of the ancients, is not, himself, entirely free from the same confusion.

135   It must be acknowledged, that both sides of the question are susceptible of specious arguments. Moral distinctions, it may be said, are discernible by

pure *reason:* else, whence the many disputes that reign in common life, as well as in philosophy, with regard to this subject: the long chain of proofs often produced on both sides; the examples cited, the authorities appealed to, the analogies employed, the fallacies detected, the inferences drawn, and the several conclusions adjusted to their proper principles. Truth is disputable; not taste: what exists in the nature of things is the standard of our judgement; what each man feels within himself is the standard of sentiment. Propositions in geometry may be proved, systems in physics may be controverted; but the harmony of verse, the tenderness of passion, the brilliancy of wit, must give immediate pleasure. No man reasons concerning another's beauty; but frequently concerning the justice or injustice of his actions. In every criminal trial the first object of the prisoner is to disprove the facts alleged, and deny the actions imputed to him: the second to prove, that, even if these actions were real, they might be justified, as innocent and lawful. It is confessedly by deductions of the understanding, that the first point is ascertained: how can we suppose that a different faculty of the mind is employed in fixing the other?

136 On the other hand, those who would resolve all moral determinations into *sentiment,* may endeavour to show, that it is impossible for reason ever to draw conclusions of this nature. To virtue, say they, it belongs to be *amiable,* and vice *odious.* This forms their very nature or essence. But can reason or argumentation distribute these different epithets to any subjects, and pronounce beforehand, that this must produce love, and that hatred? Or what other reason can we ever assign for these affections, but the original fabric and formation of the human mind, which is naturally adapted to receive them?

The end of all moral speculations is to teach us our duty; and, by proper representations of the deformity of vice and beauty of virtue, beget correspondent habits, and engage us to avoid the one, and embrace the other. But is this ever to be expected from inferences and conclusions of the understanding, which of themselves have no hold of the affections or set in motion the active powers of men? They discover truths: but where the truths which they discover are indifferent, and beget no desire or aversion, they can have no influence on conduct and behaviour. What is honourable, what is fair, what is becoming, what is noble, what is generous, takes possession of the heart, and animates us to embrace and maintain it. What is intelligible, what is evident, what is probable, what is true, procures only the cool assent of the understanding; and gratifying a speculative curiosity, puts an end to our researches.

Extinguish all the warm feelings and prepossessions in favour of virtue, and all disgust or aversion to vice: render men totally indifferent towards these distinctions; and morality is no longer a practical study, nor has any tendency to regulate our lives and actions.

137 These arguments on each side (and many more might be produced) are so plausible, that I am apt to suspect, they may, the one as well as the other, be solid and satisfactory, and that *reason* and *sentiment* concur in almost all

moral determinations and conclusions. The final sentence, it is probable, which pronounces characters and actions amiable or odious, praise-worthy or blameable; that which stamps on them the mark of honour or infamy, approbation or censure; that which renders morality an active principle and constitutes virtue our happiness, and vice our misery: it is probable, I say, that this final sentence depends on some internal sense or feeling, which nature has made universal in the whole species. For what else can have an influence of this nature? But in order to pave the way for such a sentiment, and give a proper discernment of its object, it is often necessary, we find, that much reasoning should precede, that nice distinctions be made, just conclusions drawn, distant comparisons formed, complicated relations examined, and general facts fixed and ascertained. Some species of beauty, especially the natural kinds, on their first appearance, command our affection and approbation; and where they fail of this effect, it is impossible for any reasoning to redress their influence, or adapt them better to our taste and sentiment. But in many orders of beauty, particularly those of the finer arts, it is requisite to employ much reasoning, in order to feel the proper sentiment; and a false relish may frequently be corrected by argument and reflection. There are just grounds to conclude, that moral beauty partakes much of this latter species, and demands the assistance of our intellectual faculties, in order to give it a suitable influence on the human mind.

138   But though this question, concerning the general principles of morals, be curious and important, it is needless for us, at present, to employ farther care in our researches concerning it. For if we can be so happy, in the course of this enquiry, as to discover the true origin of morals, it will then easily appear how far either sentiment or reason enters into all determinations of this nature. In order to attain this purpose, we shall endeavour to follow a very simple method: we shall analyse that complication of mental qualities, which form what, in common life, we call Personal Merit: we shall consider every attribute of the mind, which renders a man an object either of esteem and affection, or of hatred and contempt; every habit or sentiment or faculty, which, if ascribed to any person, implies either praise or blame, and may enter into any panegyric or satire of his character and manners. The quick sensibility, which, on this head, is so universal among mankind, gives a philosopher sufficient assurance, that he can never be considerably mistaken in framing the catalogue, or incur any danger of misplacing the objects of his contemplation: he needs only enter into his own breast for a moment, and consider whether or not he should desire to have this or that quality ascribed to him, and whether such or such an imputation would proceed from a friend or an enemy. The very nature of language guides us almost infallibly in forming a judgement of this nature; and as every tongue possesses one set of words which are taken in a good sense, and another in the opposite, the least acquaintance with the idiom suffices, without any reasoning, to direct us in collecting and arranging the estimable or blameable qualities of men. The only object of reasoning is to discover the circumstances on both sides, which are common to these qualities; to observe that particular in which the estimable qualities agree on the one hand, and

the blameable on the other; and thence to reach the foundation of ethics, and find those universal principles, from which all censure or approbation is ultimately derived. As this is a question of fact, not of abstract science, we can only expect success, by following the experimental method, and deducing general maxims from a comparison of particular instances. The other scientific method, where a general abstract principle is first established, and is afterwards branched out into a variety of inferences and conclusions, may be more perfect in itself, but suits less the imperfection of human nature, and is a common source of illusion and mistake in this as well as in other subjects. Men are not cured of their passion for hypotheses and systems in natural philosophy, and will hearken to no arguments but those which are derived from experience. It is full time they should attempt a like reformation in all moral disquisitions; and reject every system of ethics, however subtle or ingenious, which is not founded on fact and observation.

We shall begin our enquiry on this head by the consideration of the social virtues, Benevolence and Justice. The explication of them will probably give us an opening by which the others may be accounted for.

OF BENEVOLENCE

139   It may be esteemed, perhaps, a superfluous task to prove, that the benevolent or softer affections are estimable; and wherever they appear, engage the approbation and good-will of mankind. The epithets *sociable, good-natured, humane, merciful, grateful, friendly, generous, beneficent,* or their equivalents, are known in all languages, and universally express the highest merit, which *human nature* is capable of attaining. Where these amiable qualities are attended with birth and power and eminent abilities, and display themselves in the good government or useful instruction of mankind, they seem even to raise the possessors of them above the rank of *human nature,* and make them approach in some measure to the divine. Exalted capacity, undaunted courage, prosperous success; these may only expose a hero or politician to the envy and ill-will of the public: but as soon as the praises are added of humane and beneficent; when instances are displayed of lenity, tenderness or friendship; envy itself is silent, or joins the general voice of approbation and applause.

. . .

In men of more ordinary talents and capacity, the social virtues become, if possible, still more essentially requisite; there being nothing eminent, in that case, to compensate for the want of them, or preserve the person from our severest hatred, as well as contempt. A high ambition, an elevated courage, is apt, says Cicero, in less perfect characters, to degenerate into a turbulent ferocity. The more social and softer virtues are there chiefly to be regarded. These are always good and amiable.

The principal advantage, which Juvenal discovers in the extensive capacity of the human species, is that it renders our benevolence also more extensive, and gives us larger opportunities of spreading our kindly influence than what are indulged to the inferior creation. It must, indeed, be confessed, that by doing good only, can a man truly enjoy the advantages of being eminent. His exalted station, of itself but the more exposes him to danger and tempest. His sole prerogative is to afford shelter to inferiors, who repose themselves under his cover and protection.

140 But I forget, that it is not my present business to recommend generosity and benevolence, or to paint, in their true colours, all the genuine charms of the social virtues. These, indeed, sufficiently engage every heart, on the first apprehension of them; and it is difficult to abstain from some sally of panegyric, as often as they occur in discourse or reasoning. But our object here being more the speculative, than the practical part of morals, it will suffice to remark, (what will readily, I believe, be allowed) that no qualities are more intitled to the general good-will and approbation of mankind than beneficence and humanity, friendship and gratitude, natural affection and public spirit, or whatever proceeds from a tender sympathy with others, and a generous concern for our kind and species. These wherever they appear, seem to transfuse themselves, in a manner, into each beholder, and to call forth, in their own behalf, the same favourable and affectionate sentiments, which they exert on all around.

141 We may observe that, in displaying the praises of any humane, beneficent man, there is one circumstance which never fails to be amply insisted on, namely, the happiness and satisfaction, derived to society from his intercourse and good offices. To his parents, we are apt to say, he endears himself by his pious attachment and duteous care still more than by the connexions of nature. His children never feel his authority, but when employed for their advantage. With him, the ties of love are consolidated by beneficence and friendship. The ties of friendship approach, in fond observance of each obliging office, to those of love and inclination. His domestics and dependents have in him a sure resource; and no longer dread the power of fortune, but so far as she exercises it over him. From him the hungry receive food, the naked clothing, the ignorant and slothful skill and industry. Like the sun, an inferior minister of providence he cheers, invigorates, and sustains the surrounding world.

If confined to private life, the sphere of his activity is narrower; but his influence is all benign and gentle. If exalted into a higher station, mankind and posterity reap the fruit of his labours.

DISCUSSION QUESTIONS

1. What does Hume mean when he says that reason is impotent? Is reason as limited as Hume claims?
2. Is it possible to base morality on sentiment and at the same time avoid ethical relativism? Compare and contrast Hume's claim that sentiment is the source of morality with Jean-Jacques Rousseau's ethical subjectivism.

3. What does Hume mean by a moral sense? To what extent do our moral judgments depend on our moral sense? Compare Hume's description of the moral sense with James Q. Wilson's concept of the moral sense.

4. What does Hume mean when he says that "reason is, and ought only to be, the slave of passions"? Do you agree with Hume that passion is a better guide to morality than reason?

5. According to Hume, what are moral sentiments? How can we distinguish emotions that are moral sentiments from emotions that are not moral sentiments?

6. Hume's philosophy has been described as a precursor of utilitarianism. Is Hume a utilitarian? What is the connection between Hume's virtue of beneficence and utility? Is Hume more like Bentham or Mo Tzu?

7. Do you agree with Hume that morality is based in sentiment? Are there certain sentiments that are universally shared, as Hume claimed?

Nel Noddings

Caring: A Feminine Approach to Ethics and Moral Education

—liked David Hume

Nel Noddings (b. 1929) is a feminist philosopher and professor of education at Stanford University. Her interest in moral education has been influenced by Carol Gilligan's care ethics. Like Hume, Noddings believes that moral obligation is rooted in sentiment or what she calls "natural care."

In the selection from her book *Caring: A Feminine Approach to Ethics and Moral Education*, Noddings argues that the ethical self can only emerge from caring for others. She then goes on to explore what it means to care.

CRITICAL THINKING QUESTIONS

1. What does Noddings mean by the term *care?*

2. How does care motivate us, according to Noddings?

3. What is the relationship between caring for self and caring for others? Can someone care only for themselves? Can someone genuinely care for someone (or something) who does not respond to or reciprocate that care?

4. What does it mean to "grasp the reality of the other as a possibility for myself"?

5. What is the difference between the one-caring and the one cared-for? What are the important elements in the relationship between the two?

6. Why does Noddings reject the notion of universal caring as a virtue?

7. What does Noddings mean by "active virtue"? What are the two feelings required by active virtue?

8. What distinction does Noddings make between caring as a virtue and natural caring?

9. What, according to Noddings, is the connection between the "I must" and "caring" as an active virtue or ideal?

Caring: A Feminine Approach to Ethics and Moral Education (Berkeley: University of California Press, 1984), pp. 71–90.

WHAT DOES IT MEAN TO CARE?

Our dictionaries tell us that "care" is a state of mental suffering or of engross-ment: to care is to be in a burdened mental state, one of anxiety, fear, or solici-tude about something or someone. Alternatively, one cares for something or someone if one has a regard for or inclination toward that something or some-one. If I have an inclination toward mathematics, I may willingly spend some time with it, and if I have a regard for you, what you think, feel, and desire will matter to me. And, again, to care may mean to be charged with the protection, welfare, or maintenance of something or someone. . . .

. . . When I look at and think about how I am when I care, I realize that there is invariably this displacement of interest from my own reality to the reality of the other. (Our discussion now will be confined to caring for persons.) Kierkegaard has said that we apprehend another's reality as *possibility*. To be touched, to have aroused in me something that will disturb my own ethical real-ity, I must see the other's reality as a possibility for my own. This is not to say that I cannot try to see the other's reality differently. Indeed, I can. I can look at it objectively by collecting factual data; I can look at it historically. If it is heroic, I can come to admire it. But this sort of looking does not touch my own ethical reality; it may even distract me from it. As Kierkegaard put it:

> Ethically speaking there is nothing so conducive to sound sleep as admiration of another person's ethical reality. And again ethically speaking, if there is anything that can stir and rouse a man, it is a possibility ideally requiring itself of a human being.

But I am suggesting that we do not see only the direct possibilities for becom-ing better than we are when we struggle toward the reality of the other. We also have aroused in us the feeling, "I must do something." When we see the other's reality as a possibility for us, we must act to eliminate the intolerable, to reduce the pain, to fill the need, to actualize the dream. When I am in this sort of rela-tionship with another, when the other's reality becomes a real possibility for me, I care. Whether the caring is sustained, whether it lasts long enough to be con-veyed to the other, whether it becomes visible in the world, depends upon my sus-taining the relationship or, at least, acting out of concern for my own ethicality as though it were sustained.

In this latter case, one in which something has slipped away from me or eluded me from the start but in which I strive to regain or to attain it, I experience a gen-uine caring for self. This caring for self, for the *ethical* self, can emerge only from a caring for others. But a sense of my physical self, a knowledge of what gives me pain and pleasure, precedes my caring for others. Otherwise, their realities as possibilities for my own reality would mean nothing to me. When we say of someone, "He cares only for himself," we mean that, in our deepest sense, he does not care at all. He has only a sense of that physical self—of what gives him pain and pleasure. Whatever he sees in others is pre-selected in relation to his own needs and desires. He does not see the reality of the other as a possibility for himself but only as an instance of what he has already determined as self or not-self. Thus, he is ethically both zero and finished. His only "becoming" is a physical becoming. It is clear, of course, that I must say more about what is meant by "ethical reality" and "ethical self," and I shall return to this question.

I need not, however, be a person who cares only for myself in order to behave occasionally as though I care only for myself. Sometimes I behave this way because I have not thought through things carefully enough and because the mode of the times pushes the thoughtless in its own direction. Suppose, for example, that I am a teacher who loves mathematics. I encounter a student who is doing poorly, and I decide to have a talk with him. He tells me that he hates mathematics. *Aha*, I think. *Here is the problem. I must help this poor boy to love mathematics, and then he will do better at it.* What am I doing when I proceed in this way? I am not trying to grasp the reality of the other as a possibility for myself. I have not even asked: *How would it feel to hate mathematics?* Instead, I project my own reality onto my student and say, *You will be just fine if only you learn to love mathematics.* And I have "data" to support me. There is evidence that intrinsic motivation is associated with higher achievement. (Did anyone ever doubt this?) So my student becomes an object of study and manipulation for me. Now, I have deliberately chosen an example that is not often associated with manipulation. Usually, we associate manipulation with trying to get our student to achieve some learning objective that we have devised and set for him. Bringing him to "love mathematics" is seen as a noble aim. And so it is, if it is held out to him as a possibility that he glimpses by observing me and others; but then I shall not be disappointed in him, or in myself, if he remains indifferent to mathematics. It is a possibility that may not be actualized. What matters to me, if I care, is that he find some reason, acceptable in his inner self, for learning the mathematics required of him or that he reject it boldly and honestly. How would it feel to hate mathematics? What reasons could I find for learning it? When I think this way, I refuse to cast about for rewards that might pull him along. He must find his rewards. I do not begin with dazzling performances designed to intrigue him or to change his attitude. I begin, as nearly as I can, with the view from his eyes: Mathematics is bleak, jumbled, scary, boring, boring, boring. . . . What in the world could induce me to engage in it? From that point on, we struggle together with it.

Apprehending the other's reality, feeling what he feels as nearly as possible, is the essential part of caring from the view of the one-caring. For if I take on the other's reality as possibility and begin to feel its reality, I feel, also, that I must act accordingly; that is, I am impelled to act as though in my own behalf, but in behalf of the other. Now, of course, this feeling that I must act may or may not be sustained. I must make a commitment to act. The commitment to act in behalf of the cared-for, a continued interest in his reality throughout the appropriate time span, and the continual renewal of commitment over this span of time are the essential elements of caring from the inner view. Mayeroff speaks of devotion and the promotion of growth in the cared-for. I wish to start with engrossment and motivational displacement. Both concepts will require elaboration.

PROBLEMS ARISING IN THE ANALYSIS OF ONE-CARING

As I think about how I feel when I care, about what my frame of mind is, I see that my caring is always characterized by a move away from self. Yet not all instances of caring are alike even from the view of one-caring. Conditions change, and the time spanned by caring varies. While I care for my children throughout our mutual lifetimes, I may care only momentarily for a stranger in need. The intensity varies. I care deeply for those in my inner circles and more lightly for those farther removed from my personal life. Even with those close to me, the intensity of caring varies; it may be calm and steady most of the time and desperately anxious in emergencies.

The acts performed out of caring vary with both situational conditions and type of relationship. . . .

As we become aware of the problems involving time, intensity, and formal relationships, we may be led to reconsider the requirement of engrossment. We might instead describe caring of different sorts, on different levels and at varying degrees of intensity. Although I understand why several writers have chosen to speak of special kinds of caring appropriate to particular relationships, I shall claim that these efforts obscure the fundamental truth. At bottom, all caring involves engrossment. The engrossment need not be intense nor need it be pervasive in the life of the one-caring, but it must occur. . . .

Another problem arises when we consider situations in which we do not naturally care. Responding to my own child crying in the nigh may require a physical effort, but it does not usually require what might be called an ethical effort. I naturally want to relieve my child's distress. But receiving the other as he feels and trying to do so are qualitatively different modes. In the first, I am already "with" the other. My motivational energies are flowing toward him and, perhaps, toward his ends. In the second, I may dimly or dramatically perceive a reality that is a repugnant possibility for me. Dwelling in it may bring self-revulsion and disgust. Then I must withdraw. I do not "care" for this person. I may hate him, but I need not. If I do something in his behalf—defend his legal rights or confirm a statement he makes—it is because I care about my own ethical self. In caring for my ethical self, I grapple with the question: Must I try to care? When and for whom? A description of the ethical ideal and its construction will be essential in trying to answer these questions.

There are other limitations in caring. Not only are there those for whom I do not naturally care—situations in which engrossment brings revulsion and motivational displacement is unthinkable—but there are, also, many beyond the reach of my caring. I shall reject the notion of universal caring—that is, caring for everyone—on the grounds that it is impossible to actualize and leads us to substitute abstract problem solving and mere talk for genuine caring. Many of us think that it is not only possible to care for everyone but morally obligatory that we should do so. We can, in a sense that will need elaboration, "care about" everyone; that is, we can maintain an internal state of readiness to try to care for whoever crosses our path. But this is different from the caring-for to which we refer when we use the word "caring." If we are thoughtful persons, we know that the difference is great, and we may even deliberately restrict our contacts so that the caring-for of which we are capable does not deteriorate to mere verbal caring-about. I shall not try to maintain this linguistic distinction, because it seems somewhat unnatural, but we should keep in mind the real distinction we are pointing at: in one sense, "caring" refers to an actuality; in the other, it refers to a verbal commitment to the possibility of caring.

. . .

The one-caring, in caring, is *present* in her acts of caring. Even in physical absence, acts at a distance bear the signs of presence: engrossment in the other, regard, desire for the other's well-being. Caring is largely reactive and responsive. Perhaps it is even better characterized as receptive. The one-caring is sufficiently engrossed in the other to listen to him and to take pleasure or pain in what he recounts. Whatever she does for the cared-for is embedded in a relationship that reveals itself as engrossment and in an attitude that warms and comforts the cared-for.

The caring attitude, this quality of disposability, pervades the situational time-space. So far as it is in my control, if we are conversing and if I care, I remain present to you throughout the conversation. Of course, if I care and you do not, then I may put my presence at a distance, thus freeing you to embrace the absence you have chosen. This is the way of dignity in such situations. To be treated as though one does not exist is a threatening experience, and one has to gather up one's self, one's presence, and place it in a safer, more welcome environment. And, of course, it is the way of generosity.

. . .

Our logic may be summarized. A caring relation requires the engrossment and motivational displacement of the one-caring, and it requires the recognition and spontaneous response of the cared-for. When caring is not felt in the cared-for, but its absence is felt, the cared-for may still, by an act of ethical heroism, respond and thus contribute to the caring relation. This possibility, as we shall see, gives weight to our hope that one can learn to care and learn to be cared for.

FROM NATURAL TO ETHICAL CARING

David Hume long ago contended that morality is founded upon and rooted in feeling—that the "final sentence" on matters of morality, "that which renders morality an active virtue"—". . . this final sentence depends on some internal sense or feeling, which nature has made universal in the whole species. For what else can have an influence of this nature?"

What is the nature of this feeling that is "universal in the whole species"? I want to suggest that morality as an "active virtue" requires two feelings and not just one. The first is the sentiment of natural caring. There can be no ethical sentiment without the initial, enabling sentiment. In situations where we act on behalf of the other because we want to do so, we are acting in accord with natural caring. A mother's caretaking efforts in behalf of her child are not usually considered ethical but natural. Even maternal animals take care of their off-spring, and we do not credit them with ethical behavior.

. . .

Recognizing that ethical caring requires an effort that is not needed in natural caring does not commit us to a position that elevates ethical caring over natural caring. Kant has identified the ethical with that which is done out of duty and not out of love, and that distinction in itself seems right. But an ethic built on caring strives to maintain the caring attitude and is thus dependent upon, and not superior to, natural caring. The source of ethical behavior is, then, in twin sentiments —one that feels directly for the other and one that feels for and with that best self, who may accept and sustain the initial feeling rather than reject it.

We shall discuss the ethical ideal, that vision of best self, in some depth. When we commit ourselves to obey the "I must" even at its weakest and most fleeting, we are under the guidance of this ideal. It is not just any picture. Rather, it is our best picture of ourselves caring and being cared for. It may even be colored by acquaintance with one superior to us in caring, but, as I shall describe it, it is both constrained and attainable. It is limited by what we have already done and by what we are capable of, and it does not idealize the impossible so that we may escape into ideal abstraction.

Now, clearly, in pointing to Hume's "active virtue" and to an ethical ideal as the source of ethical behavior, I seem to be advocating an ethic of virtue. This is certainly true in part. Many philosophers recognize the need for a discussion of virtue as the energizing factor in moral behavior, even when they have given their best intellectual effort to a careful explication of their positions on obligation and justification. When we discuss the ethical ideal, we shall be talking about "virtue," but we shall not let "virtue" dissipate into "the virtues" described in abstract categories. The holy man living abstemiously on top of the mountain, praying thrice daily, and denying himself human intercourse may display "virtues," but they are not the virtues of one-caring. The virtue described by the ethical ideal of one-caring is built up in relation. It reaches out to the other and grows in response to the other.

Since our discussion of virtue will be embedded in an exploration of moral activity we might do well to start by asking whether or under what circumstances we are obliged to respond to the initial "I must." Does it make sense to say that I am obliged to heed that which comes to me as obligation?

OBLIGATION

. . .

The answer to this is, I think, that the genuine moral sentiment (our second sentiment) arises from an evaluation of the caring relation as good, as better than, superior to, other forms of relatedness. I feel the moral "I must" when I recognize that my response will either enhance or diminish my ethical ideal. It will serve either to increase or decrease the likelihood of genuine caring. My response affects me as one-caring. In a given situation with someone I am not fond of, I may be able to find all sorts of reason why I should not respond to his need. I may be too busy. He may be undiscerning. The matter may be, on objective analysis, unimportant. But, before I decide, I must turn away from this analytic chain of thought and back to the concrete situation. Here is this person with this perceived need to which is attached this importance. I must put justification aside temporarily. Shall I respond? How do I feel as a duality about the "I" who will not respond?

I am obliged, then, to accept the initial "I must" when it occurs and even to fetch it out of recalcitrant slumber when it fails to awake spontaneously. The source of my obligation is the value I place on the relatedness of caring. This value itself arises as a product of actual caring and being cared-for and my reflection on the goodness of these concrete caring situations.

Now, what sort of "goodness" is it that attaches to the caring relation? It cannot be a fully moral goodness, for we have already described forms of caring that are natural and require no moral effort. But it cannot be a fully nonmoral goodness either, for it would then join a class of goods many of which are widely separated from the moral good. It is, perhaps, properly described as a "premoral good," one that lies in a region with the moral good and shades over into it. We cannot always decide with certainty whether our caring response is natural or ethical. Indeed, the decision to respond ethically as one-caring may cause the lowering of barriers that previously prevented reception of the other, and natural caring may follow.

I have identified the source of our obligation and have said that we are obligated to accept, and even to call forth, the feeling "I must." But what exactly must I do? Can my obligation be set forth in a list or hierarchy of principles? So far, it seems that I am obligated to maintain an attitude and, thus, to meet the other as one-caring and, at the same time, to increase my own virtue as one-caring. If I am advocating an ethic of virtue, do not all the usual dangers lie in wait: hypocrisy, self-righteousness, withdrawal from the public domain? We shall discuss these dangers as the idea of an ethical ideal is developed more fully.

Let me say here, however, why it seems preferable to place an ethical ideal above principle as a guide to moral action. It has been traditional in moral philosophy to insist that moral principles must be, by their very nature as moral principles, universifiable. If I am obligated to do X under certain conditions, then under sufficiently similar conditions you also are obligated to do X. But the principle of universifiability seems to depend, as Nietzsche pointed out, on a concept of "sameness." In order to accept the principle, we should have to establish that human predicaments exhibit sufficient sameness, and this we cannot do without abstracting away from concrete situations those qualities that seem to reveal the sameness. In doing this, we often lose the very qualities or factors that gave rise to the moral question in the situation. That condition which makes the situation different and thereby induces genuine moral puzzlement cannot be satisfied by the application of principles developed in situations of sameness.

This does not mean that we cannot receive any guidance from an attempt to discover principles that seem to be universifiable. We can, under this sort of plan, arrive at the doctrine of "prima facie duty" described by W. D. Ross. Ross himself, however, admits that this doctrine yields no real guidance for moral conduct in concrete situations. It guides us in abstract moral thinking; it tells us, theoretically, what to do, "all other things being equal." But other things are rarely if ever equal. . . .

Our obligation is limited and delimited by relation. We are never free, in the human domain, to abandon our preparedness to care; but, practically, if we are meeting those in our inner circles adequately as ones-caring and receiving those linked to our inner circles by formal chains of relation, we shall limit the calls upon our obligation quite naturally. We are not obliged to summon the "I must" if there is no possibility of completion in the other. I am not obliged to care for starving children in Africa, because there is no way for this caring to be completed in the other unless I abandon the caring to which I am obligated. I may still choose to do something in the direction of caring, but I am not obliged to do so. When we discuss our obligation to animals, we shall see that this is even more sharply limited by relation. We cannot refuse obligation in human affairs by merely refusing to enter relation; we are, by virtue of our mutual humanity, already and perpetually in potential relation. Instead, we limit our obligation by examining the possibility of completion. In connection with animals, however, we may find it possible to refuse relation itself on the grounds of a species-specific impossibility of any form of reciprocity in caring.

. . .

One under the guidance of an ethic of caring is tempted to retreat to a manageable world. Her public life is limited by her insistence upon meeting the other as one-caring. So long as this is possible, she may reach outward and enlarge her circles of caring. When this reaching out destroys or drastically reduces her actual caring, she retreats and renews her contact with those who address her. If the retreat becomes a flight, an avoidance of the call to care, her ethical ideal is diminished. Similarly, if the retreat is away from human beings and toward other objects of caring—ideas, animals, humanity-at-large, God—her ethical ideal is virtually shattered. This is not a judgment, for we can understand and sympathize with one who makes such a choice. It is more in the nature of a perception: we see clearly what has been lost in the choice.

Our ethic of caring—which we might have called a "feminine ethic"—begins to look a bit mean in contrast to the masculine ethics of universal love or universal justice. But universal love is illusion. Under the illusion, some young people retreat to the church to worship that which they cannot actualize; some write lovely poetry extolling universal love; and some, in terrible disillusion, kill to establish the very principles which should have entreated them not to kill. Thus are lost both principles and persons.

DISCUSSION QUESTIONS

1. Noddings claims that care ethics provide practical guidelines for making decisions in real-life situations in a way that the abstract principles of deontologists, such as Kant and Ross, do not. Do you agree? Support your answer.

2. Noddings argues that "engrossment" is necessary in caring. What does she mean by this? Would Kant agree with her? Compare and contrast Noddings's concept of caring-for to Immanuel Kant's duty to always treat people as ends in themselves and never as only a means. — theories too abstract to act on —

3. Does Noddings focus too much on unequal relationships? Discuss whether her concepts of the one-caring and the cared-for offer guidance for relations between equals. Illustrate your answer with specific examples.

4. Do you agree with Noddings that our vision of our best self requires both the virtues of caring and being cared for? Discuss your answer in light of your own vision of your best self.

5. Feminist philosopher Rosemarie Tong criticizes Noddings's care ethics as being oppressive to women because of its focus on the inequality in relationships and its identification of the "one attached" with the feminine approach to ethics. Others argue, along similar lines, that Noddings's care ethics encourages women to hold up self-sacrifice as a virtue. Do you agree with these criticisms?

6. Does Noddings's care ethics give sufficient attention to our relations to strangers? What obligations do we have to people in foreign nations? Discuss whether Gustavo Gutierrez would find Noddings's concept of care adequate for dealing with issues of liberation ethics.

Alasdair MacIntyre

After Virtue: A Study in Moral Theory

Scottish-born philosopher and sociologist Alasdair MacIntyre (b. 1929) is
one of the foremost contemporary virtue ethicists. In this selection from his
book *After Virtue,* MacIntyre argues that the focus on duty in modern Western moral philosophy has had disastrous consequences for both society and
the individual. MacIntyre suggests instead abandoning the modern individualist concept of human nature and returning to one in which virtue and
human life as a whole are the central focus. In particular, MacIntyre is interested in the contributions that the community-oriented virtue ethics of Aristotle and Confucius have to make to contemporary moral theory.

MacIntyre—who has been affiliated with several universities, including
Oxford University, University of Essex, Boston University, and the University
of Notre Dame—is currently at Duke University in North Carolina. A pro-
lific writer and scholar, MacIntyre wrote his first book in philosophy at the
age of 23.

CRITICAL THINKING QUESTIONS

1. What is the modern concept of the self in Western philosophy?

2. What, according to MacIntyre, are the philosophical obstacles to
   envisioning a more wholistic view of human nature?

3. What does MacIntyre mean by an "intention"? Why are intentions important? What is the relation between our intentions and
   our actions?

4. Why is it incorrect, in MacIntyre's view, to consider a person's
   actions in isolation from those of others?

5. What does MacIntyre mean when he describes life as a narrative?
   How does narrative unify our lives?

6. What is the relation between our narrative and virtue?

7. Do we exercise virtues solely as individuals? Why does MacIntyre
   regard individualism as destructive to the concept of morality?

8. Do virtues differ from culture to culture? How does tradition and
   our cultural history influence what virtues are relevant to a person's life?

After Virtue: A Study in Moral Theory (Notre Dame, IN: University of Notre Dame Press, 1984).

The Virtues, the Unity of a Human Life and the Concept of a Tradition

Any contemporary attempt to envisage each human life as a whole, as a unity, whose character provides the virtues with an adequate *telos* encounters two different kinds of obstacle, one social and one philosophical. The social obstacles derive from the way in which modernity partitions each human life into a variety of segments, each with its own norms and modes of behavior. So work is divided from leisure, private life from public, the corporate from the personal. So both childhood and old age have been wrenched away from the rest of human life and made over into distinct realms. And all these separations have been achieved so that it is the distinctiveness of each and not the unity of the life of the individual who passes through those parts in terms of which we are taught to think and to feel.

The philosophical obstacles derive from two distinct tendencies, one chiefly, though not only, domesticated in analytical philosophy and one at home in both sociological theory and in existentialism. The former is the tendency to think atomistically about human action and to analyze complex actions and transactions in terms of simple components. Hence the recurrence in more than one context of the notion of a "basic action." That particular actions derive their character as parts of larger wholes is a point of view alien to our dominant ways of thinking and yet one which it is necessary at least to consider if we are to begin to understand how a life may be more than a sequence of individual actions and episodes.

Equally the unity of a human life becomes invisible to us when a sharp separation is made either between the individual and the roles that he or she plays . . .

. . . The liquidation of the self into a set of demarcated areas of role-playing allows no scope for the exercise of dispositions which could genuinely be accounted virtues in any sense remotely Aristotelian. For a virtue is not a disposition that makes for success only in some one particular type of situation. What are spoken of as the virtues of a good committee man or of a good administrator or of a gambler or a pool hustler are professional skills professionally deployed in those situations where they can be effective, not virtues. Someone who genuinely possesses a virtue can be expected to manifest it in very different types of situation, many of them situations where the practice of a virtue cannot be expected to be effective in the way that we expect a professional skill to be. Hector exhibited one and the same courage in his parting from Andromache and on the battlefield with Achilles; Eleanor Marx exhibited one and the same compassion in her relationship with her father, in her work with trade unionists and in her entanglement with Aveling. And the unity of a virtue in someone's life is intelligible only as a characteristic of a unitary life, a life that can be conceived and evaluated as a whole. Hence just as in the discussion of the changes in and fragmentation of morality which accompanied the rise of modernity in the earlier parts of this book, each stage in the emergence of the characteristically modern views of the moral judgment was accompanied by a corresponding stage in the emergence of the characteristically modern conceptions of selfhood; so now, in defining the particular pre-modern concept of the virtues with which I have been preoccupied, it has become necessary to say something of the concomitant concept of selfhood, a concept of a self whose unity resides in the unity of a narrative which links birth to life to death as narrative beginning to middle to end.

Such a conception of the self is perhaps less unfamiliar than it may appear at first sight. Just because it has played a key part in the cultures which are historically predecessors of our own, it would not be surprising if it turned out to be still an unacknowledged presence in many of our ways of thinking and acting. Hence it is not inappropriate to begin by scrutinizing some of our most taken-for-granted, but clearly correct conceptual insights about human actions and selfhood in order to show how natural it is to think of the self in a narrative mode.

It is a conceptual commonplace, both for philosophers and for ordinary agents, that one and the same segment of human behavior may be correctly characterized in a number of different ways. To the question "What is he doing?" the answers may with equal truth and appropriateness be "Digging," "Gardening," "Taking exercise," "Preparing for winter" or "Pleasing his wife." Some of these answers will characterize the agent's intentions, other unintended consequences of his actions, and of these unintended consequences some may be such that the agent is aware of them and others not. What is important to notice immediately is that any answer to the questions of how we are to understand or to explain a given segment of behavior will presuppose some prior answer to the question of how these different correct answers to the question "What is he doing?" are related to each other. For if someone's primary intention is to put the garden in order before the winter and it is only incidentally the case that in so doing he is taking exercise and pleasing his wife, we have one type of behavior to be explained; but if the agent's primary intention is to please his wife by taking exercise, we have quite another type of behavior to be explained and we will have to look in a different direction for understanding and explanation.

. . .

Where intentions are concerned, we need to know which intention or intentions were primary, that is to say, of which it is the case that, had the agent intended otherwise, he would not have performed that action. Thus if we know that a man is gardening with the self-avowed purposes of healthful exercise and of pleasing his wife, we do not yet know how to understand what he is doing until we know the answer to such questions as whether he would continue gardening if he continued to believe that gardening was healthful exercise, but discovered that his gardening no longer pleased his wife, *and* whether he would continue gardening, if he ceased to believe that gardening was healthful exercise, but continued to believe that it pleased his wife, *and* whether he would continue gardening if he changed his beliefs on both points. That is to say, we need to know both what certain of his beliefs are and which of them are causally effective; and, that is to say, we need to know whether certain contrary-to-fact hypothetical statements are true or false. And until we know this, we shall not know how to characterize correctly what the agent is doing.

. . .

I spoke earlier of the agent as not only an actor, but an author. Now I must emphasize that what the agent is able to do and say intelligibly as an actor is deeply affected by the fact that we are never more (and sometimes less) than the co-authors of our own narratives. Only in fantasy do we live what story we please. In life, as both Aristotle and Engels noted, we are always under certain constraints. We enter upon a stage which we did not design and we find ourselves part of an action that was not of our making. Each of us being a main character in his own drama plays subordinate parts in the dramas of others, and each drama constrains the others. In my drama, perhaps, I am Hamlet or Iago or at least the swineherd who may yet become a prince, but to you I am only A Gentleman or at best Second Murderer, while you are my Polonius or my Gravedigger, but your own hero. Each of our dramas exerts constraints on each other's, making the whole different from the parts, but still dramatic.

. . .

To be the subject of a narrative that runs from one's birth to one's death is, I remarked earlier, to be accountable for the actions and experiences which compose a narratable life. It is, that is, to be open to being asked to give a certain kind of account of what one did or what happened to one or what one witnessed at any earlier point in one's life than the time at which the question is posed. Of course someone may have forgotten or suffered brain damage or simply not attended sufficiently at the relevant time to be able to give the relevant account. But to say of someone under some one description ("The prisoner of the Chateau d'If") that he is the same person as someone characterized quite differently ("The Count of Monte Cristo") is precisely to say that it makes sense to ask him to give an intelligible narrative account enabling us to understand how he could at different times and different places be one and the same person and yet be so differently characterized. Thus personal identity is just that identity presupposed by the unity of the character which the unity of a narrative requires. Without such unity there would not be subjects of whom stories could be told.

The other aspect of narrative selfhood is correlative: I am not only accountable, I am one who can always ask others for an account, who can put others to the question. I am part of their story, as they are part of mine. The narrative of any one life is part of an interlocking set of narratives. Moreover this asking for and giving of accounts itself plays an important part in constituting narratives. Asking you what you did and why, saying what I did and why, pondering the differences between your account of what I did and my account of what I did, and *vice versa,* these are essential constituents of all but the very simplest and barest of narratives. Thus without the accountability of the self those trains of events that constitute all but the simplest and barest of narratives could not occur; and without that same accountability narratives would lack that continuity required to make both them and the actions that constitute them intelligible.

It is important to notice that I am not arguing that the concepts of narrative or of intelligibility or of accountability are *more* fundamental than that of personal identity. The concepts of narrative, intelligibility and accountability presuppose the applicability of the concept of personal identity, just as it presupposes their applicability and just as indeed each of these three presupposes the applicability

virtues of self define your narratives

of the two others. The relationship is one of mutual presupposition. It does follow of course that all attempts to elucidate the notion of personal identity independently of and in isolation from the notions of narrative, intelligibility and accountability are bound to fail. As all such attempts have.

It is now possible to return to the question from which this enquiry into the nature of human action and identity started: In what does the unity of an individual life consist? The answer is that its unity is the unity of a narrative embodied in a single life. To ask "What is the good for me?" is to ask how best I might live out that unity and bring it to completion. To ask "What is the good for man?" is to ask what all answers to the former question must have in common. But now it is important to emphasize that it is the systematic asking of these two questions and the attempt to answer them in deed as well as in word which provide the moral life with its unity. The unity of a human life is the unity of a narrative quest. Quests sometimes fail, are frustrated, abandoned or dissipated into distractions; and human lives may in all these ways also fail. But the only criteria for success or failure in a human life as a whole are the criteria of success or failure in a narrated or to-be-narrated quest. A quest for what?

Two key features of the medieval conception of a quest need to be recalled. The first is that without some at least partly determinate conception of the final *telos* there could not be any beginning to a quest. Some conception of the good for man is required. Whence is such a conception to be drawn? Precisely from those questions which led us to attempt to transcend that limited conception of the virtues which is available in and through practices. It is in looking for a conception of *the* good which will enable us to order other goods, for a conception of *the* good which will enable us to extend our understanding of the purpose and content of the virtues, for a conception of *the* good which will enable us to understand the place of integrity and constancy in life, that we initially define the kind of life which is a quest for the good. But secondly it is clear the medieval conception of a quest is not at all that of a search for something already adequately characterized, as miners search for gold or geologists for oil. It is in the course of the quest and only through encountering and coping with the various particular harms, dangers, temptations and distractions which provide any quest with its episodes and incidents that the goal of the quest is finally to be understood. A quest is always an education both as to the character of that which is sought and in self-knowledge.

The virtues therefore are to be understood as those dispositions which will not only sustain practices and enable us to achieve the goods internal to practices, but which will also sustain us in the relevant kind of quest for the good, by enabling us to overcome the harms, dangers, temptations and distractions which we encounter, and which will furnish us with increasing self-knowledge and increasing knowledge of the good. The catalogue of the virtues will therefore include the virtues required to sustain the kind of households and the kind of political communities in which men and women can seek for the good together and the virtues necessary for philosophical enquiry about the character of the good. We have then arrived at a provisional conclusion about the good life for man: the good life for man is the life spent in seeking for the good life for man, and the virtues necessary for the seeking are those which will enable us to understand what more and what else the good life for man is. We have also completed the second stage in our account of the virtues, by situating them in relation to the good life for man and not only in relation to practices. But our enquiry requires a third stage.

For I am never able to seek for the good or exercise the virtues only *qua* individual. This is partly because what it is to live the good life concretely varies from circumstance to circumstance even when it is one and the same conception of the good life and one and the same set of virtues which are being embodied in a human life. What the good life is for a fifth-century Athenian general will not be the same as what it was for a medieval nun or a seventeenth-century farmer. But it is not just that different individuals live in different social circumstances; it is also that we all approach our own circumstances as bearers of a particular social identity. I am someone's son or daughter, someone else's cousin or uncle; I am a citizen of this or that city, a member of this or that guild or profession; I belong to this clan, that tribe, this nation. Hence what is good for me has to be the good for one who inhabits these roles. As such, I inherit from the past of my family, my city, my tribe, my nation, a variety of debts, inheritances, rightful expectations and obligations. These constitute the given of my life, my moral starting point. This is in part what gives my life its own moral particularity.

This thought is likely to appear alien and even surprising from the standpoint of modern individuals. From the standpoint of individualism I am what I myself choose to be. I can always, if I wish to, put in question what are taken to be the merely contingent social features of my existence. I may biologically be my father's son; but I cannot be held responsible for what he did unless I choose implicitly or explicitly to assume such responsibility. I may legally be a citizen of a certain country; but I cannot be held responsible for what my country does or has done unless I choose implicitly or explicitly to assume such responsibility. Such individualism is expressed by those modern Americans who deny any responsibility for the effects of slavery upon black Americans, saying "I never owned any slaves." It is more subtly the standpoint of those other modern Americans who accept a nicely calculated responsibility for such effects measured precisely by the benefits they themselves as individuals have indirectly received from slavery. In both cases "being an American" is not in itself taken to be part of the moral identity of the individual. And of course there is nothing peculiar to modern Americans in this attitude: the Englishman who says, "I never did any wrong to Ireland; why bring up that old history as though it had something to do with *me?*" or the young German who believes that being born after 1945 means that what Nazis did to Jews has no moral relevance to his relationship to his Jewish contemporaries, exhibit the same attitude, that according to which the self is detachable from its social and historical roles and statuses. And the self so detached is of course a self very much at home in either Sartre's or Goffman's perspective, a self that can have no history. The contrast with the narrative view of the self is clear. For the story of my life is always embedded in the story of those communities from which I derive my identity. I am born with a past; and to try to cut myself off from that past, in the individualist mode, is to deform my present relationships. The possession of an historical identity and the possession of a social identity coincide. Notice that rebellion against my identity is always one possible mode of expressing it.

Notice also that the fact that the self has to find its moral identity in and through its membership in communities such as those of the family, the neighborhood, the city and the tribe does not entail that the self has to accept the moral *limitations* of the particularity of those forms of community. Without those moral particularities to begin from there would never be anywhere to begin; but it is in moving forward from such particularity that the search for the good, for the universal, consists. Yet particularity can never be simply left behind or obliterated. The notion of escaping from it into a realm of entirely universal maxims which belong to man as such, whether in its eighteenth-century Kantian form or in the presentation of some modern analytical moral philosophies, is an illusion and an illusion with painful consequences. When men and women identify what are in fact their partial and particular causes too easily and too completely with the cause of some universal principle, they usually behave worse than they would otherwise do.

What I am, therefore, is in key part what I inherit, a specific past that is present to some degree in my present. I find myself part of a history and that is generally to say, whether I like it or not, whether I recognize it or not, one of the bearers of a tradition. It was important when I characterized the concept of a practice to notice that practices always have histories and that at any given moment what a practice is depends on a mode of understanding it which has been transmitted often through many generations. And thus, insofar as the virtues sustain the relationships required for practices, they have to sustain relationships to the past—and to the future—as well as in the present. But the traditions through which particular practices are transmitted and reshaped never exist in isolation for larger social traditions. What constitutes such traditions?

We are apt to be misled here by the ideological uses to which the concept of a tradition has been put by conservative political theorists. Characteristically such theorists have followed Burke in contrasting tradition with reason and the stability of tradition with conflict. Both contrasts obfuscate. For all reasoning takes place within the context of some traditional mode of thought, transcending through criticism and invention the limitations of what had hitherto been reasoned in that tradition; this is as true of modern physics as of medieval logic. Moreover when a tradition is in good order it is always partially constituted by an argument about the goods the pursuit of which gives to that tradition its particular point and purpose.

So when an institution—a university, say, or a farm, or a hospital—is the bearer of a tradition of practice or practices, its common life will be partly, but in a centrally important way, constituted by a continuous argument as to what a university is and ought to be or what good farming is or what good medicine is. Traditions, when vital, embody continuities of conflict. Indeed when a tradition becomes Burkean, it is always dying or dead.

The individualism of modernity could of course find no use for the notion of tradition within its own conceptual scheme except as an adversary notion; it therefore all too willingly abandoned it to the Burkeans, who, faithful to Burke's own allegiance, tried to combine adherence in politics to a conception of tradition which would vindicate the oligarchical revolution of property of 1688 and adherence in economics to the doctrine and institutions of the free market. The theoretical incoherence of this mismatch did not deprive it of ideological usefulness. But the outcome has been that modern conservatives are for the most part engaged in conserving only older rather than later versions of liberal individualism. Their own core doctrine is as liberal and as individualist as that of self-avowed liberals.

A living tradition then is an historically extended, socially embodied argument, and an argument precisely in part about the goods which constitute that tradition. Within a tradition the pursuit of goods extends through generations, sometimes through many generations. Hence the individual's search for his or her good is generally and characteristically conducted with a context defined by those traditions of which the individual's life is a part, and this is true both of those goods which are internal to practices and of the goods of a single life. Once again the narrative phenomenon of embedding is crucial: the history of a practice in our time is generally and characteristically embedded in and made intelligible in terms of the larger and longer history of the tradition through which the practice in its present form was conveyed to us; the history of each of our own lives is generally and characteristically embedded in and made intelligible in terms of the larger and longer histories of a number of traditions. I have to say "generally and characteristically" rather than "always," for traditions decay, disintegrate and disappear. What then sustains and strengthens traditions? What weakens and destroys them?

The answer in key part is: the exercise or the lack of exercise of the relevant virtues. The virtues find their point and purpose not only in sustaining those relationships necessary if the variety of goods internal to practices are to be achieved and not only in sustaining the form of an individual life in which that individual may seek out his or her good as the good of his or her whole life, but also in sustaining those traditions which provide both practices and individual lives with their necessary historical context. Lack of justice, lack of truthfulness, lack of courage, lack of the relevant intellectual virtues—these corrupt traditions, just as they do those institutions and practices which derive their life from the traditions of which they are the contemporary embodiments. To recognize this is of course also to recognize the existence of an additional virtue, one whose importance is perhaps most obvious when it is least present, the virtue of having an adequate sense of the traditions to which one belongs or which confront one. . . .

. . . Unsurprisingly it is the lack of any such unifying conception of a human life which underlies modern denials of the factual character of moral judgments and more especially of those judgments which ascribe virtues or vices to individuals.

I argued earlier that every moral philosophy has some particular sociology as its counterpart. What I have tried to spell out in this chapter is the kind of understanding of social life which the tradition of the virtues requires, a kind of understanding very different from those dominant in the culture of bureaucratic individualism. Within that culture conceptions of the virtues become marginal and the tradition of the virtues remains central only in the lives of social groups whose existence is on the margins of the central culture. Within the central cultural of liberal or bureaucratic individualism new conceptions of the virtues emerge and the concept of a virtue is itself transformed. To the history of that transformation I therefore now turn; for we shall only understand the tradition of the virtues fully if we understand to what kinds of degeneration it has proved liable.

DISCUSSION QUESTIONS

1. What does MacIntyre mean by "the good of a whole human life"? Relate this to Aristotle's and Confucius's concept of human nature and the good life.
2. Do you agree with MacIntyre's criticism of modern individualism? Discuss whether individualism makes it harder for us to be virtuous people, as MacIntyre claims. Illustrate your answer with examples.
3. Like Confucius, MacIntyre regards virtues as having meaning within a cultural context. Do you agree with them that virtue cannot be separated from our culture and traditions? Does college life demand a different set of virtues than your life prior to attending college? To what extent do these sets of virtues overlap?
4. Would MacIntyre be satisfied with Noddings's care ethics as a corrective to duty-based ethics? Support your answer.
5. Is MacIntyre a conservative? In what ways does his virtue ethics differ from cultural relativism?

Chapter Applications

1. Jackie Robinson: An American Hero

In 1946 African Americans who wanted to play professional baseball had to play in segregated leagues. Branch Rickey, president of the Brooklyn Dodgers, was outraged at this injustice. His dream was to break the color barrier by finding an African American baseball player with the strength of character to withstand the inevitable abuse he would encounter, on and off the baseball field.

Rickey decided that 26-year-old Jackie Robinson of the Kansas City Monarchs might be the man for the job. During their first interview, Robinson asked, "Mr. Rickey, do you want a ball player who's afraid to fight back?"

"I want a player with guts enough not to fight back," Rickey responded.

This was a hard request because Robinson was in the habit of fighting back. When his family had moved to a mostly white suburb in Pasadena, California, they were often the target of racial harassment. Now Robinson was being asked to change for the sake of a greater good. After a long silence, Robinson replied, "If you want to take this gamble, I will promise you there will be no incident."[1]

Robinson's first team was the Montreal Royals. Although it was love at first sight for the Canadian fans, in the United States the spectators as well as the other players yelled racial slurs, booed, and threw objects and dead animals at Robinson.

Although the torrent of hatred sent Robinson into a depression, he refused to retaliate or give up. In 1947 Rickey moved Robinson to the Brooklyn Dodgers. The heckling continued. Rickey watched Robinson suffer in silent dignity over the next few years. "This young man," Rickey once remarked, "had come through with courage far beyond what I asked."[2]

In 1957 Jackie Robinson retired from baseball and began working in political campaigns and fighting for civil rights.

Discussion Questions

1. What does it mean to be a hero? Was Robinson a hero? What is the relation between being a virtuous person and being a hero?
2. Applying Aristotle's concept of the role of habituation in virtue, discuss Robinson's transition from someone who fought back to someone who could rise above others' insults.
3. Robinson was greatly admired for his courage. What is courage? Discuss the virtue of courage in light of Aristotle's and Confucius's Doctrine of the Mean.
4. Because of Robinson's example, many people who had been prejudiced changed their views. Do we have a moral obligation to be a role model to others, or is how we act our own business as long as we aren't hurting anyone?
5. Rickey's efforts in fighting racial discrimination earned him the title "Mahatma" after the Indian leader Mohandas "Mahatma" Gandhi. Compare and contrast the lives of the two men.
6. Are some cultures more conducive to the virtuous life than others? In particular, is there something about the culture of the United States that makes us more prejudiced against African Americans than the Canadians?
7. Discuss the following quote by Jackie Robinson in light of Kant's concept of the good will and the Confucian notion of the superior man.

   I had to deny my true fighting spirit so that the "noble experiment" could succeed. But I never cared about acceptance as much as I care about respect. . . . The most luxurious possession, the richest treasure anybody has, is his personal dignity.[3]

2. The Bigoted Judge

Judges are generally appointed because they are considered to be fair and just— virtuous qualities. Recently, however, the moral character of judges and potential judges has been coming under scrutiny.

In 1992, for example, Justice Stewart L. Ain, a New York Supreme Court Justice, was censured for making anti-Arab remarks. After asking attorney Paul Saqqal to spell his name, Justice Ain retorted, "You're not an Arab, are you?" Saqqal replied that he was of Arab ancestry, at which Justice Ain shot back, "You're our sworn enemies." He then turned to Mr. Saqqal and, extending his middle finger, added, "Here's what I have to say to you. . . . What the f—k do you people want anyway?"[4]

Following this scene, Justice Ain turned to the opposing lawyer and asked if he was Jewish. When the lawyer replied "yes," Justice Ain expressed his admiration for General Sharon's "hawkish view toward Arabs."[5]

Although Justice Ain was censured by the New York State Commission on Judicial Conduct, he received little more than a slap on the wrist. Justice Ain still sits on the bench in Nassau Country.

Discussion Questions

1. What does it mean to be a bigot? Is bigotry always a vice?

2. Was Justice Ain's response to Saqqal morally justified, given that he regarded Arabs to be enemies of Jews? Discuss how a virtuous person would most likely treat someone whom they or others regard as an enemy.

3. What if Justice Ain had restricted his bigoted behavior to outside the courtroom? Is it morally acceptable to be prejudiced against a certain group of people as long as we don't act on it? Discuss how a virtue ethicist would respond to these questions.

4. Do people in positions of power have a moral obligation to model virtuous behavior, or is their private life their own business? In particular, do college professors and student leaders have an obligation to lead virtuous and exemplary lives both on and off campus? Support your answer.

5. Most virtue ethicists maintain that happiness and virtue are closely linked. Do you agree? Discuss whether a person who is bigoted, such as Justice Ain, can be truly happy in the sense that Aristotle uses the term.

6. Aristotle argues that virtue is not a feeling but rather willing the good for its own sake. Is it possible to separate our feelings and our actions? To what extent do our feelings and actions shape each other? How would Hume and Buddha, respectively, answer this question?

7. Confucius emphasized the importance of sincerity in the virtuous life. Wasn't Justice Ain being sincere by openly expressing his views toward Arabs? Wouldn't it be worse for him to pretend he didn't hate Arabs? Support your answer. How might Confucius have responded to these questions?

8. Was the response of the New York State Commission on Judicial Conduct to Justice Ain's behavior appropriate? What is the policy on your campus for handling similar incidents? What action would a virtue ethicist most likely suggest for handling complaints about bigoted remarks from people in positions of power, such as judges, politicians, or teachers? Support your answer.

3. Callie Smartt: The Wheelchair Cheerleader

Fifteen-year-old Callie Smartt was a popular freshman cheerleader at her high school in West Texas. The fans didn't seem to mind that she was confined to a wheelchair because of cerebral palsy. "She had plenty of school spirit to go around," wrote journalist Sue Anne Pressley in the *Washington Post*. "The fans seemed to delight in her. The football players said they loved to see her dazzling smile."6

At the end of the season, however, she was kicked off the cheerleading squad. Fair is fair, the school officials said in justification of their decision. From now on, if Callie wanted to be on the cheerleading squad, she would have to try out like anyone else. The tryouts, however, required performing splits and other gymnastic feats that were impossible for Callie given her physical limitations.

The father of the head cheerleader, it turned out, had spearheaded Callie's dismissal. He, along with the parents of some of the other cheerleaders, had resented Callie receiving an honor that they felt she didn't deserve. If cheerleading could be done from a wheelchair, then those who could do the splits and tumbles were not given the honor they deserve for their achievements.

Journalist Michael Sandel disagrees. "What does it mean," Sandel asks, "to perform well in the role of a cheerleader?" To him the answer is about virtue and excellence, not merely physical prowess. "The case for Callie is that, by roaring up and down the sidelines in her wheelchair, waving her pompoms and motivating the team, she does well what cheerleaders are supposed to do: inspire school spirit."

Discussion Questions

1. To what extent should a virtuous character be considered in choosing people for positions such as cheerleaders, or even in college admissions? Relate your answer to the selection in Chapter 1 by Robert Coles, "The Disparity Between Intellect and Character."

2. Resentment, also known as righteous indignation, is considered a moral virtue by most ethicists. "People who are not angered by the right things," Aristotle writes, "or in the right way, or at the right times, or towards the right people, all seem to be foolish. . . . Since he is not angered, he does not seem to be the sort to defend himself; and such willingness to accept insults to oneself or to overlook insults to one's family and friends is slavish."7 Do you agree that resentment is a moral virtue? In the case study, was the parent of the head cheerleader "angered by the right thing" or was his anger inappropriate? Support your answer.

3. Resentment or righteous indignation, like most virtues, involves hitting the mean between deficiency (malice) and excess (envy). Discuss the virtue of resentment in the context of the head cheerleader's father's resentment of Callie's position on the cheerleading squad.

4. Is it degrading to others when apparently unqualified people, such as Callie Smartt, receive the same benefits or honors as those who have earned the rewards? Journalist Michael Sandel tentatively draws an analogy between Callie's situation with that of the resentment some feel toward people collecting welfare. Compare and contrast the two situations.

5. Does fairness necessarily require treating everyone equally? Discuss a social policy for recruiting cheerleaders using Rawls's two principles of justice from Chapter 7.

4. Heinz and the Drug[8]

A woman was near death from a rare form of cancer. There was one drug, however, that might save her. It was a form of radium that a pharmacist in the town had recently discovered. Although the drug was expensive to produce, the pharmacist was selling it for far more than it cost him. He was charging $4,000 for a small dose—ten times the cost of making it.

Heinz, the sick woman's husband, went to everyone he knew to try to borrow the money for the drug but could only raise $2,000. He told the druggist that his wife was dying and asked if he could pay him the rest in installments. The pharmacist said, "No, I discovered the drug and I have a right to make a profit from it."

Heinz, at his wit's end, contemplates stealing the drug for his wife.

Discussion Questions

1. According to virtue ethicists, the primary concern of virtuous people is to live the good or righteous life. Accordingly, virtuous people place moral values above nonmoral values when there is a conflict between the two. What values are in conflict in the Heinz case? Which of these values are moral values and which are nonmoral values? Discuss how a virtuous person might go about resolving the dilemma facing Heinz.

2. Care ethicists, such as Noddings, argue that the concepts of the "one-caring" and the "caring-for" offer better guidelines for making decisions in cases such as Heinz's than do abstract moral principles. Apply the concepts of care ethics to the Heinz case in coming up with a solution to his dilemma. Are you satisfied with the solution? Does care ethics take sufficient account of the concerns of the pharmacist and the wider community?

3. Is the virtue ethics of the Egyptian Ptahhotep relevant to decision making in contemporary life? Discuss how the Ptahhotep might have advised Heinz regarding his duty to his wife.

4. What would you have done had you been in Heinz's predicament? Discuss how you would morally justify your decision.

5. Alasdair MacIntyre is critical of the modern individualist approach to virtue ethics. According to him, virtue ethics need to take into account a more holistic view of humans as social beings rather than viewing humans as beings acting in isolation. Do you agree with MacIntyre? In your answer to the previous question, did you focus more on individualist or on wider community concerns? Discuss how the two types of concerns might be balanced in the Heinz case.

6. Officer Flannagan, who is on the beat at the time, sees Heinz leaving the pharmacy in the middle of the night with a package under his arm. Flannagan, who has a reputation of being a good person who cares deeply about the well-being of the people in his precinct, has heard about Heinz's situation and sympathizes with his plight. What should Flannagan do? Explain.

5. Gossip

"Joanne has herpes!" The rumor spread through the small Midwest campus like wildfire. Joanne had enrolled in the college at the beginning of her sophomore year after her father had been transferred to St. Louis from Seattle. By the time the small canker sore on her lip had healed, brought on by the stress of the move, the whispers and innuendoes had left an indelible mark on Joanne and her reputation.

Although Joanne protested that the rumor was untrue, no one believed her. Very few people spoke to Joanne. Those who did were soon ostracized and teased as well. Despite the fact that she was attractive and outgoing and had been popular at her previous college, no one asked Joanne out. Her grades began to drop, and she became depressed and withdrawn. Shortly before the semester ended, Joanne was found dead in her dorm room from an overdose of drugs.

Discussion Questions

1. We've probably all heard the saying, "Sticks and stones will break your bones, but words will never hurt you." Do you agree? Does this absolve us of any responsibility for engaging in or tolerating gossip?

2. Do we have a moral right, based on freedom of speech, to engage in gossip? What are the moral limits of freedom of speech? Does the other students' freedom of speech impinge on Joanne's privacy rights in this case? Support your answer.

3. Discuss this case in light of the Buddhist concepts of right speech and right action. Does right speech require that we always refrain from gossip? For example, would the rumors have been morally justified if the perpetrators of the rumors thought they were protecting innocent parties from a health risk?

4. What is the right action or the proper moral response if we find ourselves either privy to gossip or the target of gossip? How would you respond if you were in Joanne's position?

5. Is gossip consistent with the Confucian virtue of benevolence, as well as the principle of reciprocity? Discuss how Confucius would most likely have responded to hearing the rumor about Joanne.

6. David Hume argues that it is empathy, rather than reason, that motivates us to behave morally. However, is empathy sufficient for moving us to act when it comes to strangers or newcomers like Joanne, or do we need more abstract moral principles of beneficence and justice to move us in cases like this? Support your answer using examples from your own experience.

7. Who bears the moral responsibility for Joanne's suicide? Is suicide, as a response to a painful situation, ever morally acceptable? If so, under what circumstances? Support your answer.

6. Albert Schweitzer: Sharing Our Talents

In 1896, at the age of 21, Albert Schweitzer made the most important decision in his life. He decided that he would continue to study the subjects he enjoyed most —philosophy, theology, and music—until the age of 30. But from then on he would devote his life and talents to the service of humanity. For the next nine years, Schweitzer struggled with how he could best serve others. In 1904 he came across an article, "The Needs of the Congo Mission," about the desperate need for doctors. Schweitzer had found his answer. He enrolled in medical school, graduating in 1912.

In 1913 Schweitzer and his wife Helene sailed for Lambaréné in French Equatorial Africa (now Gabon). Here they set up a hospital in an abandoned chicken coop. Schweitzer wrote in a letter to his sister, "The misery is greater here than anyone can describe. . . . Evenings I go to bed dead-tired, but in my heart I am profoundly happy that I am serving at the outpost of the Kingdom of God."[9]

The following year, with the outbreak of World War I, the German-born Schweitzers were placed under arrest by the French government. They were eventually deported and sent to a prison camp in France. During this time Schweitzer developed his philosophy of reverence for life. Upon his release Schweitzer gave lectures on his philosophy as well as organ concerts to raise money to return to Africa.

When Schweitzer returned, he built a new hospital where he treated animals as well as people. In 1952 Schweitzer won the Nobel Peace Prize for his humanitarian work. He used the prize money in the fight against leprosy.

Discussion Questions

1. Do we have a moral obligation to share our talents? Answer this question in light of Aristotle's notion of excellence and its relation to performing our proper function as humans.

2. Schweitzer was profoundly influenced by Judeo-Christian ethics and the teachings of Jesus of Nazareth. To what extent do religious ethics promote the sharing of talents as a moral duty? What is the basis of this obligation? Discuss your answer in light of the passages in Chapter 3 from Matthew 5:13–16 as well as from the Qu'ran and the Bhagavad Gita.

3. Schweitzer believed that people mistreat each other because they do not care enough for each other. Only by caring for and respecting one another can we treat others and all living creatures better. Compare and contrast Schweitzer's concept of caring with that of Nel Noddings.

4. Like Aristotle and Confucius, Schweitzer believed that living a life of virtue was important to happiness. Are people who share their talents happier and more self-fulfilled? Answer this question in light of your own experience.

5. In Buddhist ethics, the virtue of alms-giving requires us to share our talents as well as our material wealth with those less fortunate. Discuss whether people who are virtuous—like Schweitzer, Jackie Robinson, and Suzie Valdez—are more likely to share their talents as well as their material wealth with others.

6. Being virtuous, according to Buddhists, entails seeking "right livelihood." Relate the concept of right livelihood to Schweitzer's life as well as to your own career and life choices.

NOTES

[1]Richard Scott, *Jackie Robinson* (New York: Chelsea House Publishers, 1987), p. 18.

[2]Ibid., pp. 55–56.

[3]Ibid., p. 101.

[4]Alan M. Dershowitz, *The Abuse Excuse* (Boston: Little, Brown, 1994), pp. 213–214.

[5]Ibid., p. 214.

[6]Michael J. Sandel, "Honor and Resentment," *The New Republic,* 214 (26): 27.

[7]Aristotle, *Nichomachean Ethics,* translated by Terence Irwin (Indianapolis: Hackett Publishing, 1985), Book V 1126a, 44.

[8]This case study is adapted from one of the moral dilemmas in James Rest's Defining Issues Test, which is used to measure stages of moral development. For more information on the test, contact James Rest, Center for the Study of Ethical Development at the University of Minnesota.

[9]Quote on the cover of *Reverence,* newsletter of the Albert Schweiter Center, No. 17, May 1994.

Credits

Chapter 1

Page 3 Robert Coles, "The Disparity Between Intellect and Character," *The Chronicle of Higher Education*, September 22, 1995. With permission of the author. **Page 13** Christina Hoff Sommers, "Where Have All the Good Deeds Gone?" Hastings Center Report, August 1982. Copyright ©1982 The Hastings Center. Reproduced by permission. **Page 17** Sheila Mullett, "Shifting Perspective: A New Approach to Ethics," in *Feminist Perspectives: Philosophical Essays on Method and Morals*, Lorraine Code, Sheila Mullett and Christine Overall, eds., University of Toronto Press, 1988. With permission of the publisher. **Page 23** Kosho Mizutani, "Buddhist Tradition and Modernity," in *Buddhist Ethics and Modern Society*, Charles Wei-hsun Fu and Sandra W. Wawrytko, eds., Greenwood Press, 1991. Copyright ©1991 Chung-Hwa Institute of Buddhist Ethics. Reproduced with permission of the publisher.

Chapter 2

Page 31 Jean-Jacques Rousseau, *Émile*, translated by Barbara Foxley, J. M. Dent & Sons, 1974, Book V. Reprinted by permission of Everyman's Library, David Campbell Publishers, Ltd. **Page 44** A. M. Rosenthal, "Study of the Sickness Called Apathy." Copyright ©1964 by The New York Times Company. Reprinted by permission. **Page 51** Stephen A. Satris, "Student Relativism," *Teaching Philosophy* 9(3):193–200. Used with permission of the Philosophy Documenation Center, publisher of *Teaching Philosophy*. **Page 62** Ruth Benedict, "A Defense of Cultural Relativism," from "Anthropology and the Abnormal," *The Journal of General Psychology* (10):59–82. Reprinted with permission of the Helen Dwight Reid Educational Foundation. Published by Heldref Publications, 1319 Eighteenth Street, N.W., Washington, D.C. 20036-1802. Copyright ©1934 Helen Dwight Reid Educational Foundation. **Page 67** Ibn Khaldun, "The Moral Corruption of Sedentary Cultures," in *The Muqaddimah*, translated by Franz Rosenthal, Princeton University Press, 1969. Copyright ©1958, 1967 by Princeton University Press. Used with permission of the publisher. **Page 71** Marilyn Frye, "Oppression" in *The Politics of Reality: Essays in Feminist Theory*, Freedom, CA: The Crossing Press, 1983. Copyright ©1983 The Crossing Press. Reprinted with permission of the publisher. **Page 80** Daniel Jonah Goldhagen, *Hitler's Willing Executioners*, Alfred A. Knopf, 1996. Copyright ©1996 by Daniel Jonah Goldhagen. Reprinted by permission of Alfred A. Knopf, Inc. **Page 87** Dr. Martin Luther King, Jr., "Letter From a Birmingham Jail." Reprinted by arrangement with the Heirs to the Estate of Martin Luther King, Jr., c/o Writers House, Inc. as agent for the proprietor. Copyright ©1963 by Martin Luther King, Jr., copyright renewed 1991 by Coretta Scott King. **Page 92** William H. Shaw, "Relativism in Ethics." Copyright ©1980 William H. Shaw. This is part of a longer essay, "Relativism and Objectivity in Ethics," originally published in John Arthur, ed., *Morality and Moral Controversies*, 1980.

Chapter 3

Page 110 Mohandas Karamchand Gandhi, "Teaching of Hinduism," "The Teaching of the Gita," and "Central Teaching of the Gita" in *Hindu Dharma*, Navajivan Publishing House, 1959. Used with permission of Navajivan Trust; Verses: Kees Bolle, *Bhagavadgita: A New Translation*, Berkeley, CA: University of California Press, 1979, pp. 53–72. Copyright ©1979 The Regents of the University of California. Used with permission of the publisher. **Page 118** From the *Revised Standard Version of the Bible*. Copyright ©1946, 1952, 1971 by the Division of Christian Education of the National Council of the Churches of Christ in the USA. Used by permission. **Page 124** Lippman Bodoff, "God Tests Abraham, Abraham Tests God," *Bible Review*, October 1993. Used with permission of the Biblical Archaeology Society. **Page 154** Kai Nielsen, "Religious Ethics Versus Humanistic Ethics," in *Philosophy and Atheism: In Defense of Atheism*, Prometheus Books, 1985. Copyright ©1985 Prometheus Books. Reprinted by permission of the publisher.

Index

Abdulla, Muhammad, 217
abnormality, 63–64, 66
abortion, 93, 95, 358–359
Abraham and Isaac, 118, 119–120, 124–127
absolute monarchy, 364, 366, 369
abstinence, 218
academic freedom, 91
achievement, 243–244
Adam and Eve, 194, 242
adultery, 69, 120, 432
The Adventures of Huckleberry Finn, 171, 208–210
affirmative action, 360–362
African Americans, 48–49, 76, 87–91, 217, 255, 257, 361, 386–387, 410, 477–478
After Virtue: A Study in Moral Theory, 421, 469–477
aggression, 60, 201, 309. *See also* violence
agriculture, 299, 372–373. *See also* property rights
ahimsa (nonviolence), 110–113
AIDS, 310–311
Ain, Justice Stewart L., 478–479
Akedah. See Holy Bible, Genesis 22:1–18
alcoholism 443, 447
alienation, 25–26, 46, 251
altruism
  college students and, 1
  corporate, 270
  ethical egoism and, 244–246
  hard core, 237–239
  heroes and, 271
  lying and, 237
  Rand, Ayn, criticism of, 241, 244–246
  reciprocity and, 237
  sociobiology and, 225, 234–240
  soft core, 237–239
  sympathy and, 175–177
Amazon rain forests, 411
America, colonial, 372–373

American Academy of Pediatrics, 168
American civil rights movement, 87–91, 170
American College Health Association, 311
American Express, 270
American Friends Service Committee, 100
American Medical Association, 312
American Revolution, 166
The Analects of Confucius, 314, 326–330, 342
analytical philosophy, 470
Andreasen, Alan, 270
An Enquiry Concerning the Principles of Morals, 420, 453–458
anger, 21, 72, 78, 115, 173–174, 330, 409, 430, 431, 480
Animal Liberation, 274, 295–301
animals, nonhuman
  altruism and, 225, 234, 235–236, 238–239
  Aristotle on, 426
  Buddhism and, 23, 446–447
  cruelty toward, 297, 299
  equality and, 295–297
  evolution of, 55
  killing of, 299–300
  Locke, John, on, 367, 371
  morality and, 180, 239
  Noddings, Nel, on 467
  pleasures of, 290–292
  respect for, 211
  sacrifice of, 111, 119
  Social Darwinism and, 57–58
  speciesism and, 296–297, 299
  utilitarianism and, 274, 290–291
annihilationism, 445
anthropocentrism, 118
anthropology, 62, 320
Anthropology and the Abnormal, 62–66
anti-Semitism, 56, 83–86
  See also Holocaust
anxiety, 178–179
apathy, 21, 30, 44–50

approval, 9, 187
a priori, 319, 321
Aquinas, Thomas
  background,140
  Nielsen, Kai, critique of, 155–156
  Summa Theologica, 90, 140–146
  war, on, 167
Arabs, 68–70, 478–479
Arendt, Hannah, 357
aristocracy, 149–150
Aristotle
  background, 421
  ethics education and, 1
  justice, on, 350
  lying, on, 337
  MacIntyre, Alasdair, on, 469, 470, 472
  Nicomachean Ethics, 419, 421–433
  political goods, 398–399
  resentment, on, 480
  virtue, definition of, 142, 143
Arjuna, 110–115
asceticism, 284
assembly, right to peaceful, 392, 398
assimilation, 75
asylum, 100–101
athletes, 219–220
AT&T, 270
attachment, 178, 183, 444. *See also* sociability
Augustine, Saint, 90, 142, 338, 339
autonomy
  lying and, 103, 334, 358
  capitalism and, 383
  care ethics and, 207
  ethical egoism and, 225
  moral development and, 186
  Prozac and, 222
  will of God and, 162
  See also liberty rights

Bangladesh, 237
Bauer, Bruno, 377
Beauvoir, Simone de, 14, 16
Bedouins, 68–70
behavior. *See* moral behavior
behaviorism, 170
Ben and Jerry's, 270
Benedict, Ruth
  background, 62
  A Defense of Cultural Relativism, 55, 62–66
  social Darwinism, critique of, 55
beneficence, duty of, 316, 344, 345
  See also benevolence
beneficiary, 402–403, 407
benevolence, 9, 16, 173, 175–176, 352, 438,
  457–458
Bengalis, 237

Bentham, Jeremy
  background, 281
  *An Introduction to the Principles of Morals
    and Legislation,* 274, 281–286
  utilitarianism, 274, 281–286, 288, 296–297
berdache, 63
Beyond Good and Evil and The Joyful Wisdom,
  106, 147–153
Bhagavad Gita, 106, 110–113, 113–116
Bible. See Holy Bible
Bill of Rights, 364, 388
Birmingham, Alabama, 87–91
Black Elk, 212, 214
black theology, 386–387
blame, 340, 398, 431
Bloom, Allan, 29, 249
Bodoff, Lippman
  God Tests Abraham, Abraham Tests God,
    106, 124–127
Bok, Sissela
  background, 331
  Lying, 314, 331–342
boredom, 448
Bosnia, 84
bourgeoisie, 147
The Boys from Brazil, 166
Branch Davidians, 363
Brandt, Professor, 409
Brazil, 411
Brooklyn Dodgers, 477
Brown, Dawn, 221
Brown, Kimberlee, 221
Brunner, Emil, 158–160
Buber, Martin, 90
Buddha, 441, 442–443
Buddhism
  altruism, 236
  Christianity, compared to, 23–24
  criticism of, 23–25
  ethics education and, 2, 23–26
  noble eightfold path, 419, 441, 442, 443–448
  nonviolence and, 112
  religion and, 105
  social ethics and, 2, 23, 25–26
Buddhist Tradition and Modernity, 2, 23–26
Bullock, Scott, 27
Burke, Edmund, 397
Burundi, 84
business, 379, 424. *See also* capitalism

California Proposition 187, 101
Cambodia, 335
Cameron, Nigel, 166
campus speech codes, 412–413
Canada, 101, 167, 478
cannibalism, 99–100

Can't We Make Moral Judgements? 225, 248–251
capitalism
  Buddhism on, 25
  egoism and, 268–271
  international, 25, 98, 269, 382–384, 447
  multinational corporations, 98–99
  Rand, Ayn, and, 241
  volunteerism and, 270–271
capital punishment, 362
Capuano, Michael, 27
care ethics
  care perspective, 171, 203–207
  family and, 204, 205
  Gilligan, Carol, on, 201–202
  individualism and, 206–207
  Mullett, Sheila, on, 17–22
  Noddings, Nel, on, 461–467
  obligation and, 466–468
  positive caring, 19–20
  public morality and, 205–207
Caring: A Feminine Approach to Ethics and Moral Education, 420, 460–467
Carter, President Jimmy, 270
caste system, 218, 236
categorical imperative, 189, 258, 262, 265, 320–324, 356–357, 362, 466
censorship, 412
Center for Bioethics and Human Dignity, 166
Center for Disease Control, 310
Centerwald, Brandon, 309
cerebral palsy, 479
character. *See* moral character
charity, 205, 244, 398. *See also* community service and volunteerism
chastity, 37
cheating, 68, 272–273
cheerfulness, 72
cheerleading, 479–480
Chekhov, Anton, 194
The Cherry Orchard, 193–194
children
  AIDS and, 311
  caretaking and, 205
  child labor, 98–99
  gender identity and, 195–196
  medical experiments on, 308–309
  moral development in, 180–181, 186–187
  moral responsibility and, 98
  parents and, 9, 11, 120, 130–131, 168, 393
  rights of, 393
  Rousseau, Jean-Jacques, on, 32, 37–38
  sympathy in, 182
  violence and, 309–310
  Wollstonecraft, Mary, on, 41–42
  See also motherhood

China, 359
Chodorow, Nancy, 195–196
Christ for Mexico Mission, 164
Christianity
  Catholic ethics, 93, 140, 155–157, 165
  fundamentalism, 105
  liberation ethics, 384–387
  missionaries, 100
  morality and, 106
  Nietzsche, Friedrich, critique of, 147, 152
  Protestant ethics, 159
  social Darwinism on, 55
  war and, 166
Christian Scientists, 167–168
church bombings, 45
Churchill, Winston, 403
Cicero, 457
circumcision, 100–101
Citadel, the, 28
cities, 45–49, 68–69
citizenship, 354, 378–380, 398, 410
"The City" (Mecca), 108
civic duty, 30, 270
civil disobedience, 56, 87–91, 218
civility, 27–28
civilization
  agriculture and, 58
  Benedict, Ruth, on, 63, 65
  Christian, 58–60, 385
  Khaldun, Ibn, on, 67–70
  Nietzsche, Friedrich, on, 150
  Rand, Ayn, on 246–247
  Rousseau, Jean-Jacques, on, 32
  sedentary culture and, 67, 69–70
  social Darwinism on, 55, 58–60
  Wollstonecraft, Mary, on, 39–41
Civil Liberties Union, 414–415
civil rights, 236–237, 377–380, 478
civil rights movement. *See* American civil rights movement
claims, rights and, 401–403, 407–410
Cleckley, Hervey, 178
Clinton, President Bill, 100, 270
cloning, 166–167
coercion, 333, 334, 335, 340, 405–406
Colby, Anne, 164–165
Coles, Robert
  background, 3
  The Disparity Between Intellect and Character, 1, 3–6
collectivism, 241, 245–247
college students
  academic cheating, 272–273
  AIDS and, 310–311
  altruistic behavior and, 1
  athletes, 219–220, 362

college students (*continued*)
  character development and, 3–6, 170
  community service and, 5
  moral development of, 55, 191
  ontological shock and, 22
  parental attitudes and, 179–180
  Rand, Ayn, and, 249
  relativism and, 30, 51–53
  ROTC, 416–417
  violence and, 220
Collins, Kevin, 97
colonialism, 55
common good, 69, 142, 246, 368
  See also goodness
commitment, duties of, 402–403, 407
communism (Soviet), 241
communitarianism, 270, 326, 388, 469, 474
community, 88–90, 142–143, 282–283, 286,
  394, 474–475
community membership, right to, 405
community service, 5, 14, 26–27, 220, 270
  See also volunteerism
compassion, 24, 69, 111, 173, 236, 262,
  446–447, 470
compelling appropriateness, duties of, 406
Cone, James H., 386
confidentiality, 336
conformity, 186, 187, 424
Confucianism, 23, 105, 275
  See also Confucius
Confucius
  The Analects of Confucius, 314, 326–330,
    342
  background, 326
  Doctrine of the Mean, 419, 435–439
Congo, 483
conscience, 84, 174, 176–180, 188, 208–210,
  213, 368, 378, 393
  See also innate moral sense
consequences, intentions and, 396, 398
consequentialism, 259, 274, 302
conservatives, 102, 395, 476
Constitution, United States, 91, 361, 399, 412,
  417
contemplation, 424
cooperation, 58, 237, 245, 350, 351,409
corruption, 68–69, 148, 244, 336, 337 448
courage, 34, 127, 242–247, 249, 254, 329,
  428–429, 457, 478
cowardice, 429, 433
Crips, 216
Critique of Practical Reason, 356–357
A Critique of Utilitarianism, 274, 302–305
Crito, 346
Croats, 84
cruelty, 297

cults, 163–164
cultural life, right to participate in, 393, 397
cultural relativism, 54–104
culture. *See* society
Curren, Frank, 312
Curren, Judith, 312
customs, 54, 63–66, 92–95
  See also tradition

Daly, Father C.B., 155, 157
Damon, William, 27, 164–165
Darwin, Charles, 57, 180–181
Davila, Mario, 100
Dead Man Walking, 362
death penalty, 362–363
Decalogue, 118, 120, 188, 345
deception, 231, 278, 333–334, 340. *See also*
  lying
Declaration of Independence, 182, 364,
  378–379
Declaration of the Rights of Man and Citizen,
  364
defense mechanisms, 30, 52–53
A Defense of Cultural Relativism, 62–66
degradation, 78
Delaware Supreme Court, 168
delinquency, 179
De Man, Paul, 4
de Mello, President Fernando Collor, 411
democracy, 90–91, 152, 375, 394, 398–399
deontology, 259, 314–363
depression, 222, 448
Descartes, Rene, 297
Desdemona, 333, 334
The Descent of Man, 180
despair, 90
determinism, 335, 446
development, right to economic, 397–398
developmental theory. *See* moral development
dharma (righteous living), 24, 110
DiAngelo, Rio, 163
Diaz, John Anthony, 221
Dictionary Hill, California, 413
dignity, human, 162, 166, 188, 245, 339, 370,
  388–389, 392
dilemmas, moral, 191, 208–210, 481
diligence, 151, 330
disapproval, feeling of, 9
discrimination, 72–73, 76–77, 194, 218, 353,
  361, 390, 416–417. *See also* prejudice.
The Disparity Between Intellect and Character,
  1, 3–6
dispositions, virtue and, 427–432, 470, 473
divine command theory, 105, 124–127,
  159–160
disorder, 276–278

Dobu (New Guinea), 64, 65
docility, 72
doctrine of the mean, 428–433, 435–439
Doctrine of the Mean, 419, 435–439
Doe v. University of Michigan, 412–413
dogma, 444
Dole, Bob, 361
domination, 245, 299, 386
Dostoevski, Feodor, 307–308
double bind, 72
drug addiction, 443, 447, 448
dupes, 335–337, 342
duty, 43, 179, 245, 253, 267–268, 314–318,
    394, 401–408, 438, 455
    See also specific duties

Eagle Man
    background, 211
    We are All Related, 171, 211–216
ecology. *See* environmental ethics
economics
    crises, 382
    international economy, 98–99, 382–384
    Gutierrez, Gustavo, on, 382–384
    Khaldun, Ibn, on, 68–69
    Marx, Karl, on, 377
    Social Darwinism and, 250–251
    See also capitalism and Marxism
Ecumenical Association of Third World Theolo-
    gians, 387
education
    equal opportunities, 412
    girls and, 255
    public education, 54
    right to, 393, 397, 408–409
    Rousseau, Jean-Jacques, on, 32–38
    Wollstonecraft, Mary, on, 41–42
    See also ethics education and college students
egocentrism, 239
ego development, 199
egoism, 445, 379–380. *See also* ethical egoism
egotism, 378, 244–246, 259, 448
Egypt, 420
Eichmann, Adolf, 356–357
Eichmann in Jerusalem, 357
elderly people, 13–16, 25, 204–215, 279
Eliot, George, 259–264
El Salvador, 100–102
Embodying Forgiveness, 220
Emerson, Ralph Waldo, 3, 5–6
Émile, 30, 31–38
empathy. *See* sympathy
employment, duties and, 405–406
Endangered Species Act, 415
ends. *See* goals
enemies, 121, 151, 452, 479

energy, virtue of, 437–438
England, 474
engrossment, care ethics and, 462–464
enlightenment, 444–445
Enlightenment period, 364
An Enquiry Concerning the Principles of
    Morals, 420, 453–458
entitlements, 398, 401, 404
environmental conservation, 415–416
Environmental Defense Fund, 411
environmental ethics, 211–216, 411–412,
    415–416, 443
envy, 432
Epicurus, 289, 290
equality
    original position and, 351–353
    in pay, 392
    principle of, 295–298. *See also* justice
equilibrium, 60, 435, 436
escapism, 23, 25. *See also* pessimism
Establishing a Viable Human Rights Policy,
    365, 395–399
eternal law, 140, 156
eternalism, 445
ethical egoism, 225–273
    capitalism and,
    critique of, 248–251, 274
    definition,
    ethical relativism and,
    Hampton, Jean, on, 259–268
    Rand, Ayn, and, 242–247
    virtue and, 260–262
ethical naturalism, 155
    See also natural law theory
ethical relativism, 29–104
    Buddhism and, 443
    critique of, 92–97
    definition, 29
    divine command theory and, 105
    moral development and, 170, 187
    natural law theory and, 157
    student relativism, 30, 51–54
    types of, 29
    See also cultural relativism and ethical
        subjectivism
ethical self, the, 461–462,
ethical subjectivism
    definition, 29–30
    critique of, 93, 96–97
    moral judgments and, 172
    Price, Craig, and, 97–98
    Rousseau, Jean-Jacques, and, 31–39
ethics education, 1–28
    Aristotle, on, 1, 427–429
    civility and, 27–28
    community service and, 27–28

ethics education (*continued*)
  indoctrination approach, 191
  habituation and, 455, 427–429
  Kohlberg, Lawrence, on, 171, 185, 191
  moral development and, 170
  United States and, 1
  values clarification, 191
ethnocentrism, 56
European Common Market, 382
euthanasia, 312–313
Euthyphro, 106, 129–138
evil, 112, 150–151, 328, 432, 442, 446, 451
evolution, theory of, 57, 234, 236–240
excess. *See* doctrine of the mean
excuses, 340
expectations, 396, 398
experiments
  learning, 357–358
  lies in, 358
  medical, 299, 308–309
exploitation, 149–150, 244, 246, 381–382

Facism, 4
fairness. *See* justice
faith, 125, 127, 155, 385–387, 398
family
  altruism and, 236, 238
  Buddhism on, 25
  children and parents, 9, 11, 69, 120, 126,
    130–131, 168
  Confucianism on, 327
  cultural relativism and, 94
  Decalogue on, 120
  Frye, Marilyn, on, 72, 75–76
  "generation gap," 179–180
  Held, Virginia, on, 204–205
  Holocaust rescuers and, 179
  Khaldun, Ibn, on 69
  justice and, 204, 206
  Mo Tzu, on, 276–278
  Native American views, 215
  Rousseau, Jean-Jacques, on, 37–38
  Universal Declaration of Human Rights, on,
    391
fanaticism, 444–445
farming. *See* agriculture
faults, 328. *See also* vices
fear, 47, 49, 64, 114, 179, 284, 382, 388–389,
    428, 431
Federal Communications Commission, 309
feelings. *See* sentiments
Feinberg, Joel
  background, 401
  Rights, Justice, and the Bounds of Liberty,
    365, 401–410
feminist ethics, 17–22, 203–204, 467.

  See also care ethics
feudalism, 407
fidelity, duty of, 37, 345
filial piety, 277–278.
  See also family
First Amendment, 91, 412
foolhardiness, 429
Ford, President Gerald, 270
Ford, Richard, 163
The Fountainhead, 225, 241, 242–247, 249–250
Fourteenth Amendment, 361
Fox, George, 166
Frank, Robert, 176
Federalist Papers, 399
freedom, 152, 162, 204–205, 212, 335,
    354–355, 367, 399. *See also* specific
    freedoms
free-riders, 336
French Revolution, 149, 397, 399
Freud, Sigmund, 177–178
friendship, 20–22, 151, 182, 183, 329, 451, 458
Frye, Marilyn
  background, 71
  Oppression, 55, 71–78
*Fundamental Principles of the Metaphysic of
    Ethics,* 314–324

Gabon, 483
Gallup poll, 27
Gandhiji, *See* Gandhi, Mohandas
Gandhi, Kasturba, 217–218
Gandhi, Mohandas
  background, 110
  The Moral Teachings of the Bhagavad Gita,
    106, 110–113
  pacifism, on, 167
gangs, 216–217
generosity, 214, 235–236, 451, 457, 458. *See
    also* sharing
genocide, 81–85
Genovese, Kitty, 44–50
gentleness, 37, 437
George Washington University, 165
Germans, holocaust and, 80–86, 474
ghettos, 48–49, 75
Gifford, Kathie Lee, 98
Giles, Dr. Joan, 308
Gilligan, Carol
  background, 193
  In a Different Voice, 171, 193–202
  Kohlberg, Lawrence, critique of, 171, 193
  Noddings, Nel, influence on, 460
  women's moral development, 181–182,
    193–202, 205
goals
  ends as, 423, 425

rights and, 395–398
  See also telos
God
  Abraham and, 119–120, 124–127
  Allah, 107–109
  bliss and, 116
  "death of," 147–148
  Divine Reason, 141
  Euthyphro on, 132–138
  the Great Spirit, 212–213
  Judeo-Christian concept of, 161
  justice and, 231–232
  moral law and, 106, 125–127, 141, 154, 159
  natural rights ethics and, 306, 367, 370
  nature of, 125–127
  obedience to, 124, 158
  reason of, 156
  Rousseau, Jean-Jacques, on, 32, 40–41
  as *summum bonum,* 156
  will of, 158–160, 162, 165
  Wollstonecraft, Mary, on, 40–41
  See also Holy Bible
God Tests Abraham, Abraham Tests God, 106,
    124–127
Golden Rule, 264, 293, 342
Goldhagen, Daniel
  background, 80
  Hitler's Willing Executers, 56, 80–96
goodness
  Aristotle on, 421–425, 427, 431–432
  Confucius on, 328, 329
  egoism and, 264
  Euthyphro, definition of, 129, 131–138
  God and, 158, 161
  MacIntyre, Alasdair, on, 473
  as the normal, 155
  Nietzsche, Friedrich, on, 152
  utilitarianism and, 293
Good Will, the 316–317, 419. *See also* intentions
Gordon, Milton, M., 239
gossip, 482
Gough, Harrison, 179
government
  authoritarian regimes and genocide, 84
  purpose of, 367, 369–370, 374–375
  legislation, 283, 288, 352
  rights to participate in, 392
  tyrannical laws and, 143
  universal love and, 278
gratitude, duty of, 345–346, 403–404, 406,
    409, 458
Great Mystery, the, 215
Greatest Happiness Principle. *See* utilitarianism,
    principle of utility
greed, 373, 442, 446, 448, 451
gregariousness, 58–59

  See also sociability
Gregg v. Georgia, 362
Groeger, Larry, 272
group morality, 89.
guilt, 21, 178, 340
  See also shame
Gutierrez, Gustavo
  background, 381
  critique of natural rights ethics, 364
  The Power of the Poor in History, 364,
    381–387
Gyges ring, 227–229

habituation, 455, 427–429
Haiti, 102
Hale-Bopp comet, 163
Hampton, Jean
  background, 252
  The Wisdom of the Egoist, 226, 252–268
Hanger, Charles, 362
happiness
  Aristotle on, 423–427
  Bhagavad Gita on, 114–116
  Buddhism on, 448
  Confucius on, 329, 436
  justice and, 230–232
  Kant, Immanuel, on, 316–318
  moral development and, 170
  Nietzsche, Friedrich, on, 152
  utilitarianism and, 283, 289–292, 303
  virtue and, 231, 456
  Wollstonecraft, Mary, on, 40
harassment, 28, 78, 478
Hare, Robert, 178
harmony
  Bhagavad Gita on, 114–116
  Confucius on, 435–437
  family, 277
  global, 237, 275
Harper, John, Jr., 413–414
Harvard University, 3–5
Harvard University Center for Moral Develop-
    ment, 185
Hasbro, 268–269
hate, 101, 213, 242, 277–278, 329, 412, 442,
    448
headhunting, 99–100
Heaton, Joan and family, 97
Heavens Gate (cult), 163–165
Hegel, Georg, 396
Heidegger, Martin, 4
Held, Virginia
  background, 203
  Gilligan, Carol, on, 205
  The Meshing of Care and Justice, 171,
    203–207

hepatitis, 308–309
heroes, 271, 472, 477–478. *See also* samaritans
hierarchies, 55, 257, 263–265, 405
Hillel, Rabbi, 342
Hinduism, 105, 110–113, 218, 236. *See also Bhagavad Gita*
Hitler, Adolf, 81, 82
Hitler's Willing Executioners, 56, 80–86
HIV. *See* AIDS
Holmes, Larry, 220
Holocaust, 56, 80–86, 177, 179, 474
    See also anti-Semitism and Nazism
Holy Bible
    Exodus 20:1–17, 120
    Exodus 32:1–14, 126
    Genesis 1:26–31, 119
    Genesis 22:1–18, 119–120, 124–127
    Matthew 5:1–20, 120–121
    Matthew 5: 38–48, 121
    Matthew 6:19–23, 121–122
    Matthew 7:1–5, 122
    Matthew 7:15–10, 122
    Psalms 115:16, 370
    See also Christianity and Judaism
homelessness, 415–416
homeless shelters, 415
homosexuality
    American Indians and, 63–64
    ancient Greece and, 63
    Khaldun, Ibn, on, 69
    military and, 416–417
    natural law ethics and, 417
    Plato's *Republic* and, 63
honesty, 176, 231, 337, 447
    See also lying
honor, 424, 425
hope, 284, 386, 398
Hopwood, Cheryl, 360–361
hospitals, 19–20, 414, 483
Huck Finn, 171, 208–210
human law, 141–142
human life
    cycle, 194
    as an end in itself, 324–325
    killing, 84, 299–300
    purpose of, 162
    right to life, 390, 397
    unifying concept of, 476
    value of, 165, 189–190
human nature
    Aristotle on, 421, 425–426
    Buddhism and, 26, 442
    faith and, 160–161
    Held, Virginia, on, 206–207
    Hume, David, on, 457
    Khaldun, Ibn, on, 69

Mencius, on, 8–11
    natural law theory on, 156–157
    natural rights ethics and, 364
    sociobiology and, 235–240
    Universal Declaration of Human Rights on, 389
Hume, David,
    background, 453
    An Enquiry Concerning the Principles of Morals, 420, 453–458
    hard-core altruism and, 237
    Noddings, Nel, on, 464–465
humiliation, 65
humility, 53, 151
Hundt, Reed, 309
Hurston, Zora Neale, 253–256
Hussein, King, 236
Hutus, 84
hypothetical imperatives, 320–323

Iago, 334, 472
IBM, 270
ideas, rights and, 396–397
ideology, 83, 85, 443, 444–445
individualism, 474–477. *See also* liberalism
ignorance, 444
immigrants, 101–102
immortality, 162,
impartiality. *See* justice
In a Different Voice, 171, 183–202
indebtedness, duties of, 402, 404, 407
identity, 472–475
independence, 244–245, 250. *See also* individualism.
India, 218, 359
Indians. *See* Native Americans and India
indignation. *See* anger
individualism, 244–246, 249, 251, 410
Indochina, 98
indulgence, 291, 442
industrialization, 281, 373–374, 382–384
injustice, 88, 90–91, 227–232, 354
innate moral sense,
    Aristotle on, 427
    children and, 180–181
    gender and, 181–182
    Germans and, 83
    language and, 180–181
    moral development and, 180–181, 184
    moral reasoning and, 180
    sociobiology on, 235–239
    sympathy and, 173–178
    See also conscience
in personam rights, 402–404, 407
in rem rights, 404–405, 407, 408–409
insincerity, 69

institutions, rights and, 396–399
The Instruction of Ptahhotep, 420, 450–452
integrity, 77, 249, 302, 305, 335–337
intentions, 187, 307–308, 314, 338, 339, 396, 398, 419, 471.
interests, 296–297
intolerance. *See* tolerance
intrinsic moral worth, 258, 264
An Introduction to the Principles of Morals and Legislation, 274, 281–286
intuition, 96, 182, 240, 346–347, 353
Islam, 105, 107, 217, 237. *See also* Qu'ran

Japan, 93, 382–383
Javits, Jacob
  background, 44
  A Study of the Sickness Called Apathy, 30, 44–45
jealousy, 221
Jefferson, Thomas, 296
Jesus of Nazareth, 118, 120–122, 147, 293, 385
Jews, 49, 80–86, 239, 479
John Paul II, 165
Jonah's Gourd Vine, 253–256
Jones, L. Gregory, 220
Jonestown, Guyana, 164
Jordan, Michael, 98–99
The Joy Luck Club, 218–219
Judaism, 124–127
judgment. *See* moral judgment
Jung, Carl, 4
justice
  Aquinas, Thomas, on, 141
  Aristotle on, 350, 429–430, 433
  Buddhism and, 23
  distributive, 64, 345–346, 354–355
  as equality, 257–258, 267, 392, 413
  evolution of, 57–60
  as fairness, 351–355
  family and, 204, 206, 253
  happiness and, 230, 232, 345–346
  Held, Virginia, on, 204–207
  honors and, 230
  inequalities and, 353–355
  impartiality and, 253, 278–279, 303–305
  moral development and, 188, 196–199
  Rawls, John, on, 349–355
  self-interest and, 227–232
  vigilante, 413–414
justice perspective. *See* moral development

ka, 450
Kagawa, Dr., 111–113
kamma, law of, 445–446
Kansas City Monarchs, 477
Kant, Immanuel
  background, 315
  capital punishment, on, 362
  Critique of Practical Reason, 356–357
  Fundamental Principles of the Metaphysic of Ethics, 314, 315–324
  human value and, 265–267
  Kohlberg, Lawrence, and, 183, 185
  lying, on, 319, 323–324, 331, 338–341
  MacIntyre, Alasdair, on, 475
  Philosophy of Law, 362
  Wilson, James Q., on, 183
Kanter, Rosabeth Moss, 270
karma. *See* kamma
Kasinga, Fauziy, 100
Kevorkian, Dr. Jack, 312
Khaldun, Ibn,
  background, 67
  The Muqaddimah, 55, 67–70
Kierkegaard, Soren, 461
To Kill a Mockingbird, 257
kindness, 410
King, Martin Luther, Jr., 165
  background, 87
  Letter from a Birmingham Jail, 56, 87–91
Kingdom of Heaven, 121
Kirkpatrick, Jeane,
  background, 395
  critique of human rights ethics, 365, 397–399
  Establishing a Viable Human Rights Policy, 365, 395–399
Klineberg, Otto, 180
Klugman, Dr. Saul, 308
knowledge
  applied, 431
  of God, 158
  moral, 155, 346–347, 438, 439, 444, 454
  power and, 334, 335
  principle of, 9
  scientific, 442
Koch, Mayor Ed, 414
Kohlberg, Lawrence
  background, 170, 185
  Gilligan, Carol, critique of, 196–199
  The Philosophy of Moral Development, 171, 185–191
  Wilson, James Q, on 185–186
Koran. *See* Qu'ran
Kramer, Peter, 222–223
Krishna, 110–116
Ku Klux Klan, 412
Kwakiutl, 64

labor, 371–374
laissez-faire capitalism. *See* capitalism
language, 297
Latin American, 381, 382–385

Latinos, 310
law of Nature, 32, 35–36, 367–369, 371, 374
laws, unjust, 90–91
Lebanon, 84
Lee, Harper, 257
legal duties, 407
legitimate interests, 388
leisure, right to, 393
Lepkowski, Teresa, 165–166
Letter from a Birmingham Jail, 56, 87–91
Let's Take Back Our Space, 77
Levi Strauss, 270
Levin, Ira, 166
Levin, William, 414–415
Levine, Helen, 19–20
lex talionis, 121, 166
liability, 406
liberalism, 52, 102, 204–205, 476–477
liberation ethics, 381–387
liberty rights, 27, 353–355, 367, 378–379, 388,
    397, 414. *See also* specific liberty rights
lie detectors, 178
Listening to Prozac, 223
Locke, John
    background, 366
    natural rights ethics, 364, 366–375, 388
    Two Treatises of Civil Government, 364,
        366–375
Loevinger, Jane, 199
logging, 411
love
    Buddhism on, 23
    Confucianism on, 329
    duty of, 406
    Golden Rule, 264
    Hinduism on, 111
    Jesus of Nazareth on, 121
    Kant, Immanuel, on, 317, 323
    Mo Tzu, on, 275–280
    self, 34
loyalty, 329–330. *See also* fidelity
luxury, 67–69
lying
    autonomy, 103
    Bok, Sissela, on, 314, 331–342
    Buddhism on, 446
    to children, 102–103
    coercion and, 333–335, 340
    consequences of, 334–337
    cultural customs and, 94
    dignity and, 339
    fidelity, duty of, and, 345, 346
    free-rider status, 336
    Kant, Immanuel, on, 319, 322–323, 324
    physicians and, 332
    power and, 334, 335–337

psychopaths and, 178
lying in research, 359
Santa Claus and, 102–103
sedentary cultures and, 68
self-defense and, 340
soft-core altruism and, 237
war and, 334
Lying, 314, 331–342
Lynch, Aaron, 164

Machiavelli, 335
machismo, 76
MacIntyre, Alasdair
    After Virtue: A Study in Moral Theory, 420,
        469–477
    background, 469
magic, black, 64
Mahabharata, 111
malice, 433
marriage, 34–37, 100, 218–219, 261–263, 391,
    397
martyrs. *See* self-sacrifice
Marx, Eleanor, 470
Marx, Karl
    background, 377
    On the Jewish Question, 364, 377–380
    natural rights ethics, critique, 364, 377–388
Marxism, 251, 381
masochism, 245
"master morality," 147, 150–152
materialism, 214–215, 445–446, 448
Matsch, Judge Richard, 362–363
Mattel, 268–269
maxims, moral, 319, 322, 475
McGaa, Ed. *See* Eagle Man
McVeigh, Timothy, 362–363
"Mean World Syndrome," 309–310
Meinhold, Keith, 417
Meinhold v. US Department of Defense, 417
Melanesia, 64–65, 99–100
men
    justice perspective and, 181–182
    moral development, 181–182, 186
    Oedipus complex, 177
    oppression and, 71–78
    Rousseau, Jean-Jacques, on education of,
        32–34
    self-worship and, 254–255
    superego, 177
    value theory and, 263
    violence and, 310
Mencius
    background, 8
    Works of Mencius, 2, 8–11
Mentavlos, Jeanie, 28
The Meshing of Care and Justice, 171, 203–207

Messer, Kim, 28
Mexican Americans, 361
Mexico, 164
Middlemarch, 259–264
Middle Ages, 405
middle path. *See* noble eightfold path
Midgley, Mary
  background, 248
  Can't We Make Moral Judgements? 225,
    248–251
  Rand, Ayn, critique of, 248–251
midrash, 125
Mignonette (yacht), 306–307
Milgram, Stanley, 357–358
Mill, James, 288
Mill, John Stuart,
  background, 288
  innate moral sense, on 180
  Utilitarianism, 258, 274, 288–293
  security, right to, 310, 313
  women, on, 254–255, 257
Miller House, 13–14
mining, 411
missionaries, 100
MIT, 416
Mitzutani, Kōshō
  background, 23
  Buddhist Tradition and Modernity, 2, 23–26
modesty, 9, 36, 43, 68
money, 374, 383–384, 423. *See also* wealth
"Monster" Kody Scott, 216–217
Montana State University-Northern, 310–311
Montreal Royals, 477
Moore, G.E., 343–344
moral agency, 19, 267, 303–305, 346, 358, 430,
    447, 471–472
moral beauty, 456
moral behavior, 63–66, 158, 187, 239–240,
    259, 264, 451, 455, 467
moral character
  college and, 3–6, 170
  cultivation of, 292, 419
  experience and, 17–22
  Good Will and, 316
  happiness and, 292
  honest and, 176
  moral judgment and, 174
  relationships and, 175–176
  See also virtue ethics
moral development
  attachment and, 178
  baboons and chimpanzees and, 239
  Buddhism on, 444, 448
  care perspective, 203–207
  children and, 186–187, 189, 201, 203–207
  college students and, 55, 191

conventional stages, 186–187
  Freud, Sigmund, on, 177
  gender and, 181–182, 186, 194–199, 202
  Gilligan, Carol, 193- 202
  jealousy and, 221
  justice perspective, 181, 196–199, 203–207
  Kohlberg, Lawrence, on, 170, 185–191
  moral maturity, 200–202, 261
  postconventional stages, 182, 186, 188,
    197–199, 221
  preconventional stages, 186, 187
  sports and, 220–221
  Wilson, Edward O., on, 239–240
  Wilson, James Q., on, 180–184
moral education. *See* ethics education
moral force, 327–329
moral judgment
  anger and, 173–174
  cultural relativism and, 55, 97
  intuition and, 347
  Jesus of Nazareth on, 122
  MacIntyre, Alasdair, on, 470–471
  public education and, 54
  sociability and, 179
  sympathy and, 173–175
  women and, 197, 200
moral law, 189, 258, 262, 265, 318. *See also*
  categorical imperative
moral motivation, 83, 173, 175–177, 432,
    445–446, 463–464
moral order, 346–347
moral progress, 444–446. *See also* Social Darwinism and reform
moral reasoning, 180, 96–97. *See also* moral
  development and moral judgment
moral regard, 253
moral responsibility, 98
moral sense. *See* innate moral sense
The Moral Sense, 171, 172–184
moral sensitivity, 17–18, 20–21
moral speculations, 455
Morgan, Charles, Jr., 45
mortality rates, 58
Moseley, Winston, 47
Moses, 126
Mother Earth, 211–216
motherhood, 37–38, 75–76, 195–196, 199,
    204, 253–256, 311, 393, 464–465
Mo Ti. *See* Mo Tzu
motivation, 83, 284
  See also moral motivation
Mott, Lucretia, 199–200
Mo Tzu
  background, 275
  Universal Love, 274, 275–280
movement, freedom of, 391

Mudd, Judge, 412
Mullett, Sheila
  background, 17
  *Shifting Perspectives: A New Approach to
    Ethics,* 2, 17–22
The Muqaddimah, 55, 67–70
murder
  Akedah and, 125–127
  altruism and, 246
  cities and, 46, 48–49
  Crime and Punishment, 307–308
  Euthyphro on, 130–132, 138
  of God, 147–148
  Gyges ring and, 229
  jealousy and, 221
  Kitty Genovese, 45–50
  Locke, John, on, 369
  lying and, 339–340
  Price, Craig and, 97–98
  vigilante justice and, 413–414
  witnesses of, 45–50
  Yanömami Indians, of the, 411
  See also genocide

NAACP, 48
narrative quest, 472–475
nationality, right to, 391, 397
Native Americans, 75, 211–216
The Natural Goodness of Humans, 8–11
natural law ethics
  Akedah and, 124–127
  cloning and, 165
  civil disobedience and, 90–91
  definition, 105, 143
  homosexuality and, 417
  natural inclinations toward, 144
  Nielsen, Kai, critique of, 155–159
  practical reason and, 143–145
natural rights ethics, 364, 377–380, 404
natural selection, 236–240
nature, 383,
Nazism, 4, 80–86, 153, 80–85, 339–340,
    356–357, 474
need-fulfillment, duties of, 407
need, rights and, 381, 408
nepotism, 237
New Guinea, 99
Newmark, Colin, 167–168
New Testament. *See Holy Bible*
New York City, 48–49, 414
New York State Commission on Judicial Con-
    duct, 479
Nicomachean Ethics, 419, 421–433
Niebuhr, Reinhold, 89
Nielsen, Kai
  background, 154

Religious Ethics Versus Humanistic Ethics,
    106, 154–162
Nietzsche, Friedrich
  background, 147
  *Beyond Good and Evil and The Joy of Wis-
    dom,* 106, 147–153
  ethical egoism and, 249, 251
  Noddings, Nel, on, 466
Nike (footware), 98–99
Noah, 126
"noble man," the. *See* "overman"
Noble Eightfold Path, 419, 441, 442, 443–448.
    See also Way, the
Noddings, Nel
  background, 460
  *Caring: A Feminine Approach to Ethics and
    Moral Education,* 420, 460–467
"no harm principle." *See* non-maleficence,
    duty of
non-maleficence, duty of , 345
nonviolence
  Buddhism and, 112
  care ethics and, 201
  Gandhi, Mohandas, on 110–113, 218
  King, Martin Luther, Jr., on, 87–91
  See also ahimsa
normative ethics, 16, 266–267

obedience
  to authority, 356–358, 407
  duties of, 407–408
  God and, 158–160
  laws and, 346
  children and, 33, 407
  Milgram, Stanley, experiments on, 357–358
  moral development and, 187
obligation, care ethics and, 465–467
obligation, imperfect, 343, 346
obligation, perfect, 339, 343, 346
obscenity, 68
Oedipus complex, 177–178
Oklahoma City bombing, 362–363
Old Testament. *See Holy Bible*
Oliner, Sam and Pearl, 176
On Human Nature, 234–240
On the Jewish Question, 364, 377–380
ontological shock, 17, 18, 20, 22
opinion, 54, 96, 187–188, 392, 432
oppression
  care ethics on, 22
  Frye, Marilyn, on, 71–78
  Gutierrez, Gustavo, on 382, 386–287
  helpfulness and, 73–74
  lack of universal love and, 278
  Nietzsche, Friedrich, on, 151
  racism and, 89–91

structure of, 75–77
theories of self-worth and, 257, 267
women and, 71–78
Oppression, 55, 71–78
original position (Rawls), 349, 351–353
Othello, 333, 334
Orwell, George, 218
Osbourne, Tom, 220
ought, 160, 283
"overman," the, 147, 148–152
Owen, Robert, 396

pacifism, 111, 113, 166–167
pain, 284–286, 297–300
Paine, Thomas, 399
Pakistan, 237
Palm, Danny, 413–414
Paris, John, 166
partiality. *See* justice, impartiality and
passions, 146, 237, 428, 448. *See also*
    sentiments
passivity, moral, 15–16
patience, 37, 151
pay, duty to, 407
peace, 115–116, 275, 444
Pelican Bay State Prison, 217
People's Temple sect, 164
perfection, 406, 457
Persephone, 199
personal morality, 396, 398–399. *See also* pri-
    vate morality
personality, right to development of, 397
personhood, 90, 208, 360
pessimism, 23, 25
philanthropists, 316–317. *See also* volunteerism
Phillips, Lawrence, 219–220
Philosophy of Law, 362
The Philosophy of Moral Development, 171,
    185–191
Piaget, Jean, 185, 196–197
"piety", definition of, 132–138
    See also goodness
Pigden, Charles, 358
Plato
    background, 129
    political goods, 398–399
    Euthyphro, 105, 129–138
    Republic, 225, 227–232
pleasure
    Aristotle on, 423, 425, 429, 432
    Bhagavad Gita on, 114–116
    quality of, 290–292
    sedentary cultures and, 68–69
    sensual, Buddhism on, 442, 445, 447–448
    utilitarianism on, 282, 284–286, 288–293
police, 48–49, 89, 97, 407, 414

political morality, 396, 397, 398–400. *See also*
    public morality
political power. *See* government
political rights. *See* civil rights
politics, 423. *See also* government
The Politics of Reality: Essays in Feminist The-
    ory, 55, 71–78
pollution, 214–215
poor, rights of the, 384–387
Potter, Nancy, 414
Pound, Ezra, 4
poverty, 68, 89, 214, 381, 448
Powell, Colin, 270
power, 334, 335–337, 381, 398
powerlessness, 76, 78
The Power of the Poor in History, 364,
    381–387
praxis, 17–20, 387
Prejean, Sister Helen, 362
prejudice, 40, 55, 89–90, 96, 101–102, 183,
    296, 478–479.
    See also discrimination and racism
Premasiri, P. Don
    background, 441
    The Relevance of the Noble Eightfold Path to
        Contemporary Society, 419–420,
        441–448
prenatal diagnosis, 359
Pressley, Sue Anne, 480
Price, Craig, 97–98
prima facie
    duties, 343–348, 467
    rightness, 346–348
    See also specific duties and rights
primitive (simpler) cultures, 55, 57–60, 63,
    64
principle of utility. *See* utilitarianism
principles, moral. *See* specific moral principles
Principles of Ethics, 55
prison, 76, 98, 217
privacy, right to, 247, 391, 417
private morality, 13–16, 204–207, 327, 458. *See*
    also personal morality
procreation, 165
progress
    civilization and, 41
    social Darwinism on, 55, 59–60
Prometheus, 242
promises, 318–319, 322–323, 324, 327, 344,
    345–346, 348, 402–403
property rights, 354, 370- 374, 377–379, 391,
    404, 415–416, 476
propriety, principle of, 438
Prozac, 222–223, 270
psychoanalytic theory. *See* Freud, Sigmund
psychopaths, 178, 239

Ptahhotep, Vizier
  background, 450
  The Instruction of the Ptahhotep, 420,
    450–452
public, good. *See* common good
public health, 269
public morality, 180, 204–205, 327, 355, 424
public policy, 13–16, 355
publicity, test of, 340–342
Puerto Rico, 239
punishment, 60, 136, 187–188, 220, 232,
  362–363, 368–369, 389, 452

Quakers. *See* Society of Friends
Qu'ran, 105, 107–109

Rabinowitz, Dr. Bernard, 311
racism, 89–91, 96, 296, 297, 387, 474,
  477–478
Ramayana, 111
Rand, Ayn
  background, 241
  The Fountainhead, 225, 241, 242–247
  Midgley, Mary, critique of, 248–251
rationalization, 96, 174, 397
Raveh, Judge, 356
Rawls, John
  background, 349
  Kohlberg, Lawrence, and, 185
  publicity, test of, 341
  A Theory of Justice, 314, 349–355
reason
  a priori, 319
  Aristotle on, 426
  Buddhism on, 24, 445
  divine, 141, 156
  ethical egoism and, 243, 245
  ethical relativism and, 96–97
  happiness and, 290–292
  imperatives and, 320–324
  human, 141, 389
  moral law and, 143, 258, 318–322, 323–324
  moral worth and, 297, 299, 301, 320,
    323–324
  natural law and, 141–145
  original position and, 351
  practical, 141, 143–145, 158, 318–321
  sentiment and, 237, 454–457
  speculative, 141, 145
  will and, 320, 323–324
  women and, 39, 40, 43
reasonable persons standard, 341
reciprocity, 11, 187, 235, 237, 342, 403–404,
  407, 439, 467
Rector, Margaret, 415–416
reform, 87–91, 94–95, 110, 199–200, 288, 352

relationships, 19–21, 24–26, 196, 201,
  244–245, 300, 338, 344, 461–467,
  474–475
  See also family and friendship
relativism. *See* ethical relativism
Relativism in Ethics, 56, 92–97
*The Relevance of the Noble Eightfold Path to
  Contemporary Society,* 419–420, 441–448
religion, 105–169
  Huck Finn and, 209–210
  Native American, 213
  right to practice, 378, 379, 392
  sedentary cultures and, 68, 69
  service and, 165
  See also divine command theory and natural
    law theory
  See also specific religions
Religious Ethics Versus Humanistic Ethics, 106,
  154–162
reparation, duty of, 345, 346, 368–369, 403, 407
repentance, 346
repression, 177
Republic, 225, 227–232
reputation, 231
rescuers. *See* Samaritans
research, on humans, 308–309, 357–358,
  359–360. *See also* experiments
Research and Educational Associates, Ltd, 272
resentment, 249, 335, 480
Reserve Officer Training Corps (ROTC),
  416–417
respect, 206, 211–216, 318, 327, 330, 389, 404
  See also self-respect
responsibility, 406
rest, right to, 393
retaliation, 60, 166
retribution, 60, 121
  see also lex talionis
revelation, 160–161, 370
revenge, 60
revolution, 239, 370, 389, 476
rhetoric, 395, 397
Rickey, Branch, 477–478
right action, 446–447
The Right and the Good, 314, 343–348
right contemplation, 447–448
right effort, 447–448
righteousness, 9, 121, 438
right livelihood, 447
right mindfulness, 447–448
right speech, 446–447
right thought, 446–447
right to exist and to think, 385–386
rights ethics, 56, 188, 364–418
  See also natural rights ethics and specific
    rights

Rights, Justice, and the Bounds of Liberty, 365, 401–410
Roark, Howard, 241–247, 249
Robinson, Jackie, 477–478
Romantic Sentimentalism, 30
Rosenthal, A.M.
  background, 44
  Study of the Sickness Call Apathy, 30, 44–45
Ross, William David
  background, 343
  The Right and the Good, 314, 343–348
ROTC Campus Access Act, 416–417
Rousseau, Jean-Jacques
  background, 31
  Émile, 30, 31–38
  Wollstonecraft, Mary, critique of, 30, 39, 40–42
rudeness, 27
  See also civility
rule of law, 354, 389
Rutgers College, 273
Rwanda, 84

Sabbath, 120, 126
sacrifice, 111,119–120, 124–127, 149, 445
  See also self-sacrifice
safety. *See* security
sainthood, 114, 218, 239
samaritans, 50, 177, 179, 271, 405
sanctity of life, 299
Sandel, Michael, 480
Santa Claus, 102–103
Saqqal, Paul, 478–479
Sarah, 127
Sardanapalus, 424
Sartre, Jean Paul, 251, 474
Satris, Stephen
  Student Relativism, 30, 51–53
"savages," 31, 55, 57–60
  See also "primitive" societies
Schwartzman, Dr. Stephen, 411
scientific humanism, 445
scientific progress, 442–443
Schweitzer, Albert, 483
Scott, Job, 166
Scott, "Monster" Kody, 379
second-handers, 243–247, 248–249
secular humanism, 161–162
security, right to, 310, 313, 379, 390, 397
segregation, 75, 89–91, 96
self, unity of, 470–474
self-assertion, 260–262,
self-awareness. *See* self-consciousness
self-completion, 439
self-consciousness, 292, 300–301
self-denigration, 256–257

self-destructiveness, 337
self-esteem. *See* self-respect
self examination, 9
self-improvement, duty of, 345
self-interest, 175–177, 225, 228–232, 253, 266–267, 323, 352
selfish genes, 236, 240
selfishness
  altruism and, 234, 238–239
  Bhagavad Gita on, 114, 116
  egoism and, 260–261
  Gyges ring and, 227–229
selflessness, 113, 151, 244, 267
self-mortification, 441, 445
self-pity, 21
self-preservation, 368–369
self-respect, 221, 253, 265–266, 314, 327, 354, 410. *See also* self-worth
self-sacrifice, 235, 241, 245, 261, 263, 406
self-sufficiency, 425
self-worth, 256–259, 264–267. *See also* self-respect
Seneca Falls Declaration, 199–200
sentience, 292
sentiments
  Aristotle on, 430, 431–432
  Bhagavad Gita on, 112, 114–116
  care ethics and, 181
  Hume, David, on, 420, 453, 454–456
  Nietzsche, Friedrich, on, 149–151
  Noddings, Nel, on, 466–467
  Smith, Adam, on, 173
  utilitarianism and, 282
  Wilson, James Q., on, 175–182
  See also specific sentiments
Serbs, 84
Sermon on the Mount, 118, 120–121
servility, 219, 244
servitude, 9, 75–76, 390
sexism, 296, 297, 412. *See also* discrimination and women, oppression
sexual misconduct, 447
Shakur, Sanyika, 217
shame, 9, 11, 178, 346, 409, 432
sharing, 64, 214, 405–406
  See also generosity
Shaw, William
  Relativism in Ethics, 56, 92–97
Shifting Perspective: A New Approach to Ethics, 2, 17–22
simpler cultures. *See* primitive societies
Sidgwick, Henry, 296
sincerity, 11, 438, 439
Singer, Peter
  Animal Liberation, 274, 295–301
  background, 295

Sitting Bull, 214
skepticism, 335
slander, 447, 451
"slave morality," 147–153
slavery, 94, 98, 101, 208–209, 297, 387, 390, 474
Smartt, Callie, 479–480
Smith, Adam, 173–174, 180
sociability, 174–176, 179–180, 183, 234, 235–238
social class, 21, 382, 386, 405
social contract, 238, 349, 351, 375
social Darwinism, 55, 57–60, 250–251
social gospel, 386–387
socialism, 377. See also Marxism
socialization, 39
social order, 187, 393, 436, 444
social security, 270, 392
society
    Bedouin, 68–70
    lying, effect on, 333–334, 336
    family and, 391
    moral development and, 191
    morality and, 62–66
    normalcy and, 64–66
    Rawls, John, on, 350, 351–355
    See also cultural relativism and "primitive" society
Society of Friends, 166–167
sociobiology, 234–240
sociology, 476
sociopaths. See psychopaths
Socrates
    background, 129
    civil disobedience, 89, 91, 346
    Crito, 346
    Euthyphro, 130–128
    Republic, 225, 227–232
Sodom and Gomorrah, 126, 127
Sojourner Truth, 296
Solomon Islands, 99
Sommers, Christina Hoff
    background, 13
    Where Have All the Good Deeds Gone? 2, 13–16
Sophy, 31
South Africa, 218, 387
Soviet Union, 4, 241
speciesism, 296–297, 299
speech, freedom of, 354, 388, 392, 398, 412–413
Spencer, Herbert
    background, 57
    The Principles of Ethics, 55, 57–60
    social Darwinism and, 55, 250–251
spirituality, 165, 446, 448

sports, 219–220, 477–478
stages of moral development. See moral development, stages
standard of living, right to adequate, 393, 397
Stanton, Elizabeth Cady, 199–200
starvation, 443
state of nature, 32, 39, 40–41, 367–373, 375
status, duty of, 405, 407
Stoics, 291
Stoller, Robert, 195
Student Relativism, 51–53
Study of the Sickness Called Apathy, 30, 44–50
The Subjection of Women, 254
suffering, 8–9, 18, 228, 244, 297–300, 442, 444, 446, 448. See also pain
suicide
    altruistic, 225
    cults and 163–164
    jealousy and, 221
    Kant, Immanuel on, 322, 324
    Locke, John, on, 367
    physician assisted, 312–313
Summa Theologica, 106, 140–146
Super Bowl Sunday, 216
super ego, 177
"superior man," the, 280, 436, 437, 439
survival, 243, 299, 336
sweatshops, 98–99
sympathy
    children and, 182–183, 195
    Darwin, Charles, on, 180–181
    Hampton, Jean, on, 261–262
    Hume, David, on, 458
    Kant, Immanuel, on, 316–317
    moral judgment and, 173–175
    moral motivation and, 175–177
    Nietzsche, Friedrich, on, 150–151
    Smith, Adam, on, 173, 180
    sociability and, 174–175, 178
    Wilson, James Q., on, 173–177, 180–182

Tan, Amy, 218
Tao. See Way, the
Taoism, 275
tautologies, 157, 161
Taylor, Thomas, 296
technology, 25, 214–215, 242, 383–384, 442–444
teleological theories, 146
television, 309–310
telos, 470, 473. See also goals
temperance, 428–430, 433
temptation, 291, 446
Ten Commandments. See Decalogue
terrorism, 362–363, 446
Tertullian, 235

theft, 68, 120, 432, 481
A Theory of Justice, 314, 349–355
Third World nations, 98–99, 270
Thought Contagion, 164
tobacco industry, 269–270
tolerance, 24, 214–215, 353, 444–445
Torah, 124, 342. *See also Holy Bible*
torture, 85
trade unions, right to join, 393
tradition, 397, 475–476
  See also customs
trespassers, 406
trial, right to, 390
Trivers, Robert L., 239
trust, 207, 336, 338, 450
truth, 145, 332–333, 337, 338–339, 451, 456
Twain, Mark
  The Adventures of Huckleberry Finn, 171, 208–210
  background, 208
Two Treatises of Civil Government, 364, 366–375

Union of Indian Nations, 411
United Nations, 364, 388–394, 397
United Nations Commission on Human Rights, 397
United States
  apathy and, 49
  asylum and, 100–101
  expansionist policy, 55
  diversity in, 95
  foreign policy, 397, 399
  homosexuals in the military, policy on, 416–417
  immigrants, 101–102
  international capitalism, 382–384, 411
  moral development in, 55
  Native Americans, policy on, 75
  racism in, 474, 478
  Rand, Ayn, on, 246
  Social Darwinism and, 251
  Supreme Court, 90, 361, 415–416
  wealth, distribution of, 375
Universal Declaration of Human Rights, 364–365, 388–394, 397
Universal Love, 274, 275–280
universality, 279–280, 318–319, 322–324, 357, 466–467, 475
University of California, Berkeley, 273
University of Michigan, 412–413
University of Texas, 360–361
Unsolved Mysteries, 221
utilitarian calculus, 281, 284–286
utilitarianism, 274–313

animals, non-human, and, 274, 290–291, 296–299
critique of, 284, 302–305, 362
definition, 274
happiness and, 274
human value and, 265
legislation and, 283–284
pleasure, 288–293
principle of utility, 151, 282–284, 352, 355
Ross, William David, on, 343, 344–346
scientific humanism and, 445
theories of worth and, 258, 267
virtue ethics and, 419
Utilitarianism, 274, 288–293
utopianism, 397–398

Valdez, Suzie, 164–165
Valium, 222
valuable commodities, rights and, 409
values
  cultural relativism and, 55
  humans as creators of, 54–55, 150
  institutions and, 396
  Native American, 212
vanity, 152–153, 446
vegetarianism, 218
veil of ignorance, 351, 353
vegetable kingdom, 426
Venezuela, 411
veracity, principle of, 338–340
vigilante justice, 413–414
A Vindication of the Rights of Brutes, 296
A Vindication of the Rights of Woman, 39–43, 200, 295–296
violence
  Bhagavad Gita on, 112
  Buddhism on, 443, 446–447
  lying and, 335
  sports and, 220
  television and, 309–310
  victims of, 18, 220, 271, 310, 312
  See also murder and war
virtue ethics, 419–484
  Aristotle on, 422–433
  Aquinas, Thomas, on, 142, 145
  Confucianism on, 329, 435–439
  definition, 419, 430, 470
  doctrine of the mean, 435–439, 428–433
  habit and, 427, 429, 455
  Hume, David, on, 454–458
  intellectual virtues, 427, 432
  justice as, 349
  liberty and, 220
  MacIntyre, Alasdair, 469–477
  Nietzsche, Friedrich, 151
  Noddings, Nel, 464–465

virtue ethics (*continued*)
  Rand, Ayn, on, 244
  Rousseau, Jean-Jacques, on, 34
  unity of virtue, 470
  Wollstonecraft, Mary, on, 40–41, 200
  See also specific virtues
volition, principle of, 317–318
volunteerism, 13–14, 270–271
  See also community service

Waco, Texas, 363
Wakan Tanka. *See* God, the Great Spirit
war
  Aquinas, Thomas, on, 167
  Bhagavad Gita on, 113
  Buddhism on, 443–444, 446–447
  Christianity and, 166–167
  defensive, 58–59
  draft resistance, 167
  Eagle Man on, 213–214
  Gulf War, 363
  lack of universal love and, 278
  lying and, 335, 339–340
  offensive, 58
  prejudice and, 183
  profit and, 214
  self-sacrifice and, 235
  social Darwinism on, 59–60
  sociobiology on, 225, 236–237
  state of nature and, 369
  tax refusers, 167
  Vietnam War, 167, 170, 335
  World War I, 483
  World War II, 167, 363
Wasserstrom, Richard, 408, 410
Way, the, 326, 327–329, 435, 438
wealth, 64, 328, 354–355, 375, 424, 425,
  See also justice, distributive
We Are All Related, 171
welfare programs, 204, 270
welfare rights, 204, 388
  See also specific welfare rights
West Bank, 237
Wex, Marianne, 77
Where Have All the Good Deeds Gone? 2,
  13–16
will, principle of, 317–318, 320, 323–324. *See
  also* Good Will, the
"will to life," 149–150
"will to power," 147, 149–150
Williams, Bernard

background, 302
  A Critique of Utilitarianism, 274, 302–305
Wilmut, Ian, 165
Willowbrook State School, 308–309
Wilson, Edward O.,
  background, 234
  On Human Nature, 225, 234–240
Wilson, James Q.
  background, 172
  The Moral Sense, 225, 234–240
Wilson, Governor Pete, 101
wisdom, 9, 23, 114–116, 144, 328, 436,
  443–444
The Wisdom of the Egoist, 226, 252, 253–268
Wittgenstein, Ludwig, 341
Wollstonecraft, Mary
  background, 39
  A Vindication of the Rights of Woman, 30,
    39–43
  Rousseau, Jean-Jacques, on, 30, 39, 40–42
women
  Freud, Sigmund, on 194–195
  Frye, Marilyn, on, 71–78
  gender identity and, 195–196
  Gilligan, Carol, on, 193–202
  life cycle of, 193–202
  moral development, 171, 181–182, 194–199
  oppression of, 71–78, 387
  Prozac and, 222
  rights movement, 199–200, 295–296
  Rousseau, Jean-Jacques, on education of,
    35–38
  self-worth and, 254–257
  service and, 75–76
  "slave morality" and, 153
  violence against, 18, 78, 220, 310, 312
  Wollstonecraft, Mary, on, 39–43
  See also motherhood
Woodward, C. Vann, 412
work, right to, 392
The Works of Mencius, 2, 8–11
World Anti-Slavery Convention, 200
worth, theories of, 256–259
Wright, Frank Lloyd, 249

Yale University, 417
Yanömami Indians, 411–412
yoga, 114–116
Young American's Foundation, 416–417

Zamora, Ronny, 309–310